For Cathy

The Persian Gulf
TV War

◆

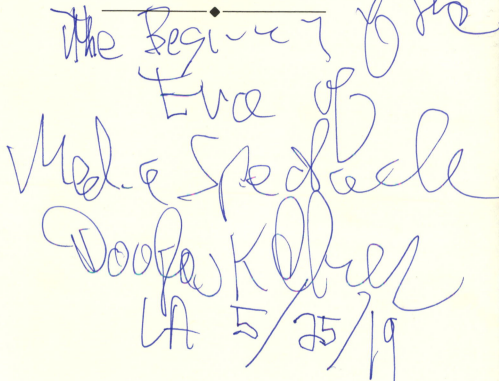

The Beginning of the
Era of
Media Spectacle

Douglas Kellner

LA 5/25/19

Critical Studies in Communication and in the Cultural Industries

Herbert I. Schiller, Series Editor

◆

The Persian Gulf TV War, Douglas Kellner

Triumph of the Image: The Media's War in the Persian Gulf—A Global Perspective, edited by Hamid Mowlana, George Gerbner, and Herbert I. Schiller

Mass Communications and American Empire, Second Edition, Updated, Herbert I. Schiller

FORTHCOMING

The Panoptic Sort: The Political Economy of Personal Information, Oscar Gandy, Jr.

Intellectual Property in the Information Age: A Political Economy of Film and Video Copyright, Ronald Bettig

The Communications Industry in the American Economy, Thomas Guback

Media Transformations in the Age of Persuasion, Robin K. Andersen

The Dallas Smythe Reader, edited by Thomas Guback

The Social Uses of Photography: Images in the Age of Reproduction, Hanno Hardt

Introduction to Media Studies, edited by Stuart Ewen, Elizabeth Ewen, Serafina Bathrick, and Andrew Mattson

A Different Road Taken: Profiles of Five Critical Communication Scholars, John A. Lent

Hot Shots: An Alternative Video Production Handbook, Tami Gold and Kelly Anderson

Music Television, Jack Banks

The Persian Gulf
TV WAR

———————— ◆ ————————

Douglas Kellner

Westview Press

BOULDER • SAN FRANCISCO • OXFORD

Critical Studies in Communication and in the Cultural Industries

Copyright © 1992 by Douglas Kellner

Published in 1992 in the United States of America by Westview Press, Inc., 5500 Central Avenue, Boulder, Colorado 80301-2877, and in the United Kingdom by Westview Press, 36 Lonsdale Road, Summertown, Oxford OX2 7EW

Library of Congress Cataloging-in-Publication Data
Kellner, Douglas, 1943–
    The Persian Gulf TV War / by Douglas Kellner.
        p.   cm. — (Critical studies in communication and
in the cultural industries)
    Includes bibliographical references and index.
    ISBN 0–8133–1614–6. — ISBN 0–8133–1615–4 (pbk.)
    1. Television broadcasting of news—United
States.   2. Persian Gulf War, 1991—Journalists.   I.
Title.   II. Series.
PN4888.T4K45   1992
070.1′95—dc20   92–3818
                                                                              CIP

Printed and bound in the United States of America

 The paper used in this publication meets the requirements of the American National Standard for Permanence of Paper for Printed Library Materials Z39.48-1984.

10   9   8   7   6   5   4   3

THERE IS NO DOCUMENT of civilization which is not at the same time a document of barbarism. And just as such a document is not free of barbarism, barbarism taints also the manner in which it was transmitted from one owner to another. A historical materialist therefore dissociates himself from it as far as possible. He regards it as his task to brush history against the grain.

—*Walter Benjamin*

IN THE HISTORY OF civilization there have been not a few instances when mass delusions were healed not by focused propaganda, but, in the final analysis, because scholars, with their unobtrusive yet insistent work habits, studied what lay at the root of the delusion.

—*T. W. Adorno*

[THE TASK OF critical theory] is to call things by their true names.

—*Max Horkheimer*

IT IS THE RESPONSIBILITY of intellectuals to speak the truth and expose lies.

—*Noam Chomsky*

Contents

Introduction

DURING THE GULF WAR, the mainstream media were cheerleaders and boosters for the Bush administration and Pentagon war policy, invariably putting the government "spin" on information and events concerning the war. By all accounts, the U.S. government was extremely successful in managing public opinion and engineering consent to their Gulf war policies. As Reagan's media manager Michael Deaver put it, "If you were to hire a public relations firm to do the media relations for an international event, it couldn't be done any better than this is being done." Veteran *New York Times* reporter Malcolm Browne compared the press's role in the Gulf war to that of the Nazi propaganda agency Kompanie, claiming: "I've never seen anything that can compare to it, in the degree of surveillance and control the military has over the correspondents."[1]

In this book, I shall argue that in an attempt to manage public opinion, the Bush administration and the Pentagon produced a barrage of propaganda, disinformation, and outright lies that covered over the more unsavory aspects of the Gulf war and that legitimated U.S. policies. The mainstream media helped mobilize public support for the U.S. war policy, and after the war George Bush's popularity surged to an all-time high. The media also promoted a euphoric celebration of the war as a great triumph for U.S. technology, leadership, and military power. Yet, in retrospect, it is not clear what positive benefits the Gulf war produced. Kuwait has been returned to its previous form of authoritarian government without significant reforms and with billions of dollars worth of damage done to the country. Iraq's economic infrastructure has been ruined and the Iraqi death count has been estimated as high as 243,000 as a result of the war.[2] The Kurds and other groups seeking to overthrow Saddam Hussein were betrayed by the United States, and Iraq continues to suffer under Baath Party dictatorship. Millions of people in the region became refugees during the war and were forced to leave their jobs for uncertain futures. The ecology of the area was ravaged by the war, which threatened devastation from the oil well fires that took months to put out, and the Persian Gulf has been heavily polluted from oil spills. The Middle East is more politically unstable than ever, and the Gulf war failed to solve its regional problems, creating new divisions and tensions.

Economically, the war cost billions of dollars; it threatened the economies of many countries and, arguably, the world economic order, which could have been thrown into chaos by an expanded conflagration and rising oil prices. The *Australian Financial Review* (March 1, 1991) reported that although it was not possible to quantify all of the environmental and human destruction, as a conservative estimate the total costs of the war range in the hundreds of billions of dollars including: $60 billion for coalition war costs; $60 billion for Iraqi war costs; $255 billion for the destruction of the infrastructure in Iraq; $100 billion for the destruction of the state infrastructure in Kuwait, with over $150 billion additional private sector losses; $90 billion of lost economic production in Kuwait and Iraq; $80 billion worth of losses due to burning oil; and $40 billion worth of debt reduction and aid to coalition allies in the region.

In retrospect, it therefore appears that the Gulf war was a disaster for the region and an immense waste of life and resources. Consequently, in the following pages, I shall attempt to show that the Gulf war was little more than a brute display of U.S. military power. Using a variety of sources, I offer a different account of the war than that which appeared in the mainstream media and attempt to expose the propaganda, disinformation, and lies with which the Gulf war was successfully sold to the public in the United States and elsewhere. I argue that the mainstream media complicity with U.S. government policies in the Gulf war has intensified the crisis of democracy in the United States, which I described in a recent book (Kellner 1990).

A democratic social order, as conceived in classical democratic theory, requires a separation of powers so that no one institution or social group dominates the society and polity. Thus, the U.S. Constitution divided the political system into the executive, legislative, and the judicial branches to create a balance of powers between the major political institutions. Yet democracy also requires an informed electorate. In order for a free people to govern themselves, they must be adequately informed and able to participate in public debate, elections, and political activity. The Bill of Rights therefore guaranteed freedom of the press to ensure that the press would be free from state domination and so that it could criticize the government and promote vigorous debate on issues of public concern.[3]

Consequently, the press was to provide a check against excessive power. A free press is vital to democratic society, and proponents of democracy often claim that freedom of the press is one of the features that defines the superiority of democratic societies over competing social systems. The concept of a free press in the United States was also extended to the broadcast media, which were assigned a whole series of responsibilities necessary to the furtherance of democracy in the Federal Communications Act of 1934 and subsequent legislation and court decisions (Kellner 1990). Accordingly, the democratic functions of the press and then the broadcast media are to provide information, ideas, and debate concerning issues of public significance in order to promote a democratic public sphere. It is my view that because democracy requires a separation of power, checks and balances, and an informed electorate, democracy in the United States is now in profound crisis and its very survival is threatened.[4]

No doubt many articles and books will be written analyzing in depth the reasons and ways in which the United States orchestrated and pursued the Gulf war. There will be scholarly studies that will reveal the background and hidden history of the precrisis machinations between the United States, Kuwait, and Iraq, as well as studies of the crisis in the Gulf and of the Gulf war itself.[5] Initially, however, most of the books published on the topic merely reproduced the Bush administration's propaganda line.[6] My book, by contrast, analyzes the role of the mainstream media, especially television, in transmitting, promoting, and legitimizing U.S. Gulf war policy and actions. Accordingly, I shall provide an analysis and critique of how the media represented the crisis in the Gulf and then the Gulf war. The version of the war presented on television and the corporate media will be systematically compared with alternative media sources in order to reveal the distortions, disinformation, and outright lies presented in the mainstream media, especially television.[7]

Alternative media sources utilized include the *Nation, In These Times,* the *Village Voice,* the *Progressive, Z Magazine,* the *New Yorker,* the *National Catholic Reporter,* and other investigative journals. I have also drawn on the British, Canadian, Irish, French, German, and other countries' media sources in order to deploy a wide range of positions against the version of the Gulf war presented by the mainstream media in the United States. Yet during and especially after the war there was also critical coverage in the U.S. mainstream media. The Gulf war was controversial, and some critical discourse was present in the mainstream—particularly after the war, when more complex perceptions of the event began to emerge. Although the mainstream media were overwhelmingly supportive of the Bush administration war policy during the war, occasional critical voices and information appeared that can be used to put in question the official version of the war by the U.S. government and military.

In addition, I systematically monitored various computer data bases for alternative information, including the "bulletin boards," or "conferences," in the PeaceNet information service. PeaceNet has more than 650 conferences where members enter data from various sources and from different parts of the world. The Persian Gulf conferences were an especially rich source of information, though, like any information source, they had to be utilized selectively and critically.[8] I also extensively used various computer data bases such as Dialog and Lexis/Nexis. The latter provides transcripts of ABC News programming and the Public Broadcasting System's (PBS) "The MacNeil/Lehrer News Hour." Thus computer data bases have proven to be a useful source for access to both print material and to transcripts of television broadcasting.

Above all, however, I have critically interrogated the version of the Gulf war presented on U.S. television. Previously, written texts were the crucial sources of historical knowledge, but I would suggest that television now provides indispensable sources for critical historical research. In a sense, television now writes the first draft of history that was previously the province of the press. It is widely acknowledged that television is now a full news cycle ahead of the press, and this was certainly evident during the Persian Gulf TV war. As soon as the television networks received information from the wire services, their correspondents, or other sources, they immediately broadcast the information—or misinformation, as was often the case.

Most people related to the war through TV images and discourse, receiving their concept of the Persian Gulf region and the war from the mainstream media, especially television. Because few people in the audience had direct knowledge of the region and its conflicts, television was of key importance in producing the public's views of the war, just as it is of fundamental importance in producing an individual's view of the world. But above all the Gulf war was a TV war in that it was largely through television that people lived through the drama of the war and received their images and beliefs about it. For the most part, much of what appeared in the newspapers reproduced more or less what had been reported the previous day on television. Thus TV by and large maintained the initiative in reporting the war and in directly transmitting primary news through military briefings, press conferences, reports from the front, and direct transmission of TV perspectives on the events of the war as they were happening.

Yet some newspapers provided context and views frequently ignored in television and engaged in some investigative reporting that put in question official views.[9] The TV networks, by contrast, tended merely to reproduce what they were told or shown by the U.S. government and military. In addition, newspapers presented more critical opinion pieces, letters to the editor, cartoons, and other material critical of the official version of the war.

Many academic scholars and antiwar activists have questioned whether one can learn anything significant from television, arguing that it is intrinsically superficial and unreliable as a source of historical evidence. In some ways, this charge is true, and I shall be sharply critical of the television version of the war in this book. But in another sense, television provides a new source of direct, immediate, and important visual evidence of how the war was played out in military press briefings and live reports from Saudi Arabia, Iraq, Israel, and other parts of the world affected by the war. Many speeches and press conferences by political and military leaders, pool footage from the front, and TV interviews with participants also provide primary documentary evidence. Some TV material was transcribed into print sources, but the TV version of the war contains much material that never found its way into print. Video recorders make it possible to tape TV coverage of political events and to cite it in scholarly works. TV archives contain videocassettes of much TV news, and texts of TV news often are available from the networks, transcription services, or computer data bases.

Thus scholars are now forced to view television as an important source of historical knowledge. Yet TV is admittedly superficial and in its lust for instant information is often a source of disinformation, easily manipulated by officials with specific agendas to promote. The challenge to critical media analysis is to decode the manifest political pronouncements and media discourses to attempt to analyze the political content behind the masks of disinformation and propaganda. This requires analysis of: (1) the version of the Gulf war presented on television and the mainstream media contrasted with more reliable accounts; (2) the political maneuvers and struggles behind the scene; (3) the disinformation and lies concerning official policies and the events of the crisis and war; and (4) the effects of the war, some of which were visible in the mainstream media and some of which were hidden.

In this book, I concentrate on how the mainstream media in the United States presented the Gulf war, though I am also interested in "what really happened" and thus draw on a variety of sources to put in question the mainstream account of the war. Accordingly, I analyze some of the political, economic, and military interests and agendas at play in the Gulf crisis and war and attempt to discern the political decisions and interests behind the various official pronouncements, briefings, leaks, disinformation, and events. I also draw on a wide range of alternative media sources. One cannot be certain that alternative sources and views are always correct, but direct contradictions between the official U.S. version and other versions at least raise some questions for thought, discussion, and further inquiry. In any case, one should always distinguish between the manifest media content and the political interests and agendas behind it. The media are often used to advance specific policy positions and agendas; through decoding media texts, critical analysis attempts to discern which interests and agendas are at play in specific official pronouncements, leaks, policies, or actions. Sometimes the media serve as a smokescreen or cover to divert attention from what is really happening or what actual interests and policies are in play. On other occasions, the media attempt to mobilize consent to certain policies through rhetoric and argumentation. In an era of media management of political discourse and imagery, the ruling political forces have strategies for manipulating the media and in an era of instant information, the media, especially television when it is in the crisis mode, tend to transmit directly what their sources tell them, without much skepticism or analysis.

Critical analysis of the television version of the war also is important because people's images of contemporary politics and history are shaped by television—and particularly during the Gulf war, with the whole world watching and following the events of the day, television directly constituted the viewers' conception of the war. Because television coverage played a key role in producing the public image of the war and, arguably, mobilizing support for Bush administration policies, analysis of how television presented the war is an important part of historical analysis of the Gulf war that was primarily a media propaganda war. In this work I analyze a series of propaganda campaigns orchestrated by the state and the military and the ways that these campaigns used television to promote popular support for the war. By "propaganda" I mean discourse that is aimed at mobilizing public opinion to support specific policies.[10] As Harold Lasswell put it:

[P]ropaganda is one of the most powerful instrumentalities in the modern world. It has arisen to its present eminence in response to a complex of changed circumstances which have altered the nature of society. Small, primitive tribes can weld their heterogeneous members into a fighting whole by the beat of the tom-tom and the tempestuous rhythm of the dance. It is in orgies of physical exuberance that young men are brought to the boiling of war, and that old and young, men and women, are caught in the suction of tribal purpose.

In the Great Society it is no longer possible to fuse the waywardness of individuals in the furnace of the war dance; a new and subtler instrument must weld thousands and even millions of human beings into one amalgamated mass of hate and will and hope. A new flame must burn out the canker of dissent and temper the steel of bellicose enthusiasm. The name of this new hammer and anvil of social solidarity is propaganda. Talk must take the place of drill; print must supplant the dance. War dances live in literature and at the fringes of the modern earth; war propaganda breaches and fumes in the capitals and provinces of the world. (1971, pp. 220–221)

We shall see that during the Gulf war it was the tribal drum of television that turned the population into often frenzied supporters of the U.S. military intervention in the Middle East. "Propaganda," as I am using the term, is thus a particular mode of persuasive discourse that mobilizes ideas, images, arguments, rhetoric, and sometimes disinformation and lies to induce people to agree with specific policies and actions. In particular, propaganda attempts to overcome divisions of opinion and to persuade people that policies they might have opposed, such as war, are right, good, and just. Propaganda produces enemies, sanctifies and hallows one's own leaders and policies, and produces a simple-minded dichotomous vision that is one-sided, limited, and distorted.

In the following chapters, I am concerned to uncover *how* television presented the war by analyzing the dominant images, frames, and messages transmitted and the ways in which the TV audience bought into the Bush administration/mainstream media version of the war. My study combines critical media analysis with cultural criticism of the forms and conventions through which the text of the Gulf war was produced and presented to the public. I thus draw on the resources of critical social theory, cultural studies, and media criticism to debunk the version of the Gulf war presented on television and to situate the Gulf war within the broader context of U.S. society and culture.

Acknowledgments

Beginning in August 1990, I videotaped and analyzed the television and print media coverage of the Iraqi invasion of Kuwait, the U.S. military intervention in the region, and the ensuing crisis in the Gulf. I had hundreds of hours of videotape of the TV coverage of the crisis and a large manuscript analyzing the mainstream coverage by the time that the war actually began. During the war I videotaped and analyzed at least sixteen hours of television a day. Since then I have reviewed my own tapes of the crisis and war as well as tapes received from friends and colleagues. I have also systematically studied mainstream print coverage of the war, including the *New York Times, Washington Post, Wall Street Journal, Time, Newsweek, Business Week, U.S. News and World Report,* and many other U.S. and foreign newspapers and journals. As mentioned earlier, I have drawn extensively on computer data bases and am indebted to the University of Texas for grants covering data base and photocopying expenses. Finally, I have engaged in many teach-ins, lectures, conferences, and debates on the Gulf war and discussed the issue with friends and colleagues from many disciplines and perspectives.

For providing research assistance for this book I am grateful to a large number of students and colleagues who contributed material and to a group of students who carefully checked my analysis of the television presentation of the war against my videotapes. For Canadian media sources I am grateful to Valerie Scatamburlo and Jim Winter; for Irish sources, my thanks to Ronan Lynch; for British sources, I am indebted to PeaceNet, Les Levidow, and Taisto Hunanan; and for U.S. media sources I am especially grateful to David Armstrong, Michael Burton, and Beth Macom for sharing their extensive files and tape collections. Thanks to the University Research Institute at the University of Texas for a grant that enabled me to search various data bases for material. Thanks to Brian Koenigsdorf for help in getting me set-up with PeaceNet; to Sarina Satya for helping me with Dialog searches; to Paul Rascoe for setting me up with Lexis/Nexis; and to Keith Hay-Roe for general computer guidance and help with frequent computer quandaries and emergencies. For critical comments on the manuscript that helped with the revision, I would like to thank Robert Antonio, David Armstrong, Oded Balaban, Steven Best, Stephen Bronner, Noam Chomsky, Harry Cleaver, Michael Emery, Scott Henson, Richard Keeble, John Lawrence, Les Levidow, Tom Philpott, Ellen Sharp, and Steve Reece. For superlative copyediting and editorial suggestions that were extremely useful in revising the manuscript I am indebted to Jeanne Remington and Michelle Asakawa.

To keep alive the tradition of critical thinking I dedicate this book to the group of thinkers associated with the Frankfurt School who strived to preserve the traditions of critical social theory and cultural critique during similarly dark periods of contemporary history: Max Horkheimer, Herbert Marcuse, T. W. Adorno, Walter Benjamin, Erich Fromm, Leo Lowenthal, Jürgen Habermas, and others associated with the tradition.[11]

Notes

1. The Deaver quote is cited in *The Fund for Free Expression,* February 27, 1991, p. 1, and the Browne quote is cited in the *Village Voice,* February 5, 1991. In this book, I shall provide references in the bibliography for the sources that I draw on more than once, or that were important in shaping my interpretations. Sources that merely reference quotes or facts will be given in the text or notes.

2. Greenpeace estimated in a press release that as of December 1991, the war and its aftermath had caused between 177,500 and 243,000 Iraqi deaths, including third-country nationals resident in Iraq who may have also been killed. Casualty figures are highly controversial, however, and I shall discuss the various estimates in section 10.2. For some accounts of the devastation wrought by the

Gulf war, see the articles by Hooglund and Hiltermann in *Middle East Report,* July/August 1991; Cainkar in Bennis and Moushabeck 1991; Middle East Watch 1991b; and Clark et al. 1992.

3. I should note that this model of democracy is a normative one that can be used as a standard against which one can measure the extent to which social orders are or are not democratic. Although I am producing this model of democracy from the constitutional order proposed in the French and American revolutions, to a large extent popular sovereignty was rarely realized in the United States (see Kellner 1990, pp. 173–174). In this book I shall argue that the growing concentration of corporate power whereby transnational corporations control the state, media, and other institutions of society threatens the separation and balance of powers necessary to a democratic social order, thus undermining democracy at the expense of capitalist hegemony. I am engaging in the strategy of "immanent critique" where I take the existing norms and constitutional framework as standards to criticize deviations from these norms and framework; on the development of immanent critique by the Frankfurt school, see Kellner 1984 and 1989.

4. I am using the term "crisis" here in the medical sense in which "it refers to the phase of an illness in which it is decided whether or not the organism's self-healing powers are sufficient for recovery" (Habermas 1975, p. 1). A crisis is a disruption of a state of affairs that threatens to produce a decisive and catastrophic change in the existing institutional order. A "crisis of capitalism" in Karl Marx's theory describes a situation in which the survival of capitalism is threatened, and a "crisis of democracy" describes a state of affairs in which the survival of democracy is in jeopardy.

5. Not enough is known of the complex relations between Iraq, Kuwait, and the United States to write a definitive analysis of the prehistory of the war. Valuable material, however, is found in Salinger and Laurent 1991, Emery 1991, the articles by Murray Waas in the *Village Voice,* Frank 1991, and Yousif in Bresheeth and Yuval-Davis 1991.

6. Pro–Bush administration books on the Gulf war began appearing immediately. Friedman (1991) focuses primarily on the military aspects of the Gulf war and is full of disinformation. For instance, he claimed that Iraq was offered "a series of last-minute, face-saving offers" that it "rejected" (p. 147), a claim for which there is no evidence whatsoever. He accepts at face value the U.S. military claims about the Iraqi baby-milk factory being a chemical warfare factory and the civilian shelter being a bunker, lies that I shall expose in the course of this book. Friedman claimed that much of the damage visible in Iraq was due to "Iraq's own spent antiaircraft projectiles falling back to earth" (p. 143), another piece of disinformation. Friedman asserted: "The dismal performance of the Iraqi national air-defense system soon led Saddam to retire its chief by killing him" (p. 162); this piece of disinformation was refuted a short while later by the appearance of the chief in Baghdad. Friedman also privileged the theory that Iraqi planes that went to Iran were defectors (pp. 162ff.), a theory that was also discredited later. The book, published by the Naval Institute Press, is full of propaganda for the indispensability of naval forces in the Gulf war and future

operations. Thus the author assumed the mode of disinformation, lies, and propaganda dominant during the war itself as well as evoking constant threats of future Third World military interventions.

Cable News Network (CNN) military consultant James Blackwell (1991) churned out a book that is extremely superficial, poorly written, and solely advances the military point of view; his CNN colleague retired General Perry Smith (1991) followed with a book that brags about how he fought to advance the pro-Pentagon view of the war in the CNN Atlanta "war room." Producer Robert Weiner (1992) published his diaries which provide an insightful account of how CNN operated in Iraq. A predominantly military history was published by NBC military consultant James Dunnigan and coauthor Austin Bay (1991). This book is a useful source of official military information and it also deflates some of the official myths of the Gulf war, though it perpetuates other myths and disinformation.

By 1991 books that focused on the political background and unfolding of the war began to appear. Bulloch and Morris (1991) provide background on Saddam Hussein, the Baath state, and the events leading up to the war, drawing on their journalism experience and sources. British Broadcasting Company (BBC) journalist John Simpson (1991) produced an account of his own experiences in the region and provides a generally reliable account of the crisis and war. Sciolino (1991) is useful on background to the crisis and war but accepts the Bush administration and Pentagon line on Iraq and the Gulf war. Although Sciolino has often done excellent critical reporting for the *New York Times,* her chapter on "The Drift to War" totally blames the Gulf war on Saddam Hussein, failing to even consider the evidence that I shall set forth in 1.2 that the Bush administration systematically blocked diplomatic initiatives. Sciolino's chapter on "The Degradation of Iraq" blames the Iraqis' suffering solely on the policies of Saddam Hussein, ignoring the killing of its people and destruction of the country by Bush's decision to wage all-out war against Iraq, utilizing the most massive destructive military power ever assembled. And she fails to criticize the longtime U.S. support for Saddam Hussein or the role of the media in the crisis in the Gulf and the Gulf war. Yant (1991) deploys mainstream press sources to put into question the Bush administration/Pentagon version of the war, which he describes as Desert Mirage. Fialka (1992) sarcastically describes the press as "desert warriors" and provides an insider glimpse of the manipulation of the media by the U.S. military in Saudi Arabia with some appropriately nasty swipes at deserving members of the U.S. military and their generally compliant press corps. Graubard (1992) and Smith (1992) provide critical perspectives on George Bush's manipulation of the war to serve his own narrow political purposes. *U.S. News and World Report* published a book (1992) that provides primarily a military and political history of the war from the standpoint of the Bush administration and Pentagon, though there is some criticism of the Bush administration and media.

Many books more critical of the role of U.S. policy and the role of the media in the Gulf war are beginning to appear as I conclude my study, including MacArthur 1992; Mowlana, Gerbner, and Schiller 1992; Miller 1992; and Taylor 1992.

Valuable print sources also include a series of readers that mobilize background material and criticism of U.S. policy supplemented with reports by various organizations that have undertaken to document the effects of the Gulf war in the Middle East. The readers include Bresheeth and Yuval-Davis (1991), Brittain (1991), Bruck (1991), Ridgeway (1991), Briemberg (1992), and Peters (1992). Reports on the war include Arkin, Durrant, and Cherni (1991), Middle East Watch (1991a and 1991b), and Clark et al. (1992). Fox (1991) presents critical perspectives on the Gulf war from a progressive Catholic standpoint.

7. The "mainstream media" are legitimately defined as "corporate media," first, because they are owned by big corporations like The Radio Corporation of America (RCA) and General Electric (GE), which control the National Broadcasting Company (NBC); Capital Communications, which owns the American Broadcasting System (ABC); and the Tisch Financial Group, which controls the Columbia Broadcasting System (CBS). Second, the mainstream media express the corporate point of view and advance the agendas of the corporations that own them. More and more, the mainstream media are run like corporations whose primary responsibility is to maximize profit, and thus they function like other major corporations. The mainstream media include the major television networks, national news magazines like *Time* and *Newsweek,* and national newspapers like the *New York Times* and the *Wall Street Journal.* In this book, I shall thus use the terms "corporate media" and "mainstream media" interchangeably and contrast them with "alternative media" that undertake investigative reporting and follow journalistic ethics of providing factual information from a variety of sources and perspectives; see the analysis in Kellner 1990, pp. 225ff.

8. All PeaceNet sources will be referenced according to the conference cited (such as "mideast.gulf," or "mideast.forum) and the date of its posting. Most PeaceNet sources can be accessed through the archive of the conference, using the date as a reference.

9. In the United States, the reporting of Knut Royce, Susan Sachs, and Patrick Sloyan of *Newsday* was distinguished, and some critical coverage appeared in other mainstream newspapers like the *New York Times, Boston Globe,* and *Washington Post.* In Britain, Robert Fisk and Patrick Cockburn did some excellent reporting, putting in question the lies and disinformation of the U.S.-led coalition. For a good selection of British press coverage, see MacArthur 1991.

10. I am using the term "propaganda" in the sense of Lasswell (1971), who uses it to describe the techniques used to manufacture consent to specific policies like war, and not in the more general sense of Ellul (1965), who uses it to describe the general climate of thought and public opinion in technological societies. For an overview of the literature on propaganda see Jowett and O'Donnell 1992.

11. On critical theory, see Kellner 1984, 1989a, and 1990.

CHAPTER ONE

———————◆———————

The Road to War

ON THE WEEKEND OF July 21, 1990, Iraq moved 30,000 troops, tanks, and artillery to its border with Kuwait. Iraq was angry that Kuwait had been selling its oil below the agreed-upon OPEC figure, thus driving down the price of oil and costing Iraq many billions of dollars. In addition, Kuwait had refused to negotiate a long-standing border dispute with Iraq and had declined to cancel debts incurred by Iraq during the Iran-Iraq war of 1980–1988. In that war, Iraq claimed to be fighting for Arab interests against the threats of Iranian Islamic fundamentalism.

During the Iran-Iraq war, the United States entered into a strategic relationship with Iraq, which was perceived as a secular bulwark against the spread of radical Islamic fundamentalist revolution.[1] The United States presented Iraq with military equipment and intelligence, agricultural credits, and "dual use" technology that could be used for building highly destructive weapons systems.[2] With the sudden end of the Iran-Iraq war in August 1988, Iraq continued buying massive amounts of arms from the West and Iraqi President Saddam Hussein persisted in building up his military machine with Western help. Despite the fact that Iraq brutally suppressed the Kurds who lived in northern Iraq and that his human rights record was atrocious, Hussein continued to receive aid and favored treatment from the Bush administration. The State Department talked of the importance of the U.S. relationship with Iraq and U.S. senators visited Iraq for Saddam Hussein's birthday in 1990, advising him that his image problem was merely a product of the Western media that could be corrected with a better public-relations (PR) policy.[3]

On July 25, the U.S. ambassador to Iraq, April Glaspie, met with Saddam Hussein and indicated sympathy for his desire to raise oil prices to rebuild his country after the war with Iran. Glaspie told him that the United States had "no opinion" on the border dispute and other disputes with Kuwait.[4] On the same day, the U.S. State Department stopped the Voice of America from broadcasting an editorial stating that the United

States was "strongly committed to supporting its friends in the Gulf" (*Newsweek,* October 1, 1990, pp. 24–25). On July 31, in a talk on Capitol Hill, John Kelly, the assistant secretary of state for Middle Eastern affairs, stated that the United States had no formal commitment to a defense of Kuwait (in Ridgeway 1991, pp. 57–58). He also stated that the invasion of Kuwait by Iraq was "a hypothetical," which "I can't get into" (Ridgeway 1991, pp. 57–58). Finally, Kelly stated that events since February had "raised new questions about Iraqi intentions in the region," but that "sanctions would decrease the [U.S.] government's ability to act as a restraining influence" (*Economist,* Sept. 29, 1990, pp. 19–21). The scene was set for Iraq's invasion of Kuwait.

The question arises as to whether the United States purposively led Iraq to believe that there was no major U.S. objection to invading Kuwait or whether the Bush administration was simply incompetent. On the conspiracy account (suggested by Agee 1990, Becker in Clark et al. 1992, Emery 1991, Frank 1991, and Yousif in Bresheeth and Yuval-Duvis 1991), the United States encouraged Kuwait to lower its oil prices and to refuse to settle its disputes with Iraq in order to provoke Iraq into military action that would legitimate U.S. military intervention in the Gulf and even the destruction of Iraq. At the same time, in this account, the United States sent signals to Iraq that it would not object to an Iraqi invasion of Kuwait and some believed that this was a trap that would enable the U.S. to mobilize a coalition against Iraq. Such an action against Iraq would enable the United States to become a permanent military presence in the Gulf and to assert itself as the number one military superpower. A triumph would help protect the military from budgetary cutbacks and fuel another cycle of arms spending to pick up the failing economy. A successful Gulf intervention and war would also promote the interests of George Bush, whom most interpreters of the complex events leading up to the war depict as the chief promoter of a military option to the crisis.[5]

The conspiracy theory explains why Kuwait would stand up to an extremely belligerent and dangerous Iraq and why Iraq would risk invading Kuwait. For without a prior U.S. pledge of support it is implausible that Kuwait would provoke Iraq and refuse to negotiate what were arguably reasonable issues. The theory that the United States was enticing Iraq to invade Kuwait also helps explain the seeming appeasement of Iraq by the Bush administration, but other accounts are also plausible. Waas (1991) described U.S. diplomacy leading up to the Iraqi invasion of Kuwait as a result of the "Bush administration's miscalculations" and "sheer incompetence," which he describes as "the worst diplomatic failure by any modern president" (p. 60). Salinger and Laurent (1991, pp. 56–79) do not explicitly advocate the conspiracy theory, though they believe that, inadvertently or not, Glaspie and Kelly gave a "green light" to Saddam Hussein to invade Kuwait. Commenting on Kelly's July 31, 1990, testimony to Congress, where he confirmed that the U.S. had "no treaty, no commitment which would oblige us to use American forces" to drive Iraq out of Kuwait were a hypothetical invasion to take place, Salinger and Laurent claimed:

> John Kelly's statements were broadcast on the World Service of the BBC [British Broadcasting Corporation] and were heard in Baghdad. At a crucial hour, when war and peace hung in the balance, Kelly had sent Saddam Hussein a signal that could be read as a pledge that the United States would not intervene.
> In the recent history of American diplomacy there had been only one other example of such a serious miscalculation, and that was Secretary of State Dean Acheson's statement to Congress in 1950 that "South Korea was not part of the United States' zone of defense." Soon afterwards North Korea had invaded the South. (1991, p. 69)

Because the Bush administration has a record of both incompetence and Machiavellian machinations, it is not possible at this point to know for sure why the United States failed to more vigorously warn Iraq against invading Kuwait, why Kuwait refused to settle its disputes with Iraq, or why Iraq finally decided to invade its neighbor. Mediating the conspiracy theory and incompetency interpretation, Edward Herman argued:

> This failure to try to constrain Hussein by diplomatic means, and de facto invitation to invade, reflects either staggering incompetence or a remarkably sophisticated conspiracy to entrap him. The failure of the U.S. mass media to consider this set of facts and issues as worthy of front page reporting and intense debate is prime evidence of their irresponsibility to the public and service to the state. My own view is that the Bush gang invited Hussein into Kuwait through sheer incompetence, but were not only deeply annoyed, they also saw that he could usefully be set up as a naked aggressor who must be taught a lesson. . . . The banking, oil, pro-Israel, and military-industrial complex constituencies could be mobilized to support this new thrust, but in my view this is a presidential war *par excellence* with the causes to be found in the parochial and self-serving calculations of Bush and his security state coterie. (*Z Magazine,* March 1991, p. 16)

Herman's argument is persuasive though it may underestimate the Machiavellian proclivities of Bush and his circle, who might well have engineered the crisis and the war. In any case, the events leading up to the invasion are highly suspicious and require further investigation and scrutiny. Furthermore, it is worth noting that whichever interpretation of the causes of the Gulf crisis one accepts, the Bush administration was largely responsible for both Iraq's invasion of Kuwait and the war, as it could easily have warned Iraq that the United States would not tolerate an invasion of Kuwait and could have urged Kuwait to satisfactorily negotiate its problems with Iraq, thus avoiding the Gulf crisis and war. For weeks there were clear signals that Iraq was planning an invasion of Kuwait and despite the Central Intelligence Agency (CIA) and military intelligence indicating that an invasion was imminent, the United States continued to appease Iraq.

For instance, on August 1, 1990, the day after Kelly's testimony, there were reports that Iraq had amassed 100,000 troops on the Kuwaiti border. Both the CIA and Defense Intelligence Agency (DIA) claimed that Iraq was ready to invade Kuwait, but still the Bush administration took no action.[6] Representatives of Iraq and Kuwait met on August 1 at the Saudi resort town of Jidda to negotiate their problems and the Saudis and others seemed to believe that these negotiations would resolve the Kuwaiti/Iraqi disputes. They did not, and *Time* magazine claimed that the failure of the negotiations was due to "the Iraqis, who demanded Kuwait's total capitulation on every count" and who "were determined to see the negotiations break down" (Aug. 13, 1991, p. 19).[7] Other observers, however, blamed the breakdown on the Kuwaitis: "[T]he reportedly contemptuous and dismissive attitude of the Kuwaiti delegation during the first round of meetings prompted the Iraqi team to walk out before a second session could be convened. Iraqi forces crossed the border into Kuwait early the next morning" (Fred Dawson, *Middle East Report,* Jan.-Feb. 1991, p. 35).[8]

During the night of August 2, Iraqi tanks and troops rumbled unchallenged down the 37 mile superhighway from Iraq to Kuwait City and quickly seized control. Key elements of Kuwait's small army were on vacation and many Kuwaiti troops and the royal family fled immediately. After sporadic fighting, the Iraqis gained control of the whole city, including government buildings, military posts, and radio and television facilities. Suddenly the Iraqi invasion of Kuwait became the number one story on the news agenda and remained so for many months.

Cockburn and Cohen speculate that the United States did not send a stronger warning to Iraq because of its strategic relationship with Iraq, but that Saddam Hussein went too far in seizing all of Kuwait (1992, p. 17):

Unless one espouses the conspiracy theory that the United States wanted Iraq to invade Kuwait as an excuse to crush Saddam Hussein, then surely the simplest explanation is that the Bush administration was trying to shove Kuwait into a more tractable posture with regard to the price of oil and possibly to the leasing of the two islands so desired by Iraq for the construction of a deep harbor in the Gulf. Iraq, after all, was a U.S. ally and already a serious trading partner. Nor would the Administration, strongly orientated to the oil lobby, have been at all averse to seeing a hike in prices, which had drifted in real terms below their 1973 level. By seizing the whole of Kuwait, Saddam Hussein overplayed the hand allowed by the United States.

In a *New York Times* interview (September 12, 1990, p. 19), the U.S. Ambassador to Iraq, April Glaspie, hinted that the United States was surprised that Iraq had seized the entirety of Kuwait, as if they expected Iraq to merely take the off-shore islands and disputed oil field. The question arises, however, why Saddam Hussein believed he could get away with invading Kuwait. The mainstream media never discussed in any detail the complex relations between Iraq, its Arab neighbors, and the West that apparently led Iraq to conclude that it could seize and keep Kuwait, or at least bargain its way out in a manner that would benefit Iraq.

In any case, Saddam Hussein grossly miscalculated the world response to his invasion of Kuwait. During the past decade, the dominant Western powers had beaten a path to his door to give him military information and support during the Iran/Iraq war, to sell him the latest military technology, to enter into economic arrangements with Iraq, and, of course, to buy Iraq's oil. In the light of this attention and support, it is not surprising that Hussein would think that his Western friends would let him get away with his robbery of Kuwait (which might, in the last analysis, merely have been a way to get Kuwaiti attention in order to extort financial and territorial concessions from the greedy Kuwaitis, who simply refused to negotiate what were serious problems). But Iraq miscalculated the effects of the collapse of the Soviet Union and the void that would be filled by the United States. Iraq failed to perceive that the United States would neither allow any threat to its two key interests in the Middle East, Saudi Arabia and Israel, nor would it allow an independent country like Iraq to wield political influence and help control oil prices in the region. The Iraqis also failed to see that George Bush and the U.S. military-industrial establishment desperately needed a war to save Bush's failing presidency and to preserve the military budget and U.S. defense industries at the end of the cold war (see 1.3).

The Iraqi seizure of Kuwait was of immediate interest to the western capitalist societies because Iraq and Kuwait together would control approximately 20 percent of the world's known oil reserves. With the potential wealth generated from future oil sales and control over oil prices, Saddam Hussein could play a major role on the world's political and economic stage. Consequently, Iraq's invasion of Kuwait produced a crisis for the world capitalist system, for U.S. and European economic interests, and for the stability of the Middle East. Iraq was not able to get control of Kuwaiti investments because much of their money had been transferred out of the country. Yet, rather than encouraging a diplomatic solution to the crisis that would return Kuwait's sovereignty and secure the region, George Bush responded with a military intervention, which inexorably led to the Gulf war itself.

1.1 Big Lies, Compliant Media, and Yellow Journalism

Interest in the crisis increased when the U.S. claimed that Iraq might also invade Saudi Arabia, which was said to control 25 percent of the world's known oil reserves and an investment portfolio even larger than Kuwait's.[9] George Bush, who had initially attacked the invasion as "naked aggression," heated up his rhetoric and declared on August 5 that the invasion "would not stand." Two days later, he sent thousands of troops to Saudi Arabia. The Bush administration had thus set the stage for the Gulf war by failing to warn Iraq of the consequences of invading Kuwait and then by quickly sending troops to Saudi Arabia while, as I shall argue in the next section, undercutting diplomatic efforts to resolve the crisis.

Although the United States constantly accused Iraq and Saddam Hussein of lying and compared the Iraqi leader to Hitler, the Bush administration itself systematically disseminated Big Lies to promote its war policy. Suspicious claims by the administration began with reports that the Iraqis had positioned an offensive force on the Saudi Arabian border, poised to invade that country. On August 3, for instance, Forrest Sawyer reported on ABC's *Nightline* that: "tens of thousands of Iraqi troops are reportedly massed along the Saudi Arabian border, and there is still fear that Saddam Hussein will carry his blitzkrieg across Saudi territory. It would not be much of a fight. Iraq's million-man battle-seasoned army against the nearly 66,000 Saudi troops, 5,500 Iraqi tanks, 10 times as many as Saudi Arabia."

There is no compelling evidence that Iraq did have large numbers of troops on the Saudi border and the same day ABC news reported the Iraqi ambassador's claim that Iraq had no intention whatsoever of invading Saudi Arabia and that it was "just a big lie" that there were Iraqi troops preparing to invade Saudi Arabia. Moreover, as I shall show, there are indications that from the beginning the Pentagon and Bush administration consistently exaggerated the Iraqi threat to Saudi Arabia, or even manufactured it, to justify their intervention. There is also reason to believe that the Bush administration deliberately overestimated the size and competency of the Iraqi army in Kuwait and that the mainstream media uncritically reproduced the Administration's (dubious) figures repeatedly. On August 4, the *New York Times* headline read: "Iraqis Mass on Saudi Frontier" and the story indicated that: "Pentagon officials said that more than 60,000 Iraqi troops were massing in the southern part of Kuwait, not far from a major oilfield in Saudi Arabia. A State Department spokesman, Richard A. Boucher, said Iraqi troops were within five to ten miles of the frontier. The British foreign secretary, Douglas Hurd, said that Iraqi troops were massing on the border. . . . There were conflicting reports about the size of the Iraqi military force in Kuwait, but one Pentagon official estimated late today that it was approaching 100,000 troops, or more than Iraq needs to pacify and occupy Kuwait" (p. A4).

The television networks dutifully repeated these figures day after day without a modicum of skepticism. There is no reason, however, why one should have accepted these figures or the claim that the Iraqis were gathering on the Saudi Arabia border as if to invade. On the contrary, compelling evidence suggested that U.S. claims concerning the imminent Iraqi threat to Saudi Arabia were pure disinformation designed to legitimate a U.S. military intervention in the Gulf. In particular, the claim that Iraqis were ready to invade Saudi Arabia served to scare the Saudis into allowing a major U.S. troop deployment on their soil and to convince the U.S. and world public that serious interests (i.e., the flow of oil) were being threatened. The Iraqis claimed repeatedly that they had no designs on Saudi Arabia, no intention of invading, and because there were no independent sources of information in Kuwait, it was impossible to verify if the United States was or was not telling the truth concerning the Iraqi troop formations on the Saudi border that were allegedly poised for invasion.

On August 5, the Pentagon continued to claim that Iraq was threatening Saudi Arabia. The *New York Times* stated: "Iraqi troops were reported to have gone into what is called the Neutral Zone, an area from which Kuwait and Saudi Arabia share oil earnings. Baghdad denied those reports as 'false news' " (p. A1). In addition, the *Times* disclosed:

> A Pentagon official said that any quick Iraqi attack on Saudi Arabia would have to be without the logistical support usual for a major operation.
> "They have not brought a lot down to Kuwait for a large-scale drive into Saudi Arabia," said an official.
> "A long-term drive would require more of a logistical tail—more water, gas, fuel, ammunition, spare parts and all of that," the official said. (p. A10)

Despite this disclaimer, buried in a story on page 10, the Bush administration and mainstream media were sending out signals that an Iraqi invasion of Saudi Arabia was an imminent and dangerous threat.[10]

On August 6, the message of the Bush administration was that the Arab countries were "not serious enough" concerning the Iraqi threat and were prepared to capitulate to Iraqi demands and accept its takeover of Kuwait. The *New York Times* commented:

> Administration officials are increasingly concerned about the unwillingness of Saudi Arabia and the other leading Arab countries to stand up against Mr. Hussein. Officials say they detect a strong tendency in the Arab world to try to appease Baghdad by letting it swallow Kuwait in hopes that this will spare Iraq's neighbors from a similar fate. Privately, American officials are expressing contempt and disgust with most of the Arab leaders.
>
> "The habits of centuries die hard," said a senior Administration official about the seeming instinct of Iraq's oil-rich neighbors to try to buy Baghdad off rather then forcefully confront it." (August 6, 1991, p. A6)

Note how the sources for every sentence of this story are "Administration officials" who are obviously using the media to put out a propaganda line. Journalists are dependent on official sources to get leads, leaks, and background information that will help them in the highly competitive business of journalism. The system of news production and competition thus forces journalists to rely on official sources who reward journalists who convey the information and line that they wish promoted with further inside information, while punishing journalists who question their positions. Thus, in a crisis situation, without independent sources of information, mainstream journalists tend to rely on official sources who are able to manipulate them.

Precisely such a process of manipulation was evident in the crisis in the Gulf as the Bush administration used the mainstream media to conjure up an Iraqi threat to Saudi Arabia and to legitimate the deployment of U.S. troops in the region. The *New York Times* headline on August 6 read: "Bush, Hinting Force, Declares Gulf Impasse 'Will Not Stand'" and the subheadline pointed to a mission by Secretary of Defense Dick Cheney to Saudi Arabia to try to persuade the Saudis to let the United States use military installations in their country. There is evidence that, early on, the Bush administration decided on the use of military force to resolve the crisis and chose the road to war. Henceforth, there would be no serious talk within the administration of a negotiated settlement; instead, the administration planned step by step its relentless march to war.[11]

The media helped the Bush administration by beating the war drums and producing an atmosphere where it was all too likely that military force would be used to resolve the crisis in the Gulf. In particular, the *Washington Post* not only privileged the Bush administration line during the crucial early days of the crisis, but itself promoted a military option. On August 3, Patrick Tyler, who had previously written an article on Saddam Hussein as a "pragmatic" Arab leader (May 13, 1989, p. A13) suddenly discovered that Hussein was a "brash and brutal leader, whose tactics have terrorized his neighbors, incited the Israelis with threats of chemical retaliation and made the superpowers look like helpless giants" (p. A25). Also on August 3, George Will attacked the "Wolf of Babylon" while two *Post* Op-Ed (opinion-editorial) page writers discovered Iraq's "Nuclear Specter"; neoconservative Charles Krauthammer deplored the "festival of appeasement" and a *Post* editorial attacked the "Aggression in the Gulf" and the "dictator Saddam Hussein." A business article noted that Hussein is now "OPEC's Most Important Member," claiming that he now controlled world oil prices.[12]

The August 7 edition of the *Washington Post* aggressively promoted a military solution, while demonizing the Iraqi leader. Before Bush even announced his decision to send U.S. troops to Saudi Arabia, the *Post* was calling for a U.S. military response to Iraq's invasion. On p. A2, Mary McGrory, in a column titled "Bush and the Beast of Baghdad," urged Bush to bomb Iraq. She assured Bush that "Americans, faced with the specter of high oil prices and new hostage-grabs, are emotionally involved in getting rid of the beast" and that the "best thing Bush has going for him is the just about unanimous approval to do whatever is necessary." Note that McGrory referred to Saddam Hussein as a "beast"—perhaps the ultimate dehumanizing epithet. Not only did she demonize the Iraqi leader, but she suggested—falsely—that Bush had a mandate from the public to bomb Baghdad and to do "whatever is necessary," thus urging and legitimating ruthless military action. After producing a litany of Hussein's bestial acts, McGrory evoked the Munich analogy, recalling the appeasement of Hitler in the 1930s at the Munich conference, implicitly warning against similar treatment of the Iraqis.[13]

Note, however, the reasons, such as they are, that McGrory recommended bombing "the beast" and how she identifies Iraq with its president as if bombing Iraq were equivalent to bombing Hussein. She claimed that "Saudi Arabia is in imminent danger of being invaded by Saddam" and then asked rhetorically if bombing Baghdad will "move up his timetable on the invasion of Saudi Arabia?" McGrory assumed that Saddam Hussein *will* invade Saudi Arabia and that therefore he should be bombed to punish him for his transgressions. This absolutely irresponsible call for violent military action disregarded all of the good reasons why it was unlikely that Iraq would invade Saudi Arabia. Indeed, had that been the Iraqi plan, the only rational way to carry it through would have been to do so immediately, although there is not a shred of evidence that Iraq ever had this in mind.

This striking example of yellow journalism was supplemented in the *Washington Post*'s August 7 edition by both an opinion piece and a front-page article which suggest that the *Post* was being used in a disinformation campaign to legitimate a U.S. intervention in Saudi Arabia and was engaging in "yellow journalism" to promote a military solution.[14] On that day, the *Post*'s associate editor and chief foreign correspondent Jim Hoagland kicked in with a column: "Force Hussein to Withdraw" (p. A19). As certain as McGrory of Iraq's imminent invasion of Saudi Arabia, Hoagland opened by proclaiming that "Saddam Hussein has gone to war to gain control of the oil fields of Kuwait and ultimately of Saudi Arabia. The United States must now use convincing military force against the Iraqi dictator to save the oil fields and to preserve American influence in the Middle East." According to Hoagland, Saddam Hussein "respects only force and will respond to nothing else."

The rest of the article consisted of false analysis, questionable analogies, and bellicose banality. Hoagland claimed that the "Iraqi dictator's base of support is too narrow and too shaky to withstand a sharp, telling blow." Yet some six weeks of the most vicious bombing in history were unable to dislodge Hussein whose support, or staying power, was obviously much stronger than Hoagland could imagine. Hoagland also believed that "he [Hussein] is so hated at home that his defeat, even by foreign forces, will be greeted as deliverance by his own nation and by much of the Arab world." As it turned out, both Iraq and the Arab world were deeply divided over Hussein and the sweeping generalities that Hoagland employed were totally off the mark.

Hoagland bordered on overt racism when he claimed that the Arab nations were too weak to "deliver that blow themselves" (one wonders what blow the hot-penned warrior at the *Post* had in mind). He also claimed that Ronald Reagan's decision to bomb Libya was the right model for Bush to follow. This example was revealing because Moammar Gadhafi preceded Saddam Hussein as a symbolically constructed Arab enemy upon which national hatred could be projected and thus served as an object lesson for Third World countries that refused to submit to domination by the neoimperialist superpowers.[15] Likewise, it is far from certain that the terrorist incident for which Gadhafi was "punished" (i.e., the bombing of a Berlin disco) was carried out by groups affiliated with Libya.[16] But facts have little relevance for an ideologue's brief for bombing.

In his opinion piece, Hoagland lectured George Bush on why he must take urgent and forceful action to save his presidency and, like McGrory, urged military action against Iraq. Hoagland assumed both that Iraq planned to invade Saudi Arabia and that only a military blow from George Bush could save the day. In fact, as I shall soon discuss, there were important Arab diplomatic initiatives underway, blocked by the United States, but these efforts were ignored by the war-mongering Hoagland. Letting his reactionary beliefs slip through, Hoagland interpreted Iraq's invasion of Kuwait as a challenge to "the legitimacy of all remaining monarchies in the Arabian Peninsula, where Britain established most existing boundaries and political systems in the colonial era." Hoagland thus defined the principles at stake as the legitimacy of some of the most reactionary monarchies in the world, with borders arbitrarily drawn by British colonialists who deprived Iraq of a viable seaport and robbed national groups like the Palestinians and the Kurds of their homelands.

Indeed, Hoagland's whole article manifests what Edward Said (1978) described as an "Orientalist" mentality in which white Westerners establish their superiority by vacuous generalizations about people in the Arab world. Hoagland characterized Arabs as understanding only force, too weak to respond to aggression, and incapable of defending themselves and solving their own problems. For him, the Gulf crisis is thus the locus of "a rare case where the United States would be unwise not to use force." Analyzing such intellectually bankrupt pleas for a military strike against Iraq would not be worth the time and energy except that administration officials paid close attention to Hoagland's columns. Further, his poorly written, badly argued, and banal punditry was highly acclaimed in political circles; indeed, he was awarded a Pulitzer prize "for searching and prescient columns on events leading up to the Gulf War." In addition, his and McGrory's columns are significant because they were published in the *Washington Post,* supposedly a bastion of liberal enlightenment, and read by U.S. policymakers and the mainstream media. Further, McGrory's demonization of Hussein was retooled and republished in *Newsweek* (Sept. 3, 1990), part of the Washington Post Company.

In fact, the *Washington Post* in their August 7 edition almost seemed to be prodding Bush to send troops to Saudi Arabia and to use force to resolve the crisis. The *Post*'s banner headline across the top of page 1 stated: "Saddam Says Seizure of Kuwait Is Permanent" and a lead story by Patrick Tyler[17] claimed:

> Saddam called in the ranking U.S. diplomat in Baghdad, and told him categorically that Kuwait now belongs to Iraq and there was no going back, according to Administration officials. "It's a done deal," one U.S. official said, characterizing Saddam's message.
>
> Another official said Saddam appended a specific warning that if Saudi Arabia shuts down the Iraqi crude oil pipelines that cross the Saudi desert to the Red Sea, Iraq will attack the kingdom. The warning further stated that if American forces intervene in the region, Iraq will "embarrass" the United States, the official said.

In retrospect, this story is sheer disinformation and the *Washington Post* reported once again merely what Bush administration officials told them as if it were fact, making Hussein sound as belligerent and threatening as possible. And although Iraq did in fact keep hold of Kuwait, according to other sources (Salinger and Laurent 1991 and Emery 1991), it was seeking to cut a deal to resolve the crisis, but from the beginning the Bush administration simply refused to negotiate. Other accounts of the meeting of Saddam Hussein with the U.S. *chargé d'affaires* in Baghdad, Joe Wilson, provide a quite different story. According to Karsh and Rautsi (1991):

> During the [August 6] meeting [with Joe Wilson], Hussein was far more affable than in his bellicose encounter with Ms. Glaspie a fortnight earlier. "Iraq is firmly willing to respect the United States' legitimate international interests in the Middle East," he told Mr. Wilson, "and is interested in establishing normal relations with the United States on the basis of mutual respect." Dismissing the reports on Iraqi military deployments along the Saudi border as fabrications, aimed at providing "pretexts to interfere in the region's affairs and to justify an aggression against Iraq," he reassured his interlocutor that Iraq harbored no evil intentions whatsoever against Saudi Arabia, with which it was tied in a bilateral treaty of non-aggression. (P. 220)[18]

The authors claim that such conciliatory gestures under duress are typical of Hussein and that he was making every effort possible to assure the world that he had no intention of invading Saudi Arabia:

> Even a cursory examination of Saddam's political record would reveal that his instinctive inclination, whenever faced with overwhelming opposition, was to appease rather than to confront, to try to defuse tensions, rather than to escalate. His initial response to the buildup of international pressures following the invasion of Kuwait was no exception. While threatening to turn the Gulf into "a graveyard for those who think of committing aggression," he took great care to emphasize the temporary nature of the Iraqi intervention, reiterating his pledge to withdraw the Iraqi forces "as soon as the situation settles down and the evil grip is loosened on Arab Kuwait."
>
> Moreover, within less than 36 hours of the invasion, the Iraqi public learned, through a special announcement of the RCC [Revolutionary Command Council], that their valiant armed forces had completed "their honest national and pan-Arab duties" of defending Kuwait, and were to begin withdrawing from the principality on August 5, "unless something emerges that threatens the security of Kuwait and Iraq." . . . A special emphasis in Saddam's conciliating campaign was placed on denying any possibility of an impending Iraq act of aggression against Saudi Arabia. "Some news agencies have reported fabricated news about what they called the approach of Iraqi forces toward the Saudi border," read an official Iraqi statement. "Iraq categorically denies these

fabricated reports. Causing confusion between the Kingdom of Saudi Arabia, which is a fraternal country with which we have normal cordial relations, and Kuwait's case is tendentious." This message was quickly conveyed to the heads of Arab states, Egypt and Saudi Arabia in particular, by high-ranking officials. More importantly, it was directly relayed to President Bush in an oral message from Saddam Hussein, transmitted at a meeting with the U.S. *chargé d'affaires* in Baghdad, Joseph Wilson. (Karsh and Rautsi 1991, pp. 219–220).

The transcript of the conversation on August 6 between Wilson and Hussein (published in Salinger and Laurent 1991, pp. 137–147 and Sciolino 1991, pp. 284–293) supports the Iraqi version and suggests that the *Washington Post* version was fabricated by the Bush administration and dutifully transmitted by the *Post*. The key issues concern: (1) whether Iraq was really planning to invade Saudi Arabia, as it was the threat of such an invasion that Bush used to justify sending U.S. troops to the Gulf on August 7; and (2) whether Iraq was or was not prepared to negotiate a settlement to the crisis. The transcript of the Wilson meeting with Hussein suggests that rather than being aggressive and intransigent, Hussein made it clear from the beginning that he was willing to negotiate a solution to the Gulf crisis and had no intention whatsoever of invading Saudi Arabia. The *Post* story, by contrast, indicated that Hussein was not prepared to negotiate a settlement. Furthermore, two *Post* columnists on August 7 insinuated that an Iraqi invasion of Saudi Arabia was imminent and that only bombing Iraq could deter Iraqi aggression. In a summary article on the invasion, one of the *Washington Post*'s top reporters, Patrick Tyler, wrote: "The initial move to seize Kuwait was relatively painless. But the next step that Saddam reportedly threatened yesterday—a possible invasion of Saudi Arabia—would pose immense difficulties for the Iraqi leader, forcing his army to operate far from home, at the end of long supply lines, in the intense summer heat of the desert" (p. A9).

This passage repeats the claim that Saddam Hussein threatened to invade Saudi Arabia, despite the lack of any compelling evidence. Moreover, Tyler's own text indicated the extreme unlikelihood that Iraq would invade Saudi Arabia right after taking Kuwait because of the logistical difficulties that such an invasion would entail (to say nothing of the political response of the West that obviously would not tolerate such a move). Indeed, during this period, the American Friends Service Committee put out a report that concluded:

Prior to the deployment of the multinational forces to Saudi Arabia many informed analysts believed that Iraq would not continue past Kuwait to the Saudi oil fields, for at least five reasons: (1) Whereas Kuwait had angered Iraq by exceeding its OPEC oil quota, Iraq and Saudi Arabia had been coordinating their oil pricing policies before the invasion, in opposition to Kuwait; (2) It will take some time for Iraq to absorb Kuwait and assess the situation; (3) Saudi Arabia's military forces, while still small compared to Iraq's, are much larger and more capable than Kuwait's were; (4) Supply lines for Iraqi forces would become overstretched and vulnerable to Saudi air attack; and (5) An attack on Saudi Arabia would almost certainly prompt military intervention by the United States and other countries. (August 8, 1990; in PeaceNet mideast.gulf archive)[19]

Other informed observers also doubted that Iraq ever had any intention of invading Saudi Arabia. Bulloch and Morris (1991) argue that "For all the talk of Saddam's plans to attack the kingdom, it never seemed likely. The Iraqi deployment, once Kuwait was taken, was entirely defensive, and the much-cited move towards the Saudi border was merely the pushing out of frontlines and tripwires which any prudent commander would undertake when setting up a defensive line. All the evidence was that suggestions of possible moves into Saudi Arabia by the Iraqis were merely propaganda designed to support the huge build-up of forces by America and its allies" (pp. 169–170). Martin Yant concluded that, "many analysts now question whether Iraqi tanks were ever poised to roll into Saudi Arabia. Historians may someday compare this claim to the 1964 Gulf of Tonkin incident, in which a clash between U.S. destroyers and Vietnamese torpedo boats was apparently blown out of proportion by President Johnson in order to gain congressional authority to expand the Vietnam War" (1991, p. 90).

But the Bush administration and *Washington Post* disinformation concerning the Iraqis' readiness to invade Saudi Arabia worked effectively to shape media discourse and public perception of the crisis and to legitimate U.S. policy, as did Tyler's front-page story concerning Hussein's meeting with Joe Wilson and Iraq's alleged refusal to negotiate a solution or leave Kuwait. The same day as the *Washington Post* article, the Iraqi news service denied the report that Iraq was massing troops on the Saudi/Kuwaiti border and claimed that it had no intention of invading Saudi Arabia; this report was cited in the Japan Economic Newswire, the Xinhua General Overseas News Service, and some Reuters reports on August 7, but was generally disregarded by the U.S. mainstream media. Also, on August 7, State Department spokesperson Margaret Tutweiler described the Iraqi troops massing on the border and presented Joseph Wilson's meeting with Saddam Hussein negatively, building on the *Washington Post* disinformation campaign. The Bush administration and media thus produced an image on the very day that the U.S. was sending troops to Saudi Arabia that Iraq was not going to leave Kuwait, would not negotiate, and was about to invade Saudi Arabia.

This discourse dominated the news coverage for the day. On an August 7, PBS discussion of the proper U.S. response to Iraq's invasion of Kuwait, co-anchor Judy Woodruff stated: "Iraq's leader Saddam Hussein was quoted today [in the *Post* story—D.K.] as saying the invasion of Kuwait was irreversible and permanent." Later on the same show, former national security adviser (and Iran/Contra criminal) Robert McFarlane quoted the story as evidence that Hussein was not going to leave Kuwait and that therefore a U.S. military intervention in Saudi Arabia was necessary. And in a discussion with Arab-American leaders as to whether a U.S. military intervention was justified, Woodruff interjected: "the U.S. chargé in Baghdad did have a two hour meeting with Saddam Hussein yesterday which by all accounts was very unsatisfactory as Saddam Hussein insisted that he was going to stay in Kuwait and made what were reported to be veiled threats against other nations in the area"—all lies which Bush administration officials fed to the *Post* which were then disseminated by other mainstream media.[20]

On the morning of August 8, presidential press secretary Marlin Fitzwater told reporters that in a tense, two-hour session between Hussein and the highest-ranking American official in Iraq, *chargé d'affaires* Joseph Wilson, the Iraqi president "indicated he had no intention of leaving Kuwait and had every indication of staying and claiming it as his own." This false account of the conversation with Wilson was printed the same day in the *Boston Globe, Newsday,* the *Jerusalem Post,* the *New York Times,* the *Daily Telegraph,* the *Toronto Star, The Times* (of London), and the *Washington Times.* Summaries of the first week of the crisis in the *Los Angeles Times* (Aug. 9, 1990) and the *Sunday Times* of London (Aug. 12, 1990) presented the false Bush administration version of the Hussein/Wilson meeting as the turning point in the crisis, which seemingly indicated that Iraq was not going to pull out of Kuwait or negotiate a solution to the crisis.

The United States was thus able to produce the impression that Iraq had no intention of leaving Kuwait and negotiating a solution to the crisis by distorting the discussion between Iraq and Joseph Wilson and the mainstream media served as a compliant conduit for the U.S. disinformation campaign. In his early morning television speech on August 8, which announced and defended sending U.S. troops to Saudi Arabia, Bush claimed that "the Saudi government requested our help, and I responded to that request by ordering U.S. air and ground forces to deploy to the kingdom of Saudi Arabia." This was a lie as accounts of the Saudi-U.S. negotiations later indicated that the United States pressured the Saudis to allow the U.S. military intervention into their country (Woodward 1991, pp. 241ff. and Salinger and Laurent 1991, pp. 110ff.).[21] Bush repeated the dubious claim that "Iraq has massed an enormous war machine on the Saudi border," and his administration emphasized this theme in discussion with the media, which obediently reproduced the argument. At 9:24 A.M. on August 8, for instance, Bob Zelnick, ABC's Pentagon correspondent, dutifully reported that the Pentagon informed him that Iraqi troop presence had doubled since the invasion of Kuwait, that there were now more than 200,000 Iraqi troops in Kuwait with a large force poised to invade Saudi Arabia.

Yet it is not at all certain how many troops Iraq actually deployed in Kuwait during the first six weeks of the crisis. All preinvasion reports produced by the Bush administration indicated that Iraq had amassed about 100,000 troops on the border of Kuwait. Initial reports during the first few days after the invasion suggested that Iraq actually had between 80,000 and 100,000 troops in Kuwait, more than enough for an occupation, as the Bush administration liked to point out and as the mainstream media diligently reported; once the U.S. forces were on their way to Saudi Arabia, the Iraqi forces suddenly doubled. But these figures invariably came from Bush administration or Pentagon sources, and it was later claimed that Iraqi troops were actually being withdrawn from Kuwait at the very moment when the Bush administration and Pentagon asserted that they were doubling their forces. After the war, Pentagon officials told *U.S. News and World Report* writers that the divisions positioned furthest south in Kuwait were not the elite Republican Guard forces, which were moved back to Iraq during the first week of the invasion (1992, pp. 97–98). A senior Central Command officer conceded that "We still have no hard evidence that he [Saddam] ever intended to invade Saudi Arabia. We believe that he did. But none of the captured documents or prisoner debriefs has come up with anything hard [indicating an attack on the Saudi oil fields]" (U.S. News and World Report 1992, p. 98).

After the war, it was evident that the U.S. had vastly overestimated the number of Iraqi troops in Kuwait (see 10.3), and there is reason to believe that the U.S. estimates were highly flawed from the beginning. *St. Petersburg Times* reporter Jean Heller published two stories (Nov. 30 and Jan. 6) suggesting that satellite photos indicated far fewer Iraqi troops in Saudi Arabia than the Bush administration claimed (the Jan. 6 story was republished in *In These Times,* Feb. 27, 1991, pp. 1–2). Heller's suspicions were roused when she saw a December 3, 1990, *Newsweek* "Periscope" item that ABC news had never used several satellite photos of Saudi Arabia and southern Kuwait taken in early September (p. 6). Purchased by ABC from the Soviet commercial satellite agency Soyez-Karta, the photos were expected to reveal the presence of a massive Iraqi troop deployment in Kuwait, but failed to disclose anything near the number of troops claimed by the Bush administration. ABC declined to use them and Heller got her newspaper to purchase the satellite photos of Kuwait from August 8 and September 13 and of Saudi Arabia from September 11. Two satellite experts who had formerly worked for the U.S. government failed to find evidence of the alleged buildup. " 'The Pentagon kept saying the bad guys were there, but we don't see anything to indicate an Iraqi force in Kuwait of even 20 percent the size the administration claimed,' said Peter Zimmerman, who served with the U.S. Arms Control and Disarmament Agency during the Reagan administration" (Heller, *In These Times,* Feb. 27, p. 2).

Both satellite photos taken on August 8 and September 13 showed a sand cover on the roads, suggesting that there were few Iraqi troops on the Saudi border where the Bush administration claimed that they were massed, threatening to invade Saudi Arabia. Pictures of the main Kuwaiti airport showed no Iraqi planes in sight, though large numbers of U.S. planes were visible in Saudi Arabia. The Pentagon refused to comment on the satellite photos, but to suggestions advanced by ABC (which refused to show the photos) that the pictures were not high enough quality to detect the Iraqi troops, Heller responded that the photograph of the north of Saudi Arabia showed all the roads swept clean of sand and clearly depicted the U.S. troop buildup in the area. By September, the Pentagon was claiming that there were 265,000 Iraqi troops and 2,200 tanks, which posed a threat to Saudi Arabia, deployed in Kuwait, but the photographs reveal nowhere near this number and, so far, the U.S. government has refused to release its satellite photographs.

Indeed, Woodward (1991) noted that the Saudis had sent scouts across the border into Kuwait after the Iraqi invasion to see if they could detect the Iraqi troops that the United States claimed were massed for a possible invasion of their country. "The scouts had come back reporting nothing. There was no trace of the Iraqi troops heading toward the kingdom" (Woodward 1991, pp. 258–259). Soon after, the U.S. team arrived with photos of the Iraqi troops allegedly massed on the Saudi border and General Norman Schwarzkopf explained to the Saudis that the Iraqis had sent small command-and-control units ahead of the mass of troops, which would explain why the Saudi scouts failed to see them (Woodward 1991, p. 268).[22] Former CIA officer Ralph McGehee told journalist Joel Bleifuss: "There has been no hesitation in the past to use doctored satellite photographs to support the policy position that the U.S. wants supported" (*In These Times,* Sept. 19, 1990, p. 5). Indeed, Emery (1991) reported that King Hussein of Jordan was sent similar pictures of tanks moving along roads near the Saudi/Kuwaiti border and that King Hussein claimed that the Saudis "pressed the panic button" when they saw the photographs (p. 15). King Hussein was skeptical and "argued that if Saddam Hussein had wanted to invade the Saudis, he would have moved immediately, when the only thing between him and the Saudi capital was a tiny and untested—if expensively equipped—Saudi army" (Emery 1991).

This account is supported by Dunnigan and Bay's diagram of Iraqi defenses in August 1990 when U.S. forces arrived in Saudi Arabia (1991, p. 248). Iraqi troops are presented in a defensive posture around Kuwait City and not poised on the border ready to invade. Later diagrams by the authors (1991, pp. 256–257) show Iraqi troops located in defensive positions on the border but there is no evidence that they ever planned to invade Saudi Arabia. Thus, there are reasons to believe that the Bush administration exaggerated the number of Iraqi troops in Kuwait and the threat to Saudi Arabia to scare the Saudis into accepting the U.S. troops and to justify its own troop buildup in the region and eventual military action. The mainstream media reproduced the U.S. claims and figures as facts with newspapers like the *Washington Post* and the television networks serving as conduits for the Bush administration disinformation campaign. Moreover, the *Washington Post* followed the tradition of yellow journalism by urging Bush to military action on the basis of disinformation. The difference, however, between classical yellow journalism and the promotion by the *Post* of military action against Iraq was that William Randolph Hearst's papers had produced the lies themselves to help sell papers and to push a policy line desired by the newspaper publisher, but during the Gulf crisis and war the mainstream media simply reproduced the lies and disinformation of the Bush administration and Pentagon.[23] Yet *Post* editorial writers and columnists actively promoted a military solution, urging an attack on Baghdad even before Bush announced that he was sending troops to Saudi Arabia.

Crucially, the major newspapers, news magazines, and television networks did not criticize Bush's deployment or debate whether it was wise to send so many U.S. troops to Saudi Arabia in the first place. The alternative press argued against the deployment and for a UN peace-keeping force to be sent to the area, rather than a massive U.S. military force, but this position got almost no hearing in the mainstream media. Furthermore, the leaders of the Democratic party also failed to criticize the U.S. military deployment, which points again to the crisis of liberalism. Yet there were many oppositional voices to the Bush administration's policies that were simply excluded from the mainstream media, thus precluding serious debate over the proper U.S. response to Iraq's invasion of Kuwait. But the mainstream media only draw on an extremely limited repertoire of voices and privilege the same administration officials and top Democratic Party leaders, thus freezing significant views out of public policy debates—a topic that I return to in Chapter 2 and throughout this book.

1.2 The Subversion of Diplomacy

In addition to disinformation concerning the Iraqi threat to Saudi Arabia, another of the Big Lies was that the United States sought a diplomatic solution to the crisis in the Gulf. Many diplomatic attempts were made throughout the crisis to avoid war and the Bush administration did not actively encourage any of these efforts; in fact, it energetically blocked such efforts or ignored them, as I shall document in this section.

On August 3, for example, it was announced that there would be a meeting between Iraq, Kuwait, and Saudi Arabia over the weekend in Jidda, Saudi Arabia, aimed at resolving the crisis, but nothing came of this. There were rumors that Iraq was willing to withdraw for concessions on the disputed Rumaila oil field, its debt to Kuwait, and access to Kuwaiti islands, which would guarantee clear access to the Gulf. But the August 5 *New York Times* had the headline "Arab's Summit Meeting Off; Iraqi Units in Kuwait Dig In." The story did not really analyze why the summit was called off, stating merely: "Apparently one reason that the Arab mediation summit meeting . . . was postponed was that President Hussein was not prepared to attend and the Saudis did not want to meet without him for fear that he would perceive this as an anti-Baghdad initiative" (p. A8). The same story, however, was subheadled "U.S. Is Seeking to Forestall Any Arab Deal for Kuwait," thus raising the question of whether the U.S. itself was blocking diplomacy from the beginning, perhaps because it already envisaged and desired a military solution to the crisis.

Salinger and Laurent (1991) observed that at precisely this moment the Bush administration was actively subverting an Arab attempt to reach a diplomatic solution to the crisis. These authors claimed that on August 3, King Hussein of Jordan visited Saddam Hussein in Baghdad and that the "Iraqi President gave his guest the impression of a benevolent leader prepared to make major compromises" (p. 108). Saddam told King Hussein that he had signed a nonaggression pact with Saudi Arabia, indicating that he had no intention of invading it, and that he would be at the minisummit the coming weekend. Moreover, he suggested that he would be willing to negotiate a solution to the crisis that would involve his pulling out of Kuwait. At this juncture, the Bush administration was telling the Saudis that Saddam Hussein was about to invade their country, but King Fahd first refused the U.S. offer of troops, saying that "he still had confidence in King Hussein's efforts to reach a negotiated settlement and to persuade the Iraqi president to withdraw from Kuwait. He reminded Bush that an Arab mini-summit was due to be held the following day, August 4" (Salinger and Laurent 1991, pp. 110–111).

But, according to Salinger and Laurent (1991, p. 112), despite U.S. promises not to intervene until the Arabs had a chance to settle the problem on their own, John Kelly of the State Department sent Egypt a note threatening them with the loss of foreign aid unless they immediately condemned the Iraqi invasion and supported the U.S. line at a meeting of the Arab League which was meeting in Cairo. Egypt's President Hosni Mubarak quickly put out a statement condemning Iraq and engineered an Arab League condemnation of Iraq, thus subverting the planned minisummit. Salinger and Laurent claimed:

> Highly placed figures within Iraq told us that during the course of his meetings with King Hussein, the Iraqi President had agreed to go to Jeddah for a mini-summit on August 4 to negotiate with King Fahd and, if the negotiations were successful, to withdraw from Kuwait. Just before the war broke out, when Saddam Hussein was meeting with UN Secretary General Pérez de Cuéllar in Baghdad, he re-emphasized his decision to pull out of Kuwait on August 5 if the mini-summit planned for August 4 in Jeddah were successful (1991, p. 114).

But because Egypt managed to pass a resolution condemning Iraq's invasion at the Arab League meeting in Cairo on August 3, Iraq canceled the minisummit that had been scheduled for the next day (Salinger and Laurent 1991, p. 117). Emery's account (1991), based on an interview with King Hussein of Jordan and other Arab sources, indicated that Saddam Hussein was indeed ready to negotiate a solution to the crisis in the Gulf and was prepared to pull out immediately, but that the United States blocked the early attempt to negotiate the crisis.

On August 5, though bitter about the sabotage of the minisummit, Saddam Hussein reportedly told Yasir Arafat that he should contact the Saudis and tell them that he was ready to talk. Two days later Arafat gave a letter from Hussein to a Palestinian businessman who had contacts in the White House. The letter was addressed to George Bush and confirmed that Iraq was ready to pull out of Kuwait but needed to resolve its problems with Kuwait first. According to Salinger and Laurent: "The businessman called John Sununu, White House chief of staff, and told him he was forwarding the message. 'It's OK, but I don't want anyone to know such a message has been passed on,' Sununu said. When the message got to Washington, there was no reply" (1991, p. 127).

On August 12, Iraq agreed to withdraw from Kuwait if Syria and Israel withdrew from occupied Arab lands in Lebanon and the occupied territories; although this move was clearly an opening to begin a negotiated settlement, the United States derisively dismissed the initiative. As Noam Chomsky (1990) explained: "Television news that day was featuring a well-staged presentation of George Bush the dynamo, racing his power boat, jogging furiously, playing tennis and golf, and otherwise expending his formidable energies on important pursuits, far too busy 'recreating' (as he put it) to waste much time on the occasional fly in Arab garb that he might have to swat. As the TV news clips were careful to stress, the President's disdain for this irritant was so great that he scarcely even broke his golf stroke to express his contempt for what the anchorperson termed Hussein's 'so-called offer,' not to be regarded as 'serious.' The proposal merited one dismissive sentence in a news story on the blockade in the next day's *New York Times*" (p. 22).

Chomsky pointed out that in England the *Financial Times* thought that the Iraqi peace initiative "may yet serve some useful purpose" by offering "a path away from disaster . . . through negotiation" (1990, p. 22). The *Financial Times* also conceded that Iraq's demand to link the resolution of the Kuwaiti question to other Middle East issues such as Arab/Israeli relations and Lebanon was also rational. Yet the Bush administration rejected such "linkage," which they tried to make into a dirty word, although any negotiator knows that linkages often provide solutions to crises. The *Financial Times* concluded: "The 'immediate issue' is for 'Iraq to get out of Kuwait'; but in the light of Iraq's proposal, 'the onus is now on everyone involved, including Middle Eastern and Western powers, to seize the initiative and harness diplomacy to the show of political, military and economic force now on display in the Gulf'" (1990, p. 22).

In addition, investigative reporter Robert Parry later revealed in the *Nation* (April 15, 1991, pp. 480ff.) that on August 9, the United States received a back-channel offer from Iraq to withdraw from Kuwait in return for settlement of some border disputes. The proposal was considered by the National Security Council on August 10 and rejected as "already moving against policy," according to the retired Army officer who arranged the meeting. Former CIA director Richard Helms attempted to carry the initiative further, with no success. In addition, later efforts by high Iraqi officials and U.S. interlocutors elicited no response. "There was nothing in this [peace initiative] that interested the U.S. government," according to Helms (quoted in Parry, April 15, 1991). A Congressional summary concluded that a diplomatic solution might have been possible at that time.

Further, during a much-heralded visit of King Hussein of Jordan to the United States on August 15 there were rumors that the king was delivering a peace message from Saddam Hussein to Bush at his Kennebunkport summer-vacation home. Suddenly, however, there was no message, no proposed solution, and Bush could return to playing golf and driving his speedboat. Several days later, however, the London-based

Mideast Mirror reported that King Hussein had indeed brought Bush a peace proposal from Iraq. As David Armstrong put it, "According to the *Mirror,* Saddam relayed his willingness to negotiate a withdrawal of Iraqi troops from Kuwait, to be followed by the lifting of U.N. sanctions and an end to the U.S. military buildup in Saudi Arabia. The only point on which the Iraqi president was unwilling to negotiate, the *Mirror* said, was the restoration of the al-Sabah clan in Kuwait" (*Random Lengths,* Aug. 30, 1990, p. 3). Alexander Cockburn pointed out at the time that "even if the king did not carry such a message, he must have known before his arrival in Kennebunkport that America has no interest in any deals. He was kept waiting 24 hours before getting his audience with Bush, who took good care to let it be known that he was only interested in discussing the blockade of shipments to Iraq through the Jordanian port of Aqaba" (cited in Armstrong, *Random Lengths,* p. 3).

Consequently, the repeated U.S. claim that its troop deployment was merely a defensive force was a highly suspicious cover. There is good reason to believe that the United States planned an offensive military strike from the beginning, systematically building up its forces until it possessed enough power to easily destroy Iraq. Despite their Big Lie that they constantly "went the extra mile" for a peaceful resolution to the crisis, the U.S. repeatedly blocked all efforts at finding a diplomatic solution, failing to respond to all Iraqi peace efforts as well as initiatives sponsored by other countries.

On August 19, Saddam Hussein proposed that the status of Kuwait be settled by the Arab states alone, without external interference, much as the Syrian occupation of Lebanon and Morocco's attempt to take over the Western Sahara had been dealt with. Once again, Washington refused to countenance such effrontery, even though it had long been U.S. policy not to tolerate outside interference in matters in Latin America or the Caribbean. On August 21 the major TV network newscasts showed Iraqi Foreign Minister Tariq Aziz at a news conference in Amman indicating an Iraqi readiness to talk, but the United States refused. On "ABC World News Tonight," Tariq Aziz reported that he told the U.S. *chargé d'affaires* in Baghdad, Joe Wilson: "Look. If you are ready to talk, we are ready to talk." But ABC noted that Bush wouldn't even bother himself to answer, explaining: "The President, who was golfing, refused to comment. His spokesman, Marlin Fitzwater, says it is the same kind of rhetoric that we've heard before in a daily litany." ABC then presented the Yemeni ambassador saying that he did not understand why the U.S. would not talk to its adversary and Tariq Aziz's complaint that the U.S. will not listen to Iraqi proposals. Then, putting the Bush administration spin on the refusal to engage in diplomacy, ABC noted that the State Department answered that they listen to all Iraqi proposals, but dismissed negotiations, declaring that "as long as Iraq is holding thousands of hostages, pretending they are human bargaining chips, it is impossible to take any Iraqi proposals seriously." This is a questionable justification for not negotiating, as even after Saddam Hussein agreed to release all hostages some weeks later, the Bush administration still refused to negotiate.

On August 21, CBS also presented Tariq Aziz's offer to begin negotiations, stating: "The Iraqi's offer to talk brought only scorn and Marlin Fitzwater says that there is nothing to negotiate; 'there is very little to talk about when we get only negative responses.' " The next day on CBS News, Dan Rather explained that President Bush in Maine was determined, even confrontational, about the showdown with Iraq, giving the back of his hand to any diplomacy with Saddam Hussein. "I don't rule in or rule out the use of military force," Bush stated. CBS reported that the United States would defy Iraq's order to shut down the U.S. embassy in Kuwait and might fire on Iraqi ships even without a UN resolution allowing this action, which the Soviets were blocking. According to CBS, President Bush held the strongest hand he would ever hold and saw no need to give Saddam Hussein any hope that the crisis could be peacefully settled. In this way, CBS justified Bush's refusal to negotiate and his bellicose militarist gestures.

On August 22, Thomas Friedman published a column in the *New York Times* outlining State Department reasoning on the need to block the diplomatic track because Arab states might be tempted to "defuse the crisis" with "a few token gains" for Iraq, such as the islands of Warba and Bubiyan, which would give them secure access to the Gulf, or adjustment of the borders on the Rumaila oil field. The *Times*'s best source on State Department thinking thus revealed once again that the Bush administration was uninterested in diplomatic solutions and was actually blocking those that were circulating.

On August 23, a former high-ranking U.S. official reportedly delivered another Iraqi offer to Bush's national security adviser Brent Scowcroft; the proposal was confirmed by the emissary and accompanying memoranda, and published by Knut Royce in *Newsday* on August 29. In this peace offer, Iraq agreed to withdraw from Kuwait and to allow foreigners to leave in return for the lifting of the economic sanctions, guaranteed access to the Gulf, and control of the Rumaila oil field. There were also proposals for the United States and Iraq to negotiate an oil agreement "satisfactory to both nations," to jointly work to secure stability of the Gulf, and to develop a plan "to alleviate Iraq's economic and financial problems." Royce quoted a Bush administration official as saying that the "terms of the proposal are serious" and "negotiable." Yet despite the fact that the proposal did not even demand that the United States withdraw from Saudi Arabia, or have any preconditions, the Bush administration ridiculed the Iraqi peace feeler, stating that "there was nothing in this particular proposal that merited its pursuit" (reported by Royce in *Newsday,* August 30, p. 6).

The *New York Times* also received a copy of the Iraqi message, but declined to take it seriously, following the lead of the Bush administration in dismissing all attempts at a negotiated settlement. As Chomsky pointed out:

> the *New York Times* noted the offer briefly on page 14, the continuation page of an article on another topic, citing government spokespeople who dismissed the *Newsday* report as "baloney." After framing the matter properly, the *Times* report concedes that the story was accurate, quotes White House sources who said the proposal "had not been taken seriously because Mr. Bush demands the unconditional withdrawal of Iraq from Kuwait." The report also noted quietly that "a well-connected Middle Eastern diplomat told the *New York Times* a week ago [August 23] of a similar offer, but it too was dismissed by the Administration." That news had not been published. (1990, pp. 22–23)

And so, during the first month of the crisis, the mainstream corporate media either ignored the Iraqi peace overtures or explained them away, taking the U.S. position that negotiation with Iraq was unacceptable. The mainstream media only began taking negotiations seriously when the Bush administration began leaking hints that they were ready to negotiate a settlement. For instance, the three major U.S. news magazines—*Time, Newsweek,* and *U.S. News and World Report*—either failed completely to report on Iraqi efforts at negotiation, or briefly dismissed them, during the first weeks of the crisis. On September 10, however, these weeklies began to discuss the possibility of a diplomatic solution but did not discuss the actual Iraqi initiatives that were on the table. A story in *U.S. News and World Report* opened by stating that the Joint Chiefs of Staff and the National Security Council had concluded that "a full-scale war against Iraq, with its almost certain use of chemical weapons, could cost 20,000 to 30,000 American combat casualties." For this reason, the article suggested, Bush was trying diplomacy. Interestingly, the article intimated as well that Bush's current pose could be a smoke screen to give him time to marshall his forces for a deadly strike, a suggestion which, in retrospect, appears likely. Apparently, the Pentagon discerned that it needed more time to put together overwhelming military force to minimize casualties and the Bush administration periodically sent out rumors that they were preparing diplomatic initiatives. Such rumors of peace assured a naive antiwar Congress and public that war might be avoided, while at the same time the administration hinted that if diplomatic efforts failed, a military solution would be necessary. The September 10 *U.S.*

News and World Report stated, for instance: "Privately, one senior administration official predicts that if diplomacy has borne no fruit in a month, Bush will review his military options."

In October, the plans were reportedly finalized for a January air war against Iraq (see Friedman and Tyler, *New York Times,* March 3, 1991, p. A12 and Woodward 1991, pp. 300ff). Meanwhile, the Bush administration was relentlessly orchestrating the eventual war by doubling the number of U.S. forces sent to Saudi Arabia after the November 7 election and then mobilizing UN resolutions against Iraq, including one on November 29 that authorized the use of force to eject Iraq from Kuwait. Shortly after, Bush proposed talks with Iraq, and Iraq ordered all foreign hostages to be released on December 6. Yet no date could be arranged for talks until January 9, and by then it was clear that the Bush administration had no intention whatsoever of seeking a diplomatic settlement.

As late as January 2, 1991, U.S. officials revealed an Iraqi offer "to withdraw from Kuwait if the United States pledges not to attack as its soldiers are pulled out, if foreign troops leave the region, and if there is agreement on the Palestinian problem and on the banning of all weapons of mass destruction in the region" (in Knut Royce, *Newsday,* Jan. 3). Some administration officials indicated that the offer was "interesting" because Iraq renounced all territorial claims here and signaled "interest in a negotiated settlement." Chomsky noted: "A State Department Mideast expert described the proposal as a 'serious prenegotiation position.' The U.S. 'immediately dismissed the proposal,' Royce continues. It passed without mention in the *Times,* and was barely noted elsewhere" (1991, p. 50).

Thus, two weeks before the deadline for Iraqi withdrawal from Kuwait there were strong signs that the Iraqis were ready to negotiate a settlement, but the United States did not respond at all positively and, in fact, blocked a negotiated solution by delivering the Iraqis a blunt ultimatum during the Geneva meeting between James Baker and Tariq Aziz on January 9, 1991. Although it was clear that the Iraqis were making reasonable offers for negotiation, it appears in retrospect that the Bush administration wanted war and did everything possible to block a negotiated diplomatic settlement.

Consequently, throughout the crisis in the Gulf, there was a series of viable proposals for negotiation. From the beginning of the crisis, King Hussein of Jordan made a number of diplomatic initiatives, which were all undercut by the United States (Salinger and Laurent 1991 and Emery 1991). The Palestine Liberation Organization (PLO) campaigned hard for a diplomatic resolution and floated a series of peace initiatives. The Algerians made some serious attempts at negotiation and some observers believed that they were in a particularly good position to resolve the crisis as they had done so in previous situations and were not seen as allied closely with either Iraq or Saudi Arabia and Kuwait.[24] And both François Mitterand and the French and Gorbachev and the Soviets proposed diplomatic initiatives that were ignored by the Bush administration.

France made two major diplomatic proposals that the U.S. scorned and rejected and that the mainstream media failed to discuss. On September 24, 1990, French President Mitterrand advanced a four-point peace proposal at the UN that would have Iraq declare that it would withdraw from Kuwait, mandate UN supervision of the withdrawal, call for the restoration of Kuwaiti sovereignty with the people having an opportunity to decide on their form of government, and propose an international peace conference on the Middle East. Finally, on January 14, the French proposed—in a last minute attempt to avoid war—that the UN Security Council call for a "rapid and massive [Iraqi] withdrawal from Kuwait and commit itself to an 'active contribution' to the settlement of other regional problems, particularly the Palestinian problem, by 'convening, at an appropriate date, an international conference.' Belgium on the Security Council, as well as Germany, Spain, Italy, Algeria, Morocco, and Tunisia supported the proposal. Britain and the Soviet Union joined the U.S. in rejection" (Briemberg, in Briemberg 1992, p. 26). In George Bush's New World Order, it would thus be the military power of the mighty that would settle disputes and not reason or diplomacy.

1.3 Hidden Agendas and the Logics of War

There was no single reason why the United States relentlessly pursued the military option in the crisis of the Gulf. Dissection of the underlying forces that led the Bush administration to pursue the war option reveals a complex web of political, economic, and military considerations. The Gulf war was not solely a war for oil, for the greater glory of George Bush and the Pentagon, or for the promotion of U.S. geopolitical supremacy in order to bolster a faltering U.S. economy, although all of these factors played a role in producing the war. Instead, the Gulf war was "overdetermined" (see Althusser 1969) and requires a multicausal analysis.[25]

Although the Gulf war was arguably overdetermined in its origins and causes, there was a remarkable coincidence between the interests of the Bush administration, the Pentagon, and powerful economic forces. This convergence is itself no accident. George Bush is the first U.S. president in recent years who is himself part of both the corporate economic establishment and the National Security State. Bush was an oilman and his family continues to have important oil interests.[26] In addition, Bush was also a director of the CIA and has consistently supported the use of military force and covert operations to promote U.S. foreign policy and U.S. interests—as perceived by those in power who actually had interests to promote. The Gulf war is therefore correctly perceived as Bush's war and analysis of the causes of the war can legitimately begin with him.

In 1990, Bush's presidency was facing severe domestic economic and political problems, including: a sky-rocketing deficit caused by Reagan's and Bush's astronomical defense-spending; a severe S&L, banking, and insurance crisis caused by Republican deregulation policies; and proliferating public squalor marked by growing homelessness, unemployment, economic deprivation, deteriorating cities with epidemics of crime and drugs, health problems such as AIDS, cancer, and the absence of a national health insurance program. These and many other problems were in part caused, or aggravated, by the policies of George Bush and his predecessor Ronald Reagan.

Consequently, it was in George Bush's interest to divert attention from current crises and the deteriorating economy with a scapegoat for the economic imbroglio produced by Republican economics. That is, Bush could claim that the economic problems were caused by Saddam Hussein's invasion of Kuwait and the ensuing crisis that drove up oil prices. This response diverted inquiry from seeking the origins of the crisis in Reagan-Bush economic policies. Not surprisingly, in mid-November Bush actually interpreted the current recession as a function of rising oil prices from the Gulf crisis (a position repeated by Federal Reserve Chairman Alan Greenspan; see *New York Times,* Nov. 29, 1990, p. 1).

In fact, questions concerning the S&L crisis were already haunting Bush, whose son Neil and other associates were deeply involved in the scandal. Indeed, Bush himself and other top Republicans had been friendly for many years with S&L criminal extraordinaire Charles Keating, whose collapsed financial empire bankrupted many investors. The S&L crisis dramatized the economic disaster of the Reagan-Bush years in an especially striking fashion. It indicated the fallacies of the free-market deregulation strategy and of the unleashing of free-wheeling entrepreneuralism upon which the Reagan-Bush economic strategy was based. The Gulf crisis not only put this story off of the front pages for months, but also short-circuited the debate over economic policy that intensified during the U.S. budget crisis in July and August before the Iraqi invasion.

The Gulf war also diverted attention from the failures and potential collapse of Bush's domestic policies. *Time* magazine named Bush their Man of the Year in 1990 and, in a cover story on the "two George Bushes," claimed that Bush was a whiz in foreign policy and uninterested and incompetent in domestic policy. During the fall congressional budget debates that raged while Bush was playing his Gulf war games, he lost his budget battle with the Democrats and led his party to an embarrassing defeat in the mid-term 1990 elections. Indeed, Bush was seen as such a liability that many Republicans would not allow him to campaign for them and many sharply criticized him. Weiner (1991) argued that Bush was suffering a "domestic political collapse of historic proportions" and needed a war to reverse his political fortunes. Gathering together an impressive number of mainstream media quotes indicating that Bush's presidency was in serious trouble, Weiner suggested that a successful war was a necessary step to save his presidency.

Bob Woodward's book *The Commanders* (1991) suggested that it was George Bush himself who was the most aggressive promoter of the military solution to the crisis in the gulf. This argument also was advanced by Graubard (1992) and Smith (1992). During the crisis, many speculated that Bush's peculiar psychology might also be part of the reason for the U.S. military action: Arm-chair psychologists speculated that he was highly obsessed with overcoming his "wimp" image, that he was deeply insecure about his manhood, and that these insecurities drove him to prove that he was tough and manly.[27] Perhaps other factors in Bush's biography, however, might be more significant in motivating him to choose the military option, such as the fact that his father, former Senator Prescott Bush, was a strong supporter of the military and the use of military power to advance U.S. interests.[28] George had a moment of early heroism in World War II, headed the CIA in 1976, and always strongly identified with the National Security State, U.S. military power, covert operations, and the use of force to achieve U.S. policy goals.[29] During the Reagan administration, Bush was a strong supporter of the sometimes illegal contra war against the democratically elected Nicaraguan government, and there were even speculations that an illegal contra supply operation was run out of his office by his close associates.

Bush, therefore, had long been a part of the National Security State and his role in the Gulf war was arguably an extension of a life spent serving the interests of the military, the intelligence apparatus, and an aggressive U.S. foreign policy. Likewise, his national security adviser Brent Scowcroft pushed hard for the military option.[30] Scowcroft had been a lieutenant general in the Air Force, a deputy to Henry Kissinger, Gerald Ford's national security adviser, and a member of Kissinger Associates. It was alleged that Scowcroft "owns stock in forty companies that took advantage of the let's trade with Iraq policy backed by the N.S.C. [National Security Council, which Scowcroft headed]. Several of these firms are also clients of Kissinger Associates" (David Corn, *The Nation*, May 27, 1991, p. 692). Kissinger Associates has been connected with Saudi Arabian, Kuwaiti, and other Middle East forces that had a deep interest in destroying Iraq's regime, which they perceived as a threat to their interests. Corn also reported that Henry B. Gonzalez (D-Tex.), head of the House Banking Committee, was "deeply concerned" about "the influence Kissinger may exert over his former lieutenants" and was "especially troubled" by "Scowcroft's ability to set policy that affects his portfolio" (p. 692).

Furthermore, Scowcroft had served on the board of directors of Santa Fe International, a Kuwaiti corporation that controlled several U.S. corporations, including the company that was accused of slant-drilling into the Iraqi Rumaila oil field.[31] Scowcroft was thus thoroughly compromised by apparently using U.S. foreign policy to push a Gulf policy that would advance his—and his associates'—economic and political interests. It might also be noted that Brent Scowcroft was one of three individuals on the Tower Commission, which looked into the scandals of the Iran/Contra affair and exonerated George Bush. If, as many believe, Bush was deeply involved in the scandal, Tower and Scowcroft would know, and it probably was no accident that Bush immediately named John Tower as Secretary of Defense, despite the fact that Tower had been the subject of constant rumors concerning his alcoholism and sexual improprieties.[32] Nor was it a coincidence that Bush named Brent Scowcroft his national security adviser. Better to have someone with possibly damaging knowledge on your team rather than outside, where he might cause some problems. In any case, Scowcroft has not been thoroughly investigated, and his possible role in covering up the Iran/Contra scandal should be looked into, as well as the ways that his economic and military interests may have influenced his action in the Gulf war.

Brent Scowcroft was thus a flagrant representative of the military-industrial complex who had served in the military and on boards of corporations active in the defense industry, and had investments in oil and defense companies whose interests were involved in the Gulf. Scowcroft had also lobbied hard to have Dick Cheney appointed as Secretary as Defense, as he had worked with Cheney in the Ford administration and "wanted a known commodity in the Pentagon" (Woodward 1991, p. 62). As Bush's national security adviser, Scowcroft pushed hard to replace General Frederick Woerner as CINCSOUTH (i.e., Commander-in-Chief of the U.S. Southern Command) because Woerner was opposed to aggressive U.S. military intervention in Latin America (Woodward 1991, p. 83); Cheney later blamed the decision to remove Woerner in "its suddenness and finality" on Scowcroft (p. 97). Woerner was replaced by gung-ho General Maxwell Thurman, thus paving the way for the Panama invasion that Thurman and the Pentagon enthusiastically pushed and participated in.

Indeed, the U.S. military establishment, as well as the Bush administration, had compelling reasons for wanting to fight a Gulf war. The

Panana invasion attempted to demonstrate the need for effective U.S. military forces to enforce U.S. interests,[33] but it was a small-scale operation against a small country with little military force. In general, the military in a high-tech weapons environment needs a major war every twenty years or so to test their new weapons systems, to gain prestige to justify the vast amount of resources that go into military spending, and to produce a situation in which its officers can gain promotion and honor through military action. It had been more than fifteen years since the military had been engaged in Vietnam, its last major war. In that war, the military lost a tremendous amount of prestige from its inability to defeat a Third World peasant-guerrilla army and from the intense conflict over the war that tore apart the country. In addition, there had been a massive military buildup during the Reagan administration, which helped double the national deficit. This buildup had created heated controversy over alleged waste, cost overruns, ineffective high-tech weapons, and resentment over the phenomenal amount of the U.S. federal budget that the military controlled, while domestic programs were being slashed or underfunded. The Pentagon wanted to prove that its weapons systems were indeed useful, even essential, to national security, and that the gigantic investment in the military was justified.

In addition, important segments of the U.S. military wanted to fight a war in which the country was behind it, in which their prestige would be restored, and this was the war. From the beginning of the crisis in the Gulf, the Bush administration and Pentagon managed a skillful public relations campaign and the compliant media produced a positive image of U.S. military troops, weapons systems, and policy. Indeed, with the collapse of the Soviet empire and end of the cold war it was not certain that such tremendous investment of resources in the military was justified, and there was much talk of scaling down the military and producing a "peace dividend" by reordering U.S. priorities. As Barbara Ehrenreich put it, "The current war was ostensibly triggered by the Iraqi invasion of Kuwait and the apparent threat of further invasions throughout the region. But the real threat may well have been the potential redundancy of the vast U.S. military enterprise, which had been fattening, throughout the 1980s, on unprecedented levels of peacetime military spending, only to find itself, in 1990, without a credible enemy to confront" (*Z Magazine*, March 1991, pp. 24–25).

There was a variety of other motivations for the U.S. intervention in the Gulf and eventual war. Members of the Bush administration wanted to assert the United States as the number one superpower after the collapse of the Soviet empire. This assertion required a demonstration of the use of U.S. military power to effectively defend "national interests." As Gabriel Kolko (1991) pointed out, since the end of World War II, the

U.S. military was deeply concerned with its "credibility." The United States apparently wanted its "enemies" to believe that it would use military power when U.S. interests were at stake and was afraid that its defeat in Vietnam had created the impression that the United States was a paper tiger, unable to use its military power effectively. The goal of restoring Pentagon credibility was coded as "overcoming the Vietnam syndrome." This goal was interpreted by members of the Bush administration and their conservative supporters as overcoming the reluctance to use U.S. military power after the humiliation of Vietnam, in which there was no decisive victory after years of heavy investment and troop deployment. In fact, the "Vietnam syndrome," interpreted literally, points to a propensity for U.S. policymakers to use military force to solve problems all over the world and to assert its military might as the policeman of the world. In this sense, the Gulf war was merely another expression of the Vietnam syndrome. Genuinely overcoming this pathological syndrome in U.S. policy would require seeking diplomatic and political solutions to problems, not military ones.

From another perspective (Klare 1990), reestablishing U.S. military supremacy was the goal of a group of individuals tied to the military-industrial complex who envisaged the nation's future as the number one military superpower. Individuals who urged this military "geostrategic" policy were opposed, according to Klare, by those who sought cuts in the U.S. military establishment and "a greater investment in science, technology, education and trade development. If we are to compete successfully in world markets, this position holds, we must become more like Germany and Japan—that is, we must spend less on military forces and more on domestic industrial revitalization" (p. 416). Proponents of these positions had been debating America's future since the first evidence of the collapse of the Soviet empire in 1989, and the Persian Gulf crisis gave those seeking a stronger military a splendid opportunity to push their agenda by pointing to the need for expansion of the military in a dangerous world.

Obviously, there were also powerful economic interests involved in the Gulf region that influenced U.S. policy. Many policymakers and their corporate allies were concerned with the flow and control of Middle East oil and many believed that U.S. military presence in the region would allow the United States to help dictate energy prices, production quotas, and distribution. There were many in the foreign policy establishment who for years wanted a U.S. military presence in the Gulf.[34] Since the 1970s, there were attempts to build a "rapid deployment force" that would be able to intervene in the Middle East, and after the Iranian revolution of 1979 President Jimmy Carter issued in his 1980 State of the Union address what was to be known as the Carter Doctrine: "An attempt by any outside force to gain control of the Persian Gulf will be regarded as an assault on the vital interests of the United States of America, and such an assault will be repelled by any means necessary, including military force."

The Carter administration attempted to convince the Gulf states to allow the United States to build up naval and air bases in the region, but only Oman agreed to a permanent U.S. military presence. During the Reagan administration, the Central Command was established to facilitate a U.S. intervention in the Middle East and the United States gained access to a large number of bases in the region, in exchange for military and/ or economic aid. Norman Schwarzkopf became the head of Central Command in 1987, and in 1989 Joint Chiefs of Staff Chairman Colin Powell directed Central Command and the Joint Chiefs to revise the plan, which had assumed that a Soviet invasion of the Gulf would be the major threat to U.S. interests. The new plan assumed that Iraq would be the primary threat to the region, and on the eve of the Iraqi invasion Schwarzkopf was engaged in war games rehearsing U.S. military response to an Iraqi invasion of Kuwait (Blackwell 1991, pp. 84ff.).[35]

Thus, the military itself had long been preparing for a Gulf war to reestablish its prestige and this area was precisely where the Bush administration wanted the war to be fought. Bob Woodward reported that Central Command had a top-secret contingency plan, Operations Plan 90–1002, ready "for moving about 100,000 ground troops to the region over three to four months" (1991, p. 220), and this is indeed the plan that was eventually used. The United States also had a military infrastructure in place. Although Saudi Arabia would not allow U.S. troops to be stationed on their soil prior to the crisis in the Gulf, the U.S. helped build a massive military infrastructure in the country. Scott Armstrong (1991, pp. 30ff.) contended that protection and justification for a $200 billion military infrastructure in the Middle East was one of the underlying causes of the Gulf war.

Another economic and military motivation for the war was to promote U.S. arms sales to the region. One of Cheney's first acts during his initial meeting with the Saudis was to secure a multibillion dollar arms contract and shortly thereafter new arms deals were secured with Egypt, Syria, Turkey, Bahrain, and other countries in the region. A 1991 congressional report asserted that U.S. weapons sales to the Third World more than doubled in 1990, reaching $18.5 billion, which included $14.5 billion in sales to Saudi Arabia; another multi-billion dollar arms package to Saudi Arabia was held up in November 1991 because of the Mideast peace conference. In fact, perhaps one of the reasons that Saddam Hussein was allowed by the U.S. to remain in power after the war was because his presence created a climate to secure further U.S. arms sales and military intervention in the region (see 10.5).[36]

There were also other economic reasons for a U.S. military intervention in the Gulf connected with the control and pricing of oil, although obviously the politics of oil was important. For those who think in terms of world global-power struggles, an intervention and successful war would perhaps give the United States increased power over Japan and Germany, whose economies were doing much better than that of the United States, and would thus reverse the U.S. economic decline. A U.S. military presence in the Middle East would allow the United States to influence the pricing of oil and it would therefore have increased leverage over its Japanese and European competitors who were more dependent on Middle East oil.

There was also concern over the flow of petrodollars, those Middle East oil dollars derived from immense oil profits. It was estimated that Kuwait had invested between $100 and $250 billion in the economies of Britain and the United States alone.[37] The tremendous federal deficit needed to be funded, and the Middle East oil states purchased a substantial portion of U.S. government treasury bonds, thus providing a crucial economic contribution. But although Saudi Arabia and Kuwait invested heavily in the U.S. and Western economies, Iraq invested its wealth in other projects and areas; taking Kuwaiti petrodollars out of the U.S. bond market would threaten U.S. economic stability, and if Saudi Arabia was also taken over by Iraq and its petrodollars were spent elsewhere, catastrophe could ensue. Indeed, in a speech at a meeting of the Arab Cooperation Council in Amman, Jordan, on February 24, 1990, Saddam Hussein told his Arab brethren not to invest money anymore in the United States and to invest instead in Eastern Europe and the Soviet Union.[38]

There were, then, a large number of economic, political, and military motivations for the United States to intervene in the Middle East, though most of the major reasons were not discussed in the mainstream media. Moreover, as Thomas Ferguson noted (*The Nation,* Jan. 28, 1991, pp. 1ff.), the Bush administration did not have an unlimited amount of time to force Iraq out of the Gulf through sanctions because of the tremendous costs of Operation Desert Shield, which were overburdening an already strained economy. Consequently, the rush to war was hastened by a declining economy, from which a successful war would deflect immediate attention. Indeed, some economists were claiming that a successful war could pull the United States out of recession, as well as improve the country's economic position in comparison to Japan and Western Europe.

In the light of the complex economic, political, and military logics of war, most of Bush's official rationale, which vacillated from week to week, was mere ideological camouflage for the real reasons for the military deployment, which had to do with the economic and political interests of a small group of people who planned and would benefit from the war and had little to do with the lofty principles in the name of which the war was executed. The Gulf war was thus a media propaganda war in which the Bush administration managed to cover over the key reasons for the U.S. intervention. In the remainder of this book, I shall continue developing the argument that instead of assuming its responsibilities for furthering democracy by debating issues of public concern, the main-stream media uncritically promoted the policies of the Bush administration and military, thus strengthening the power of the National Security State. I argue that during the Gulf war, the nation fell prey to one of the best-managed media propaganda campaigns in history. The military had learned its lessons from Vietnam and studied techniques to manage the press and the flow of information based on the British experience in the Falkland Islands and their own experiences in Grenada and Panama (see 2.2).

Notes

1. On the Iran/Iraq war see Hilop 1990 and Farouk-Sluglett and Sluglett (1990). The latter wrote: "The human and economic costs of the war were staggering. Diro Hilop cites Western estimates of nearly 400,000 dead, roughly a quarter Iraqi and three-quarters Iranian, and perhaps 750,000 wounded. Kamran Mofid has calculated the total cost of the war as $452.6 billion to Iraq and $644.3 billion to Iran, based on a combination of 'damage to the infrastructure; estimated oil revenue losses; and the estimated GNP losses.' He notes that this total exceeds by $678.5 billion the entire oil revenues of Iran and Iraq since they started to sell their oil on the world market, in 1919 and 1931 respectively" (p. 20).

2. On the U.S. role in building up the Iraqi military machine, see Klare 1990; Waas 1990; Darwish and Alexander 1991; Henderson 1991; Karsh and Rautski 1991; and Timmerman 1991. As it turned out, the Reagan administration was also secretly supplying Iran with military parts and weapons and, according to some accounts, had been providing weapons to Iran since 1981. Persistent stories have circulated that in a trade-off for holding the U.S. diplomats hostage in Tehran during the 1980 election campaign, the Reagan election team promised the Iranians arms and spare parts for their war against Iraq, which they began delivering, via Israel, upon assuming office. The Reagan team feared an "October Surprise" from the Carter administration, that is, a release of the U.S. hostages, which would help to reelect Carter; see Sick 1991. Whatever the truth of this story, it is documented that U.S. arms and spare parts began arriving in Iran immediately after Reagan's inauguration and secret arms deals continued to be made with Iran throughout the decade until their exposure in the Iran/Contra

affair, which only scratched the surface of the incredible secret policies of the Reagan administration. On the exposure of early arms deliveries to Iran via Israel, which was serving as intermediary, see the report concerning the Israeli chartered plane with U.S. arms bound to Iran that crashed in Turkey (*The Nation,* June 20, 1988, p. X). In addition, the Report of the Congressional Committees Investigating the Iran/Contra Affair notes that Oliver North told the Iranians that "the United States would help promote the overthrow of the Iraqi head of government" and that in Reagan's view "Saddam Hussein is a [expletive]" (Government Printing Office: Washington D.C., 1987, pp. 12f.). On Iran/Contra and allegations of Bush's involvement in this scandal, see Kellner 1990.

3. In August 1984, Peter Galbraith, Senator Claiborne Pell's (D-R.I.) Foreign Relations Committee aide, submitted a staff report warning that Saddam Hussein was running a neo-Stalinist state. The Reagan administration ordered this report to be watered down; see *The New Republic* (Nov. 5, 1990, p. 13). By 1990, the State Department had compiled a human rights abuse report on Iraq, but this report did not seem to have much influence on State Department policy toward Hussein and Iraq. On Hussein's birthday party visit by U.S. senators, see the documents in Ridgeway 1991, pp. 35ff.

According to articles published in the *Los Angeles Times,* George Bush himself intervened as Vice-President during the Reagan administration to secure controversial loans to Iraq that totalled over $5 billion, and he pushed hard to allow the export of dual use technology to Iraq that had military uses. Moreover, the *Times* reported that "in October 1989, nine months before Iraq invaded Kuwait, Bush signed a top-secret directive ordering closer ties with Baghdad and opening the way for $1 billion in loan guarantees to finance the purchase of U.S. agricultural products by Iraq. Officials in the Agriculture Department and other agencies objected to granting Iraq the loan guarantees but were overruled after Secretary of State James A. Baker III telephoned Clayton K. Yeutter, then secretary of agriculture, and asked for the aid 'on foreign policy grounds,' according to classified documents." Iraq has already defaulted on over $2 billion, and the Bush administration attempted to block Congressional inquiry into their earlier relations with Iraq (Douglas Frantz and Murray Waas, "Attempted cover-up of aid to Iraq to be probed," March 8, 1992; see also the stories of February 26, 1992; February 25, 1992; February 24, 1992; and February 23, 1992).

4. For the transcript of Glaspie's conversation with Hussein, see Ridgeway 1991; Sciolino 1991; and especially *The New Combat* 1 (Summer/Autumn 1991), which has detailed annotations and articles on both Glaspie's July 1990 testimony and postwar March 1991 testimony. In this latter testimony, Glaspie claimed that she had taken a very tough approach with Hussein and that passages in which she spoke of a "vital" U.S. relationship with Kuwait and warned Hussein that "we can never excuse settlement of disputes by other than peaceful means" were omitted from the publication of the transcripts of her talk. Later, when some senators saw the cable that she had sent to Washington after her talk, they claimed that Glaspie had misled them in her March testimony, with Senator Alan Cranston (D-Calif.) charging that, "April Glaspie deliberately misled the Congress about her role in the Persian Gulf tragedy." (*New York Times,* July 13, 1991, pp. 1 and 4, which contain excerpts from her cable).

5. See Graubard 1992 and Smith 1992. Woodward's *The Commanders* (1991) suggests that Bush was the main force pushing for war, supported by his national security adviser Brent Scowcroft, his chief of staff John Sununu, and his secretary of defense Dick Cheney. Woodward's account makes it appear as if the Pentagon sought peaceful solutions and had severe reservations about going to war. Joint Chief of Staff Colin Powell was presented by Woodward as the "reluctant warrior" who had serious doubts about seeking a military solution to the crisis in the Gulf; on Woodward's account, General Norman Schwarzkopf was also shown to have reservations about the rush to war favored by Bush and his inner circle. This interpretation appears somewhat naive, for obviously it was in the Pentagon's interest to fight a successful war and many top military officials must have been pushing this option, though one would not glean this information from Woodward's book. A book published during the same period suggests that Woodward has always been promilitary, since Reserve Officers Training Corps (ROTC) training at Yale and an early internship in the Pentagon in the 1960s, and that he has systematically covered over his close connection with the military and his conservative views (Colodny and Gettlin 1991).

6. Both Salinger and Laurent 1991 and Woodward 1991 document the CIA and defense intelligence analyses claiming that by August 1 an Iraqi invasion of Kuwait was imminent. The *International Herald Tribune* reported that on July 31, 1990, "a Defense Intelligence Agency analyst, Pat Lang, bluntly warned in a memo that Saddam Hussein intended to invade. Mr. Lang intended his memo as a 'thunderclap' to top policy makers . . . but it drew virtually no reaction" (May 3, 1991). The *New York Times* reported that CIA analyst Charles Eugene Allen, whose job is to warn the government when crises are emerging, had urgently warned the U.S. government that Iraq was about to invade Kuwait (Jan. 24, 1991, p. A9). Allen reportedly walked into the offices of the National Security Council's Middle East staff and told them: "This is your final warning" and that by day's end, Kuwait would be invaded by Iraq. Allen had also reportedly crossed over bureaucratic lines previous to August 1, warning a senior State Department official and two National Security Council experts that an invasion was imminent. He was rewarded for his vigilance by having his biweekly reports on trouble spots suspended and his staff cut. Finally, Woodward claims that General Colin Powell concluded that Iraq was not bluffing and was about to invade Kuwait and that Powell told Cheney to warn the president. Nothing was done, however, and as "far as Powell could tell, either the White House had another idea about how to handle the problem, or the suggestion just fell through the cracks" (1991, p. 221). Thus, Bush could have easily prevented the Iraqi invasion of Kuwait, either by directly contacting Iraq or making a public statement warning Iraq of the consequences of invading its neighbor.

7. Throughout this study, we shall note how time and again the mainstream media uncritically presented Bush administration positions as "facts" while independent journalists and scholars offer different and usually more compelling versions. I might also note that various sources spell Middle Eastern sites like "Jidda" differently and I am following the standard U.S. usage, while Salinger and Laurent 1991 in the passages cited use the British spelling "Jeddah."

8. Independent investigative sources tend to blame the Kuwaitis for subverting the Jidda summit (Salinger and Laurent 1991, pp. 64–77; Emery 1991, pp. 6ff.; and Simpson 1991, pp. 107–109). Emery cited a hand-scrawled note from the emir of Kuwait to the crown prince, who would be representing Kuwait at the meeting, which advised him not to listen to requests of Arab solidarity from the Saudis or the Iraqis, nor to submit to Iraqi threats; this was the advice of "our friends in Washington, London and Egypt." The Emir closed by stating that: "We are stronger than they think." According to Emery, King Fahd of Saudi Arabia told King Hussein of Jordan that the failure of the conference was "all the Kuwaitis fault" and that King Hussein believed that indeed the Kuwaitis sabotaged the summit and that the note was authentic (Emery 1991, pp. 9–12).

9. See *The Economist* which claimed that with Iraq's invasion of Kuwait it controlled twenty percent of the "world's known oil reserves" and would rival Saudi Arabia as OPEC's "swing" producer (Aug. 4, 1990, p. 13). *Time* magazine asserted that Iraq doubled the oil under its control to some twenty percent of the world's known reserve and that only Saudi Arabia, with twenty-five percent, had more (Aug. 13, 1990, p. 16). In fact, there were arguments that the claims concerning the amount of oil controlled by Kuwait, Saudi Arabia, and Iraq were greatly exaggerated and that the phrase "known oil reserves" was misleading because there are vast oil resources that have not been developed in the United States, Soviet Union, and off the Falkland Islands. Vialls (1991) claimed that the undeveloped oil reserves off the Falkland Islands are much larger than the Saudi Arabia oil reserves, but the cost of developing the off-shore oil resources, far from refineries and distribution, would require a much higher per-barrel oil price than the market is currently yielding. He suggested that the Gulf war might have been in part a cynical ploy to help exhaust Saudi, Kuwaiti, and Iraqi oil supplies so that oil prices could go up enough to make it pay to develop the Falkland off-shore oil resources, thus producing a bonanza for the U.S. and Britain which would control these oil resources.

10. The *Washington Post* also reported on August 4, 1990, that "U.S. intelligence yesterday monitored a new buildup of 100,000 Iraqi troops in Kuwait south of the capital and near the border with Saudi Arabia." On August 5, the *Post* published a story by Charles Babcock on the possibility of an Iraqi invasion of Saudi Arabia and the inability of the Saudis to defend themselves; editorial writer Jim Hoagland contributed an article on "Stopping Saddam's Drive for Dominance," arguing against "appeasement" of Iraq.

11. A *New York Times* summary of the genesis of the war by Thomas Friedman and Patrick Tyler on March 3, 1991, claimed that the Bush administration had decided on the path to war in September; the *Times*'s analysis, however, suggested that Bush and Scowcroft were pushing the military option from the beginning (p. A12). Emery (1991, p. 19) wrote that King Hussein told him that Margaret Thatcher blurted out on August 3 that "troops were halfway to their destination" before the official request came for them to go to the Middle East. In addition, I met a soldier on an airplane in December 1990 who told me that he had been sent to the Gulf some days before the official U.S. deployment had been announced.

12. The *New York Times* also began attacking Iraq and Saddam Hussein, publishing stories and columns on August 5, 1990, with headlines: "Arab of Vast Ambition—Saddam Hussein," "Iraq Makes Its Bid to Run the Show in the Middle East," "Stopping Saddam's Drive for Dominance," and "Stop Hussein with Force if Necessary." For a comparative analysis of *New York Times* and *Washington Post* coverage of the crisis in the Gulf, see Malek and Leidig 1991.

13. On the Saddam-as-Hitler theme, see 2.1.

14. "Yellow journalism" is a term associated with the sensation-mongering journalism that began in the late 19th century with Joseph Pulitzer's *World* and William Randolph Hearst's *San Francisco Examiner* and *New York Journal*. Hearst and other "yellow journalists" produced a war hysteria and campaigned for a war against Spain in Cuba, often trumping up false threats against the United States. See the chapter on "The Age of Yellow Journalism" in Emery and Emery 1992, pp. 226ff.

15. On August 6, 1954, the *New York Times* published an editorial celebrating the overthrow of the Mossadegh government in Iran and the restoration of the shah, accompanied by a takeover of 40 percent of the Iranian oil by U.S. corporations, breaking a British monopoly. The editors wrote: "Underdeveloped countries with rich resources now have an object lesson in the heavy cost that must be paid by one of their number which goes berserk with fanatical nationalism. It is perhaps too much to hope that Iran's experience will prevent the rise of Mossadeghs in other countries, but that experience may at least strengthen the hands of more reasonable and more far-seeing leaders." Namely, those who will have a clear-eyed understanding of the U.S.'s overriding priorities (thanks to Noam Chomsky for this reference). In this context, the U.S. military intervention and Gulf war was an object lesson to Third World leaders who do not follow U.S. priorities and policies.

16. Some West German government reports indicated that it was really Syrian connections and not Libyan ones who were responsible for the bombing. On Oct. 29, 1986, John Laurence on ABC News quoted top German officials as attributing the disco bombing to Syria. See also the article by Elaine Sciolino, *New York Times,* Nov. 20, 1986, who reported that a number of administration officials said privately that the disco bombing was carried out by the same organization responsible for the bombing of an Arab social club in West Berlin, and that pretrial testimony linked Syria, not Libya, to that attack. A few days later, *Der Spiegel* reported suspicions that the perpetrators were actually double agents working for the Israeli secret services (Dec. 1, 1986), a story reproduced in the *Boston Globe,* Dec. 1, 1986; see the discussion in Chomsky 1987, pp. 113ff. A report, broadcast Sept. 14, 1990, on Radio Deutsche Welle, suggested that the CIA knew that a terrorist bombing of the disco was in the works, but failed to maintain proper security, perhaps to give the Reagan administration a pretext for bombing Libya; see the discussion in Joel Bleifuss, "The First Stone," *In These Times,* Sept. 26, 1990, p. 5.

17. This same Patrick Tyler in the same *Washington Post* had published a puff piece on Saddam Hussein on May 13, 1989 (p. A13) describing how Hussein was pursuing the "politics of pragmatism," moderating Iraq's previous radical tradi-

tion "in favor of friendly overtures to Arab moderates and the West." Christopher Hitchen noted that the *New York Times* also characterized Iraq as "pragmatic" and "cooperative," attributing these virtues to Hussein's "personal strength" (*Harper's,* Jan. 1991, p. 72). Yet the same Hussein had suddenly become the *Post's* "beast of Baghdad" and the previously bestial Hafez al-Assad of Syria had become "pragmatic." Obviously, bestiality is in the eyes of the beholder and the policies of the current administration, which opportunistic journalists are only too eager to serve.

18. Karsh and Rautsi (1991) has been received as the most reliable book on Saddam Hussein and Iraq yet to appear; see the review in *Middle East International,* August 30, 1991, p. 22.

19. James Atkins, Nixon's former ambassador to Saudi Arabia and a career diplomat, told *In These Times*: "The U.S. deployment is totally unnecessary. There is going to be no invasion. Saddam Hussein is a rational person; an invasion of Saudi Arabia would have been an irrational act." Atkins explained that since the Carter Doctrine was a major tenet of U.S. foreign policy, Hussein would know that any attack on Saudi Arabia would have brought a swift U.S. military response (Aug. 29, 1991, p. 5). In addition, after the war, *Los Angeles Times* reporter Jack Nelson stated in a symposium sponsored by the Gannett Foundation: "The reports of Iraqi troops massed at the Saudi border were certainly intended to tell the American people that there was a threat of invasion, when in fact there weren't that many [Iraqi] troops at all. I think today most government people will tell you that nobody really thought that Saddam Hussein was going to go into Saudi Arabia; but the story helped marshall public opinion behind the war effort" (in LaMay et al. 1991, pp. 73–74). In fact, the mainstream media were saying that there *was* a threat that Iraq was going to invade Saudi Arabia and that the U.S. military deployment was thus necessary; see the clips from editorials from the major U.S. newspaper in LaMay et al. 1991, pp. 54–55.

20. Reuters transmitted the *Washington Post* version of the Hussein/Wilson meeting, and it was published in newspapers such as the *Toronto Star, USA Today,* and *Newsday.* ABC and the other TV networks also bought into the *Washington Post* version of the meeting between Saddam Hussein and Joe Wilson. In explaining why the Bush administration was sending troops to Saudi Arabia, ABC White House correspondent Brit Hume noted on the August 7 edition of "ABC World News Tonight": "of course, there was a meeting yesterday in Baghdad in which the United States *chargé d'affaires* was told in no uncertain terms by Saddam Hussein that not only did he not intend to leave Kuwait, he intended to claim it as his own. Finally, intelligence reports overnight indicated what the White House is calling an 'imminent threat to Saudi Arabia' from the very positioning of the Iraqi forces in Kuwait." That evening on ABC's "Nightline," host Ted Koppel informed the audience that he'd just received information "from my colleague Bob Zelnick over at the Pentagon, who quotes sources over there as saying that there is strong evidence that the Iraqis are now massing along the border with Saudi Arabia and that there is some fear that they may launch an invasion even before U.S. troops get there." This disinformation was obviously intended to legitimate the U.S. deployment and to create anxiety that could be utilized to mobilize consent to the Bush administration policy.

21. The *Washington Post* cheerleader for the war, Jim Hoagland, dutifully attacked "Saddam's Big Lie" (that dispossessed Arabs would supposedly profit from his seizure of Kuwait's oil) in the August 9 edition, failing to note that it was Bush who was producing a really Big Lie concerning Iraq's alleged threat to Saudi Arabia—a lie reproduced by Hoagland. Hoagland also attacked CBS for interviewing Jordanians who were sympathetic towards Saddam Hussein and who opposed the U.S. military intervention and war, as if it was the duty of journalists simply to parrot the line of the administration rather than providing a range of viewpoints on controversial and important issues.

22. Interestingly, there was a report that the Soviets launched a new photo reconnaissance spy satellite within 48 hours of the invasion of Kuwait whose orbit was identical to the U.S. satellite (PeaceNet, mideast.gulf, Aug. 15, 1990). But there have been no release of pictures or information from the Soviet government, so we have only the visual evidence of the Soviet commercial satellite pictures against the claims of the U.S. government.

23. For the record, I might note that the *New York Times* slavishly followed the Bush administration line through the early days of the crisis rather than actively promoting the military solution à la the *Washington Post*. When, on the day of the invasion of Kuwait, Bush attacked Iraq's "naked aggression" of Kuwait but did not call for a military intervention, the *Times*'s R. W. Apple titled his front-page story "Naked Aggression" and the *Times*'s editorialist opined: "The U.S. has no treaty obligation to come to Kuwait's aid. But the gulf states and most nations still look to Washington for leadership and help in organizing action. President Bush has responded with the right lead—a strong national stand and a strong push for collective diplomacy" (Aug. 3, 1990). When, shortly thereafter, Bush sent U.S. troops to Saudi Arabia, the *Times* quickly got on board, writing in an August 9 editorial appropriately titled "The U.S. Stands Up. Who Else?": "President Bush has drawn a line in the sand, committing U.S. forces to face down Saddam Hussein. . . . On balance, he has made the right choice in the right way."

24. United Press International (UPI) reported that Algerian President Chadli Benjedid was "one of the few Arab leaders still on speaking terms with both Saddam and the Saudi Arabian leadership," noting that he was "known for successful mediations, including the release of U.S. hostages in Iran in 1980" (Dec. 13, 1990, from clarinews). In a Dec. 18, 1990 UPI report, it was claimed: "Diplomatic sources said Benjedid has tried to arrange a meeting between Saddam and King Fahd of Saudi Arabia. But the [Saudi] kingdom put a damper on his efforts when it failed to invite him to Riyadh." Finally, President Chadli was planning to fly to Washington on January 13 to carry through a last-minute negotiating mission, but as he arrived at the airport he received the message that U.S. officials would refuse to meet him when he arrived in Washington (Briemberg 1992, p. 27). On the Algerian initiative, see also Salinger and Laurent 1991.

25. "Overdetermination" signifies a coexistence of multiple causes operating together on different levels to explain complex historical events. Althusser (1969) introduced the concept of overdetermination to avoid reductionistic readings of Marxism as a form of economic determinism in which economics was taken to

be the sole important causal factor in history. The relevance of this concept for interpreting the causes of the Gulf war is to avoid interpreting it solely as a war for oil, as did many in the antiwar movement, or on economic or narrowly political grounds alone. Obviously, economics were important, but so were a variety of other political, military, cultural, and psychological factors; thus a multicausal model is necessary to explicate the causes and aims of the Gulf war.

26. During the war, the *Village Voice* published an article (Feb. 5, 1991) on George Bush, Jr.'s oil interests in Bahrain and there were also indications that Brent Scowcroft, Bush's national security adviser who pushed hard for the military option, also had oil interests. *Houston Post* investigative reporter Pete Brewton discovered, in the course of Savings and Loan (S&L) scandal research, that George Bush, Jr., the president's son, had interests in Harken oil, which had an exclusive contract to drill for oil in Bahrain. Moreover, Brewton learned that George, Jr., sold his stock in the company some weeks before the Iraqi invasion of Kuwait. Furthermore, he failed to report the transaction until March 1991, nearly eight months after the federal deadline for disclosing such transactions. This episode raises the question of whether George, Jr., was guilty of "insider trading" and whether his father was planning for a war in the Gulf in the summer of 1990 when George, Jr., conveniently sold his stock. One week after the invasion of Kuwait, Harken traded for just $3.03 per share, down nearly 24% from the price that George Bush, Jr., received for his shares seven weeks earlier. So far, there has been no SEC investigation of this transaction; see the discussion in David Armstrong, "Oil in the Family," *The Texas Observer,* July 12, 1991, p. 12.

27. For years, there had been media presentations of Bush as a "wimp"; see, for example, the October 19, 1987, *Newsweek* cover story "Bush Battles the 'Wimp Factor,'" (pp. 28ff.); and Eleanor Clift, "The 'Carterization' of Bush," *Newsweek* (Oct. 22, 1990, p. 28). Many speculated that Bush's insecurities might have helped drive him to war. It may be worth mentioning that after the Panama invasion, "President Bush exulted that no one could call him 'timid'; he was at last a 'macho man.' The press, in even more primal language, hailed him for succeeding in an 'initiation rite' by demonstrating his 'willingness to shed blood.'" (Barbara Ehrenreich in Bennis and Moushabeck 1991, p. 130). Later, after Bush's fluttering heart condition and diagnosis of a hyperthyroid condition in May 1991, pundits speculated that Bush's overactive thyroid might have driven him to pursue military action; see William Safire's column in the *New York Times* Op-Ed page on May 18. Actually, such complex decisions are always overdetermined and no doubt there were a complex set of psychological, physiological, political, economic, and other factors which explain why Bush undertook his second major military action in the second year of his presidency.

28. An accurate and complete biography of Bush remains to be written. It would trace his background in an Establishment family with deep roots in big business, government, and military intelligence; his own career in the military and CIA; his possible involvement in the October Surprise, perhaps the crime of the century; his longtime involvement with Manuel Noriega and other unsavory dictators around the world; his involvement in the Iran/Contra affair and other scandals of the Reagan era; and his role in promoting the Gulf war. These episodes should make for an interesting project. See the pieces about Bush's life

collected from mainstream and alternative news sources in Kellner 1990, especially the appendixes.

29. By "National Security State" I mean the set of political, military, and intelligence institutions that promote an aggressive foreign policy, including covert operations, military intervention, and war as an instrument of state policy. These institutions include the Pentagon, the CIA, and other intelligence agencies. During the Reagan and Bush Administrations the White House itself became an instrument of the National Security State which carried out covert operations, military actions, and war, sometimes secretly and sometimes with the complicity of Congress. A National Security State sees the promotion of "national security," as defined by those in power, as the primary goal of the state and advocates the use of military action when the interests of dominant political and economic groups are at stake. To justify and maintain its existence, it produces enemies, promotes tensions, and carries out covert and overt wars to legitimize the vast amount of wealth and resources it commands. During the forty-plus years of the cold war, the war against communism was used by the National Security State to justify its aggressive actions. Since the demise of the communist threat, new enemies have had to be found, such as drugs, terrorism, or governments alleged to be hostile to the United States such as Libya or Iraq. With the end of the cold war, serious debates began to arise as to whether the National Security State was really necessary and the Gulf war was arguably undertaken to justify continuing its existence. Finally, the National Security State is aligned with what has been called the military-industrial complex that produces the weapons and products which it commands.

30. Andrew Rosenthal quoted an unnamed White House official, who stated, "It was Brent's presentation at one of the meetings on August 3, that Friday after the invasion, that made clear what the stakes were, crystallized people's thinking and galvanized support for a very strong response" (*New York Times,* Feb. 21, 1991; see also Elizabeth Drew, *The New Yorker,* Dec. 3, 1990, p. 178, and Woodward 1991, pp. 300–301, passim).

31. See Bob Feldman's article in *Downtown,* Jan. 23, 1991. When Andrew Rosenthal profiled Scowcroft in the *New York Times* on February 21, 1991, he skipped over Scowcroft's economic connections and years in the private sector, even though the *Standard and Poor's Register of Corporations* listed Scowcroft in 1984, 1985, and 1986 as a member of the board of directors of Santa Fe International, a subsidiary of the Kuwait Petroleum Corporation. Furthermore, I checked several data bases encompassing mainstream media sources and none of them had articles connecting Scowcroft with Santa Fe International, which highlighted his economic relationship with the Kuwaiti government whose interests he pushed throughout the crisis in the Gulf and the Gulf war.

32. John Tower died in a plane crash after the Gulf war, and the media never investigated *why* Bush would nominate such a thoroughly discredited individual as secretary of defense. During a television interview that I did with University of Texas history professor Tom Philpott on boy prostitution, shown on *Alternative Views,* Philpott mentioned that Tower's name often came up as a client of young boy prostitutes and claimed that Tower had filled out a deposition to this effect

with the FBI. Despite all of the sexual scandals and alcohol abuse stories concerning Tower, well-known in Washington circles, Bush nominated him—after Tower had chaired an important committee that had helped cover over Bush's involvement in the Iran/Contra scandals. Despite all of the media wallowing in the Tower scandal during his failed confirmation hearing, few, if any, official media commentators made this connection, symptomatic of the mainstream media failure to investigate George Bush's motivations, background, and character.

33. When responding to a reporter's question after the Panama invasion concerning the impact of the operation on the debate on the cuts in the defense budget, Powell answered: "Thank you for the question. I hope it has a great effect. I hope it has enormous effect. . . . And as we start to go down in dollars and as we see the world changing, don't bust this apart. . . . Don't think that this is the time to demobilize the armed force of the United States because it isn't. There are still dangers in the world" (Woodward 1991, p. 194). Thus the Panama invasion was obviously in part an attempt on behalf of the Bush administration and Pentagon to save the military from extensive budget cuts and to demonstrate the usefulness of U.S. military force. The Gulf war, from this perspective, was a more spectacular venture to advance the interests of the U.S. military and the National Security State.

34. See Stork and Wenger in Sifry and Cerf 1991, pp. 34ff.; Scott Henson, "Entangling Alliances," *The Texas Observer,* Jan. 25, 1991, pp. 5ff.; and Sheila Ryan, "Countdown for a Decade: The U.S. Build Up for War in the Gulf" in Bennis and Moushabeck 1991, pp. 91–102. Actually, the United States had ten bases in Oman before the war even started and had the infrastructure for about sixteen bases in place in Saudi Arabia; Armstrong argued (1991) that altogether $200 billion had been invested in Saudi military bases. So the U.S. was definitely ready for its Gulf war with policy and military infrastructure already at hand.

35. In addition, a National Security Council White Paper was prepared in May 1990 that asserted: "Iraq and Saddam Hussein are described as 'the optimum contenders to replace the Warsaw Pact' as the rationale for continuing cold war military spending and for putting an end to the 'peace dividend'" (John Pilger, *The New Statesman,* Feb. 8, 1991). In July 1990, Schwarzkopf played a computer war game under the code name "Exercise External Look 1990" (J. Der Derian, "War Games May Prove Deadly," *Newsday,* Dec. 9, 1990). In an October 8, 1990, interview with *USA Today,* Schwarzkopf revealed that the U.S. military was ready for war in the Gulf because two years earlier they had learned that Iraq "had run computer simulations and war games for the invasion of Kuwait." Schwarzkopf noted in the same interview that he programs "possible conflicts with Iraq on computers almost daily." These examples suggest that the United States had been planning for a war with Iraq for some time.

36. *The Toronto Star* reported on August 12, 1991 (p. A3) that "U.S. weapons sales to the Third World more than doubled last year, making America the world's top arms supplier." The growth in U.S. arms sales from nearly $8 billion in 1989 to $18.5 billion in 1990 was attributed to the Iraqi threat in the Gulf. It was the first time since 1983 that the United States ranked at the top of the list of arms suppliers to Third World nations.

37. See Peter Dale Scott, "U.S. Needs Kuwaiti Petrodollars—Not Just Oil," *San Francisco Chronicle,* Jan. 2, 1991, pp. C1–2.

38. See *The Economist,* Sept. 29, 1990, p. 20, and April Glaspie's congressional testimony, March 20–21, 1991, broadcast on C-SPAN; see also the account in Waas 1991, pp. 60ff. and, Ridgeway 1991, pp. 25ff.

CHAPTER TWO

———————◆———————

The "Crisis in the Gulf" and the Mainstream Media

IN EARLY AUGUST 1990, the "crisis in the Gulf" threatened the political economy and order of the Middle East and the United States quickly responded with the threat of military force. In this chapter, I discuss how the mainstream media constructed "the crisis in the Gulf" through analysis of the primary frames, images, and discourse by which the crisis was presented to the public; I put the phrase in quotation marks to highlight that the crisis was a media construct, as was "Saddam Hussein," "Iraq," "Arabs," and "the Middle East." Thus, although the West presented the events as a "crisis in the Gulf," Arabs spoke of "the annexation" or the "gulf build-up" (Ivan Solotaroff, "Lines in the Sand," *Village Voice,* Oct. 30, 1990, p. 28). Moreover, most people had no direct experience or knowledge of these phenomena so their pictures of the events in the Gulf were a product of the Bush administration discourse and media frames through which the crisis was constructed. My argument is that the mainstream media fostered the military solution through its framing of the images and the discourse of the crisis, through its omissions, and through the ways that the media were manipulated and controlled by the Bush administration and Pentagon to manufacture consent to its policies.

2.1 The Media and Hegemony

Ruling elites use the mainstream media to promote their own agendas and to advance their own interests. I explored a classic case of media manipulation in section 1.1 whereby the Bush administration leaked disinformation to the press to legitimate sending U.S. troops to Saudi Arabia and to mobilize public support for this action. Once the Bush administration announced that it had sent a huge number of troops to

Saudi Arabia on August 7, the mainstream media applauded these actions and became a conduit for mobilizing support for U.S. policy. For weeks, only a few dissenting voices were heard in the mainstream media, and no significant debate took place over the validity and dangerous consequences of the initial U.S. military response to the Iraqi invasion. During the first three months of the crisis, TV coverage, in particular, favorably portrayed all U.S. policy actions, presented the U.S. military intervention in an extremely positive light, and privileged those voices seeking a military solution to the conflict.

As the U.S. military juggernaut occupied Saudi Arabia, television commentators spoke of the inevitability of war and of the necessity for a military solution. For example, on ABC's "Nightline" on August 20, correspondent Forrest Sawyer indicated that he believed that the United States was moving toward a military resolution of the crisis. ABC reported on August 21, after citing a 75 percent approval rating for Bush, that "Americans appear to be rallying around the president and to support military action"; later in the same broadcast ABC cited French President Mitterrand claiming that "Saddam Hussein has led the world to a war mentality from which it will be hard to get out." On August 23, NBC Pentagon correspondent Fred Francis reported that the Pentagon had promised the Saudis that they would not leave Saudi Arabia and allow Saddam Hussein to remain in place and that unless he pulled out of Kuwait immediately, there would be war in three to six weeks.

When the Iraqis began floating diplomatic initiatives on August 12, they were shot down one by one by the Bush administration, which was inexorably orchestrating the march to war (see 1.2). The media rarely criticized the Bush administration's failure to negotiate a diplomatic settlement to the crisis in the Gulf and served to cover over their relentless progress toward a military solution. In fact, the mainstream media consistently privileged whatever strategy the Bush administration favored and were little more than public relations managers for the White House and Pentagon. On the other hand, there was eventually some debate precisely because of differences in ruling circles and the public concerning the advisability of a war in the Middle East. Many members of the political establishment had grave doubts concerning the wisdom of getting involved in the turbulent politics of the region and there were many economic sectors that were concerned that a war in the Gulf would harm their interests. From the early days of the crisis, there were frequent and intense discussions in the mainstream media concerning the impact on the economy of a Gulf war and many sectors of the economy were indeed harmed by the crisis and war, including the travel industry, the automobile industry, retail and consumer goods industries, and the housing industry. Many economists feared that the rising oil prices and uncertainty concerning war would induce a recession, which eventually occurred, and the stock and commodity markets were jittery and erratic throughout the crisis and war.

In addition, there was great concern in the public over the wisdom of getting involved in a Middle East war. Memories of the Vietnam debacle were still strong and there was a reluctance among sectors of the public to support a military solution to the crisis. There was also a strong peace movement that organized during the crisis which consisted of veterans of the 1960s antiwar movement; members of the antinuclear, environmental, feminist, and other social movements opposed to war; and members of a younger generation who themselves did not want to be involved in war. While this antiwar movement was rarely seen or heard from in the mainstream media, it was well organized, large, and vocal and had at least some influence on public opinion (see Paley 1991 and Cagan 1992).

In view of the division of opinion over the proper response to the crisis in the Gulf, I believe that it is better to utilize a hegemony model of the media which explains media discourse as articulating positions within or against an established hegemony, or as an attempt to establish hegemony within society. Thus, rather than seeing the media as instruments of the state or business which are merely used to manipulate individuals to support the state or the established economic system, it is better to analyze how the media function within varying struggles for hegemony. Different groups and social forces are constantly struggling for hegemony within society in order to control the direction, policies, and future of the society. During the 1950s, a conservative hegemony formed in the United States during the cold war and a period of relative affluence and social conformity. This hegemony was challenged by Kennedy liberalism in the 1960s and then by a variety of countercultural and social movements the same decade. The 1970s was a period of contestation between liberal and conservative forces with the marginalization of more radical forces. The elimination of Nixon during the Watergate affair and 1976 victory of Jimmy Carter suggested an uneasy liberal hegemony during the era.

From the 1980s to the present, however, a conservative hegemony has been in place, though it has been and continues to be contested (see 10.5 on the latter point and for the historical analysis presented here see Kellner 1990 and Kellner and Ryan 1988; Ferguson and Rogers [1984] analyze which particular corporate forces, groups, and institutions supported the opposing political factions during the 1970s and early 1980s). Yet U.S. society continues to be divided, contested, and full of contradictions which makes possible the space for critical discourse and oppositional politics. The advantages of a hegemony model over an instrumental model are that it recognizes contradictions within ruling elites, between ruling groups and the public, between professional journalistic ethics and serving the interests of corporate elites, and between genuine information and mere propaganda (see Kellner 1990, pp. 16–20 and Chapter 3). The hegemony model also represents society and culture as a contested terrain and depicts various social groups and movements struggling for power, rather than seeing society merely as a site of manipulation and domination (though, as this book will document, such manipulation of the public does obviously occur).

From this perspective, the Gulf war was a hegemonic project organized around the use of military force to resolve political conflicts and to assert U.S. interests in a "New World Order" with the U.S. as the world's number one superpower. Such a project would highlight the importance of the military for U.S. foreign policy in which the U.S. would use its military might to become the policeman of the world. This project was supported by Bush, Scowcroft, Gates, and many in the U.S. military and would promote the continuation of a National Security State (see 1.3). Bush's Gulf war policies were able to enlist the support of old Cold Warriors looking for new enemies, as well as military-industrial complex interests, big oil, banking and finance, and other interests directly served by a strong U.S. role in the Middle East and other hot spots of the world. Because an aggressive interventionist policy and war in the Gulf was opposed by powerful forces, it was crucial that the Bush administration enlist mainstream media support in establishing their Gulf intervention as a hegemonic project and, as I argue in this chapter, they were on the whole successful.

Not all mainstream media voices supported without reservation the Bush administration policies, however, and critical discourses that appeared during the crisis in the Gulf can thus be explained through conflicts within society over the viability of a military solution.

There were structural reasons concerning the ownership and structure of the media which help explain why the mainstream media supported the military solution. As Scott Henson argued, the interlocking connections between the military and television networks are striking: General Electric (GE), which owns NBC, derived $9 billion of its $54.5 billion in revenues from military contracts in 1989 (while NBC only provided $3.4 billion in revenue). Lee and Solomon (1991, p. xvii) pointed out that GE "designed, manufactured or supplied parts or maintenance for nearly every major weapon system employed by the U.S. during the Gulf war—including the Patriot and Tomahawk Cruise missiles, the Stealth bomber, the B-52 bomber, the AWACS plane and the NAVSTAR spy satellite system. In other words, when correspondents and paid consultants on NBC television praised the performance of U.S. weapons, they were extolling equipment made by GE, the corporation that pays their salary."

Many GE board members sit on the boards of other corporate media like the *Washington Post* and are connected with U.S. government agencies and oil corporations as well. ABC's board of directors is involved with oil companies and the defense industries, and CBS also has connections with big oil and the defense industries (see Henson 1991 and the charts compiled by Doug Henwood in Kellner 1990, pp. 83–87). Greg LeRoy pointed out in an August 4, 1991, *Houston Post* article that: "The chair of Capital Cities/ABC-TV sits on the board of Texaco. And CBS's board includes directors from Honeywell and the Rand Corp. (both of which are major military contractors). NBC is owned by General Electric, the same GE that had aircraft engines in more than 20 different types of combat aircraft serving in the Gulf."

Hence, there were strong corporate forces connected to the "Big Three" TV networks which would benefit from a war in the Middle East. Consequently, when the networks were boosting military technology, a military solution to the crisis, and U.S. intervention to promote corporate interests, they were acting in the interests of the corporate elite who controlled the networks. Indeed, we shall see that there were many examples of blatant bias in favor of corporate interests during the coverage of the Gulf war that have once again compromised the mainstream media's functions of providing accurate and unbiased information to make a working democracy possible.

In addition, the mainstream media tend to support administrations whose political policies and agendas correspond to their own interests. During the Reagan administration, the networks were extremely uncritical of Reagan and his policies in part because they supported his tax program, his deregulation, and his lax enforcement of antitrust policies which allowed the networks to merge with big corporations and which tremendously benefitted them economically (see Kellner 1990 for documentation). For similar reasons, the corporate sector has largely supported Bush, though if his economic policies fail and a viable alternative emerges, they may abandon him (see 10.5).

Furthermore, the discourses of the state are usually privileged by television news in particular, especially in times of crisis. The press and broadcast media journalists regularly get their news and information from official sources and thus attempt to maintain good personal relations with their sources. Thomas Friedman of the *New York Times* plays tennis with U.S. Secretary of State James Baker, receives frequent leaks of information and briefings from high State Department officials, and is considered an important source of State Department thinking on various issues. George Bush invites reporters to go jogging or walking with him and plays tennis with ABC White House correspondent Brit Hume; Bush and his staff often favor sympathetic reporters like Hume with information or interviews. John McWethy of ABC news has had close links with the Reagan and Bush administrations and all of the Pentagon correspondents depend on inside connections for information and perspective, and thus are easily manipulated by their sources.

If reporters turn on their sources, or are too critical of official policies, they disrupt their connections and lose important conduits of information. Furthermore, as a matter of convention, the mainstream news media usually include views from the current administration and present administration positions as fully and sympathetically as possible. During times of crisis, especially with late-breaking stories, the media are especially dependent on official sources which are thus able to manipulate and control the agenda. If the public, as in the case of the crisis in the Gulf, tends to support official policy, this is another incentive for the mainstream media to privilege the views of the administration in power, for going against popular policies could lead to loss of audience and revenue. Conversely, if administration policies are unpopular, the media may gain audiences and thus revenues by criticizing these policies, which provides structural economic reasons for occasional critical discourse.

In fact, it is another convention of mainstream media coverage that they usually cite the opinion of leaders of the opposing political party. If the Democratic leadership agrees with Republican policies, as frequently happened during the past decade, then the hegemonic policies or ideas are strengthened. Yet if there is significant establishment opposition to administration policies, there is usually someone in a high position who on or off record will provide information or critical opinions to journalists who may choose to go with oppositional views and information embarrassing to the established administration. In the highly competitive world of the mainstream media, there are also rewards for breaking stories and for presenting novel or challenging views as well as official ones. While on the whole the ethos of investigative and oppositional reporting, which had a brief vogue even within the mainstream media during the 1970s, has been on the decline, there are still some journalists who follow the ethic of balance, objectivity, presenting various sides of a story, and even articulating views or information that may oppose official policies and spokespeople.

Hegemony thus involves conflict, opposition, and shifting configurations of power and ideology. The media do not construct hegemony through imposing a one-dimensional, dominant, shared set of ideas which are then absorbed by a passive public. U.S. society itself is divided into competing groups, ideologies, and political agendas which play themselves out in the media. Hegemony is constructed when a coalition of social groups imposes its agenda on the public and it attains dominance. Since most people get their ideas and opinions through the mainstream media it is a crucial site of hegemony. But hegemony is usually contested and hegemony shifts, develops, and mobilizes opinion according to the vicissitudes of the situation.

During the crisis in the Gulf and the Gulf war, the Bush administration achieved hegemony by successfully carrying out its war policy and selling it to the public. Although there was opposition to Bush administration policies, this opposition was marginalized in the mainstream media and ultimately silenced. In the following sections, I analyze how the Bush administration constructed hegemony for its military adventure by shaping the discourses, frames, and images through which the crisis was interpreted and ultimately accepted by the public. The media aided in the construction of Bush administration and Pentagon hegemony through transmitting its positions and discourses and through omission of what issues it did not discuss and what alternatives to the war policy it did not pose. I argue that during this fateful episode of world history, the mainstream media in the United States failed to serve the public by providing a wide range of opinion on issues of great importance during the crisis in the Gulf. In particular, they failed to inform the public concerning what was at stake in the crisis, what the consequences of war would be, what alternatives there were to a military solution to the crisis, and who would primarily benefit from a Gulf war. Yet the fact that there was occasional questioning of Bush administration and Pentagon policies within the mainstream media, which I draw on in this book, indicates that there were divisions within the policy establishment and public over the wisdom of U.S. Gulf policy. However, as I shall indicate in the following sections, the mainstream media framed their coverage of the crisis in ways that supported Bush administration policies and that thus helped mobilize support for the Gulf war.

Frames, Images, and the Construction of the Enemy

The media mobilize public opinion according to frames through which they present events and individuals. The frames utilized to present possible U.S. military intervention or war involved producing an image of the enemy. As Sam Keen puts it, "In the beginning we create the enemy. Before the weapon comes the image. We *think* others to death and then invent the battle-axe or the ballistic missiles with which to actually kill them. Propaganda precedes technology" (1986, p. 10). From the outset of the crisis in the Gulf, the media employed the frame of popular culture that portrays conflict as a battle between good and evil.[1] Saddam Hussein quickly became the villain in this scenario with the media vilifying the Iraqi leader as a madman, a Hitler, and worse, while whipping up anti-Iraqi war fever. Saddam was described by Mary McGrory (see 1.1 above) as a "beast" (*Washington Post,* Aug. 7, 1990) and a "monster" that "Bush may have to destroy" (*Newsweek,* Oct. 20, 1990, and Sept. 3, 1990). George Will called Saddam "more virulent" than Mussolini and then increased Hussein's evil by using the Saddam-as-Hitler metaphor in his syndicated columns. *New York Times* editorialist A. M. Rosenthal attacked Hussein as "barbarous" and "an evil dreamer of death" (Aug. 9, 1990). *The New York Post* described Hussein as "a bloodthirsty megalomaniac" and headlined tabloid fashion the epithet "UP YOURS!" when word emerged on August 7 that Bush was sending troops to Saudi Arabia. *The New Republic* doctored a *Time* magazine cover photo on Saddam to make him appear more like Hitler by shortening his mustache. The Saddam-as-Hitler metaphor, of course, would be one of the dominant images of the crisis and war. According to a study by the Gannett Foundation, there were 1,170 examples in the print media and television of linking Saddam Hussein with Hitler (see LaMay et al. 1991, p. 42).[2]

Cartoonists had a field day presenting images of a demonized Saddam Hussein and television resorted to cartoon techniques itself as when a NBC "war game" simulation on August 8, 1990, had a U.S. colonel pretending to be Hussein and threatening, "I'll hang a hostage every day!" The media eagerly reported all of Hussein's alleged and actual crimes (suddenly focusing on actions and events that had gone unreported when Saddam was a U.S. ally, such as his use of chemical weapons against Kurdish rebels in his own country). There was even speculation on Iraq's plans for future terrorism when no current atrocities were on hand (see *Christian Science Monitor,* September 21, 1990) and countless TV segments on Iraqi terrorism, which, along with chemical weapons, were oft-repeated threats that never materialized.

Saddam's negative image was forged by a combination of rhetoric, popular culture demonology, and Manichean metaphysics that presented the Gulf crisis as a struggle between good and evil. The "naked aggression" of the Iraqi leader was continually denounced by the Bush administration, and from the beginning Bush demonized Hussein and personalized and simplified the conflict as that between the "good" U.S.-led coalition and "evil" Iraqis. In Michael Rogin's view, the United States regularly constructs political enemies "by the inflation, stigmatization, and demonization of political foes" (1987, p. xiii). The effect of the demonization of Saddam Hussein was to promote a climate in which the necessity to take decisive military action to eliminate him was privileged. The mainstream media endlessly repeated stories of Hussein's brutality and made countless reports on Iraqi chemical weapons, its potential nuclear capacity, and its ability to mobilize terrorist attacks on the United States and its allies. TV networks broadcast news segments about radio stations playing records that simulated rock classics with new lyrics vilifying Saddam and about T-shirts with vicious images of Saddam Hussein and the Iraqis. It is as if U.S. popular and political culture needed demonized enemies to ensure its sense of its own goodness and the media responded with the demonology of the Iraqi dictator.

Generally speaking, the United States is perpetually "in search of enemies," to use John Stockwell's phrase,[3] and constructs enemies with propaganda campaigns that paint some leaders, or countries, as absolute villains, while painting other leaders, who may be just as bad, or worse, as "allies." Indeed, the attack on Hussein was especially hypocritical as the United States and other "allied" powers had built up Hussein's military machine with almost unlimited military equipment and sided with him in the Iran/Iraq war.[4] The caricature of Hussein and the Iraqis, however, was one-sided and hyperbolic, substituting cliché and image for analysis and debate. Hussein is a brutal dictator, but he is also a pragmatist with a history of cutting deals with the West. His Baath party did torture and murder its opponents, but it also produced one of the best welfare states in the Middle East, was one of the few states in the region to give rights to women, and utilized its oil resources to provide social programs as well as weapons. Some Iraqis tortured and murdered Kuwaitis, but many were themselves drafted into the military and opposed the regime and invasion of Kuwait—as would be perfectly clear at the end of the war by scrutinizing the pitiful, surrendering Iraqi conscripts.

The Bush administration and media personalized the crisis as the result of the actions of one man, Saddam Hussein, the Iraqi president who was identified with his country throughout the war. Richard Keeble (forthcoming) points out that during the Iran/Iraq war, the media invariably referred to "Baghdad" and "Iraq" as the agents in the war, but during the Gulf crisis and war the dominant mode of reference was to "Saddam Hussein," who was presented as the sole agent of all Iraqi actions, thus collapsing Iraq into Saddam. This was misleading and dishonest as the Iraqi people were themselves victims of Saddam Hussein and his regime, but the media images of the evil Hussein reduced the Iraqis to an evil essence embodied in the Iraqi leader. Yet constructing Saddam Hussein as an absolute villain, as a demon who is so threatening and violent that he must be destroyed and eradicated, precluded negotiations and a diplomatic solution. One could not sensibly talk with such a villain or seek common ground or a diplomatic solution. Instead, one must exterminate such evil to restore stability and order in the universe. This vision appears in Hollywood movies and popular television entertainment and structured the political discourses and dominant media frames of the U.S. intervention into the complex politics of the Middle East.

Mainstream media coverage of the crisis in the Gulf tended to personalize the crisis as a conflict between George Bush and Saddam Hussein. Although Hussein was presented in purely negative terms, Bush's actions, by contrast, were praised as "decisive," "brilliant," and "masterly." On August 7, CBS correspondent Leslie Stahl spoke of Bush's "unique" diplomatic style, and the same day in the *New York Times* Maureen Dowd flatteringly portrayed Bush as a man of decisive action. A few days later, the *Times* dubbed Bush "the leader of all countries" (Aug. 12, 1991, editorial). U.S. motives were described as good and pure, as when the *Times* pontificated that U.S. politicians "appeal to high moral values and the lessons of history. . . . [D]eep down the United States understands that many of its partners are in the coalition only because of a coincidence of interests, not because they share a common sense of moral purpose" (Sept. 23, 1990). Few questions were raised concerning more base U.S. motives like the desire to control the flow of oil and petrodollars, to establish a permanent military presence in the area, to discipline Third World countries that refuse to submit to U.S. hegemony, or the domestic political motivations of Bush and the military (see 1.3 and 2.5). Instead, the United States was presented as the good protector of small countries against vicious bullies, while countries like Germany and Japan, which had reservations about pursuing a military solution to the crisis, were presented as weak and lacking in resolve.

Although the Iraqis were portrayed as brutish bullies, Bush and the United States were presented as strong and honorable defenders of international law and order. *Newsweek* proclaimed that "the president's grand plan for the post-cold war world can be summed up simply: Stop International Bullies" (Sept. 3, 1990). Many newspapers and TV commentators praised the United States as the only superpower able to stand up against aggression and enforce international law. Such fulsome praise overlooked the fact that Bush and the United States recently violated international law during the Panama invasion. Moreover, U.S. allies in the multinational coalition included Syria, which seized parts of Lebanon in the 1980s; Turkey, which invaded Cyprus, seizing half of the island; Morocco, which invaded Somalia; and, on the sidelines, Israel, which held Arab lands seized in several wars. Double standards, however, were necessary to frame the conflict as a simple struggle between good and evil.

In sexual terms, the narrative of the Gulf war was that Saddam/Iraq were raping Kuwait, refused to pull out, and must be destroyed, with the United States threatening to "cut it off and kill it," to employ General

Powell's brutal but accurate phrase. The Bush administration and media also played on sexual and racial fears in constructing their image of Saddam Hussein. The rhetoric of Iraqi "rape" and "penetration" was employed from the beginning of the crisis throughout the war.[5] The media demonized Saddam's Big Gun and chemical weapons, as well as his missiles that could hit Cairo and Tel Aviv. His very name was mispronounced as Sad-dam, evoking sadism and damnation, and Sod-dom, evoking sodomy. Bush constantly referred to Hussein as "Saad'm"— a mispronunciation evoking Satan, damnation, and Sodom. Using both racist and sexual rhetoric, Bush claimed that the United States went to war against the "dark chaos" of a "brutal dictator" who followed the "law of the jungle" and "systematically raped" a "peaceful neighbor" (quoted in Joel Bleifuss, "The First Stone," *In These Times,* March 20–26, 1991, p. 4). Undersecretary of Defense Paul Wolfowitz asked rhetorically if you would "let a man like that get his hands on what are essentially the world's vital organs?" (Bleifuss 1991, p. 4).

Throughout U.S. history, vengeance for rape—especially the rape of white women by men of color—has been used to legitimate U.S. imperialist adventures and military action. Captivity-drama narratives of white women captured and raped by Native Americans were a standard genre of colonial literature, and during the Spanish-American war, the Hearst newspapers popularized the story of Spanish kidnapping of an upper-class and light-skinned Cuban woman as a pretext for U.S. intervention. John Gottlieb reminded us in *The Progressive* that: "Bush not only used rape as a justification for the war against Iraq, but also . . . cited the sexual assault of an American officer's wife by a Panamanian soldier as a reason for invading that country, and . . . used the rape of a white woman by black convict Willie Horton to attack Michael Dukakis in 1988" (April 1991, p. 39).

The demonization of Hussein and the Iraqis was also orchestrated by their alleged possession of exotic weapons (none of which actually materialized in the Gulf war). There was perhaps as much coverage of Iraqi chemical weapons as any single topic during the crisis and war. On August 8, the television networks reported that the Iraqis were loading chemical weapons onto planes en route to Kuwait and that there would thus be Iraqi chemical weapons in the field. Henceforth, there were countless segments on Iraqi chemical weapons, the need for protective gear and antidotes, and the absolutely evil nature of the weapons. As it turned out, the Iraqis never used these weapons, in part because they did not have adequate protection against them and in part because they feared U.S. retaliation with even worse weapons. In fact, the Iraqis had never used chemical weapons in close combat with an opposing army, yet the military and the media constantly emphasized the danger from an Iraqi chemical weapons attack. Such constant evocation of Iraqi threats and atrocities intensified the demonization of the "enemy" and produced a fearful mood which prepared the public for war and ultimately the destruction of the Iraqis.

When the Iraqis began holding foreign nationals in Iraq and Kuwait as hostages in the middle of August, this story became the major focus of the crisis for some months. The Gannett Foundation found that the term "human shields" was referred to 2,588 times in broadcast and print media from August 1, 1990, to February 28, 1991, second only to Vietnam with 7,279 mentions (LaMay et al., p. 42). Almost every night television networks broadcast ritualistic reports depicting the plight of the hostages, negotiations for their release, the suffering of hostages' relatives, and the happy homecoming of those released. The nightly horror stories of returning "hostages" tearfully describing the barbaric actions inflicted on foreigners in Kuwait by the Iraqis provided images of innocent Americans suffering at the hands of the savage Arabs. The hostage stories personalized the crisis and provided figures of identification for U.S. audiences. Hostages were featured guests on talk shows and were interviewed in some depth for the TV news presentations. The hostage dramas presented morality tales depicting the Iraqis as evil hostage takers and the Americans and other foreign hostages as innocent victims. This scenario also replayed the primal captivity drama, one of the mainstays of U.S. popular literature that began with Indian captivity narratives and continued through media coverage of the Iran hostage crisis (see Slotkin 1973 on the captivity narrative).

The Baby Incubator Atrocity and the Hill and Knowlton PR Campaign

But perhaps the most outrageous propaganda ploy by the Bush administration and the Kuwaiti government concerned fallacious stories about Iraqi atrocities in Kuwait. In October 1990, a tearful teenage girl testified to the House Human Rights Caucus that she had witnessed Iraqi soldiers remove fifteen babies from incubators and had seen them left to die on the floor of the hospital. The girl's identity was not revealed, supposedly to protect her family from reprisals. This baby-killing story helped mobilize support for U.S. military action, much as Bush's Willie Horton ads had helped him win the presidency by playing on primal emotions. Bush mentioned the story six times in one month alone and eight times in forty-four days; Vice-President Dan Quayle frequently referred to it, as did Schwarzkopf and other military spokespeople. Seven U.S. Senators cited the story in speeches supporting the January 12 resolution authorizing war.

In a January 6, 1992, Op-Ed piece in the *New York Times,* however, John MacArthur, the publisher of *Harper's* magazine, revealed that the unidentified congressional witness was the daughter of the Kuwaiti ambassador to the United States. The girl had been brought to testify to Congress by the PR firm Hill and Knowlton, who had coached her and helped organize the Congressional Human Rights hearings. In addition, Craig Fuller, Bush's former chief of staff when he was vice-president and a Bush loyalist, was president of Hill and Knowlton and was involved with the PR campaign. In addition, Robert Gray, who had served as co-chair of Reagan's inaugural committee in 1981, worked on the Free Kuwait account (Miller 1992). Thus it is likely that together the U.S. and Kuwaiti governments developed a propaganda campaign to manipulate the American people into accepting the Gulf war. According to reports, the Kuwaiti account was one of the most expensive PR campaigns in history, costing $5.6 million from the period from August 20 to November 10; eventually it was estimated that the total account was $11 million (see Ruffini 1991, p. 22, and Rowse 1991, p. 20). Hill and Knowlton organized a photo exhibition of Iraqi atrocities displayed at the UN and the U.S. Congress and widely shown on television; assisted Kuwaiti refugees in telling stories of torture; lobbied Congress; and prepared video and print material for the media. There were also reportedly six other U.S. PR firms working for the Kuwaitis (Rowse 1991).

Hill and Knowlton put out over thirty "Video New Releases" (VNRs) that were distributed free to television stations. Rowse (1991) claims that, "One video, based on a film of destruction in Kuwait, [reached] 61.4 million viewers. Another on human rights violations in occupied Kuwait reached 35.3 million. Viewers had no way to tell that the source was a PR firm." The two VNRs were among the top ten most successful VNRs distributed from July 1 to December 31, 1990. "Free Kuwait" also released tapes of Westerners supposedly hiding in Kuwait, denouncing atrocities and calling for U.S. military action; CNN, in particular, frequently played these tapes. For instance, CNN played on October 28 a tape in which a Western man in hiding told of Iraqi atrocities, including the baby incubator story, and called upon the U.S. to intervene militarily. In retrospect, this appears to be part of the Hill and Knowlton/Free Kuwait propaganda campaign that duped CNN and the other networks. So video too was manipulated by the PR firm that faked photo evidence to dramatize its demonization campaign, and the TV networks were conduits for this propaganda.

On January 17, 1992, ABC's "20/20" disclosed that a "doctor" who testified that he had "buried fourteen newborn babies that had been taken from their incubators by the soldiers" was also lying. The doctor was a dentist who later admitted that he had never examined the babies and had no way of knowing how they died, nor did Amnesty International which published a report based on this testimony (Amnesty International later retracted the report, which had been frequently cited by Bush and other members of his administration). ABC also disclosed that Hill and Knowlton had commissioned a "focus group" survey, which gathers groups of people together to find out what stirs or angers them. The focus group responded strongly to the Iraqi baby atrocity stories and so Hill and Knowlton featured this in their PR campaigns for the Free Kuwait group.

Furthermore, reporter Morgan Strong revealed that Hill and Knowlton also used the wife of Kuwait's Minister of Planning who was "herself a well-known TV personality in Kuwait" in the UN hearings (*TV Guide*, Feb. 22, 1992, p. 12). The woman, Fatima Fahed, appeared just as the UN was debating the use of force to expel Iraq from Kuwait and she provided "harrowing details of Iraqi atrocities inside her country." Fahed claimed that her information was firsthand, stating, "Such stories . . . I personally have experienced." But Strong claims that when the woman was interviewed before the UN appearance, "she told me that she had *no* firsthand knowledge of the events she was describing" (1992, p. 13). After her Hill and Knowlton coaching, however, her story changed.

Strong also tells of how a tape from inside Kuwait, edited by Hill and Knowlton, "purported to show peaceful Kuwaiti demonstrators being fired upon by the occupying Iraqi troops." But Strong had interviewed a Kuwaiti refugee who was present at the demonstration who "said that no demonstrators were injured, and that gunshots captured on tape were, in fact, those of Iraqi troops firing on nearby resistance fighters, who had fired first at the Iraqis" (Strong 1992, p. 13). So video too was manipulated by the PR firm working with the Kuwaiti government, Bush administration, and Congress. Hill and Knowlton's behavior led some members of the industry to complain that, "There's a wide-spread feeling within the industry that Hill and Knowlton has brought some discredit on our industry." The firm is also under investigation for its role in covering over the criminal activities of the Bank of Credit and Commerce International (BCCI) (see the discussion in Gary Emmons, "Did PR firm invent Gulf War stories?" *In These Times,* Jan. 22, 1992, p. 2).

In addition, MacArthur revealed that Rep. Tom Lantos (D-Calif.), co-chairperson of the Congressional Human Rights Caucus, has a close relation with Hill and Knowlton who provide low-rent office space for the Caucus and contribute money to a foundation that fronts for the Caucus and to Lantos' election campaign. Moreover, Citizens for a Free Kuwait, largely funded by the Kuwaiti government, gave $50,000 to Lantos' foundation. Hill and Knowlton also represent Turkey and Indonesia, two countries with dismal human rights records, and they "were notably absent from the foundation's 1991 list of human rights concerns" (MacArthur 1991, p. A17). Lantos defended concealing the identity of the witnesses and his financial arrangements with Hill and Knowlton and Citizens for a Free Kuwait, though in an editorial shortly thereafter the *New York Times* said that Lantos' "behavior warrants a searching inquiry by the House Ethics Committee" (Jan. 17, 1992, p. A20).

At the time of the Hill and Knowlton Kuwaiti propaganda campaign, the majority of the public in the United States was against a military intervention in the Middle East and Congress was also tending against the military option. Hill and Knowlton's campaign, however, helped turn things around, mobilizing public opinion in favor of the use of military force against Iraq. Two of the primal images employed by the campaign were the Iraqi "rape" of Kuwait and the baby atrocity story. Rape and the murder of babies are two primal images of evil that have frequently been employed in propaganda campaigns. For instance, World War I propaganda campaigns often featured stories or images of German rape and murder of babies (see Figure 2.1). In particular, British and U.S. propaganda teams produced copious atrocity stories of the dasdardly deeds of German "Huns" against innocent Belgiums during World War I; these atrocity stories helped mobilize an indifferent and isolationist American public to support U.S. entry into the war against Germany (Jowett and O'Donnell 1992 and Miller 1992).

Following the model of the World War I "rape of Belgium" campaign, Hill and Knowlton discerned that the rape metaphor was powerful and carried through a "rape of Kuwait" campaign replete with a book (Sasson 1991), newspaper articles, packaged videos, pictures, press releases, news conferences, and demonstrations. There were frequent media events such as National Free Kuwait Day, National Prayer Day (for Kuwait's liberation), and National Student Information Day; local events were also organized (see MacArthur 1992 and Miller 1992 for a detailed account of the campaign).

Bush, Schwarzkopf, and the media pundits used the rape metaphor continually and also repeatedly disseminated the baby atrocity story. On November 28, the television networks transmitted images of the UN testimony and focused on the killing of premature babies by the Iraqis who had allegedly taken away their incubators (the incubators were found in Kuwaiti hospitals after the war and medical personnel there denied that the Iraqis had killed the premature babies; see 10.1 for further details). The UN "testimony" was accompanied by a photo exhibition of torture victims and other exhibits staged just before the UN was to vote on whether to legitimate the use of military force if Iraq did not withdraw from Kuwait by January 15; the exhibition was set up

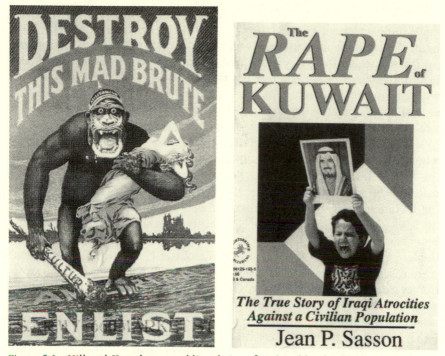

Figure 2.1   Hill and Knowlton, a public relations firm hired by the Kuwaiti government, replicated a World War I "Rape of Belgium" campaign (poster at left) by demonizing the Iraqis as rapists and murderers of innocent children. The propaganda book, *The Rape of Kuwait,* features an innocent child as victim on the cover and celebrates the Emir, whose government helped distribute the tract.

again for the benefit of the House Foreign Affairs Committee on January 8 as it prepared to vote on Bush's request to Congress for a resolution authorizing the use of force against Iraq.

This baby atrocity story was, therefore, a classic propaganda campaign to manufacture consent for the Bush administration policies. It was part of an elaborate web of deception, disinformation, and Big Lies to sell the war to the public. It revealed the U.S. president and vice-president and the top U.S. military leaders to be propagandists who did not hesitate to repeat Big Lies over and over in order to win support for the war effort. The media which repeated these lies without skepticism or inquiry also revealed itself to be a naive instrument of U.S. propaganda. Such lying polluted political discourse and continued the trend toward the politics of lying that has been a recurrent feature of U.S. politics in recent years—a theme that I explore in later chapters.

Technology, Troops, Race, and Gender

In their coverage of the largest U.S. military intervention since Vietnam, the mainstream corporate media concentrated much of their focus on the logistics of the operation and its impact on families at the home front rather than on whether or not the deployment was a good idea and where it might lead. For the first weeks of the deployment, there was almost no discussion of whether Iraq really planned to invade Saudi Arabia, whether the situation required the massive U.S. troop deployment to stop Iraqi aggression, or, crucially, whether the U.S. force was primarily a defensive or an offensive force. In general, the media repeated endlessly the rationalizations offered by the Bush administration for its successive military deployments. In the early days of the crisis, the mainstream media dramatized the Iraqi threats to Saudi Arabian and other Gulf State oil fields, which legitimated the U.S. military presence and the economic blockade of Iraq. Instead of analyzing what was at stake in the U.S. troop deployment, night after night the details of the U.S. military deployment were discussed. TV reports centered on desert maneuvers and the depiction of shiny and powerful new high-tech weapons. These positive images of the U.S. deployment were contrasted with frequent news reports warning against Iraqi chemical weapons and the one million strong, experienced, well-armed, and highly trained Iraqi military forces. The numerous military experts and media commentators never questioned these figures, though now there are good reasons to doubt these claims concerning the Iraqi military (see 9.3).

Against the "evil" Hussein and threatening Iraqis, the media thus posed images of the "good" American soldier and powerful U.S. technology. In the nightly repetition of these positive images of U.S. troops valiantly protecting a foreign country from aggression, the need for a strong military was repeatedly pounded into the public's psyche. "Desert dispatches" from troops in the front allowed young men and women to send greetings home. These images of wholesome young Americans in the desert to fight an evil and dangerous enemy bonded the American people with the troops and helped create positive feelings about the patriotic troops in the field. The audience was also able to identify with the plight of the troops through the frequent episodes on TV news which dealt with the calling up of reservists to serve in the Gulf, ranging from working class, to middle class, to professional groups with whom the audience could identify and empathize.

Likewise, the frequent visuals of planes, tanks, artillery, and more exotic high-tech items provided splendid images of U.S. military technology. The U.S. intervention took place in the context of debate over the cutting back of the budget of the military and CIA, and defenders of these institutions used the crisis in the Gulf to support their arguments against military cutbacks. For instance, Congress killed the B-2 bomber before the invasion; within days, Congress reinstated the funding (sanity ultimately reigned, however, and the aircraft was canceled in January 1992). The images of the military hardware and troop deployment thus functioned as advertisements for a strong military and prepared the public for the rigors of all-out war while building support for the U.S. intervention and Middle East policies. The U.S. military could not have asked for better advertisements or PR. While the military prepared for war in the Middle East, urged on by hawks like Henry Kissinger, William Safire, and columnists and editorialists in the *Wall Street Journal, Washington Post, New York Times,* and *National Review,* the media built up a consensus for Bush administration positions, no matter how dangerous and potentially catastrophic.

In addition to the promilitary rhetoric, television provided racist imagery and discourses to position the public against the Iraqis.[6] Repeated images of Saddam Hussein, of mobs of Arabs demonstrating and shouting anti-U.S. slogans, and repeated associations of rich, corrupt Arabs with oil—and other Arab leaders with terrorism—provided a negative set of Arab images. Television coverage of the frequent Arab conferences during September and October, which sought Arab solutions to the problem, almost always focused on the more radical Arab leaders and featured scenes of Arab anti-American demonstrations where U.S. flags were ritualistically burned. When Secretary of State Baker visited Syria, for instance, to recruit Syrian support and troops for the anti-Iraq mobilization, the television networks stressed the links between Syria and terrorism and employed negative stereotypes of Arabs.

Although the United States was presumably intervening on behalf of Kuwait and Saudi Arabia and included Arab allies in its coalition, TV coverage frequently associated Arabs with terrorism, anti-American flag burning demonstrations, and oil. Other images portrayed Arabs as premodern nomads, wandering about in the vast Middle East deserts, and thus as utterly different from "civilized" Westerners. Throughout the crisis, the dichotomy between foreign and uncivilized Arabs and civilized Westerners was drawn upon, thus replicating the racist discourse analyzed by Edward Said (1978), which founded western ideology on a distinction between the civilized and rational West and the barbaric and irrational Orient.

To be sure, there were also several TV news reports dealing with racist stereotypes of Arabs and anti-Arab images in the United States, but these segments invariably featured Hollywood film images of Arabs and neglected analysis of the range of standard TV images of Arabs, how they were framed, and with what they were associated on TV news and entertainment. Consequently, although television pointed to the perniciousness of anti-Arab violence in the United States and elsewhere during the crisis in the Gulf and then the ground war, it never disclosed its own complicity in anti-Arab racist imagery.

The presentation of race and U.S. troops was highly delicate as a large percentage of the U.S. forces serving in the Gulf were people of color; 23 percent of the U.S. military as of June 1990 were black, while the total minority percentage was 32.3 percent (Ronald Brownstein, *Los Angeles Times,* Dec. 6, 1990, pp. 1 and 3). It was later reported by the *New York Times* that 33 percent of enlisted military women and 21 percent of enlisted men serving in the Gulf were black while 47 percent of active-duty enlisted personnel were black women and 29 percent were black men; it was also estimated that 30–35 percent of those on the frontline, who would be the first to be killed, were non-Caucasian. Although some black opponents of the war made this point, generally television avoided the question of the military and race. The media mainstream ignored discussing the hypocrisy of the Bush administration, which attempted to remove federal scholarship programs based on race and vetoed a civil rights bill at a time when a disproportionate amount of people of color were risking their lives for their country in the deserts of Saudi Arabia.

TV images of the military and their families pointed to the cohabitation of traditionalist images of gender and the family with more liberal images (which also, as we shall see, had an ideological function).[7] On one hand, the construction of gender of U.S. military families was extremely conventional, with the male soldiers going off to war, while the wife and children stayed behind. This frame reproduced the conservative division between the public sphere as the domain of male activity with the private sphere reserved for women. The frame also privileged the sexist picture of men as active and virile and women as passive and helpless. Constant pictures of wives breaking into tears as their men marched stoically to war reinforced this traditional picture, as did the juxtapositions of the men active in the desert while the women at home sought help from psychiatric counselors or support groups. As Enloe pointed out (1992), the fusion of images of "womenandchildren" as released hostages or domestic victims on the home front reinforced images of women as helpless and dependent.

Yet the media also fixated on the new "women warriors" sent to the Gulf. *Newsweek* featured a September 10, 1990, cover story on women and the military (see Figure 2.2), as did *People* magazine (September 10, 1990). As the crisis proceeded, images of women troops appeared ever more frequently in the TV news coverage. These images also helped with military recruitment by presenting exciting images of work in a foreign country. The images of women in the military also replicate the

Figure 2.2 Women were represented either as domestic protectors of the home or as warriors putting their lives on line for the country, as in this *Newsweek* cover from September 10, 1990.

images of women warriors, which have been popularized in film and television since the volunteer army allowed women to join. In addition, images of U.S. women in the desert were often juxtaposed with pictures of Arab women in veils, thus presenting pictures of "modern," "progressive" customs contrasted to "backward," "reactionary" regimes that continued to oppress women. Such a juxtaposition legitimated U.S. intervention in the region as a progressive force. This contrast was highlighted in mid-November, when Saudi women protested a ban on their driving automobiles with a "drive-in" during which they defiantly drove autos in Saudi cities. The Saudi women were harshly criticized by the regime and in some cases fired from their jobs; the U.S. media focused on the story for several days, contrasting the plight of Saudi women with U.S. women soldiers driving jeeps and participating actively in military life—presenting the message that the United States was bringing a progressive "modern" influence into backward Saudi Arabia.

The whole television coverage of the Persian Gulf war was detrimental to women through the constant bombardment of images of male culture and masculine values. Supporters of the war, from George Bush and Norman Schwarzkopf to troops in the desert and their supporters at home, constantly talked about "kicking ass," and when the war started, rarely has brute violence been so positively portrayed. Feminists argue that war culture helps validate brutality, which ultimately promotes violence against women (Roach 1991) and, one might add, people of color. Pilots watched porn movies before their bombing runs, thus fusing sex and violence. Throughout the Gulf war, military images and discourse totally dominated television programming and in general promoted a war culture that is primarily a male culture, thus devaluing women. Women were positioned as either devoted wives, serving as cheerleaders for the military, or women warriors—hardly an attractive array of gender ideals. Although many women actively opposed the war, they were for the most part excluded from media discourse (see Roach 1991 and Paley 1991 for documentation).

Consequently, war culture simultaneously promotes sexism and militarism. War culture devalues women, but by legitimating violence it brutalizes the whole culture, thus contributing to the militarization of U.S. society (see 10.5). The Gulf war was thus an important and dangerous cultural event, as well as a military one, promoting a military culture that had been discredited since Vietnam and had been on the defensive. Indeed, the project of winning a decisive war and the validation of the military as an important part of U.S. society was part of what the Gulf war was all about, and TV was decisive in producing precisely the images and discourses that would promote the military after a long period in which they had been discredited and on the sidelines of U.S. society.

The Absence of Critical Voices

During the first days of the U.S. intervention in early August, there were some critical voices in the press. Conservative columnists Roland Evans and Robert Novak attacked the rhetorical "Overkill on Saddam" in the August 8, 1990, *Washington Post* and cited Bush's lack of outrage when his "old Chinese friends" murdered students in Tiananmen Square. The August 9 *Washington Post* carried a critical overview of the media demonization of "Saddam Hussein: Monster in the Making" by Marjorie Williams. The *Los Angeles Times* ran a critique of Bush's war policy by radical Alexander Cockburn on August 6 and by conservative Tom Bethell on August 8. The "CBS Evening News" broadcast reports from Jordan on August 6 and 7 that ran interviews providing the Arab point of view— earning them an attack by warmongering *Washington Post* columnist Jim Hoagland on August 8. Four Arab-Americans were allowed on the "MacNeil/Lehrer News Hour" on August 7, though the next night the guests were almost all pro-Bush administration conservatives.

The few criticisms voiced on the television networks during the first weeks of the deployment concerned the timing of Bush's intervention; families of hostages wished he'd given them time to get out before sending in U.S. troops. For the most part, the only critical voices allowed on television specifically concerning the deployment were Arabs in the United States, Egypt, Jordan, and other countries where television networks stationed crews—and their criticisms were sometimes framed, or perceived, as "anti-American" hostility rather than rational arguments. One of the few critiques of Bush's military response from a major political source on the television networks during the first several weeks involved ABC reporter Cokie Roberts citing former UN Ambassador Jeane Kirkpatrick's questioning of whether the magnitude of the U.S. response was in line with the degree of U.S. interests ("Sunday Morning with David Brinkley," August 26, 1990); soon after, however, Kirkpatrick reverted to her usual militarism and by September was defending the Bush administration and calling for a military solution.

During the early weeks of the crisis, the dominant debate in the media concerned whether the United States should begin bombing Iraq immediately to destroy their military and eliminate Saddam Hussein or continue with the UN-sanctioned economic blockade, which might produce a long deadlock and indefinite deployment of U.S. troops in Saudi Arabia. On August 19, for instance, in a syndicated column, Henry Kissinger argued that it would be a disaster to get U.S. troops bogged down in the Middle East desert and urged a "surgical strike" against Iraq—a position that he repeated on an August 24 CNN panel and continued to defend in the following months. Similar military solutions were urged on August 27 in a *New York Times* Op-Ed piece by William Safire and this was the line advocated by editorialists in the *Wall Street Journal* and *National Review,* and by many Israelis, military "experts," and pundits who appeared on talk shows and wrote editorial "opinion" pieces.

Zbigniew Brzezinksi argued on television and in the August 16 *Washington Post* and August 27 *Newsweek* for the economic blockade strategy, "to slowly strangle them." He wrote: "My greatest fear about the ongoing crisis is that it could get out of hand. The way it has been played in the media, and even by some officials, will create a mass hysteria." Brzezinski was almost alone in advocating a "moderate" approach during the first several weeks of coverage, against those who wanted to begin the bombing. By late August, however, the war hysteria subsided somewhat and finally talk of possible negotiated settlement to the crisis, or of a long-term stalemate, began appearing during the weekend of August 25–26—a moderate discourse denounced by Safire in the *New York Times* as the "new pacificism" (Aug. 27, 1990, Op-Ed column).

Thus, the major debate visible on television during the first month of the crisis was between the "stranglers" (who advocated sanctions) and the "butchers" (who advocated immediate military action), thus ignoring the question of whether it was a good idea for the United States to send so many troops to the region in the first place. There were, to be sure, Op-Ed pieces in the major newspapers warning about the dangers of the U.S. intervention and a Gulf war, but these views rarely appeared on television. Moreover, the dominant critical discourse found in the corporate media in the early weeks of the crisis was from the right. In addition to Brzezinski's and Kirkpatrick's misgivings, conservative columnists Evans and Novak warned against portraying "Saddam Hussein as a Hitlerite madman thirsting for world conquest [which] endows the Iraqi strongman with powers he does not possess" rather than presenting him as a rational individual with whom the United States must and can deal. Patrick Buchanan and other right-wing commentators on CNN warned against the costs of war and criticized those who promoted the military solution.[8]

The right-wing critique of the U.S. military buildup provided further evidence of splits within the Right in the United States. While Kissinger, some core spokespeople for the military-industrial complex, and key members of the Bush administration urged a military solution, other conservatives argued that the benefit would not equal the costs. This split replicated the division between traditionalist isolationist conservatives and more interventionist ones. The isolationists represented sectors whose interests would be harmed by war and the potentially higher oil prices if the war dragged on, which would fuel inflation, while the interventionists tended to represent military-industrial and other interests that would benefit from war (though some interventionists were also, no doubt, primarily hardcore macho militarists who represented no specific economic interests but incarnated a military mentality).

No significant antiwar voices were allowed on mainstream television during the first months of the troop buildup in Saudi Arabia and there was almost no criticism of Bush's deployment by the supine Democrats, pointing once again to the profound crisis of liberalism in the United States (Kellner 1990); exceptions include discussions on PBS's "The MacNeil/Lehrer NewsHour" in August with George McGovern and Barbara Jordan, who urged the diplomatic route, and Edward Luttwak and Brzezinski, who argued against immediate military action. The overwhelming majority of voices, however, supported Bush administration positions and many called for a military solution.

The few images of antiwar demonstrators in the United States that appeared during the first months of the U.S. intervention coded antiwar demonstrators as Arabs, as irrational opponents of U.S. policies. Demonstrators were portrayed as an unruly mob of long-haired outsiders; their discourse was rarely allowed and coverage focused instead on slogans, or images of marching crowds, with media voice-overs supplying the context. Major newspapers and newsmagazines also failed to cover the burgeoning antiwar movement. Thus, just as the media constructed a negative image in the 1960s of antiwar protestors as irrational, anti-American, and unruly, so too did the networks frame the emerging antiwar movement of the 1990s in predominantly negative terms.

There was consequently little significant debate in the mainstream media from the time that Bush first sent troops to Saudi Arabia on August 8, 1990, and little criticism of his policies. A study by the media watchdog group FAIR (Fairness and Accuracy in Reporting) indicated that during the first five months of TV coverage of the crisis in the Gulf, ABC devoted only 0.7 percent of its total gulf coverage to opposition to the military buildup. CBS allowed 0.8 percent, while NBC devoted 1.5 percent, a hearty 13.3 minutes to all stories about protests, antiwar organizations, conscientious objectors, religious dissenters, and the like. Consequently, of the 2,855 minutes of TV coverage of the Gulf crisis from August 8 to January 3, FAIR claimed that only 29 minutes, roughly 1 percent, dealt with popular opposition to the U.S. military intervention in the Gulf.[9]

Not only was the large antiwar movement ignored, but "[n]one of the foreign policy experts associated with the peace movement—such as Edward Said, Noam Chomsky, or the scholars of the Institute for Policy Studies—appeared on any nightly news program" (FAIR 1991, press release). Instead media "experts" came from conservative think tanks like the American Enterprise Institute and the Center for Strategic and

International Studies, with the centrist Brookings Institute providing "the 'left' boundary of debate." Moreover, not only were most TV commentators conservative and pro-Pentagon, but they were overwhelmingly white and male. FAIR indicated that Caucasians made up 98 percent of "Nightline's" guests and 87 percent of "MacNeil/Lehrer's"; the proportion of women was the same proportion as people of color. A *Times-Mirror* poll, however, that was recorded in September 1990 and January 1991 discovered "pluralities of the public saying they wished to hear more about the views of Americans who oppose sending forces to the Gulf" (Special *Times-Mirror* News Interest Index, January 31, 1991). Furthermore, the voices of troops who were alarmed at their deployment in the Saudi desert and who objected to primitive living conditions there were silenced, in part by Pentagon restrictions on press coverage, in part by a press corps unable or unwilling to search for dissenting voices.

Thus, the TV debate on the crisis of the Gulf was marked by an absence of critical voices and vigorous debate. Although the country at large was deeply divided and serious debates went on all over the country, this debate was largely absent in the mainstream media, especially television. Indeed, TV failed to adhere to even the most basic journalistic standards and provided by and large a one-sided, highly biased range of voices that favored the Bush administration's war policy. Once again, television failed to vigorously debate issues of national importance and thus contributed to the continuing decline of democracy in the United States.

2.2 Media Pools and Pentagon Control

From the beginning of the U.S. deployment, the press was prohibited from having direct access to the troops. Journalists were instead organized by the military into pools that were taken to sites selected by the military itself, and then reporters were allowed only to interview troops with their military "minders" present.[10] Laird Anderson, a journalism professor with experience in both the press and military, stated: "These rules are terribly restrictive. If I were a reporter in Saudi Arabia, I would not want to be in the hands of an Army public information officer. They are conservative by nature and their answer to any request will be 'No.' As the old saying goes, truth will be the first casualty" (cited in *Contra Costa Times,* Jan. 18, 1991). Press and video coverage were also subject to censorship, so that, in effect, the military tightly controlled press coverage of the U.S. military deployment in the Gulf and then the action in the Gulf war.

Consequently, no independent access to the troops was allowed and reporters were only able to visit troops when escorted by public affairs officers. The president of CBS News, Eric Ober, wrote in the *Wall Street Journal* (Jan. 17, 1991): "As journalists, we need to seek out the story and relay it to the public. If we interview a soldier, we want to obtain frank, unpackaged responses that give people a better feel for the story at the front. But if Bob Simon, CBS News' veteran war correspondent, interviews the soldier with a military escort by his side, will the soldier really tell the truth? Will we really find out what is happening in the desert? I have to conclude that the answer is no." Yet CBS and the other mainstream media submitted to the pool system, encouraging William Kovach, curator of Harvard's Nieman Foundation, to note: "Since 1970, the military has worked on plans [to control the press during a war]. I blame the press for not making as careful plans as the military" (cited in Nan Levinson, *Index on Censorship,* April/May 1991, p. 27).

Reporters without escort who ventured out on their own were detained or told to leave upon arrival at bases and some were even roughed up (see Fialka 1992). During the war, credentials were lifted if reporters broke the rules of the pool system; *New York Times* reporter Chris Hedges had his credentials temporarily lifted for interviewing Saudi shopkeepers fifty miles from the Kuwaiti border (Schanberg 1991). Reporters were not allowed to forward their material until it had been subjected to "security review," in other words, military censorship.

Such control of press coverage was unprecedented in the history of U.S. warfare. Historically, journalists have been allowed direct access to combat troops and sites, and frontline reporting was distinguished during World War II and Vietnam (see Knightly 1975). The military organized the pool system, however, because they perceived that reporting had been too critical in Vietnam, and they blamed the press for helping erode public support for the war. Following the example of British censorship of the press during the Falkland Islands/Malvinas war, the United States controlled press access during the Grenada invasion and instituted the pool system during the Panama invasion. The pool system allowed the U.S. military to keep the press completely away from the battle action in Panama during the decisive first day of the invasion and to keep most of the press interned on a U.S. military base during the next days. Because the press was prevented from discerning the extent of civilian deaths and the destructiveness of the invasion, the military used this strategy of information management as the model employed during the Gulf war.

Although the press was unable to adequately cover the Panama invasion, failing to get any pictures of U.S. destruction of Panamanian barrios that purportedly supported Noriega or of the Panamanians killed by the invasion, they generally went along with the restrictions and capitulated as well to the pool system during the crisis in the Gulf and then the Gulf war. On January 10, a New York–based public law firm, the Center for

Constitutional Rights, filed a federal lawsuit against the Pentagon in an effort to overturn press restrictions. Filed on behalf of the *Nation,* the *Village Voice,* the *Progressive,* and other alternative media and progressive journalists, the suit claimed that military "escorts engaged in arbitrary censorship of interviews, photography, and altered the activities of soldiers when reporters come into their presence, not for security reasons, but to ensure favorable coverage of their military presence" (cited in Anderson 1991, p. 23). In addition to First Amendment arguments, the suit held that the press pools organized and controlled by the military provided preferential treatment of select news organizations; indeed, the *New York Times* was only assigned one reporter to the pools while the military newspaper *Stars and Stripes* was awarded several. The military paid travel expenses and facilitated visa arrangements for some correspondents, "anticipated to favor the U.S. military," while the French were excluded completely from the pools, leading to a protest and threatened lawsuit from Agence Presse de France.

The major media outlets, however, neither joined the suit, nor adequately covered it, and the war started and finished without any real challenge to the pool system. After the war, U.S. District Judge Leonard Sand dismissed the suit on April 17, claiming that the issues were "too abstract and conjectural" and that the suit was irrelevant because the war was over. As we shall see in the following chapters, the pool system worked to manage the news flow during the Gulf war and to ensure support for the Bush administration policies.

When the Pentagon suggested giving the major news organizations more time in the field in October, General Schwarzkopf vetoed the suggestion (*New York Times,* May 5, 1991, p. A8) and the military tightly controlled both access and content of the news in one of the most thoroughgoing exercises in news management and the manufacture of public opinion in U.S. history. During the crisis in the Gulf, there were thus few reports of dissenting soldiers or critics of the war. An article in the December 9, 1990, *Washington Post,* however, suggested that a large number of troops expressed "reservations over U.S. involvement in what they see as an internal Arab conflict." When President Bush visited the troops in Saudi Arabia on Thanksgiving Day, "a truckload of soldiers drove past television cameras and shouted to reporters, 'We're not supposed to be here! This isn't our war! Why are we over here?'" An Army lieutenant told the *Post* that "this is not worth one American losing his life. If they [Iraqis] were threatening us, I'd be ready to lay down my life in a minute—but this is different."

Consequently, although there was a pointed debate among the U.S. troops in Saudi Arabia concerning the wisdom of their deployment, the U.S. public was not allowed to hear this debate. Any information that might have raised questions concerning Bush administration policy was considered off limits. Reporters critical of the deployment were not given access to top military brass or allowed to join the pools, while compliant reporters were rewarded with pool assignments and interviews. According to Fialka (1992), different generals had their pet reporters who they provided with special favors. Schwarzkopf's favorite was Joseph Galloway of *U.S. News and World Report* (pp. 33–34); Gen. Paul Funk favored Copley reporter Susan Walter (p. 41); and General Walter Boomer allowed *Washington Post* reporter Molly Moore to ride with his "mobile command post throughout the war" (p. 28). In particular, the Pentagon favored local reporters sympathetic to the military, allowing them access to troops from their region to write puff pieces that positively portrayed the troop deployment (see the *Progressive,* Feb. 1991, pp. 25ff.). As the *New York Times* put it: "The military, assuming that correspondents from the small-town press would write sympathetic articles, provided free transportation to Saudi Arabia and special access to servicemen and women from their areas. Aides also analyzed articles written by other reporters to determine their interests and to screen out interview requests from those likely to focus on mistakes by the military" (May 5, 1991, p. A8).

Clearly the military was concerned primarily with its image and with avoiding criticism rather than with legitimate national security concerns. Thus, reporters who were critical of U.S. policy found themselves without access to sources or sites. For two months, *New York Times* reporter James LeMoyne requested an interview with General Schwarzkopf, but his request was denied because his articles "were not 'liked'" by the U.S. military (*New York Times,* Feb. 17, 1991). Lemoyne had written a story that included quotes from soldiers who criticized President Bush and "emotionally questioned the purpose of their being sent to fight and perhaps die in Saudi Arabia." LeMoyne was later told that "all hell broke loose" after the article was published, and senior commanders chastised the soldiers who had expressed critical views. After the LeMoyne story, for "six weeks almost all print news reporters were denied visits to Army units," though television personalities like NBC weatherman Willard Scott and sports announcer O. J. Simpson were given free access to the troops because they did not "cause problems" (*New York Times,* Feb. 17, 1991).

Some television reporters also found themselves blacklisted. ABC's John Laurence was refused access to the troops after he had helped produce a segment detailing heat and sand problems with equipment in the desert and describing ammunition shortages. Laurence had previously angered the military in Vietnam when "CBS Reports" aired his footage of soldiers refusing orders in 1970. Cutting off access to critical reporters obviously has the effect of inhibiting reporters from criticizing the military, knowing that henceforth their access will be restricted.

Howell Raines, the bureau chief of the *New York Times* in Washington, claimed: "The Bush administration managed to prevent us from doing our jobs to an unprecedented extent." He claimed that the military betrayed the media, promising that the restrictions would be temporary and then keeping them in effect throughout the war. "We were had!" Raines exclaimed. "In our discussions with the administration we went over everything from a practical point of view—visas, transport, etc. The pools were not going to be more than a temporary measure. Everything was steeped in the atmosphere of a 'gentleman's agreement.'" But just before Christmas, he wrote, the Pentagon sent out a seven-page list of restrictions about which the press's representatives had not been consulted. They protested, some changes were made, but in January, the media were faced with a new document, presented as an ultimatum. "My colleagues and I discussed the idea of a legal action against the Pentagon," Raines noted. "Then, all of a sudden, the war began" (cited in Chantal de Rudder, *Le Nouvel Observateur,* No. 1387, June 6, 1991).

Hence, the military was ultimately able to control the flow of information coming from the press in the field by allowing access only to those favorable to the military and by exercising a security review of reports and video produced by the pools. This latter practice amounted to blatant censorship that attempted to block all critical commentary coming out of Saudi Arabia. A "Nightline" episode on press control showed public affairs escorts breaking in and cutting off discussion between the press and the soldiers on the front when topics were broached that the military did not want to see discussed. When an Air Force reservist from Michigan, Sgt. Dick Runels, sent his local paper letters detailing the poor living and sanitary conditions in the desert and questioning the U.S. mission in the Middle East, *Bay Voice* editor Tom Stanton said that military authorities found out about the letters and reprimanded Runels, saying that his letters would be censored in the future (United Press International, Nov. 30, 1990). During the war itself, as I shall report later, there were many other examples of press censorship by the military.

In addition, television controlled and censored antiwar advertisements. Alex Molnar, a University of Wisconsin professor and father of a twenty-one-year-old stationed in Saudi Arabia, founded a Military Families Support Network. Molnar's poignant letter, protesting the troop buildup, was published in the *New York Times* on August 23 on the Op-Ed page, but CNN and all three networks turned down a thirty-second commercial paid for by Molnar's group. CNN and ABC and CBS affiliates also turned down a paid antiwar ad produced by the Los Angeles chapter of the

Physicians for Social Responsibility, although some NBC stations and smaller affiliates ran the ad. However, pro-war commercials, sponsored by the Coalition for America at Risk and Free Kuwait group, were shown on many local stations (Clarkson, *In These Times,* Jan. 30, 1991, and Ruffini 1991, p. 22).

The lack of critical voices in the mainstream media during the first weeks of the crisis disclosed the timidity, narrowness, and fundamental subservience of the mainstream media, especially the television networks, in the United States. The broadcast media are afraid to go against a perceived popular consensus, to alienate people, or to take unpopular stands because they are afraid of losing viewers and thus profits. Because U.S. military actions have characteristically been supported by the majority of the people, at least in their early stages, television is extremely reluctant to criticize potentially popular military actions. The broadcast media also rely on a narrow range of established and safe commentators and are not likely to reach out to new and controversial voices in a period of national crisis.

The TV networks usually wait until a major political figure or established "expert" speaks against a specific policy and that view gains certain credibility as marked by opinion polls or publication in "respected" newspapers or journals. Unfortunately, the crisis of democracy in the United States is such that the leadership of the Democratic party has largely supported the conservative policies of the past decade and so the party leaders are extremely cautious and slow to criticize foreign policy actions, especially potentially popular military actions. The crisis of liberalism is so deep in the United States that establishment liberals are afraid of being called "wimps," or "soft" on foreign aggression and thus often support policies that their better instincts should lead them to oppose. Consequently, the only criticisms of a major U.S. military intervention that appeared on network television during the first weeks of the Gulf crisis came from hawks like Kirkpatrick and Brzezinski. On the other hand, it is not certain if no mainstream opposition was to be found[11] or whether television simply ignored any voices that would interrupt the manufacture of public support for the U.S. intervention.

In any case, promilitary discourse dominated the corporate media during the first crucial weeks of the U.S. buildup and many media voices subtly or not urged military solutions to the crisis: Some of the hawks argued that only an all-out war against Iraq would solve the crisis, while others suggested that it would be a long-term disaster if Saddam Hussein was allowed to survive, thus implying that the only real solution to the crisis was to remove him from power. The media privileging of military solutions and whipping up of war fever was so extreme that even some of its own representatives began noticing it. On an August 26 "David

Brinkley Show," for example, Sam Donaldson complained of war hysteria in the media, the repeated emphasis on the inevitability of war, and the failure to stress the need for negotiation and peaceful settlement. The next day on "Nightline," however, Donaldson announced that the "war psychosis that was gripping Washington has eased." Thus, from late August into the following weeks of the crisis, some media voices began indicating that the economic blockade of Iraq, international pressure, and negotiations might be able to get Iraq out of Kuwait and that it would not be necessary to fight a war to resolve the crisis.

2.3 CNN's "Crisis in the Gulf"

Yet, in some quarters aggressive militarism continued to be the norm. A new nightly program appeared, CNN's "Crisis in the Gulf," which quickly became the most jingoistic and militarist program during the first months of the confrontation. The Gulf war brought CNN into international prominence, producing higher name recognition, ratings, and advertising revenues. CNN, the creation of Atlanta entrepreneur Ted Turner, began service ten years before as the first cable news channel on the air twenty-four hours per day. Within a decade, it had developed the largest news operation in the world with a staff of 125, compared to 60 to 80 in the major networks, and with news bureaus throughout the world. In particular, CNN had established itself in the Middle East with news bureaus and broadcast outlets connected to the United States via satellite feed and was thus well positioned to provide coverage of the crisis in the Gulf and then the Gulf war.

CNN's "Crisis in the Gulf" program began as a half-hour segment on August 13 and four days later was expanded to an hour, preempting CNN's prime-time news program for news on the Middle East crisis and its domestic and international ramifications. Although, at first, coanchors Bernard Shaw in Washington and Jonathan Mann in Cairo offered more perspectives on the Gulf crisis than the "Big Three" networks, the program soon degenerated into outright military propaganda. By September, the program opened with dramatic musical chimes and titles showing pictures of U.S. troops marching across the desert, followed by images of Saddam Hussein and George Bush, the two archetypical enemies, and then images of Arabs, the desert, and oil, the symbols of the Middle East. These iconic images personalized the conflict as a confrontation between Bush and Hussein, projected clichéd images of Arabs and the Middle East (oil, camels, desert—an exotic Otherness to the West), and glorified the U.S. troops as martial music chimed in the background to dramatize the U.S. military intervention as the good U.S. warriors marched in to solve the crisis.

The news segments featured the key events of the day concerning the crisis, celebratory stories of U.S. troops in the Middle East, martial music between segments, and statistical tidbits before and after the advertising breaks posing trivia questions concerning the military intervention or citing statistics like the number of foreign nationals being held hostage within Iraq or Kuwait. The military images, music, statistics, and news stories were punctuated with discussions, usually dominated by hard-line right-wingers, on such issues as U.S. military responses, the possibilities of terrorism, and other predominantly military elements of the crisis. The program often closed with images of Saddam Hussein and Iraqi soldiers marching to military music, leaving the spectator with a notion of the threat to "the American way of life" posed by the Iraqi army.

But it was the constant flow of military images on CNN's "Crisis in the Gulf" and the extremely positive images of the U.S. troop deployment that was most supportive of the military option to the crisis. Night after night, CNN, and the other networks as well, broadcast an incessant flow of pictures of troops, airplanes, ships, tanks, and military equipment, with interview after interview of the troops and their military spokespeople. Footage of the U.S. military was frequently supplemented on CNN by footage from the British and other allies' military establishments, resulting in seemingly endless images of military hardware and personnel. Interviews with the U.S. soldiers "humanized" the coverage, picturing "our boys" (and some military women as well) as innocent and heroic protectors against Arab greed and aggression. And the segments of families of the troops on the home front, suffering from divided families or economic hardship (especially for reservists), created bonds and sympathy between the military families and the public that ultimately was an important component of the construction of public support for the U.S. policies during the war itself.

Lee and Solomon (1991) have discussed the propensity of the mainstream media to use "we" in such a way to identify the media spokesperson with the government or military and both this form of discourse and the use of "our" ("our troops," "our country") were very frequent in the crisis in the Gulf and Gulf war TV coverage. The military "experts" almost always used the term "we" to describe U.S. military policies or action, and this was perfectly appropriate as they actually identified totally with the military and were no more than propaganda experts speaking on behalf of the Pentagon. TV "journalists" such as Barbara Walters, Tom Brokaw, and Dan Rather also used "we" and "our" to bind themselves to the military and the nation. "We" and "our" also binds the audience into an intimate relation with the troops and nurtures a sense of shared national purpose (and dangers, once the war started). In this way, the military was identified with the nation and the TV audience was fused into a unitary bond with the United States and its (our) troops. The media thus became propaganda organs for the military state to ensure that "we" support "our" troops—and consequently submit to the policies of the Bush administration and Pentagon.

Further, the audience was prepared daily throughout the crisis for the rigors of war. From September through January, there were frequent TV network presentations of possible scenarios for a U.S. invasion of Iraq and all-out war in the region. During the weekend of September 15–16, there were reports on Air Force General Michael Dugan's claim that only an aggressive air war against Iraq would succeed in getting Saddam Hussein out of Kuwait. *Time* magazine published a report in the same period citing a State Department official saying: "If we are serious about going beyond getting Saddam out of Kuwait—and we are damn serious about it—then war is just about inevitable" (cited in *In These Times,* Sept. 26, 1990, p. 4). Dugan was fired for telling reporters that Saddam Hussein's government and key Iraqi installations were targeted for bombing—all of which turned out to be true.

Yet General Dugan merely said in public what administration officials were saying in private and even ultrahawk Pat Buchanan attacked the "clowns" who were calling for bombing Iraq (CNN "Crossfire," Sept. 13, 1990). Two weeks later, an aide of Defense Secretary Dick Cheney indicated that the United States was planning a massive invasion of Iraq to remove Saddam Hussein and that casualties were estimated to be over 20,000 U.S. troops and hundreds of thousands of Arabs (*International Herald Tribune,* Sept. 28, 1990, p. 1). Other estimates indicated that the casualties would be even higher, but there was little discussion of the extent of the casualties in the mainstream media or speculation of what would really happen in an all-out war (see the analysis by James Bennet in Sifrey and Cerf 1991, pp. 355–367).

War scenarios, however, continued to be leaked to the media, and CNN and the other networks willingly broadcast them: During the weekend of September 22–23, there were reports, with diagrams, charting the course of a U.S. invasion and all-out war. Such reports possibly created the impression that war was inevitable and helped prepare the public for the coming campaign against Iraq. Indeed, the constant projection of war scenarios could have created a desire for war to resolve the situation or to relieve the tension built up by the frenzied reporting which, especially in CNN's "Crisis in the Gulf," merged reports, military statistics, speculation, music, and images of war into a nightly spectacle that normalized, and perhaps created a desire for, war.

Thus, CNN's nightly "Crisis in the Gulf" report was especially hawkish, privileging promilitary discourses and imagery. The main emphasis of the coverage was on U.S. troop deployment, and military spokespeople were the most frequent commentators. Although some exmilitary officials warned against the dangers of war and urged a peaceful solution, the overall tone of the nightly report was highly militaristic and chauvinist. Previously, Ted Turner used his broadcasting networks during the cold war with the Soviet Union to plead the case of détente, friendly relations with the U.S.S.R., world peace, nuclear disarmament, environmental protection, and other worthy issues. But during the Gulf crisis, CNN was little more than a propaganda organ for the military, promoting almost without exception U.S. military intervention in the Middle East and a military solution to the crisis.

Yet CNN also presented more Arab points of view and a broader range of commentary than the other networks, in part because they had opened bureaus throughout the Middle East and in part because they had so much air time to fill, as their twenty-four hour news operation focused almost exclusively on the Gulf crisis and war from early August through mid-March. Exceptions to the hegemonic military discourse in the CNN nightly broadcast included appearances by former Attorney General Ramsey Clark and a conservative opposing the U.S. intervention on CNN's "Crossfire" on September 13, though the "liberal" Michael Kingsley replied in response to Clark's alleged "pacificism" that on this one he was in agreement with rightist Pat Buchanan. The other break with militarist discourse during the first two months of the CNN "Crisis in the Gulf" came on September 27–28 when a two-part program "Waging Peace" brought together individuals to discuss possible peaceful resolutions to the crisis. By October, the coverage was somewhat more balanced and an October 25, "Special Assignment: The Invasion Files" featured military experts discussing the difficulties of desert warfare and in some cases arguing against the military option.

2.4 Omissions, Silences, and Unasked Questions

When the U.S. policy turned from a defensive posture to an aggressive one, after Bush doubled the number of troops sent to the Gulf in mid-November, the media dramatized Iraqi brutality toward Kuwait and alleged mistreatment of U.S. and foreign hostages. On the other hand, there was for the first time a debate over U.S. Gulf policy after Bush, arguably, turned the Desert Shield into a Desert Sword aimed at Saddam Hussein and Iraq. From November through January, coverage veered back and forth from discourses suggesting the inevitability of war or positively urging an immediate military solution to cautionary warnings about the dangers of war and the desirability of a diplomatic solution. Efforts of

Mitterrand and Soviet leaders to mediate the crisis and to seek a diplomatic solution were covered, as were continuing hawk discourses and arguments that only a military intervention could get Iraq out of Kuwait. Members of the U.S. Congress began speaking out against the administration policy and Congress held hearings on the war that were usually televised in their entirety by the congressional C-SPAN channels and covered by CNN and more sporadically by the three mainstream networks. The Big Three TV networks failed, however, to present any special reports on the hearings or to interrupt their daily commercial programming as they often did during the Vietnam war in the 1960s and the Watergate hearings in the 1970s.

In the Senate hearings on U.S. Middle East policy in late November, Sam Nunn, chair of the Senate Armed Services Committee holding the hearings, noted in his opening statement: "The question is whether military action is wise at this time and in our own national interest. Is it in our vital interest to liberate Kuwait through military action by a largely American military force?" (*New York Times,* Nov. 28, 1990, p. A8). A number of witnesses from previous administrations advised against military action in the immediate future but did not raise many of the crucial economic, ecological, political, and military questions concerning what would actually happen in a Middle East war. Although the witnesses and senators made some good arguments about the dangers of a war in the Middle East, they failed to ask many of the key and hard questions concerning the dangers of the military option that I shall pose in this section.

Furthermore, the mainstream media failed to adequately cover the hearings and debate the key issues of war and peace. A study by Malek and Leidig (1991) concluded that the week of November 25 to December 1 "saw coverage of congressional dissent in the press largely replaced or overshadowed by news which supported the Administration's position. Sources from the State Department, the Defense Department, and the Central intelligence Agency led the discussion. Headlines reflecting official policy objectives dominated the scene, while editorials favored the Administration's opinion" (p. 18).

One of the key issues that a nation faces is the choice between war and peace to resolve difficult crises threatening its national interests. When a nation is confronted with a challenge to economic interests and international law, such as Iraq's invasion of Kuwait, basically there are two ways to resolve the crisis: war or diplomacy. For the mainstream media, however, the options were reduced to waiting for sanctions to work or going to war immediately. There was never any real push for a diplomatic solution to the crisis evident in the mainstream media which sharply restricted the terms of debate; nor did key congressional leaders push for a diplomatic solution urging instead the sanctions option. Furthermore, there was never a serious debate in the media concerning precisely what U.S. interests and political principles were at stake in the crisis in the Gulf; nor was there adequate discussion of what was involved concerning the competing options for getting Iraq to withdraw from Kuwait. A democratic social order would necessarily engage in intense debate concerning precisely what was at stake in the crisis in the Gulf and whether a military or a diplomatic resolution to the crisis was preferable. Reflecting on the media's failure to adequately debate the issue of war and peace, Ruffini wrote: "[D]uring the months when the Bush administration was maneuvering us relentlessly from economic sanctions and the defense of Saudi Arabia toward the crushing of Iraq's military power and probably ground warfare, the mighty American press refused a fair hearing to the case for peace. With some notable exceptions, the media chose to ignore clear and early signs that the administration was preparing for a full-scale war against Iraq—and when that prospect could not be denied, helped make it appear to be inevitable through the business-as-usual transmission of the war whoops of the administration" (1991, p. 21). Ruffini also reported: "Of the 25 largest U.S. newspapers . . . only one—the *Rocky Mountain News* in Denver—has argued for the most part against military action even as a last resort to dislodge Saddam Hussein's troops from Kuwait" (1991, p. 22).

Although before and after the outbreak of the Gulf war, it was argued repeatedly that "the use of force was inevitable," in fact, nothing in history is inevitable. Such a dubious doctrine conceals the U.S. blocking of any possibility of a negotiated settlement and its active promotion of the rush to war. The argument of the Bush administration against diplomacy was that "aggression should not be rewarded." This argument, however, was hypocritical, obtuse, and beside the point. The U.S. and its coalition had been engaging systematically in aggression for decades and to follow such a rigorous and absolutist principle in the case of Iraq, while disregarding the aggression of the United States, Israel, Syria, Turkey, or other countries in the alliance against Iraq, is hypocritical, a perfect instance of the double standard that marked the Bush administration and media Gulf policy from the beginning. In fact, the phrase "we will not reward aggression" was really a code word for "we refuse any diplomatic solution" and thus lacked cognitive and moral content. Furthermore, one could have engaged in a diplomatic process that did not reward Iraq, but which facilitated their exit from Kuwait. There is significant evidence that such a course could have worked, but it was never pursued by the Bush administration.

The Failure of Contextualization

The media generally fail to adequately contexualize historical events, tending to simplistic explanations which omit complexity and history. Failure to adequately contextualize the Gulf crisis, I submit, contributed to the eventual military resolution of the crisis and intensified the crisis of democracy. To begin, the mainstream media did not discuss how it was that U.S. policy toward Iraq created the crisis in the first place. As noted in Chapter 1, the United States tilted toward Iraq in the Iran-Iraq war and helped build up Saddam Hussein's military machine, continuing to give Iraq economic aid and material used to build up the Iraqi military right up to the invasion of Kuwait. There was no discussion about how failures of U.S. policy had contributed to the crisis nor how the U.S. intervention and a subsequent war would be primarily in the interests of the Bush administration and Pentagon.

Furthermore, there was a failure to contextualize the Gulf crisis within a broader Middle East frame. Obviously, the crisis in the Gulf was related to the political economy of oil in the region, the division between rich and poor Arab nations, and the complex inter-Arab relations as well as the U.S. relation to the region and its relations with Iraq and Kuwait. Further, the crisis in the Gulf also concerned the relations between Iraq, Syria, Egypt, Saudi Arabia, and Iran and their battles for hegemony in the region. In addition, relations between Israel and the Arab states, as well as the Palestinian Intifada for an independent Palestinian state, were involved. The crisis was influenced by the conflicting pan-Arab ideologies contrasted with Islamic fundamentalist ones and by combinations of these tendencies in several countries. The Middle East was thus a complex cauldron of seething rivalries with competing interests, ideologies, and power struggles (the articles in Bennis and Moushabeck 1991 and Bresheeth and Yuval-Davis 1991 help clarify this context). The situation was intensified by the vast oil resources of the region and its extreme militarization. Indeed, the United States contributed heavily to the arming of the Middle East, which had become one of the most militarized regions of the world (see Tilly 1991, pp. 38–40).

Instead of attempting to clarify this complexity, the media constructed a highly simplistic narrative: Saddam Hussein invaded Kuwait; he wouldn't leave; and war was necessary. This narrative leaves out the crucial fact that the United States and the other Western coalition powers built up the military machine of the Iraqis; that Kuwait and Iraq had an extremely complex and conflictual relation; and that U.S. policy had long asserted its interests in controlling the flow of Gulf oil and in maintaining a military presence in the region. It failed to clarify why Saddam Hussein refused to leave Kuwait and why it was in the interests of George Bush and the U.S. military to have a war.

The Bush administration and the mainstream media often mentioned Saddam Hussein's "miscalculations" but never discussed in any detail why Hussein felt that he could not pull out of Kuwait without being humiliated and losing face and perhaps his life. British author Roger Owen believes: "Saddam was almost certainly expressing a deeply held conviction when he told Tony Benn and other visitors that withdrawal would mean the collapse of Iraqi civilian and, most importantly, military morale" (1991, p. 160). Helga Graham wrote in the British *Guardian* that Hussein feared his military and was certain that he would be overthrown if he withdrew from Kuwait (Jan. 6 and 13, 1991). Others speculated that Hussein did not believe that the United States would actually attack Iraq and did not believe that the U.S. could sustain heavy casualties in an all-out war. Yet others speculated that Hussein was prepared to take heavy losses, believing that he would be an Arab hero if he survived a U.S. attack and would thus be a winner politically even if he lost the war in military terms.

Thus, there was no context to understand the crisis and no Big Picture or overview of the issues involved. In some ways, what was not shown or discussed in the mainstream media was as significant as what was portrayed. There was almost nothing in the mainstream media on the geopolitical history of the Middle East region where the confrontation was occurring: there was little discussion of the history of the borders in the region or of the complex relations between colonial powers and Arab states, between Israel and the Arab states, or between the Arab states themselves. The media also avoided analysis of the history of U.S. involvement in the region, the precise nature of U.S. interests in oil production, the political economy of oil, and the relations between U.S. oil companies and the governments of the region. Nor was the question raised as to why the United States reacted so aggressively to the Iraqi invasion of Kuwait, while accepting the earlier Iraqi invasion of Iran, the Israeli invasion of Lebanon, Syrian and Israeli occupations of Lebanon, and Israeli occupation of land claimed by the Palestinians and others. Although there were many Israelis and their supporters on television attacking Iraq and calling for a military solution to the crisis, there was no discussion of why Israel was promoting the military option and why it was in their interest to do so. And there was almost no discussion of the interesting parallels between the U.S. invasion of Panama and the Iraqi invasion of Kuwait.

The only attempt to contextualize the events by the major networks during the crisis in the Gulf was an ABC special, "A Line in the Sand" (Sept. 11, 1990). Note that the title of this program parrots Bush's own phrase denoting his resolve that U.S. forces would draw "a line in the sand" to protect U.S. interests in the region. The program glossed over the complex geopolitical history of the Middle East in moments, without addressing the issues that I posed above. Peter Jennings mentioned in passing that the borders of the states involved in the crisis were imposed by Britain earlier in the century, but he provided no real historical analysis. Jennings constantly mentioned that "geography is important" as he walked on a simulated map, from one country to another, an imperial televisual colossus of the West stomping on Middle Eastern countries, but he seemed unaware that history was also important.

Jennings ended his special, moreover, on a disturbingly hawkish note. After mentioning the spectrum of possible resolutions to the crisis, ranging from U.S. air strikes to peaceful negotiations, he claimed that the "worst option of all" might be for Saddam Hussein to withdraw intact to Iraq, preserving his military machine, chemical weapons, and potential nuclear weapons for future mischief in the area. Jennings's implication was that it would be better to take the route of eliminating Hussein completely; thus he implicitly made the argument for a U.S. military attack on Iraq.

The ABC special did present some interesting information in a historical montage of the 1990 events that led up to the Iraqi invasion and put some (no doubt warranted) blame on Bush administration officials for failing to give Saddam Hussein clear signals before his invasion that the United States would resolutely oppose his intervention into Kuwait. Articles in the *New York Times* and some television newscasts took similar positions, pointing out that State Department officials and the U.S. ambassador to Iraq, April Glaspie, indicated that the U.S. had no treaties with Kuwait and no position on the disputes between Iraq and Kuwait (see 1.1). The ABC program and subsequent newspaper stories suggested that the Bush administration thus might have given the green light to the Iraqis to invade Kuwait—promoting speculation that the U.S. might have suckered Saddam Hussein into invading, precisely to deploy the show of force of the U.S. military and to reassert the U.S. claim to military superpower status.[12]

Although the mainstream media positively presented the diplomatic moves toward a peaceful resolution of the crisis in early December, for months the corporate media failed to criticize Bush's obvious reluctance to negotiate a peaceful diplomatic solution to the crisis. It was obvious that the Bush administration was doing everything possible to block any negotiated settlement (see 1.2), but there was no major analysis of the reluctance of the Bush administration to negotiate a peaceful solution nor was there discussion of the reasons that the military option was in the interests of the Bush administration and Pentagon (see 1.3). Whereas a *Newsweek* poll on October 29 indicated that 69 percent of Americans thought that "President Bush should pay more attention to a diplomatic solution to the crisis," the mainstream media rarely criticized his refusal to negotiate and usually legitimized his unwillingness to directly seek a diplomatic solution with the Iraqis (see 1.2). Instead, the corporate media reproduced the Bush administration rationale for its policies and thus contributed to the march toward war.

In addition, there was little questioning of the Bush administration's claim that it was its hard line that forced Saddam Hussein to accept proposed negotiations between the countries and Iraq's subsequent agreement to release all foreign hostages in early December. There are, however, strong arguments that it was precisely the growing opposition to his bellicose Middle East Policy by the U.S. public that forced Bush to agree to negotiations. In light of the later public support for the war it is useful to recall that before and after the November 29 UN resolution that legitimized force as a potential resolution to the crisis, Bush's approval rating for his handling of the crisis was falling dramatically. This drop was in part due to the emerging antiwar movement that television finally recognized by December and presented some sympathetic reports of the opposition to administration policies. The release of foreign hostages by the Iraqis in December shifted the network focus from military to diplomatic solutions, but during the stalemate in the talks during December and January, the networks swung back and forth between military and diplomatic solutions to the crisis.

And yet the anti-Iraq propaganda was so developed in the mainstream media that even Saddam Hussein's stated willingness to negotiate with the United States and his surprising offer to release all foreign hostages was portrayed negatively. The December 1 NBC newscast used soldiers and a mother of a soldier about to go to the Middle East to express skepticism over whether Saddam Hussein could be trusted and whether one could negotiate with him. Sgt. Brian Callum stated: "I'm skeptical if Saddam Hussein will budge an inch." Interestingly, the identical clip was aired the same night on the CNN "Crisis in the Gulf" report, raising questions whether the U.S. military was staging seemingly spontaneous soldier-in-the-field reactions. On the other hand, such response did not need to be rehearsed because the media had created such a negative image of Saddam Hussein that people naturally and spontaneously thought the worst of him and mistrusted all gestures, however promising. Both the NBC and CNN reports on December 1, however, continued to present Bush's moves favorably and failed to ask why Bush had taken so long to consider diplomatic negotiations with Iraq (which, in retrospect, appear as a smokescreen to appease domestic fears of war and antiwar public opinion).

The Nuclear Threat, Congressional Debate, and Media Blindspots

During the weeks preceding the war itself, the Bush administration attempted to deflect attention from the growing concern about the advisability of war by producing stronger reasons why war might be necessary. "Focus group" interviews and a *New York Times* poll indicated that U.S. citizens were most disturbed by reports that Iraq might possess a nuclear weapons capacity. During Bush's Thanksgiving visit to the U.S. troops in the Saudi desert, he dramatized the dangers of Saddam Hussein having a nuclear capacity as a justification to fight and eliminate him. This argument was repeated over the Thanksgiving weekend by Secretary of Defense Dick Cheney and national security adviser Brent Scowcroft. According to them, recent intelligence information revealed that Iraq might have a nuclear capacity within one year, dramatizing again the dangers of the Iraqi president and implicitly supporting the need to totally eliminate him and his military capacity through decisive military action.

For some days, the television networks failed to question the claim advanced by the Bush administration concerning Iraq's nuclear capability. Despite a *New York Times* Op-Ed piece on November 27 by Richard Rhodes concerning "Bush's Atomic Red Herring," which stated that "[e]xpert estimates put Iraqi acquisition of a limited nuclear arsenal at least 10 years away,"[13] and despite reports from experts at the International Atomic Energy Agency that the small amount of nuclear fuel possessed was not being used in a nuclear weapons program (*New York Times,* Nov. 28, 1990), the television networks and other mainstream media outlets continued to use the argument that Iraq's possession of a nuclear weapons capacity was a compelling argument to destroy Saddam Hussein immediately in an all-out military invasion. This argument was suggested by William Safire in a November 26, 1990, *New York Times* Op-Ed column, was repeated by Wolf Blitzer in a November 27 CNN report, and frequently appeared as a rationale for war expressed by those on talk shows or "person in the street" interview segments. When the reports questioning Iraq's nuclear capability started gaining attention, the Bush administration put out a statement saying that the International Atomic Agency report that doubted such a capacity was false and the statement was aired on CNN on November 28, 1990.

Eventually, some media critique appeared that addressed the Bush administration's claim that Iraq was close to producing a nuclear bomb. The December 1 "Larry King Live" program featured a discussion between nuclear weapons expert Richard Rhodes, who argued that the nuclear threat was a red herring, and a prowar advocate from the Heritage Foundation, David Silverstein, who argued that the Iraqi nuclear threat was immediate and real. Silverstein violently attacked Saddam Hussein, the Soviet Union, and Palestinians, disclosing the venom and aggression that the media was unleashing. The "MacNeil/Lehrer News Hour" and "Nightline" also had shows during the first week of December that questioned whether Iraq could develop a nuclear capability in the immediate future. In the face of this questioning, the Bush administration backed away from this rationale, at least for the moment.

In January, the Senate resumed hearings in which a series of expert witnesses urged restraint and the continuation of sanctions rather than the use of military force to resolve the crisis. Two former heads of the Joint Chiefs of Staff and seven former secretaries of defense argued in the hearings that it would be preferable to pursue the policy of sanctions rather than exert the military option. Henry Kissinger and other die-hard militarists who continued to call for a military solution were the exceptions. The media finally began circulating these discourses, and Bush acted quickly to stem criticism and to help deflate the increasing questioning of his policies by promising negotiations. He announced a meeting between James Baker and Iraqi Foreign Minister Tariq Aziz in Geneva on January 9.

Yet, despite rising opposition to Bush's war policy and signs of peace negotiations in December and January, no peaceful solution to the crisis resulted. The negotiations had stalled by mid-December and the Bush administration never really seriously engaged in direct diplomacy with Iraq to seek a peaceful resolution to the crisis. Although Ted Koppel's "Nightline" had planned to air a "town meeting" on December 7, with an impressive array of antiwar speakers, the program was "postponed" after Bush proclaimed a willingness to negotiate with the Iraqis. No negotiations resulted, though the Bush administration continued to insist that it had "gone the extra mile" to seek a negotiated settlement, that it had "left no stone unturned" in the search for peace, and that the Iraqis simply refused to negotiate. In fact, the Bush administration did everything possible to undermine serious negotiations, leading some in the alternative media to speculate that they actively sought the military option.[14]

In any case, the television networks and mainstream media simultaneously failed to adequately discuss why the United States had committed so many troops and resources to the Gulf and transmitted little serious criticism of the Bush administration policy. There was inadequate analysis of the enormous expenses incurred by the U.S. military intervention and the impact of this spending on a faltering U.S. economy, which might not have been able to stand such excessive strain on its resources. There was little or no analysis questioning the timing of Bush's intervention during an era when the federal deficit, the savings and loan scandal, and possible collapse of the financial system, linked with growing recession, might require a scapegoat and diversion from the economic woes that threatened to become greater as time went on. Nor were the immediate political advantages to Bush and the Republican party from a military intervention discussed (i.e., the inevitable rush of patriotism that boosted the president's popularity ratings, the advantages to incumbents and hawks in the 1992 election if Bush was able to triumph in a Gulf war, and the downplaying of domestic issues, potentially damaging to Bush and the Republicans, in favor of focus on foreign politics and a Gulf war).

Consequently, the media failed completely to offer anything like an analysis of why it was in Bush's immediate political interests to undertake a vast military adventure which would certainly unleash political turmoil throughout the region, disrupting the political ecology of the Middle East, just as it was certain to wreak havoc on the environment. Nor did the mainstream media point out that Bush was a longtime champion of the military-industrial complex and National Security State, and that his actions during the crisis strongly promoted the interests of these institutions.

Indeed, the Gulf intervention by the United States was primarily in the interests of those groups whose representatives were crucial in encouraging Bush to undertake such a risky adventure. Bush's national security adviser Brent Scowcroft, his assistant, ex-CIA Deputy Director Robert Gates (now CIA director), Secretary of Defense Dick Cheney, and others in Bush's war team were all ardent defenders of the military-industrial complex and argued consistently for a military solution to the crisis in the Gulf. But the mainstream media failed to discuss how it was the military-industrial complex that would benefit enormously by the Gulf crisis and war, providing the defense industries the possibility of gleefully looking forward to immense profits just when they feared sharp cutbacks.[15] On August 6, the *Los Angeles Times* reported that "in a single stroke, Saddam Hussein's foray of tanks and troops has blunted the momentum in Congress toward making deep cuts in the American military establishment and has redrawn the debate about the shape and size of the nation's future military force. Since Iraq's troops marched into Kuwait City, Saddam Hussein's actions saved the B-2 on the Senate floor and rescued a pair of Navy battleships from going into mothballs." On the eve of the crisis of the Gulf, there was intense pressure to cut back the military budget to produce a "peace dividend" for increased domestic programs that would cut into the profits of the military-industrial establishment. In fact, a former member of Reagan's Council of Economic Advisers was told in mid-October, "We owe Saddam a favor. He saved us from the peace dividend" (*New York Times,* Oct. 16, 1990).

Yet there was little analysis in the mainstream media of the specific political and economic interests in the United States who would benefit from and which were promoting such expensive and dangerous involvement in the region. Oil corporations benefitted tremendously from the crisis; Lewis Lapham told of a Texas oilman buying bottles of champagne in a restaurant and reading aloud a telegram that he'd just sent to Saddam Hussein: "Warm congratulations on your well-earned victory. Every good wish for your continued success" (in Sifrey and Cerf 1991, p. 460). Bush and his family had oil interests in the region, and Brent Scowcroft was connected with both oil and defense interests.[16] Although there was discussion of the role of oil in motivating the U.S. troop deployment, there was little in the corporate media on the history of U.S. dependency on Middle East oil. The mainstream media ignored the fact that during the Carter administration, the U.S. drastically reduced dependency and attempted to develop a coherent energy policy, but under Reagan and Bush the United States increased dependency on foreign oil supplies and ceased developing an energy policy. There was little analysis of how the Republican administrations first sought cheap oil prices at the expense of oil dependency, leaving price and supply to the "magic of the marketplace," and then sought higher oil prices to benefit the U.S. oil industry (see Cleaver 1991). Nor was there much discussion of the fact that by 1990 the United States imported about 25 percent of its oil from the Middle East or that the dependency figure had been down to about 7 percent by the end of the Carter presidency.

There was also inadequate discussion pointing out that it is mostly Western Europe and Japan that were directly dependent on Iraqi and Kuwaiti oil (the United States was only receiving about 5 percent of its oil from these two countries), or that the U.S. has been reduced to a mercenary force supplying troops and weapons to intervene on behalf of its capitalist allies. There was almost nothing in the mainstream media on the need to develop sane energy alternatives, and what discussion of this issue there was focused on the need to rethink the nuclear energy option and to loosen restrictions on oil drilling in environmentally sensitive areas (rather than on the need to develop solar energy or renewable and ecologically safe energy alternatives). Instead, the corporate media took advantage of the crisis to promote the failing nuclear energy industry and also urged the loosening of environmental restrictions on oil production.[17]

Other blindspots in the media and Congress concerned the actual consequences of a Middle East war and the few speculations were rather tentative and limited. In a *New York Times* article on "Iraq's Aim: High Toll for G.I.s," Patrick Tyler outlined some of Iraq's military strategy (Nov. 27, 1990, p. A8) but failed to analyze what might actually happen in a war. A *New York Times* Op-Ed piece by Anthony Lewis took on the rightist arguments that democracy was hindering Bush in his attempt to intimidate Saddam Hussein into unilaterally withdrawing from Kuwait (Nov. 26, 1990). Lewis asked: "How would a war be fought? How many American casualties could be expected? What vital U.S. interests would be vindicated? What would be the consequences of a war? How stable would pro-Western Arab governments prove to be? Might Israel be threatened?" Although Lewis raised these questions, little effort was exerted in the mainstream media to seriously discuss them.

Crucially, almost nothing was explored on the political and ecological effects on the region if there actually was a war. There was little discussion of the economic consequences and potential environmental holocaust that would ensue if the Kuwaiti, Iraqi, or Saudi oil fields were bombed or set on fire. The Iraqis claimed that they had mined the Kuwaiti oil fields and would set them on fire if attacked, thus causing an environmental disaster—an event that came to pass, though, as we shall see, its origins were more complex than the media let on (see 5.3). Environmentalists argued before the war that such fires would be difficult to put out and that pollution from the burning oil would be extremely lethal and would cause tremendous environmental damage. Although there was an international environmental conference in London to discuss the environmental effects of a Gulf war in early January, CNN only managed a brief report on the conference, which suggested that there might be an ecological catastrophe from the soot and smoke resulting from a thousand burning oil wells in Kuwait and that the fires might produce a "nuclear winter" effect, blocking out the sun, lowering temperatures, and wreaking havoc with global weather patterns. It was also suggested that oil spills in the Gulf would be many times worse than the *Exxon Valdez* oil spill in Alaska. However, the *New York Times* and most mainstream news sources neglected this story completely.[18]

The political instability of the Middle East that might result after an all-out war was rarely discussed. Although there was some criticism of Secretary of State James Baker's visit with Syria's President Assad and some speculation that Syria might invade and take over parts of Iraq after a Gulf war, little attention was given to the turmoil that might emerge in the region during the eruption of major warfare—upheaval evident in Iraq immediately after the end of the ground war. There was almost nothing on a possible Israeli response to a U.S.-led war against Iraq. Would Israel enter the war with its chemical and nuclear weapons against Iraq, and might Iraq attack Israel? If so, how would Israel respond and what impact would Israel's response have on the U.S.-led coalition? Would Israel utilize the confusion to produce a final solution to the Palestinian question and use the state of emergency to drive Palestinians and Arabs out of the West Bank and out of Israel entirely? Would Syria or Iran attack their enemy Iraq and seize territory? How would the various Arab regimes survive such chaos? Might there not be a reaction against the regimes that sided with the United States, resulting in mass upheaval and the overthrow of regimes involved in the U.S.-led coalition against Iraq? How would U.S. interests be served in such turmoil?

Furthermore, given the absence of critical Arab voices in the mainstream media, there was no discussion of how Arabs perceived the coming war and how it would impact on the Arab world. Obviously, the crisis had divided the Arab world and some sectors wanted the U.S.-led coalition to forcibly expel Iraq from Kuwait. Many other Arabs, however, feared that a war would seriously disrupt the political ecology of the region and would be a disaster for the Arab world—as it arguably was. In fact, neither the Bush administration nor voices in the media really articulated any vision for a post-war Iraq or what would happen to the region after the war during the crisis in the Gulf. It was not clear how the United States envisaged driving the Iraqis out of Kuwait. It was not certain if the Iraqis would flee if attacked, as happened, or if it would be a bloodbath with house-to-house fighting in Kuwait City. If the U.S.-led coalition succeeded in driving the Iraqis out of Kuwait, it was unclear if the goal was to eliminate Saddam Hussein and his regime or merely a large part of his army. The U.S. had not publicly connected with any Iraqi opposition groups and if Saddam Hussein was overthrown or eliminated by U.S. military action, there was no indication of which forces in Iraq could form a government. Indeed, both the Bush administration and the media neglected the democratic Iraqi opposition, failing to discuss the positions of oppositional Iraqi forces on the issues of war, peace, and democratization in Iraq (Chomsky 1992).

Thus, it was not clear what sort of societies could be created out of the rubble if an all-out war destroyed most of the oil, cities, industrial capacity, people, and resources of Iraq and Kuwait. Consequently, neither the Bush administration nor anyone urging military action expressed what sort of a postwar order they envisaged in the Middle East. Although some (i.e., Admiral William Crowe in the November 28 Senate hearing) speculated that anti-American backlash throughout the region might haunt and threaten U.S. interests in the region for decades, there was little discussion of how the United States would guarantee oil supplies, maintain peace and order, and provide stability to a region that has been wracked with instability and seemingly unsolvable problems for decades.

It was not TV alone that failed to adequately discuss the issues of war and peace. Although the December 10, 1990, *Time* magazine cover story was titled "What Would War Be Like," the story itself did not raise the questions concerning the impact of a war on oil supplies, the potential ecological crisis, and the question of a postwar order in the region. *Newsweek,* in its December 10, 1990, issue, also featured a discussion of Bush's "Plan for All-Out War," but failed as well to raise the key questions. Furthermore, *Time*'s coverage omitted even a mention of the Senate Armed Service Committee hearings that overwhelmingly warned against the military option; because this event was of crucial importance, *Time*'s failure to cover it provides a clear indication of the extent to which key corporate media privileged the military discourse.

Even when important congressional hearings took place during the last weeks of the crisis, the networks for the most part ignored these debates, taking at most a snippet from the day's testimony for their evening news programs. There were almost no in-depth discussions concerning the hearings on talk shows, no news specials to highlight their importance, and no extended analysis of the hearings in the weekly newsmagazines. By contrast, interviews with released hostages during the same period were a frequent feature of the mainstream media. This preference clearly indicated the extent to which human interest stories are privileged over political debate in commercial corporate media, which are primarily dedicated to ratings, profits, and promoting the interests of the corporate class.

Finally, there was little discussion of the ways that the United States manipulated the UN to sanction the use of force against Iraq.[19] In mobilizing support for its resolution, the U.S. bribed, bullied, and coerced members of the Security Council to support the use of force and publicly punished those who refused to submit to its will. The U.S. paid off all the countries who had key votes in the Security Council with massive loans or debt forgiveness, threatening punishment for those who did not go along. When Yemen, for instance, refused to support the U.S. resolution authorizing the use of military force against Iraq, its Ambassador was informed that this would be "the most expensive 'no' vote you ever cast." Three days later, the U.S. eliminated its $70 million aid package to Yemen, "one of the poorest countries in the region" (Bennis 1991, p. 7). This action violated the charter and spirit of the UN which was supposed to be dedicated to peacefully resolving conflicts, to using diplomacy to resolve conflicts.

Many key issues were therefore not posed or adequately discussed before the war broke out and one could argue that inadequate debate of the issues of war and peace in the mainstream media might have been decisive in pushing the country into the Gulf war. The lack of an adequate critical discussion in the media regarding its Gulf policy enabled the Bush administration to prepare for eventual war and triumph by giving it time to slowly but inexorably build up the U.S. war machine and military strategy. The mainstream media aided Bush by employing the forms of popular culture to demonize Saddam Hussein and the Iraqis, by glorifying U.S. troops and technology, and by submitting to the pool system that allowed the military to control images and information. Saddam Hussein was presented so negatively and the massive U.S. troop deployment so positively that the only logical solution to the crisis was decisive military action and unquestioning support for the U.S. troops. The nightly images of the U.S. troops in the desert bonded viewers to the soldiers and created a basis of support. One could also argue that the use of the Saddam-as-Hitler theme and the demonization of the Iraqis especially prejudiced the public against a negotiated, diplomatic solution. Obviously, one cannot negotiate with a Hitler who is such a threat to the peace of the world that he must be destroyed.

Thus the extremely negative framing of Saddam Hussein and the Iraqis helped rule out a peaceful and diplomatic solution to the crisis by conditioning significant segments of the public to support war. In addition, the constant war talk created a climate in which only military action could resolve the crisis. The media's representation of the confrontation as a struggle between good and evil, with the evil Saddam Hussein unwilling to negotiate and threatening the allies, produced tension and the need for a resolution that war itself could best provide. Consequently, the mainstream media failed to meet their democratic responsibilities of providing a wide range of opinion on issues of public importance and informing the public concerning contemporary events. Because democracy requires a separation of powers and an independent media, the combination of the Bush administration, military, and media all pushing for war undermined the democratic system of checks and balances, failed to discuss issues of key importance, did not adequately inform the public, and thus intensified the crisis of democracy in the United States.

*   *   *

On November 28, the United States passed a UN resolution authorizing the use of force if the Iraqis did not unilaterally withdraw from Kuwait by January 15. On January 12, Congress narrowly approved the UN resolution authorizing force to resolve the crisis. The momentum toward military confrontation then escalated rapidly, creating a situation in which war could erupt at any minute when Iraq did not accept the U.S./ UN January 15 ultimatum. Headline stories in the January 15 *New York Times* reported that "U.S. and Iraq Prepare for War as Tonight's Deadline Nears; Diplomacy Remains Fruitless. Early Attack Seen." Other front-page stories were headlined: "Final Iraqi Preparations Indicate Hussein Wants War, Officials Say," next to a story headlined: "Iraqi Parliament Votes to Defy U.S." Another story noted in headlines on page 1: "On the Verge of

War, G.I.'s Are Anxious." On Wednesday, January 16, war was indeed to come.

Notes

1. On the Manichean frames of U.S. popular culture, see Jewett and Lawrence 1988 who describe the way that popular culture replicates the metaphysics of the ancient Manichean Christian sect that portrayed human existence as a struggle between good and evil. See also Rogin (1987) who analyzes how Reagan manipulated these frames and used political demonization to manufacture consent to his policies; political demonization involves the rhetorical construction of political opponents as demons who threaten the existing order. Both of these studies were influenced by Slotkin (1973) who analyzed the theme of regeneration through violence in American culture and the role of captivity dramas in which the capture of white women by people of color was utilized to justify extermination of colonized people—a theme utilized in the rape discourse of the Gulf war, as I shall note below.

2. To compare Hussein to Hitler and the Iraqis to Germany presupposes a false analogy in terms of the military threat to the region and the world from the Iraqi army—whose threat was hyped up from the beginning. Iraq's 17 million population can hardly compare with Germany's 70 million and its military could hardly be compared with Hitler's military machine, which was the most powerful in the world in the 1930s. Nor could Iraq, which depends on oil for over 95 percent of its exports, be compared with an industrial powerhouse like Germany. Such comparisons also trivialize the holocaust and Hitler's wave of aggression in Europe. The Hitler metaphor also serves to cover over the fact that the Middle East was, in fact, colonized by Western powers, which drew the borderlines of the region. Such decontextualization, hyperbolic metaphor, and sloppy argumentation would, however, characterize the discourse of the Gulf war.

3. See Stockwell 1978 and 1991 on the U.S. search for enemies to legitimate an aggressive foreign policy and national security state and Keen 1986 on the construction of political enemies. Popular biographies of Saddam Hussein were also villainizing him in hyperbolic terms; see Miller and Mylroie 1990 and Sciolino 1991. For more scholarly and balanced critical studies of Hussein, see Karsh and Rautsi 1991; Henderson 1991; and Darwish and Alexander 1991.

4. The initial media coverage of the Iraqi invasion of Kuwait and U.S. intervention in Saudi Arabia validates the argument of Herman and Chomsky (1988) that the corporate media tend to picture adversaries of the U.S. as evil while overlooking crimes of U.S. allies. While Saddam Hussein was a U.S. ally in his war against Iran and the recipient of U.S. aid and arms sales, he was presented positively and his crimes were ignored; when he became U.S. enemy number one, his every evil deed was magnified. Likewise, when the United States invaded Panama, its actions were defended by the same corporate media that later attacked Iraq for similar aggression. See the documentation of media bias toward the Bush administration during the Panama invasion in Kellner 1990; Chomsky 1990; Lee

and Solomon 1991, pp. 316–317; and Mark Cook and Jeff Cohen, "The Media Go to War: How Television Sold the Panama Invasion," *Extra!*, Jan./Feb. 1990.

5. The rhetoric of "rape" was encouraged by the Free Kuwait group and their U.S. public relations firm, Hill and Knowlton, which I discuss below. One of the first books on the crisis was titled *The Rape of Kuwait* and was funded and distributed by the Kuwaiti government (see Sasson 1991). There was, however, a double standard operative in which the Iraqi intervention into Kuwait was characterized as "rape" and "naked aggression" (i.e., sexual crimes), whereas the U.S. military intervention into Saudi Arabia was described as a totally justified undertaking to protect U.S. interests and the "American way of life." Ann Norton noted the sexual innuendoes in the media discourse constructing Saddam Hussein in a November 26 Teach-In at the University of Texas and suggested that this discourse presented him as a sexual monster and threat, and thus as abnormal. In contrast, she continued, Bush's "incursion" into Panama was presented as "normal," as consensual intercourse whereby the territory solicited the U.S. incursion, accepting its penetration, even though several barrios were largely destroyed and much damage was suffered.

6. For criticism of the bias against Arabs and Islam in U.S. media presentations, see Said 1981; on the anti-Arab stereotypes that dominate U.S. popular culture, see Shaheen 1984.

7. For feminist analysis of the media presentation of the Gulf crisis and war that I draw upon, see Enloe 1992 and Roach 1991.

8. Buchanan was attacked by A. M. Rosenthal in the *New York Times* Op-Ed page for claiming that Israel, its supporters, and U.S. hawks were leading the country to war (Sept. 14, 1990). Rosenthal accused Buchanan of anti-Semitism, which might be seen as a legitimate charge in view of Buchanan's record of defending ex-Nazis, but such an attack suppressed the issue of what the Israeli policy actually was and what influence it actually exerted on U.S. policymakers and public opinion leaders like Rosenthal. After this controversy, Buchanan disappeared from his CNN "CrossFire" post for a brief period, but soon returned; Rosenthal went to Israel during November to make sure that he continued to accurately portray the Israeli point of view in his Op-Ed pieces.

9. Studies by FAIR (1990) document that such discussion shows as ABC's "Nightline" and the PBS's "The MacNeil/Lehrer News Hour" characteristically contain only a small range of views from establishment sources, drawing on the same small pool of white conservative males from conservative Washington "think tanks" and former government officials. FAIR also argued that PBS features only conservative talk shows, with no liberal or left alternatives. An initial FAIR study of the Gulf crisis revealed that once again "Nightline" and "MacNeil/ Lehrer" drew on the usual small pool of "experts": Not one critic of the U.S. military intervention appeared on either program during the first month of the crisis; about half of the guests were current or former government officials and two-thirds of these were Republican; almost all were white males. See *Extra!* (Nov.-Dec. 1990), p. 4.

10. On the pool system, see the articles by Ruffini 1991; Schanberg 1991; Browne 1991; LaMay et al. 1991; Anderson 1991; and Fialka 1992. See also the

articles in the *Columbia Journalism Review,* Mar./Apr. 1991, pp. 23–29; *Index on Censorship,* Apr./May 1991; *Le monde diplomatique,* May 1991, pp. 11–18; and the *New York Times,* May 5 and 6, 1991.

11. Jesse Jackson managed to get to Iraq for an interview with Saddam Hussein, which won him a few minutes of airtime to criticize the U.S. intervention, though he later complained: "Since [the invasion of Kuwait on August 2] I have talked with Saddam Hussein for six hours, two hours on tape. Longer than any American. I met with Tariq Aziz for almost ten hours. I took the first group of journalists into Kuwait, negotiated for the release of hostages. And when we got back, there was not one serious interview by a network. A categorical rejection. Now why is there no interest in what we saw, observed, and got on tape?" (*Columbia Journalism Review,* Mar./Apr. 1991, p. 28). One of the few critiques by members of Congress during the first month of the crisis was that of Rep. Henry B. Gonzalez (D.-Tex.) who blamed the U.S. government and banks for funding much of Hussein's military buildup and who called for immediate withdrawal of U.S. troops from the Middle East (*Austin American-Statesman,* Aug. 4, 1990, pp. 1A and 4A). Later, during the Gulf war itself, he produced a resolution to impeach Bush, but this, too, was ignored by the mainstream media.

12. The position that the United States manipulated Iraq into thinking that it would not oppose its invasion of Kuwait is discussed in 1.1. It should be noted, however, that ABC did devote more stories to diplomatic efforts to resolve the crisis than the other networks. According to an analysis in the Tyndall Report, during the 45 days before the UN deadline, ABC had 23 reports on diplomacy compared to 13 for CBS and 11 for NBC; during the war itself, ABC featured 18 reports on attempted diplomatic resolutions of the war compared to 9 for CBS and 3 for the military-industrial network, NBC, which apparently favors war over peace, weapons over diplomacy.

13. Rhodes is author of *The Making of the Atomic Bomb,* which won a Pulitzer Prize in 1988. In the Senate hearings, James Schlesinger also stated that the Iraqis probably wouldn't have the nuclear capacity for five to ten years (*New York Times,* November 30, 1990, p. 1) and this view was held by others as well (see the *Bulletin of Atomic Scientists,* March 1991, pp. 16ff.). During the war, General Schwarzkopf and his minions would claim repeatedly that they had destroyed Iraq's nuclear capability with their bombing campaign; after the war, however, there were conflicting stories as to the extent of Iraq's nuclear capability and whether it had or had not been eliminated.

14. See *Z Magazine,* January 1991, pp. 3 and 56; *The Nation,* Dec. 24, 1990, pp. 1ff; *In These Times,* Nov. 21, 1990, pp. 1 and 14; and *The Progressive,* January 1991, pp. 8ff. The *New Yorker* featured a sharp analysis of how the nation was "sleep-walking toward war" in its "Talk of the Town" column of December 10, 1990, p. 43. These and other publications correctly discerned that Bush was proceeding to war, but the mainstream media either failed to note this or urged him to do so.

15. See 1.3. In September, *In These Times* reports, there was a meeting in Milwaukee of military contractors called by the Procurement Institute; when its cochairman Jim Roberts opened the meeting with the words: "Thank you,

Saddam Hussein!" the crowd reportedly cheered (November 21, 1990, p. 5). Manfred Sadlowski, who publishes *Military Technology,* headlined an editorial in the October issue "Well Done, Saddam!" Villains like Saddam, he observes, have "a very useful function" in that they provide the justification for not reducing military spending "without the need for too much propaganda effort by our governments." "At the very moment," Sadlowski noted, "when too many people were beginning to label our armed forces as useless relics of the long past Cold War age, we have suddenly found . . . a new mission for them" (cited in the *Sydney Morning Herald,* Oct. 9, 1990). On August 19, the *Los Angeles Times* reported that the proposed sale of 24 F-15 fighter jets to Saudi Arabia could earn the McDonnell-Douglas corporation an estimated $1.2 billion. Indeed, it was estimated that deals were cut with the Saudis in August 1990 for the purchase of over $40 billion dollars worth of military equipment, the largest single package in history. Although there were frequent news reports about the increased defense spending and occasional discussion of the costs of the intervention, there was little or no analysis in the mainstream media of the way that this was primarily benefiting the military-industrial complex.

16. Curiously, Bush's Zapata Oil company had operated in Kuwait in the 1960s. On the Bush family oil connections in the region, see the discussion in 1.3 and sources in Chapter 1, Note 26; Scowcroft was on the board of Santa Fe International, a subsidiary of the Kuwait Petroleum Company from 1984–1986 (see *Extra!,* May 1991, p. 16).

17. See *New York Times* editorial pages for August 7 and 9, which argued for reconsidering the nuclear option and loosening energy restrictions; this position was also frequently presented on NBC. Alternative media, by contrast, argued that the Persian Gulf crisis dramatized the need for energy conservation and renewable energy sources and energy independence so that the U.S. would not depend on Middle East oil to run its economy. See David Moberg, "Hussein's Moves Raise Energy Security Questions" (*In These Times,* August 15–28, 1990, p. 2) and Dwight Holing, "America's Energy Plan: Missing in Action" (*The Amicus Journal,* Winter 1991). It may be worth noting that oilman George Bush removed environmental restrictions on oil drilling and signed an executive order removing the necessity of the Pentagon to produce an environmental impact report on their actions and policies—a point that I shall draw on later. Thus Bush unleashed a war on the environment at the same time that he carried out a war against Iraq.

18. Once again it was the alternative and local press that stressed the environmental dangers from a Gulf war. See Joni Seager, "Tigris, Tigris, Burning Bright: Is the Middle Eastern Desert a Wasteland? . . . No, But It Will Be," *Village Voice,* December 25, 1990, and Glennda Chui, "Desert Wounds: The Environment Could Also Become a Casualty of War," *San Jose Mercury News,* January 15, 1991. On the day that Bush began bombing Baghdad, the *New York Times* published a story indicating that military scientists had concluded that a Gulf war would not constitute a threat to the environment of the Persian Gulf region (January 16, 1991, p. C3).

19. Although some argued that the passing of the UN resolutions against Iraq showed the positive potential of the organization as a force for global peace,

others argued that the U.S. shamelessly manipulated it, turning an organization dedicated to peace into a body that legitimated a brutal war. For documentation of the U.S. abuse of the UN, see Phyllis Bennis, "Bush's Tool and Victim," *CovertAction Information Bulletin,* Number 37 (Summer 1991) and Barbara Rogers, "Wanted: A New Policy for the United Nations," in Brittain 1991, pp. 143–158.

CHAPTER THREE

◆

Bush Bombs Baghdad

ON THE EVE OF the Gulf war, the public, the U.S. Congress, and the military and political establishment were deeply divided on the question of whether war or diplomacy was the best way to resolve the crisis in the Gulf. In congressional hearings, two former joint chiefs of staff and seven former secretaries of defense argued against the military option in Senate hearings; one of the most influential promilitary senators, Sam Nunn (D-Ga.), had deep reservations about fighting a Persian Gulf war. Congress was also strongly divided in an emotional debate over what turned out to be a war resolution. In addition, the citizens of the United States were split into those favoring or opposing a military solution to the crisis in the Gulf. A strong antiwar movement was already in place and was carrying out large peace demonstrations; in many parts of the country, antiwar strategies were set to begin if the war broke out (see Figure 3.1). But there were many who just as strongly supported a war to drive Iraq out of Kuwait and to destroy its military machine. Debates took place in communities throughout the country and the United States was extremely tense and uneasy as the deadline for Iraq to leave Kuwait passed.

Despite the intense division over a military solution to the crisis in the Gulf, the Bush administration was able to achieve strong backing for its war policy once the war started. Early polls pointed to overwhelming approval for the military adventure, and the Bush administration successfully promoted a propaganda line that all good Americans should support their troops, whatever their opinions on the war. Coverage of the war by the mainstream media, especially television, mobilized support behind Bush's decision to go to war; during the rest of the war the media would continue to be used by the Bush administration and Pentagon to manufacture consent to their war policies.

109

IF WAR BREAKS OUT

If the Bush administration ignores common sense and goes to war, we must be prepared to respond with clarity and a united purpose.

That evening at 7 pm there will be two gathering points - the South Mall (below the Tower) of the University of Texas and the parking lot of Palmer Auditorium. Marches from each location will begin at 8 pm and proceed to the capitol. We will encircle the entire Capitol Building, shoulder to shoulder, with light. Bring flashlights, candles, or lighters. Our demand will be that all elected representatives of the State of Texas work for an immediate end of the war.

After the circle of light we will proceed into the Capitol Rotunda for an open microphone expression of feeling.

For information, suggestions or comments, call 445-3063. Peace.

Figure 3.1   The antiwar movement was well organized and prepared to demonstrate. The above example is from Austin, Texas.

3.1 TV War

Because the Persian Gulf war was perhaps the first war ever orchestrated for television, it was appropriate that it broke out during the prime-time television news.[1] On "ABC World News Tonight" at 6:32 P.M. EST,[2] Bill Redeker gave an early indication from eastern Saudi Arabia that something was up: There was an unusual amount of nighttime flight activity and he had counted about twenty fighter jets taking off. At 6:39 P.M., ABC's Gary Shepard from Baghdad reported live from his room in the Al-Raschid Hotel that:

> throughout the entire sky there are flashes of light. It appears to be some sort of antiaircraft fire, a couple of flashes on the horizon now, something is definitely underway here, something is going on. The whole sky lit, lit up with these flashes continually. . . . tracers in the sky, planes, planes now coming toward this hotel and flashes. The sound of flak and flares. Obviously an attack is underway of some sort. It appears that there is tracer fire coming up from the ground. An incredible panorama of flashes continuing as I speak.
> . . .
> We now see an entire stream of red tracer fire and now sirens, air raid sirens are beginning to sound over Baghdad. The lights of the city itself continue

to burn on the ground, streetlights, houselights and as this occurs the flashes continue throughout the sky. . . .

Sorts of antiaircraft fire now rising up from the ground going up into the sky in all directions. . . . You can hear the firing as well, explosions in the distance and the echoes of them.

CNN reported live from Iraq at 6:35 P.M. that antiaircraft fire was lighting up the night sky over Baghdad where it was 3:35 A.M. About the same time, "CBS Evening News" reported that their correspondent in Baghdad sighted flashes in the distance and Dan Rather added that there was also heavy air traffic around bases in Saudi Arabia where troops had been engaged in drills during the day. From Baghdad, CNN correspondents Bernard Shaw, John Holliman, and Peter Arnett began giving live accounts of the bombing of Baghdad around 6:50 P.M. EST. Holliman described antiaircraft fire lighting up the sky, but he saw no signs of bombing. Veteran Vietnam war correspondent Peter Arnett asserted: "There has been an attack. The antiaircraft fire began twenty minutes ago. There were loud explosions, obviously bombing. Perhaps near the airport, and a military barracks. The attack started at 2:30 Baghdad time. Perhaps they are seeking out Iraqi radar sites." The CNN reporters took turns looking out the window on two sides of the hotel and reported via telephone connections what they saw. Ironically, the TV war was employing what was basically telephone/radio technology to provide some of the most dramatic live reporting of the war.[3] Consequently, the CNN "boys from Baghdad" were simply replicating the mode and style of journalism that Edward R. Murrow and others made famous during World War II, reporting live by radio during an actual bombardment.

The live CNN broadcast was highly dramatic and riveting.[4] Loud explosions interrupted their account of the bombing, and one could hear exclamations of "ooh" and "oow." Continuing his report, Holliman said: "An airburst, the telecommunications center. Bombs are now hitting the center of the city. War has begun in Baghdad." According to the *New York Times*: "When there was a large explosion at 7 P.M., heard blasting through the phone line that a CNN reporter had left hanging out the window of his Baghdad hotel room, the President looked relieved to be back on the timetable he had approved. 'That's the way it was scheduled,' he nodded to others" (Jan. 17, 1991, p. A8). At that time, Bush turned to Fitzwater and told him to "go ahead and do it," referring to the press announcement that would ratify that the "liberation of Kuwait has begun." Bush's "thousand points of light," celebrated during his 1988 campaign, were indeed flashing over Iraq and would continue to do so for the next six weeks.

There were some media accounts that Bush and his team were surprised at reports around 6:32 P.M. of the war beginning in Baghdad, as the first bombs were not scheduled to hit until 7:00 P.M. (see *U.S. News and World Report* 1992, p. 218). On *60 Minutes* in April 1992 it was reported that the Apache helicopters, which were supposed to take out key Iraqi radar in the attack path leading to the city, failed in their mission and that the Iraqis were therefore prepared when the bombing started and indeed began firing their anti-aircraft artillery early in anticipation of an attack, or out of panic; this story was told by General Buster Glosson in the *Air Force Times* (June 2, 1992, p. 1). Thus the early reports of bomb attacks on the city might have been false, identifying the Iraqi anti-aircraft defense shooting with bombing. The *60 Minutes* story also deflates the Pentagon myth that the Apache helicopter attacks on Iraqi radar sites and all of the missions leading to the bombing of Baghdad functioned perfectly. *U.S. World and News Report*'s *Triumph Without Victory,* for example, presents the Apache helicopter attacks on two Iraqi radar sites as perfect missions and the true beginning of the war (1992, pp. 219–221). If the Glosson story and *60 Minutes* account are true, however, the official story of the war begins with a myth and a lie.

By 7:00 P.M. EST, other networks were also reporting that the war had started. ABC's Gary Shepard, on the telephone from Baghdad, reported that he heard a communications tower being blown up and saw "an incredible panorama of flashes." NBC's Tom Aspell, also reporting by telephone from Baghdad, exclaimed: "Red tracers! White tracers! It's going up all over the place!" The words were as dramatic as pictures and made evident that war with Iraq had erupted. Moments later communications were cut off in Baghdad and only CNN was able to provide live reports during the rest of the evening. Subsequently, when Secretary of Defense Dick Cheney was asked what was happening in Iraq, he replied, with a smile, that the best information that he had about Baghdad came from CNN—a sound-bite later used in CNN commercials. CNN's management had spent much time negotiating with the Iraqi government for the special four-wire telephone, which cost them $16,000 per month and the investment paid off with first night's live scoops of the bombing of Baghdad.

By 7:30 P.M., CNN's John Holliman reported from Baghdad that the first waves of the attack had ended. "The sky is pitch black. There is a pallor of smoke over the whole city" produced by the "big explosions" earlier. Arnett summed up the attack at that point: "There were four or five waves of bombing. I think they were F-15Es. It has been deathly quiet for the last 15 or 20 minutes. It seems the first wave is over." Arnett concluded: "This was a surprise attack," explaining how reporters who had remained in Baghdad had not expected an attack so soon and that many of them, including Shaw, had planned to take a charter flight out of the city the next day. After the first day's bombing, the Iraqi government expelled almost all foreign journalists except Peter Arnett, and CNN soon managed to produce a live satellite TV feed that enabled Arnett to provide live telecasts from Baghdad throughout the war.

During the opening days of the war, CBS was the most cautious network in reporting the outbreak and progress of the war. At a time when other networks were reporting that U.S. planes were bombing Baghdad, CBS Pentagon correspondent David Martin noted that he did not believe that there were any U.S. aircraft currently over Baghdad. Instead, he suggested the reports might be describing Cruise missiles, which have a range of 1,200 miles. This would be a likely first strike weapon, Martin reasoned, because by using missiles you are not risking pilots' lives and you can target the missiles against sites that threaten U.S. air power. These missiles, however, only carry a small warhead, so more powerful weapons would be needed, such as aircraft that carry 2,000-pound bombs of the kind carried by F-117A Stealth fighters. The thrust of Martin's report, however, was that he thought that the beginning of a major air campaign was under way, using Cruise missiles to soften up Iraqi air defenses so that larger planes could then accelerate the bombing.

Throughout the evening, CBS anchor Dan Rather promised that his network would provide "steady, reliable reportage," and CBS military expert, former Air Force General Michael Dugan, warned that there is always disinformation at the start of the war and that some of the initial reports may be spurious (Dugan had been fired by Dick Cheney in mid-September when he leaked too many salient details of the planned U.S. air attack on Iraq to reporters; see 2.3). Rather agreed and the CBS reporting through the evening would be somewhat more skeptical of the official government version of the war than other networks, with Rather and some of his colleagues pointing out that the only sources of information so far were the Bush administration and Pentagon. But CBS also deployed a logo "Showdown in the Gulf" for its coverage, utilizing the codes of the Western, and employed the codes of entertainment for the entirety of the war.[5] In the two weeks previous to the January 15 deadline, CBS dramatized their newscasts as a "Countdown to Confrontation," ticking off the days one by one.

In fact, TV presented the Gulf war primarily as entertainment, complete with dramatic titles, graphics, and music. In Chapter 2, I discussed how TV utilized the codes of popular entertainment by personalizing the villain of the scenario, and presenting the conflict as that between good and evil. Throughout the war, the Bush administration continued to deploy this rhetoric and the media not only failed to criticize its applicability to the Gulf war, but employed the codes of popular culture which reinforce such rhetoric. In its presentation of the war, the TV networks used the codes of the war movie, Western, action/adventure, and miniseries to present the war as a dramatic conflict with exciting events, ups and downs, and threats and triumphs. The events themselves produced a happy ending and a restoration of order—though disorder would soon enough reappear (see 10.4). Thus the audience was positioned to watch the events as dramatic entertainment and to cheer for victory.

The CBS drama accelerated shortly after 7:00 P.M. when Bob Simon reported from Dhahran, Saudi Arabia, that there was an air-raid siren on, and that Iraqi Scud missile attacks were expected. Simon opened up the mike to pick up the air-raid siren, which Rather described as "the sound of war in Saudi Arabia." Immediately thereafter CBS lost its signal to Dhahran, and Rather explained that they did not know if there was an Iraqi air strike in Saudi Arabia, creating the specter that perhaps Saudi Arabia was under Iraqi air attack. Rather observed that there may be "retaliation" from Iraq's "so-called Scud missiles, the best that Iraq has." These missiles have a short range, he noted, but can reach targets in Saudi Arabia. "They are inaccurate, but . . . ," and Rather broke off his analysis by announcing that there were now air-raid sirens going off in Riyadh, Saudi Arabia, its capital in the center of the country. Rather reiterated that it was not certain if Dhahran or Riyadh were under attack, as he played the sound of the blaring air-raid sirens.

These live moments were genuinely thrilling and constituted the most compelling TV drama of the Gulf war. It was not clear yet if Iraq did or did not possess the capacity for an air or missile attack on Saudi Arabia and the U.S. forces, so that the suspense was particularly acute this first evening. ABC correspondent Barrie Dunsmore reported in a chemical weapons protection suit from Riyadh that the air-raid sirens had gone off again and when Jennings gave him the option to put his gas mask on or to continue talking, Dunsmore chose the prudent response and the line went dead, accelerating the drama. In a sense, the network correspondents in Saudi Arabia, Baghdad, and Israel provided the most engaging moments of live drama, rather than the combat troops, who were rarely seen. The correspondents under fire from Iraqi Scud attacks provided an illusion of audience participation in the drama of the war, and the fact that the TV personalities could actually be hit involved the audience in a new kind of live drama. The immediacy of the live broadcasts, I believe, helped mobilize public antipathy against the Iraqis, who were threatening the TV correspondents as well as the U.S. troops and people of Saudi

Arabia and Israel with the Scud attacks, which were a central aspect of TV coverage during the first weeks of the war (see Chapter 4).

The live reports were, at first, uncontrolled by the military censors, though each country quickly moved to control the flow of information and even cut off satellite communications when they did not approve of the live reports. Yet the moments of live drama produced a genuinely exciting situation where it was not certain what was happening, what would be the outcome, and what destruction might follow. At these moments, the discourse and images were not controlled by the Pentagon and the Bush administration, which struggled to manage the flow of information and images reaching the public through the media. On the whole, most experts would agree that the government carried out the most effective media management and control campaign in history, but the moments of live TV showed a situation out of control and provided real excitement and drama, capturing a large TV audience for the duration of the war.

The network anchors, correspondents, and experts, however, put their own spin on events and coded the drama of the war in ways that were sympathetic to the Bush administration and Pentagon. ABC's anchor Peter Jennings came through with the Freudian slip of the evening, announcing that "Operation Desert Cloud, I mean Storm, is now under way." Indeed, the mainstream media's function throughout the war was to provide a cloud of propaganda and disinformation over the brutal Desert Storm unleashed against the Iraqis. Throughout the war, ABC military correspondent Tony Cordesman praised the wonders of U.S. military technology and frightened the audience with his tales of Iraqi horror.[6] Cordesman and other military consultants told repeated tales of Iraqi chemical weapons, support of terrorism, and prowess on the battlefield. These tales of future terror, little of which actually materialized, helped scare the audience and position it against the Iraqis (see 6.1).

Tom Brokaw and his colleagues at the military-industrial network, NBC, provided steadily prowar and promilitary coverage, which no doubt pleased their corporate bosses at GE and RCA who were among the biggest defense contractors in the United States. Brokaw produced no memorable comments or insight, and as the hours moved on he became increasingly partisan. At one point, for instance, Brokaw and the NBC military adviser, General William Odum, chuckled about Saddam Hussein's merely having words and not weapons to hurl, and flashed triumphant smiles. The NBC correspondents and "experts" exposed their partisanship by constantly saying "our" and "we," obviously strongly identifying with the U.S. troops and war effort. Moreover, Brokaw soon discredited his news organization with his emotional and biased reporting of the major event of the second day of the Persian Gulf war, the

Iraqi Scud missile attacks on Israel (see 4.4). In addition, NBC was the only network that totally submitted to the pool system, and media critics after the war agreed that it provided the most undistinguished coverage (see LaMay et al. 1991, pp. 69–70).

NBC's military "expert," James Dunnigan, competed with Tony Cordesman of ABC in concocting Iraqi horror stories and radiated with glee as he described the ways that the U.S.-led coalition was destroying Iraq. With menacing, glowering eyes, Dunnigan's function seemed to be to terrorize the public into submitting to the Bush administration's war policies by producing images of unspeakably horrible atrocities that would occur unless the Iraqis were soundly defeated. Indeed, as we shall see, all of the network military analysts were totally pro-Pentagon and for the Bush administration, serving more as propaganda instruments for the military than as dispassionate and objective analysts of events.

CBS's Dan Rather wavered between, at first, critical and skeptical reporting and then promilitary reporting. After it was clear the first night that a major attack was underway, Rather went into the sentimental mode that he would periodically assume, telling the audience with a lump in his throat that there are young American men on the planes, who might be dying, hyping up the drama and evoking sympathy for the military (though he rarely, if ever, elicited any sympathy for dead Iraqis). Throughout the evening, Rather played the theme of Americans in peril and that the U.S. public should support the troops whether or not they agreed with Bush's policies or his handling of the Gulf crisis. Rather also played amateur war historian with references to Joshua, Alexander, and Caesar, to properly mythologize the war and elevate it to a higher stature than that of a slaughter of a Third World country by the most advanced technological military machine in history.

The live "real time" reporting made the TV coverage prey to wild rumors as well as carefully plotted disinformation. Early in the evening the first night, CBS's Rather breathlessly stated that an Associated Press (AP) reporter had just telephoned saying that "we are seeing activity within the hotel from Dhahran," suggesting a terrorist attack or some such danger, which turned out to be a mere rumor. Throughout the war, the networks reported almost anything that came over the wire services or that they received from their various sources in the theater of war.

The networks also dutifully and immediately reported whatever the Bush administration and Pentagon chose to tell them. When Marlin Fitzwater told reporters that President Bush would address the world in an hour and a half, the White House correspondents of all the major networks eagerly repeated the same PR line that the Bush administration fed them: that President Bush himself wrote the speech, after putting it through many drafts; that the president called major world and congressional leaders to tell them of his decision to begin the war; that when the war started, the president had been accompanied by John Sununu, his chief of staff, Vice-President Dan Quayle, and national security adviser Brent Scowcroft; and that President Bush was calm, expectant, and waiting for military reports. These reports extolled the President, making him a hero. The almost identical, straightforward transmission of White House reports, which would continue through the war, revealed the networks, especially the White House correspondents, to be mere transmission belts for the Bush administration, which controlled the discourse of the war by leaking information at key moments, which inevitably put the Bush administration "spin" on events.[7]

The networks also took the point of view of the military families, who they lavished with sympathy and attention. Dan Rather told how military people were pulling together in Norfolk, Virginia, and stated that it was important for military families to know how strongly people felt about U.S. troops abroad. However people may feel about the war policy, or about how President Bush has handled it, people feel great sympathy for the troops in peril, Rather pontificated, purporting to speak for the public itself. So, Rather continued, the military families should know how strongly everybody wants to bond with you and say "we're with you." Rather repeated this line over and over through the night and through the long days and nights to come, expressing a combination of heartfelt emotion and an opportunistic attempt to bond the military and prowar audience to *him* and CBS.

Throughout the night, the other networks utilized similar clips of emotional scenes with military families. CNN's Tom Mintier was at a church service in Norfolk with a distraught and tearful navy wife, who made painfully clear how upset she was with the outbreak of the war. In San Diego, CNN's Robert Vito met with wives crying for their husbands; one tearful woman blamed everything on "this crazy man Saddam Hussein," failing to perceive that it was George Bush who started the bombing that triggered the war. She and another woman took the view that they just wanted to get the war over now so that their families could come home. As the military families got control of their emotions in the days to come, they dutifully reproduced whatever line the Pentagon fed them. But that night emotions were raw and one segment on CBS even showed a military wife attacking Bush for starting the war.[8]

CNN's Pentagon correspondent Wolf Blitzer indicated that the initial reports from the Central Command (Centcom) in Saudi Arabia were very positive. There were no reports that any U.S. planes were destroyed and the Pentagon was confident that the assault was going just fine. Blitzer was interrupted by a report from Charles Jaco in Dhahran, Saudi Arabia, who explained that the earlier air-raid sirens were a false alarm by the

Saudi civil defense and that the electricity had then been cut off, explaining why the TV satellite feeds had gone dead. The Saudi military claimed, according to Jaco, that the U.S. and allied assault was massive and that no missiles had been sighted coming toward Saudi Arabia. Thus it appeared that Iraq had not yet responded militarily to the U.S.-led attack.

Returning to his upbeat assessment, Wolf Blitzer reported that the U.S. assault was moving along very smoothly. Initial targets in Iraq and Kuwait, he explained, were anything that could endanger U.S. aircraft. The United States had sent in its Wild Weasel and Raven aircraft to zap all communications in and around Iraq, making it difficult for the Iraqis to hit U.S. aircraft. So far everything had proceeded exactly according to the "game plan" that had been crafted "very, very carefully" over the last few months. As the days went by, we would hear much about this plan, one of the key features of technowar.[9]

Throughout the evening, Blitzer was the most gullible conduit for Pentagon propaganda, as he eagerly conveyed every rumor and piece of disinformation as the revealed Word of Truth. During the opening night at least, CBS periodically warned against accepting all reports from the Pentagon at face value, but Blitzer simply reported whatever he was fed, and emerged by the end of the evening as the most compliant and naive Pentagon disinformation tool among the military reporters. A former reporter for the *Jerusalem Post,* Blitzer identified with the Pentagon completely and never raised the slightest doubt that what he told his audience was factual information, never pointing out how the Pentagon was attempting to manage a positive consensus for the war and military.

To provide the proper Pentagon spin on the evening's events, former Reagan Secretary of Defense Casper Weinberger noted on CNN that the U.S. military had achieved "tactical surprise," as in Libya. Weinberger believed that the first wave of attacks was intended to draw radar and antiaircraft fire, and that "defense suppression" was the primary goal. He speculated (or did the Pentagon brief the military "experts," telling them what to report?) that the second wave of planes hit their targets, and that the targets had been specifically chosen. Weinberger was the first to put out the official Pentagon propaganda line that the U.S. military sought to avoid civilian damage and that it carefully selected targets and appropriate weapons to avoid harming civilians. Throughout the war, CNN and the other networks saturated their war coverage with guests and commentators who were former military or political officials who almost invariably put a pro-Pentagon, pro-Bush administration, prowar spin on events in their commentary. Thus, most TV commentators were really conduits for the Pentagon-Bush administration point of view and served to reinforce the view of events that the U.S. government promoted.

Weinberger believed that the bombing of Baghdad would continue well into the morning hours and, confirming his analysis, CNN broke in live to let their reporters describe another wave of attacks on Iraq. From their hotel in Baghdad, Shaw and Holliman described skies lit up with antiaircraft fire, and the audience heard firing in the background. Helping U.S. defense analysts, they described a blast to the east side of their location and, out to the west, bright lights on the horizon. Throughout the evening, "the boys from Baghdad" provided explicit descriptions of where the bombs were landing, which would help inform the Pentagon and anger the Iraqis; CNN military analyst James Blackwell described the "boys" as "good scouts." John Holliman crawled to the window to let the audience hear the sounds of the bombing of Baghdad and the antiaircraft fire. Peter Arnett described three enormous explosions that shook the hotel, and he claimed that the bombing was continuing in "wave after wave." Providing helpful information for the Pentagon planners, he stated that the Iraqis had new antiaircraft defenses that were more impressive than before. Holliman, who presumably heard Weinberger claim that the United States was not aiming at civilian targets, helpfully repeated that civilian targets were not being hit. Yet it is difficult to know how he could have known this from his hotel room.

The first mention that there might have been some opposition to the war came when Charles Kuralt of CBS stated that President Bush was not leading a united country into war. Kuralt, CBS's avuncular "human interest" reporter, pointed out that 46 percent of the people in the latest *New York Times* poll urged President Bush not to begin the war. Accompanying video pictures showed a demonstration outside of the White House and arrests of demonstrators there. Kuralt predicted that the next day there would be protests all over the country and that the United States was a divided nation. Dan Rather kicked in saying that he didn't know when a country was ever fully united during a war going all the way back to prebiblical times, although perhaps World War II was the exception. Continuing in the pro-U.S. ideological mode that he would frequently employ, Rather said that "for a democratic people like ourselves, divisions are out in the open" (though CBS and the other media would do much to hide these divisions in the days to come and would, in fact, help mobilize public opinion in favor of the war). Kuralt noted that many relatives of the troops thought that the best thing to do would be to bring them home, perhaps revealing himself to be the covert peacenik in the CBS camp.

CBS's veteran war correspondent and venerable anchor, Walter Cronkite, was brought out of retirement to provide some "perspective" on the war. Cronkite made a plea for supporters of the war to tolerate dissent, arguing that those against the war were "also patriots" with deep convictions that should be respected. This point was well taken, but it quickly became apparent that Cronkite was out of place. Responding to early Iraqi reports that there was "wave after wave" of U.S. aircraft over Baghdad, Cronkite chuckled and with that famous gleam in his eye noted: "That's just typical Iraqi, Arabic overstatement. We don't attack in 'waves and waves.'" Cronkite explained that U.S. planes fly solo, or in pairs, on their bombing missions to avoid heavy antiaircraft fire or being attacked by enemy planes. But he didn't seem to get the message that this was not the kind of war that he was used to covering; rather it was a high-tech massacre, with U.S. planes flying in groups with impunity above Iraqi antiaircraft systems, meeting little resistance from Iraq's hopelessly out-gunned air force and inadequate air defense systems.

CBS's Pentagon correspondent David Martin noted that reporters in the Pentagon had just been given a copy of a brief speech that General Schwarzkopf gave to the troops in Saudi Arabia. The general announced that he had launched Operation Desert Storm—"an offensive campaign that will enforce the United Nations resolutions that Iraq must cease its rape and pillage of its weaker neighbor and must withdraw its forces from Kuwait." Assuming a false unity and homogeneity, Schwarzkopf claimed: "The President, the Congress, the American people and, indeed, the world stand united in their support for your actions." In fact, almost half of Congress voted against Bush's war resolution, more than half of the American people were against the military option on the eve of war, and the world was likewise deeply divided on the issue of U.S. Gulf war policy. Throughout the war, Schwarzkopf purveyed lie after lie, seasoned with propaganda, and the compliant media rarely criticized a word that he uttered. It was as if Schwarzkopf believed that all he had to do was to proclaim something and it was true, and, pitifully, the media rarely contradicted him.

Schwarzkopf went on to tell his troops that they were "the most powerful force our country . . . has ever assembled in a single theater." Schwarzkopf typically spoke the language of raw power, and the war as a whole would legitimate his brutal discourse. Trying further to boost his troops morale, Schwarzkopf intoned: "You have trained hard for this battle and you are ready. During my visits with you, I have seen in your eyes a fire of determination to get this job done quickly so that we can all return to the shores of our great nation." The general combined here an autocratic order to get ready and do your job with the pragmatic suggestion that the troops will not be able to leave until they defeat the Iraqis. He ordered his forces to be the "lightning and thunder of Desert Storm" and proclaimed: "Our cause is just!"—a debatable proposition at best. Binding together God, the troops, families, and homeland, Schwarzkopf concluded: "May God be with you, your loved ones at home, and our country." All the networks obligingly read Schwarzkopf's text, and his positive media coverage elevated the general to the status of a popular hero by the end of the war.[10]

At 9:00 P.M., President Bush was ready to give his speech in the Oval Office, and Dan Rather told the CBS audience that no decision that a president has to make is any harder than the decision to go to war. President Bush made it, Rather explained, in response to Iraq's invasion, occupation, and "rape" of Kuwait, and at this hour the full scope of U.S. air power was being directed at Iraq and Iraqi forces in Kuwait with the goal of driving them out of Kuwait. Rather utilized the privileged metaphor of "rape" that Schwarzkopf had also employed and that Bush was constantly using, thus positioning Iraqis as rapists deserving punishment—a metaphor also privileged during the crisis in the Gulf (see 2.1). The CBS anchor described the August Iraqi invasion of Kuwait as a "blitzkrieg," which coded the Iraqis as fascists and the "massive air strikes" against them as just retribution. Positioning himself as an omniscient Voice of Truth, Rather informed his audience: "The plan is for the air war to go as long as necessary and then to go to a ground war." In effect, Rather was playing president, giving the essence of Bush's speech, making it simple for the simple minded to get Bush's message that the Iraqis were getting their due for their "blitzkrieg" and "rape" of Kuwait.

The relentless TV apparatus caught the last numbers of the countdown and on cue President George Bush began his speech, his thin lips pursed into a slight smile, and his face attempting to look determined and resolute. "Just two hours ago, allied air forces began an attack on military targets in Iraq and Kuwait. These attacks continue as I speak. Ground forces are not engaged." Employing emotional and loaded rhetoric, Bush noted: "This conflict started August 2nd when the dictator of Iraq invaded a small and helpless neighbor." Kuwait was "crushed . . . [and] brutalized . . . [in] a cruel war. . . . Tonight the battle has been joined." The implication was that Iraq already started the war and that Bush was merely "joining" it, a rather dubious assertion when, clearly, Bush had started the war himself with his bombing of Baghdad, joining Hussein's aggression with his own.

Framing his speech in the Big Lie which he had employed for months and continued to employ, Bush insisted that the military action was only taken after "months of constant and virtually endless diplomatic activity." He claimed that Arab leaders had pursued "an Arab solution—only to conclude that Saddam Hussein was unwilling to leave Kuwait." This claim was a double lie as Bush did everything possible to block all diplomatic solutions (see 1.2) and many Arab leaders still wanted to pursue a diplomatic solution, hoping, with the exception of a couple of the U.S. Arab allies, to avoid war altogether. Bush alluded to Secretary of State James Baker's "historic meeting in Geneva" where he was "totally rebuffed"—blaming the failure of diplomacy only on the Iraqis, even though the U.S. had never seriously pursued diplomatic negotiations. Bush never personally contacted Saddam Hussein and the U.S. turned down every single peace feeler and offer from the Iraqis, month after month. Hypocritically blaming the war on Saddam, Bush intoned that "[w]hile the world prayed for peace, Saddam prepared for war." Yet Bush had also relentlessly prepared for war and was now unleashing the results of this preparation against the Iraqis. The lies and hypocrisy that radiated through Bush's speech would mark his discourse throughout the war and would never be even slightly criticized by the spineless media commentators.

"Now the 28 countries with forces in the Gulf area," Bush continued, expanding his lie, "have exhausted all reasonable efforts to reach a peaceful solution, [and] have no choice but to drive Saddam Hussein from Kuwait by force. We will not fail." And so George Bush officially declared war against Iraq, identifying the country with its president. Indeed, Bush would constantly refer to Saddam Hussein as both the subject of Iraqi action and the object of the U.S. attack, thus personifying the Iraqi nation in the figure of its president. Obviously, it was Saddam and not the Iraqi people who were the target of public animosity, and Bush constantly exploited this by identifying Saddam with Iraq.

Revealing his true goals, he disclosed that "[w]e are determined to knock out Saddam Hussein's nuclear bomb potential. We will also destroy his chemical weapons facilities. Much of Saddam's artillery and tanks will be destroyed." Thus, Bush admitted that he was targeting Iraq's vast military arsenal and that the destruction of the Iraqi military was the goal of the effort. Later, many in the Bush administration and Pentagon would insist that they were merely attempting to drive Iraq out of Kuwait and to enforce the UN mandates. However, at the end of the war General Schwarzkopf confessed that the destruction of Saddam Hussein's military was the real goal of the operation (see 9.3).

Bush acknowledged Schwarzkopf's report that the assault was going according to plan and that Saddam Hussein would be driven out of Kuwait and its "legitimate government" restored, following the UN resolutions. Bush announced that "Kuwait will once again be free," returning to the "family of free nations." Such rhetoric suggested that Kuwait was once "free" despite the dissolving of its parliament and autocratic control of its public life by the al-Sabah family. Bush insisted that he had to act now because the sanctions "showed no signs of accomplishing their objective." "While the world waited," Bush stated, employing the Hill and Knowlton/Free Kuwait propaganda line, "Saddam

Hussein systematically raped, pillaged, and plundered" Kuwait, submitting its people to "unspeakable atrocities, and among those maimed and murdered, innocent children." In addition, Hussein continued to add to his chemical weapons arsenal and attempted to add nuclear weapons. As Saddam "dug in and moved massive forces into Kuwait," Bush argued, harm was being done to the economies of the Third World, the emerging democracies of Eastern Europe, and our own economy. Here Bush blamed the economic problems of rising oil prices solely on Iraq, whereas, arguably, his own failure to negotiate a diplomatic solution so as to return oil markets to normal was responsible for the world's economic woes.

After blaming the war solely on Saddam Hussein, Bush insisted that he had "no argument with the people of Iraq" and indeed prayed for their safety, hypocritically trying to atone for the fact that he had given the orders that would cause the deaths of tens of thousands of Iraqis. In a phrase that he would later repeat and that would come to haunt him after the war, Bush indicated that he hoped the Iraqi people would dispose of their "dictator" and "rejoin the family of peace-loving nations"—suggesting to the Iraqi people that they ought to overthrow Saddam Hussein. Playing a patriotic note, Bush quoted Thomas Paine's famous line: "These are the times that try men's souls." The implication was that just as all true Americans joined the revolution against the British, so too would all good Americans unite behind George Bush and his bloody fight against the Iraqis.

Bush concluded by quoting four soldiers who articulated their reasons to fight, implying that the country should follow the lead of these wise warriors, support the troops, and pull behind the president and his policies. The next day it was reported that there had been a giant TV audience for Bush's speech, that 78.8 percent of the people in homes with televisions watched Bush's speech. Only in 1963, during the live telecast of President John Kennedy's funeral, was there a higher viewing level. Because people all over the world watched the speech, the event probably had the largest viewership in the history of television. TV thus emerged from the Gulf war as the producer of a global village which, when significant events occur, presents similar words and images to people all over the world.

Furthermore, it was clear during the Gulf war that television provides the president with a powerful tool with which to govern. Throughout the war, almost every single videotaped word of George Bush was broadcast live or immediately rushed to the air. Clips from his speeches and comments were broadcast repeatedly, so he had an unparalleled opportunity to shape the image and discourse of the war to the interests of his policies. White House correspondents dutifully reported whatever they were fed by the Bush administration, without any skepticism or criticism, and commentary after Bush's war declaration was invariably positive, serving to highlight Bush's main points and to amplify his positions.[11]

After his speech, for instance, CBS's Leslie Stahl praised Bush for "conveying the air of calm determination." Bush's tennis and jogging partner, ABC's Brit Hume gushed: "Tonight President Bush had a vision, a long view of the world. . . . As one who has heard virtually every word that he has spoken on this issue from August 2nd forward, it struck me that he did save his most organized and most persuasive case for the night when he needed it most." This comment was blatant nonsense, for it was totally unclear what Bush's "vision" was, or even what he meant by his "New World Order." Assuming the pose of knowledgeable insider, NBC's Pentagon correspondent Fred Francis reported that the air attacks would continue for at least ten days before ground troops would be deployed. Francis explained that Iraqi radar had been knocked out, guaranteeing U.S. air superiority. Apparently, the critical faculties of the television commentators were also knocked out, providing the Pentagon with air superiority on the television channels as well.

Pentagon press spokesperson Pete Williams came on around 10:00 P.M. EST to introduce Secretary of Defense Dick Cheney and Chairman of the Joint Chiefs of Staff General Colin Powell, who would make some brief remarks and would take a few questions. Cheney noted that he, at the direction of the president, had signed the order the previous day to execute the battle plan and that proper notice had been given to Congress. The focus of the operation, Cheney insisted, was to hit military targets, to minimize U.S. casualties, and to do everything possible to avoid injury to civilians in Kuwait and Iraq; obviously, the Pentagon's line was that they were conscientiously trying to avoid harming civilians, though in the light of the extensive damage to civilians and nonmilitary targets, this propaganda line would turn out to be sheer hypocrisy. The ultimate goal of the war, Cheney implied, was the destruction of Saddam Hussein's offensive military capabilities that enabled him to seize control of Kuwait and now to threaten U.S. and allied forces in the Gulf. Reverting to the party line, he claimed: "Our goal . . . is to liberate Kuwait and enforce the resolutions of the UN Security Council." Cheney's own text, however, made it clear that there were two goals: to liberate Kuwait and to destroy Saddam Hussein's military; as we shall see, in the future, the Bush administration and Pentagon would not be as forthcoming concerning its goals as it was that night.

Cheney insisted on the need to limit the flow of information, and then claimed: "We had hoped to settle this peacefully" and that the decision to utilize forces was "agonizing." But, he added, assuming a more threatening posture, his nostrils flaring, "no one should doubt our ability and our resolve to carry out our mission and to achieve our objective."

Repeating Schwarzkopf's declaration of confidence in the troops, Cheney bragged that the U.S. force consisted of the finest troops "ever sent in harm's way" and that they will carry out the president's orders as quickly and efficiently as possible "and at the lowest cost possible." The "lowest possible cost" was a code word for maximum destruction of Iraqis, though this would not be clear until later.

General Powell noted that so far there had been no Iraqi air resistance and both Powell and Cheney told reporters and the public that preliminary reports have been "very, very encouraging." The operation appeared to have gone "very, very well" and although there had been a number of reports of Scud missile attacks, they had all been false. General Powell insisted that they had not been targeting Saddam Hussein, but were going after command and control of Iraqi armed forces and other military targets, such as air defense sites. Cheney claimed that they had attained a "fairly high degree of tactical surprise" and that they had already hit Iraqi chemical and nuclear facilities, though they could not assess the degree of damage at this point.

These military briefings, which would be a daily staple of the television war, were intended to produce an image of control and to manage the flow of information. Throughout the war, the TV frame would oscillate from control to out of control, from U.S. control and management of the war to uncontrollable chaos, produced by the unpredictable Iraqis. Just after the briefing, Dan Rather interrupted his summary to provide a live report from David Green of CBS, who was on the phone in Khafji, in northern Saudi Arabia. He had witnessed an attack on a Saudi Arabia oil refinery and told Rather that the Saudi military left the town when the Iraqi artillery opened fire on the refinery, which they had hit about five times.

This report was the sole "scoop" of the night and the only piece of negative news to emerge. Interestingly, it had been uncovered by a CBS reporter who, breaking the rules of the pool system (2.2), had gone up to Khafji on his own to try to get some news from the front. Dan Rather complained that the Saudi Arabian troops who were supposed to be the "tripwire" in case of an Iraqi invasion had pulled out about an hour ago, leaving the town of Khafji, which was north on the road to Dhahran. Green then reported that another artillery round had just gone into the oil refinery, about three miles from him. Rather commented that the Iraqis had good artillery, Argentinean artillery, with good range, that was better than U.S. artillery. CBS's Bob Simon came on from Saudi Arabia and noted that it was predicted that the Iraqis would target U.S. lives, Arab oil, and Israel and that it appeared that "the beginning of that prophecy is coming true." But the primary mood of the evening, especially on the other networks, was upbeat, even euphoric.

3.2 Euphoria

Indeed, there was no negativity or uncertainty on CNN, where the reporting on the first day's results was steadily upbeat, thanks to Wolf Blitzer, CNN's Pentagon reporter, who took every Pentagon rumor and piece of disinformation and quickly relayed them to the public. Around 11:00 P.M., Blitzer came on to report a growing sense in the Pentagon that Iraqi Scud missile bases H2 and H3, in western Iraq, had been destroyed by U.S. fighter aircraft in the initial assault, thus saving Israel from possible Scud attacks. According to Blitzer, the United States informed Israel one hour before the start of the war that Israel should not participate. The Israelis agreed, and it appeared that Iraqi threats to bomb them had not been realized, as there were no reports of any Iraqi retaliation (a bit premature as it would turn out).[12] Moreover, the initial attack on Iraq was "a blowout." It was the "most massive, concentrated U.S., or any, air strike in history," certainly the most highly coordinated, using the most sophisticated high-tech weaponry. Furthermore, there was no Iraqi resistance and the Iraqis appeared to have been caught by surprise on the ground. As Dick Cheney and Colin Powell had said, Blitzer explained, there was "tactical surprise." Although the Iraqis had always boasted that they could deal with such an assault, Blitzer concluded triumphantly that they obviously did not know what the United States had in store for them.

Shortly thereafter, Blitzer came on the air again with additional euphoric news, reporting that "high Pentagon officials" now claimed that the entire Iraqi air force was destroyed in the bombing assault and that the elite Republican Guard units, on the Iraq/Kuwaiti border, were "decimated" as well. Blitzer also remarked that he was told that with the decimation of much of the Republican Guard, "there is clearly a hope that the balance of Iraqi troops in Kuwait will surrender, bringing the war to an end." Thus, Blitzer was systematically purveying the view that the war was as good as over the first night.

Blitzer was joined a bit later in the evening by CNN's military expert James Blackwell, who presumably was to comment on Blitzer's euphoric revelations. Blackwell, a former military officer and defense industry executive who was currently an analyst at a Washington military think tank, marveled at Blitzer's "remarkable descriptive terms." The total destruction of anyone's air force was quite impressive, Blackwell noted, as was the destruction of all of the Scud missile sites. But, he believed, perhaps the most impressive report was the decimation of the Republican Guard forces, "the center of gravity" of the Iraqi military. If all of this happened, Blackwell concluded, this war will be over soon. But Blackwell noted, "that's a mighty big if." Bringing some realism to the naive

Blitzer, Blackwell pointed out that bomb damage assessment was needed before such conclusions could be drawn. Refusing to come down to earth, Blitzer asked Blackwell if the reports reflected U.S. overconfidence or if the United States and others had overestimated Iraq's military capability. Blackwell believed that the U.S. had underestimated their own capability. Such a massive assault had never been done before, so they probably and prudently used "military conservativism."[13]

Blitzer insisted that his information was "from well-placed Pentagon officials," who had told him that U.S. air assaults over Iraq had now stopped. The pause, Blackwell explained, was to assess battlefield damage. Indeed, he warned, they may need to hit targets again because sometimes the targets are not completely destroyed. But if the destruction described by Blitzer had happened, Blackwell noted, it surpassed anything estimated in advance. If a big chunk of the Republican Guards was destroyed as well as most of the tanks that were dug in, Saddam Hussein had lost the ability to utilize his forces in Kuwait and had lost the ability to threaten his neighbors. The key to U.S. success, Blackwell claimed, was coordination, battle field management, information processing, assessment, and the skills of the fighters.

Blitzer again recapped his information from "well-placed officials in the Pentagon" who told him that U.S., British, and Saudi forces undertook a massive and highly successful air strike with no losses. Blitzer's euphoria was based on pure disinformation and signaled that the Persian Gulf war would be a media propaganda war with the TV networks serving for the most part as propaganda agents for the Pentagon and Bush administration.[14] Agence France Presse also published a report asserting that the U.S. Defense Department claimed that four hours after the first attack the allied forces had "almost totally" wiped out the Iraqi air force and the elite Republican Guards. Reuters and the Chinese Xinyua General News Service also circulated the CNN disinformation the night of the war, as did the following papers and wire services the next day: the *Atlanta Journal and Constitution,* the *Boston Globe,* Japan Economic Newswire, Press Association Newsfile, the *Toronto Star,* and *USA Today.* The Pentagon disinformation campaign thus created the false impression that the U.S. and its coalition partners were scoring a brilliant opening night knock-out.

The Pentagon was also claiming that in the first wave of bombing, 18,000 tons of explosives were dropped, which makes it "the heaviest bombing in history" (Luostarinen 1991, p. 10). The Finnish military expert Pekka Visuri, however, estimated later that the tonnage numbers were exaggerated tenfold and that the Pentagon reports were disinformation—as they indeed turned out to be. Luostarinen speculated that the purpose of the disinformation campaign was to convince oil markets, the world stock exchanges, Israel and Western opinion of the success of the attack. The tactic worked because on 18 January the news agencies were reporting, "Oil prices underwent the greatest drop in history on Thursday . . . As the markets opened in Europe, the first news of the allied's successful attacks had spread around the world and this calmed the traders . . . The stock exchanges everywhere responded to the Gulf War with substantial rise in prices" (1991, p. 11).

Oded Balaban, however, speculated that perhaps the Pentagon officials who leaked disinformation were opponents of Bush's policy; they wanted to bring an end to the war and their message was that "the war has in fact finished" (pers. com., Jan. 13, 1992). Or it could be that the disinformation was leaked to intimidate, confuse, and demoralize the Iraqis by exaggerating their losses. On another level, the disinformation reports of a first-night "blowout" produced a picture of a technowar totally controlled by the U.S. military. Luostarinen points out that the very beginning of a war is especially important for the propagandists and that the Pentagon was especially eager to manipulate international news agencies and CNN the very first night of the war to shape the public's initial image of the action (1991, p. 11). Indeed, throughout the war the mainstream media were used by officials with specific agendas and many so-called "journalists" were nothing more than conduits for Pentagon and Bush administration propaganda.

David Martin, CBS's Pentagon reporter, by contrast, was somewhat more restrained. Martin reported around 11:00 P.M. EST that the briefing by Powell and Cheney had been short on specifics. The initial casualty reports were very positive, and apparently there were no reports on missing or destroyed airplanes, which was "to say the least, very encouraging." Apparently, no Iraqi airplanes succeeded in getting off the ground; there was no air-to-air combat. Iraqi response was limited to artillery shelling at Khafji and shooting surface-to-air missiles over Baghdad without radar guidance, and they apparently all missed. As to how successful the air attacks were, Martin insisted that the situation was "still up for grabs," which is why Cheney and Powell didn't make any assessments. They were waiting to view videotapes from the gun-cameras and to get satellite photo evidence. Martin, too, however, intimated that the United States had obviously hit the Scud missile sites very hard and perhaps all of the Scud missile sites were destroyed.

Soon after, Dan Rather of CBS summarized the evening's news by stating that in the first hours of the war, the Iraqis had seemingly refused to fight, either because the allied attack was so overwhelming and they were caught off guard, or, perhaps, they were holding back. However, in the early stages of war, Rather warned, one has only a tiny amount of information. Not only is little known, but much of the information is not accurate. Throughout the evening, Rather would constantly warn about accepting early assessments at face value and insisted on being careful in assessing official government claims.[15] In a discussion with Rather, Walter Cronkite made light of the claims that the Iraqi Scud missile bases, Republican Guard, and air force were all "decimated," saying that if the term "decimated" was to be taken literally, this may have meant that the coalition planes had only destroyed one of every ten of the Iraqi "assets," which is a long way from the opening-night victory that was being claimed by some in the Pentagon and media. Peter Mansbridge of the Canadian Broadcasting Corporation (CBC) also was skeptical, telling his viewers: "Keep in mind that in the early moments of war, there is a great deal of disinformation on both sides." He noted that truth is a casualty of war and that the viewers should be "very careful" of early official reports. In fact, by the next day it was clear that Blitzer's euphoria was totally misguided and eventually it would take forty days of bombing to demolish what Blitzer and some Pentagon "sources" claimed was destroyed in the first night of the war.

ABC also tended to buy into the first-night euphoria, though with some qualifications. At 11:30 P.M., hosting ABC's "Nightline," Peter Jennings reported that the sun was up in Baghdad and the Iraqis were emerging to see what the U.S. and multinational forces had done to their country in the last several hours. ABC correspondent Forrest Sawyer in Saudi Arabia tended to display the euphoria. He described the U.S. assault on Iraq as "a brilliantly coordinated attack" that has "struck apparently, the Scud missiles in western Iraq, which they were very concerned about striking Israel, seem to have been knocked out at this point." The strategy was called the "suppression of enemy defense tactics." The goal was to "knock out the eyes and ears" of the enemy by destroying Iraqi command-and-control facilities. The attack also tested Iraqi radar, jamming it and knocking it out. The initial assault was "a spectacular run for the allied forces" with no U.S. casualties "and with no reports of Iraqi planes challenging U.S. air forces." Furthermore, "there are at least some people who feel that a lot of that air force may have been knocked out on the ground."

ABC Pentagon correspondent Bob Zelnick later provided a very revealing analysis of what the United States was attempting to achieve in the Gulf war. Ted Koppel noted to Zelnick that the United States had been trying to convince Saddam Hussein that he truly does not understand the destructive capability of American weapons systems. Zelnick then described some of these systems. The Cruise missiles are weapons, he explained, that could be fired off in Boston Harbor and put through the goalpost of RFK stadium in Washington, D.C. These weapons had an enormously destructive capability because of their accuracy. This was a totally different situation than in Vietnam where "a bunch of guys wearing black pajamas, winding down the Ho Chi Minh trail with 30 days' supply of food in a sock or something, and ammunition that could ambush and pick off Marines or Army men at the time and place of their choosing." This was the "worst-case basis," and since then the Pentagon has "been looking for something which could really demonstrate the fact that technology does count, that these things do matter, that the money that we've spent on these sophisticated systems is not in vain."

This analysis suggested that the United States desired a war to demonstrate their new high-tech weapons and that the Gulf war provided the perfect terrain for such a demonstration. The air force and those using the weapons, Zelnick said, were looking for a situation that demonstrated that their bombing was highly accurate and effective. In World War II, he said, bombs could hit targets within a radius of three thousand feet. Today, by contrast, the circle is five to ten feet; this makes the bombs thousands of times more destructive as they are that much more accurate. Zelnick's analysis also suggested that the Vietnam war was, in part, an attempt to test new weapons systems (Gibson 1986), and the flawed outcome of the war put in question high-tech weapons systems and the honor and prestige of the military. In order to regain this prestige, and the budget to keep developing their weapons systems, the military needed to demonstrate that their weapons worked and that a high-tech military was needed to defend the national interest and to regain the prestige lost in the jungles of Vietnam.

Later that night, while providing headlines of the day's events, CBS's Dan Rather reported on the seeming success of the first night's bombing raids but cautioned that this information consisted of "censored reports" from "official sources." This was one of the few qualifications that network correspondents made in describing their information from Pentagon and Bush administration sources. Indeed, throughout the war, the media received their information from "official sources," which gave out a highly propagandistic and biased flow of information. Moreover, reports from the theatre of operations were literally censored, as the military required that all reporters on their pool assignments submit their words and images for government approval. The network correspondents in Washington were also getting censored information handed out by the government and for the most part were reproducing it without skepticism or qualifications, à la Wolf Blitzer. As we shall see, the official sources continued to lie throughout the war and the mainstream media tended to reproduce these spoon-fed words and images without the qualifications and skepticism that Rather and some of his colleagues exhibited the first night.

After twelve midnight, the networks began getting the pool footage that the Pentagon censors released via satellite; the networks, greedy for pictures, immediately played these images. Pool video was taken by crews in the pools (see 2.2) and subjected to U.S. government censorship, though it was rarely labeled as such. One segment, shown around 1:00 A.M. the first night, found a CNN reporter in Saudi Arabia describing the "sweet, beautiful sight" of bombers taking off. CBS demystified these highly aestheticized images when Bob Simon noted that the pictures were specifically chosen to produce the image of a neat, methodical, sleek, clean war, "beautiful planes taking off in the darkness for Iraq." These were precisely the images that the Pentagon wanted the public to have of this war, Simon noted, and it would be some time before we had any idea what they did when they got to Iraq.[16] Simon himself would soon risk his life to try to get uncensored pictures of the war with a CBS camera crew, which some days later was captured by Iraqis in Kuwait and held captive until the end of the war (see Simon 1992).

The general tenor of the reporting was upbeat the first night, with many predictions of a quick victory. Fred Francis of NBC reported that officials in the Pentagon were saying, "seven to ten days and it's over" while Tom Brokaw hoped for a "short and sweet war." To demonstrate the lunatic euphoria that was sweeping the nation, CBS treated its late-night audience to the fascinating spectacle of Representative Bob Dornan (R.-Calif.) telling Dan Rather that he had flown every "army asset" except the latest Stealth and that he believed that "by before sunset tomorrow," the war would be over. We had so dominated the skies and we used our "assets" so properly that the war will be over in less than two days, Dornan predicted. Moreover, we may never use our ground troops, Dornan asserted, suggesting that the war could be won by air power alone. The major difference from Vietnam, in Dornan's view, was that this time we used our assets properly to "destroy everything." Saddam is now down in his bunker like Hitler, Dornan snarled, adding, "This man is not a head of state"; he is in a separate category of criminal mass murderer, like Idi Amin and Pol Pot and Stalin and Hitler. "And that's what's not getting across to those people out in the streets. . . . It's going to be over soon and a lot of people are going to have to make some apologies."

Rather tried to refocus the discussion in a less extreme direction, but Dornan wouldn't be controlled and exclaimed that he hoped that the media would go in and tell the story of how Saddam Hussein had "raped this small country and gutted his own country, killing 500,000 of his own people." Lacking any charity, Dornan wished that Saddam "dies in a rat hole . . . [and that he] took the first bomb right here," Dornan hissed as he gestured wildly at his nose.

Positive images of public support began emerging late in the evening. On ABC, Ted Koppel revealed the results of an ABC News/Washington Post poll, taken in the immediate hours after the war in the Gulf began, which showed "overwhelmingly strong support for the President's actions. Asked if they approve of the United States going to war with Iraq, 76 percent said yes, they approved, while 22 percent said they disapproved. And asked if they thought the U.S. would win the war against Iraq, Americans by an 89 to one percent margin said they thought that the United States would be victorious." Thus Koppel concluded that "the President has what he needs: strong domestic support." To prove this, ABC then showed clips of support from the House and Senate with Tom Foley (D-Wa.), Al D'Amato (R-N.Y.), Alan Simpson (D-Wy.), Donald Riegle (D-Mich.), among others, indicating their support of the war. ABC correspondent Jim Wooten on Capital Hill reported that there were dissidents in Congress, "but they are few and far between." Ron Dellums (D-Calif.) was "outraged" by the war, but "by and large, both sides" were "supportive of the President and backing the troops." NBC's John Chancellor spoke of the "American people's great support" for the bombing, which was "quite justified." In the days to come, the media indeed helped mobilize an impressive consensus of support for the Bush-Pentagon TV war.

3.3 Disinformation, Media Management, and Technowar

For the first forty-two hours of the Gulf War, all of the three major networks jettisoned their regular programming and broadcast continuous live coverage of the war, for the most part without commercial breaks. With so much time to fill, the networks scurried around for military and political "experts" to comment on the war and depended on their correspondents to provide instant perspective on complex events with inadequate information. In addition, the network prime-time news anchors spent long hours before the camera during the early days of the war, trying, with mixed success, to manage the confusing welter of information and disinformation and to provide what they euphemistically described as "perspective" and "context," the latter being precisely what TV rarely provides (see 2.4). The news segments anchored by the TV morning show hosts were particularly painful. The "Big Three" network morning shows are characteristically happy talk programs, intended to make their audiences feel good and mobilize their energies for the day's work. The hosts are happy talkers, pleasant looking folks without any particular credentials or qualifications in journalism. Hence, once CBS's Dan Rather surrendered his role as anchor in the early morning hours of

January 17, he was replaced by happy talkers Paula Zahn and Harry Smith of "CBS This Morning." A confused and slightly dazed Smith recounted that just as he tried to catch a little sleep, a spontaneous antiwar demonstration broke out in front of his apartment in New York City. Longtime CBS early morning pundit Charles Osgood gave some deliciously bourgeois perspectives on the war breaking out from his apolitical dinner guests, who were shocked that war would erupt and upset their dinner; in addition, his seven-year-old daughter wanted immediately to know who was winning and when the war would be over, as if it were a TV movie. Paula Zahn was inappropriately perky, providing peppy summaries of sound bites from the evening's CBS coverage with a rather too pleasant smile; her happy-talk demeanor had become a behavioral constant and she didn't seem aware of the gravity of the events she was reporting.

During the early hours of January 17, the CBS morning team repeated the same headlines endlessly, brought in correspondents who had no real new information to report, and gamely tried to make it through the long hours until more competent commentators and correspondents could be brought on board. They also reproduced instantly any rumor or report that would come down the wire service, including much disinformation. The most interesting (dis)information of the first day of the war concerned some rumors, probably floated by the Kuwaitis, that the liberation of Kuwait City was beginning. CBS reported that French sources claimed that all Iraqi command posts in Kuwait had been destroyed, but Kuwait City was not hit. Shortly thereafter, reproducing some Kuwaiti disinformation, Steve Crofts said that the BBC had reported that Kuwait radio claimed that ground troops were moving toward Kuwait City and that Iraqi troops were surrendering; this report was played repeatedly through the night by CNN. In fact, the U.S. plan was to totally destroy the Iraqi military and infrastructure and they did not begin the liberation of Kuwait until forty days of merciless bombing of Iraq and Iraqi positions within Kuwait had occurred. Kuwaiti disinformation was already being disseminated and the networks were buying into it, as they would continue to do throughout the war.

In the early morning of January 17, ABC's Peter Jennings reported that over fifty Iraqi tanks had driven across the border and surrendered to the Saudis, and this too would turn out to be false. Throughout the day, Kuwaiti resistance sources insisted that there had been many Iraqi defections, although Saudi General Khalid bin Sultan denied the report. By contrast, Dan Rather was skeptical, noting, in response to Bob Simon's report that Iraqi soldiers were knocking on doors and defecting in Kuwait, that sometimes these reports were false. "In our very best hour," Rather cautioned, "we can only get a smidgeon, a sliver of information" and "in the early stages most of the information turns out not to be correct," because we are operating under "military censorship."

There was little caution at CNN, however, which aired a call from Kuwait City from an "Ali Salem," who described the situation in the city, reporting bombings near an Iraqi military hospital, other bombing raids on Iraqi targets in Kuwait City, attacks by Kuwaitis against some Iraqi soldiers, and Iraqis defecting. "Mr. Salem's" English was perfect and he was totally calm, articulate, and well rehearsed, as if he were possibly a Kuwaiti propaganda plant. Both CNN and ABC featured these highly suspicious phone calls from Kuwait City throughout the war, which raised the question of whether they were dupes once again of Kuwaiti propaganda (see the further discussion in 10.1).

Obviously, the Kuwaiti propaganda mill was churning, and the gullible and compliant networks picked up every rumor and piece of disinformation, instantly turning it into "news." Throughout the war, almost everything that Kuwaiti "sources" disseminated was pure disinformation and pure propaganda. Yet the network anchors and correspondents continually gave credence to these reports and circulated them, making the networks dupes of a foreign government and propaganda agents for the Kuwaitis.

CBS also fed rumors of an impending ground war throughout the day of January 17. Their Saudi Arabia correspondent Scott Pelley took a two hundred mile tour to see how the ground units were doing. He saw these forces massing toward the Saudi/Kuwaiti border at sunset and observed an almost endless convoy of fuel trucks going toward Kuwait, signaling imminent movement there. Paula Zahn announced that the ground war to liberate Kuwait was about to begin immediately, that the U.S. commanders were putting soldiers and matériel in place for the ground offensive. Later in the afternoon, Jim Stewart, CBS's Pentagon correspondent, reported that U.S. forces were now very close to the Kuwaiti border and were moving forward in attack position, though they needed to bring up more big armored tanks. In regard to the claims that the ground war was about to begin, CBS military adviser General George Crist warned that the U.S.-led coalition needed to hit the Iraqi ground troops with artillery and bombs for more than two nights and then assess the damage before a ground campaign could begin.

Obviously, the U.S. military was assembling its troops for a ground war, but it needed several more weeks to put everything in place. Thus, perhaps the military was suggesting to the media that ground war was imminent to throw the Iraqis off guard or to create the impression that the war was going to be over soon with a fast and easy victory. Or perhaps the media were drawing false conclusions on their own. Many members of Congress, the media, and the public were worried about getting stuck in another Vietnam quagmire and the euphoric reports of an easy victory were probably a Pentagon disinformation move to relieve such worries.

Reports of casualties did not drift in until late in the morning after the opening night bombing. The French were the first to report that four of their planes were hit and slightly damaged, but none went down; later, they said one pilot was slightly injured. The British reported that all of their planes had returned safely, though wire services claimed that one U.K. plane was shot down. Moreover, Baghdad radio claimed that Iraqi antiaircraft units shot down fourteen allied planes, and the government ordered people to take POWs; they also claimed that the U.S. had bombed civilian neighborhoods. Harry Smith explained that "we absolutely have to expect that the Iraqis will use their radio for propaganda, yet we feel the obligation to report what we hear." Smith did not seem aware that the Pentagon, Bush administration, and Kuwaitis were using U.S. media for propaganda and would continue to do so throughout the war, thanks to willing accomplices like Harry Smith.

The other interesting material from the first day of war concerned the pool footage that gave the world the first pictures of the faces and words of the U.S. flight crews who were involved in the bombing of Baghdad. One of the first clips involved pool footage from a pilot who—sounding like John Holliman on CNN—reported that the bombing of Baghdad looked like Fourth of July fireworks, with the sky "lighting up like a Christmas tree." These reports tended to aestheticize war, turning the high-tech war into an aesthetic spectacle. It also elevated the pilots who carried out the successful bombing runs into mythical heros, without questioning the effects of their bombing on the Iraqi people. The younger warriors were especially excited; one exclaimed: "We launched out and we were pumped. We had a lot of good adrenalin going." Another said that they had the "same adrenalin that a young hunter has after his first hunt or a young athlete has after his first game." It was "good to have one under my belt, that's behind us now."

Another pilot related how they initially watched the groundfire come up and "we said, 'hey it's neat,' but it's aimed at me . . . . You're just so high, on adrenalin, but you can't get overconfident." He described the antiaircraft fire as "exactly like the movies," and noted that the antiaircraft fire and the air bursts below were "exciting." Also intepreting their experience in the aesthetic mode, a young flyboy told of the "flickering lights when triple-a [i.e., antiaircraft artillery] comes up," which then "looks like Christmas lights" when the bombs explode. "It's awesome," he concluded. This coding of the air war as an exciting war movie points to the complicity between technowar culture and Hollywood movies. Indeed Hollywood films like *Top Gun,* the top grossing film of 1986, produced extremely positive images of air warrior heroes, while films like *Iron Eagle* I and II created Arab enemies who were destroyed by U.S. airpower. Films like *Star Wars* used Hollywood special effects to produce libidinal pleasure at the destruction of evil enemies, charges of pleasure that these airmen evidently felt upon returning from their initial bombing runs.[17]

A pool picture aired later on January 17 showed the support personnel chanting "woof! woof! woof!" as the U.S. planes came back triumphantly, and one pilot said: "It was an ugly high." Another cocky airman returned swaggering and bragging: "Been a very fortunate fellow. Led a really swell life. The Lord blessed me with a good woman and made me an American fighting pilot. God bless America." Assuming the Pentagon propaganda mode, another pilot justified the Gulf war by stating: "We've waited as long as we can. We hope that the American public supports the President. . . . We want to do a good job and get it over as soon as possible."

The first officially sanctioned military information came during the military briefings, which would become a daily feature of the Gulf war. At the first briefing at Riyadh, the United States announced that so far they had carried out over 750 "sorties" (i.e., air assaults over the Iraqi/ Kuwaiti "theater of war"). The briefing described the astonishing array of weapons used—Cruise missiles, F-18s, B52s, F-111s, Apache helicopters, and so on—which were deployed in two waves of strikes that hit 159 Iraqi targets. The military affirmed that there was no ground combat. The possibility that Iraq had dispersed its air fleet to sixty air bases around the country, with hardened shelters, was discussed, putting in question the previous night's claim that the entire Iraqi air force was destroyed.[18] Although the U.S. military still asserted that they had destroyed all the fixed Scud-missile launchers, they admitted that Iraq might still have mobile missile launchers, which made doubtful the claim that Iraq's Scud missile capacity had been destroyed.

CBS's military correspondent Jim Stewart said that the fact that Apache helicopters, which are primarily short-range "tank killers," were used suggested that there had been a probing of Iraqi troops inside of Kuwait. Yet Stewart did not raise the question of whether or not the Iraqi Republican Guard troops were "decimated," as was claimed the previous evening. Stewart repeated the report that Iraq had moved its chemical weapons into Kuwait and noted that "some people think that this precipitated the attack"—an obvious piece of disinformation, as Bush and the Pentagon had plenty of other reasons for beginning the Persian Gulf war, reasons that were never discussed by the mainstream media. In fact, chemical weapons were never used during the war nor were they found in the Kuwaiti theater of operations after the war.

At around 8:00 A.M. EST Dick Cheney and Colin Powell arrived for another briefing. Pentagon spokesman Pete Williams announced that Cheney would open with some brief remarks and a couple of questions but had to leave shortly for a White House meeting. Cheney confirmed that to date the operation was going very well but emphasized the importance of being cautious in comments on the war. He especially cautioned "our friends in the press corps" to avoid euphoria and to be aware that "we are in the early stages of an operation that will run for a considerable period of time." There would be casualties and everyone should "be careful about claiming victory or making assumptions about the ultimate cost of this operation in terms of casualties."

This message would be the message of the day from the Bush administration and Pentagon. The administration followed the strategy of the Reagan administration (see Kellner 1990) by putting out one message per day that would be circulated to the media through all government agencies and spokespeople, ranging from top officials to middle- and low-level bureaucrats, who were supposed to give out the same message to the press when they encountered them. The previous night the message was that things were going extremely well, but the Bush administration then concluded that there was an excess of euphoria, which could raise unrealistic expectations for a quick and clean victory. Thus, the White House and Pentagon throughout the day tried to dampen this euphoria and to get people to accept the necessity of a longer and more painful war than the initial commentary suggested. Indeed, the goal was to destroy the Iraqi military and industrial capacity and this would take many days of bombing that the public would have to tolerate.

Yet Cheney and Powell's report was generally upbeat. Cheney noted that the allies had fired over 100 Tomahawk Cruise missiles and flown over 1,000 sorties, with only one U.S. and one U.K. aircraft lost. The military was assessing the bomb damage, Cheney said and then decisions would be made about restriking certain targets. Such retargeting, he explained, was a normal part of the operation, which would continue until Saddam Hussein was out of Kuwait and the UN resolutions were implemented. In a question-and-answer session, Cheney and Powell confirmed that there had been no Iraqi Scud launches and that, so far, all activities were part of an "air phase," though ground forces may be introduced as part of the plan. The early stage of the air portion of the campaign could run "for some period of time" and the allies would maintain the campaign as long as necessary to carry out their objectives. The United States rejected the notion of a bombing pause to commence negotiations, and the only Iraqi action so far had been hitting an oil refinery with artillery that had been quickly "silenced." The Pentagon was pleased that they had achieved "tactical surprise," but did not rule out the possibility of Iraqi action on the ground or in the air. They claimed that 80 percent of their sorties were "effective," which meant that percentage of planes went to their target, dropped bombs and fired missiles, and returned. The U.S. assessment of damage to Iraqi command-and-control and other units indicated that the coalition had been effective in attacking air fields and Scud missile sites, though Powell admitted that there might have been mobile missile sites that they missed. The targets also included the Iraqi elite Republican Guards forces, though there was no bomb damage assessment of strikes on this target (putting in question CNN's Blitzer's claim the previous night that the Republican Guard had been "decimated"). Finally, Powell pointed out that a tremendous number of planes from the U.S., U.K., Saudi, and Kuwaiti air forces were used, as were Cruise missiles that were deployed against a variety of targets needing precise hits.

Powell claimed that their success was made possible by an "extremely detailed, well thought out plan," through which Generals Charles Horner and Schwarzkopf coordinated the multinational forces under a single commander. Powell stressed that they would carry out a "comprehensive campaign with air, land, and sea components [that] would unfold over a period of time." In the following days Powell, Cheney, Schwarzkopf, and others repeatedly referred to their "plan," which was obviously the linchpin of a complex technowar. Exposing the technocratic mentality undergirding the project, Powell explained that they plan "to use all of the tools in the toolbox that we've brought."

Technowar thus involves a coordinated plan, tools, and their application. The technowar in the Gulf was integrated and comprehensive, under a single commander. The failure of U.S. military operations undertaken to rescue the hostages in Tehran in 1980 and many problems with the Grenada invasion, as well as other U.S. operations in the previous decade, were attributed to lack of successful coordination between the services. This time the military was resolved to have a more integrated leadership. The emphasis on a "single commander" was also intended to signal that General Schwarzkopf was in charge, making clear that this was a U.S.-led operation.

Technowar was developed in Vietnam as a strategy for deploying new high-tech weapons systems and bringing managerial science to the practice of warfare (see Gibson 1986). It thus combines science, technology, and comprehensive planning to control the battlefield and to destroy the enemy. It was impossible, however, to control the battlefield in the jungle terrain of Vietnam, against well-organized and armed peasants and soldiers, and the U.S. military suffered a humiliating defeat by a Third World guerilla army. Consequently, the military was desperately in need of a war that would give it the opportunity to demonstrate that its expensive weapons systems work, that would legitimate the expense involved, and that would justify production of more high-tech weapons systems. The Gulf war, we shall see, was the perfect war for this endeavor (see 9.5).

At bottom, however, technowar involves the use of high-tech weapons and coordinated planning to maximize the killing of the enemy and minimize casualties on one's own side. Killing is a nasty business and so the technowar in the Persian Gulf also involved a sophisticated program of media management to organize consensus in favor of the war. The result was the most carefully managed flow of information and brilliantly packaged disinformation in the history of modern warfare. The initial strategy of the war managers was to present an image of a war that was clean, precise, and effective. At the briefing described above, General Powell insisted that they had been very sensitive to collateral damage in the Baghdad area and joked that the best source of how careful they had been were the CNN reporters who reported precise hits with no visible destruction of surrounding areas. He claimed that the military was very sensitive to civilian damage and to religious and cultural sites in the area, stressing repeatedly that they were employing precision bombing, a theme that would become the leitmotif of technowar in the days to come. The images of precision, coordination, effectiveness, and cleanness of the war were replayed day after day, until images of the suffering and devastation put in question this technocratic ideology (see Chapters 4–7).

The network commentary after Powell's speech reflected U.S. chauvinism and military pride in the technowar. CBS military correspondent George Crist, a former Marine general, said that at least five nations were in the air, flying thousands of sorties "and it's all being put together under one commander, the American leader, General Schwarzkopf." Crist then praised the "incredible command and control apparatus," which was keeping everything together. Turning somber, Crist categorically stated that "there will be a ground portion of this" campaign. He noted that the "talk of an air portion" presupposed a ground portion, and, indeed, Powell had stressed that the plan involved a single operation containing an air campaign, a ground campaign, and an amphibious one. Later this coordinated campaign would be referred to as AirLand war (see Chapters 8–9).

3.4 Surrender

And so the Bush administration and the Pentagon wanted to present an image of total control and a positive, optimistic view of the military campaign. However, as noted, they were concerned to puncture premature euphoria and to prepare the nation for the fighting and dying ahead. The other message of the day was that Saddam Hussein should not expect any mercy or deals. The Bush administration and Pentagon had already made clear that there would be no bombing pause that could lead to a diplomatic solution. Around 1:50 P.M. on January 17, CBS's White House correspondent Leslie Stahl came on after a Marlin Fitzwater briefing to the press with the news that the United States had called on Saddam Hussein to surrender; Fitzwater, however, refused to define "surrender." This ultimatum heated up the rhetoric and would make a diplomatic settlement all the more difficult, as obviously Saddam Hussein was not going to surrender. Stahl reported that Senator Bob Dole also used the word "surrender" in talking to reporters about the meeting with Bush and the Congress. Indeed, the White House soon released the footage from this meeting where a haggard and testy George Bush said that he "didn't want to get into semantics," but insisted that "we are going to prevail" and that "he'll have to get out of Kuwait" and there will be "no concessions, no conditions." He blustered that "we're using force and we are not going to stop until he moves out of Kuwait," resulting in "full compliance with the UN resolutions."

ABC's White House correspondent Brit Hume explained that the demand to surrender was to preclude a maneuver by Saddam Hussein to call for a cease-fire or to partially withdraw from Kuwait, which "in the eyes of the administration would be the worst thing possible."[19] The call for caution and lower expectations came, Hume explained, because public support would have a lot to do with what the public expects; if the public expects a quick victory and then the war drags on, the war would lose support. On the January 17 "CBS Evening News," Leslie Stahl interpreted Bush's call on Saddam Hussein to surrender as a message designed to prohibit Iraq from making a "partial move" that might call for diplomatic initiatives. Moreover, ABC reported that day that the talk around the UN was that the United States wanted "capitulation" from Iraq—that nothing less would do.

In effect, then, the Bush administration sent out a tough message that it would accept no solution to the crisis except Iraqi defeat and surrender, making clear that Bush intended to carry out his threat to destroy the Iraqi military capacity. None of the network pundits that I observed picked up on the significance of Bush's call to surrender or criticized his intransigence and total refusal to even contemplate a diplomatic solution, a posture that he would assume throughout the war when various peace initiatives were floated. The cumulative White House message of the day, therefore, was that the country should prepare itself for an extended and bloody war that would not end until Iraq was soundly defeated.

Notes

1. The Libyan bombing, approved by Ronald Reagan in 1986, had been planned to take place during the prime-time news, and one suspects that George Bush and his advisers followed their Republican predecessors in paying as much attention to media strategy as to the political and military dimensions of the event.

2. Throughout this book, I shall use eastern standard time (EST) as the temporal measure because the major U.S. TV networks originate in this time zone and frequently put the eastern standard time on the video that I have analyzed.

3. CNN had negotiated with the Iraqis to allow them to use a "four-wire" telephone "on a military communications network which ran in hardened gulleys to the Jordanian border" (Simpson 1991, p. 282). Thus, when regular telephone service and electricity went out, CNN had its own communications system that it used to transmit live broadcasts from Iraq. Later, CNN was able to negotiate bringing in a satellite TV transmitter and generator and provided live TV pictures from Baghdad, to the anger of their media competitors and those who argued that CNN was transmitting Iraqi propaganda. Officials from ABC even claimed that CNN was allowing the Iraqis to use the satellite phone for political purposes, a charge that CNN strenuously denied (*New York Times,* Jan. 21, 1991, p. B1). It was reported that Iraq monitored CNN twenty-four hours a day and that Saddam Hussein was an avid CNN viewer.

4. According to the Nielsen ratings service, CNN's overnight rating from twenty-five major cities jumped 27.1 percent Tuesday evening, the night before the war broke out, compared with the same night a week before (*Wall Street Journal,* Jan. 17, 1991, p. A6). The CNN audience the first night of the Gulf war was by far its largest in history. During the prime-time hours, CNN had a 19.1 rating among households with cable television. This was fairly astonishing because of the three major networks ABC had a 19.5 audience share in the overnight ratings, NBC had a 15.1 share, and CBS had an 11.3 share. Each rating point represents 931,000 homes, and CNN usually averages less than one rating point nationally during the prime-time hours (*New York Times,* Jan. 18, 1991, p. A13). CNN's moment of glory had arrived; for a lively but uncritical version of the CNN story, see Whittemore 1990, and for background on how the war played out in the CNN studios in Atlanta, see Smith 1991. Weiner 1992 tells the inside story of CNN's adventures in Baghdad.

5. Curiously, ABC also employed the same "Showdown in the Gulf" slogan the opening night, but would soon change its logo to "The Gulf War." CBS would continue to utilize Western motifs, especially hyping the drama of the *High Noon* showdown on the eve of the ground war (see 8.2), while ABC played it more like a war movie. NBC logoed the event as "America at War" and played up the nationalist elements and the triumphs of U.S. military technology, which its parent companies GE and RCA happened to produce.

6. Cordesman was a former Pentagon employee and aide to right-wing Senator John McCain (R-Ariz.), and both are strong supporters of the U.S. military.

Proving decisively that he was an apologist for the military-industrial complex, the day after the Gulf war was over, Cordesman published an Op-Ed piece in the *New York Times* arguing against any cuts for defense spending (Feb. 28, 1991).

7. The term "spin control" referred to how the White House put its own "spin" on events, making negative events appear positive and positive events brilliant. More and more, the mainstream media seemed vulnerable to manipulation by White House spin control. Indeed, the format of the White House correspondents largely reporting and amplifying administration positions render the television networks little more than public relations organizations for their political masters.

8. One would rarely see military families criticizing the Bush administration or the war thereafter. The Pentagon made it clear that such remarks would ruin the careers of those whose family members spoke out, and the U.S. military took to coaching family members who appeared on talk shows, even writing their scripts, as was painfully obvious in some cases as nervous spouses turned to read prepared statements. Just before the war broke out, a touring group of military spouses appeared at an antiwar rally in Austin, Texas, that I attended and told how their civil rights were being violated by the military, which was attempting to repressively control antiwar speech. The same thing happened to soldiers in the Gulf who were not allowed to articulate antiwar sentiments or to criticize the Bush administration or military (see 2.2). Thus members of the military and their families lost their freedom of speech during the Gulf war and those members of the military who resisted the war–the true heroes of this sordid episode— were subject to harsh treatment and trials (see 10.5).

9. The term "technowar" is taken from William Gibson's (1986) book *The Perfect War: Technowar in Vietnam,* which described the organization of military strategy according to a highly rationalized mode of warfare. The Gulf war constituted a higher stage of technowar in which computerized plans deployed high-tech weapons for daily U.S. military action. My analysis is deeply influenced by Gibson's superb study, the best single book to be written on the mode of warfare employed in Vietnam, but I shall suggest later that the Gulf war, and not Vietnam, was the "perfect war" to test and demonstrate the efficacy of high-tech electronic warfare (9.5). Indeed, Vietnam turned out in retrospect to have been a flawed laboratory to test the Pentagon's new weapon systems. Yet, as with Gibson's analysis of the Vietnam war, the Gulf war, too, was motivated by the administration's desire to try out new weapons systems and to utilize U.S. military power to maintain U.S. economic and political hegemony.

10. Schwarzkopf ripped off General Bernard Montgomery's call to battle in World War II in these remarks; see Cohen and Gatti 1991, pp. 260ff. During the Vietnam war, Schwarzkopf had been responsible for the deaths of many of his troops because of his zealous and often incompetent pursuit of enemy death counts; see Anderson and van Atta 1991, pp. 28ff., and Cohen and Gatti 1991, pp. 106ff. During the Grenada invasion, Schwarzkopf was part of a team that bungled incredibly a simple operation against a powerless and defenseless "enemy"; see Chapter 5, Note 1.

11. Richard Nixon complained vociferously about "instant analysis" after his speeches in which the network correspondents often made critical comments.

By the time Bush had become president, the norm was merely to summarize what the leader had said in a totally uncritical and usually positive and supportive tone. Hence, TV commentary moved from critical discourse to becoming public relations instruments of the White House.

12. Interestingly, shortly before on ABC, Peter Jennings reported that: "an Israeli diplomatic source . . . told ABC News just a short while ago that all the Iraqi Scud missile sites that are within range of Israel have been destroyed or put out of action in some form. That all known—this is quoting the Israelis now—that all known Iraqi atomic and chemical weapon plants have been destroyed." Obviously, certain Israeli "sources" had an agenda in leaking this disinformation to the U.S. media and I analyze this issue in the next chapter.

13. Blackwell later wrote (1991, pp. 133–134) that Blitzer "was fairly new to his beat" and that "some of his sources betrayed him." According to Blackwell, Blitzer had found a "highly placed source" who told him that the Iraqi Air Force and Republican Guards had been "decimated" and that all Scud launcher sites had been destroyed during the first night's bombing, with all of the sites capable of launching Scuds at Israel obliterated. Blackwell claimed that he pleaded with Blitzer not to use the term "decimated," yet, as we see from their CNN exchange, Blackwell did not sharply contradict Blitzer, so his later disclaimer at Blitzer's expense is disingenuous and dishonest.

14. On a February 2 CNN special on the media and the war, Blitzer claimed mendaciously that the first night of the war he had qualified his reports by claiming that "these are initial, sketchy reports" and that he had claimed that "large chunks" of the Republican Guards were being decimated. Although he may have said this sometime in the evening, I have on tape three times when he said, without this qualification, that Pentagon officials were claiming that the Scud missile sites were knocked out, that the Republican Guard was decimated, and that the Iraqi Air Force was destroyed, all totally specious claims.

15. CBS generally got the worst reviews and ratings for the first day's coverage, however. The *Washington Post* TV critic Tom Shales complained that CBS was "sketchier" than other networks and "just didn't have enough reportage" (Jan. 17, p. C6). This is simply false, for, in fact, no network had much solid information the first night of the war. In retrospect, CBS presented the most accurate and reliable reportage, as well as breaking one of the few scoops in the night in reporting the bombing of the Khafji oil refinery. The January 28 *Time* magazine story on TV coverage of the war generally praised the networks' performance, with the exception of CBS: "Only CBS, led by the unnerving and overly cautious Rather (with his constant admonitions: 'Let me underline for you what we don't know . . . '), seemed creaky and slow on its feet" (p. 20). Yet Rather should be praised rather than condemned for his caution, and CNN should be criticized for its Pentagon disinformation. Interestingly, the *Time* analysis does not mention the most significant event of the first night: the extent to which several networks, especially Blitzer and CNN, transmitted the Pentagon propaganda concerning its opening night knockout of the Iraqi forces; nor does Smith (1991) mention the Blitzer episode in his history of CNN at war.

16. Bernard Shaw of CNN also criticized his enthusiastic and inexperienced colleague John Holliman, who raved about the "beautiful red and orange" bombs

exploding and "beautiful tracer fire" aimed at the U.S. planes. Shaw admonished him, "You keep using that word 'beautiful'—it's not beautiful to me."

17. On how Hollywood films transcode militarist ideology, see Kellner and Ryan (1988) and on how *Top Gun* and a series of Middle East action/adventure films helped prepare the audience for the Persian Gulf war and the apotheosis of military culture, see Kellner (forthcoming).

18. Later in the day, Pentagon sources would intimate that 50 to 80 percent of the Iraqi Air Force was destroyed, and a French source would claim that 50 percent was taken out. Later, it would be revealed that only a small percentage of the Iraqi Air Force was destroyed during the opening night bombing, high-lighting the lies and disinformation that the U.S.-led coalition spoon-fed reporters.

19. Throughout the war, any Iraqi or other peace initiatives were "the worst thing possible" and the Bush administration "nightmare scenario" was the possibility of an Iraqi unilateral withdrawal from Kuwait. The mainstream media never commented on peace initiatives as "the worst thing possible" and ending a war as a "nightmare scenario." Such language, however, revealed the Bush administration's lust for all-out war and a decisive military victory that would destroy and humiliate Iraq.

CHAPTER FOUR

◆

Out of Control

THE PENTAGON AND the Bush administration were concerned with creating an image of themselves as being totally in control of events, waging a well-planned, coordinated, and effective war. Around 7:00 P.M. EST on January 17, however, with the first reports of Scud missile attacks on Israel, a picture suddenly emerged of a dangerous and chaotic war with unpredictable results that might elude administration and Pentagon control. For the rest of the evening, the relentless allied bombing attack was ignored as the TV focus became the Iraqi missile attack on Israel and whether this would lead Israel to retaliate and broaden the scope of the war. It was feared that Israeli retaliation might engulf the entire Middle East in an Arab-Israeli war, which would shatter the fragile U.S.-dominated coalition and perhaps envelop the Middle East in flames. Consequently, Bush's Gulf war could have exploded into Armageddon at any minute.

The television presentation of these compelling events was extremely dramatic, highlighting again that this was a live "You are There" TV war which was binding together the world as fascinated and often frightened spectators of military spectacle. It was claimed during the evening that Bush, Baker, and other members of the war team first learned of the Iraqi attack on Israel via television and it seemed that television was providing direct access to the suspenseful events unfolding. But more significant events were going on behind the scenes concerning whether Israel would retaliate against the Iraqi Scud missile attacks. As we shall see in this chapter, the media became an actor in the drama of whether Israel would or would not enter the Gulf war, expanding it to a Middle East and perhaps Israeli/Arab war. Bombing Israel was Saddam Hussein's greatest gamble and how it played out would determine the fate of the war.

4.1 Israel

During the first twenty-four hours of the war, the networks presented occasional interviews with Israelis and Middle East "experts" concerning Israel's potential role in a Gulf war. Initial reports indicated that there was tremendous enthusiasm for the war in Israel, which for months had been goading the United States in public and private to commence hostilities against their enemy Iraq. Israel immediately called a state of emergency in the country when the war erupted and urged its citizens to keep their gas masks and chemical weapons antidote kits with them at all times. This kit was given out free to Israeli citizens. After a fierce public debate and Israeli Supreme Court order, the gas masks were given out to Palestinians as well, but they were kept under a tight curfew that was maintained for weeks.

Initial media focus on Israel related to the Israeli response to the reports that the United States had destroyed Scud missile sites. Around 5:35 A.M. on January 17, for instance, CBS broadcast an interview in Israel with author Dore Gold, who stated that Israel was manifesting "guarded relief" because "it is very likely" that the H2 and H3 air bases in Iraq had been destroyed by allied air forces the previous night. Yet, there was concern that Iraq also had a lot of mobile air missile launchers that might be located in protected hangers, concrete bunkers, or other sites hidden from view. Thus Israel was still on a high state of civil defense alert. Gold explained that near the end of the Iran-Iraq war, the Iraqis took a Soviet-made Scud missile and extended its range from 280 kilometers to over 650 kilometers, which made it possible to hit Tel Aviv from Iraq. There was a debate in Israel, he noted, over whether these missiles could carry chemical weapons, but Israel was prepared for the worst. Much more would be heard about the Scud missiles that night and the following days.

Throughout the afternoon of January 17, it was reported that the Iraqi ambassador to Belgium threatened that Iraq was still planning to attack Israel. In a talk with ABC's Ted Koppel, the Iraqi ambassador to France reiterated that there would be an Iraqi attack against Israel, emphasizing that Iraq indeed had the capacity to strike Israel. ABC pundit Judith Kipper said that this "threat to strike Israel doesn't sound credible" and that "it's very, very doubtful." Around 4:00 P.M. Kipper repeated this position, stating that the threat of an attack on Israel was posturing, that the Iraqis are just "trying to scare us." Kipper couldn't have been more wrong, as it turned out.

Indeed, most of the military experts and media commentators bought the line that the United States had destroyed Iraq's Scud missile capacity during the first night's air strikes. On the CBS morning show, Senator

Sam Nunn (D-Ga.), reputedly the Senate's premier defense expert, said that the U.S. war effort had accomplished "main strategic goals" in the initial phases, including the protection of Israel through the knocking out of Iraqi Scud missiles. ABC's Jerusalem correspondent, Dean Reynolds, reported that the destruction of the Scud missile launchers removed the main threat to Israel, according to Israeli military authorities. However, they believed that there might be some hidden weapons, such as missile launchers out in the desert. Tonight would be the litmus test, Reynolds stated; if Israel could get through the evening without going on emergency status, there would be a feeling that Israel would escape "scot free."

Concluding this upbeat report, Reynolds noted that for months there had been discussion of the threat to Israel from the "Iraqi military colossus" and Israelis "are surprised concerning the lame Iraqi response," which they explain as a result of "total incompetence." Some Israelis, Reynolds reported, said that they never considered "this fellow Hussein" a threat to their country. Reynolds also noted that the Israelis were "enjoying the fact that Americans are doing the fighting" and that the Israelis were watching; they were happy to be "on the sidelines of a Middle Eastern war." This pleasure would, however, soon disappear and the Israelis would shortly be subjected to an extremely traumatic set of attacks on their country.

Later in the afternoon, Bob Zelnick, ABC's Pentagon correspondent, pointed out that bomb damage assessment analysis showed that 60 to 80 percent of the Iraqi air force was destroyed. This claim turned out to be totally false, as was Zelnick's claim that stationary Scud missile launchers were largely destroyed. He admitted the possibility that mobile Scud missile sites "could get one or two missiles off at Israel," yet, following his Pentagon masters, he downplayed the threat, claiming that the Scud was not a militarily effective weapon. Obviously, the Pentagon and Bush administration were concerned to put out propaganda about the lack of a serious threat to Israel from Iraq, and its compliant media servants helped by conveying the messages fed to them.

The January 17 "CBS Evening News" reported that Iraq had plans to attack Israel, but reporter Bob Simon stated that it was hard to imagine how Iraqi offensive capability could do anything but decrease. He was skeptical that Iraq could indeed seriously threaten Israel, or anyone else for that matter. But at 7:04 P.M., Dean Reynolds of ABC News broke in to report that air-raid sirens were going off in Tel Aviv. Shortly thereafter, Tom Fenton on CBS explained that sirens had begun blaring, followed by a huge blast. Israelis were told to go into their chemical weapons protection rooms, which were sealed rooms above ground level. The satellite connection then broke off with Fenton putting on his gas mask, intensifying the drama and suspense. Dan Rather explained that "this is live. We don't know what is happening," and then concluded that an Iraqi missile attack on Israel might be under way.

ABC's Peter Jennings announced that: "The Associated Press is now reporting that three missiles hit in Tel Aviv." Soon after, a video appeared of Reynolds and his crew in Jerusalem, looking rather rattled and without gas masks on. Reynolds and the others were told to put on their gas masks, and all the crew frantically began to do so. As the Israeli crew members rapidly put on their masks, Reynolds was flustered and had trouble getting his on; the camera rather indelicately focused on him as his crew helped him put the mask on. Suddenly, there were explosions in Tel Aviv and Jennings commented: "These are the worst fears realized, of course, of Israelis and Americans. Saddam Hussein had said from the outset that he was going to try to engage the Israelis if the war came and of course now that the war is in its 24th hour, perhaps people were beginning to relax. They expected him to counterattack or attack against the Israelis early on. Very much a worst case scenario for Israel and for the Middle East in general."

Reynolds noted in response: "I would point out that this would . . . that if this is really what we think it is that it will prompt virtually a certain Israeli retaliation and the potential now for a wider conflict, I dare say is there." The TV drama was electrifying; on the ABC live report, the sounds of explosions in the background could be heard and Reynolds reported that Israeli radio confirmed that a missile attack was on. A crackling sound then began erupting every few seconds, giving the impression that bombs and missiles were exploding everywhere. But it was concluded that the sounds were the sharp breathing of Reynolds in his gas mask with an open mike! The TV coverage thus added to the drama and perhaps even created panic.

The air-raid sirens went off again, and a technician noted that this was not an all-clear signal and that Israeli radio was giving instructions on how to put on gas masks and what to do in case of a chemical weapons attack. Peter Jennings commented: "I cannot tell you how in the middle of the night this comes as an enormous shock to people." Jennings then switched to a live phone call from Tel Aviv, where a hysterical voice, barely understandable, told of hearing missiles explode nearby. Soon after, CBS correspondent Tom Fenton from Tel Aviv came on, speaking through a gas mask, and reported that city officials admitted that there had been three hits on Tel Aviv by Iraqi missiles and that there was still no knowledge of whether there had been any casualties or whether the warheads were chemical or conventional. To add to the drama and the sense that the Gulf war was rapidly careening out of control, it was announced that in Dhahran, Saudi Arabia, there were reports of air-raid sirens. ABC cut to Saudi Arabia live at 3:42 A.M., local time, where their correspondent, Forrest Sawyer, reported that the hotel alarm had sounded, but the national air-raid alert had not gone off yet, so that it was uncertain whether or not Saudi Arabia was under attack (the previous night there were two false alarms).

Air-raid sirens wailed again in Tel Aviv, which suggested that another missile attack might be underway. CBS's Tom Fenton in Tel Aviv related that there was just a radio message from an Israeli army representative who said that they did not have information yet regarding the kind of attack it was, so people should stay in their shelters. Fenton thought that Israel was much less likely to respond "after the astounding performance last night and early this morning by the U.S. Air Force." He then announced that there were casualties in the south of Tel Aviv, in Holon, a working-class suburb that was hit by a missile, and that there were reports that three more missiles struck the north of Israel. Altogether, there had been six missile attacks, he summarized: three in Tel Aviv, two in Haifa, and one in Spak. They still did not know the extent of the damage or whether the missiles held chemical weapons. "But" Dan Rather concluded, "Saddam Hussein has been able to make good on one of his threats: He has hit Israel with some Scud missiles."

A bit later, Rather spoke to CBS correspondents in Jerusalem and Tel Aviv, with Fenton reporting that there were a number of Israeli jets seen in the air after the attack. Fenton had heard reports that there were ten casualties in one hospital, but it was still not clear whether there had been a chemical attack. Jim Jensen from Jerusalem broke in to report via telephone that the Israelis were in the process of attacking Iraq; he had heard on Israeli radio that retaliation was under way. On that dramatic note, CBS then moved to Saudi Arabia where Bob Simon added that they had just gotten word from Saudi officials that missiles had been fired at Dhahran, but that the United States had Patriot missiles to protect them against the Scuds. The Israelis, however, Simon explained, did not trust Patriot missiles and did not trust the U.S. to defend them. Dan Rather recalled that the first night there had been reports from Bahrain that Scuds had been fired, but that they missed their targets (the BBC, Agence France Presse, and other news sources had also announced that several Scud missiles had been launched the previous night). This was interesting because U.S. Secretary of Defense Dick Cheney had claimed that morning that the Iraqis had not fired any Scud missiles. As we shall see, U.S., Israeli, and Saudi authorities would continually lie about the number, location, and extent of damage of the Scud missile attacks, in part so as not to give the Iraqis important information, but also to keep the illusion of control and because the Bush administration was concerned to keep Israel out of the war. CBS's State Department correspondent Bill

Plante reported that Israel had turned down U.S. requests that it not retaliate if hit by Scuds; Secretary of State James Baker, however, had been assured that the Arab allies in the coalition would not bolt if Israel retaliated. Plante noted that evidence was building that the Israelis were retaliating, though it was believed that they were not flying over Jordanian air space (which would reduce the risk of Jordan becoming involved in the war). Thus, for some time CBS reproduced the story of Israel's retaliation, and it and other networks continued until later in the evening to make these claims.

Meanwhile, CBS cut live to Saudi Arabia about 8:30 P.M. and Bob Simon reported that air-raid sirens had stopped, but then there had been an explosion and Saudi officials announced that they were in imminent danger. The video images showed people fleeing from an explosion toward bomb shelters, and Simon commented that they were now being told to put gas masks on. Shortly thereafter, Forrest Sawyer reported that he heard something like an explosion in the distance and that a very nervous situation existed in and around Dhahran. ABC's satellite picture went down at this point, accelerating the tension, though anchor Peter Jennings explained that losing the satellite feed "happens from time to time." It appeared that events were careening more out of control by the minute.

ABC's Dean Reynolds indicated from Jerusalem around 8:45 P.M. that there were reports of at least ten missiles hitting Tel Aviv and Haifa. There were some casualties, but it was not yet confirmed how many and whether the missiles had chemical warheads. The all-clear sirens went off at 3:32 A.M. local time and the Israelis were told that they could take their gas masks off. General Bernard Trainor broke in and said that "if these reports that we're getting from the Israelis, and indeed the United States, of something like 10 Scud missiles hitting Israel, my understanding of Israeli doctrine and my knowledge of the Israeli armed forces, I can't believe for a moment that the Israelis are not in the process of launching not only a strike against possible Scud sites, but a full-scale retaliatory mission against the Iraqis." CBS correspondent Tom Fenton stated that he was not surprised that the Israelis were retaliating since they were "a hard-line government" and have always responded immediately and decisively to attacks on their territory.

On CBS, Dan Rather announced that in Dhahran, Saudi Arabia, air-raid sirens were on again, and a video appeared showing bright lights exploding in the sky as Rather explained that they did not know if they were missiles exploding or flares. CBS Pentagon reporter David Martin claimed that the Pentagon insisted that there were not now, nor had there been, Scud missiles fired at Saudi Arabia and CBS's Bob Simon in Dhahran claimed that a report from Bahrain that a missile hit Dhahran "is absolutely untrue." Instead, they were told that the explosion was a Patriot missile that misfired and exploded. Simon explained that the Patriot is an antimissile defense system that destroys airplanes and short-range missiles. General Dugan added that the Patriot missile was designed to knock airplanes out of the sky and was modified to fire at incoming missiles, but it had not been tested in battle. Its drawback was that it had only a small arc and close range within which it could attack incoming missiles with computer guidance systems. Dugan believed that the Patriot system would not be adequate to defend Israel because of the wide circumference of the defense perimeter. Shortly thereafter, ABC's Bob Zelnick reported that the Pentagon now believed that an Iraqi Scud missile had been intercepted by a Patriot missile in eastern Saudi Arabia. Only one missile was fired, but the Pentagon was worried that perhaps it was fired by the Iraqis to get their range and bearings in order to follow with a volley of missiles. As Zelnick spoke, the video showed an explosion of lights in the sky and the audience was treated to what was reported as the first Patriot hit of a Scud missile.

In Tel Aviv CBS's Tom Fenton broke in and breathlessly announced that they had been told to put gas masks back on, as air-raid sirens blared in the background. Fenton said that they had just heard two more bangs, and Israeli radio reported that there were some casualties, but it was still not clear if it was a chemical or conventional attack. Some new video footage from Tel Aviv came on and CBS played the sounds of air-raid sirens going off on Tel Aviv streets, accompanied by a picture of a middle-class family coping with the attack. The mother was shown with her yawning daughter and a sleeping baby, with gas masks and other equipment next to them; the video then cut to the mother strapping on gas masks to her boy and girl who were then shown having gas masks and plastic wrapped over their faces; next the video moved to a baby in a baby carriage with a plastic protective cover over it. Dan Rather stated "that's the reality in Israel tonight," but it is possible that these were pretaped pictures prepared as a masterpiece of propaganda and ready to broadcast in case of a Scud attack. Rather noted that these pictures "put into perspective" Israel's response, which was that "we are going to strike back at Iraq," and he reported that Israeli jets were heading for retaliation to Iraq.

CBS played the footage of the mother and children with gas masks repeatedly, using it as a paradigm of Israeli suffering. Such footage created instant empathy, for it employed primal scenes of the mother protecting her children and evoked the images of Jews suffering gas attacks. I suspect it was propaganda because it was so perfectly packaged and framed, and because this was among the first satellite footage from Israel, evoking the possibility that the footage was planned and sent up to the satellite when the attack started to elicit world wide sympathy for Israel. It was becoming clear that the Persian Gulf war was a media propaganda war, and all interested parties were operating at full throttle to produce words and images to aid their own causes (see Chapter 5).

Yet the television coverage of the Gulf war created the illusion of seeing a real war in real time. In fact, one could only see and hear live what was shown or reported from the places in Saudi Arabia, Israel, and Iraq where the networks had functioning satellite feeds and here too the words and images were subject to government control. Moreover, the various governments censored words and images that did not please them and the networks themselves chose what images to play and what not to play. Hence, although some of the moments of live drama provided a compelling sense of realism, that one was really and directly perceiving the war itself, nonetheless, the Gulf war, as presented by the media, was a symbolic construct produced by the government, media, and military, which presented a highly selective and controlled image of the war. There were, of course, real political struggles and military events going on behind the TV screen, but these were usually invisible in the TV war.

Indeed, the words and images produced were often a cover for a battle of specific political interests, agendas, and policies. The media, for political players, are instruments to shape public opinion. I argued in the Preface that critical media theory must attempt to discern what positions and agendas lie behind the various official pronouncements or leaks. This requires decoding the political meaning of media words and images: Which policy and interests are being articulated? Who is advancing this position and why? Why are the media disseminating this position and what interests are at play here? Things are rarely what they seem to be in complex events like crises and wars and all players use the media to advance their own interests and agenda. Therefore, critical media analysis must decode the media pronouncements and attempt to discover what is behind the facade of media discourse and images.

The question of chemical weapons use against the Israelis was a highly emotional one that dominated much of the coverage of the Iraqi Scud attacks on Israel and in the following analysis I shall attempt to detect what lay behind the various U.S. and Israeli pronouncements and leaks on the Scud attacks. During the first attack, the networks reported that chemical weapons were used, though these reports ultimately turned out to be false. Dean Reynolds broke in at 9:01 P.M. to report that as many as twenty people had been taken to the hospital suffering from the effects of nerve gas, although Israeli radio reports said that only seven people had been hospitalized. At 9:31 P.M., ABC's Pentagon correspondent Bob Zelnick said that "the Israelis have informed the U.S. that at least some of the missiles that landed in Israel were of the nerve gas variety" and, in response to a query by Peter Jennings, he asserted that his Pentagon sources were "sure of it." Yet this claim could not be confirmed because the Israeli government had not officially authenticated how many attacks there had been, whether the warheads were conventional or chemical, what specific damage had been wrought, and whether they were or were not retaliating. Thus, speculation ran rampant, and figuring out who to believe was difficult.

On CBS, Tom Fenton reported around 9:30 P.M. that one area on a highway north of Tel Aviv had been roped off because there was danger of nerve gas from a missile attack. There were accounts of buildings burning in a small town outside of Tel Aviv. But Fenton now admitted that there was no confirmation whatsoever that Israel was retaliating for the attack, and Rather cautioned that Israeli retaliation "is not absolutely confirmed yet." ABC's Peter Jennings discussed with correspondent Chris Wallace in Jerusalem whether Israel would use nuclear weapons to retaliate against Iraq! Wallace replied that Saddam Hussein should be very frightened by the possible response if he used chemical weapons against Israel. CBS's Rather reported a bit later that James Baker had discussed the Iraqi missile attack on Israel with the ambassadors of Israel, Saudi Arabia, Egypt, and Syria, and the U.S. State Department claimed that the Bush administration was "working on the problem," and trying to keep Israel from retaliating.

In Dean Reynolds' next report from Israel, he announced that "the Israeli army chief spokesman has come on the air and denied reports that chemical weapons were used against Israel." Concerning the conflicting reports as to whether chemical weapons had or had not been used in the attack, and whether Israel was or was not retaliating, ABC's Peter Jennings wondered at one point if there was a disinformation campaign on in Israel, speculating that the Israeli government might not want their public to know what had happened. Dean Reynolds said that his report was from a "reliable source" who was "100 percent certain" that a hospital was treating more than twenty victims of a nerve gas attack. He also commented that military reporters on TV tended to report what the government wanted the public to hear; soon after, Israel instituted military censorship of TV reports and such critical remarks were no longer allowed.

At 9:49 P.M., Reynolds returned on camera, saying that it was now believed that no nerve gas had been involved in the Scud attacks and he apologized for conveying the misinformation earlier; probably someone had fed him the misinformation as part of an internal Israeli struggle over retaliation. Obviously, Israel was getting attacked by Iraqi Scud missiles, and there was a furious debate going on concerning whether the country should immediately retaliate. It was Israeli military orthodoxy that when Israel was attacked, it should respond immediately and violently. Many in Israel shared this perspective, so it was possible that those individuals created reports that chemical weapons were used in order to accelerate and legitimate an Israeli response. Those who, for political reasons, were against immediately retaliating against Iraq had an interest in reporting that casualties were minimal. Consequently, it was possible that different Israeli officials with different agendas and goals were giving the U.S. government and media correspondents information that furthered their own agendas.

All the networks cut live at 10:45 P.M. to a press conference with the Israeli ambassador to the United States, Zalman Shoval, who began by reporting that there was an unprovoked attack on Israel by Iraqi Scud missiles aimed at "purely civilian targets." Shoval detailed some of the consultations between the United States and Israel, and he concluded by stating that the government of Israel, fully supported by the opposition, reserved the right to respond in any way that it deemed fit, without indicating what the decision of the Israeli government would be. He noted that Israel chose not to undertake a preemptive strike at Iraq, on Washington's request, and commented that Israel had now paid a price for its forbearance. In his commentary, Dan Rather underscored that the fact that the Ambassador specifically did not mention any retaliation indicated that, for the moment at least, Israel was not striking back at Iraq. David Martin at the Pentagon then reported that the allied forces in Saudi Arabia had done "some retaliating of their own" against these Scud missile launchers. This news was repeated through the night and became a major motif of General Schwarzkopf's briefing the next day, to reassure Israeli hardliners that the U.S. was carrying out the agenda of destroying Saddam Hussein's military and protecting Israel.

About 12:30 A.M. on January 18, CBS ran some footage of Foreign Minister David Levy of Israel, who noted that Israel was in contact with the United States but that it was Israel's right and responsibility to retaliate for this attack. Shortly thereafter, CBS reported that Prime Minister Yitzhak Shamir would have a cabinet meeting to debate the Israeli response. Israel needed to decide if it was satisfied with assurances from President Bush or should retaliate on its own. Throughout the day— and for the days to follow—there was feverish speculation on the possible Israeli retaliation. If Israel did attack Iraq, would its planes fly over Jordan, risking war with that country? What would Israel hit if it chose to retaliate? How would Arab members of the coalition respond to Israeli retaliation? Would this unravel the coalition or could it withstand such pressures? How would the Palestinians respond if Israel waged war against Iraq? What, if any, Arab countries would join a Jihad against Israel and the West? Every network brought on pundits who discussed every nuance of these questions.

Many of the leaks and opinions expressed, however, were in support of very specific policies and actions. As noted, those wanting retaliation may have leaked the nerve gas report to legitimate an Israeli military response, or even to create a panic that would drive Israel to retaliate. But such is the complexity of the situation that an Israeli theorist, Oded Balaban, suggested that some of those who were urging retaliation might have been precisely those who wanted the war to end (pers. com., Jan. 13, 1992). On this reading, Israeli retaliation would lead to an immediate demand in the UN for a cease-fire to prevent a Middle East conflagration, consuming the whole area. Thus some of those inciting Israeli retaliation might have been doing so precisely to bring the war to an end. Needless to say, this was also the goal of Saddam Hussein, who was firing missiles regularly at Israel in order to elicit an Israeli response which would either, or so he might imagine, lead to an Arab/Israeli conflict, which would split the coalition against him, or would accelerate calls for a cease-fire and negotiations. Consequently, precisely the Israeli hard-liners who previously would have responded to an Iraqi attack immediately with gusto and maximum force were resisting the call to retaliate on the grounds that the maximum destruction of their Iraqi nemesis would likely be furthered by a prolongation of the war that might be curtailed by Israeli interventions.

This episode raises the question of sources, disinformation, and propaganda. The network correspondents rely in times of crisis on official sources who feed them information. In a crisis situation, there is usually not time to check the validity of the reports and in the highly competitive TV news business the networks tend to go on air with whatever information their correspondents receive. Much of this information, however, may be disinformation in a crisis situation. The night before, CNN's Wolf Blitzer repeatedly reported that he had been told by "highly placed Pentagon officials" that the Iraqi Air Force was destroyed, their Scud missile sites knocked out, and the Republican Guards decimated, all disinformation that someone in the Pentagon had chosen to disseminate. I suggested that this disinformation might have been aimed at creating a euphoria to reassure a nervous public, Congress, and financial markets, or it might have been a desperate attempt to end the war quickly by raising the sense that it was already over.[1]

During the Scud attacks on Israel, various sources were also leaking disinformation and trying to manipulate the media. Some sources were leaking disinformation concerning the alleged Iraqi chemical weapons attack on Israel and the next morning the television networks were transmitting various reports that announced that Israel was retaliating against Iraq, just when the Israeli cabinet was meeting to decide their response. CBS News was citing through the early morning of February 18 one "unconfirmed report" that two groups of Israeli warplanes were flying toward Iraq, and another that eight Israeli jets were sighted in Lebanon on the way to Iraq. CBS also quoted an Agence France Presse report that Israel had decided on a "measured response" to the Scud attacks. All of these reports were disinformation, supporting specific Israeli policy choices which were leaked to the press to encourage or support the policy of retaliation.

Peter Jennings of ABC had raised some questions concerning the "information" being disseminated and alluded to the possibility of disinformation campaigns, but on the whole the mainstream media largely transmitted whatever their sources fed them without much skepticism or critical analysis. Consequently, it was hard to make out what was really going on behind the scenes concerning the debates over the proper Israeli response to the Scud attacks. Moreover, it would prove extremely difficult to ascertain what actually happened during the Scud missile assaults as the countries under attack frequently provided blatantly false accounts of what happened, as did the U.S. government. Ultimately, the seemingly "moderate" Israeli line prevailed (i.e., that Israel not retaliate) and official information was generally tailored to fit this line, playing down the extent of Scud missile damage (though this "moderate" policy might have ultimately expressed hardline interests which sought the maximum destruction of Iraq and its military).

Therefore, one had to be extremely careful in appraising information from "official" sources. Often certain network correspondents are regularly used as disinformation conduits; during the Grenada invasion and Libyan bombing the Pentagon and Reagan Administration used ABC's John McWethy as a reliable source of disinformation.[2] During the Persian Gulf war, CNN's Wolf Blitzer was a regular source of Pentagon disinformation, with Blitzer eagerly reproducing on the spot whatever he was told, although often his information turned out to be false. The TV networks' military "experts" for the most part put a pro-Pentagon spin on their "analyses," explaining and defending the Pentagon line of the moment. Dan Rather started off critical of official sources, but ended up becoming one of the most blatant defenders of the military, for reasons that will be explained later (Chapter 8). Thus, two of the most deplorable aspects of the media coverage of the Persian Gulf war were the uncritical use of reports from official sources and the narrow range of sources and "experts" and commentators employed in framing and analyzing the complex events of the war.

4.2 A Clean War?

The TV public, quickly addicted to the drama of the war, became entralled with images, spectacle, and fascination with a new type of high-tech video. Images of the bombing of Baghdad taken by night cameras produced an eerie, surreal vision of the war as an aesthetic phenomenon. Images of buildings, bridges, and military targets (but never civilians) being destroyed by laser-guided bombs were photographed by cameras on the planes and on the bombs themselves, which conveyed the images to satellites where they were downloaded and recorded on videocassettes and then shown to a captivated audience. These images literally took the TV viewers into a new high-tech cyberspace, a realm of experience with which many viewers were already familiar through video and computer games, the special effects of Hollywood movies, and cyberpunk fiction. Fascination with video and computer images provided an aura of magic and power for the military that produced such spectacles and enhanced their credibility with a public eager to believe whatever they would claim. Not surprisingly, the media themselves were mesmerized by these images, which they played and replayed repeatedly; Dan Rather spoke with awe when he presented "more remarkable video just released by the Defense Department," and CNN seemed to open each news segment with the videos of the astonishing high-tech bombing. The images of "clean" bombing seemed to give credence to military claims that they were avoiding civilian casualties and endowed these high-tech wizards with power as well as credibility, providing an aura of veracity to whatever claims they would make, which were seemingly grounded in technological omnipotence and evidence too compelling to doubt.

Around 11:00 P.M. on January 17, ABC, using a British ITN report by Brent Sadler and footage shot by ABC cameraman Fabrice Moussus,[3] provided the first footage of the bombing of Baghdad. The film was shot with a special night lens and showed explosions of light over the sky of Baghdad with antiaircraft fire, tracer bullets, and bombs exploding in the sky, which produced a spectacular sound and light show. The pictures were genuinely dramatic and engaging, with Iraqi antiaircraft installations on roofs and gunners firing wildly in the air; cars sped through the night and people ran for shelter on the ground; a bomb hit a communications tower in a nuclearlike explosion; and outgoing antiaircraft fire and explosions lit up the sky.

Reinforcing the Pentagon line that the U.S. military was engaging in a precise and clean technowar, Peter Jennings related, while the footage was on, that Brent Sadler and Gary Shepard of ABC said that there wasn't much damage visible in Baghdad, though Sadler's report included Iraq's claim that there were "barbaric raids on Iraqi towns and villages" that had left 23 dead and 66 injured. Immediately after the broadcast of the video, John McWethy came on the air and described the video as "truly an awesome display of ground fire in Baghdad" at U.S. and allied planes. He explained that "one thing that is a little misleading" was that the camera had a nightscope lens so that everything going up, whether lead, tracers, or missiles, all looked the same. Jennings commented that this was how it appeared to pilots with night-vision goggles who were forced to fly into "a wall of fire."

Jennings was then suddenly reminded of a remark by General William Westmoreland, head of U.S. forces in Vietnam, who told him in 1965 that the camera gets a very narrow view of things. Jennings further noted that the video in question was a narrow view of the war from a camera near the western edge of Baghdad during the first night's air attack. This was a point well-taken and, in fact, about the only images that the Pentagon and networks circulated were high-tech video of aestheticized war, of technowar as a video game spectacle, that produced a narrow range of images within the vast array of weapons and sites of death and destruction.

One might add that these video images covered over that the bombs were being dropped on *Baghdad,* one of the centers of civilization, a city full of archaeological treasures that were in danger of being destroyed. It was also one of the largest cities in the Middle East with a population of over four million inhabitants. The fact that the bombs were also falling on Iraqi civilians and destroying their homes and social infrastructure was also hidden by the Nintendo-like video images of the pyrotechnics of modern warfare. The media, however, focused on the aesthetics of the images, or the military factors involved, without discussing the human dimension of the bombing.

Shortly thereafter, CBS played the same footage and Dan Rather commented that the "two most dramatic images of the night" were the Israeli mother and her daughter putting on gas masks and the pictures of the bombing of Baghdad, which Rather noted, "shows the kind of courage it takes to fly into this kind of defense." Rather also gushed to Ed Bradley, that the exciting images of Patriots hitting Scuds and the bombing of Baghdad "take my breath away." This disclosure revealed the fascination with images that permeate the network television mindset and how they bought into the military propaganda, reproducing the discourse of a clean and precise technowar.

The image of technowar was more sharply defined during a January 18 briefing that General Schwarzkopf and General Horner held in Saudi Arabia, which provided the first videotapes of the high-tech precision bombing. Schwarzkopf opened with a brief statement on the progress of the war and Horner made some banal opening remarks, but the hit of the day was the videotapes of the actual bombing footage. Articulating the principles of technowar, General Horner described their "very complex and very large campaign plan" and the integration of all the technological and national forces. Waxing metaphorical when asked to describe the coordination of the campaign in more detail, Horner enthused:

> It is an enormous effort. Of course, now we have a lot of computers, and you can bring together the tens of thousands of minor details, radio frequencies, altitudes, tanker rendezvouses, bomb configurations, who supports who, who's flying escort. . . . There are thousands and thousands of details and we work them together as one group, put them together in what we call a common air-tasking order, and it provides a sheet of music that everybody sings the same song off.

The song, of course, is that of death and destruction, and technowar in its essence is the use of advanced technology to destroy its targets. Indeed, Horner admitted in his opening remarks: "It has been in some respects a technology war, although it is fought by men and women." The highlight of the briefing, however, was technology as Horner turned on his videos to demonstrate precision bombing at work. The world was treated to videos of Air Force F-111 fighter bombers using laser-guided bombs to destroy an Iraqi airfield runway and a suspected storage bunker for Scud missiles. Horner then presented a video of a F-117 Stealth fighter bomber dropping its load down the air shaft of Iraqi air defense headquarters. Finally, Horner showed a Stealth bomber dumping another smart bomb into the Iraqi air force headquarters, destroying the building (see Figure 4.1).

These videos were replayed for days, producing the image of a precise bombing and coding the destruction as positive. Norm Schwarzkopf's video cassette shows demonstrated that U.S. bombs always hit their targets, do not cause collateral damage, and only take out nasty military targets. This was intended to change the public perception of war itself, that the new technowar was clean, precise, and surgical, that the very nature of war had changed. War was thus something that one could enjoy, admire, and cheer about. War was fun, aesthetic, and fascinating. The videos created a climate of joy in destruction in its audiences, as when reporters clapped and laughed when Horner said: "And this is my counterpart's headquarters in Baghdad," as a video showed a bomb blowing up the Iraqi air force headquarters. Just as video and computer games—or special-effects movies like *Star Wars*—produce a positive

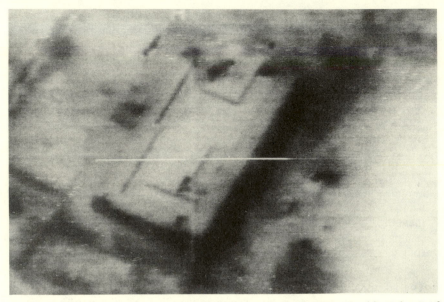

Figure 4.1 The hyperspace of technowar. A U.S. Air Force F-117 "Stealth Fighter" of the 37th Tactical Fighter Wing performs a precision attack on an Iraqi air defense sector headquarters during early stages of Operation Desert Storm, January 17, 1991. The dark spot at the upper right quadrant of the sighting cross is the entry point of a bomb dropped moments earlier by a preceding aircraft. (Official Department of Defense photo. Reprinted by permission.)

libidinal pleasure in destruction, so too did the videos of high-tech bombing produce pleasure in the destruction of Iraq—at least among the audience that bought into the spectacle of high-tech destruction.[4]

The illusion was projected that only machines and not people were involved in the new high-tech warfare, which was bloodless and antiseptic. The targets of the released footage were always ugly buildings, usually serving military functions. The austere buildings were seemingly always deserted, devoid of humans, so the bombing was coded as a positive surgical operation that was removing methodically the instruments of Iraqi war—medical discourse and imagery of clean surgery removing evil disease.[5] This image proved to be quite untrue (see Chapters 6 and 7), yet the constant replaying of these tapes, and their power to produce images of a clean and precise technowar, created the impression that the military desired. Only after the war were figures released showing that most of the bombs dropped were not "smart" computer- and laser-guided bombs. Instead, most of the bombs missed their targets altogether and even the so-called smart bombs often produced a lot of dumb "collateral" destruction (see the documentation at the end of this section). In fact, it was claimed that the best explanation for the accuracy of some of the initial bombing raids, in contrast to the imprecision of the latter ones, is that the ability of the first bombs "to hit their targets would have been enhanced by homing devices at or near their targets, planted by U.S. agents in Iraq before the war started."[6]

Early on, one military analyst attempted to puncture the myth of a clean and precise technowar. Pierre Sprey, a longtime critic of high-tech military systems, claimed: "They're retargeting a lot of the places where they already claimed great success. The bombing just isn't that accurate. In the future, the ineffectiveness is going to become painfully obvious" (*New York Times,* Jan. 21, 1991, p. A6). Indeed, the Pentagon's admitted need to retarget some of their bombing raids indicated that the bombs were not all that precise, and a great debate broke out in defense circles concerning bomb damage assessment and the effectiveness of the U.S.-led coalition bombing campaign. In the days to come, many pictures of the "collateral damage" suffered by Iraqi civilians became evident (see Chapters 6 and 7). Thus, the material reality of the technowar was that the Iraqi civilian and economic infrastructures were being destroyed, along with military targets, and, eventually, it was clear that many innocent victims were maimed and killed as well.

The Pentagon, however, tried to create an image of control, efficacy, and humaneness, and the videos seemed to prove that. Schwarzkopf's opening statement during the briefing with General Horner on January 18 indicated that the U.S.-led coalition was flying "about 2,000 air sorties of all types each day" and "[m]ore than 80 percent of all of those sorties have successfully engaged their targets." Whereas General Powell previously defined the 80 percent success rate in terms of ordinance delivered, independent of whether or not it destroyed its target, Schwarzkopf created the false impression that they actually destroyed their targets ("successfully engaged" them). Horner amplified this impression when he answered a reporter's question concerning whether the planes were hitting 50 percent or 80 percent of their targets: "The combined percentages you see are a function of the number of targets targeted versus the number hit"—as if the 80 percent referred to the hits. Actually, the later figures revealed that only 30 percent of the targets were hit (see below), and the Pentagon later admitted that it was forced to constantly return to retarget earlier "assets" that they had bombed.

In fact, even in terms of Powell's definition of success rate in terms of delivery, Schwarzkopf's figure of "80 percent" was dubious. Minutes before he began his briefing, Scott Pelley of CBS News reported that a group of planes had just returned to base with bombs intact under their wings because of bad weather. Furthermore, Dunnigan and Bay attest: "Uncharacteristic bad weather in the Gulf caused forty percent of the bombing missions to be canceled during the first two weeks of the war" (1991, p. 161). Thus bad weather was forcing the cancellation of flights, or preventing the crews from dropping their bombs, so that Schwarzkopf's 80 percent "success rate" was pure bluster.

The Schwarzkopf and Horner briefing was a bit odd and might have been the first time that such videotapes were ever played at military briefings. General Schwarzkopf appeared tired and subdued and not as arrogant and bullying as usual. Warrior Schwarzkopf was basically a ground soldier who was perhaps not comfortable or at home with the high-tech spectacle of video display. For Schwarzkopf, war was serious business and there was something frivolous about playing videos at a military briefing. Horner, by contrast, cool and relaxed, was evidently enjoying playing the videotapes and answering questions, the perfect technomanager for assuring the public that a new type of clean and precise war was being waged.

The media could not resist falling prey to the images and ideology of technowar that became the dominant mode of presentation and discourse for the rest of the campaign.[7] The high-tech weapons were endlessly praised throughout the war by network commentators. CBS's Charles Osgood acclaimed the high-tech bombing of Iraq as a "marvel," and his colleague Jim Stewart extolled "two days of almost picture-perfect assaults" (both on Jan. 17, 1991). On January 19, NBC's Katherine Couric at the Pentagon described how the videos were taken and praised the high-tech planes, weapons, and strategies deployed. Her descriptions of the specifications and capabilities of the weapons provided excellent PR for the high-tech weapons that her employer GE/RCA (which owned NBC) produced. NBC and the other networks constantly played videos of the weapons systems on display provided by their manufacturers, thus furnishing attractive images and free advertisements for the U.S. weapons—many of which NBC had a financial stake in.

CBS's Harry Smith watched the videotapes with the CBS military adviser, General Dugan, and described the precision bombing as "stunning." And the CNN military analysts interminably praised the wonders of high-tech warfare. Reinforcing this image, on the January 19 "ABC World News Tonight," Jim Hickey in Dhahran reported that U.S. pilots claimed that they were "very exacting, very precise" in their bombing and that if they did not see their targets they would return home. On the same program, Bob Zelnick reported that in World War II, weapons missed by half a mile, but in this war Cruise missiles and laser-guided bombs scored direct hits. NBC's Tom Brokaw explained, "So far the U.S. has fought this war at arm's length with long-range missiles, high-tech weapons. This is to keep casualties down." *Newsweek*'s February 18 cover read, "The New Science of War," with a subheading, "High-Tech Hardware: How Many Lives Can It Save?" This myth of technowar continued to dominate the media discourse for days and helped fix the public's image of a new era of high-tech warfare.

After the war, it was revealed that U.S. bombing was highly imprecise and overwhelmingly low-tech. In a March 15 press conference after the war, Air Force Chief of Staff General Merrill McPeak (1991) admitted that only 6,520 out of 88,500 tons of bombs dropped by U.S. planes on Iraq and occupied Kuwait were precision bombs, merely seven percent of the total. He claimed 90 percent of these "smart bombs" hit their targets. Former Assistant Secretary of the Navy, John Lehman, however, doubted whether the smart bombs had such a high accuracy rate, citing his own experience of many misfires when the weapons were being tested (Lehman made the point on CNN on Jan. 26 and elaborated the point in an article by Fred Kaplan in the *Boston Globe,* Jan. 29, 1991). Lehman was told by Pentagon officials that only 60 percent of the so-called smart bombs hit their target—a figure repeated in a later story in the *Philadelphia Inquirer* (Feb. 11, 1991, p. 12A).

More startling, "a senior Pentagon official" told *Washington Post* reporter Barton Gellman that only 25 percent of the conventional bombs hit their targets and that cumulatively U.S. bombs missed their targets at least 70 percent of the time (*Washington Post,* March 16, 1991, p. A1). Shortly thereafter, General McPeak admitted in an interview with *USA Today* that the U.S. made targeting mistakes in their massive bombing campaign against Iraq, "indicating that U.S. pilots hit and destroyed civilian targets" (March 19, 1991).[8] Furthermore, the U.S.-led coalition dropped a large variety of "area-impact munitions" that were imprecise and extremely lethal (see Paul Rogers, "The Myth of the Clean War," *CovertAction Information Bulletin,* No. 37, pp. 26–30). Thus, the discourse concerning precise bombing and the clean war was pure propaganda designed to sell the war to the public and, as noted, the mainstream media were instrumental in promoting this ideology which covered over the brutal reality of the U.S.-led coalition air war.

4.3 Scuds and Patriots

The seeming success of the Patriot missile against the Iraqi Scud missiles was one of the most potent advertisements for the precision and magic of U.S. high-tech weapons. The images of Patriots apparently intercepting Scuds thrilled the TV audience and, as I shall document in this section, led the mainstream media to celebrate the Patriot as the ultimate example of U.S. military superiority. The Scud missile, by contrast, was presented as evidence of Iraqi military inferiority and immoral terrorist bombing of civilian targets.

The Scud missile attacks, however, embarrassed the U.S. military, which wanted to maintain an image of total control of the battlefield, and greatly worried the Bush administration, which wanted to keep Israel out of the war. Schwarzkopf admitted in his January 18 briefing that trying to find a mobile Scud launcher "is like trying to find a needle in a haystack," and later in the day pundit Edward Luttwak noted on CBS that "you can put a Scud launcher in a truck, a barn, a church, anywhere." The problem in war, he claimed, was to see things and then to hit them. Mobile Scud launchers, he explained, were simply hard to see. Thus, although Schwarzkopf bragged about how they were constantly destroying Scud launchers, no one really knew how many Scud missiles and missile launchers Iraq had and where they were deploying them. Nonetheless, the pundits constantly speculated on the number of missiles and launchers that Iraq possessed and what percentage were already destroyed.

Scuds over Israel

All through the day of January 18, Israeli officials and media commentators put out the line that if Israel was not attacked again, it would probably not retaliate for the first Scud assault, but if they were attacked again and took high casualties and losses, they would retaliate. In mid-morning EST, the TV commentators noted that the Israeli cabinet meeting was over and it appeared that Israel was holding off on retaliation. It was also announced that two people in Israel had died of heart attacks and two others died of suffocation when they frantically put on gas masks and forgot to pull off the seal. Thus, the Scud attacks were taking a lethal toll on the Israeli public.

A bit after 11:00 A.M., George Bush gave a news conference to comment on the progress of the war. Repeating the phrase of the day, which would be reproduced from New York to London to Tel Aviv, Bush called the progress, "so far, so good." He cautioned against euphoria and said that it "will take some time" to destroy Saddam Hussein's military assets. But, he was "outraged" by Iraq's "act of aggression" against Israel and appreciated Israel's "restraint." Consultations were continuing with Israel and other allies, and Bush affirmed that he was determined to "safeguard" Israel, promising that "[w]e are going to be redoubling our efforts in the darndest search-and-destroy effort that's ever been undertaken in that area."

Bush's performance was lackluster and he only summoned emotion when Helen Thomas of UPI asked him why he should be "outraged" when the Iraqis engaged in an "act of retaliation." Otherwise, he failed to understand some of the questions and kept talking about the unity of the nation behind him and the troops, and the unity of the world behind him and the UN resolutions, although both the country and the world were deeply divided over Bush's war against Iraq. Bush's war team rushed him out of the press room and over to the Pentagon for an afternoon briefing and then off to Camp David for the weekend.

The rest of the networks broke off their war coverage midafternoon, returning to their soap operas, and the world turned to CNN to get news of the unfolding events. In a remarkable segment on CNN with Israeli Deputy Foreign Minister Benjamin Netanyahu, an air-raid siren went off in the middle of the interview. Voices in the background indicated that there was an air attack and that the Israeli government had promised them that there would be no air-raid drills or false alarms. "Israel is being bombed again," Netanyahu categorically concluded. Reid Collins asked him from CNN headquarters if "it is an attack or a warning," and Netanyahu answered: "It's an attack." CNN continued to interview Netanyahu until the producer in Jerusalem, Larry Register, broke off the interview, saying that they had to "get protected." The crew started to put on their gas masks and Wolf Blitzer continued trying to question Netanyahu while he and the CNN crew put on their protective gear. Blitzer was trying to make the point that the Israeli government had said that if they were attacked again they would immediately retaliate, while at the same time Register was giving a report through his gas mask on the facts of the supposed air attack; finally CNN cut Blitzer off.

CNN then turned to its correspondent Richard Blystone in Tel Aviv, who said that the sirens had ceased, and next the screen showed Netanyahu making a call from the CNN studio, no doubt to get information. Blystone reported that the Israeli radio announced a missile attack, yet he had not heard any sound of it in Tel Aviv. The radio, he claimed, ordered people to put on their protective gear and to go into a sealed room, as there was fear of a chemical attack. CBS broke into its soap operas and Tom Fenton reported that Israeli radio announced that an attack was underway; Fenton thought that he had heard a bomb drop, but wasn't sure. CBS reported that they believed that a Scud alert was on in Saudi Arabia and broke to correspondent Scott Pelley, but his satellite link was abruptly cut off just as he started to report, intensifying the drama.

CBS's Pentagon correspondent Jim Stewart relayed the Pentagon's statement that they were fairly confident that there were no Scud attacks, but in Israel there was suddenly another warning siren, so it was hard to know exactly what was going on. Meanwhile, CNN's Linda Sherzer and Netanyahu were conducting an interview in their gas masks before the all-clear signal sounded. Then, in a fascinating exchange with Larry Register, Netanyahu explained why Israel had to retaliate against such "terrorism." When a map of the area was brought out, he put his hands one after another on the Arab world and his thumb on Israel, to demonstrate how vastly outnumbered Israel was by its Arab enemies. Register told Netanyahu how people had told him that Israel shouldn't respond, that "Israel should let America respond for us." In response, Netanyahu launched into his usual demonization of Saddam Hussein, Arafat and the PLO, and the other Arabs who he claimed wished to destroy Israel, repeating his hawkish line that national survival dictates that they must destroy these enemies first. Netanyahu warned of the danger to Israel if a Palestinian state were formed right on its border, making it able to fire even more accurate short-range missiles at them. Never before had the Israeli hard-line right wing gotten a more sympathetic hearing on U.S. television.

The prime-time news programs centered on the false alarms of Scud attacks on Israel and Saudi Arabia, and through the evening a now-dominant technowar discourse settled in, focusing on the high-tech wonders of the U.S. military and speculating on when a ground war would be necessary, thus providing an aura of control and normality. However, late in the evening, events careened out of control once again. ABC's "Nightline" was having a report on the antiwar movement when suddenly, around midnight, the show was interrupted by correspondent Chris Wallace in Israel, saying that there had been a series of explosions in downtown Tel Aviv. Wallace reckoned that there were between three and five explosions close to the ABC bureau. The crew was in a sealed room, and radio confirmation had been given that there was a missile attack in Tel Aviv that, Wallace claimed, hit in the center of the city in a highly populated area.

On CBS, Tom Fenton reported through a gas mask to Susan Spencer that a series of missiles fired together hit Tel Aviv at dawn. He also reported that a CBS cameraman in Jerusalem claimed that there were seven hits in Jerusalem and four in Tel Aviv! Tom Brokaw broke in on NBC to move live to correspondent Larry Weidman in Tel Aviv, who, also talking through his gas mask, claimed that he heard three explosions on the northern side of the city and had heard reports of one explosion in the south side of Tel Aviv. The sound volume of the explosion was about the same as last night, he claimed, though this time the missile hit at dawn. A bit later, Weidman said that there may have been as many as six or seven explosions in the Tel Aviv area. It appeared that a major missile attack was happening which could determine the fate of the war. Once again, the drama of the Persian Gulf TV war was gripping.

The attack raised speculation regarding whether chemical weapons had been used and how many casualties the attack had produced. Well before these facts were ascertained, NBC's Tom Brokaw stated almost immediately that this attack "will remove every doubt whatsoever whether Israel will respond. . . . No government, no matter how liberal or understanding, can allow its society to come under an attack of this kind without doing something about it. And Israel has always operated under the principle of an eye for an eye. The Israelis will feel compelled to strike back despite the overtures to hold back of President Bush." Brokaw then speculated that Bush, too, may accept the now inevitable Israeli retaliation. Thus, Tom Brokaw stepped back from his function as reporter to become public policymaker, legitimating what he believed would be an Israeli retaliation and advising President Bush to accept the inevitable!

At least four times in the next hour, Brokaw repeated his assurance that Israel would now retaliate and throughout the evening would push the retaliation line; Tom Brokaw was obviously out of control. At one point, NBC's White House correspondent John Cochran produced an argument against retaliation, suggesting that it did not seem that this attack was big enough to trigger a response. Later, when it was announced that there were only slight casualties, Cochran indicated that Washington would have a hard time accepting such an insignificant attack as justification for retaliation. Nonetheless, Brokaw continued to push the retaliation line, arguing against Cochran, Middle East expert Gary Sick, and others who thought that Israel would not and probably should not retaliate. Instead, Brokaw agreed with U.S. and Israeli interviewees that Israel should retaliate immediately. One cannot be certain why Brokaw took such a strong and emotional position in favor of retaliation, but it was clear that he overstepped his function as journalist and became a public policy advocate, pushing what, in retrospect, was a particularly stupid policy. During several Israeli Scud attacks, in fact, he became extremely emotional about the viciousness of the Iraqis, though he never seemed to summon any sympathy for dead Iraqis, bombed by the U.S-led coalition.

By contrast, NBC White House correspondent John Cochran was pushing the White House line that Israel should not retaliate, doing the bidding of the Bush administration upon whom he depended for his "information." On the whole, however, the other network commentators followed Brokaw, citing the inevitability and rightness of Israeli retaliation. Dan Rather noted on CBS that "there are going to be an awful lot of people . . . who [will] say: 'Look, there is no way to keep the Israelis out of the war now. They're going to retaliate. It's only a question of time.'" CBS military adviser General Crist stated categorically: "I don't see how they can allow this to happen. I think the only option . . . is for Israel to try to handle the missile problem themselves." CBS White House correspondent Leslie Stahl, however, had some reservations: "If Israel does react, they hand Saddam Hussein the very victory that he is looking for. . . . Now we will wait and see if Israel will continue to show the restraint they have shown so far." ABC's Ted Koppel, however, predicted that: "It seems almost inevitable that the Israelis will respond."

Thus, while the network anchors generally took the line that Israel would and should retaliate, the White House correspondents took the position of the Bush administration that Israel should show restraint. This example indicates once again the extent to which the White House correspondents just parrot the line of the moment of the administration that they are covering, while the TV anchors respond to a variety of influences and thus might support policies at odds with the government. In any case, it was revealing to see the major White House correspondents arguing for the policy that the Bush administration was pushing—that Israel not retaliate—whereas the anchors were urging, justifying, or predicting Israeli retaliation.

In one of the most interesting exchanges on the Iraqi Scud attack, Joshua Epstein, a defense analyst for the Brookings Institution, said on ABC that Israel would clearly respond and that he was afraid that it would spread the war and break up the multinational coalition. Israeli retaliation, he feared, could roll out of control and cause the coalition to accelerate the combat and perhaps begin the ground war prematurely. Moreover, it was not clear what the endgame would be: There were still many Iraqi divisions north of Baghdad, so the total destruction of the Iraqi military and overthrow of the regime of Saddam Hussein could involve quite a bloodbath. Epstein did not see that the Bush administration had projected any clear end to the war, and it appeared to him in retrospect that starting a war in the Middle East was "a rather rash act." The possibility of bringing in Jordan could also intensify and complicate the war and cause a serious split in the coalition. Moreover, Epstein warned, the status of the Iraqi air force was still unknown; it is conceivable that they could assemble a large armada, perhaps loaded with chemical weapons, and some might get through to Israel. In any case, it appeared that events were spinning out of control, he warned. Epstein's was one of the few critical voices to emerge in the mainstream media that questioned the rationality of the war itself, pointing out that it was not clear where the war was going, how it would evolve, what the terminus might be, and how it might be widened, causing a further escalation into the unknown and uncontrollable.

Around 2:15 A.M., CBS correspondent Tom Fenton reported that the Israeli Red Cross told him that there had been casualties, but the all-clear signal had just gone off, and he was told that the weapons were conventional warheads and that poison gas was not used in this attack. In Fenton's next report, he stated that by monitoring police radios in Jerusalem, his team had concluded that there were no missile hits in

Jerusalem and that the noises reported there might have been reverberations or echoes. Fenton noted that there were hits in Tel Aviv and that they had pictures of a crater five feet across. Illustrating Fenton's report was video footage of an Israeli civil defense team with chemical suits checking out sites for damage and for evidence of chemical weapons while spraying water on the crater.

Throughout the night, the networks aired footage from the missile attack as soon as it appeared on their satellite feed, much of it of very poor quality and obviously unedited. It appears that in a crisis the networks would show any picture that came down the satellite feed, as quickly as they could get it on the air. Their aesthetic in these situations might be described as a "neorealist minimalism" in which they throw out all aesthetic and technical standards and show whatever video images they are fed. Hungry for pictures, they are potential dupes for governments who want to feed them certain words or images that serve the interests of the government in question, thus rendering the networks propaganda agents for foreign governments.

Around 3:15 A.M., NBC broadcast a statement live from an Israeli embassy spokesperson who reported that all the warheads in the Scud missiles that hit Israel were conventional and that there were about ten light injuries and heavy property damage. The most interesting point of the briefing, however, was that the Israeli government stated that it would no longer comment on the number, accuracy, or location of the missile strikes. This briefing thus signaled a new Israeli policy that would make it increasingly difficult to chart the trajectory of the Scud wars. The decision was made for military and political reasons. Militarily, Israel obviously did not want the Iraqis to know which missiles hit and caused damage and which did not. Politically, the Israeli government wanted to manipulate the information concerning the damage of the Scuds for its political purposes: to exaggerate damage if it decided to retaliate or to cover up damage if it chose not to retaliate.

In fact, it was not certain how many Scuds hit in this attack and what damage they caused. CBS claimed during the morning of the attack that their crew confirmed that there were four Scud hits with heavy property damage, but light casualties (the latter point was also asserted by the Israeli embassy in the United States). The following morning the *New York Times* reported: "Four Iraqi missiles slammed into heavily populated areas along Israel's coastal heartland early this morning . . . and slightly injured 15 civilians." The U.S. military, however, claimed at their briefing in Riyadh, Saudi Arabia, the next morning that only three Scuds hit Israel. One wonders, however, if there were really more serious Scud hits and if the Israeli and U.S. governments were covering over the extent of the damage, thus enabling Israel to avoid retaliation. Baghdad radio claimed that it fired eleven missiles and an Israeli, David Halevey, also reported that Iraq might have fired as many as eleven missiles at Israel. There were reports by both CBS and NBC that there were multiple missile hits in Jerusalem,[9] and although these reports were later denied, one might be suspicious of these denials. In fact, CBS's correspondent Doug Tunnell in Jordan said that they received an unconfirmed report that at least one of the missiles fired at Israel landed in Jordan! Jordanian officials were not commenting on the report, he said, yet they did not deny it either.

And so it was not really clear how much damage the Iraqi Scud attack produced or what the Israeli response would be. I indicated earlier how the network commentators for the most part believed that retaliation was inevitable. Some of those who took this position were pundits, who simply thought that Israel would immediately retaliate, while a large number were Israelis or their ideological champions, who wanted Israel to retaliate. Others took the Bush administration position and urged Israel not to retaliate, claiming that this action would simply play into the hands of Saddam Hussein. In any case, throughout the next several weeks, this issue was endlessly debated. As it turned out, Israel did not retaliate during the Gulf war itself, at least as far as is known, nor has it yet retaliated despite constant bluster that it would definitely retaliate, but at a time of its own choosing.[10]

Scud Wars in Saudi Arabia

Part of the reason that Israel did not retaliate against Iraq was that the U.S. sent Patriot missile batteries to the Jewish state to protect it against Scud attacks. During the weekend of January 19 and 20, there was much media attention focused on the bringing of Patriot missile batteries to Israel which were supposed to protect the country from Scud attacks. After the relatively calm weekend of January 19 and 20, the U.S. military began to assert that they had the Scud situation under control. A Saudi military official told the BBC that the Iraqis no longer had the capacity to hit Saudi Arabia with Scud missiles, and the media reported repeatedly that U.S. Patriot missiles, sent to Israel over the weekend, would protect Israel against future Scud attacks. At the U.S. military briefing in Riyadh, Saudi Arabia, Captain Robert Johnson observed that the Scud attack trend was obviously down, declining from eight hits the previous night to three that night (figures in themselves contestable), and other U.S. officials and their allies in the media continuously repeated this inane argument, one that was soon literally shot down by new rounds of Scud attacks.

Throughout that weekend the Patriot missile system, which so far had only performed once, was praised to the skies—despite the fact that the media also reported that two Patriot missile systems had misfired and the missiles had to be exploded in the area, costing taxpayers more than one million dollars for each misfire.[11] This rather dubious track record did not, however, interfere with fulsome Patriot propaganda. On the "CBS Evening News," for instance, Pentagon correspondent David Martin reported that the first of the Patriots were operational in Israel and described the Patriots as "[t]he single most important weapon in the American arsenal," which was obviously total nonsense. Martin did note the accidental firing of two Patriots that day and that it was still not certain why they misfired: "But finding out is essential because these missiles are capable of shooting down American planes flying back from Iraq or Kuwait."

Around 1:56 P.M. EST on January 20, CNN correspondent Charles Jaco reported from Dhahran, Saudi Arabia, that there were claims of five Scud missiles in the air coming toward Saudi Arabia. A frantic Jaco breathlessly informed the world that Patriot missiles were just fired at the Scuds, and everyone had been told to scramble off the platform. Jaco and his crew remained, however, and described the confusion live for some time. A CNN crew member saw Patriots going up and then saw streaks of light and sparks in the sky. There was no warning of this raid at all, Jaco remarked; it came as a complete surprise and "the first warning we might get is the explosion of the missiles going off." Air sirens screamed in the background and a very nervous Jaco looked from side to side and calculated whether he should stay on the scene or seek shelter as advised.

At the same time, the Big Three networks' broadcasting of sports events was interrupted by announcements of Iraqi Scud attacks on Saudi Arabia. During the broadcast of a playoff for next week's Super Bowl, NBC's Saudi Arabia correspondent, "Scud stud" Arthur Kent, reported that Iraqi Scud missiles had been fired at Saudi Arabia and subsequently attacked by Patriot missiles; footage was shown of Kent ducking and saying: "There goes a Patriot. Let's go!" Shortly thereafter, reporting live on NBC, Kent nervously dashed his head from side to side, looking for the next Scud, as he gave his report, obviously rattled by the large number of Scuds aimed at Saudi Arabia. Remaining cool in New York, Tom Brokaw reported: "It now looks like the worst was over" and "the American investment in that anti-missile missile is certainly paying off. . . . This is the second time that it intercepted Scuds."

But on CNN, Charles Jaco kept repeating: "We still don't know anything at all." The CNN crew had seen three to five Patriots going up, and one crew member reported an explosion of a Patriot hitting a Scud. But Jaco and his crew got no information from the military, who were "hunkering down in the sealed room of the hotel bomb shelter." He said that military officials had told the CNN crew that it was "in or out" before they sealed off the shelter and it was evidently "out" for Jaco and his CNN crew. Jaco noted that there was no official confirmation of missile hits or information concerning the dangers of a chemical attack because there were no officials in Saudi Arabia accessible to the media. Consequently, rumors ran rife.

During halftime of the football game, NBC broke in for a live report by Arthur Kent, who announced that four Scuds had been fired at Dhahran and that Patriots had intercepted them. On CBS, Connie Chung related that U.S. pool technicians saw two Patriots destroying the Scuds, though Scott Pelley in Saudi Arabia stated that "it is hard to get precise information about what's going on." Meanwhile, Jaco was becoming increasingly angry that he could get no official information from the military. Indeed, one wondered why the military was not giving out any information, as people in Saudi Arabia and those closely following the war throughout the world probably became increasingly anxious as the uncertainty grew and the rumors flew, perhaps leading many to fear the worst.

Around 2:35 P.M., Jaco was describing the quiet in Dhahran when the CNN newsreader broke in to say that they had just been handed a report of a missile firing and an explosion in Bahrain. Moments later it was claimed by the Saudis that two Scuds had been fired at their territory and intercepted by Patriots. Shortly thereafter, CNN's Greg LaMotte reported that Patriots shot down the Scuds and that allied airplanes hit the launchers. At 3:00 P.M., Pete Williams of the Pentagon said that the "best information" from preliminary reports was that there were launches of two Scud missiles toward Saudi Arabia from southern Iraq and in response the U.S. fired five Patriot missiles from batteries near Dhahran, which destroyed all the Scuds. The Pentagon did not know yet what sort of warhead it was; there were no reports of injuries nor were there reports of any missiles aimed at Riyadh—despite the media reports just given. Williams praised the Patriot missile system and answered some questions. As usual, CNN Pentagon correspondent Wolf Blitzer summarized the report as if we were finally getting accurate information concerning the Scud attack. This practice of immediately summarizing official briefings or press conferences creates what might be called a "redoubling effect" in which the message (often propaganda) is doubled by the correspondent who summarizes the event, lending an extra dimension of credibility and objectivity to what is usually highly self-interested discourse of the parties putting it out. Then, the military experts reproduce once more the same "information" as facts, usually putting as pro-military a spin as possible on whatever information was produced. But in this case, CNN quickly undercut the Pentagon propaganda line on the Scud battle of the day by switching to Charles Jaco in Saudi Arabia, who said that they had information that "contradicts everything that Pete Williams of the Pentagon just said." According to Jaco, a U.S. government official stated that there were four Scuds fired and two were hit and two got through, "landing with ground explosions." Furthermore, a civilian saw two Patriots launched with no explosion, although Saudi sources claimed that there were five Scuds launched and that all of them were destroyed.

CNN's military adviser James Blackwell noted that it would be important to resolve the contradictory information because a lot was riding on the accuracy of the Patriots. Indeed, precisely because the defense of Israel and Saudi Arabia seemed to depend on the Patriots, it was highly probable that U.S. and Saudi officials chose to cover over failures of the Patriot missile system, as they continued to do throughout the war. At 4:02 P.M., Wolf Blitzer broke in with some "new information," reporting that Pete Williams had claimed that there were three and not two Scuds that were fired and that five Patriots were fired, resulting in the destruction of all three Scuds; the Pentagon stuck with this story in the days to come, despite reports to the contrary.

Around 4:45 P.M., CNN cut to Dhahran, Saudi Arabia, where a siren was audible, along with hysterical background talking, but no one on camera. Finally, technician Chris Turner appeared on camera wearing a gas mask, reporting that they had just seen two Patriot launchings and heard two explosions, with one Patriot going up and crashing straight down. CBS's Scott Pelley, also in gas mask, said that the air base in Dhahran was under attack and that Saudi authorities told everyone to put their gas mask and suit on because "there was reason to believe that there has been a chemical attack." ABC broke in with a live report from Morton Dean, without gas mask, who nervously explained that he had to leave to seek protective gear. NBC's Arthur Kent, also without protective gear, reported, with head bobbing from side to side nervously, that they had heard two thumps and rumbles, which sounded like the impact of a missile on the ground, but the explosion seemed to be in the direction of a neighboring city.

Shortly thereafter, CNN correspondent John Sweeney broadcast live from the capital city of Riyadh that it was under attack by Iraqi missiles. He claimed that they had seen a dozen or more Patriot missiles fired at the Scuds and observed how some Patriots appeared to hit Scuds in the sky, exploding in a fireworks display of sparks and lights, while another missile seemed to come down unimpeded and exploded. Greg LaMotte then called CNN from his hotel room in Riyadh, saying that his heart was pumping like it had never pumped before. LaMotte said that a bit after 1:00 A.M. local time, he felt a heavy explosion that shook the hotel and then heard many other explosions one after another. During the following minutes the CNN crew in Riyadh continued to claim that they had seen a dozen of what appeared to be Patriot missiles shooting into the sky and saw one that they believed had crash-landed.

The confusion continued during the rest of the afternoon. There had obviously been two rounds of Scud attacks, the first hitting at least Dhahran and the second hitting Dhahran and Riyadh, but it wasn't certain what damage had been done, if the Patriots either missed Scuds or even went up and crashed into the city, as would later be reported. A media pool video of the second Dhahran attack appeared showing panic in the streets with people running for shelter and yelling. Something that looked like a missile came down and crashed on the horizon as people put on gas masks and ran into a shelter. CNN transformed the earlier CBS report that there *may* have been chemical weapons in the second Dhahran attack into a report that there *were* chemical weapons involved, and then retracted this, saying that CBS had reported that chemical weapons may have been used and not necessarily were used. Later in the evening, pool video of a large crater in Riyadh appeared. This video also showed destroyed adjacent buildings, though the Pentagon and Saudis continued to insist that the Patriots intercepted all Scuds. False alarms continued to go off, rumors continued to fly, and all the while commentators kept praising the Patriot system though it really wasn't clear if it had worked or not.

Henceforth, there were frequent contradictions between the Scud war figures concerning the number of Scud launches, Patriot intercepts, and the extent of damage. At a press conference broadcast at 9:15 P.M. EST by CNN, U.S. military spokesperson Mike Gallagher claimed that during the first attack on Dhahran three Scud missiles had been fired into eastern Saudi Arabia (i.e., Dhahran) at about 9:50 P.M. local time and were blown up by five Patriots. Most television reports, by contrast, announced that four Scud missiles had been fired at Dhahran and also reported that an explosion had been heard in Bahrain that had sounded an air alarm. Gallagher also claimed: "In the second attack, about 12:45 A.M. this morning, January 21, Saudi time, Iraq fired seven Scud missiles: four at Riyadh, two at Dhahran, and one in the waters off Dhahran. Six of these Scuds were shot down by Patriot missiles and one crashed harmlessly in the water." When asked, Gallagher denied that the military had any information concerning an errant Patriot or a Scud hit in Riyadh, or any information concerning a crater caused by a missile hit (CNN, in an effective use of montage, cut to pictures of the crater while Gallagher spoke, putting in question his denials). Gregg LaMotte of CNN then imparted that he just returned from a scene where a Scud "blew out the back side of a building and left a hole in the ground about ten feet deep and thirteen feet wide. There were pieces of a missile all over the place around a mile and a half down the road."

The U.S. military thus asserted that the Iraqis had fired a total of ten Scud missiles in the January 20–21 assault on Saudi Arabia and that the Patriots had intercepted nine of the missiles, with one Iraqi missile falling into the sea, not having been engaged by the Patriots. But the French army headquarters said that eighteen Scuds were fired at Saudi Arabia. TV reports constantly mentioned that witnesses saw missiles crashing to earth in both Dhahran and Riyadh, and television had clearly shown images of a large crater from one missile hit. Jeffrey Lenorovitz, an editor of *Aviation Week and Space Technology,* said that he witnessed the launching of a Patriot missile and then saw the missile crash after traveling horizontally less than two miles (*New York Times,* Jan. 21, 1991, p. A1). To the reports that a crater was visible in Riyadh, the U.S. military first claimed not to know of it, and then, after it was telecast repeatedly, claimed that it was the result of debris from an exploded Scud hit by a Patriot. The next day, however, CNN played what they described as "an amateur video," which showed a Patriot going up and then crashing. Furthermore, the same day at the daily Pentagon military briefing, Pete Williams admitted that one Scud got through the Patriots. Despite this information, the Big Three networks continued circulating the official Pentagon version that all Scuds were successfully intercepted by the mighty Patriots. Moreover, Bush, Schwarzkopf, and other military briefers would continue to claim a 100 percent success rate for the Patriots for some time to come, in spite of evidence to the contrary.

Indeed, the contradictions in the account of the big Saudi Arabian Scud/Patriot exchange were smoothed out when the major networks processed the story and magically transformed a very negative event for Saudi Arabia into a triumph of U.S. technology. CBS, which gave no extended report the day before on the Scud attacks, opened their "CBS This Morning" program on January 21 with the headline: "Patriot missiles protect Saudi Arabia from Scud attacks." Then Scott Pelley reported from Saudi Arabia that the previous night Iraq launched its largest missile barrage ever in Dhahran and Riyadh. U.S. Patriot missiles were launched, and the Pentagon said that nine Scuds were knocked down, with the tenth crashing into the water. The Pentagon claimed that damage from falling debris was relatively minor. Pelley indicated that a crater was found in Riyadh where there were reports of damage from debris, but it was not certain if the crater and damage were from a Scud missile or an errant Patriot. CBS did not show the footage of the crater and evidently did not have anyone on the scene the previous day. Moreover, in a report that closely followed Pelley's (which raised some question concerning the level of protection provided by the Patriots), CBS supported the Pentagon version by assuring its audiences of the Patriot's efficacy.

The segment in question featured Jeffrey Lenorovitz, who previously said that he saw a Patriot shoot straight up in the air and then suddenly swerve horizontally to crash in the distance. This was earlier perceived as the errant Patriot that might have caused the crater, but now he said that after examining the site he believed that the Patriot carried out a low intercept of the Scud as pieces of both missiles were found in the site. Thus, the contradiction between the media reports and the military reports was smoothed out, allowing the military to triumphantly claim that its Patriots had successively intercepted all Scuds, in a show of U.S. technological superiority and even omnipotence. For the rest of the day the major networks repeated the Pentagon version as the gospel truth, although occasionally CNN reports questioned whether a Patriot had misfired or a Scud had actually gotten through the Patriot defenses.

Patriot Propaganda

Later, it was revealed that many of the missiles that the military said had been intercepted by Scuds were only partially hit, with the warhead crashing to earth. Many Patriots hit the fuel storage part of the Scud, causing spectacular explosions, while the warhead continued toward earth unimpeded. In other cases, clearly seen on video but denied by the military, the Patriot fired and then crashed to earth. In some cases, the combined debris from Patriot and Scud explosions fell to earth, causing serious damage. The crater in Riyadh, for example, seemed to have been caused by a low-level Patriot intercept that had arguably compounded the explosive damage of the Scud by scattering more debris over a larger area than a Scud hit alone would have caused. The Patriot was thus something of a fraud, celebrated by the Bush administration and its media boosters but often causing more damage than a Scud hit alone.

But for weeks during the war, one "expert" and commentator after another praised the Patriots' 100 percent intercept record, creating the deceptive impression that the Patriots constituted a shield of total security. For example, on January 21, "NBC Nightly News" correspondent Katherine Couric commented: "Every war supplies a hero above all others and this one has produced the Patriot missile." In an episode titled "The Protector," she argued that the Patriot is "ten for ten" and that "every Scud missile that threatened Saudi Arabia . . . has been smashed to bits by the Patriot," which she eulogized as "the king of air defense systems." The segment concluded by noting that "star wars technology is expected to be revitalized, thanks to the Patriot's success."

In assessing these claims, note that Couric simply accepted at face value the U.S. military claim that all Scuds were intercepted by Patriots

(Schwarzkopf and other military briefers were making similar claims). Later analysis, however, showed that many Scuds got through despite military claims that they had intercepted the Iraqi missile. Furthermore, serious questions had already been raised concerning whether the Patriot was "ten for ten." But the networks almost always followed whatever the Pentagon reported, privileging its sources above all others, even when contradicted by their fellow reporters' eye-witness accounts and media footage that seemed to corroborate these contrary accounts. In addition, Couric's claim that the Patriots had "smashed to bits" all the Scuds was obviously false in the light of the picture of the crater and the shattered Saudi insurance company building, which was shown periodically through the day by CNN. Moreover, as noted, the Patriot often hit some of the Scud, while the rest proceeded on its destructive way, so Couric's "smashed to pieces" claim was false.

Furthermore, not only did Couric mythologize the Patriot's technological omnipotence, but she connected it to "star wars" (SDI) technology, a connection that experts later called highly misleading.[12] It may be relevant to point out that GE and RCA, NBC's parent companies, have billions invested in military space technology, so NBC's constant promotion of the Patriot was boosting its own defense industry interests, providing advertising for a strategic antimissile defense system that GE/RCA was strongly interested in, showing once again the acute problems inherent in corporations owning TV networks and using them to promote their own economic and ideological interests. But it is unlikely that the Raytheon corporation, which produces the Patriot, would criticize such coverage, as its stocks soared as a result of the free advertising for its wares (perhaps the Federal Communications Commission should undertake a study of the TV networks' Patriot PR to see if deceptive advertising practices were violated!).

In retrospect, the Patriot was more of a propaganda weapon than a military one. In his January 21 briefing, General Schwarzkopf claimed that the Patriot had intercepted ten out of ten Scuds fired at Saudi Arabia. During a February 15 visit to the Raytheon Patriot missile factory, Bush claimed that the Patriots had destroyed 32 of 33 Scuds fired (see 6.2 for further details of Bush's visit). "Official" U.S. figures after the war asserted that Patriots succeeded in knocking out forty-five out of the forty-seven Scuds they went after (Dunnigan and Bay 1991, p. 186). And throughout the war, the Patriot was praised as the ultimate high-tech weapons system without a word of dissent from this standard view—which greatly aided Patriot missile sales around the world.

Yet some weeks later, it was admitted that only 49 of the 60 Scud missiles launched by Iraq had been destroyed by Patriot missiles and that 160 Patriots, at a cost of $1.3 million each, were fired and that most of them destroyed themselves after unsuccessful attempts to find the Scuds (*Der Spiegel*, March 25, 1991 and *Science*, Vol. 252, May 3, 1991, pp. 640–641). Furthermore, at an April 16, 1991, House Armed Service Committee Defense Policy Panel hearing, MIT defense analyst and former Pentagon consultant Theodore Postol contended that reliance on the Patriot in Israel and Saudi Arabia may have resulted in more damage from debris than if the system had never been deployed. Drawing on an Israeli study, Postol (1991) claimed that before the Patriots were used in Israel thirteen Scuds fell unopposed near Tel Aviv; they wounded 115 people and damaged 2,698 apartments. After the Patriots were deployed in Israel, another eleven Scud attacks occurred, killing 1 person, injuring 168, and damaging 7,778 apartments. So although the number of attacks dropped 15 percent, the figures show that Israeli casualties per Scud fired increased by 50 percent after the Patriots started "defending" Israel. The number of buildings damaged per Scud tripled. Consequently, Postol concluded that Israel might have been better off if it had never fired any Patriots at all.

Postol argued that there were several serious problems with the Patriot's performance in Israel: the Patriot's "homing device" seems to have been confused by pieces that broke away from the Scuds as they reentered the atmosphere and thus failed to target consistently the warheads. Furthermore, the Patriot system was designed to fire more than one interceptor missile against each incoming Scud, thus multiplying the number of missiles fired at fragmenting Scuds. In addition, Patriots would occasionally explode in the air, scattering their debris, and sometimes even crashed to earth. For example, Postol noted a video recording by an ABC News crew of four Patriots launched against incoming Scuds over Tel Aviv on January 25 which showed that one Patriot self-destructed in midair while two others crashed into residential areas and the fourth climbed and then dived into a warehouse district. House Armed Service Committee Chairman Les Aspin thus concluded that the Patriot "was not as effective as we originally thought," after hearing the testimony about the missile and reviewing secret information about its performance. Aspin concluded that the interceptors' greatest contribution "was in fact psychological," rather than military (*Washington Post*, April 17, 1991).

During the fall of 1991, further Israeli studies raised questions about the Patriot's performance. The *New York Times* reported: "Senior Israeli scientists and military officers have disclosed new information indicating that the American Patriot missiles used in Israel in the Persian Gulf war destroyed far fewer Scud missile warheads than previously believed, Israeli and Defense Department officials said today" (October 31, 1991). The Israelis claimed that the Patriots destroyed far fewer than the 44 percent of the Iraqi Scud missile warheads claimed by the U.S. government and that estimates now ranged between zero and 20 percent Scud warheads destroyed. Reuven Pedatzur, a research fellow at the Tel Aviv University-based Jaffee Center for Strategic Studies, claimed in a preliminary report published in an October 24, 1991 issue of the Israeli daily *Ha'aretz* that the Israeli team of missile scientists demonstrated "beyond a shadow of a doubt that the Patriot missiles failed totally in the mission of intercepting the Scuds" (*Defense News,* November 18, 1991). Israeli sources were now claiming that the Patriot missile failed to destroy even one Scud warhead during 39 missile attacks, despite damage to parts of the Scud missiles which produced spectacular explosions.

In a later paper on his and Israeli research, Postol (1991–1992) argued that the visual pyrotechnics of dramatic explosions in the air only produced an illusion of antimissile success. The Scuds, he explained, were so poorly designed that they broke into pieces before landing and the Patriots were often merely hitting pieces of the missile, or exploding in the air without significantly impacting on the Scud, creating a fireball often mistaken as a successful interception. Postol claimed that close inspection of publicly available videotapes showed Scud warheads hitting the earth unscathed by Patriots. In an analysis of videotapes of fourteen missiles fired in Saudi Arabia, for instance, Postol counted thirteen misses and one probable hit. In addition, Postol continued to argue that ground damage was greater than would have probably occurred if the Patriots had not been fired. Finally, he noted reports of a widespread lack of data-recording equipment at Patriot sites, suggesting that the government has poor records of what actually occurred. Postol thus concluded that: "Our first wartime experience" with antimissile defense resulted in what seems to be "an almost total failure to intercept quite primitive attacking missiles."

On the January 16, 1992, ABC News, the TV networks finally exposed the Patriot fraud. Defense expert Pierre Sprey noted: "No doubt if they released the complete data you would see, in fact, what a failure the Patriot has been." ABC Correspondent Morton Dean explained that: "The complaints have reached Congress. John Conyers of Michigan has directed his government operations subcommittee to investigate the Patriot's performance." Conyers (D-Mich.) admitted: "What I'm beginning to feel is that this wonderful system wasn't so wonderful after all." Dean concluded: "The Patriot's apparent success helped win a billion dollars for the Star Wars program and Raytheon expects five billion dollars in foreign sales. So appraising the Patriot's performance is not just an historical exercise." And on a January 30, 1992, "MacNeil-Lehrer NewsHour," it was reported that the Pentagon itself was now admitting that fifty percent of the Patriots missed their targets.

Furthermore, in the postwar assessment of high-tech weapons performance, serious questions were raised concerning some of the other stars of the Gulf war. At an April 22, 1991, hearing of the House Armed Services Committee, Pierre Sprey, a weapons expert and former Pentagon official, accused the Defense Department of "shamelessly doctoring statistics" on the performance of U.S. arms in the Gulf war. He sharply criticized the use of videos which only portrayed hits, claiming that these images of picture-perfect precision bombing provided a totally misleading image of the accuracy of high-tech weapons systems. Using official U.S. government statistics, Sprey argued that it had taken an average of 24 laser-guided "smart bombs" to hit each Iraqi bridge in the first two weeks of the air war. He attributed the success of the F-117A Stealth fighter to its ability to fly above the range of Iraqi air defenses, claiming that the F-117A was "probably not so stealthy" and had been tracked during the war on British-, French-, and Chinese-made radars (Sprey and Perry 1991).

Sprey also claimed that the old-fashioned low-tech "Warthog" A-10 jet was responsible for destroying far more Iraqi vehicles than the highly praised and expensive "tank-killing" Apache helicopter.[13] Questions were also raised about the highly-praised Cruise missile system. At the same April 22 hearing, Former Defense Department official Bill Perry claimed that the missile did not make a significant difference in the war (Sprey and Perry 1991). Although the Navy fired around 200 Cruise missiles at Iraqi targets, Perry claimed that bombs dropped by jet airplanes could have done just as well—at much less cost. Cruise missiles cost about $2 million a piece, Perry explained, while a one thousand pound bomb costs about ten thousand dollars. Experts also questioned the accuracy claims for the Cruise missile, doubting Navy claims of an "over 90% combined mission success rate" (Marc S. Miller, "Patriotic blindness and anti-truth weapons," *Index on Censorship,* No. 10, 1991, p. 32).[14] In addition, Sprey repeated the claims that the Patriots had caused more damage in Israel than before their deployment and concluded: "The country has been poorly served by . . . hand-selected video clips of isolated successes that were pumped out to the media during the war in order to influence postwar budget decisions."

An April 10, 1992, Pentagon report, "The Conduct of the Persian Gulf War," admitted that poor bomb damage–assessment information led to unnecessary retargeting of Iraqi facilities that caused excessive damage to civilian targets such as Iraq's electrical system. The Pentagon also conceded that it had overestimated the number of Iraqi armored personnel vehicles destroyed, revising the number from claims of 2,400 destroyed to 1,450. The study acknowledged that the air campaign failed to destroy parts of Iraq's nuclear weapons program: "Iraq's nuclear weapons program was more extensive than previously thought and did not suffer as serious a setback as was desired." The report indicated that military planners believed that the initial air campaign would last about 18 days and that the ground assault would take about 2 weeks more. In fact, the air campaign lasted 6 weeks and the ground offensive lasted 100 hours.

The same day, the *Washington Post* reported that classified Pentagon sources indicated that the F-117A Stealth attack jet and the Navy Tomahawk cruise missile struck considerably fewer of their targets than military officials had earlier claimed (April 10, 1992, p. A1). The *Post* reported that according to current Pentagon classified analysis, the F-117As placed laser-guided bombs on their primary targets in about 60 percent of the missions flown, in contrast to the 90 percent success rate estimated by the Air Force after the war. The Tomahawk Cruise missiles hit their intended targets only slightly more than half the time, in opposition to earlier Navy claims that the missile had an 85 percent success rate. Although the Apache helicopter was praised for having achieved a 90 percent "mission capable rate," the report fails to note extraordinary maintenance efforts required to keep them flying and includes little discussion of combat performance.

Other stories emerged concerning the failures of the new high-tech equipment. More than 2,000 Bradley fighting vehicles carried Army infantry units into the battle, but many crews complained that "vehicle exhaust tended to blow into the vehicle commander's face." Gunnery accuracy was hampered by poor sighting systems; so were "detection, recognition and identification of targets" (*The New York Times,* April 11, 1992). British sources noted that the U.S. Abrams A1M1 tank used four times as much fuel as its British counterpart, the Challenger, and that although the Abrams was not really tested adequately (because the Iraqis hardly fired on it), some U.S. tanks were blown apart by unsophisticated rounds from an Iraqi T-62 tank during the Gulf war (*The Independent,* June 11, 1991).

Regarding helicopters, the April 1992 Pentagon report said the Army sent nearly half of its fleet of Apaches to the Persian Gulf, where the "harsh desert environment, especially sand, adversely affected aircraft components." Also, the limited radio transmission range of the helicopter hindered the ability of commanders to communicate with crews flying at low altitudes or while they were conducting "deep interdiction" missions. Furthermore, a separate General Accounting Office report shortly thereafter said that the Apache helicopter experienced various shortcomings, including five accidental missile launches and complaints from two-thirds of pilots that the chopper's 30mm Gatling gun had jammed (Gannett News Service, April 25, 1992). Later in the month, *60 Minutes* did a segment on the Apache helicopter that described its many operational failures both in the Panama invasion and the Gulf war. Apparently, its navigation systems, guns, blades, and motor frequently failed to function and thus it only flew 83 missions in the Gulf war, while the older Cobra helicopter flew twice as many missions with only one-third the number of copters.

An April 23, 1992, report by the House Armed Services Committee noted several serious deficiencies with U.S. equipment and performance during the Gulf war, among them late and inaccurate battlefield intelligence, poor communication between units and services that led to "friendly fire" casualties, continuing difficulties in dealing with low-technology land and sea mines, and the inability of support forces to keep pace with high-speed combat units. Evidently, there were fierce battles going on within the Pentagon concerning budget lines for various weapons systems, and proponents of certain systems were leaking failures of opposing systems to Congress and the press in order to influence budget decisions during an era of shrinking defense revenues.

*   *   *

For the rest of the Gulf war, there were contradictions between official reports concerning the Patriot/Scud conflicts, and frequent contradictions between what the audience saw on television the night before and what was heard the next day in the briefing room. Ultimately the Patriot was a propaganda weapon more effective in creating the illusion of U.S. technological brilliance than in protecting people from missile attacks, in spite of praise from George Bush and Dan Quayle. Consequently, by the end of the first weekend of the war it was clear that the Persian Gulf war was rapidly becoming a media propaganda war as much as a military adventure.

Notes

1. In terms of reassuring the markets, the opening night euphoria was a smashing success. It was reported on January 17 that sweet crude oil prices dropped a record ten dollars per barrel and the stock market went up 114 points, the biggest one-day jump in more than three years.

2. See the discussion in Kellner 1990, pp. 171 and 236. Once again, McWethy proved himself to be a loyal servant of power. When asked to respond to the State Department response to the war, McWethy obsequiously replied on the first night of the war: "Secretary [of State James] Baker is here in the State Department tonight. He is watching the reports as things unroll, the man who is very much responsible for putting the coalition together and making it work in these final days, so that when this finally happened the different countries would come

together without a problem." When anchor Peter Jennings noted that the outbreak of war represented a failure of diplomacy, McWethy responded in defense of Baker: "I'm sure that Secretary Baker would argue that diplomacy was successful in bringing about a coalition to try and reverse what Saddam Hussein had done, first peacefully, if he could, Baker would argue, or by force, which is of course happening tonight."

3. On January 18, Moussus and ABC reporter Gary Shepard appeared in Amman, Jordan, with the story of how they shot the footage during the first night of the war. Apparently the cameraman and his soundman hid in the closet of the Al-Raschid Hotel in Baghdad. When the bombing started, they went to the window of the hotel to tape the footage, using a special night lens that produced an odd phosphorescent quality to the images. They were among the media personnel who left Iraq the next day, traveling on the road from Baghdad to Amman, where they experienced several bombing raids, saw Scud missiles being loaded and moved down the highway, and hid under a bridge when flak from U.S. bombing was dangerously close. The footage was initially broadcast under the rubric of a British ITN report by Brent Sadler and it turned out that Moussus had given a copy of his footage to Sadler to help assure that it could be gotten out of the country and telecast; it was broadcast and every network used it, robbing ABC of an "exclusive" ("Nightline," Jan. 18, 1991).

4. Through the first weeks of the war, the TV pool footage showed hand-written inscriptions on the bombs that included such literary wit as: "To Saddam With Love," "Saddam, You're Going to Die Soon," "Bend Over Saddam" (a masterpiece of homoerotic sadism), "Saddam, this one's for you" and "To Saddam. A 2,000 pound kiss from Flaherty." Another hand-scrawled dedication read: "When I've been over here for five and a half months it's personal," thus revealing the resentment building up in the troops and their desire for revenge for the disruption of their lives.

5. On the use of medical metaphors in war and military metaphors in medicine, see Montgomery 1991. I shall discuss the use of language and metaphor in the Gulf war in more detail in 6.1.

6. From *Anti-War Briefing Week Four,* cited in the *Covert Action Information Bulletin,* No. 37 (Summer 1991), p. 11. For further documentation of how the Special Forces placed locator devices by targets, see the article by James Adams, "Secret War" in MacArthur 1991, pp. 250ff. There were several reports of a U.S. commando team hitting Baghdad to perform secret operations just as the war was starting; for example, the episode of ABC's "Primetime Live," Feb. 28, 1991; Michael Gordon, "Desert Missions by Commandos Aided in Victory," *New York Times,* March 1, 1991, p. A1; and two *Newsweek* cover stories on "The Secret History of the War" (March 18, 1991) and "Secret Warriors" (June 17, 1991).

7. By "ideology," I mean a mode of discourse that legitimates certain forms of domination and destruction. Ideologies utilize language, images, narratives, and other cultural forms to cover over domination, inequality, and oppression, or attempt to render it natural and just. In this case, the ideology of technowar legitimates a high-tech military and its right to control a tremendous amount of the country's resources and to utilize military assets as an instrument of foreign

policy. The ideology of technowar thus legitimates domination of the polity by the military and the exercise of a certain form of modern warfare as rational and beneficial to the public. Ideologies of technowar present it as rational, good, just, and beyond critical questioning. (For more on the concept of ideology that I am employing, see Kellner 1978, 1979, 1989a, and 1990.) The Gulf war was thus an attempt to sell the military as a whole and its new high-tech weapons systems, as well as to legitimate specific practices and policies in the war.

8. I return to the McPeak interview in 5.2 and 7.3 in further discussion of U.S. claims concerning their precision bombing and will debunk the U.S. military denials of significant damage to civilian targets throughout the book.

9. CBS claimed for some time that there were missile hits in Jerusalem before denying the report. NBC's Larry Weidman also stated that "there was a report that there were a series of missiles shot into the occupied territories in Jerusalem." CBS asserted initially that it was their monitoring of Jerusalem police radio reports that led them to conclude that there were no missile hits in Jerusalem, but NBC disclosed that its monitoring of police radio reports led it to conclude that there were missile hits in the city! The *New York Times* wrote on January 21, 1991: "There were reports that another fell near Jerusalem at the same time, but they were never confirmed" (p. A1). Of course, the reports claiming Scud hits in Jerusalem could have been disinformation by those who wanted to rush Israel into immediate retaliation—or perhaps Jerusalem was hit and those Israelis favoring nonretaliation covered this over.

10. Iraq claimed that Israel sent planes and troops to join the coalition that attacked Iraq, but I have encountered no independent evidence for this claim.

11. Misfires were common and expensive. In addition, Dunnigan and Bay (1991, p. 186) estimate that at least two Patriots were fired at each Scud and after the war, as I indicate below, there were many that argued that the Patriot missile did not really provide protection and was a colossal waste of money.

12. Vice-President Dan Quayle claimed that those who did not believe Star Wars would work should look at the Patriot, disregarding the fact that the technologies were fundamentally different and that a Patriot hitting a nuclear warhead close to its target would hardly provide protection. Quayle and his PR team stressed throughout the war that he was responsible for saving the Patriot from cancellation in the Senate, and neither Bush nor Quayle missed an opportunity to praise the Patriot. Ideologue George Will argued (ABC, Jan. 20, 1991) that the Patriot proved the virtues of Ronald Reagan, SDI, and the military-industrial complex, and most of the network military "experts" never missed a chance to praise the Patriot's wonders. After the war, however, it was revealed that the Patriot's record was less than sterling, though by then it was already mythologized in the popular consciousness as the symbol of U.S. technological brilliance. For exposés of the Patriot fraud, see *Science,* Vol. 252, May 3, 1991, pp. 640–641; *Aviation Week & Space Technology,* April 22, 1991, pp. 90–91; *New York Times,* May 26, 1991, p. E10; *Scientific American,* June 1991, pp. 26–27; and other sources that I shall draw upon in the following discussion. Indeed, even military apologist Perry Smith questioned the efficacy of the Patriots (1991, pp. 20–21), as did a January 16, 1992, episode of "ABC World News Tonight" and a January 30, 1992, episode of "The MacNeil/Lehrer News Hour."

13. A report by the Government Accounting Office (GAO) supported Sprey's allegations, stating that "the average Apache had been able to spend less than 37 hours in the air during the six weeks of allied offensive operations in the Gulf. In contrast, the study noted that the average Air Force A-10 Thunderbolt attack plane had been able to spend about 130 hours in the air during the war. (The Army and Air Force credited the aging A-10s, nicknamed 'Warthogs,' with destroying more than 1,000 Iraqi tanks). The report contended that the Army had been forced to make extensive use of civilian technicians to keep the Apaches flying, and had been forced to cannibalize spare parts from Apaches based outside of the gulf region" *(Facts on File World News Digest,* May 30, 1991).

14. Recall that "success rate" was defined by General Powell simply as delivering ordnance and "combined mission success rate" refers to the fact that two Cruise missiles were fired at each Iraqi target which were followed up by attacks by piloted aircraft. MIT's Postol finds it "surprising the Pentagon didn't have anything more to say if the Tomahawk [Cruise missile] did well" (Miller 1991, p. 32).

CHAPTER FIVE

◆

The Media Propaganda War

IN THE MOST RELENTLESS bombing campaign since World War II, the U.S.-dominated multinational coalition systematically destroyed Iraq's military and economic infrastructure and inflicted terrible suffering on the Iraqi people. The Pentagon worked to project an image of a clean, precise, and efficient technowar war, in which the U.S. military was controlling events and leading the coalition inexorably to victory. The Pentagon disinformation "leaks" of a quick victory the first night of the war, disseminated by members of the media and political establishment, created a euphoric sense that the coalition forces were scoring a quick knockout victory, or "blowout" as certain media commentators called it. The videotapes of the precise bombing reinforced the image of a new era in high-tech warfare and the claims of a 100 percent Patriot intercept rate of Scud missiles were used to extoll U.S. technological superiority.

But events began to turn sour. Iraq maintained its Scud missile capacity and almost drove Israel into the war, an event that held unforeseeable results. The Scud attacks and the fear of chemical warheads created panic in Saudi Arabia and Israel. The dramatic coverage of these developments projected TV images of a war out of control. The spectacle of the Scud/Patriot conflicts dominated TV war coverage during the early stages and produced a sense of anxiety in the media commentators and the TV audience. Worst of all from the standpoint of the Pentagon and Bush administration, the Scud attacks made the military look bad. On Sunday, January 20, General Schwarzkopf said in a TV interview that the coalition had destroyed all fixed Scud missile launchers and had destroyed twenty of twenty-four mobile launchers. The same day Iraq fired ten missiles at Saudi Arabia (see 4.4) and would continue almost daily Scud attacks for the duration of the war. The U.S. military's failings in the Vietnam war, the Iran hostage rescue mission, the occupation of Lebanon, the Grenada invasion, the Libyan bombing, and the Panama invasion all spoke to the possibility that they might make a mess of things in the Gulf as well.

To be sure, Grenada, the Libyan bombing, and the Panama invasion had been presented as military victories, but, in fact, key weapons systems failed to work in all three actions. Troops failed to fight in Grenada, and there were serious coordination flaws and many mistakes in all of these attempts to flex military muscle and to use force as an instrument of foreign policy.[1] Indeed, the past military blunders constituted part of the military rationale to control the flow of information during the Gulf war. The credibility, prestige, and budget of the military establishment were at stake and the Pentagon did not want to risk another defeat in the arena of public opinion and thus tightly managed all news and information.

During the first days of the war, Hussein's "evil" and "madness" were downplayed by the Bush administration, Pentagon, and media in favor of the ideology of the efficient technowar. But it soon became clear that the war could not be sold to the public as an easy victory for the U.S. military, and so a renewed propaganda effort was necessary to mobilize support for the war effort. The military discourse of control and precision was not going to sustain support for the war in the face of embarrassing "collateral damage," Scud attacks, and Iraqi military and propaganda initiatives. Stronger measures were needed and the propaganda machine of the Pentagon and Bush administration geared up to produce a strategy that turned out to be highly successful: the demonization of Saddam Hussein and the Iraqi "enemy."

The Bush administration and media had already demonized Hussein and dramatized Iraqi atrocities (see Chapter 2).[2] Throughout the crisis in the Gulf and the Gulf war, Saddam Hussein and the Iraqis were presented as the foreign "other" to the moral, rational, and civilized coalition forces. This dichotomy between the irrational Iraqis and rational West builds on the "orientalist" discourse dissected by Edward Said.[3] "Rational" is equated with "just" and "moral" in this Western discourse, and "irrational" is connected with the "unjust" and "immoral" because justice and morality are grounded in "reason." Further, reason is identified with civilization and modernity, while its "other" is equated with "barbarism." This "orientalist" perspective also legitimated violence against the "barbaric" non-Western foreign other. During the Gulf war, the characterization of the barbaric, irrational, and immoral Iraqis was used to legitimate and conceal the arguably barbaric saturation bombing of Iraq by the United States and its coalition allies, who were driving Iraq back to a preindustrial era through their systematic destruction of its economic base.

During the war, Iraq engaged in activities that the U.S. propaganda machine could exploit. Totally overpowered militarily, Iraq fought what was largely a propaganda war itself. Its Scud missiles were more instruments of propaganda and terror than of war and the daily Iraqi press campaign used the crudest instruments of propaganda, which were easily ridiculed in the Western press: grotesque exaggerations of allied casualties and Iraqi victories, outright lies, and a bellicose nationalist, pan-Arab, and Islamic fundamentalist rhetoric that sounded quaint and eccentric, to say the least, to Western ears. Indeed, Hussein's propaganda war was not in the least directed toward the West but rather toward the Arab world. His Scud missile attacks on Israel were an attempt to galvanize Arab support in a holy war against Israel and the West; his Scud missile and rhetorical attacks on Saudi Arabia were an attempt to humiliate the Saudis, who had invited Western troops to their soil; and the vintage Khomeini-Islamic rhetoric channeled religious sentiments into support for war against the infidels.

But Iraqi propaganda directed to the Arab world was a dual-edged sword. Although Iraq's Scud attacks on Israel might have thrilled some in the Arab world, they disgusted most of the West; the parading of the captured POWs through Baghdad and their display on television may have excited some people, but the sight appalled others. Likewise, Hussein's propaganda and Islamic/Pan-Arabic rhetoric produced a negative resonance in the West. The U.S. propaganda campaign exploited all of these negatives to mobilize public hatred of Hussein and the Iraqis. Heating up the rhetoric of the Iraqi Hitler, however, had both political and military costs. Creating public desires for the elimination of Hussein generated the expectation, and even demands, for his overthrow and the destruction of his regime, thus significantly upping the military and political ante.

Both the United States and Iraq thus constructed an enemy that was inflated to represent absolute evil, constituting the other as satan, or the evil infidel. Both propaganda rhetorics were highly simplistic and merged religion, patriotism, and the forms of popular culture. Both propaganda strategies dehumanized the adversary and manipulated people's needs and fears into support of the government's official policies and both channeled aggressive impulses toward the enemy. Such manichean patriotism thus promotes a culture of militarism, which is to say, a culture of death and violence (see 10.5 for further discussion). The propaganda of Bush and Hussein were thus the mirror image of each other. Both denied their own aggressive actions and projected all belligerence and evil onto the other, blaming their enemy for all the inevitable horrors of war, while absolving themselves. Both denied their own responsibility for the war and sacrificed their people and nation's resources to advance their own interests, covering over their self-serving and destructive policies with propaganda.

5.1 POWs

The demonization of Saddam Hussein as a primary Bush administration focus intensified with Iraq's treatment of U.S. POWs. Iraq's air defense forces began shooting down coalition airplanes and taking prisoners of war (POWs). The January 18 NBC "Today" program announced that an unconfirmed report stated that Iraq had captured two U.S. pilots and that they planned to parade them before the foreign press. Throughout the day of January 19, CNN's Peter Arnett revealed that the Iraqis were holding POWs, whom they promised would be made available to the foreign press. Soon after, the Iraqis would make good on that promise. On Sunday morning, January 20, CNN reported an Iranian TV claim that Iraqi TV had shown films of two U.S. soldiers who were blindfolded and paraded through the streets of Baghdad. CBS ran the same story but cautioned that Iranian television was not known for its veracity, so independent confirmation was needed.

Shortly thereafter, however, Peter Arnett reported live on CNN that seven allied POWs had been interviewed that evening on Iraqi TV, dressed in military uniforms and sitting in front of a white wall. "One man had a bandaged hand. And two others had bruised faces." Each submitted to a series of questions and Arnett summarized their answers, quoting several of the POWs. U.S. Warrant Officer Guy Hunter was heard to say: "I think this war is crazy and should never have happened. I condemn this aggression against peaceful Iraq." Navy Lieut. Jeffrey Zaun said, "I think our leaders and our people have wrongly attacked the peaceful people of Iraq." Arnett remarked that the episode reminded him of the scenes from Hanoi during the Vietnam war where pilots and POWs were seen in films criticizing the war.

Immediately thereafter, the notorious Iran-contra felon, Richard Secord, came on CNN, introduced as an "anti-war expert"! Secord had been thrown out of the military for shady business connections and had run Oliver North's secret operation "the Enterprise," which purchased guns for the Nicaraguan contras from money obtained from illegal Iranian arms sales (and illegal drug sales according to many; see Cockburn 1988). Yet Secord seemed eager for a couple of minutes more of international fame and the chance to serve in the propaganda war, commenting that it is "sad to see this [display of POWs], but not surprising. These things are used for propaganda purposes." Indeed, but Secord and other military experts were also serving "propaganda purposes," and his very presence on CNN revealed that the media were instruments of U.S. propaganda.

CNN broadcast the audio portion of the Iraqi TV interviews with the POWs around 3:30 P.M. EST, a long, tedious transmission with questions in Arabic and then English and answers in English and then translated back to Arabic. A former POW in Vietnam, Daniel Pitzer, came on CNN afterwards and claimed that "these people have been coerced" in some way. Upping the rhetoric, Sen. John McCain (R-Ariz.), a former Vietnam POW, observed that "it's patently obvious that these men have been subjected to torture and physical beating . . . That's the only thing that would lead them to say anything against their country." The American people "must assume," McCain insisted, that "these people have been tortured."[4]

During the POW-propaganda campaign, McCain served as the Bush administration "point man," slickly conveying the administration line of the day to the media in countless appearances. For the next several days, the media debated whether the POW's injuries, evident in the televised version of the events that the Iraqis released, were a result of torture, or ejection from crashing airplanes. Around 8:30 P.M. on January 20, CNN announced that the United States was formally protesting Iraq's treatment of the POWs, claiming that coercing statements with mistreatment was a war crime. The U.S. appealed to Iraq to adhere to the Geneva Conventions and demanded immediate access to the POWs by the International Red Cross. Shortly thereafter, the Iraqi UN ambassador appeared on CNN's "Larry King Live" and claimed that the coalition POWs had not been abused and were being treated according to the Geneva Conventions. He also made the point that while Iraq held twelve unhappy coalition POWs, eighteen million Iraqis suffered from U.S. "inhumanity."

On January 21, the POW issue was the top story of the news and was widely discussed for days to come. The video portion of the interviews and clips were shown repeatedly throughout the day, focusing on the bruised and scarred faces, especially that of Navy Lt. Jeffrey Zaun, whose puffy and scared features became the symbol of the POWs plight; it was featured hourly on TV news (see Figure 5.1), prominently in newspapers, and even on the cover of a national news magazine (i.e., *Newsweek*, Feb. 4, 1991). CBS News led off its morning show with pictures of Zaun's face, accompanied by the headline that Iraq was releasing pictures of the POWs and that they will be used as "human shields." Dick Cheney appeared and denounced their treatment as a "war crime" on the morning talk shows and, one after another, former POWs appeared on all the networks to denounce the Iraqi treatment of the POWs. At 9:32 A.M., Deborah Norville of NBC's *Today* stated that "some American families can't believe their eyes and don't want to believe their ears after Iraq put

Figure 5.1 The bruised face of Jeffrey Zaun became the symbol of alleged Iraqi brutality against U.S. POWs. After the war, Zaun admitted that his injuries resulted from ejection and that he punched himself in the face a couple of times so that he wouldn't be put on Iraqi TV.

American POWs on TV with words put in their mouths by the Iraqis," words, she explained, "that sounded like previous Iraqi propaganda."

Radio, TV, and the press presented similar discourses on the POWs and thus contributed to the success of the Bush administration propaganda campaign. The PR model of media management was highly developed by the Reagan administration, which used a "message of the day" that was decided on in early morning strategy sessions. The message was then sent through the White House so that whenever reporters would appear, the various White House sources fed them the line that the administration wanted transmitted to slant the news toward its agendas. The president often appeared in a "photo opportunity" to dramatize the message, providing an image and "sound bite" for the evening's news (see Kellner 1990, Chapter 4).

The Bush administration continued this practice and even faxed its "talking points" every day to political allies, business executives, religious leaders, media figures and other "friendlies" who could be counted on to promote the administration's message. When the administration had a big message to get out, they would trot out their chief spokespeople in a carefully orchestrated campaign. On January 21 they wanted to get out the message that Saddam was torturing POWs and should be tried for war crimes. This message was articulated early in the morning by Secretary of Defense Dick Cheney, who appeared on the morning talk shows. It was the top message of the day in Marlin Fitzwater's briefing and was dramatized in a "photo opportunity" with George Bush, high-lighting its importance. The "message" was amplified by British Defense Secretary Tom King and Prime Minister John Major, both of whom provided rousing attacks on the alleged Iraqi violation of the Geneva Conventions and produced excellent sound bites for coalition television.

Returning from a weekend in Camp David, Bush departed from the presidential helicopter, coughed, yawned, and walked up to a microphone stating: "Let me say a quick word about the, uh, brutal parading of these allied pilots. . . . This is a direct violation of the, uh, every convention that protects prisoners. The International Red Cross, understand, certified to that today. . . . This will not make a difference in the prosecution of the, of the, uh, war against Saddam. . . . I would make the strongest appeal that these people be treated, uh, properly. . . . America is angry about this. . . . Everybody is upset about it." Bush was accompanied at Camp David by the Speaker of the House, Thomas Foley, who had spent the weekend with Bush to produce an image of bipartisan support for the war. Speaker Foley stood by Bush as he spoke and then concurred that the Iraqis were violating the Geneva Conventions concerning treatment of prisoners of war. A reporter shouted to Bush: "Will he [i.e., Saddam] be held accountable?" and the testy Bush replied: "Count on it."

And so Bush and Foley repeated the current propaganda line in the photo opportunity of the day to control prime-time news coverage and news briefs. They arrived just in time for the midday news programs and, of course, Bush's statement dominated the news for the rest of the day. This episode showed how the president can control news frames and the flow of news. We live in an era of news management where the state manages the media to get its line across and usually succeeds, especially in times of crisis. "Instant commentary" tends to be supportive, parroting what official spokespeople say, and this was precisely what happened during the POW event.

After Bush's statement, ABC's Peter Jennings brought out Bush administration point man Sen. John McCain, via satellite, for commentary. He and ABC Pentagon spokesperson Bob Zelnick repeated the Pentagon line concerning the violation of the Geneva Conventions and war crimes. John McWethy at the State Department added that the United States had warned Iraq concerning treatment of POWs and may call in the Iraqi *chargé d'affaires* today. And so, the TV parrots squawked the line of the day. McWethy and Peter Jennings emphasized the president's "strong message" that the allied military war effort would not be deterred by Iraq's threat to make the POWs "human shields" in their prosecution of the war. CNN anchor Reid Collins interpreted Bush's emphasis that

Saddam was "*dead* wrong" if he believed otherwise as an implicit threat on Saddam's life if the POWs were mistreated.

We see here an example of how the White House developed a propaganda line, fed it to the press, and the network correspondents dutifully reproduced the lines fed to them by their official "sources," usually without criticism or qualification. The Bush administration campaign worked brilliantly and the news, discussion shows, and media agenda were dominated by the POW issue for the next several days. Commentator after commentator followed John McCain's line that the appearance and discourse of the POWs proved that they were beaten or tortured, though occasionally an honest voice suggested that the injuries could have been sustained by ejection from the downed planes, but these cautionary voices were overwhelmed by the hysterical demonization of the Iraqis. Radio and television talk shows were dominated by discussion of the topic, with caller after caller insisting that the POWs were indeed beaten, tortured, and brutalized by the Iraqis, views which demonstrated the success of the Bush administration propaganda campaign.

After the war, the POWs appeared healthy and admitted that they had been well-treated by the Iraqis. Jeffrey Zaun confirmed that most of his injuries were sustained from his ejection from his plane, adding that he had punched himself in the face a few times so that the Iraqis wouldn't put him on TV.[5] McCain, Bush, and the many media commentators who claimed that the POWs were beaten and tortured had thus disseminated disinformation, and the public, which passionately bought into the Iraq torture discourse, was duped.

The Bush administration also raised the specter of war crimes trials of Saddam Hussein and the Iraqis at the end of the war. The networks focused on this topic repeatedly and the Bush administration and media continued to threaten Iraq and Hussein with war crimes trials for some time, threats which, in retrospect, appear to have been pure propaganda for, so far at least, there have been no inquiries or public moves in this direction. Perhaps the talk about war crimes stopped when former U.S. Attorney General and peace activist Ramsey Clark began holding international tribunals on U.S. war crimes in the Gulf starting in May 1991, a topic ignored by the mainstream media.[6] In any case, the rhetoric of Iraqi war crimes circulated by the Bush administration and media during the war now appears as part of a propaganda campaign to mobilize hatred against the Iraqis and to justify the slaughter of their people and the destruction of their civilian infrastructure, both of which became visible by the end of January (see the analysis in Chapters 6–10).

A propaganda war also involves the fabrication of disinformation and "white propaganda," which, like little white lies, are used to negatively portray the enemy or to boost one's own side. In late January, for instance, the networks circulated the story that Saddam Hussein's family had fled to Mauritania, and CNN, in particular, played the story repeatedly. Sen. Bob Dole (R-Kan.) used the story in interviews on CBS and NBC as evidence of the collapse of the Iraqi regime, although Tom Brokaw was forced to tell him that the story wasn't confirmed. CBS's pundit Fouad Ajami used the story to illustrate the evil of dictators, how they plunder and destroy countries and then flee from their crimes when events turn against them. When this story was deflated, the propaganda apparatus claimed that Hussein's family fled to Gambia.

In the next section, I provide some examples of "white propaganda" propagated by General Schwarzkopf and the U.S. military and spread daily through the media. Yet "propaganda" does not merely refer to fictional stories concocted to embarrass one's enemy, but also to constantly repeated codewords and claims, such as the oft-repeated description of "precision" or "surgical bombing." Indeed, the concept of propaganda is not self-evident and obviously the TV audience did not understand how the public was being manipulated by the U.S. government with military propaganda on a daily basis. In the popular mind, propaganda is simply outrageous and transparent deception and blatant falsehoods, such as the Iraqi claims that they were shooting down a large number of allied planes or winning the war. Such discourse was manifestly false and provided the impression that everything the Iraqis said was sheer lies and that their state was a propaganda machine in its very essence.[7] U.S. propaganda, by contrast, was more subtle and often had some basis in fact, though the United States also told some outrageous lies, which were, however, generally believed by the public (see 5.2, 6.3, 6.4, and 7.3).

For the propagandist, what matters are the effects of the discourse and not its truth. Propaganda is a mode of discourse intended to persuade, to manipulate, and to indoctrinate its audience into accepting policies and personnel that they might not otherwise support. It attempts to squash questioning and criticism by dramatizing evil and concealing facts that might be embarrassing for the forces disseminating the propaganda. It is important to note, however, that propaganda might not be purely false, but is rather a discourse that legitimates certain interests and policies while providing a one-sided, simplified, and distorted, but not necessarily totally untrue, view of events, people, or institutions. As Ellul (1965) pointed out, propaganda is not mere lies and must appeal to facts, though often selectively. The Iraqi regime *was* violating the Geneva Conventions by not immediately reporting the POWs' capture, by presenting them on TV, and by not allowing immediate access to the International Red Cross. This was rather common practice in the Middle East, however, and, in fact, in most of the world. But later evidence revealed that the POWs were not tortured and were, for the most part (there will always be exceptions), treated according to the Geneva Conventions. The Bush administration POW discourse intended to picture the Iraqi "enemy" (which was, don't forget, itself a symbolic construct of the Bush administration and media) as barbaric and savage and the coalition forces as civilized and humane.

In fact, the United States was also systematically violating Geneva Conventions while it was self-righteously condemning the Iraqis. Sources later revealed that the U.S. had run commando raids into Kuwait and Iraq before the war, using troops disguised in Iraqi uniforms and equipment—a clear violation of the Conventions.[8] U.S. forces allegedly kidnapped Iraqi ground troops and grilled them for intelligence and showed pictures of the captured troops on U.S. television, also violations of the Conventions. The United States systematically violated Article 56 of the Geneva Protocol 1 of 1977, which states, "Works or installations containing dangerous forces, namely, dams, dikes and nuclear electrical generating stations, shall not be made the object of attack, even where these objects are military objectives, if such attack may cause the release of dangerous forces and consequent severe losses among the civilian population." In addition, during postwar hearings Ramsey Clark and his colleagues presented nineteen charges of war crimes committed by the United States and its allies in violation of the UN Charter, Geneva Conventions, and international law in hearings after the war (Clark et al. 1992, pp. 11ff.).

The Bush administration effectively manipulated the mainstream media on the POW issue, which tended to follow Bush's propaganda line perfectly. Indeed, for the rest of the war the Bush administration continued to play its highly successful trump card of the demonization of Saddam Hussein and the Iraqis, mobilizing people's hatred for the bad guys of their propaganda scenario. Both sides, however, were guilty of heinous crimes, as those who engage in warfare and utilize and depend on propaganda for public support usually are. One of the functions of propaganda is to cover over one's own evil actions and the amount and excessiveness of propaganda that a regime employs is one measure of its own viciousness and mendacity. For propaganda is employed most readily by regimes having unpleasant actions to hide, which they dissemble with lies and disinformation that divert attention from their actions and focus attention on their opponent's evil ways. The utilization of systematic propaganda often suggests that a group is trying to hide something and to deflect attention from its own misdeeds and in the next sections we shall examine some U.S. attempts to cover over the effects of their bombing.

The anti-Hussein propaganda ploy, inaugurated during the first days of the crisis in the Gulf, worked effectively to mobilize a growing number of people to support the Bush administration war policy while splintering its opposition. Who could speak with sympathy of the suffering of Iraqis if they were brutes who were getting what they deserved? The Bush administration had found an excellent PR strategy to manage public opinion and to gain consent to its increasingly destructive war policies, and they carried this propaganda strategy through to the end of the war.

5.2 Disinformation and the Numbers Game

The Bush administration thus began orchestrating a campaign to mobilize hatred against the Iraqis, utilizing the negative image-making of their opponent that had served Bush so well in the 1988 election (see Kellner 1990). The Pentagon, by contrast, at first tended to utilize its technocratic ideology of control and efficiency in managing public opinion and projected a positive image of its endeavors. This effort involved the use of statistics in the daily briefings, reports on the progress of the war, and videos serving as visual evidence that supported their claims. Thus, Gulf war propaganda combined words and images that enhanced the U.S. military while demonizing the Iraqis. Yet the military's discourse on the POWs, for example, was circumspect and cool in contrast to the heated rhetoric of the Bush administration and its media allies.

The military had to overcome its Vietnam legacy in the briefing room as well as the battlefield. During Vietnam, military officials constantly juggled numbers and soon lost all credibility. The military news briefings became known as "The Five O'Clock Follies" and the daily body counts of dead Vietnamese appeared increasingly farcical and absurd (see Herr 1967 and Halberstam 1973). During the Grenada and Panama invasions, the military also lied day after day, but they successfully covered over their mistakes and lies, and the mainstream media did not seriously question the official accounts. The Gulf war was perceived as popular, and the cowardly mainstream media avoided any positions that might lose their audience shares and thus produce a decline in advertising revenues based on the number of viewers.

Technowar measures its successes and its ability to control the situation through numbers by means of quantitative measurement. The numbers game in the Gulf war focused on the number of sorties, planes shot down, and equipment destroyed. During the last days of the war there was a daily count of remaining Iraqi tanks, artillery, and ground vehicles rather than body counts. Although the United States provided running tallies, dutifully reproduced in graphics and charts by the media, of those missing in action (MIA), and occasionally noted that someone was "killed in action" (KIA), they never disclosed a running tally of those U.S. soldiers who died in the Persian Gulf war. There were over 100 casualties before the war even started, but these were rarely mentioned. Moreover, the military didn't list those who died by accident, as when the bunkers of soldiers in the desert collapsed or a helicopter crashed into a sand dune. And, of course, the Special Forces troops who died in covert actions were never mentioned. Consequently, the "killed in action" figures literally referred only to those who were killed in fighting with Iraqis. Thus, the total number of U.S. casualties was never really a part of the discourse of the war.

The U.S. military also renounced the numbers game of citing their estimates of Iraqi civilian and military casualties by claiming that they could not be certain of these figures. Of course, the military had estimates of Iraqi troop casualties, which they utilized to plan the ground war, but to this day these figures have never been released. The U.S. government's reluctance to release Iraqi casualty figures followed from one of the primary propaganda lines from the early days of the war—that the Gulf war was clean, precise, bloodless, and avoided civilian targets and casualties. Over and over, the Pentagon claimed that they were only focusing on military targets and did everything possible to avoid harming civilians. This line was soon refuted by images and facts (see Chapter 6 and 7), but at least for the first week, when consent was being formed, the war appeared to be relatively bloodless.

Of course, the military did everything possible to make sure that this image was transmitted and part of the media management strategy known as the pool system (see 2.2) was intended to keep out of the public eye all images of the inevitable injuries and death that war produced. The Pentagon, wanting to suppress memories of Vietnam and the human costs of war, forbade images of wounded Americans to appear and even made the U.S. reception center for dead soldiers at Dover, Delaware, off limits to the media.[9] The Iraqi government helped out by not allowing any images of human casualties of war during the first week. The Iraqis at first seemed intent on avoiding images of damage to their civilians and soldiers, and viewers thus saw very few images of the suffering, mutilation or death caused by the U.S.-led multinational forces' daily bombing runs. The Gulf war therefore at first appeared to be peculiarly antiseptic, a video war consisting of images of smart bombs and spectacular antiaircraft fireworks displays.

The pool system went way beyond censoring images of blood and death and attempted to assure that nothing in the least bit critical of the military would circulate. For example, early in the war, Frank Bruni of the *Detroit Free Press* used the adjective "giddy" to describe the returning F-117A fighter pilots after their first night's action; the military censor changed the word to "proud." Pilots aboard the aircraft carrier USS *John F. Kennedy* told an Associated Press reporter that they watched pornographic movies before their bombing missions, according to *Philadelphia Inquirer* reporter Carol Morello. She said that the censor deleted the information, claiming that it "would be too embarrassing" and also excised one pilot's use of an obscenity (Browne 1991, p. 44). Military censorship was thus actively involved in image-making and not just preventing information helpful to the Iraqis.

Schwarzkopf's Prevarications

The U.S. military also provided copious disinformation during the Gulf war and one of its top propaganda managers was the chief of the operation, Stormin' Norman Schwarzkopf. Although the cowardly media never exposed his constant prevarications, he continually provided disinformation and outright lies in his many official and unofficial meetings with the press. It is not certain in some cases, however, whether Schwarzkopf was simply lying or transmitting mis- or disinformation fed him by intelligence sources. Obviously, his figures were coming from official sources and he may or may not have consciously doctored them in specific cases. Yet the amount of disinformation conveyed by him suggests that in some cases he was consciously transmitting propaganda and even lying, as we shall see in this and succeeding chapters.

Propaganda works through the manipulation of misleading numbers and "facts," as well as deceptive generalizations and blatant lies. At the videotape briefing with General Horner on January 18, for instance, Schwarzkopf claimed that the allied bombing missions had an 80 percent success rate, repeating that number on ABC's "David Brinkley Show" on January 20. Schwarzkopf failed, however, to explain—as General Powell did on January 17—that the success rate was measured by the percentage of flights able to deliver their weapons and not by percentage of targets hit. Furthermore, it would be hard to believe that, even in Powell's weaker sense, the figure was still a "success" rate of 80 percent on January 20 because there were reports all weekend that bad weather had caused a large number of planes to return without delivering their weapons. Schwarzkopf, however, was obviously attempting to maintain the myth of a precise and effective war, and thus misled the public by failing to qualify what was meant by "success rate" and by inflating the figures of early coalition "success."

In fact, both sortie and success rate figures were fundamentally misleading. *Newsweek* reported on February 4, 1991, that by the time that the allies claimed that they had flown 20,000 sorties, only 11,000 or so were combat missions; "the others were flights by tankers, transports, radar planes and other nonfighting aircraft. Most of the 11,000 combat sorties did not attack ground targets. Only about one plane in four carried 'strike munitions.' The others were responsible for missions like air cover, electronic jamming and reconnaissance" (p. 32). Furthermore, of the one-fourth of the planes intending to deliver bombs or missiles, "success" merely meant that the planes dropped their loads. This figure, however, did not indicate how many targets were actually damaged, and *Newsweek* claimed that "the satellite pictures suggested an effectiveness rate of 'somewhere between 66 and 75 percent'" (p. 32)—a rate that declined significantly as the war grinded on, since the Pentagon admitted at the end of the war that 70 percent of the bombs missed their targets (see 4.2).

In addition, Schwarzkopf constantly underestimated the number of Scud missile sites remaining, producing figures to meet the needs of his political agenda. On the January 20 NBC's "Meet the Press," Schwarzkopf asserted that: "Our initial estimates were that they had approximately thirty fixed launchers and more than twenty mobile launchers. Today we're very confident that we have managed to neutralize the fixed launchers. Of course, the problem is the mobile launchers and the difficulty in targeting them. We have estimates that say that we may have killed as many as sixteen mobile launchers." Other military officials were, however, more accurate and honest than Schwarzkopf. The same day, in an NBC interview, Dick Cheney reported: "I would put their overall level at this point at perhaps thirty or forty launchers, but that's just a rough guesstimate."

Also on the same day as Schwarzkopf's number-cooking, NBC's Pentagon correspondent Fred Francis announced that the Iraqis had been buying Saab trucks from Sweden and converting them into Scud launchers. He disclosed that they may have as many as seventy of these highly mobile and hard-to-find launchers, deployed throughout the country. According to Wolf Blitzer of CNN, Israeli sources claimed that Iraq still had more than 100 mobile Scud launchers. During the weekend, it was also revealed that Iraq had been deploying decoy Scud launchers, which the multinational forces bombed and then claimed as a hit. Evidently Schwarzkopf didn't get these reports or he chose to disseminate disinformation in order to meet the propaganda need of the moment, which was to keep Israel out of the war by assuring them that the Scud threat was under control. The next day, after a harrowing night of Scud attacks on Saudi Arabia (see 4.4), Maj. Gen. Burton Moore, operations officer of the U.S. command in the Persian Gulf, admitted that the allies were "nowhere near" eliminating either the fixed or the mobile Scud missile launchers (*New York Times,* Jan. 22, 1991, p. A1). Thus, on this account, Schwarzkopf's "facts" were pure disinformation.[10]

Schwarzkopf also seriously misrepresented the extent to which the allied bombing had incapacitated Iraq's nuclear, chemical, and biological warfare programs during the early days of the war. On January 20 on CNN, Schwarzkopf insisted that there was "absolutely no question about the fact that the campaign to date has done a lot of damage to his chemical, nuclear and biological capacity." Then on NBC's "Meet the Press," Schwarzkopf made known his "high confidence that those nuclear reactors have been thoroughly damaged and won't be effective for many years." Next, on ABC, he claimed: "We've gone after his nuclear capability, his chemical capability, and his biological capability. . . . I can assure you that it's had a considerable setback, if not a total setback by this point in the game." More honestly and accurately, Britain's Defense Minister Tom King stated to BBC television the same day: "We have made the nuclear, biological, chemical facilities part of the first priorities for the attacks in the air campaign. We think there has been some significant damage done in those capabilities, but it would be very difficult, and we're not yet ready to certainly publish any assessment as to just how significant is 'significant.' . . . They've certainly been hit but the overall assessment [is] too early to make." And Britain's Armed Forces Minister, Archie Hamilton, gave a more realistic assessment of the effects of allied bombing on Iraq's chemical and biological weapons program when he told the BBC on their "Breakfast News" program of January 21 that it would be "a complete exaggeration" to say that "we've taken it all out" and he admitted that the allies had only done "some damage to his chemical establishments and so forth."

Throughout the war, the British would be far more honest and forthright than their U.S. counterparts, who constantly exaggerated their successes and minimized their failures and errors (see 7.3). Although the United States asserted early on that they had destroyed Iraq's unconventional weapons capacity, after the war these claims were put into question. General Powell, for instance, declared in a January 23 briefing that the U.S. had destroyed all of Iraq's nuclear reactors and General Schwarzkopf asserted in a January 30 briefing that "we have destroyed all of their nuclear reactor facilities." But by July 1991, there were claims that the bombing had failed to destroy Iraq's nuclear program, and Bush had to threaten bombing Iraq again to force Iraq to allow UN inspectors to examine its nuclear facilities. Sources claimed that Iraq had managed to hide some of its nuclear, chemical, and biological facilities altogether and to take crucial material out of the facilities bombed before the war. In August 1991, there were revelations that Schwarzkopf's bombers had failed to detect the "Big Gun" that Iraq was building to shoot missiles at

Israel, and TV showed pictures of the giant gun being built on the side of a mountain.[11]

Thus, in retrospect U.S. claims to have destroyed the Iraqi nuclear weapons program in the opening days of the war stand as empty bragging. Likewise, it is questionable whether the United States destroyed Iraq's biological weapons program as Schwarzkopf repeatedly claimed. Lt. Gen. Charles Horner, who was in charge of the coalition bombing campaign, was quoted in *Time* (Aug. 5, 1991, p. 31) as saying that "a strike by a conventional bomb could have spread a deadly agent across the countryside, killing millions. As a result, Iraq's biological stocks are largely intact, and a U.S. attack poses the same risks that it did during the war." So either General Schwarzkopf and his associates were lying when they claimed to have eliminated Iraq's biological weapons capability or Horner was telling a story that could legitimate renewed U.S. military action against Iraq.

Horner and Bush's assertions after the war that Iraq's nuclear, biological, and chemical weapons program had survived the bombing may be equally dubious, intended to coerce Iraq into allowing inspection of its facilities, or to legitimate renewed bombing, as Bush threatened. In any case, such claims should be seen as propaganda, intended to achieve certain effects and not as factual discourse. Propagandists adjust their "facts" to the political ends of the moment, totally disregarding truth. Such a daily rewriting of history is reminiscent of Orwell's *1984*, where a Ministry of Truth rewrote history to serve the political exigencies of the moment. "Ministries of Truth" in the so-called Western democracies consist of both the governments and the mass media, which rarely questioned the claims, facts, figures, and disinformation constantly served by the Bush administration and Pentagon.

During the Gulf war, the mainstream media rarely questioned the statements of George Bush and General Schwarzkopf as to their veracity or validity. Yet Schwarzkopf's exaggerated claims and doctoring of figures reveal interesting aspects of the authoritarian mind that he so perfectly exemplifies and the extent to which the U.S. military was continuing its practice of dissembling and lying for political ends. It was intolerable to authoritarians, who like to project an image of knowledgeability and control, not to be able to reveal in public how many Scud missile sites remained, what the extent of damage to Iraqi weapons capacity was, or what percentage of bombs dropped were successful. Technowar involves control over events that presupposes factual knowledge. Knowledge is a form of power for technowar managers and when they do not have accurate knowledge, they become desperate and deceptive. For example, bomb damage assessment was extremely difficult the first weeks of the war because of the bad weather, and the U.S. military obviously did not have complete information, as many of them admitted. Schwarzkopf, however, projected an image of certainty and control whenever he put his massive ego on line in front of the press and he would respond with anger and even rage when questioned or criticized concerning the obvious disinformation that he dished out regularly.

On the other hand, systematic disinformation and dissembling was typical of the U.S. military and has been the standard practice since Vietnam. The brilliance of the PR campaign of the Gulf war was that military lies, especially those of Schwarzkopf, were believed despite their often palpable contradiction by countervailing information. This was in part because people were so caught up in the war that they simply believed everything that General Schwarzkopf and the military told them and in part because the compliant media never criticized the duplicity and lies. Consequently, the Pentagon continually claimed that during this war they were telling the truth and were praised at the end of the war for being more forthright and honest than the military of the past. Dan Quayle made these points on a CNN "Newsmakers Saturday" on February 2, and General Powell and General Schwarzkopf made these claims repeatedly, as did CNN military "expert" retired General Perry Smith. These military officials and defenders endlessly asserted that the U.S. military was telling the truth and was avoiding disinformation. The excessive repetition of claims of truthfulness, however, is itself a sign that they might be attempting to conceal that they were not really telling the truth.

Indeed, to the claim that war *always* involves propaganda and lies, one could respond that during the Gulf war, the Bush administration and Pentagon were constantly making claims that they were telling the truth and thus could legitimately be investigated as to whether their claims were or were not true. With few exceptions, official U.S. discourse was accepted as true by the media and public during the war, though after the war the magnitude of U.S. propaganda and lies became apparent.

In addition to giving out false military information, Schwarzkopf and others in the media and military establishments continually circulated and in some cases created a spate of wild rumors concerning the Iraqis and Saddam Hussein: Hussein's wife and family had fled the country; Hussein had executed his top air force and antiaircraft commanders for their failure to fight; and Hussein was becoming mentally imbalanced and depended on heavy drug dosages to keep him functional. Schwarzkopf himself helped circulate these rumors as when he told *U.S. News and World Report* on February 11, 1991, that: "I would also tell you that we have several reports that Saddam is a very distraught man, that he has three doctors treating him with tranquilizers, which may say something about his mental state" (p. 36). Schwarzkopf also claimed that although some reports had Saddam on tranquilizers, "others have noted he has taken to pulling out his pistol and shooting some of his people—which isn't necessarily calm, by my definition" (Anderson and van Atta 1991, p. 161). Hence, did a U.S. general descend to the level of discourse of the *National Enquirer* and tabloid newspapers, disgracing the U.S. military and his country with his petty lies and propaganda.[12]

Civilian Casualties, the Infant Formula Factory Bombing, and Pentagon Lies

The biggest lie, repeated over and over by everyone from General Schwarzkopf to the lowliest briefer, was that the U.S. bombing campaign was precise and relatively bloodless, avoiding civilian targets and casualties. Initially, the Iraqis played into this propaganda line by not allowing pictures of the damage of coalition bombing or of civilian casualties. The first blood of the war was visible in the image of a badly injured man in a hospital in Tel Aviv, the victim of the second Scud attack on January 19. The visual images of the POWs were also extremely shocking because these were the first images of combatant injuries. But the first images of injuries and death were evident in the January 22 bombing of Israel, in which the Iraqi Scud missile attacks took their first casualties. A Scud missile hit an Israeli suburb of Tel Aviv and at least seventy people were wounded and three were killed. Ironically, the Scud missile was hit by a Patriot that evidently exploded at its tail, "sending it off the intended trajectory but leaving the warhead intact" (*New York Times,* Jan. 24, 1991, p. A). The diversion sent it crashing into an apartment, causing severe casualties and raised serious questions concerning how much protection the Patriot missile actually provides. But again there was little discussion of this key issue in the mainstream media, which had already elevated the Patriot to the status of technological hero. Yet some gruesome footage of heavily wounded Israelis was shown on television and *Newsweek* published on February 4, 1991, a large color photo of a woman covered with blood. With the sight of blood and death, the media propaganda war heated up.

Detecting a propaganda boon from images of casualties, Iraq began showing pictures of civilian damage on January 22, as they circulated images of a bombed Iraqi mosque, and soon began disseminating images of civilian casualties as well. In one of the most revealing battles of the propaganda war, the Iraqis affirmed that the United States had bombed an infant-formula factory, which the U.S. claimed was a biological weapons factory. The Pentagon had been asserting daily that the coalition forces were not bombing civilian targets, so this seeming refutation of its strategy was highly embarrassing. It reacted with a fierce campaign to discredit the report, which embroiled Peter Arnett and CNN in heated controversy.

This battle in the propaganda war began at 3:38 A.M. EST on January 23 with a report from Peter Arnett in Baghdad via telephone concerning "the bombing of what Iraqis claim is a baby-formula milk factory." Arnett announced that the Iraqis claimed that now, on the seventh day of the bombing, the multinational coalition was targeting not only strategic and military targets but civilian installations. The previous day, the Iraqi information ministry took Arnett to the western outskirts of Baghdad to visit an infant formula–factory that produced milk for infants. The Iraqis said that the plant was destroyed by coalition bombing, and Arnett added that the force of the explosion had torn the aluminum sheets from the side of the factory and scattered them all over the countryside. The steel girders that had supported the building were twisted and blackened and the machinery inside was a molten pile. CNN had visited it in 1990 and the sign in front of the plant read "Baby Milk Plant" in English and Arabic. CNN's 1990 footage accompanied Arnett's 1991 report and showed bottles of milk formula coming down an assembly line, with employees wearing white uniforms that said "Baby Milk Plant" on them in English.[13] The plant was producing 200,000 tons of formula a day and was the only source of instant formula for infants in Iraq. The plant was valued at $150 million; the Iraqis said it was destroyed in two airplane missile attacks on January 20 and 21, with four missiles used in each attack.

Within hours of Arnett's report, at the January 23 military briefing in Riyadh, Saudi Arabia, Pentagon spokesperson Mike Gallagher claimed that the plant was a "valid military target": "Apparently this facility, by what we've just learned has, uh, military guards around it, barbed wire fence. It has a military garrison outside and numerous sources have indicated that the facility is associated with biological warfare production." Gallagher read the report with a smirk, raising his eyebrow for emphasis as he read. On a live CNN report at 10:25 A.M. from Baghdad, Arnett was asked by anchor Bob Cain to respond to the Pentagon claim that the infant formula factory was heavily guarded and was a biological warfare plant. Arnett replied that there was only one guard at the gate and when he visited it previously he recalled seeing powdered milk from Britain coming in that was to be made into baby formula. "It looked innocent enough from what we could see," Arnett concluded and his report broke off at that point.

Around 2:00 P.M., Frank Sesno of CNN reported on the daily White House briefing and said that "unfortunately CNN's reporting out of Baghdad . . . came into question with Peter Arnett reporting earlier today that a baby milk plant had been destroyed." President Bush responded angrily to the report and Marlin Fitzwater subsequently went out of his way to discredit it, claiming that the United States had prior intelligence that the site was a biological weapons facility, ringed with barbed wire and heavily guarded. Fitzwater insisted that everything that Peter Arnett reported was subject to Iraqi censors. When asked if CNN was a propaganda arm of the Iraqis, Fitzwater replied that it was not, that CNN was free to report what it wanted, but any broadcast coming out of Baghdad was coming out of a totally controlled Iraqi government.

Colin Powell also commented on the baby formula plant (see below), clearly showing that a full-scale propaganda war was on between Iraq and the United States over the extent of damage to civilian targets from the U.S.-led coalition bombing. The campaign unfolded, first, when U.S. military spokespeople in Saudi Arabia attacked what they claimed to be Iraqi propaganda. Then the attack was repeated by the White House and the Pentagon (interestingly, Fitzwater alluded to Bush's anger, without bringing the president directly into the fray). As the *New York Times* reported the next day, "Mr. Fitzwater said that the plant was heavily guarded and surrounded by barbed wire, but refused to say what other evidence there was that the facility was used for germ warfare, or how it was obtained" (Jan. 24, 1991, p. 4).

As it turned out, this was a disinformation campaign: The U.S. command in Saudi Arabia, the White House, and the Pentagon were lying. The *Washington Post* later reported that the French firm that had built the factory insisted that it was a milk factory and that the equipment there could not produce biological weapons (Feb. 8, 1991, p. A1); the French contractor, Pierre Guerin, who built the plant insisted that it solely produced infant formula. New Zealand technicians who visited the plant repeatedly said that they saw powdered milk being produced there and questioned the U.S. military account, denying that there was a military garrison or special security around the plant (Feb. 8, 1991). In addition, a representative from the Nestlé corporation claimed: " 'We know this was a state-built infant-formula plant.' Company officials said they had regularly observed its construction in the last few years, 'because we like to be aware of the competition' " (cited in the *Village Voice,* Feb. 5, 1991). Yet the mainstream media went along with the White House version, with the exception of CNN, which broadcast reports of the return of Peter Arnett and other reporters to the milk factory; they showed that there was no evidence whatsoever that biological weapons were produced there, reports that intensified White House attacks on Arnett and CNN.[14]

After the war, however, on a BBC documentary on Operation Desert Storm that was shown on the A&E cable channel, the former director of defense intelligence, Lt. Gen. Leonard Perroots, admitted that "we made a mistake" and that the United States had faulty defense intelligence.[15] In a *USA Today* interview after the war, Gen. Merrill McPeak, head of the Air Force responded to a question concerning whether the bombing of the infant formula factory was a mistake by stating: "Time will tell what kind of factory that factory was. There is no doubt that we made some mistakes about what we bombed" (Mar. 20, p. 12). During the war, however, the U.S. military never admitted making mistakes and lied consistently to hide the fact that they were regularly hitting civilian targets. On February 8, Iraq asked the United Nations to send a fact-finding mission to determine if the infant formula factory was a biological weapons facility and the UN reported "that no biological capabilities or facilities existed" (Arkin, Durrant, and Cherni 1991, p. 104).

Obviously, reports of civilian damage represented a legitimation crisis for the Bush administration and Pentagon, who were claiming that the bombing campaign was precise, aimed only at military targets, and avoided all civilian damage. Almost every day for the rest of the war, the Iraqis asserted civilian damage from U.S. bombing and often confirmed it with graphic pictures of the destruction of nonmilitary sites and the mutilation and murder of innocent civilians. The Bush administration and Pentagon constantly dismissed these reports and often presented lies and disinformation as counterpositions. Military lies were sometimes accompanied by brutal admissions of the true intentions and philosophy of the U.S. military. In a January 23 Pentagon briefing, Colin Powell stated that, "Our strategy to go after this army is very, very simple. First, we're going to cut it off, and then we're going to kill it."

Technowar is clean and precise, but it is also brutal and deadly. At another point, Powell admitted that so far they had "killed" only 41 Iraqi aircraft out of 809, deflating earlier excessive claims (recall that the first night, when Wolf Blitzer reported continually that the allied military had totally destroyed the Iraqi air force, and network Pentagon correspondents debated the next two days whether 50 percent or 70 percent of the Iraqi Air Force was destroyed). Yet Powell revealed technocratic faith in the ability of coalition forces to destroy all Iraqi military material, asserting that, "[t]hese numbers will rise over time as we continue the campaign to go after shelters, go after bunkers, and essentially rip up the air force in its entirety." As it turned out, much of the Iraqi Air Force escaped to Iran and most of the rest of it hid throughout Iraq, thus reducing Powell's predictions to empty boasting.

Later that day a pool interview was released in which General Schwarzkopf also boasted: "Eventually we will destroy his air force." The war planners stressed over and over that they had concocted a comprehensive plan to totally destroy the Iraqi military, an aim made manifestly clear in Powell's briefing. In another revealing and oft-quoted phrase Powell stated that, "we have a tool box that's full of lots of tools, and I brought them all to the party, General Schwarzkopf has them all at the party." So war is a "party" for the techno-managers, who systematically will use their "tools" to annihilate the Iraqis and to "rip up" their military assets. In fact, the Persian Gulf war was a proving ground for these tools, many of which were untested in battle. It was also a project in which the overpowering superiority of the U.S. military would demonstrate that it could cut off and kill any army in the world—or at least a Third World army in the desert.

The total destruction of the Iraqi military was thus revealed as the goal of the technowar managers. Their vision entailed the methodical and systematic destruction of the Iraqi weapons facilities, tanks, artillery, armored vehicles, air force, and as many soldiers as necessary to humiliate Saddam Hussein and to defang Iraq as a military power. Over and over, the technomanagers used the words, "kill," "destroy," and "annihilate," or the more sanitary "attrit," an abbreviation of "attrition" that became one of the favorites of the Pentagon briefers (see 6.1), though Powell and Schwarzkopf preferred the harsh "kill." Their vision of a technowar that would totally destroy the Iraqis replicates the insane Nazi plan to systematically annihilate the Jews, and indeed the U.S.-led coalition would "kill" as much of the Iraqi military as they were able to get away with (although after the war General Schwarzkopf bemoaned the fact that he wasn't able to "annihilate" more of it). These technokillers became national heroes, to the shame of the nation.

One of the major points of Powell's briefing was that although the Iraqis had a lot of troops, so far all they had used were their inaccurate Scud missiles, which were weapons of terror, in contrast to the totally precise U.S. weapons, which were allegedly avoiding civilian casualties. Justifying the claim of precision bombing and avoiding civilian targets led Powell into denying the Arnett report, stating categorically: "There was a story earlier today about the infant formula factory. It is not an infant formula factory, no more than the Rabta chemical plant in Libya made aspirin. It was a biological weapons facility, of that we are sure, and we have taken it out." Note the combination of arrogance and certainty in Powell's mode of discourse: He was sure that the plant produced biological weapons and that it had been totally destroyed. Powell also claimed that the Iraqi nuclear facilities were destroyed: "I think I can confirm for you that the two operating reactors they had are both gone, they're down, they're finished, and the one that the Israelis took care of some years ago remains down."

This claim, too, was highly questionable, and the British press pointed out that the two reactors at Tuwaitha, near Baghdad, had nothing to do with Iraq's nuclear weapons program, as Powell implied. " 'The reactors have no military significance at all; they are of no significance for Iraq's nuclear programme,' said Dr Frank Barnaby, a nuclear physicist and defence analyst. 'They produce radioactive isotopes for medical purposes'" (*Observer,* Jan. 27, 1991, p. A11). Later, the International Atomic Energy Authority indicated that the reactors were only research establishments, "but if the reactors have been fractured there is a possibility of radioactive spillage and release into the atmosphere" (Vidal 1991, p. 136). The mainstream media in the U.S., however, seemed to be unaware that the Pentagon was handing them one piece of disinformation after another, articulated as categorical assertions, affirming certainty for claims that later turned out to be bogus. At one point, as General Powell showed a series of complicated graphs, doctored to confuse the Iraqis, he said, "Trust me, trust me." The press laughed, but this was exactly what most of them did and reports the next day indicated how Powell had "the press eating out of his hand" (*New York Times,* Jan. 24, 1991, p. A5).[16]

Yet it was certain that by carrying out enough daily bombing sorties, sooner or later the Iraqi army would collapse. Even if the Pentagon missed most of its targets (which it did), the daily carpet-bombing, cluster bombs, daisy cutters, and fuel-air explosives would sooner or later "attrit" the Iraqi army and force it to surrender or flee Kuwait (this matter is discussed further in Chapters 7–10). Powell's briefing, coupled with the unfolding of the bombing campaign itself, the most savage in history, should have made clear the brutality of the U.S. technowar. As it turned out, not only were the Iraqi people and their economic and military infrastructure the target and victim of U.S. bombing, but so was the delicate environment of the Persian Gulf, which would experience one of the greatest ecological catastrophes in history.

5.3 Environmental Terrorism

In a *New York Times* Op-Ed piece at the beginning of the war (Jan. 17, 1991, p. A15), Leonard Spector begged the Bush administration not to bomb Iraq's nuclear plants because of the dangers of lethal environmental contamination. A conference in London the first week in January, almost totally ignored by the U.S. mainstream media, warned against environmental holocausts either through the burning of oil wells or oil spills in the Gulf. John Vidal notes: "for all the justification given for combat, the possible environmental consequences were wilfully ignored by the United Nations, the European Community, all participating governments and the oil industry, before and during the conflict. Even though Saddam Hussein had warned the West in October 1990 that he would set fire to the wells and create and light 'a sea of oil', and the industry knew that he had mined the wellheads, the forces of government chose not to listen" (1991, p. 134).

The media also ignored the possible devastating threats to the environment from a Gulf war. The destruction of nature seemed to matter neither to the war managers nor to the media. When the devastation eventually became public it was processed as an event in the propaganda war with the U.S.-led coalition and their compliant media boosters blaming the environmental holocaust solely on Saddam Hussein and the Iraqis. Yet, as we shall see in this section, both Iraq and the coalition forces share blame for the wanton destruction of the environment that took place during the Gulf war.

The War on the Environment

The environmental effects of the Gulf war were largely suppressed by both the military and the media during the opening days of the fighting. In his January 18 military briefing in Saudi Arabia, General Schwarzkopf was asked if oil refineries were a target and he blandly noted that: "We have made it a point to not hit targets that are not of a military nature." This was a typical Schwarzkopfian evasion and soon after, the military briefers openly admitted that they were bombing oil refineries, claiming that these targets were of military significance. During the Pentagon briefing in Washington the same day, a reporter asked if damage had been done to the chemical, biological, and nuclear sites that the military had claimed were high priority targets. Again the briefers ducked the question.

ABC's "World News Tonight" on January 18 had the first comprehensive report on the war and environment, and Ted Koppel developed the theme further on "Nightline" that evening. The ABC News report noted that because the Kuwaiti oil fields were right on the Gulf, their destruction could be disastrous. Imagine, the report suggested, that after the war, the Iraqis could blow up one thousand oil wells, which would produce a mind-numbing environmental threat—a horror show illustrated by pictures of black, sooty smoke erupting from just one Kuwaiti oil well ablaze from U.S. bombing. ABC explained that Saddam Hussein had booby-trapped the wells and their torching could create a terrible smoke cloud affecting the climate and environment all over the world. Dr. Paul Crutzen from the Max Planck Institute in Germany claimed that temperatures could drop 10 to 15 degrees Celsius and cause an environmental disaster. A British scientist countered that it would be nothing more than a local event. Another scientist feared radioactive contamination after attacks on Iraq's nuclear facilities and toxic fumes from the wreckage of their chemical weapons facilities. Taking up the prophetic mode again, the ABC report also noted that Iraq may use oil as a weapon, as it did in the Iran/Iraq war, causing spills in the Gulf.

In a chilling NBC report on January 20, Pentagon correspondent Fred Francis made known the U.S. military belief that they had taken out most of the Iraqi chemical sites, but concluded that they had not totally destroyed the nuclear development or research facilities because their sensors had not picked up any radiation! The Pentagon thus admitted that it was prepared for nuclear contamination and was indeed seeking it as positive confirmation that they had destroyed Iraq's nuclear program! When, after the horrific environmental destruction of Vietnam after years of U.S. bombing, the Pentagon was forced to follow an environmental code, the Bush administration signed an order exempting the Pentagon from all environmental restrictions (see *New York Times,* Jan. 30, 1991, p. A14). When environmental issues came to the fore in the Gulf war, the Bush administration passed along an order on January 25 that no government agency could release any environmental information to the press or public.[17]

Oil fires and environmental destruction were evident, however, early in the war. One of the first skirmishes of the war involved a fight over eleven oil platforms near Kuwait that the Iraqis were using to mount antiaircraft attacks against allied planes. In a fight with U.S. troops, twenty-three Iraqis were taken prisoner and five were killed. In a pool report on the incident, broadcast by CNN on January 20, Lt. Cdr. Mark Jensen recounted that the ship accompanying the operation, the USS *Nicolaus,* was close to Kuwait and he could see a fire burning in an oil refinery. He described "burst oil tanks," presumably from allied bombing as this had occurred before there were claims that Iraq had torched oil wells and refineries. The results were "a big fire," Jensen said with a giggle, which made the "Louisiana oil fire [which had broken out in the Gulf of Mexico the previous year] look small." Furthermore, in a British military briefing telecast by BBC television on January 23, it was claimed by Maj. Gen. Alex Harley that Iraq's oil-refining capacity had been reduced by 50 percent as a result of allied bombing. Pictures of flames coming from Iraqi refineries outside of Baghdad were some of the first images to emerge from Iraq during the early days of the war, so there was no doubt that bombing Iraqi oil facilities was an important priority of the U.S.-led coalition war plan.

Thus, early on, there was confirmation that coalition bombing was producing oil fires in both Iraq and Kuwait. The stated coalition aim of destroying Iraqi nuclear, chemical, and biological weapons facilities also raised the issue of the environmental effects of the Gulf war. This concern, however, did not surface in the mainstream media until the United States claimed that Iraq was torching oil wells and refineries. When reporters and scientists began questioning the military and government in regard to the environmental effects of the multinational forces' bombing, they usually got evasive answers. For instance, in the January 21 military briefing in Riyadh, Gen. Burton Moore took the Schwarzkopf line, claiming that Iraqi nuclear and chemical facilities had been largely destroyed, but there was no response to the inquiry concerning the potential environmental effects of this destruction.

Yet accounts began to emerge in the foreign and alternative press concerning potential environmental damage. In a January 24 British Channel 4 report, Dr. Tom Wilkie claimed that the area of Iraq around these bombed chemical and biological weapons facilities "must be rather unpleasant and contaminated with, presumably, with mustard gas and other noxious chemicals. . . . I certainly wouldn't like to be in the neighborhood of the chemical plants that have been attacked." Journalist Randy Thomas reported on January 26 to the Environment News Service that a Gulf Peace Camp volunteer, who just arrived in Jordan from Baghdad, "told of fleeing a 'chemical cloud' in one section of the city. 'You could see and smell it,' he said. We ran for our lives." Dr. Abdullah Toucan, science adviser to King Hussein, told Thomas that he was concerned about the release of Seranian, mustard gas, and other chemical warfare agents following the destruction of an Iraqi chemical warfare factory. Toucan feared even more nuclear contamination from the bombing of a five-megawatt nuclear plant near Baghdad.

In a January 30, 1991, briefing General Schwarzkopf claimed that the coalition forces were using precision weapons to bomb Iraqi weapons facilities and were being "very, very careful in the method of attack and the munitions used, to ensure that we didn't have any contamination." Arkin, Durrant, and Cherni noted, however, that *Aviation Week & Space Technology* reported on April 22, 1991, that a "massive (and seemingly disorderly and unsuccessful) attack by some 32 F-16 fighters carrying unguided general purpose bombs preceded a later attack by F-117 stealth aircraft carrying laser-guided weapons" on the heavily guarded nuclear research facility on the outskirts of Baghdad (1991, p. 97). A later *Aviation Week* report noted that, "[s]mokepots around the facility obscured the target, and antiaircraft fire was too intense to linger in the area" (1991, p. 97). Lt. Col. Robert Maher, commander of the 417th Tactical Fighter Training Squadron of F-16s, claimed that, "[t]hey lofted bombs from a fairly great distance and did little damage with a large number of aircraft." This refutes Schwarzkopf's specious claims concerning the precision used in bombing nuclear, chemical, and biological warfare facilities and raises the question concerning the degree of environmental contamination from coalition bombing.

Schwarzkopf claimed during the January 30 briefing that coalition forces had "destroyed over eleven chemical and biological storage areas" and had "destroyed or heavily damaged three chemical and biological production facilities." He also noted that, "we're going to continue a relentless attack on this very, very heinous weapon system," and by February 11, Lieutenant General Kelly stated that "very, very little NBC [nuclear, biological, and chemical] production was going on in Iraq." Concerning chemical contamination, Arkin, Durrant, and Cherni report:

> On 18 January, the chief of Soviet Chemical Troops warned that an attack on Iraqi chemical facilities would release dangerous concentrations of sarin and tabun, spreading to several dozen kilometers. On 22 January, the *Washington Times* reported that a Czech chemical reconnaissance unit in Saudi Arabia detected trace quantities of chemical weapons in the air. On 3 February, French military officials stated that the allies had detected traces of nerve gas fall-out as a result of allied bombing. 'We have found traces,' Gen. Maurice Schmitt said on Channel 4 TV in the UK on 4 February. 'We think that they could only come from chemical weapons and what we've picked up was along the border as well as in the sea' (1991, p. 100).

I would add that on January 26, ABC and CNN reported that coalition forces had detected chemical contamination in Saudi Arabia (see Chapter 6, note 13). Later, the Environment News Service reported on February 11, 1991, the spread of an unknown and rapidly progressing disease, after a biological weapons production plant near Baghdad was bombed. Fifty Iraqi soldiers mysteriously died from exposure to biological agents around these bombed-out plants. The U.S. military came close to admitting responsibility for nuclear or chemical contamination when Lt. Gen. Thomas Kelly replied in a January 29 briefing: "The initial assessment I saw was that, if there was any [nuclear or chemical contamination], it would be very localized. Precisely what it is, I don't know the extent of it." Other U.S. military briefers also admitted the possibility of environmental contamination, raising the issue that the Geneva Convention prohibits attacks on installations containing "dangerous forces" (see Arkin, Durrant, and Cherni 1991 and Clark et al. 1992). But despite the significance of the issue, the mainstream media almost completely ignored the issue of environmental contamination from coalition bombing.

On January 22, however, the corporate media focused on the environmental damage to the Gulf when the Iraqis were reported to have deliberately set Kuwaiti oil wells and refineries on fire. CNN reported during the early morning hours of January 22 that allied military authorities claimed that Iraq had deliberately torched oil wells and storage tanks at the al-Wafra oil field in the south of Kuwait and that there were reports of oil fires at two refineries as well. A bit later, during the early morning CNN "Business Day," it was announced that Iraqi forces had blown up Kuwaiti oil facilities and that the Iraqis might have been trying to keep the United States from starting a ground war by fouling the battlefield with dark smoke that would hamper U.S. high-tech military activity. Earlier in the day, Dr. Abdullah Toucan appeared on a CNN segment claiming that such oil fires could influence target detection, hamper air support, and thus could be a military tactical weapon. Without going into the environmental threats that he had earlier described in the CBS and ABC segments, Toucan darkly hinted that the tremendous amount of carbon monoxide in the fires might be a more effective weapon than the chemical weapons that had been the focus of so much media attention.

According to CNN, Iraq was making good on a threat to make the Middle East an inferno, and pundit Lawrence Korb of the Brookings Institute speculated that Saddam Hussein knew that he would eventually lose the war and wanted Kuwait to be left with nothing and make it more difficult to bomb his troops as they departed. This alleged "scorched earth" policy was interpreted as evidence of how badly things were going for Iraq, and how malicious Hussein and the Iraqis were. Nothing was said, of course, concerning all the oil fires that allied bombing had produced. The other morning TV news programs also interpreted the oil fires as expressions of Iraqi evil, without mentioning the equally pernicious effects on the environment of the U.S. bombing, which had caused an oil fire in Kuwait two days before as well as producing oil fires in Iraq, and the potential chemical, biological, and nuclear contamination caused by coalition bombing. There was no real discussion the entire day of the new environmental threats from the oil fires, which resulted from the actions of both sides. Instead, Bush administration and media attention still focused on the POW issue, which was reaping such a fabulous bonanza in demonizing the enemy.

Another ominous environmental event was revealed on January 24 when ABC's Forrest Sawyer reported from Saudi Arabia that Baghdad radio claimed that two Iraqi oil tankers were hit and were leaking a huge amount of oil into the Persian Gulf. Later that morning, at the U.S. military briefing at Riyadh, Saudi Arabia, Col. Greg Pepin reported that two Iraqi oil tankers doing intelligence work had been attacked and disabled by U.S. naval air operations, setting off secondary explosions. There were fires on the deck, he noted, and during the questioning Pepin admitted an oil spill of one-half mile of refined rather than crude oil, which he claimed burns faster. The story was given little exposure and probably would have been forgotten were it not for a massive oil spill that appeared the next day and that produced one of the more significant battles of the propaganda war.[18]

The Middle East News Network reported on January 25, 1991, that: "Saudi environmental authorities yesterday spotted two oil slicks off the coast of Kuwait, hours after Iraq claimed oil was spilling from two of its tankers attacked by Allied planes." Moreover, "A U.S. military spokesman said U.S. Navy A-6E Intruder fighter jets had hit one Iraqi tanker and one hovercraft in the Gulf and that a small oil spill occurred, probably because of the attack. The Meteorological and Environmental Protection Agency said one slick was just off the coast of the Saudi town of Khafji on the Kuwait border and another was near Saudi Arabia's Safaniya offshore oil field." U.S. Air Force Master Sgt. Jack Siebold admitted, "We assume the oil spill was caused by the attack on the tanker." *Platt's Oilgram News* reported a similar story on January 25, 1991, and the question would arise later in the day whether this was the source of the oil seen splashing on the beach near Khafji.

At the U.S. military briefing in Riyadh, Saudi Arabia, on January 25, Maj. Gen. Robert Johnston responded to a question from a reporter who asked if fires reported around Kuwait City were caused by U.S. bombings by stating, "the answer to that is no." Discussion then turned to questions concerning what caused the massive oil slick that had just appeared. When asked if this was caused by coalition combat operations, Johnston replied that "I can't respond to that." Nobody brought up Pepin's briefing of the previous day, when he admitted that the United States had caused an oil spill by bombing two Iraq oil tankers, which they claimed were sending out intelligence communications. Johnston speculated that "it's a lot of oil to pump in there accidentally" and suggested that it was possible that the Iraqis blew up the oil storage station, but he seemed edgy and evasive.

During the Saudi military briefing, National Public Radio reporter Deborah Wong asked about the oil spill and the Saudi military briefer, Col. Ahmed al-Robayan, said that Saudi General Khalid had been at a meeting with scientists from the Ministry of Petroleum and Mineral Resources to study the problem and to find solutions. The Saudis believed that the Iraqis had deliberately caused the oil spill and that they expected this based on their knowledge of the Iran/Iraq war, where there had been "oil spilling." The oil was moving from the north to south, al-Robayan explained, and the spill was about fifteen kilometer's long and was following the water movement and weather. It had begun three days earlier, he claimed, and had moved fifteen kilometers south from its origin at the Sea Island Terminal, the main Kuwaiti offshore loading station. When asked if the oil spill threatened the desalination plant in Khafji, the Saudi military briefer answered that the "oil is going out away from Khafji." This point of information would be extremely interesting, as we shall soon see.

At 11:24 A.M., CBS's regular programming was interrupted by a live report from Pentagon correspondent David Martin, who said that the

Pentagon claimed that it has reports of a massive oil slick, though there were different claims concerning its origin. The spill was comparable to the *Exxon Valdez* disaster and was estimated to be two miles wide and twenty miles long. Martin speculated that the oil spill could be a major Iraqi military operation intended to impede an allied amphibious operation and foul up a Saudi desalination plant, an action that could threaten the water supply. Martin's report was illustrated with pictures of oil splashing on the shore and birds dripping with oil, conveniently provided to dramatize the report, which would eventually turn out to come from another oil spill altogether.

Around 1:40 P.M. CNN's Frank Sesno announced from the White House that Marvin Fitzwater had indications that Iraq was dumping large amounts of crude oil from a Kuwaiti oil storage tanker into the Persian Gulf. Fitzwater said that he had "no particular read" on Saddam Hussein's motivations for doing this: They may be military or just meanness. Bush was briefed on this spill, which had been developing for three days. Moreover, the Department of Defense was assuming primary responsibility to control the oil flow. In addition, experts from the Environmental Protection Agency and other government agencies and environmental groups were being assembled to discuss how to deal with the problem.

Technowar requires control of all contingencies, of being totally in control of the situation, so the Bush administration and Pentagon constantly stressed their plans to control the disaster. They repeated that the spill had no military significance and would not interfere with their war plan. Such a blatantly specious claim, repeated over and over, raised the suspicion that this was a propaganda line and honest military commentators pointed out that obviously the oil spill would be of military significance in days to come, despite what the Pentagon and Bush administration claimed.

Throughout the day, CNN played a British ITN report narrated by Peter Sharp that covered the oil spill. Interestingly, the ITN team got the footage outside of the pool system. It was later revealed that there was a pool team present in the Khafji area when the spill was discovered, but they were not told about it by their military escorts and thus were not able to photograph the spill or inquire into its origins. In any case, the ITN tape turned out to be of great propaganda value to the Bush administration and Pentagon; it provided pictures to mobilize disgust against Saddam Hussein, who had allegedly caused the spill that was polluting the beaches and killing the wildlife. However, as we shall see, there were claims that the oil spill and devastation that was shown throughout the day was the result of U.S. bombing.

Sharp's extremely powerful ITN report documented in words and images the environmental holocaust that the Gulf war produced. "Looking across enemy lines into occupied Kuwait this morning, smoke from the al-Wafra oil field set alight by the Iraqis clouds the horizon. Oil analysts and scientists believe that setting fire to the Kuwaiti fields and storage facilities could bring environmental catastrophe to the region," Sharp narrated as the images showed burning oil wells. Sharp next described a new disaster. "It was the cormorants stumbling across the highway near the beach that signalled something was wrong." Images of oil-soaked birds were followed by images of thick oil washing onto the shores. "Neither side is admitting responsibility for this disaster, but these scenes will be repeated in the days and weeks ahead. . . . No one should be surprised at this. It's exactly what environmentalists said would happen if war broke out." The cleanup will be very difficult, he stated, because it is in the war zone, and thus pollution threatens the entire Persian Gulf which was now "a major casualty of this war."

At 3:00 P.M., George Bush held an unscheduled press conference and the questions centered on the oil spill. When the president himself intervened there was obviously a major propaganda campaign on. Indeed, both the White House and the Pentagon mobilized their top spokespeople and propaganda apparatus throughout the day to blame the oil spill on the Iraqis. When asked by UPI reporter Helen Thomas to comment on the oil spill, Bush replied:

> Well, there's a lot of activity going on right now, trying to figure out what the best course of action is to clean this mess up, to stop this spill. Saddam Hussein continues to amaze the world. First, he uses the Scud missiles that have no military value whatsoever. Then he uses the lives of prisoners of war, parading them and threatening to use them as shields. Obviously, they have been brutalized. And now he resorts to enormous environmental damage in terms of turning loose a lot of oil. No military advantage to him whatsoever. It's not going to help him at all. Absolutely not. It has nothing to do with that.

Note that Bush's rambling response was pure propaganda, mobilizing, first, the technocratic ideology of control and then quickly shifting to the propaganda lines of the previous days that cumulatively demonized Hussein and the Iraqis: the indiscriminate use of Scud missiles, the parading and brutalizing of POWs, and now the destruction of the environment. In retrospect, Bush's blaming of the oil spill solely on Hussein and the labeling of him as an "environmental terrorist" were among the most daring and hypocritical moves in the propaganda war. The hyperbolic nature of Bush's propaganda rhetoric emerged in further answers to questions in which he characterized Hussein's alleged act as a "sick" act of desperation that had outraged the entire world and that his acts were "totally irrational."

It remains for future historians to judge how rational and healthy Bush's actions in the Gulf war were, though it was immediately obvious that the labeling of Saddam Hussein as an "environmental terrorist" was another example of Bush's hypocrisy. The United States had been bragging daily in the military briefings about destroying Iraq's nuclear, biological, and chemical facilities, destruction that undoubtedly had produced environmental contamination. Moreover, the U.S. admitted destroying oil installations in Iraq and a British military briefing even stated that the allies had destroyed more than 50 percent of Iraq's oil-refining capacity. Obviously, such destruction of oil installations was going to cause oil fires, spills, and pollution, therefore it was clear that both sides were engaging in environmental terrorism, that war itself is a mode of environmental terrorism. Thus it was sheer hypocrisy for Bush to attack Hussein for what the United States did regularly in this and other wars.[19]

The media, however, did not pursue the issue of the extent of environmental destruction caused by the United States and its allies in the war and privileged the U.S. version, which became more detailed and aggressive as the day proceeded. At the 3:30 P.M. military briefing at the Pentagon, the propaganda war over the oil spill intensified. Pentagon spokesperson Pete Williams claimed in his opening remarks that Iraq had been spilling oil pumped from the Mina al-Ahmadi storage facilities in Kuwait to the Sea Island Terminal, ten miles from shore, where the oil was released into the sea. This was, Williams insisted, an act of "environmental terrorism," which was causing an oil spill likely to be twelve times bigger than the *Exxon Valdez* spill, as several million barrels of oil had already been spilled and millions more were expected. As Williams spoke, the CNN viewer was treated to images from the ITN report of black oil splashing onto the beach with birds covered with oil. This was, he added, an environmental concern and not a military concern, repeating the Pentagon propaganda line that the oil spill was not of military significance.

Williams was not clear on exactly where the oil was coming from, when the spill started, or what its nature and direction was. He admitted that while at least "one-half" of the oil was dumped into the Gulf from the Sea Island Terminal, some of the oil might have come from five Iraqi oil tankers, located in the vicinity of the al-Ahmadi storage facility. Nobody asked Williams if these were among the oil tankers that the United States had admitted bombing and that the Iraqis claimed were the source of the oil spill. Although the Saudis asserted that the oil spill had started three days earlier, and the ITN report indicated that it had been underway for thirty-six hours, Williams claimed that the Pentagon had only become aware of the oil spill in the last twenty-four hours (though Marvin Fitzwater had earlier told reporters that the White House had known of the spill for several days). Either the White House was not talking to the Pentagon or a cover-up was underway. Although Williams declared that there were already several million barrels of oil dumped in the Persian Gulf, the military briefer that morning in Riyadh had stated that the Sea Island terminal was only capable of discharging 100,000 barrels a day. The facts and figures were not adding up.

The official Pentagon briefer of the day, Lt. Gen. Tom Kelly, continued to deny that the oil had any military significance and when skeptical reporters continued to ask why Iraq might have dumped the oil, he replied: "It makes as much sense militarily as shooting Scud missiles into population centers," and he called it "another act of an international terrorist." Thus, the Pentagon and Bush administration strategy was to equate the oil spill with Hussein's other allegedly irrational and terroristic acts and to present it as another instance of his "evil."

Some of the initial media reports exhibited a cautious skepticism toward the Bush administration/Pentagon version of the oil spill. At 6:30 P.M., the "CBS Evening News" opened by describing "a new ecological disaster beyond anything the world has seen." The CBS report indicated that "the facts are unclear" and it was not certain whether the oil spill was a deliberate act of environmental terrorism, as the Saudis and United States stated, or a result of coalition bombing. Dan Rather reported that George Bush and Dick Cheney were saying that the oil slick was from a deliberate oil dumping by Saddam Hussein, while others asserted that it may have been leaking from oil facilities damaged by allied bombing. The CBS report depicted Dan Rather asking Dick Cheney in a filmed interview: "What proof do we have that the Iraqis did it?" Cheney answered: "As best as we can tell, it is a conscious release of oil from one of the offshore loading terminals off the coast of Kuwait. The size of it, the fact that it continues, gives every indication that it is a deliberate release by the Iraqis of Kuwaiti oil. . . . All of the evidence that we've seen to date, it looks to me like a conscious release of oil by the Iraqis." Note the slight equivocation in Cheney's report ("As best as we can tell," "it appears to be"), compared to George Bush and Pete Williams's categorical allegations. Returning quickly to his usual propaganda mode, however, Cheney stated how he was continually amazed at Saddam Hussein's willingness to operate as an "international outlaw" with chemical weapons, hostages, Scud attacks, and the environmental terrorism of "his massive oil spill." Cheney implied—following Bush's propaganda line almost verbatim—that if Saddam Hussein had done all of these other horrible things, then he must have caused the oil spill as well.

Although CBS news claimed that there were two different explanations concerning who and what caused the oil spill, ABC bought into the official Bush administration/Pentagon line that the Iraqis were the sole culprits, not even questioning the official reports. ABC's "Nightline," for example, in their January 25 program dutifully reported the dual propaganda line that the oil spill was caused by the Iraqis, who had allegedly consciously dumped oil into the Gulf and that it had no military significance. During the evening of January 25 and the following days, there was no debate over the cause of the oil spill on any of the talk programs, and almost every person asked about the spill on discussion shows or who mentioned the spill in news reports blamed it on the Iraqis, or merely assumed that the Iraqis did it and speculated on the reasons.

Over the next few days, Iraq continued to deny responsibility for the huge oil slick and said that allied bombing had produced it, hurling back at the Americans the charge of "environmental terrorism." The Iraqis claimed, according to Baghdad Radio: "The alliance planes bombed oil installations in the province of Kuwait and targeted oil pipes which ignited a fire and led to the flow of quantities of oil" into the Gulf (*New York Times,* Jan. 29, 1991, p. A6). The Iraqi UN ambassador categorically denied that the Iraqis caused the oil spill and Iraqi Foreign Minister Tariq Aziz called for a UN team to investigate the oil spill. So far, there has been no official investigation, and it is still difficult to know who to believe, concerning who caused the oil spills.

The mainstream media, of course, privileged the U.S. version, blaming the spill on the Iraqis. Yet some media reports in the coalition countries over the next days would be more balanced in their official news summaries. CNN would frequently open a progress report on the oil spill by stating that the United States blamed the spill on the Iraqis while the Iraqis blamed it on allied bombing. Some newspapers hinted that there were two versions, but also usually privileged the U.S. account, as did the mainstream weekly news magazines.[20] On January 26, the *New York Times* reported: "Iraq filed a complaint with the United Nations saying that the United States caused the slick by bombing two tankers in the gulf, a charge the White House denied" (p. A5). The rest of the report documented the U.S. version, with no elaboration of the Iraqi claim. There was an interesting chart, however, which stated: "Millions of gallons of oil floated southeast yesterday from tankers at the port of Mina al-Ahmadi *and* [italics mine] from a nearby offshore oil loading dock" (p. A4). The "and," not discussed or analyzed in any articles in the paper, suggests that there may have been at least two sources for the Gulf oil spill.

Indeed, the U.S. military briefer on January 23 had already admitted the sinking of Iraqi oil tankers, and evidence existed that from the beginning of the war, the U.S.-led coalition had bombed oil facilities in Iraq and Kuwait, causing fires and other damage. During the morning of

January 26, the TV version of the war oscillated between categorically assuming that the Iraqis were responsible for the spill and journalistic "balance" that contrasted the Iraqi claims with the U.S. ones. The U.S. position was, of course, privileged because most reports accompanied their version with clips of Bush administration or Pentagon officials blaming the spill on Iraq and their "environmental terrorism," and the audience had been positioned to believe that anything that the Iraqis claimed was mere propaganda whereas the U.S. was telling the truth.

During the morning military briefing in Riyadh, Saudi Arabia, Lt. Col. Mike Scott indicated in his opening statement that "Iraq continues to dump oil into the Northern Arabian Gulf. . . . The resulting oil slick has now grown to approximately 30 miles by 8 miles wide. Overall, from a military standpoint, the oil slick is minimal. However, from the environmental standpoint, you can see that it's going to have a major impact." In response to a question concerning the origin of the oil spill, Scott went to a map and, pointing to the Sea Island Terminal, stated that the oil spill started ten miles off shore, and was moving south. When asked if it was moving toward the shore, Scott said it did not yet pose a threat to the shorelines. When the reporter then asked what caused the on-shore oil spill that the television images were showing, Scott knitted his brow and said that he didn't know, suggesting that the oil near the shore "might be, er, part of it, or it may be something else that's out there."

This concession suggested that there might well have been more than one source of the oil spill. The possibility of several oil spills supports parts of both the Iraqi and the U.S. versions, implying that both sides were responsible for the environmental damage and that both countries were engaging in environmental terrorism—that the Persian Gulf war itself was an act of environmental terrorism. If the oil polluting the shoreline, which had so appalled world TV audiences who viewed the ITN report, was a result of U.S. bombing of Iraqi oil tankers, this would be embarrassing for the Bush propaganda team, which had made such aggressive attacks on Iraq's "environmental terrorism" and the psychological sickness of Saddam Hussein.

Some sources were actually claiming that the United States was responsible for the oil seen pouring onto the Saudi beaches, which was killing the birds and befouling the coastline. Britain's Channel 4 News claimed on January 28 that although it seemed clear that the major oil slick in the northeastern Gulf was the result of the opening of valves on two major oil tanks in Kuwait by the Iraqis, the oil pollution on the beaches of northeast Saudi Arabia was the result of damage caused by U.S. military action. Channel 4 News said that the U.S. authorities admitted this on Friday, and it had been confirmed by Saudi oil officials. This means that all the TV pictures of dead and dying cormorants and oil washing the beaches of Saudi Arabia, which were being used as illustration for stories about Iraqi environmental terrorism, were actually the result of collateral damage to—or deliberate attacks on—oil facilities by U.S. forces.

It was thus becoming clear that there had been two oil spills. In the January 26 Pentagon military briefing in Washington, Pete Williams disclosed the Pentagon's belief that the oil was coming from both the oil storage tanks in the Sea Island Terminal and five Iraqi tankers in the port at Mina al-Ahmadi, thus admitting that there were two oil spills, but blaming both of them on the Iraqis. This would be the official U.S. line for the next several days, though it vacillated in interesting and revealing ways, and concealed the admission by the U.S. briefer on January 24 that the United States had bombed two tankers, which were spilling oil into the Gulf.

Schwarzkopf's Fable

On January 27, the Saudis were blaming both oil spills on the Iraqis, claiming that the second spill came from an oil tanker at Khafji, which the Iraqis had shelled some days before, and that this spill was befouling the beach and killing the birds, as seen on TV. Shortly thereafter, the world was treated to a somewhat different version in a briefing by Gen. H. Norman Schwarzkopf. The general began his briefing by reading, with glasses on, an "operational update" consisting of the day's statistics, just the sort of "factual data" that the military technocrat enjoys before his formal briefing. Then, Schwarzkopf took off his glasses and spun a yarn about the origins of the oil spill and his recent military action to try to stem it. Schwarzkopf began his narrative with the assurance that his story comes "from hard evidence, schematic in nature, but pretty accurate" ("pretty accurate"?). According to Schwarzkopf's fable: Once upon a time on the coastline of Kuwait near the port Mina al-Ahmadi, there were five Iraqi ships. On January 16, they were riding low in the water because they were full of oil; on January 24, they were suddenly riding high because they were empty of oil. Ergo, the evil Iraqis dumped the oil from these tankers into the sea. Ten miles out from the port there was a Sea Island Terminal that had an oil buoy next to it that fed hungry oil tankers. There was now a flood of oil coming out of the oil buoy because the Iraqis opened its spigots and pumped oil into the Persian Gulf. The general checked his records and found that "we see absolutely no indications at all, no indications at all, that any U.S. military action caused this to happen."

The general and his staff began consulting with experts concerning the damage to the environment and military action that could be taken to solve the problem. Experts advised that the oil spill should be set on fire and that the flow of oil to the buoy that was pouring the oil into the Gulf should be cut off, perhaps by bombing. Because General Schwarz-kopf was "not in the business of destroying Kuwait to liberate Kuwait," this was very tricky. But lo and behold, the fable continued, in the course of normal military actions one of Schwarzkopf's boats encountered a small Iraqi boat near the Sea Island Terminal. "This was a small boat of the type that is suspected of supporting mine-laying craft," the General explained, "also a small boat that has antiaircraft [guns] on it, and this is the type of small boat that they've been going [after]—out in the area because those boats have been shooting at them." And so, "They engaged that boat, that boat happened to be next to the Sea Island Terminal and as a result of that engagement, the Sea Island Terminal caught fire."

This admission that U.S. bombing produced the fire is interesting because the day before, Pentagon briefer Pete Williams described a fire in the vicinity of the Sea Island Terminal and categorically insisted that: "Early this morning, the fire was bigger than it appears to be now. In the past several hours, it's been getting a little bit smaller. We do not know what caused the fire. However, we can say that the United States had nothing to do with causing this fire." Now, however, General Schwarzkopf was admitting that the U.S. had started that fire and that he was happy because experts had recommended that the oil be set on fire and it was on fire. The next thing to do was to bomb the source of the leaking oil in the on-shore terminal, in which there were two oil storage units about five miles from the shore. Schwarzkopf accordingly had the manifolds bombed (these were the pipes that controlled the flow of oil from the tankers to the off-shore oil terminal). This precision bombing cut off the flow to the Sea Island Terminal. To be sure, Schwarzkopf admitted, there were about thirteen miles of oil pipes full of oil from the storage area on-shore to the off-shore terminal, so there could be leakage for a while. Schwarzkopf did not know the answer to a question concerning what happened to the oil flowing from the bombed manifold pipes as it poured onto the land, and there have been almost no mainstream media reports that followed up, or critically analyzed, Schwarzkopf's "surgical" operation.[21]

Schwarzkopf's fable was extremely interesting because he admitted that his aircraft were routinely firing at vessels in the vicinity of oil installations. In fact, there had been several well-confirmed stories of U.S. bombing setting fire to oil installations and rupturing oil tankers. Given that coalition forces routinely patrolled the area and fired on Iraqi boats, perhaps the coalition troops bombed some of the tankers, the Sea Island terminal, or its oil buoy, and began some of the fires and spills before the fire that Schwarzkopf admitted starting.

A reporter asked General Schwarzkopf if the U.S. sinking of an Iraqi oil tanker, which was admitted earlier, caused any major spill. Schwarzkopf answered that the Navy claimed that the oil from this military action was a "refined product" (and thus not crude oil) and that it had burned off, thus "there is no concern in regard to that." Hence, Schwarzkopf was claiming that there was no major spill from the allied bombing, which he indicated "took place somewhere in the northern part," but he wasn't sure where. He said that he'd get back to the reporters on that, but he never publicly returned to the incident, which some believed was the source of the oil spill that TV showed splashing on the beach in Saudi Arabia and killing wildlife.

When a reporter told Schwarzkopf that the Saudis had said that the second oil spill, lapping up on the Saudi shore, came from Khafji, but the slick began north of Khafji, General Schwarzkopf admitted that he did not know where that specific spill was coming from. He said, incoherently, it "might have been an outlet," but broke off and said, "I just don't know." Thus, there were now conflicting stories by the Saudis and the United States concerning the origin of the second slick and, interestingly, the U.S. would soon turn to the Saudi version, which claimed that the second slick (i.e., the one seen on TV with oil splashing on the Saudi shore) came from Khafji, where Iraqis had fired on oil facilities (while the Pentagon had earlier claimed that it came from tankers near Mina al-Ahmadi opened by the Iraqis; this episode consequently disappeared from the U.S. version of the spill). However, the Iraqis, British television, British and French reporters, oil company personnel, and even some coalition military officials claimed that the onshore spill was coming from Iraqi tankers bombed by the United States. As we shall see in the next section, however, it is still not clear who produced the oil spill seen on TV or where it came from.[22]

Cover-Up

The mainstream media focused attention in the following days on the oil spill and its clean-up rather than on who actually started the spill. For example, in a front-page *New York Times* article of January 28, R. W. Apple relied solely on coalition sources and failed to even consider the Iraqi version, which many other reporters were at least raising and investigating. Apple quoted Saudi officials and a "ranking American officer based here [who] spoke bitterly of 'Saddam's scorched-ocean policy'" (p. A1). Apple described the devastation of the oil spill, cited Schwarzkopf's admission that "the origin of the oil coming ashore here was not clear" and then concluded, "it hardly seemed to matter" (p. A4). It is disturbing that a top writer for the *New York Times* thinks that it doesn't matter if his own government is involved in environmental terrorism, covers it over with disinformation, and uses that writer and his once-distinguished newspaper as part of the disinformation campaign. Indeed, neither U.S. television, newspapers, nor the mainstream weekly newsmagazines that appeared on January 28 (see Note 20), went back to the January 24 U.S. military briefing where the U.S. admitted that it had bombed two Iraqi oil tankers and caused an oil spill; none investigated the extent to which allied bombing created the spill; none noted that the Saturday, January 26, U.S. military briefing made it clear that there were two spills; and none attempted to draw out the Iraqi, Saudi, and other sources which were blaming at least some of the spills on coalition bombing.

Yet, conflicting accounts continued to emerge and eventually some critical questions arose concerning the origins of the oil spill. At the Pentagon military briefing on January 28, Col. Dave Herrington reported that the major oil spill was now approximately thirty-five miles in length and ten miles in width and had not reached the shoreline in Kuwait or Saudi Arabia. He claimed that the oil seen coming onshore originated from Iraqi attacks on the Saudi refinery in Khafji, thus repeating the Saudi story that had earlier been questioned by reporters, who had seen oil splashing on the shores north of the Khafji oil refinery, while the currents were moving the oil to the south. Thus the five Iraqi tankers which the Pentagon had claimed were sources of the oil spill now disappeared from the Pentagon fable.

On January 28, CBS News raised the key question of who caused the massive oil slick in the Gulf. Alan Pizzey reported that "it still isn't clear if the oil came from a loading buoy that the U.S. said that Saddam Hussein opened on purpose, or if the Sea Island Terminal was accidentally hit by naval vessels in an engagement with Iraqi gunboats." Pizzey also indicated that the cause of the spill onto the beaches south of Khafji was still unclear. This explosive questioning of the U.S. propaganda line was done quickly and without fanfare and seemed to have passed over the heads of most of the audience. The television networks and the mainstream press did not pursue the issue and there was almost no discussion of the origin of the oil spills in the mainstream media, although reporters kept asking questions in the U.S. and Saudi military briefings in Saudi Arabia over the next few days concerning who really caused the oil spills.

On January 31, 1991, the New York Times published a story headlined "Another Oil Spill Imperils the Gulf" (p. A5). The story read:

> Even as salvage experts and environmentalists went to the Persian Gulf today to try to limit damage from the largest oil spill ever recorded, Western military officials reported that oil had begun cascading into the gulf from a new source, an Iraqi offshore oil terminal near Kuwait.

The officials said it was not clear if the Iraqis had deliberately created the new slick by opening valves at the Mina al-Bakr oil terminal . . . or if the spill resulted from an allied bombing attack. . . .

American military officials today described other, previously unreported oil spills that are adding to what is already an environmental catastrophe in the gulf. Some of the spills, they said, may have been created intentionally by the Iraqis, while others are apparently the result of allied bombing raids on oil installations in Iraq or Kuwait, or attacks on Iraqi shipping.

The *Los Angeles Times* reported on January 31, 1991, that oil was being leaked from a destroyed Iraqi tanker and a damaged oil platform in the gulf, according to Capt. Barclay Trehal of the 152nd Tactical Reconnaissance Group, which analyzes photographs taken by low-flying aircraft after allied bombing missions. "It's being spread from various sources. . . . You can see the oil spewing out into the gulf and flowing in the current." Trehal said that he was not sure who was responsible for the damage and admitted: "I don't know if it was blown up intentionally or if it happened during allied bombing."

It had thus become increasingly clear that there were multiple oil spills and that the U.S.-led coalition was causing at least some of them. On January 31, CBS had a brief segment which noted that a London news source provided partial confirmation that U.S. bombers on January 22 had attacked two Iraqi oil tankers and caused an oil spill. Apparently, a British submarine was hiding under the tankers for a commando raid that night and the British were not amused by the resulting damage to their submarine from the U.S. attack on the oil tankers. It is also interesting to note that just before General Schwarzkopf's briefing on January 30, Dan Rather dramatically announced that "Iraq has started pouring more crude oil into the waters of the Persian Gulf." During Schwarzkopf's briefing, a reporter mentioned a Reuters news agency report that the Iraqis were pouring more oil into the Gulf in the region of the Iraqi offshore ship loading terminal at Mina al-Bakr. Schwarzkopf admitted that Iraqi oil tankers there had been attacked "for several reasons in the past." He acknowledged that his staff had been watching that oil spill for several days and were prepared to attack the terminal again to stop the flow of oil into the Gulf.

The United Nations announced that they were undertaking an investigation of the oil spills, but so far no authoritative report has been published. Different sources attribute different levels of responsibility to the respective forces with the U.S. and Iraq blaming each other for the spills. The environmental journalist for the British *Guardian,* John Vidal, later wrote:

On Tuesday 21 January 1991 the Allies attacked Iraqi tankers in the Gulf. Five supertankers, each capable of holding 100,000 tonnes of crude—no one will say how laden they were—were moored at offshore terminals. Two-mile-wide slicks were reported off Khafji, and sometime between then and 25 January the oil terminal at Mina Al Ahmadi was destroyed. Then—the timing is uncertain—the Iraqis opened the pumps and millions of gallons of crude poured into the Gulf from the Al Hamaji terminal.

Whether the Allies caused more oil to be spilt into the Gulf than the Iraqis may never be known, but for a few days it became politically expedient to condemn Saddam Hussein's ecological aggression and take the sting out of any accusations that the Allies were using similar tactics in their 100,000 sorties into Iraq. The media, starved of images of death, turned to filming cormorants, albeit dying in oil spilt in Allied raids (1991, p. 137).

On February 3, the French *Journal de Dimanche* reported that "four out of five [oil spills] are the responsibility of allied forces." According to a summary of Claude-Marie Vadrot's study by Andre Gunder Frank (1991), "The first one was from the January 19 allied bombardment of three oil tankers. The second one from the January 20 bombing by French and British planes. The third one can be attributed to Iraqi bombardment. The fourth is due to allied bombardment of Al-Ahmadi, and the fifth oil spill is from the bombing of Boubyane Island by British planes" (p. 19). Saudi and U.S. sources, however, concluded that 70 percent of the oil spilled resulted from Iraqi actions (see *Aviation Week and Space Technology,* March 4, 1991, p. 24; *National Journal,* March 2, 1991, p. 536; and *Maclean's,* March 4, 1991).

In any case, it is clear that coalition bombing had caused at least some of the oil spills and fires in the Gulf and the issue of Iraqi "environmental terrorism" was dropped by the Pentagon, although occasionally those in the Bush administration would invoke the theme because the issue had never really been discussed in the mainstream media and most of the public continued to think that the environmental damage in the Persian Gulf was solely the result of Iraqi action. Yet after the war, John Horgan argued in an article in *Scientific American* (May 1991) that the United States had ordered government officials not to disclose any information concerning the environmental damage in the Gulf war because such information might raise embarrassing questions concerning the impact of the U.S.-led coalition bombing on the ecology of the region. Horgan cited John Cox, an environmental engineer and member of the Campaign for Nuclear Disarmament in Britain, who believed that satellite images would reveal that coalition bombing of Iraqi refineries and oil reserves had "created an appalling smoke cloud" comparable to the one generated by the Iraqi sabotage of Kuwait's oil fields.[23]

But the compliant corporate media never really investigated who caused the oil fires and spills and because the spills did not ultimately harm the Saudi desalination plants and thus the water supply, the story was more or less dropped for the rest of the war. The Saudis constantly revised down their estimate of the extent of the damage from 8 million barrels spilled, to 5, to 3.5, and finally to one million barrels by the end of the war, about one-twelfth of earlier claims.[24] In most media reports during the following weeks, however, it was assumed that the Iraqis had caused the oil spills, thus the media helped cover over possible U.S. complicity in one of the greatest environmental crimes in history.

Consequently, the Gulf oil spill was probably the greatest propaganda victory of the war for the coalition forces, as the public generally believed that Saddam Hussein and the Iraqis caused the oil spills and many who had been sympathetic to the plight of the Iraqis were now angry with the images of dead birds and oil pouring onto the Saudi beaches. The powerful images of environmental damage intensified hatred of Saddam Hussein and demoralized the peace movement, many of whose members were strong environmentalists. The Bush administration and Pentagon propaganda campaign thus succeeded to mobilize a large majority of the public behind their war effort.

Notes

1. Two "Frontline" PBS documentaries on Grenada (narrated by Seymour Hersh) and on Panama (narrated by Bill Moyers) demonstrated the military blunders that were left out of mainstream media reports in these two interventions. On the Grenada foul-ups, Greg Easterbrook wrote: "Invading the smallest nation in the world, the forces of the United States committed blunder after blunder. Space-age helicopters were shot down by Cuban construction workers using World War II surplus guns; a SEAL commando team drowned without being fired on; paratroopers were dropped into 'secure' areas that were in fact defended; civilian targets were bombed; interservice rivalries were highlighted by the discovery that Army and Air Force units could not communicate with each other because their radios used different frequencies. Most important, the medical students, whose rescue supposedly justified the attack, were not located until some thirty-six hours after the invasion began. Had there been a real danger that local forces would execute the students, Grenada would now stand as one of the greatest embarrassments in the history of statecraft" (*The New Republic,* Sept. 30, 1991, p. 36).

In Libya, high-tech bombs missed their targets, killing many innocent civilians, and it was not widely reported that the terrorist disco bombing of West Berlin, which was the ostensible reason for the Libya bombing, was not a Libyan operation, as the Reagan administration speciously claimed, but was, according to the West German intelligence forces who investigated it, caused by terrorist groups who had ties to the Syrian government (see Chapter 1, note 16).

2. Popular culture had firmly established Saddam as "the man you love to hate" and once the war started the media had vilified him in terms more extreme than any previous target of propaganda campaigns since World War II, employing the rhetoric of "another Hitler" to mobilize hatred of the Iraqi leader. Moreover, a cottage industry emerged of anti-Saddam artifacts, including golf balls with Saddam's head painted on them, Saddam dart boards, T-shirts and bumper stickers with anti-Saddam messages, cartoons in newspapers and magazines vilifying him, and parodies of popular songs with anti-Saddam or anti-Iraq lyrics. The tabloids published wild stories about his bizarre and vicious sexual practices with the February 12, 1991, *National Enquirer* "reporting":

His own bodyguard's terrifying story.

- Saddam executes his young lovers
- His evil sex life
- His passion for "Little House on the Prairie"

The "bodyguard" later appeared on "60 Minutes" with stories more suitable for this audience. It was later revealed by French intelligence, however, that there was no evidence that the "bodyguard" had ever worked for Hussein and they labeled him a "mythomaniac" who had frequent contacts in Paris with Saudi military and intelligence officers (see Doug Ireland, *The Village Voice,* Feb. 12, 1991). A *National Examiner* story the same week headlined a "Shocker": "Saddam's Love Child Lives in U.S. He's Joining Army to Kill His Father" (Feb. 12, 1991). Cartoonist David Levine drew a sketch on the Op-Ed page of the *New York Times* on February 1, 1991, labeled the "Descent of Man" starting with a humanoid Caucasian image of Clark Gable and passing through apes and various animals to a diminutive Saddam Hussein with flies buzzing around his head.

3. Said (1978) compiled copious documentation of Western texts that affirm the radical otherness of non-Western races by asserting that "accuracy is abhorrent to the Oriental mind," that Orientals cannot reason and are fundamentally irrational, and that they are barbaric and uncivilized (see pp. 38ff., 54ff., passim). Said claimed that Arabs were often the target of these discourses and pointed out that such doctrines legitimate domination and are thus instruments of power over subjected races. Aksoy and Robins (1991) provide some examples of Western commentary producing the Iraqis as an irrational foreign Other: " 'Their twentieth century is not our's,' wrote Alain Finkielkraut, 'They have allowed honour to prevail over democracy, and force and machismo over freedom.' According to Martin Woollacott, it was 'the problem of irrationality and fantasy in Arab life'; there is an 'Arab sickness' centred on the failure of rational thought" (p. 329).

4. Some nights later, on January 23, George Bush gave a speech to the retired officers association. He quoted an Air Force general to the effect that the pilots must have been tortured—otherwise they wouldn't say such things "because they are Americans." The crowd roared with approval.

5. See the *New York Times,* June 11, 1991, where Zaun also stated: "I don't ever want to kill anybody again." Referring to victory celebrations in Washington and New York, Zaun remarked, "This country didn't get to see the cost of war. I did." He added, "They didn't see Iraqi mothers get killed." Immediately after making these statements, Zaun was reassigned aboard a ship in the Indian Ocean and could not be reached for further comment. *LOOT* (July-August 1991, p. 9) reported that the June 11 AP dispatch was captioned, "U.S. Pilot Shot Down in Iraq Regrets Human Cost of War." The *Times* headline on June 11, however, read, "American Flier Shot Down in Iraq Recounts Horrors After Capture." The first caption, however, more accurately sums up the substance of the Zaun interview, while the other is pure propaganda.

6. Ramsey Clark and a group of international lawyers and researchers amassed a tremendous amount of evidence of war crimes by the U.S.-led coalition forces (Clark et. al 1992). The mainstream media, however, ignored these efforts, just as they ignored Clark's trip to Iraq during the war and the graphic video and reports he made of the barbaric damage to civilians and systematic hitting of civilian targets.

7. One of the more amusing examples of alleged Iraqi propaganda concerned a widespread report that "Baghdad Betty" broadcast on an Iraqi propaganda radio frequency to U.S. troops, warning: "G.I. You should be home. . . . While you're away, movies stars are taking your women. Robert Redford is dating your girlfriend. Tom Selleck is kissing your lady. . . . Bart Simpson is making love to your wife." This example was reported as evidence of the crudity of Iraqi propaganda in the *New York Times, Washington Post,* CNN, NBC, and *Time* magazine. The joke, however, was on the mainstream media because the story was originally told as a gag on the Johnny Carson show on August 22, 1990, and was taken up by a cycle of mainstream media corporations as a true story! See *Extra!,* May 1991, p. 17.

8. This and the following example come from articles in the *Covert Action Information Bulletin,* Number 37 (Summer 1991). The claims concerning the violation of the Geneva Conventions come from Clark et al. 1992.

9. The military received some mainstream media criticism for this restriction, as when NBC's commentator John Chancellor groused about the restriction on January 20, though anchor Tom Brokaw stated two days later that it was not "in the best interest of the U.S. to cover the return of dead U.S. soldiers" (note how the GE military-industrial complex booster Brokaw equates his role as "journalist" with promoting the U.S. national interest, as if he were competent to define it). A more grisly tale of dead U.S. soldiers emerged when reporter Jonathan Franklin infiltrated the Dover mortuary and provided graphic accounts of mutilated bodies, claiming that he believed there were more U.S. casualties than officially reported from his comparison of the number of dead and mutilated bodies with the official U.S. casualty figures of the time (*San Francisco Bay Guardian,* March 6, 1991).

10. In a June 24, 1992, Op-Ed piece in the *New York Times,* Mark Crispin Miller asserted that official sources were claiming that no mobile Scud launchers were destroyed during the war and that only 12 of the 28 fixed Scud launchers

were destroyed. Miller cited Scott Ritter, a former Marine captain now employed with the United Nations Special Commission and charged with supervising the destruction of of Iraq's weapons, as well as unnamed military sources who claimed that Schwarzkopf's assertions concerning the destruction of Scud launchers were bogus. According to one source, Schwarzkopf fabricated claims concerning the bombing of mobile Scud launchers, and a videocassette shown in a Schwarzkopf briefing of the destruction of what was claimed to be a mobile-launcher really depicted the bombing of a truck! The source claimed that analysts who detected this were overruled and that subsequent computer analysis revealed that the vehicles said to be Scud launchers were mere trucks. Furthermore, on June 12, 1992, in a *Jerusalem Post* article, the former commander of the Israel Air Force accused the United States of not trying to stop Iraq from launching Scud ballistic missiles against Israel during the Gulf war. "It's not that the U.S. military failed to stop Iraqi Scud launchings against Israel; they never tried," said Maj. Gen. Avihu Bin-Nun. "I know this is a very harsh accusation, but I firmly stand behind it," he said.

11. For the case that the United States had not really destroyed Iraq's unconventional weapons programs, see *Washington Post,* National Weekly Edition, October 21–27, 1991, pp. 9–11. U.S.-Canadian arms merchant Gerald Bull had been building the Big Gun and was found murdered, probably by Israeli agents; see Darwish and Alexander 1991 and Henderson 1991.

12. Propaganda analysts distinguish between "white propaganda," consisting of overt lies attributed to official sources to defame or confuse one's enemies; "gray" propaganda, in which the source is not clear and its truth or falsity is not known; and "black" propaganda, in which the source is completely hidden and the disinformation is manifestly untrue. Such distinctions are racist (equating "white" with harmless "little white lies" and "black" with mysterious and deadly lies) and do not hold up in analyzing Gulf war propaganda, which was carefully orchestrated and coordinated, mixing "white," "gray," and "black" propaganda in the same campaigns and discourses.

13. It was claimed later by apologists for the U.S. government that the sign in English in front of the plant proved that the whole episode was an Iraqi propaganda ploy. To this argument, I would counter that the uniforms shown in the 1990 video footage of the plant also had English writing on them and it was later ascertained that the uniforms had been made in England. Furthermore, one learned from careful TV viewing that signs on buildings and streets in Baghdad were frequently written in both English and Arabic, so that ideologues who claimed that the sign in English was evidence of Iraqi propaganda were themselves dupes or agents of propaganda.

14. On February 1 on a live CNN report from Baghdad, Arnett indicated that journalists had returned to the baby-milk formula plant to inspect its ruins and that it continued to appear that the plant was solely civilian and did not produce any biological weapons. In a later ITN report, Brent Sadler, who was one of the pool of foreign correspondents with Arnett at the plant, reported that the site "looked, felt, and smelt like an innocent building where milk was made," as video images showed what certainly looked like the ruins of a milk factory.

Sadler indicated that he and the other reporters were able not only to look through the wreckage of the building, but also to inspect the company's books and records, and one image showed Sadler examining what looked like company records. Sadler's segment was strongly narrated and supported by convincing visual images.

The weekly newsmagazines, however, privileged the U.S. account. *Time* claimed: "In the first days of the war, bombers concentrated on blasting Iraqi nuclear facilities, chemical- and biological-weapons plants (including one factory in Baghdad that the Iraqis said manufactured baby formula but that the White House insisted was devoted to preparations for germ warfare)" (Feb. 4, 1991, p. 24). Although this statement appears to be even-handed, giving both versions, it was included in a story on the bombing of nuclear, chemical, and biological weapons facilities and ultimately identified the milk factory with these targets; the *Time* version also posited the antithesis between Iraq and the White House, leaving out Arnett, who was to stand by his report, noting in several interviews after the war that he believed that the plant was not a military facility. *Newsweek* chimed in the same week (Feb. 4, 1991) with two references that accepted the White House version attacking "the ham-handed attempt to depict a bombed-out biological-weapons plant near Baghdad as a baby-formula factory" (p. 26) and claiming: "U.S. officials identified that facility as the country's main biological-weapons factory. According to one source, the evidence included 'human source material'" (p. 32). Propaganda works with hyperbole, so in this account the factory was elevated to "the main biological-weapons factory" and an unnamed source claimed that the evidence includes "human-source material." When propaganda is being disseminated, beware of unnamed sources, especially unnamed sources citing other unnamed sources.

15. Perroots was described by the London *Times* (March 25, 1991) as "director of the American Defense Intelligence Agency until 1989 [who] was used as a special consultant to the agency throughout the Gulf war." On an edition of the BBC show *Panorama*, Perroots admitted that, "the American intelligence community had got it wrong when bombers attacked the baby milk factory." He also questioned the official U.S. claim that the bombed sleeping shelter in which hundreds of Iraqi civilians were killed was a bunker (see 7.3).

16. After the war Powell continued to insist that the U.S. had made no mistake in targetting the infant formula factory, claiming: "Even after it was destroyed, some of the so-called baby powder that was around could not have been made there. We saw the packages and read the labels. It was made by a company that was not, to the best of our knowledge, doing business in Iraq. There was a body of evidence to suggest that we knew what we were doing." In fact, the packages and labels revealed the product to be a powdered milk product called Millac, which was produced by the Northern Ireland firm Pritchitt Foods that sold it to the Iraqis, who then produced the infant formula; see the Irish papers *Today,* Jan. 25, 1991, p. 8, and the *Daily Mirror,* Jan. 25, 1991; the latter paper stupidly assumed that the fact that the product was powdered milk proved that the Iraqis were lying, when obviously the powder was just part of the infant formula. In any case, Powell was misinformed.

17. See Tom Wicker's Op-Ed column in the *New York Times* on April 3, 1991, and the discussion in an article by John Horgan, in *Scientific American* (May 1991) which I shall discuss below.

18. The lead story in the Jan. 25 *New York Times,* for instance, mentioned the bombing of an Iraqi tanker as part of their description of naval activity but did not mention the oil spill (p. A4). Buried in another story on Iraq, however, the *Times* noted, "Baghdad radio also accused American airmen of causing a huge oil slick in the Persian Gulf by attacking two Iraqi oil tankers. The United States Navy reported Wednesday that American carrier-borne aircraft had badly damaged an Iraqi tanker and destroyed three armed Hovercraft in the gulf." Oddly, the *Times* does not mention the briefing where Pepin admitted that the United States caused the oil spill, attributing the story to the Iraqis, so it could easily be dismissed as mere Iraqi propaganda.

19. Recall the massive U.S. environmental destruction in Vietnam where the United States dropped thirteen million tons of bombs, defoliated between one-fourth and one-half of the country with deadly herbicides, "pockmarked the land with 25 million craters, displacing 3 billion cubic meters of soil and leading to disease and water shortages. . . . Vietnam's environment remains devastated from the war . . . and 'much of the damage can probably never be repaired.'" Political Ecology Group, *War in the Gulf: An Environmental Perspective* (San Francisco, Calif.: The Tides Foundation, Jan. 1991). In this context, Brian Tokar's remarks are worth citing: "The environmental consequences of war may be easy for some people to overlook. . . . But the consequences for the earth are invariably the most lasting, and they continue to plague people and their land long after hostilities have ended. Hospitals in Vietnam still report several new victims of left-over land mines from the ecocidal war every week. Much of the country's land remains unable to sustain life, as the effects of chemical defoliants dropped by United States forces continue to linger." "War Is Ecocide," *Z Magazine,* April 1991, p. 37.

20. Both sides of the oil slick story were at least mentioned on January 26 in the *Boston Globe, Japan Economic Newswire, New York Times, Toronto Star,* London *Financial Times,* and the *Washington Post.* Only the U.S. version was presented the same day in the *Atlanta Constitution, Chicago Tribune, Gannett News Service, Los Angeles Times, Reuters, Seattle Times, San Francisco Chronicle,* and *USA Today. Time* magazine opened its February 4 story "A War Against the Earth" by suggesting the concept of "eco-war": "The environment itself has become both a weapon and a victim" (p. 32). The main body of the story, however, utilized the hypothetical mode or passive voice ("U.S. and Saudi officials claimed that . . . ," "Iraq is believed to have opened . . . ," "The Iraqis may have released . . . "). Caution was thrown to the wind, however, in the concluding paragraph where *Time* evoked "the sense of horror and demoralization caused by Saddam's callous acts of environmental terrorism," concluding: "in his quixotic madness, the Iraqi strongman seems intent on waging what he calls 'the mother of all battles' against the mother of us all—the earth itself" (p. 33). This is a telling example of how propaganda and ideological rhetoric overcame journalism in the Gulf war. *Newsweek* in their February 4 story blamed the spill solely on Saddam Hussein who "ordered a massive attack against the Persian Gulf itself.

The Iraqis opened the pumps. . . . They also pulled the plugs on five Kuwaiti tankers loaded with 3 million gallons of petroleum." Note here the use of the active tense and the assumption that Iraq and Saddam Hussein are the sole culprits. The story, as we shall see, is more complex.

21. Randy Thomas reported in the *Earth Island Journal* (Summer 1991) that months after the end of the war "large quantities of oil were also seen spilling from bomb-ruptured pipes at the Ahmadi oil terminal" [which Schwarzkopf had bombed] (p. 42). John Vidal (1991, p. 137) claimed that, "Two months later more than 5,000 gallons of oil a day were still reported to be leaking out." On August 16, 1991, Australian oil expert Joe Vitalls reported on PeaceNet (mideast.gulf) that the formation of oil lakes was making it hard to put out some of the oil fires (see 10.3 for more details on the aftermath of the environmental terrorism in the Gulf).

22. It is still not clear to me who caused the oil spill that produced the images of oil flowing onto the beaches around Khafji and killing birds. The Saudis claim that this spill resulted from Iraqi shelling of Khafji early in the war, but the question arises as to why it took so long for the oil to be visible and how the spill had entered beaches north of the city when the tides were said to have been flowing to the south and east. British and French reporters, as I note in this section, claim, based on interviews with Saudi and U.S. military officials, that the oil on the Saudi beach was caused by the U.S. bombing of Iraqi tankers, as did the Iraqis who called for a UN investigation. Although the U.S. admitted bombing an Iraqi oil tanker on January 23, they claimed that the oil spilled from this was a refined product that burned quickly and that the spill was only approximately one-half mile (U.S. military briefing in Riyadh, January 24, a claim repeated by Schwarzkopf in his January 27 briefing).

23. Tokar (1991) points out that weeks before the retreating Iraqi troops set ablaze the Kuwaiti oil wells, "unusually high levels of soot in the air were being measured as far away as the observatory at Mauna Loa in Hawaii and unprecedented acid rain was observed in the mountains of Turkey and Iran. Considerable scientific evidence suggests that widespread atmospheric pollution and spillage of oil into the Gulf began with the onset of U.S.-led bombing" (p. 57).

24. There were, however, other spills and other estimates, so that the Saudis might have been downplaying the extent of the damage. Tokar (1991), for example, claimed that, "Estimates of the amount of oil spilled directly into the Persian Gulf are reaching 7.5 million barrels, and rising. This is twice the amount of oil that spilled into the Gulf of Mexico in 1979 after an accidental well blowout—until now, the largest oil spill in history—and almost thirty times as much oil as was spilled by the *Exxon Valdez*. A dozen different sources of leaking oil have been identified, challenging claims that most of the oil in the Gulf originated with the Iraqis opening valves at the Sea Island oil terminal at the end of January" (p. 58). A Greenpeace, Jan. 10, 1992, Press Release claimed that an estimated four to eight million barrels of oil was split into the sea. There will be further discussion of the environmental aftermath of the war in 10.3.

◆

TV Goes to War

THE GULF WAR WAS the first war played out on TV with the whole world watching it unfold, often live. Never before had so many people watched so much news. The nation had rarely, if ever, been so involved in a single story. There was discussion of the vicissitudes of the war throughout the TV day and there had probably never been so much concentrated TV coverage of a specific event week after week for the duration of the war. And never had the nation been exposed to and fallen prey to so much disinformation and propaganda. For the rest of the Gulf war, both the Bush administration and the military vilified Saddam Hussein and the Iraqis whenever possible while presenting their own actions, however brutal, in a positive light so that few negative images appeared of U.S. military actions.

The Big Lie that was repeated daily throughout the war maintained that the U.S-led multinational coalition bombing campaign was precise and was avoiding civilian casualties. This lie was promoted by both the Bush administration and the U.S. military. General Schwarzkopf, in a January 27 briefing, insisted that the coalition forces "are absolutely doing more than we ever have" to avoid casualties. He claimed that "I think no nation in the history of warfare" has done more to use their technology to minimize civilian casualties and to avoid hitting cultural or religious targets. George Bush echoed this in a February 5 press conference, claiming: "We are doing everything possible and with great success to minimize collateral damage. . . . I'd like to say that we are going to extraordinary, and I would venture to say, unprecedented length, to avoid damage to civilians and holy places."[1]

After the war, the Pentagon admission that 70 percent of the bombs missed their targets put in question the claims of precision bombing (see 4.2), as did the daily visual evidence coming out of Iraq, which depicted a tremendous amount of civilian casualties and destruction of nonmilitary targets in that country. In fact, the destruction of Iraq's economic infrastructure, including its electrical power, water, sanitation, industrial, and communications facilities, was an avowed goal of the allied bombing campaign, and such extensive bombing made it obvious that civilians would suffer greatly during the air war in which Iraq was systematically pounded into a preindustrial condition. And yet day after day the military insisted that they were not bombing civilian targets and concocted ever more specious stories to deny the visual evidence by claiming that the seemingly civilian targets that they had bombed, like the infant formula factory, were really military ones (see 4.2, 6.3, and 7.3).

The fact that the media commentators and the public swallowed these big lies in the face of daily conflicting evidence shows a serious moral and intellectual blindness that I examine in the next two sections. Thus, in this chapter I try, first, to explain why the public so strongly supported the Gulf war and accepted at face value whatever they were told by the Bush administration and Pentagon (6.1 and 6.2). My analysis draws on data from the media and some empirical research already produced, but is largely interpretive and speculative. Although I do not generally subscribe to the "bullet," or hypodermic, theory of mass communications which holds that the media directly influence and manipulate thought and behavior, I believe that in the Gulf war the media helped create an environment that, in conjunction with other social factors, helped mobilize consent to the Bush administration war policies.[2]

6.1 The War at Home

Part of the reason why people supported the Gulf war has to do with what might be called "territorial herd instincts." When a country is at war and in danger people tend to support their government and pull together.[3] It could be argued, however, that during the Gulf war the country was not really in danger, that a diplomatic rather than a military solution could best serve the national interests, and that support of the troops required bringing them home as soon as possible. Moreover, the country was genuinely divided at the start of the war and there was a large antiwar movement in place before Bush began the military hostilities with Iraq. Furthermore, Kolko (1991, p. 25) points out that public opinion since 1969 has been increasingly anti-interventionist and that every Rand Corporation poll had indicated that U.S. military intervention would not receive adequate public support. Yet during the Gulf war, the public was mobilized to support Bush's interventionist policies, in part at least, because of the media support for the war.

To begin, the prowar consensus was mobilized through a variety of ways in which the public identified with the troops. TV presented direct images of the troops to the public through "desert dispatches" which produced very sympathetic images of young American men and women, "in harm's way" and serving their country. TV news segments on families of the troops also provided mechanisms of identification, especially because many of the troops were reservists, forced to leave their jobs and families, making them sympathetic objects of empathy and identification for those able to envisage themselves in a similar situation. There were also frequent TV news stories on how church groups, schools, and others adopted U.S. troops in Saudi Arabia as pen pals, thus more intimately binding those at home to the soldiers abroad. As we shall see in this section, people were also bound to troops through rituals of display of yellow ribbons, chanting and waving flags in prowar demonstrations, and entering into participation in various prowar support groups.

The media also generated support for the war, first, by upbeat appraisals of U.S. successes and then by demonizing the Iraqis that made people fervently want a coalition victory. Initial support was won for the war effort through the media-generated euphoria that the war would be over quickly, with a decisive and easy victory for the U.S.-led coalition (see Chapter 3). Then, the audience got into the drama of the war through experiencing the excitement of the Scud wars and the thrills of technowar war with its laser-guided bombs and missiles and videotapes of its successes (Chapter 4). The POW issue, the oil spills and fires, and intense propaganda campaigns by both sides also involved the audience in the highly emotional experience of a TV war (Chapter 5). The drama of the war was genuinely exciting and the public immersed itself in the sights, sounds, and language of war. The media images of the high-tech precision bombing, (seeming) victories of Patriot over Scud missiles, bombing of Iraq, and military hardware and troops helped to mobilize positive feelings for the U.S. military effort in much of the audience. Military language helped normalize the war, propaganda and disinformation campaigns mobilized prowar discourse, and the negative images and discourses against the Iraqis helped mobilize hatred against Iraq and Saddam Hussein.

Polls during the first weeks of the war revealed growing support for the war effort and widespread propensities to believe whatever the media and military were saying. A *Times-Mirror* survey of January 31, 1991, revealed that 78 percent of the public believed that the military was basically telling the truth, not hiding anything embarrassing about its conduct of the war, and providing all of the information it prudently could. Seventy-two percent called the press coverage objective and sixty-one percent called it for the most part accurate. Eight out of ten said the press did an excellent job. Fifty percent claimed to be addicted to TV watching and said that they cannot stop watching news of the war. Fifty-eight percent of adults under 30 call themselves "war news addicts"; twenty-one percent of these "addicts" say they have trouble concentrating on their jobs or normal activities, while eighteen percent say they are suffering insomnia.

It was, I would argue, the total media and social environment that was responsible for mobilizing support for the U.S. war policies. From morning to evening, the nation was bombarded with images of military experts, vignettes of soldiers at home and abroad, military families, former POWs, and others associated with the military. Military figures, images, and discourse dominated the morning talk shows, the network news, discussion programs, and the twenty-four-hour-a-day CNN war coverage as well as many hours per day on C-Span and other networks. On home satellite dishes, one could sometimes catch live transmissions as the networks prepared to present their reports from the field, and one satellite transponder provided hours per day of live military pool footage from Saudi Arabia for use by the networks—propaganda provided by the military free of charge. TV news preempted regular programs for weeks on end. The result was a militarization of consciousness and an environment dominated by military images and discourses.

CNN was particularly responsible for the militarization of the American psyche during the Gulf war with its around-the-clock bombardment of images of war, including military music, endless repetition of the same headlines, images of soldiers and weapons, and incessant discussion of the war that rarely questioned Bush administration policies. All of the networks cut into regular programming if exciting events took place. Consequently, the nation was in thrall to the television war and, as noted, accepted the TV version. In Danny Schechter's words (1991), "It was a marathon, a news-athon. It hooked us into a state of addictive anxiety where we stayed tuned in to saturation updates without end. It rallied the country behind the war while promoting the illusion that what we were watching in our living rooms was what was happening in the deserts of Arabia" (p. 22).

In this section, I shall accordingly analyze some of the ways in which TV helped militarize language and consciousness to help produce a prowar constituency in the country. TV went to war and helped manufacture consent to Bush administration war policies via its uncritical war coverage, which sacrificed its democratic imperatives of providing a forum of debate and accurate information so that citizens could participate in key issues in their society. The intensity of the U.S. bombing of Iraq and its destructive effects on the Iraqi people and the environment, the obvious fact that Iraq and much of the world wanted a cessation to military hostilities, and the dangers to the world economy and political ecology of the Middle East from a protracted war should have generated a substantive debate in the political, intellectual, and media establishment. That it did not is partly the responsibility of the mainstream media that silenced critical voices and that privileged the pro-military and pro-Bush administration discourses and images. In addition, the crisis of liberalism and cowardice of opponents of the war in the Congress and intellectual establishment contributed to the prowar consensus, but exploring this theme would require a separate study. Instead, I wish to focus in the following analysis on the role of the media in mobilizing support for the war effort.[4]

Warspeak

The Bush administration and Pentagon mobilized support for the war through their discourses and images of a precision, high-tech bombing that was minimizing civilian casualties while systematically destroying the Iraqi military machine. I analyzed the mobilization of video images of the high-tech war in earlier sections (see 3.3, 4.3, and Chapter 5) and here will analyze the militarization of language. War tends to debase and destroy language as much as humans and their social and natural environment. In the novel *1984,* George Orwell developed the term "Doublespeak" to connote language that makes the bad seem good, the negative appear positive, and the unpleasant appear attractive, or at least tolerable.[5] Orwellian "Newspeak" described the production of neologisms and language to sanitize unpleasant realities. The Gulf war saw a proliferation of Orwellian language that I call "Warspeak." The coalition forces "engaged" the enemy rather than attacking it. Instead of dropping bombs or firing weapons, planes "dropped ordnance." If the bombs missed their targets, "incontinent ordnance delivery" resulted, which produced "collateral damage," a neologism used to sanitize the destruction of civilian targets and civilian deaths as accidental damage. Targets were referred to as "assets" and warplanes were described as "force packages." Targets were not destroyed, but "visited," "acquired," "taken out," "serviced," or "suppressed." Tanks and equipment were "neutralized" rather than blown up. "Cluster bombs" became "area denial weapons." Rather than destroying the Iraqi military, the goal was "assertive disarmament," to be achieved through "discriminate deterrence."

Instead of descriptive terms like "bombing targets," the military and the media therefore spoke of "servicing the target," "neutralizing targets," "suppressing assets," or "visiting enemy." Euphemisms for killing emerged, such as "eliminate," "degrade," "hurt," and, the favorite of many, "atrit," though General Powell and General Schwarzkopf preferred "kill." Many of the euphemisms used in Vietnam such as "friendly fire" (i.e., bombing your own troops) and "kill boxes" (i.e., areas subject to systematic bombing and destruction) reappeared, while the nastier terminology of Vietnam was redefined or defined away: "body bags" became "human remains pouches" and U.S. casualties were merely KIAs (killed in action). Captured coalition troops were still POWs, though captured Iraqis became EPWs (enemy prisoners of war), which lacked the sympathetic connotation of POWs. Iraqi nuclear, biological, and chemical weapons were "NBC"'s, sanitizing the deadly objects of coalition bombing to friendly initials, associated with a TV network familiar to the TV audience. Schwarzkopf denied that his troops were engaging in "carpet-bombing" Iraq, claiming that the term was inaccurate for the precise coalition bombing, though he did admit that such massive bombing was being used on Iraqi troops in the desert. In fact, the term "carpet-bombing" itself connotes a gentle, laying on of a carpet, a friendly domestic term, rather than destructive killing by a field of viciously lethal bombs.

Such euphemisms concealed the lethality of the destruction and the effects of the bombing and provided a false picture of surgical, precision bombing. Warspeak abstracts and sanitizes military activity and substitutes familiar and friendly terminology for the unpleasant activities being undertaken.

Media critic Norman Solomon described the routine destruction of common meanings of language as "linguicide." "When the slaughter of civilians is called 'collateral damage,' that's linguicide. When a dictatorship in Saudi Arabia, routinely torturing political dissenters, is called a 'moderate' government, that's linguicide. When a few missiles fired at Tel Aviv are called weapons of terrorism while thousands of missiles fired at Baghdad and Basra are called technological marvels, that's linguicide" (mideast.media, March 11, 1991). The degradation of meaning and language is not harmless for it is language that we use to make sense of the world, communicate with others, and create collective meanings, and if our language is debased or degraded, so is our consciousness, our communication, and our social interactions.

Other terms like "sorties," "Scuds," and "triple-A" became common media fare. The term "sortie" provides a nice neutral and Frenchified sound for bombing missions. The term "Scud" has a rather noxious, scummy quality to it, and its foul sound was exploited by George Bush who invariably uttered the term "Ssccudd missile" with an exaggerated sneer. The "Patriot" missile, by contrast, connoted positive virtues, associated with devotion to country. Thus, even ordinary language was absorbed by the propaganda apparatus, which reserved all positive descriptive adjectives for "our" side while the "enemy" was described in negative adjectives. The official military discourse described the "enemy" as "ruthless," "cruel," "wanton," "desperate," "surprising," and

"cunning." The U.S. forces were, however, "precise," "careful," "scru-
pulous," "tough," "decisive," and "effective," combining technological
efficacy with traditional (male) virtues. The media, of course, perpetu-
ated this manichean duality of "us" and "them," with commentators and
experts frequently using the terms "we" and "our" to describe U.S. assets
and actions (see 2.1). In these ways, language went to war as well as
television, and those who used such language served the interests of the
Bush administration and military as they normalized Orwellian Warspeak.

The Danish paper *Politiken* examined the English-language press and
documented some of the ways in which the English language had gone
to war (reproduced in *In These Times,* Feb. 13, 1991, p. 5):

The Allies have:
  Army, Navy, and Air Force
  Guidelines for journalists
  Briefings to the press
The Allies:
  Eliminate
  Neutralize
  Hold on
  Conduct precision bombing
The Allied soldiers are:
  Professional
  Cautious
  Full of courage
  Loyal
  Brave
The Allied missiles:
  Do extensive damage
George Bush is:
  Resolute
  Balanced

The Iraqis have:
  A war machine
  Censorship
  Propaganda
The Iraqis:
  Kill
  Kill
  Bury themselves in holes
  Fire wildly at anything
The Iraqi soldiers are:
  Brainwashed
  Cowardly
  Cannon fodder
  Blindly obeying
  Fanatic
The Iraqi missiles:
  Cause civilian casualties
Saddam Hussein is:
  Intractable
  Mad

The debasement of language began at the start of the U.S. military
intervention with the coining of the term "Operation Desert Shield" to
describe Bush's decision to send troops to the desert of Saudi Arabia to
engage in war against Iraq. Bush claimed that he was drawing "a line in
the sand" and providing a "shield" against Iraq's invading Saudi Arabia.
As it now appears (see 1.2), Iraq had no intention of invading Saudi
Arabia and Bush had every intention of waging war against Iraq, yet
Bush's propaganda line stating the necessity of sending troops to Saudi
Arabia to protect neighboring countries against Iraqi aggression pre-

vailed, along with a demonization of Saddam Hussein and the Iraqis. Over and over, the Bush administration repeated the Big Lie that they were attempting to negotiate a diplomatic solution to the crisis, when in fact they did everything possible to block any diplomacy. Thus lying and hypocrisy became a normalized part of political discourse during the Gulf crisis and war.

The code name "Operation Desert Storm" referred to Bush's aggression as an "operation" rather than a war, repeating the trope of the Panama invasion "Operation Just Cause." As Jim Winter suggested (1991), in the era of Reagan/Bush Newspeak, wars "are only waged on poverty and drugs, not people." By contrast, the discourse of "operation" suggests the surgical removal of malignant matter. The medical discourse pervaded the war with its rhetoric of "surgical strikes," a term that connotes both a precise, clean mode of bombing and the beneficial removal of disease and malignancy. Likewise, Bush's attempt to overcome the "Vietnam syndrome" suggested overcoming the disease of weakness of will and hesitancy in using U.S. military power.

The code for the war itself, Operation Desert Storm, also created the impression that the Gulf war was a natural event, occurring as a force of nature. The war "erupted" with "waves" of attacks the first night. Bombs continued to "rain" on their targets and planes "thundered" through the night. Scuds "showered" their debris below, Baghdad was "awash" in sounds and lights as the bombs exploded, and the "fog of war" made it difficult to ascertain if U.S. troops were killed by "friendly fire." These metaphors coded the event as a natural, inexorable force and lent an air of inevitability to it. Pentagon consultant Bernard Lewis stated: "Once a war is under way the dynamics are difficult to control." The *Dallas Morning News* headline on January 17 read "War Unfolds in the Gulf" and the *Austin American Statesman* noted that "the U.S.-led ground campaign opened Saturday" (Feb. 24, 1991). Such events are without agents, without personal responsibility, and unfold with the force of mythic inevitability. No human agency can intervene to stop the war. The "world waits" for first the air war and then the ground war to erupt; the war "is on schedule" throughout; "the end is certain" and "of this, there can be no doubt," George Bush assured us.

Technowar discourse also mythologizes technology and invests it with powerful cultural meanings. Many of the weapons systems played on the mythologies of the American West such as the Apache helicopter and Chieftain, Sidewinder, and Tomahawk missiles. CBS utilized the Western mythology in its nightly logo "Showdown in the Gulf," reducing the war to a struggle between good and evil, like the Western and the fairy tale. Many of the weapons had the implication of powerful nature like Thunderbolt, Tornado, Hawk, Falcon, Hellfire, Hornet, and, of course, Operation Desert Storm itself. Moreover, Mirage and Stealth aircraft magically targeted their "smart bombs," while General Powell and General Schwarzkopf used all their "tools in a toolbox." Honorific qualities like "smart" were thus attributed to weapons, which also absorbed the pragmatic, familiar aura of "tools." In this way, military language occupied the terrain of human intelligence, everyday life, and mythology, which together helped constitute the Gulf war as a heroic project of the mythic destruction of evil.

Curiously, military language has always used terms with a strong sexual connotation and this was evident in the war in the Gulf. U.S. bombs "penetrated" enemy radar or targets, and during the ground war coalition forces quickly "penetrated" Iraqi defenses and "thrust deeply" inside Iraq itself. Weapon systems "engaged" the enemy, and there was constant concern that Saddam Hussein had "married" chemical warheads to his Scud missiles. The enemy was "softened" by saturation bombing, and the discourse of "cutting off" the Iraqi army contained an implied threat of castration; the Iraqi torching of Kuwaiti wells and rounding up of Kuwaiti males also played on sexual fears of castration. Making the castration theme explicit, a British tabloid even featured a story of an English candy firm making Saddam balls, pictured in the smiling mouths of Brit soldiers who were about to tear into them (*Evening Chronicle,* Feb. 23, 1991. Such sexual metaphors invest the bombing of Iraq with a positive, libidinal charge, supported by the images of destruction as a thrilling demonstration of precision weapons. They also mobilize sexual fears, like castration, against the "enemy."

Warspeak circulated daily in the media and was absorbed by a public that, in turn, reproduced the debased language. Talk radio and television shows, letters to the editor and opinion pieces, and everyday discussion exhibited countless examples of individuals parroting the language and propaganda fed them by the military, state, and media. The United States seemed to have been infected by a war psychosis, which made ordinary people raving militarists and fanatic patriots. How did this happen?

Yellow Ribbons and the Culture of Fear

Part of the reason that large sectors of the public supported the Gulf war was that television coverage of the war helped produce a cumulative mass hysteria and frightened people into submission to military discourse and propaganda. Massive and oft-repeated network TV coverage of chemical weapons threats, terrorism dangers, Scud missile attacks, the torture of POWs, and environmental crimes helped terrorize people into hating and fearing Hussein and the Iraqis. The delirium resulted in broad public support for whatever policies Bush and the Pentagon carried out and whatever disinformation and propaganda they produced. When people are fearful, they support individuals and groups who promise to assuage their fears and to protect them. The Bush administration and Pentagon attempted to project an image of strong, fatherly men in control and competent to deal with the nefarious threats to the people of the United States. The media reinforced this climate of fear and submission by dramatizing and exaggerating Iraqi evil, by masking U.S. lies and crimes, and by producing positive images of Bush and military officials.

The network news featured frequent reports on the tremendous increase in sales of army surplus war merchandise. Segments showed stockbrokers buying gas masks to take to work because they feared a terrorist attack on the New York subways. Stores all over the country sold out their gas masks after the dramatization of the Scud attacks on Israel and an announcement that President Bush's bodyguards were carrying gas masks at all times. One TV news episode featured a saleswoman who told of how a frantic mother came in the store that day to buy a plastic covering for her child's crib "like they have in Israel." On January 29, NBC featured a woman buying a gas mask, telling how her child had been waking up in terror at night, fearing an attack, and that she is buying a gas mask for the child to comfort her. On February 3, CNN broadcast a segment that showed an Atlanta family buying gas masks and constructing "safe rooms" in their house in case of a terrorist attack.

It is difficult to interpret the degree of fear, and, in particular, fear of terrorism, evident in the American public during the Gulf war. Airline travel declined dramatically and many people were afraid to leave their houses, leading to loss of profit and many bankruptcies in the entertainment and service industries. Gas masks sold out all over the country, calls to police bomb squads in major cities multiplied tenfold, and security systems companies claimed that business was up over 50 percent. In his analysis of the symbolic culture of violence in the United States, George Gerbner and his colleagues in the Annenberg School of Communication argued for years that the culture of TV violence produced a "mean world" syndrome whereby people who watched heavy doses of TV violence were highly fearful and tended to submit to conservative leaders who claimed to alleviate their fear (Gerbner and Gross 1976). During the crisis in the Gulf, Gerbner and his associates (1992) did research that indicated that the amount of violence in film culture was accelerating significantly; the number of episodes of violence in sequels to popular films like *Robocop, Die Hard,* and *Young Guns* doubled or tripled in comparison to the original, showing that a culture nurtured on violence needed ever heavier doses to get their fix. Such heavy doses of violence from popular culture, however, created dispositions toward fear that led the public to seek refuge in authoritarian leaders like George Bush or General Schwarzkopf.

Psychohistorian William K. Joseph (1991) suggested that the coming of the war was forecast by *Home Alone,* one of the most popular movies of 1990.

> This movie depicted a prosperous, self-indulgent group. The hero of the story was treated quite poorly in early life by his parents and family. Finding himself at the crossroads of collapse or going into battle, he chooses to go to war against the most heinous of characters, an evil and ugly child tormentor who will stop at nothing to defeat his enemy.
>
> The scenes of battle are vivid and violent and the weapons are used in brilliant strategic fashion. Finally the foe is defeated because the hero was wise enough to create a most unlikely alliance. The jubilation and celebration at the end of the movie was indeed moving and the euphoria of the hero's supporters was unbounded. (pp. 32–33)

In addition, two of the most popular movies during the Gulf war were psychological thrillers (*Sleeping with the Enemy* and *Silence of the Lambs*), which featured threats to innocent people from psychotic killers. Both mobilized the public to desire the destruction of evil threats and legitimated violence to destroy that evil. Both radiated fear and paranoia, supplementing TV coverage of threats to the public from the evil Iraqis and helping to permeate the culture with fear. In particular, TV promoted a culture of fear by presenting nightly episodes warning about the threats of Iraqi chemical weapons, terrorism, and destruction while popular culture featured a symbolic environment of terror and destruction. The country seemed to go into a war hysteria where they simply accepted whatever lies and propaganda they were fed by the Bush administration and Pentagon, submitting their rationality and humanity to the symbolic fathers who promised to take care of them.

The war hysteria in the United States produced an infantilization of U.S. society, which was especially evident in the fetishism of yellow ribbons and the prowar demonstrations. Yellow ribbons had been broadly displayed during the Iranian hostage crisis in which U.S. hostages were held in the late 1970s by militant Iranians. The yellow ribbons go back to the Civil War and Indian wars in which the families of soldiers displayed yellow ribbons when their loved ones were away at war and held in captivity (recall John Ford's John Wayne vehicle *She Wore a Yellow Ribbon* and the popular song "Tie a Yellow Ribbon 'Round the Old Oak Tree"). The ribbons reappeared when U.S. citizens were held captive by the Iraqis in Iraq and Kuwait during the crisis in the Gulf.

The yellow ribbon symbolism in the Gulf war combined the hostage and soldiers-in-harm's-way connotation, with a popular discourse portraying the U.S. troops as the hostages of "Sad-dam In-sane." Curiously, the symbolism of the ribbons was transferred back and forth from hostages to soldiers; initially, the ribbons were displayed to commemorate the situation of the hostages but were soon transferred to the soldiers. This symbolic transference suggested that the U.S. troops in Saudi Arabia were hostages, held against their will in the desert because of the presence of an evil which had to be surgically removed (actually the troops and the entire world were the hostages of the respective Iraqi and U.S. political and military establishments which produced the war). The symbolism implied that innocent Americans abroad were victims of foreign aggression and linked the soldiers with their supporters on the domestic front.

Displaying yellow ribbons provided talismans, good luck charms, and signs of social conformity all at once. It enlisted those who displayed yellow ribbons in the war effort, making them part of the adventure. Drawing on mythological resonances, tying ribbons to trees connected culture with nature, naturalizing the solidarity and community of Gulf war supporters. The ribbons symbolically tied together the community into a unified whole, bound together by its support for the troops.[6] The ribbons thus signified that one supported the troops, that one was a loyal member of the patriotic community, that one was a team player and a good American. They also signified, however, that one was ready to give up one's faculties of critical thought and to submit to whatever policies and adventures the Bush administration might attempt.

Indeed, the sight of yellow ribbons mesmerized the media, scared Congress, and demoralized antiwar protestors. Yellow ribbons appeared everywhere in some neighborhoods and regions of the country and some individuals who refused to put yellow ribbons on their homes were threatened by their neighbors. This mode of forced conformity reveals a quasi-fascist hysteria unleashed by the Gulf war and a disturbing massification of the public.

Dehumanization, Racism, and Violence

The Gulf war involved a massive dehumanization process both on the home front and the battle front. Supporters of the war at home became parts of human flags, crowds mindlessly chanting "U.S.A!, U.S.A!," and uncritical conduits of the lies and propaganda disseminated by the government and media. Many troops in the Gulf dehumanized their Iraqi "enemy" and took pleasure in killing. A-10 pilot Captain Eric Salomonson stated: "I'm proud to have dropped some bombs on these guys. We could hardly wipe the smiles off our faces. We fired off more live ammunition than I ever have. It was great." Pilots flying over groups of Iraqi troops reported that they "ran like ants" when the bombs were dropped on them, while Susan Sachs of *Newsday* reported that Col. Dick "Snake" White stated: "It's like someone turned on the kitchen light on late at night, and the cockroaches started scurrying. We finally got them out where we can find them and kill them" (Feb. 1, 1991, p. 4). (See the discussion of the "Turkey Shoot" during the ground war in Chapter 9 for more examples of the dehumanization of the Iraqis by the U.S. troops in the Gulf.)

The mainstream media contributed to the dehumanization process through its use of euphemisms and military language, its demonization of Saddam Hussein and the Iraqi "enemy," and its serving as an instrument of U.S. government propaganda. As Norman Solomon pointed out:

> As soon as the war began, *Time* magazine defined "collateral damage" this way—"a term meaning dead or wounded civilians who should have picked a safer neighborhood." In U.S. news media, the rare mention of civilian casualties is routinely followed by immediate denial of responsibility. "We must point out again and again that it is Saddam Hussein who put these innocents in harm's way," Tom Brokaw declared on NBC, a network owned by one of the nation's largest military contractors, General Electric. "The MacNeil-Lehrer News Hour"—one of TV's leading war boosters—aired a few moments of civilian casualty footage from Iraq, only to debunk it as "heavy-handed manipulation." On CBS, reporter Ron Allen said that "Iraq is trying to gain sympathy" by showing grisly film of bombed civilian sites. Connie Chung chimed in that Saddam is "trying to break the resolve of the United States and its allies." (PeaceNet, mideast.media, Feb. 4, 1991)

Solomon, as well as Pratt (1991) and Umberson and Henderson (1991), argued that there was a massive denial underway during the Gulf war, in which the U.S. refused to take any responsibility for Iraqi suffering, blaming it all on Saddam Hussein. Pratt (1991) commented that the war hysteria evident during the Gulf war represented a displacement of fear and anxiety that led to the search for alien scapegoats and the use of brute force to establish a (false) collective feeling of power and identity. When people feel threatened and insecure, they seek scapegoats; throughout U.S. history Native Americans and other people of color, communists, and various domestic and foreign "enemies" have served as scapegoats. During the Gulf war, Iraqis were scapegoated as threats to the U.S. economy and "American way of life." Higher energy prices, inflation, the loss of jobs, and a declining economy were blamed on Saddam Hussein and the Iraqis, and Americans apparently felt satisfaction in seeing them punished and experienced empowerment through identification with U.S. military and technological might.

The personalization of the Iraqi enemy in the figure of Saddam Hussein allowed the Iraqi president to be the ultimate scapegoat. One soldier reported: "No one talks about 'the enemy.' They talk about Saddam Hussein. 'Hussein did this.' 'Hussein did that'" (cited in Anderson and van Atta 1991, p. 165). Bush, Schwarzkopf, and others also routinely blamed the war and all suffering on Saddam Hussein. This scapegoating of Hussein allowed the United States to legitimate its destruction of the Iraqis, but such transference of guilt from Hussein to the Iraqi people was hypocritical because the Iraqi people, too, were victims of Hussein's oppression yet it was they who were receiving the brunt of the violent U.S. bombing.

The denial of U.S. guilt for the slaughter of Iraqis was also aided, as Umberson and Henderson (1991) argued, by reifying the enemy and personifying things. Bombs were "smart" and equipment was "killed," thus making it a "casualty of war." "Tank units," "Scud missile launchers," Iraqi aircraft, and "assets" were killed, not people. When people were referred to they were reified and dehumanized. The "elite Republican Guard units" were reified as things and a number of euphemisms were employed for killing (see 6.11). Worse still, racist epithets such as "cockroaches," "sand niggers," "camel jockeys," and other dehumanizing terms were used to describe the Iraqis, while their slaughter was described in hunting terms as "a turkey shoot," "shooting fish in a barrel," or "clubbing seals."

Denial is often coupled with projection and throughout the crisis and the war all evil was projected onto the Iraqis while the American effort was described as "just" and "moral." Such blatant projection involved the denial of the suffering caused by the U.S.-led coalition bombing and the fact that the Gulf war was a human and ecological holocaust for the people of the Middle East. Indeed, the extent of the U.S. brutality was so great that it would be difficult for the media boosters and fans of the war to look the results of U.S. bombing in the face without shame and guilt. Thus the media and other promoters of the war regularly blamed all of the war's destruction on Iraq—a phenomenon that would be most evident in the U.S. bombing of an Iraqi civilian shelter (see 7.3).

Military socialization and a thoroughly brutal process of military training had obviously produced "a bloody good bunch of killers" (as Gen. George Patton III put it in Vietnam) ready to slaughter Iraqis in the desert sands. In the hangar at one U.S. airfield there was a giant banner of a U.S. "Superman" holding a limp and terrified Arab with a big hooked nose in his arms. As units passed through the U.S. air base in Torrejon, Spain, on their way to the Gulf, they left their calling cards on the wall that read:

Door Gunners from Hell:
If it walks, it crawls, it dies.
—QB Company, 2nd Battalion, 502 Infantry

Or:

If you kill for fun, you're a sadist.
If you kill for money, you're a mercenary.
If you kill for both, you're a paratrooper.
—Q3rd Battalion, 505 Airborne Regiment.[7]

CNN featured a segment from Fort Benning, Georgia, at the beginning of the Gulf crisis where troops chanted "one, two, three, four, Kill Hussein!" in their training exercises. There were also many examples of protofascist behavior among the U.S. population during the Gulf war. An Italian basketball player at Seton Hall University was thrown off the team when he refused to wear a U.S. flag on his uniform and eventually returned to Italy after harassment by "patriots." After Prof. Barbara Scott, at a campus rally at the State University of New York, New Paltz, urged U.S. military personnel not to kill innocent people, she was dubbed "Baghdad Barbara," was accused of treason by a state senator, was subjected to hate mail and a letter campaign aimed at the university president and Governor Mario Cuomo, urging them to fire her. In Kutztown, Pennsylvania, a newspaper editor was fired for his editorial titled "How about a Little Peace?" and an editor was fired from a Round Rock, Texas, paper for publishing an interview with a Palestinian-American expressing antiwar views.[8]

Arab-Americans were victims of government harassment and intimidation since the beginning of the crisis. Neal Saad described how Arab-Americans were visited by the FBI in their homes, places of business, and neighborhoods and were questioned concerning attitudes to U.S. policy in the Middle East, the PLO, Arab-American political activities, and terrorism (in Clark et al. 1992, pp. 188ff.). During the war harassment intensified and Pan American Airlines actually decided not to allow Arab passengers on their planes! Identifying ethnic members of a country with "the enemy" itself promotes oppression of minorities who belong to these groups. This identification happened in World War II with Japanese-Americans who were interned in concentration camps and began in the crisis in the Gulf with FBI investigations of Arab-Americans. The result was a resurgence of racism against Arabs and acts of violence against them.

Anti-Arab racism proliferated within U.S. popular culture. For years, Arabs had regularly been villainized in Hollywood films and American television entertainment (see Kellner and Ryan 1988), and during the

Gulf war anti-Arab sentiments were mobilized against Iraqis. The words "Bomb Iraq" were superimposed on the lyrics of the Beach Boy song "Barbara Ann." A radio show in Georgia proclaimed, "towelhead weekend," telling callers to phone in when they heard the traditional Islamic call to prayer; a disk jockey in Toledo, Ohio, solicited funds from listeners to buy a ticket to Iraq for an Iraqi-American professor who was critical of the war. Jennie Anderson wrote: "In the United States, anti-Arab propaganda is a hot commercial item. A widely disseminated T-shirt pictures a U.S. Marine pointing a rifle at an Arab on the ground, with the caption, HOW MUCH IS OIL NOW? Another briskly selling T-shirt shows military planes attacking an Arab on a camel, with the caption, I'D FLY 10,000 MILES TO SMOKE A CAMEL," (*The Progressive,* Feb. 1991, pp. 28–29). "KICK THEIR ASS, TAKE THEIR GAS" was a sample T-shirt slogan quoted by the *New York Times* (March 19, 1992). Another T-Shirt read: "JOIN THE ARMY, SEE INTERESTING PLACES, MEET NEW PEOPLE, AND KILL THEM."

In addition, there was much violence against Arab-Americans in the United States during the Gulf war.[9] Even before the war began, businesses owned by Arab-Americans were bombed, an Arab-American businessman was beaten by a white supremacist mob in Toledo, a Palestinian family riding in a car was shot at in Kansas City, and an Arab-American who appeared on a Pennsylvania television program received seven death threats. Later, Edward Said and other Arab-American activists received death threats, and during the Gulf war itself violence against Arab-Americans accelerated. The United States had demonized Arabs for years in the figures of the Ayatollah Khomeini (actually, a Persian and not an Arab), Yasir Arafat, Muammar Qadhafi, and the images of the Arab terrorist. The demonization of Saddam Hussein and the Iraqis heated up racist passions that exploded into violence against Arab-Americans.

Racism and dehumanizing national peoples or ethnic groups promotes violence at home and abroad. Dehumanizing individuals or groups makes them legitimate targets for violence and thus encourages and justifies social violence. One of the pernicious effects of war is that it accelerates racial violence. In order to kill members of another country or race, one must perceive them to be worthy of death and thus there is a tendency to perceive one's opponent as less than human. Schwarzkopf was constantly dehumanizing the Iraqis, indicating in a briefing at the end of the ground war that he would not want to belong to the same race as those Iraqis who had committed atrocities in Kuwait (see 9.3). Yet Schwarzkopf's own troops were at the moment he spoke slaughtering Iraqis in one of the great bloodbaths of history and from this episode one sees that one of the functions of the dehumanization of the "enemy" is to legitimate violent and destructive actions.

Wars also divide countries between those who do and do not support the official war policies and the Gulf war produced incredible division and conflict in the country. It polarized individuals into pro- and antiwar groups, it alienated people from those who did not share their views, it ruptured families, friendships, and the vestiges of communities that have survived the onslaught of television and the consumer society. Although TV portrayed the division clearly in the case of Arcata, California, a town torn between pro- and antiwar citizens (i.e., on a CBS news segment on January 24 and an NBC segment on February 3), one rarely saw the genuine divisions in the country over the Gulf war, or the antiwar voices as the war ground on. Most of the people that I spoke to, ranging from my neighbors and colleagues to students, were against the war and we had well-attended teach-ins every day at the University of Texas, so there was certainly an invisible antiwar public in the United States. In the months after the war, I talked to many people who said that in their travels and work in rural Kentucky, south Texas, Michigan, and other parts of the country there was significant opposition to the war—much more than the polls and media let on.[10] Before the war began, polls and media discourse revealed a divided nation and, as we shall see in the next section, one could see the divisions at the beginning of the war, but they became invisible in the media discourse and images as the war proceeded.

6.2 Demonstrations and Propaganda Campaigns

During the Gulf war individuals were not merely passive spectators of the media war, but there were active pro- and antiwar demonstrations and organizing. There was a large antiwar movement in place before the war even began and many prowar groups became active as the war went on. In the following pages I explore how TV presented the antiwar movement and then discuss some of the ways that prowar groups, the media, and Bush administration mobilized support for the war.

The Antiwar Movement and TV Bias

Contrary to the opinion of many in the antiwar movement, during the first ten days of the war, television provided fairly extensive and not completely unsympathetic coverage of the antiwar movement. The commercial TV networks are profit-machines and at the early stages of a war cannot be certain if the war will be successful and popular. Thus they tended to show both pro- and antiwar sentiment to please both sides of the audience. However, the protest movement soon disappeared from the media spotlight, which instead lavished attention on prowar demonstrations for the duration of the war. During the opening night of the war there were frequent reports on antiwar demonstrations in California, New York, and other parts of the country ranging from Iowa to Texas. In fact, there had been a large antiwar movement active from the beginning of the crisis in the Gulf that the media suddenly discovered in December as Congress held hearings on the war and a fierce debate broke out concerning whether force or negotiations should be used to get Iraq out of Kuwait. As noted earlier, the country had been genuinely divided, and the networks began to feature stories on the rapidly growing antiwar movement, mainly in vignettes dealing with individuals involved in the movement.

On January 15 and 16, as the deadline for Iraq to leave Kuwait approached and passed, significant coverage of the antiwar movement appeared on television. Both national and local news prominently featured stories on candlelight vigils in which large groups of individuals prayed for peace. During the first days of the war, frequent presentations of antiwar demonstrations throughout the country appeared on television, showing antiwar demonstrators in San Francisco blocking the Golden Gate bridge, high school students in Iowa and California carrying out lively demonstrations, demonstrators in Seattle taking over the state capital building, 4,000 occupying the Texas state capital in Austin, and antiwar demonstrations all over the country.

On the first weekend of the war, January 19–20, the big demonstrations in Washington, D.C., and San Francisco, in which around 100,000 people marched in opposition to Bush's war, were covered on TV.[11] On Sunday, January 20, CBS's "Sunday Morning" program featured a sympathetic segment on opposition to the war in Durham, N.C., and the local stations in Austin, Texas, presented detailed coverage of the weekend's antiwar activity. There was coverage by the networks of a sit-in at the University of California, Los Angeles (UCLA), and civil disobedience in Boston. For the next week as well, there was coverage of antiwar demonstrations, with the major TV networks also providing coverage of the antiwar movement which was national in scope.

On CNN, Ann McDermott narrated a segment on January 23 that showed that antiwar protests were more organized and diverse than in past wars. Pointing out the differences between the protests in the Vietnam era, the CNN reporter noted that protests in the earlier era were motivated by a feeling of deep alienation from the system, but the current demonstrations were often organized by people strongly integrated into the system. Many protesters had been involved in other issues and a diverse range of groups and types of activities were visible, ranging from high school and college students organizing demonstrations, to lobbying efforts, involvement in peace campaigns, education efforts like teach-ins, and prayer vigils. The segment indicated that there was much rational criticism of Bush administration policies in the movement, a worry about violence on both sides, and insistence that antiwar activity was patriotic and supportive of the troops. Indeed, antiwar demonstrators claimed that if one really supported the troops, one should work to bring them home safely.

The message of the antiwar movement was thus, McDermott concluded, the same as during Vietnam: Stop the war. Many TV reports stressed similarities with the earlier 1960s' antiwar movement such as a CBS segment featuring signs reminiscent of Vietnam: "Bring the troops home," "Peace Now," "U.S. Out of Iraq," and "Hell no, we won't go, we won't kill for Texaco!" though one demonstrator carried a sign more appropriate to the TV war currently underway: "Violence begins at breakfast." On January 25, "CBS This Morning" had an excellent segment on organized local and national efforts to stop the war. Roger Newell, representing the National Committee for Peace in the Middle East, stated that, "the American people want an end to the conflict," and he stressed that the goal of the movement was to bring the troops home safely. The organization sought to end the military conflict in the Middle East, to reshape national priorities, and to rectify the devastation caused "by the militarization of the economy" by the Reagan and Bush administrations. Actress Margot Kidder called for a ceasefire now "before the boys in the desert will be getting killed." She was working with the Friendship of Reconciliation, a religious pacifist group, and stressed that the victims in Iraq are children, innocent civilians, and refugees. A physician who was called up with the military reserves, Yolanda Huet-Vaughn, refused to go to Saudi Arabia, went AWOL, and joined the antiwar movement. She claimed that the coalition forces were dropping the "equivalent of a Hiroshima a day on Iraq." Citing German sources who estimated that there would be from 100,000 to 300,000 civilian Iraqi casualties, she warned that an environmental catastrophe in the region could take thousands of more lives. Huet-Vaughn declared that she had trained as a physician to save lives and would not now serve in an effort that was so wantonly destroying lives.

CBS also featured a segment on military recruiters in high schools who got a mixed response to efforts at recruitment; high school antiwar activists told reporters that they resented the presence of military recruiters on their campus. The report indicated that several big cities had rules against giving out addresses of high school students and had banned military recruiters from high school. Earlier, NBC covered the banning of military recruiters from high schools in Oakland and a debate over whether this violated free speech of the military.

On January 26, CNN had a segment on the image problem of the antiwar movement, which was often perceived as unshaven, countercultural, and violent. Roger Newell argued against this perception by claiming that the mainstream was directly involved in the current peace movement, which included the National Council of Bishops, the National Council of Churches, and many religious organizations. The movement also had very diverse demographics, he claimed, drawing supporters from groups ranging from students, blacks, gays, pacifists, unions, women, and so on. The movement rejected the idea that public protest is unpatriotic, though, as author Jim Miller noted, its participants had gone beyond unquestioning acceptance of what the government said was a rationale for a war. A black woman pointed out the irony that although there seemed to be billions of dollars to fight a war, there was no money for child care, health care, shelter for the homeless, or job training for the unemployed.

Yet a FAIR "Gulf War Sources Survey" of television coverage of the war from January 17–January 30, 1991, found that only 1.5 percent of the network TV sources were identified as U.S. antiwar protesters—about the same percentage of people asked to comment on how the war had affected their travel plans; only one leader of a peace organization was quoted in the broadcasts surveyed, while, by contrast, seven Super Bowl players were asked their opinions on the war; about half of the sources were connected to either U.S. or allied governments; and few intellectuals and professionals associated with the antiwar movement appeared while retired military personnel were most frequently used by the networks as "experts" (FAIR Press Release, Feb. 26, 1991).

There was a tremendous amount of coverage, invariably prowar, of the military families coping with war. These segments bonded the country to the troops and their families, serving as propaganda devices for military views because often the families appearing on television were coached by the military, told what to say—and what they were not to say. In addition, "person in the street" interviews and segments on communities dealing with the war became increasingly prowar. CNN had several units traveling around the country, sampling public opinion, and the reports were overwhelmingly prowar. With the exception of some examples discussed above, there were few segments dealing with people organizing and struggling against the war, and TV reinforced the prowar public-opinion consensus by making it appear unpatriotic to be against the war as they increasingly promoted the new patriotism.

Furthermore, the mainstream media ignored completely the theme of resistance against the war within the military. Yolanda Huet-Vaughn was able to surface on some TV programs when she went AWOL for refusing to accept her military reserve orders, and a clip of her being arrested and taken to prison for her resistance was briefly shown. During the crisis in the Gulf, there were some reports on Marine reservist Erik Larsen, who refused his orders and was an active participant in the antiwar movement, but there was little or nothing on the many other cases of troops who refused orders to fight in the Gulf. In both the United States and Germany many soldiers went AWOL when they got their Gulf orders.[12] Nor has there been TV coverage of their later trials and, in some cases, prison sentences for their resistance to the war. Yet, in retrospect, it was precisely these resisters who were the true heroes of the Gulf war, many of whom are now languishing in prison.

Nonetheless, throughout the country, antiwar demonstrations continued to unfold, despite the media attacks and the more positive coverage of prowar demonstrations. Divisions in the country became less and less visible, however, for network television gave less and less coverage to opposition to the war, and one heard almost no antiwar voices in the mainstream media as the war went on. What little one saw of the antiwar demonstrations was reduced to quick images of crowds without any discourse and there was hardly anything on the growing European or Third World antiwar movements and demonstrations. One got a quick glance at 200,000 German antiwar demonstrators in Bonn; brief images of large demonstrations in Britain, Italy, and Spain; and snippets of images of hundreds of thousands of Arabs demonstrating in Algeria, Libya, Morocco, Jordan, and other Arab, Moslem, and Third World countries as well.

TV's increasingly prowar stance and its exclusion of legitimate antiwar discourses was primarily, I believe, because commercial television is fundamentally a money machine. At the start of the war, the television machines envisaged that their audience was split and tried to portray both sides of the issue, in part to avoid alienating segments of their audiences and thus suffer declining ratings and advertising rates. As the public opinion polls showed increasing support for Bush and his war policies, and as conservative prowar fanatics began attacking the antiwar demonstrators and the media that broadcast their message, the amount of coverage given to the antiwar movement steadily declined while prowar demonstrations, however small, repetitive, and mindless, got good coverage. This is not, I would submit, because the television networks were intrinsically prowar, but because their lust for ratings and profits dictated that they follow popular opinion, which increasingly supported the war. Thus, the occasional antiwar voice heard during the first two weeks of the war was excluded from the mainstream media which turned to publicize the new patriotism, love of the flag, and prowar demonstrations.

Patriotism, the Flag, and Football

Eventually, U.S. Vice-President Dan Quayle assumed former Vice-President Spiro Agnew's role during the Vietnam era and attacked protesters and the media. Speaking to a military crowd in Texas on January 25, Quayle began attacking the antiwar demonstrations where: "some American flags were burned." En masse, the crowd booed as the demagogic Quayle continued: "And, unfortunately, the media seemed compelled to devote much more time to these protests than they've deserved." At this lie, the crowd broke into applause and Quayle, who was reportedly able to get out of active duty during Vietnam through his father's political connections, nodded his head. And thus Quayle and the Bush administration followed the Nazi leader Hermann Göring's advice that "all you have to do is tell people they are being attacked, and denounce the pacifists for lack of patriotism and exposing the country to danger. It works the same in every country."

Indeed, the Bush administration promoted the line that one was either prowar and a good citizen, or antiwar and thus not a good citizen, not a patriotic American. Call-in radio and television shows featured rabid and aggressive attacks on the antiwar demonstrators, and more and more prowar demonstrations and violent opposition to the antiwar demonstrators appeared on television. On January 17 at a basketball game in Missoula, Montana, as antiwar protesters were being dragged off the courts by police, the crowd pelted the protesters with potatoes and began chanting "U.S.A! U.S.A!" In fact, one began seeing prowar demonstrations almost every day on television, with crowds waving the flag and chanting "U.S.A! U.S.A!" Media critic Dan Quayle to the contrary, these usually small demonstrations got more coverage than the larger antiwar demonstrations. The networks quickly shifted, on cue from the Bush administration, to segments covering the "new patriotism" and love of the flag. News reports featured yellow ribbons and flags with many stories on flag factories where the managers indicated that they could barely keep up with the demand.

Carl Boggs (1991) argued that the intense nationalism, racism, glorification of violence, and militarism evident during the Gulf war was a response to growing powerlessness and insecurity, and was similar to the situation in Nazi Germany analyzed by Erich Fromm in *Escape From Freedom* (1941). The prowar demonstrations seemed to offer mechanisms through which individuals could escape their powerlessness and overcome (temporarily) their insecurities. The flagwaving and chanting pointed to individuals immersing themselves in masses and exhibiting collectivist, conformist behavior. It appeared that powerless individuals felt themselves part of something greater than themselves when they chanted and waved flags. Human flag phenomena began to appear: in San Diego, 30,000 people appeared in red, white, and blue T-shirts on January 25 to form the world's largest human flag, photographed from a blimp and dutifully broadcast by the television networks. On February 2, an even larger human flag was formed in Virginia Beach, Virginia, with 40,000 people chanting "U.S.A!, U.S.A!" as they became one with their country and flag. On February 15, CNN featured a story on the new patriotism in which flags were shown flying en masse throughout the country and TV images linked the flags to portraits of George Bush, accompanied by the 1988 Republican campaign song as background music.

All over the country, whenever there was a prowar demonstration, crowds chanted "U.S.A! U.S.A!" The lack of specific content in the chant in favor of empty patriotism contrasted with the antiwar chants and slogans that always had a specific content—attacking the war, calling for the troops to come home now, or affirming specific values like peace. Yet the masses of prowar demonstrators who chanted "U.S.A!" every time they were given the occasion were not articulating any particular values or reasons for their prowar and pro-America stance. Rather, they were simply immersing themselves in a crowd and expressing primal patriotism, national narcissism, and aggressive threats against anyone who was different. The "USA!" chant thus expressed loyalty to the home team in the Super Bowl championship of contemporary war and bound together the prowar constituency into a national community of those identifying with the U.S. war policy, becoming part of something bigger than themselves through participation.

In addition, the prowar demonstrations seemed to make people feel good through providing experiences of community and empowerment denied them in everyday life. Those who were usually powerless were able to feel powerful, identifying themselves as part of the nation proudly asserting itself in the war. Losers in everyday life, the prowar demonstrators could experience themselves as part of the winning team in the Gulf war. Participating in the prowar rituals thus gave individuals new and attractive identities that provided a sense of participation in a great national adventure. Like sports events and rock concerts, the prowar demonstrations thus provided the participants with at least a fleeting sense of community, denied them in the privatized temples of consumption, serialized media watching, and isolated "life styles." For almost 100 years, sociologists have studied crowd behavior and analyzed the mechanisms through which individuals dissolve themselves in mass behavior. During the Gulf war the phenomenon of individuals immersing themselves in mass behavior was a daily feature of the TV war. Usually, American community in the Age of the Media is a simulated TV community, whereby one becomes one with the others by watching the same images and participating in the same ritualized experience of events like the Super Bowl or Gulf war. Yet one could participate in the ritual of the Gulf war more fully by leaving one's home and joining into prowar demonstrations, in which one could become more vitally integrated into the patriotic community.

The flag-waving and chanting also provided a new form of participatory experience that enabled individuals to be part of an aesthetic spectacle. The prowar flag wavers and chanters had been immersed for years in the aesthetic of consumer culture: viewing seductive commodities in advertisements; fascinated by images of luxury, eroticism, and power in the images of popular entertainment; tempted by the dazzling display of the commodity world in malls and stores; and gratified by whatever items they could afford to buy in their everyday lives (i.e., cars, clothes, electronics, etc.). The Gulf war was packaged as an aesthetic spectacle, with CNN utilizing powerful drum music to introduce their news segments, superimposing images of the U.S. flag over American troops, and employing up-beat martial music between breaks. The audience was thus invited to participate in a dazzling war spectacle by its media presentation.

But prowar demonstrators were able to overcome the usual privatization and passivity of TV culture by more actively participating in the public celebrations of the war. Many individuals of the TV war audience were normally isolated, disempowered, and able to feel that they belonged in the consumer society only if they could afford to buy the icons and totems of social prestige. A prowar demonstration and flag waving, however, is a cheap thrill, offering anyone the opportunity to become part of an aesthetic spectacle of flag waving, rousing music, and enthusiastic chanting. Although individuals at home watching television are passive and isolated, in prowar demonstrations the participants were active and socially bonded.

Indeed, the prowar constituency rooted for the U.S. team as if it were a sports event and from the beginning there was a close relation between war and football. During a break in a nationally televised football bowl game from El Paso shown on New Year's eve, an announcer greeted U.S. soldiers in the stands who were there courtesy of The John Hancock insurance company. Then, as Haynes Johnson put it, "while the cameras panned rows of cheering, waving soldiers, the sportscaster pointed to a mural painted across the stadium wall. Depicted was an eagle swooping down on prey. Helpful as ever, while the cameras slowly played across the mural, the sportscaster read aloud the message spelled out there: 'Go Desert Shield, Beat Iraq'" (*Washington Post,* Jan. 4, 1991, p. A2).

During the Super Bowl weekend of January 25–26 patriotism, flag waving, and support for the war were encouraged by Bush and the media. Bush insisted that the Super Bowl game not be postponed and urged the nation at his Friday, January 24, news briefing to enjoy the game during the weekend. The ubiquitous television reports documented the unprecedented security at the Super Bowl, with almost 2,000 security personnel checking each spectator with metal detectors. Radios, TV sets, purses, and other items were not allowed, and spectators had to wait in line for hours to submit to the searches and gain entrance to the game. Television also reported on the brisk selling of Operation Desert Storm T-shirts, pins, hats, and other memorabilia, and especially flags, which were the best sellers of the day. The "Star Spangled Banner" was dedicated to the "half million fans in the Gulf," identifying troops with fans, war with football. Footage shown that evening confirmed the identification, showing troops in the desert staying up all night to watch the football game (it was amazing that Iraq failed to fire any Scuds that day or even to begin the ground war, which would have caught the sleepy fans in the Gulf off guard).

The football fans at home, in turn, were rooting for the troops while watching the game. One sign said: "Slime Saddam" and a barely verbal fan told the TV cameras that "he's messin' with the wrong people," while fan after fan affirmed his or her support for the troops. One of the teams wore yellow ribbons on their uniforms and the football stars went out of their way to affirm support for the troops and/or the war. Halftime featured mindless patriotic gore, with a young, blonde Aryan boy singing to the troops "you're my heroes," while fans waved flags, formed a human flag, and chanted "U.S.A! U.S.A!", reminding one of the fascist spectacles programmed by the Nazis to bind the nation into a patriotic community.

Also during the halftime, a videotaped speech by George Bush was broadcast dedicated to the men and women in the Gulf, with Barbara Bush standing next to him, beaming at her husband, and helping project a strong family image—the ultimate photo opportunity for a politician. Bush's message was that the families of the troops were the true heroes, aiming a lowest-common-denominator discourse at the narcissism of the families suffering from the loss of those currently serving in the Gulf. Yet it was simply demagogic to claim that the families at home were the heroes rather than those troops in the Gulf inhaling chemicals from the bombing of chemical plants,[13] sleeping with scorpions and deadly insects in the cold desert, ploughing through mud without the possibility of a shower for weeks on end, eating cold packaged food, and suffering god knows what fears as they were getting ready for the bloody ground war.

During the Super Bowl week, there were frequent discussions of the connections between war and football, patriotism and sports in the

American imagination. Both activities involve teamwork, coordination, and game plans, and both activities are highly competitive and violent. In both, squadrons of helmeted men seek to gain territory and try to drive their enemy back, while throwing balls, bombs, or bullets down-field. Both stress the values of discipline, training, teamwork, hitting the opposition hard, and, above all, winning. On December 19, Lt. Gen. Calvin Waller told the press, "I'm like a football coach. I want everything I can possibly get and have at my side of the field when I get ready to go into the Super Bowl" (United Press International (UPI), Dec. 20, 1990). On a news segment on the CBS morning show on January 25, a sports fan stated that he liked Buffalo in the bowl because "it's an impressive unit with powerful weapons." A U.S. soldier in a January 23 report on CNN said that "Saddam Hussein doesn't have much of a team; in comparison with football he'd be the Cleveland Browns." Army Chief Warrant Officer Ron Moring stated on the eve of the war: "It's time to quit the pregame show. We're a lot more serious about what we're doing. There's a lot more excitement in the air."[14]

Football metaphors were also employed in war rhetoric when Bush said that Tariq Aziz gave them a "stiff arm" after the unsuccessful Geneva meeting at the eve of the war. Helen Thomas asked Bush in a January 18 press briefing if the Gorbachev peace initiative was perceived as an "end run" [around Bush's desire to start the war]. A Canadian Broadcasting Corporation (CBC) Radio headline indicated that the Canadian armed forces in the Gulf were given "the green light to tackle the Iraqis." ABC's "Nightline" (Jan. 17, 1991), quoted fliers just back from the first missions of the war, enthusing: "It's just like a football game once you get airborne and you get the jet under you and you start feeling good, then you just start working—working your game plan." Another pilot exclaimed: "It's like being a professional athlete and never playing a game. Today was the first game and the enemy didn't show up, the opponent didn't show up. We went out there and ran our first play and it worked great, scored a touchdown, there was nobody home."

In addition, the military planners talked of making an "end run" around the Iraqi troops massed on the Kuwaiti border. Scud missiles were "intercepted" by Patriots and Col. Ray Davies described the U.S. air team as "like the Dallas Cowboys football team. They weren't a real emotional team. That's exactly what it's like with these pilots out here. They know exactly what they've got to do" (*Washington Post,* Jan. 19, p. C1). Furthermore, the audience processed the Gulf war as a football game. A Jesuit professor wrote in the *National Catholic Reporter* that, "A resident adviser in one of our college dorms tells me his students watched the CNN live war and cheered and took bets as if they were watching a football game. Small wonder. A sports mind-set has revved us up for the war. Some weeks ago, TV's most disconcerting image was of Defense Secretary Dick Cheney whipping the cheering troops into a fighting frenzy as if he were a coach at halftime in a locker room" (Feb. 1, 1991, p. 1). And so did the Gulf war become a game in which the U.S. emerged victorious in the Super Bowl of wars.

Bush's Propaganda Offensive

During the week beginning on Monday, January 28, the Bush administration mobilized the theme of patriotism as its major propaganda line in the war effort. It was a carefully orchestrated effort in which every day Bush carried out a propaganda offensive to generate patriotism and solidify support for the war. Analysis of this campaign reveals how Bush used patriotism, religion, and moral rhetoric to mobilize support for his war policies.

On Monday, Bush addressed a convention of religious broadcasters and presented his "just war" speech. In his State of the Union address on Tuesday, Bush mobilized patriotic rhetoric in support of Operation Desert Storm and insisted that the United States is the beacon of freedom and democracy, that U.S. leadership in the world is indispensable, that "the hopes of humanity turn to us. . . . We are Americans." Continuing the moral rhetoric of the week, Bush concluded: "Our cause is just. Our cause is moral. Our cause is right." On Wednesday, Bush spoke briefly at a congressional ceremony honoring Franklin Roosevelt and said that Roosevelt's "four freedoms" (of expression, of worship, from want, and from fear) were the moral beacons and guideposts of U.S. policy to this day and that the Gulf war was an exercise in "the work of freedom." Bush was camouflaging the fact that the Gulf war limited the freedom of expression of the press and military families more than any event in recent U.S. history, that the troops in Saudi Arabia could not practice freedom of religion because of the feudal customs of the Saudis, and that his war was producing want and fear throughout the Middle East.

On Thursday, Bush addressed another convention of religious broadcasters and uttered some banalities about war, God, and prayer.[15] On Friday, Bush took trips to three military bases in the South to generate images of flag-waving, gung-ho, prowar support. Bush got carried away, however, at Fort Stewart, Georgia, and blurted out: "The U.S. has a new credibility. What we say now—goes!" The crowd went wild in response to Bush's chauvinistic imperialism, pointing again to disturbing tendencies afoot in the land of the free and the home of the brave. At all three of his stops that day, all televised live, military wives and relatives of POWs were present to serve as part of the propaganda offensive. The morning talk shows cut live to Bush's speeches at the bases, inundating the nation with images of flag-waving supporters of Bush and the war. On his Saturday radio broadcast, Bush declared that Sunday would be a day of prayer. During news segments on both Saturday and Sunday, there were clips of Bush's speeches, trips, radio broadcast, and pronouncements throughout the week. Thus the Bush war team could legitimately conclude that they had conducted a successful propaganda campaign for a country at war.

To complement Bush's patriotic offensive, during the weekend of February 2–3, prowar demonstrations throughout the country featured the usual flag waving, chanting of "U.S.A!, U.S.A!," burning of effigies of Saddam Hussein, and unleashing aggression against the "evil" Iraqi "enemies." Television featured images of "the largest flag ever made," in which a Virginia Beach crowd formed a human flag the size of a football field, enabling those participating to become part of something bigger than themselves, part of the flag itself. The flag seemed to be becoming a totemic security blanket that gave the waver a sense of magical power, and waving the flag empowered individuals, signifying their belonging to a community. Perhaps the flag also served as a phallic fetish that gave the holder a sense of phallic power and libidinal gratification, as well as aesthetic gratification, enabling flag wavers to become part of a dazzling mass spectacle. Or perhaps flag waving and exhibition was simply a duty that good patriotic citizens performed because they were told to do so.

In any case, during the weekend of February 2–3, television broadcast clips from demonstration after demonstration of support for the troops in the Persian Gulf, providing images of a massive mobilization of civilian support, embodied in outbursts of patriotic fervor throughout the country. The antiwar movement seemed to have disappeared and the country seemed to be experiencing a simultaneous wargasm of patriotic ecstasy. CNN, for instance, had a camera crew in Fayettesville, Georgia, where most of the people in the town turned out for a demonstration in which people waved flags and cheered and chanted. In this bucolic invocation of small-town America, blacks and whites came together in patriotic enthusiasm and a chubby young boy told the crowd and the television camera why the United States was in the Persian Gulf, ending his canned speech by exclaiming, with genuine passion, "and we're going to kick some butt!" The crowd roared.

Obviously, war is the most time-honored mode of organized aggression yet devised for the channeling of aggressive energies. The spectacle of a small child wanting his country to "kick butt" raises some interesting questions about the mode of socialization and culture in the United States and the ways that war brutalizes individuals. The young boy had perhaps been raised on *Rambo* movies and other action adventure spectacles, on football and other sports, and had been socialized into a male culture of aggressivity in which being tough and "kicking butt" are part of the social construction of masculinity, of "being a man." We have observed the role of football metaphors in the Gulf war, and one often hears admonitions to "kick butt" from school gym teachers and athletic coaches. Kicking butt is part of military socialization as well, and the media popularized and naturalized the phrase during the Gulf war.

In regard to the Persian Gulf war, none other than the war leader himself, George Bush, bragged that the U.S. was going to "kick ass" and this noble sentiment was also enshrined in a piece of video in which General Schwarzkopf bragged how his troops were going to "kick Iraqi butt."[16] TV showed image after image of soldiers on the front bragging about how they were going to kick butt, while frenzied and aggressive individuals at prowar demonstrations told the TV people over and over how the U.S. was going to kick Iraqi butt. So the little Georgia butt kicker is just emulating his president, the commander of the multinational coalition, his coaches, TV, and his peer group in wanting to unleash aggressive energies against a foreign "enemy." He was not alone. Throughout the week, television portrayed young children carrying signs at Bush's visits to military bases that celebrated the victory of Patriot over Scud missiles and that threatened Hussein and the Iraqis. One could envisage little warriors sitting in front of the TV cheering every time a Patriot hits a Scud and every time the daily kill rate was announced for Iraqi planes, tanks, and artillery.

The Persian Gulf TV war thus militarized U.S. culture and throughout the United States, the media, schools, churches, circuses, athletic events, and businesses sold patriotism and mobilized support for an aggressive war. The patriotic propaganda war channeled positive sentiments into flag, country, and the military, while mobilizing negative emotions against the enemy and, especially, Saddam Hussein. This highly dangerous propaganda strategy raised emotions to a fever pitch and helped promote violence against Arab-Americans while legitimating U.S. violence against the Iraqis.

This analysis of Bush's patriotic propaganda campaign helps explain why his rationales for U.S. involvement in the gulf were so weak and vacillating concerning the reasons that the U.S. was fighting a brutal war far from home with an enemy that was, for the most part, totally unknown to the American people. Bush really had no politically justifiable reasons why the U.S. should fight a Persian Gulf war, so he fell back on blind patriotism and flag waving. In his State of the Union address, the key rhetorical point was: "We are Americans and this is what we do." By extension, if one supports the war one is patriotic and a good American, while if one does not support the war one is not a good American. It was as simple as this and this simplistic binary logic of either/or was the crux of Bush's propaganda campaign. However, the test of all propaganda is purely pragmatic—does it work?, and it appeared that Bush's propaganda, however primitive, was working in mobilizing support for his war policies.

6.3 Iraq Under Bombardment

For the first week of the Gulf war, the war itself was invisible, with the exception of the Scud wars that were a nightly drama for some time before they became routine fare. The daily bombing and skirmishes between ground and naval forces were reduced to bland statistics at the daily military hearings or headlines in news briefs. The video footage of the bombing provided excellent photo opportunities for the military to demonstrate the wonders of technowar, and the U.S. pool footage, properly seen as military propaganda, provided banal images of planes taking off, ground crews engaged in daily labor, ground troops moving to the front preparing for land war, and interview footage with the soldiers usually saying something patriotic or bellicose.

Only into the second week of the war did the audience begin to see the reality behind the statistics of the coalition bombing campaign in the form of video footage of victims of the air war. During the morning of January 25, "NBC Today" opened its news segments with the headlines that it had been a busy night for the allied forces in the Gulf, which had taken advantage of the clear weather to fly 3,000 sorties, the most of the war. NBC also reported that Iraq was claiming that the allies were bombing civilian areas, "a charge that U.S. military authorities firmly deny." Orchestrating a new propaganda theme, the Iraqis began to document daily U.S. bombing of innocent civilians and the destruction of homes, neighborhoods, religious, cultural, and other nonmilitary sites. Iraq intensified its dramatization of the horrors of war by releasing videotapes of civilian destruction by U.S. bombing. This theme became the emphasis of Peter Arnett's CNN reports out of Baghdad. Arnett, a New Zealander who had won a Pulitzer prize for his Vietnam reporting and who was generally respected as one of the world's greatest war correspondents, was the only major Western broadcast journalist left in Iraq after it expelled the press during the first week of the war. For some time thereafter, until Iraq began allowing foreign journalists to reenter, Arnett was the only Western voice in Baghdad. His descriptive and evocative reporting, subject to Iraqi censorship, became the center of a firestorm of controversy, drawing attack from the prowar coterie in the United States and elsewhere.

On January 25, at 10:01 A.M. Arnett reported on CNN that on his first trip outside of Baghdad, he had been taken one hundred miles to a residential area in al-Dour, a small town in northwest Iraq where heavy damage was caused by extensive bombing by the multinational forces. A technical institute five miles from the town had been bombed previously, Arnett was told. The southwest part of the town was hit hardest; homes there "were flattened as though shaken by a mighty earthquake." Arnett counted twenty-three homes destroyed and twenty-three bomb craters; Iraqi authorities claimed that twenty-four civilians were killed and one hundred injured in the bombing. A whole family was killed; they had a son who was a student in the local university and Arnett found a tattered copy of Thackeray's *Vanity Fair* in the house in English, inscribed by his teacher. There was no bomb shelter because the townspeople didn't believe that they were in danger of being attacked. A weeping woman said that her three brothers and many other members of her family had died. She said that there were no reasons to bomb the city because there were no military targets in the area. Arnett saw twenty-four recent graves in the cemetery.

When asked to respond to criticisms that his reports were aiding the Iraqis, Arnett answered that "viewers will have to get used to reports of this nature. . . . You can't unload this many tons of bombs on a country and not expect to get. casualties." Arnett then recalled that during the Vietnam war, *New York Times* correspondent Harrison Salisbury was taken to Hanoi in 1966 when the U.S. military was claiming pinpoint precision bombing, and he reported on civilian casualties. Salisbury was taken to places bombed, reported what he saw, and was widely criticized. Arnett explained that with such a massive bombing assault, there is bound to be "fallout on civilians."

Arnett concluded that "[t]here has been heavy bombing of this little community," documented by video that was shown later in the day by CNN and which portrayed Arnett and other reporters observing the damaged buildings and talking to townspeople. In addition, a framed photograph of a child hung from a tree in front of one rubble-strewn lot. When asked if this could have been staged, Arnett replied: "There is no way that this could have been staged; I have seen bomb damage in seventeen wars over thirty-three years. . . . The Pentagon may say that they had a reason to bomb this community, but I didn't see any." CNN anchor John Holliman, Arnett's companion during the first night of bombing, told him that people were criticizing the CNN coverage, claiming that CNN was being used by the Iraqis to transmit their propaganda. Arnett responded that he did not feel that he was being used: "Obviously, the Iraqis are going to take us to selected sites, but if all of this bombing is taking place, people should expect that there is going to be this sort of damage."

Around 12:30 P.M. CNN's Mary Ann Loughlin broke in to read a report attacking Peter Arnett's claims, stating: "We have some additional information 'from our CNN research files here." Beginning with a rather irrelevant point, Loughlin read: "What the Iraqis described to Peter Arnett as a technical school is as far as we have been able to determine, this al-Dour site, is uh, is described as, uh, a main electronics communications center." Reading from a piece of paper in front of her, rather than the usual CNN text on monitors, Loughlin continued to stumble, noting that the center was opened in 1985 and military communications and radar were being built there. "Peter Arnett," she continued, "described this as being near, uh, Sammara, which is located, ah, according to the research that, uh, we've been able to come up with, uh, producing, uh, mustard and, uh, nerve gas and agents with the annual capacity to produce 200, uh, 700 hundred tons of mustard and 200 tons of nerve agent. This building described by Iraqi authorities to Peter Arnett as a technical school is, as we have been able to determine, a chemical weapons facility."

This report is highly interesting because what is being presented as "CNN research" is obviously disinformation fed to CNN by the Pentagon. Obviously, the newsreader was handed a report that she had never seen before and read the Pentagon propaganda sheet, falsely claiming that it was from "CNN research files." A CNN report later in the afternoon indicated that it was actually Pentagon sources who claimed that there were chemical and biological weapons facilities in the area, a point repeated the same afternoon by the Pentagon briefer in Washington. The Pentagon was obviously disturbed by reports that its bombing was creating civilian casualties and was desperately attempting to discredit such reports. Yet it was becoming evident that the massive U.S.-led coalition bombing was destroying the economic infrastructure of Iraq and that there were a large number of civilian targets hit and civilian casualties from all over the country. The Pentagon continued to insist, however, that they were not hitting civilian sites and that their bombing was pinpoint and precise, a lie refuted daily by the video pictures coming out of Iraq.

On January 26, for instance, Arnett reported that he was taken to cities in southern Iraq, five hours from Baghdad, where, for the fourth day in a row, he had been taken to civilian sites that had been bombed by the coalition. This time he was taken to the Shiite religious city Najaf, one of the holiest sites for the Islamic religion. In the town, he saw the destruction of a civilian area, with five blocks of residential houses flattened. An engineer working for a Korean firm in Baghdad told Arnett that he took his family to the town because he thought it was one of the holiest places in Islam and therefore would be safe. But his house was bombed and many of his family were killed. Arnett then told of others he interviewed who told him of the bombing and destruction of their property as well as of injuries and deaths suffered by their relatives. At another site he was taken to in the town, about seven houses were flattened, seven civilians were reported killed, and about fifty were wounded. Relatives were seen going through the rubble and they were particularly angry because they thought that the holy spirit of the city had been violated and because there were no military targets in the area.

The same day CNN showed pictures from Mosul, in the north of Iraq, of an ancient Christian church that had been bombed, with tearful worshippers attending a service. The Pentagon reported that afternoon that they did not bomb religious sites and denied involvement in the bombing. More forthcoming for once, General Schwarzkopf admitted in his January 27 briefing, in response to a question concerning the bombing of the church: "These things happen. I've been bombed by our own Air Force. I don't think that they did it intentionally . . . but you have to understand that bomb racks get hung up and drop." General Schwarzkopf denied that allied forces were carpet-bombing civilian areas and rejected this nasty term from the days of Vietnam. He insisted that his bombing was not indiscriminate, that he used appropriate weapons for appropriate targets, and tried to avoid civilian targets. At this briefing, Schwarzkopf repeated that the milk factory contained a biological weapons component (see 4.2) and went so far as to claim that coalition bombing was so precise that it damaged "only that part of the facility that [was] . . . a research facility for biological warfare." This ridiculous claim was belied by the images of the milk factory reduced to rubble by Schwarzkopf's "discriminate" bombing with "appropriate weapons."

In the days to come, the networks showed picture after picture of the bombing of civilian targets in Iraq and began presenting images of civilian casualties. On January 26 CBS News broadcast images from Iraqi TV of dead children in a morgue and images of widespread damage to residential areas from the allied bombing. The video pictured at least ten dead children and presented perhaps the first images of Iraqi civilian casualties. This footage was, as NBC pointed out, given to the networks in Jordan without commentary or explanation; the images might have been images of children killed in a previous war and thus, strictly speaking, propaganda, although Iraq was to produce many pictures of dead and wounded civilians who were victims of U.S. bombing. CBS indicated that while the few foreign journalists in Iraq were prohibited from reporting on military targets, they were now allowed to report on civilian bombings. The footage showed many images of the rubble of civilian buildings allegedly caused by allied bombings and the destruction of a Christian church in northern Iraq, earlier shown on CNN. Taking the Pentagon propaganda line at face value, the CBS report noted that the town of al-Dour was a military communications site and a storage place for chemical weapons, thus changing the story fed to CNN that depicted it as a military communications center with chemical weapons produced in the nearby town of Sammara. Obviously, like Winston Smith in Orwell's *1984,* the Pentagon changed its line from day to day to meet its propaganda needs and the television networks dutifully reported whatever they were fed.

When Arnett was told that the Pentagon claimed that there were military targets close to the al-Dour area, he responded by asking "how close is close?" and insisted that he saw no military targets in or near the town. In his January 27 CNN report, Arnett told how he visited the Jerma general hospital in Baghdad, which is one of twenty that was taking care of civilian and military wounded from the coalition bombing. The hospital, according to the Iraqis, had 120 victims of the U.S. bombing and Arnett interviewed a woman who was in a car with her family when a bomb dropped near her, wounding her in the arm. Another victim was having lunch in his backyard with his family when a missile hit nearby. Arnett noted that the rush of patients had depleted the blood supply, and local papers urged citizens to donate blood. Antibiotics were also depleted and beds were in short supply. Finally, Arnett reported how members of a family profusely bleeding from the bombing were brought in and put into beds in the hallway of the hospital, as the video footage showed.

The presentation of Iraqi civilian casualties in Iraq by U.S. television was deplorable. For weeks, Arnett's reports of civilian casualties were invariably labeled as "propaganda," even when accompanied by pictures. For the first week or so of the war, Iraq refrained from releasing information or pictures of the bombing of civilian sites or damage to civilians. But then video and reports of civilian casualties started pouring out of Iraq via Baghdad TV, Peter Arnett, and other foreign correspondents. These sources sent forth picture after picture until the end of the war of destroyed buildings and injured or killed Iraqi civilians. While the media repeatedly reported as fact the wildest assertions of George Bush or the U.S. military (i.e., that the Patriot missile had a perfect intercept record against the Scuds; that the targets they were hitting were all military targets; and so on), every time a picture or report of civilian casualties came out of Baghdad, the networks went out of their way to label it as "propaganda." At the end of the "NBC Nightly News" on January 27, after a report full of pictures of civilian casualties in Baghdad, correspondent Dennis Murphy concluded: "Until we get some Western reporters and photographers in there to vouch for it, I think we'll have to call it propaganda." With a broad smile, anchor Garrick Utley replied,

"That's a pretty good name for it." Dead Iraqis were thus reduced to propaganda by the media war team.

One wonders what the network flacks thought that ten days of the heaviest bombing in the most massive air war in history were going to produce? Even military apologists like General Schwarzkopf conceded that there were going to be civilian casualties in such bombing raids, so why did the media insist that totally plausible claims from Iraq that innocent civilians were casualties of war be labeled "propaganda," while U.S. disinformation was presented as factual information? Obviously, U.S. propaganda was more clever and effective than Iraqi propaganda—at least to viewers in the United States. Iraq began by making absurd claims concerning how many planes they had shot down and claimed victory when obviously they were suffering defeat. Henceforth, all discourse that emerged from Iraq was ridiculed as propaganda discourse and pure disinformation.

Generally, in a propaganda war, everything that the other side says and shows will naturally be seen as propaganda while one's own side is seen by supporters of the war to speak the truth. But the mainstream media should have shown some skepticism and critical awareness. They should have questioned the official reports by the Bush administration and Pentagon and done a better job of labeling its management of information as propaganda, or at least as a slanted perspective opposed by a different perspective. They also should have avoided the double standard of labelling everything that came out of Iraq as subject to government censorship, as propaganda, whereas they rarely did this with reports coming out of Saudi Arabia or out of U.S. military pool footage, which was equally subject to censorship and often equally propagandistic. And they should not have allowed so many of their own "military experts" to simply serve as conduits for U.S. disinformation which put the Pentagon-spin on all controversial events and policies.

The reports coming out of Iraq were the only reports that showed the actual consequences of war, with the exception of the highly censored reports concerning Scud missile attacks on Israel and Saudi Arabia. During this period, there were descriptions on all the networks of the destruction of civilian trucks on the Baghdad/Amman road and the killing of at least four Jordanian civilian truck drivers on the road. There were interviews with other truck drivers in the hospital in Amman who described how they had been bombed by allied planes; refugees who traveled down that road told similar tales. Evidently, the road was used for the transportation of mobile Scud missile launchers and in the obsession to destroy the Scuds, the U.S.-led coalition bombed every truck in sight, killing many civilians in the process (see Arkin, Durrant, and Cherni 1991, pp. 86–87).

Arnett and his colleagues posted daily graphic and poignant reports of destruction of civilian targets in Iraq. Despite these well-documented and disturbing reports, bolstered by video images, a *Times-Mirror* survey of January 31, 1991, revealed that 78 percent of the public believed that the military was not hiding anything embarrassing about its conduct of the war and was telling everything it prudently could. When CNN began broadcasting pictures of civilian casualties in Iraq, many people criticized it for broadcasting Peter Arnett's live reports from Baghdad and allegedly articulating the Iraqi point of view. Forty-five percent of respondents to the *Times-Mirror* poll expressed disapproval of American media broadcasting of Iraqi-censored reports from Baghdad, and a large number of viewers also feared that TV would provide information useful to the Iraqi government, even claiming that there was too much information revealed in military briefings, which might aid the enemy. Although the media themselves often criticized the censorship restrictions, the *Times-Mirror* poll indicated that nearly eight out of ten Americans supported the Pentagon restrictions on the press and that six out of ten said that the military should exert more control. And as I noted at the beginning of this chapter, most respondents believed that media coverage was "objective" and "accurate," with eight out of ten saying that the press did an excellent job.

In response to these findings, Cees Hamelink commented (1991, p. 4): "If any manufacturer had put on the market a product as defective and unreliable as media performance during the Gulf War, there would have been a vast consumer uproar. However, when people were sold televised lies, they did not seem to care. This public complacency about and uncritical acceptance of disinformation and propaganda have also seriously contributed to the violation of human rights" (i.e., the media's right to seek information blocked by military censorship, the public's right to know, the prohibition of war propaganda, and so on). Thus, the public blamed the messenger for disturbing news, preferring not to know the awful truth behind the scenes of the Persian Gulf TV war.

6.4 The Battle of Khafji

On a daily basis, the Pentagon claimed that their plan was unfolding on track, although insiders claimed that, in fact, the U.S. military had planned for a ten-day air war and that bad weather, Scuds, and a more extensive Iraqi military machine than they had calculated postponed the eventual ground war.[17] In his briefing of January 30, General Schwarzkopf claimed that the U.S.-led coalition was achieving all of its objectives: "By every measure—by every measure—our campaign plan is very much on schedule." Schwarzkopf's briefing was full of bluster, videotapes of precision bombing, and a series of lies, exaggerations, and oddities. For instance, he claimed that in the Scud wars the record was thirty-three Scuds fired and thirty-three Patriot intercepts, although this was obviously false. The general stated that they had attacked thirty-eight airfields and flown 1,300 sorties against the airfields and "at least nine of them are nonoperational." Making 1,300 sorties to knock out nine airfields seemed to be rather excessive overall, especially when Iraqi planes did not seem eager to fight and were posing little, if any, threat to the coalition operations. Moreover, he claimed that "almost 1,500" sorties had been launched against Iraqi Scuds, a figure that seemed excessive from a military point of view if, as Schwarzkopf constantly claimed, the Scuds were not really a military threat or weapon. Schwarzkopf claimed further that the allies had attacked thirty-three bridges with 790 sorties, which raised the question of why it took so many sorties to knock out these bridges if, as in a couple of the videotapes he played that very day, the bombing was so precise? Schwarzkopf claimed that the bombing campaign had cut the Iraqi supply operations from about 20,000 tons per day needed to supply the Iraqi troops to 2,000 tons per day, figures that seemed rather arbitrary and unconvincing. And, as I note below, Schwarzkopf falsely claimed that it was Saudi forces that were ejecting the Iraqis from Khafji when, in fact, it was U.S. forces who were doing much of the real fighting.

The so-called "battle of Khafji" was the only skirmish in the Gulf war where troops actually shot at and killed each other and the ways that the U.S. military manipulated information concerning this minor event revealed the extent of their total control of news and information. The first reports of the fighting came via late night TV accounts of heavy fighting along the border over Saudi Arabia and Kuwait and were confirmed by Pentagon spokesperson Mike Gallagher in Saudi Arabia: "Preliminary reports indicate that there was contact with enemy forces at three different locations along the border. The contact began last night and continued until early this morning when contact was broken off. These reports indicate heavy losses of both personnel and equipment on the Iraqi side and light losses to U.S. Marines and other coalition forces." The CNN commentary disclosed that the fighting began around 9:35 P.M. Saudi time at three different spots on the border of Kuwait and Saudi Arabia, including Khafji. The Iraqis staged "probing attacks" that were countered by intense fire, resulting in heavy casualties for the Iraqis when allied forces counterattacked. According to CNN, the U.S. Marines and allies did experience some casualties, and the fighting stopped around 3:00 A.M., though air attacks on retreating Iraqi troops continued. Baghdad radio, CNN noted, claimed that their forces staged a massive ground attack on Saudi Arabia, but there was no confirmation of this.

Gallagher's briefing and the CNN gloss, based on information fed to them by the military, provides a good example of how the military managed information during the Persian Gulf war. The Khafji incident was the first ground battle of the war, the first time that Iraqi ground fighting inflicted casualties on U.S. and allied troops, the first (and only) time that Iraq had occupied, however briefly, Saudi Arabian soil. From start to finish the U.S. military attempted to manage the information of the event, providing one false report after another. Gallagher's initial report was erroneous in claiming that fighting had broken off, because Iraqi troops occupied the city of Khafji. It would be several days before they retreated, surrendered, or were killed.

For some time CNN and then the other networks repeated this story when they began their morning shows, and there was intense speculation over why the Iraqis chose to cross the Saudi border and engage the coalition troops. Discussion focused on the possibility that Iraq was trying to drive the U.S. prematurely into a ground war. Reflecting the opinion of the military, CNN Pentagon correspondent Gene Randall reported that despite the attack of the previous night, the coalition would choose the time and the place for the ground war. CNN's military "analyst," retired General Perry Smith, concurred, stating that Saddam Hussein was "trying to get us involved, he wants to draw us into combat; clearly what he would like to do is bloody us, get us bogged down."

CBS's first report of the day on January 30 from their Pentagon correspondent Jim Stewart also claimed that a battalion size incursion by the Iraqis around Khafji and other points of the Saudi border was repulsed by U.S. troops and their allies. The reports from the war front in Saudi Arabia painted a different picture, however, by midmorning. CNN's Charles Jaco explained that the initial reports that the Iraqis were driven back with heavy losses originated from a *San Diego Tribune* pool reporter. Now, he said, there were reports that Iraqi troops had driven down to Khafji and still occupied the city and had not retreated across the border. Blaming the disinformation on the San Diego pool reporter, however, was misleading because the military fed the pool reporter the same story that Gallagher and the Pentagon were feeding reporters, so clearly the Pentagon was controlling the disinformation flow. Yet Jaco did note that it was not clear why the Iraqi troops encountered little or no resistance when they came across the border and made it all the way to Khafji. The Saudis were supposed to defend the border region, with the United States behind them.

Throughout the morning, CNN's Perry Smith put a rosy glow on the reports. Earlier, he claimed that the United States used airpower and "good tactics" to repulse the invading Iraqi forces. Continuing his speculation, Smith described what tanks and planes were engaged in the battle and confidently recounted what happened. Within minutes, Jaco came back on from Saudi Arabia and gave another list of planes used in the battle, totally different from Smith's list, making it laughably clear that Smith's analysis was sheer fantasy. Later, Schwarzkopf claimed that an entirely different set of planes were used in attacking the invading Iraqi forces, suggesting how useless the military reports from Saudi Arabia were in an environment of controlled information.

Perry Smith had also praised the smart bombs that had supposedly repulsed and destroyed some of the invading Iraqi units. It was later revealed, however, that the "smart bombs" had stupidly destroyed two U.S. light armored vehicles (LAV), killing the Marines inside with "friendly fire." Thus, everything that retired General Perry Smith was saying was hot air or propaganda with no informational content, raising the question of why CNN employed pro-military flacks as "analysts." All Smith did throughout the war was to try to put a positive Pentagon spin on everything that happened.[18] Likewise, CNN military analyst, James Blackwell and Pentagon correspondents Wolf Blitzer and Gene Randall gave instant analysis after every Pentagon briefing, serving as mere Pentagon transmission belts, faithfully reporting whatever the Pentagon told them without any critical analysis or skepticism. Smith and Blackwell put a positive pro-Pentagon spin on events and thus were mere PR adjuncts of the military. Consequently, while all of the reports from Iraq were labeled "Cleared by Iraqi Government Censors," and video was sometimes labeled or described as "Iraqi government propaganda," CNN should have also labeled everything that their military analysts and Pentagon correspondents said as "Pentagon propaganda."

Some of CNN's correspondents in the field were equally as servile and uncritical as their Pentagon flacks in the United States, whereas other CNN correspondents did their best to compare government reports with other news sources, but this was difficult. For example, CNN's Charles Jaco in Saudi Arabia was trying to sort out fact from fiction in the battle of Khafji on January 30, but was continually fed disinformation from the U.S. military that he then relayed immediately in his TV accounts. In this way, the Pentagon was able to control the flow of information, but this time their disinformation came back to haunt them, as one after another of their propaganda lines were refuted. Projecting the image that the Pentagon desired, Jaco reported that Qatari and Saudi troops were currently fighting in Khafji while the Marines blocked the road to the south. It turned out that this, too, was disinformation, fed by the U.S. military for political reasons so that it would look like the Arab troops fought the Iraqis on their own. It was revealed later, however, that U.S.

Marines were heavily involved in the fighting, lobbing artillery shells into the city, bombing the Iraqis with cluster bombs and missiles, controlling the fighting within the city, and even engaging in combat.

Jaco also recounted that initially the Saudis thought that the Iraqi forces came over to surrender, but they then engaged them in battle, driving them back. There were, according to the Saudis, about eighty Iraqi vehicles with about 1,000 troops engaged. It appeared that the Iraqis fooled the Saudis by pointing the turrets of their tanks to the rear in the sign of surrender, but instead of giving up, they turned their guns on the Saudi forces and opened fire. The Saudis fled, allowing the Iraqis to move quickly to Khafji, about twelve miles from the Saudi/Kuwaiti border, and to occupy the town. Khafji, we may recall, was the site of Iraqi bombardment by artillery fire the first night of the war. An oil refinery had been set on fire, the inhabitants of the town fled, and it became a ghost town. Khafji was also the site where oil was discovered rolling in on the beaches and killing wildlife.

In any case, the Iraqis caught the Saudis and the allied forces by surprise, though, of course, General Schwarzkopf denied this in his military briefing later in the morning of January 30. NBC's Arthur Kent, however, noted in his report of January 31 that it violated every military rule to allow your enemy to take a site like an abandoned city where they could mount a defensive operation. On February 1, Kent claimed that the easy Iraqi advance toward Khafji revealed weaknesses in coalition reconnaissance and reaction. The Pentagon, however, claimed that it had purposely broken the rule book, asserting that the coalition forces were prepared to allow the Iraqis to occupy the city and were not surprised by the incursion, always trying to put a positive spin on events, however negative.

In a sense, the battle of Khafji turned out to be the only battle in the entire war where troops on both sides actually shot at and killed each other. The air war wasn't really a war at all, as the Iraqi Air Force rarely engaged the coalition planes, which bombed Iraqi targets more or less at will. And the ground war, as we shall see, was more of a high-tech massacre than actual combat between two sides. But the battle of Khafji was a potential embarrassment for the U.S.-led coalition forces. The Saudis had allowed the Iraqis to fool them and then march down the coast to occupy a Saudi town. As it turned out, the Saudis were unable to take back the town without U.S. help, but the U.S. military did their best to make it appear that the Saudis were "mopping up." In his afternoon briefing on January 30, General Schwarzkopf admitted that fighting was still going on in Khafji, but claimed that "the Saudis are moving forces into al-Khafji to eject any Iraqi that may be in that area," as if the Saudis alone were doing the fighting; later it was revealed that

U.S. forces were heavily involved, as were Qatari forces, and that Schwarz-kopf and the U.S. military were concealing U.S. involvement for purely political reasons, to create the impression that Arab forces led by the heroic Saudis did the fighting.[19]

Indeed, Brig. Gen. Pat Stevens, in the Saudi Arabia military briefing on January 31, claimed that it was solely Saudi and Qatari forces who engaged in the fighting, with Marine Cobra helicopters supporting the action. He claimed that no Marine ground units were engaged in Khafji and that Saudi forces had taken and secured the city. When skeptical reporters said that they had reports of U.S. artillery forces engaged in the action, as was seen by TV viewers, Stevens insisted again that "U.S. forces were not engaged in that action," which was simply not true. Later it became clear that the U.S. military officers did everything possible to glorify the action of the Arab forces for political purposes while down-playing the fierceness of the Iraqis. It turned out that the Saudis were rather incompetent and, according to a U.S. Marine involved in the action, Saudi armored personnel carriers had been firing "toward the Iraqis, toward our position, toward other Saudis, everywhere, at anything that moved, even at things that didn't move" (*New York Times,* Feb. 2, p. A5). It also leaked out that although many Iraqis were taken POW and some were killed, a large number got away, driving out of the city back into Kuwait.

Video footage of the "battle" had a Keystone Cops movie quality to it: U.S. Marines raced into the city to try to rescue some U.S. forces and fled when fired on. The marine in charge of the rescue, Maj. Craig Huddleston, who cockily said earlier that his marines were going to march into the city and "spank" the Iraqis who'd better "call 911 for help," was almost in tears as he told of the failure to find the missing U.S. soldiers. Iraqi radio claimed the capture of U.S. women soldiers in the fighting around Khafji, and the United States admitted that a woman soldier was missing, giving rise to spirited debate over whether women should be allowed so close to the front. TV viewers were treated to images of Saudis and U.S. forces firing at a high-rise apartment building, where the Iraqis were allegedly holed up to direct the fire of their units; eventually, the building was demolished, as allied forces were evidently prepared to destroy Saudi Arabia to liberate Kuwait. Of course, the Saudis, with the complicity of the U.S. military and media, presented the unsavory episode as a great victory for the allied forces in which the Saudis performed heroically and vindicated themselves militarily. A Saudi prince went on U.S. television to bask in the glory of victory and Saudi General Khalid bin Sultan told reporters that the Iraqi attack was a "suicide mission," although a U.S. official told the *Washington Post* that the operation "was wellplanned, even sophisticated in part" (Feb. 2, p. A16).

Media reports later revealed that two U.S. reconnaissance units were in the town, directing the fighting and fiercely engaging the Iraqis; that U.S. artillery fire, helicopters, and tactical fighter planes played important roles in the fighting; and that Schwarzkopf, Stevens, and others thus flatly lied when claiming that the United States was not engaged in the fighting. Interestingly, when a general's credibility, such as General Stevens's, suffered after being caught up in obvious lies, he was usually replaced in the morning Saudi Arabia briefing room by a fresh information manager and he soon disappeared from public view. Schwarzkopf, however, continued to lie throughout the war and was rarely challenged by the press.

The Pentagon propaganda apparatus also tried to hide another embarrassing story. The Pentagon initially fed to the press the story that the eleven marines killed in the two light-armored vehicles in the engagement to the northwest of Khafji died when their vehicles were destroyed by Iraqi tanks. Rumors began circulating that friendly fire killed the marines. When asked to comment on this during the January 31 Pentagon briefing in Washington, Lt. Gen. Thomas Kelly first insisted that the marines killed were hit by enemy gunfire, but when pushed admitted that the command in the field was looking into the possibility that friendly fire had caused their death. "I don't think it was [the cause]," Kelly said, but it was being investigated. A few days later, the U.S. military finally admitted that friendly fire had killed the marines; indeed, "friendly fire" produced most of the U.S. casualties during the ground skirmishes of the first several weeks, leading to heated debates concerning the possibility of serious operational difficulties in the U.S. war machine.[20]

The Iraqi incursion into Khafji obviously embarrassed the U.S. military. They had covered over the facts that fighting continued for days in the city, that the United States had played a key role in finally destroying the Iraqis, and that friendly fire had killed the U.S. marines and not Iraqi tanks. General Schwarzkopf played down the importance of the Khafji incident, saying that it was "about as significant as a mosquito on an elephant." Although that might have been true from a military point of view, obviously the disinformation campaign carried out by the U.S. military showed that from the standpoint of the propaganda war the incident was significant. The Iraqis celebrated the battle as a great victory, crowing that they had penetrated Saudi Arabia, captured a city, fought intensely for at least three days, and inflicted casualties on the allied forces.

Interestingly, reporters, mostly British, independent of the press pool, broke the information that the fighting continued when the U.S. military declared that the fighting was over. Independent reporters also disclosed the role of the U.S. Marines in the battle and exposed the Pentagon cover-up of the friendly fire killings. This showed that the pool system primarily functioned as a Pentagon tool of information management that kept reporters away from information that the military did not want disseminated and that used them as a conduit for the information which they wanted to circulate. The Khafji incident also revealed the complicity of the U.S. media in this system, as when reporter Robert Fisk of the British newspaper *The Independent* described how the pool was misled by their military "minders" into communicating the retaking of Khafji when, in fact, fighting continued. Fisk (in Ridgeway 1991, pp. 218–219) recounted that when British journalists, not in the pool, returned to the scene to investigate, NBC correspondent Brad Willis yelled: "You asshole! You'll prevent us from working. You're not allowed here. Get out. Go back to Dhahran." Willis then called over a U.S. Marine public affairs officer who told the reporter that he was not allowed to talk to the marines.

It was also reported that a French TV crew that arrived on the outskirts of Khafji was "greeted by angry shouts from attending pool reporters": "According to producer Alain Debos, the crew was forced at gunpoint by Marines to give up videotape it had shot of a wounded U.S. soldier" (*Time,* Feb. 18, 1991, p. 39). Above all, the U.S. military wanted to avoid images of dead or wounded U.S. soldiers. Moreover, a few days before the battle of Khafji, NBC's Arthur Kent confronted the Pentagon (dis)information officer Pete Williams and asked him why the Pentagon did not allow the pool team that was in Khafji when the oil spill story broke to visit the spill area. Brad Willis had complained to Kent that the pool managers hadn't even told the pool reporters of the oil spill in the area, which had been discovered by a British TV team doing independent reporting. Perhaps, the U.S. military was afraid that journalists would discover that the United States rather than the Iraqis, was responsible for that specific spill, as British and French reporters were indeed to argue while the U.S. media for the most part reproduced the U.S. military/Bush administration propaganda line that the Iraqis alone were responsible for the oil spills.

*   *   *

During the day of January 31, CNN reported repeatedly that 60,000 Iraqi troops were massed around the Kuwaiti town of al-Wafra; later they reported that 800 to 1,000 Iraqi tanks were on the move in Kuwait, perhaps to invade Saudi Arabia. At the end of the CBS news, Dan Rather dramatically reported stories of a convoy of 1,000 Iraqi military vehicles moving through southern Kuwait toward Saudi Arabia and that pool reporters were saying that the sounds of war, including heavy bombing, were heard around the Saudi border. The alarming story of the Iraqi concentration of troops in the border area continued to circulate through the evening. At 10:00 P.M., CNN reported that hundreds of Iraqi vehicles were heading south toward the border; reports at 11:03 P.M. indicated that a ten-mile column of Iraqi tanks and troops was snaking its way down south, suggesting that an Iraqi invasion of Saudi Arabia may have been underway. During the next day, February 1, these reports continued to circulate. The military briefers refused to comment on them, creating speculation by the press that the military was once again concealing something important. The press in Saudi Arabia was becoming increasingly testy, leading Schwarzkopf to limit the daily news briefings to a maximum of thirty minutes. But the major Iraqi attack on Saudi Arabia never materialized. CNN military analyst Perry Smith later claimed (1991) that a big Iraqi offensive was indeed under way, which, had it gained momentum, could have produced "considerable ground engagements and heavy casualties" (pp. 58–59). If this is true, it is curious that the U.S. military never disclosed this and for several days simply denied that a major Iraqi offensive was under way. Indeed, CNN reporters in Saudi Arabia claimed that officials were telling them that the Iraqi troops were moving south and west because it was apparent that the U.S. ground war offensive would take place to the west and the Iraqis wanted to locate more troops in a defensive position there. These Iraqi troops on the move were vulnerable to air attack and Iraqi tanks were destroyed in a "turkey shoot" during the troop movement. The *New York Times* related: "A pool reporter with the British Fourth Armored Brigade said he had watched all day as United States' B-52 bombers passed overhead, refueled and then pummeled the Iraqi column. He spoke of fierce fighting spread across a front stretching more than 150 miles inland from the sea and quoted intelligence reports as saying 100 Iraqi tanks had been wiped out" (Feb. 1, 1991, p. A1). The war was getting more and more brutal and its brutality will be the subject of the next chapter.

Notes

1. In a 1991 documentary produced by Bill Moyers, "PBS Special Report: After the War," Bush is quoted saying of allied bombing raids: "This has been fantastically accurate and that's because a lot of money went into this high technology weaponry—these laser guided bombs and a lot of other things—stealth technology—many of these technologies ridiculed in the past now coming into their own and saving lives, not only American lives, Coalition lives but the lives of Iraqis."

2. For an analysis of theories of mass communication, see Czitrom 1983. I would suggest that the so-called "bullet theory" is a construction of Lazarsfeld and his followers who deny direct media influence in part by setting up a straw-man model. Obviously, the media do not always directly influence the audience and audiences can always decode media texts, producing their own meanings.

On the other hand, phenomena like the Gulf war, in which a mass audience is intensely participating in media rituals, may influence audiences more deeply than does, say, normal TV viewing. Obviously, without in-depth research, one cannot know precisely what effects the media had on various audiences during the Gulf war, but I am setting forth some hypotheses and speculation which can help interpret the effects of television and the media and at least describe some phenomena which demand further exploration and interpretation. Indeed, it is a mistake to use the analytic category of "the audience" as there are always multiple audiences and were so during the Gulf war, with different audiences processing it differently.

3. In his book *The Territorial Imperative* (London: Fontana, 1967), Robert Ardrey tells how he was a young playwright in New York at the time of the Pearl Harbor bombing, thinking only of his career and personal life, when he was transformed overnight into a patriot when he perceived that his country was under attack.

4. In fact, a few in Congress and many of the intellectual establishment did speak out against the war, but their voices were rarely heard in the mainstream media. Issues like the Gulf war constitute an important test of an individual's political morality, and it would be useful to investigate the positions of members of Congress, the media, and the intelligentsia in the United States and other countries in the Gulf war. Many have a lot to answer for.

5. I am grateful to Ericka Virillo for some of the examples of the mythic and ideological resonances of the language of the Gulf war. For an earlier study of the corruption of language by politics and the military, which draws on Orwell and Marcuse, see Kellner 1989b.

6. As Elissa Marder argued in an unpublished paper, "Arbologies of Roland Barthes," the tying of ribbons to trees played on mythological resonances of the sort analyzed by Barthes in *Mythologies* (1972). The very concept of "Operation Desert Storm" is a mythology in Barthes' sense of naturalizing unnatural events, making a phenomenon of ugly history appear to be an event of nature, an inevitable desert storm bringing just retribution on the evils of Saddam Hussein.

7. The examples of the calling cards were taken from the mideast.forum in the PeaceNet bulletin board of April 19, 1991, which cites its source as "War Watch Special Report, March 1991."

8. The first three examples are from Winter 1991, while the last example is documented in *The Texas Observer,* April 19, 1991, p. 22. See also Kathy Mitchell's article in *The Texas Observer* on violence against Palestinian-Americans (Feb. 8, 1991, pp. 8–9).

9. The Arab Anti-Discrimination League reported that incidences of violence against Arab-Americans reached an all-time high during 1991, with 119 hate crimes compared with 39 in 1990 (*New York Times,* Feb. 22, 1991).

10. An empirical study in Britain revealed that support for the Gulf war was much softer and more ambivalent than the polls indicated. Martin Shaw and Roy Carr-Hill argue that "two surveys of a local population in Northern England, based on random samples of the electorate . . . [reveal] that while perceptions of the war closely reflected the pictures of the war provided by the media, there

was a great deal of anxiety not reflected in national poll findings, and 'resistance' to media coverage—reflected particularly in the finding that large minorities agreed that television and the popular press 'glorified the war too much.'" The authors also claim that their surveys indicated that people's attitude toward the war often varied according to what newspaper they read. "Mass Media and Attitudes to the Gulf War in Britain," in *The Electronic Journal of Communication,* Vol. 2, No. 2 (Fall 1991). I know of no similar in-depth empirical research in the United States that investigated how the population really felt about the war, so one must invariably speculate concerning the state of antiwar sentiment and the depth of prowar sentiment and convictions.

11. Newspaper coverage, as FAIR pointed out, tended to downplay the size of the demonstrations. The *New York Times* coverage of the January 19 national demonstration against the war in Washington, D.C., consisted of a single photo and caption, which put the size of the crowd at 15,000, as opposed to the official police count of 25,000 or the organizers' estimate of 75,000 (*Extra!,* May 1991, p. 19). Within a week, TV coverage of the antiwar movement disappeared and one hardly heard from the movement for the rest of the war on the mainstream media.

12. Over 2,500 soldiers filed for conscientious objector status during the war; many troops went AWOL; many filed for dismissal on grounds of homosexuality; and many women soldiers became pregnant; after the war, it was revealed that on one ship, 36 of the 360 women on the ship became pregnant and were sent home, obviously a form of resistance (see the *New York Times,* April 30, 1991, p. A9).

13. Interestingly, that same morning (Jan. 26), the David Brinkley program featured footage of troops in the north of Saudi Arabia in chemical protection suits and with detection devices that indicated that there were dangerous chemicals in the air, presumably from the coalition bombing of chemical and nuclear facilities in Iraq or storage sites in Kuwait. One heard a voice-over of a soldier with a detection device indicating that "we are experiencing a contamination event" and later explaining to the camera that they had detected dangerous chemicals present. One saw some of the same clips, with a barely intelligible explanation on CNN that day, but the topic suddenly disappeared without explanation.

14. Some of these football examples are from the Greenpeace Gulf Report on Jan. 18, 1991, Situation Report No. 2 from the PeaceNet mideast.gulf bulletin board. During the ground war, as I shall note in Chapter 9, General Schwarzkopf and media reporters regularly used football metaphors to describe U.S. tactics.

15. Against Bush's claim that he was waging a "just war," former Congressman Father Robert F. Drinan argued in the *National Catholic Reporter* (Feb. 8, 1991, p. 2) that the U.S. Gulf war policy only met three of the seven criteria for a just war. A minister appearing on CNN's Sonia Friedman show after the war on March 1 properly said that it was literally blasphemous for Bush to invoke the name of God in favor of his murderous war policies. But Bush continued to play the war and religion theme, telling the annual gathering of the Southern Baptist Convention on June 6, 1991, that he recalled praying at Camp David before ordering the

start of the Gulf war. According to the *New York Times* (June 7, 1991), Bush wiped tears away from his eyes as he described praying before ordering the bombing that began the war against Iraq and the 23,000 delegates roared their approval, stood up and shouted "Amen!" Bush was on a political trip, trying to cement alliances with "conservative, church-oriented Republicans whom he and his advisers see as crucial to his political strength" (p. A7).

16. General Schwarzkopf was widely quoted as saying on August 31, 1990, "Let's face it, if he dares . . . if he dares come across that border and come down here, I'm completely confident that we're going to kick his butt when he gets here." *The Independent* reported that "One Republican told members of the 82nd Airborne that they were 'to kick some ass,' and 'to kick Saddam's butt'" (September 6, 1990). On December 20, 1991, United Press International reported that "President Bush was quoted as saying that if he orders an offensive, Iraqi President Saddam Hussein would get 'his ass kicked.'" Note how Bush personalized the war as an assault against the Iraqi president and how he utilized the puerile metaphor of "kicking ass." Some years earlier, Bush bragged how he was going to "kick ass" in his Vice-Presidential debate with Geraldine Ferraro in 1984.

17. Bob Woodward's article in the *Washington Post* of January 28 (p. A1, A15) questioned whether the allied bombing campaign was really achieving its aims. Woodward pointed out that despite Pentagon claims that airfields had been 100 percent "neutralized," 65 percent were operational; the Pentagon claimed that it had destroyed 100 percent of Iraqi radar, but Woodward's sources indicated that 20 percent had been replaced; and although the U.S. had claimed that all of Iraq's fixed Scud launchers had been destroyed, Woodward's sources revealed that only eight had been damaged enough to totally disable them. A *New York Times* story of February 4 quoted Gen. Buster Glosson who stated that unseasonably bad weather had delayed the air war campaign: "Right now we're in day 23 of the overall campaign, but only day 15 or 16 in terms of where we wanted to be in the air war." Glosson confirmed that the weather had caused allied pilots to cancel more than half of their daily bombing raids on top-priority targets in Iraq and Kuwait.

18. In a book published after the war, Smith (1991) admitted that he fought hard within CNN to make sure that the Pentagon point of view got across. He also made a pitch for the importance of having military analysts work with the news networks and claimed, hypocritically, that he was not a Pentagon propagandist. But it was obvious that Smith constantly put the Pentagon spin on events and was particularly concerned to refute the information that Peter Arnett was putting out of Baghdad concerning casualties caused by U.S. bombing. In his book, Smith wondered whether Arnett was anti-U.S. and even a traitor, though he concluded that Arnett was merely a "feeler" who "felt for" the people he covered. On Smith's own account, he constantly told the news production team what to report, chose letters to be read on the air, and helped pick military "experts" as guests. His book clearly reveals his thorough-going promilitary biases and how they shaped his daily activity at CNN. Thus Perry Smith's activity and not Peter Arnett's reporting is one of the scandals of the war, and CNN should critically discuss whether they should let individuals obviously totally committed

to a specific policy shape their news operations as they allowed Smith to do in the Gulf war.

19. The *Washington Post* headlined a February 2, 1991, front-page story with "Iraqi Tactics Surprise U.S. Officials," whereas the U.S. military in Saudi Arabia constantly told reporters that it was not surprised by the Iraqi incursion. In a report on February 4, the *New York Times* noted that no pool reporters were allowed to watch the fighting at Khafji "so they had to quote staff officers far from the scene, who glorified Saudi and Qatari troops, for political purposes, and understated the fierceness of Iraqi resistance. The best accounts of the fighting at Khafji came from reporters and photographers who got there in violation of the Pentagon ground rules" (p. A6).

20. On August 9, 1991, the *New York Times* published an article revealing that 20 of 148 American war dead were killed by friendly fire—about 15 percent of U.S. casualties in comparison with a 2 percent rate in World War II, Korea, and Vietnam. Of the 458 U.S. troops wounded, 60 to 70 were wounded by their own forces. Evidently the smart high-tech weapons couldn't tell the difference between friend and foe and in the heat of battle killed everything that generated heat and moved.

CHAPTER SEVEN

◆

The Pounding of Iraq

DAY AFTER DAY, the U.S.-led multinational coalition continued the relentless pounding of Iraq. Eventually, a certain repetitive quality to the war set in and watching the TV coverage was increasingly oppressive. Everyday was the same: military headlines and war stories on morning shows; the military briefers providing the latest kill counts with the compliant reporters sparring a little but generally asking all questions within the parameters of the Pentagon discourse; Peter Arnett providing accounts of the latest damage to civilian targets and civilian casualties in Iraq from coalition bombing; CNN recycling the same images and interviewing the same military "experts" who would say more or less the same predictable things; the Big Three networks trying to squeeze the sound bites of the day into their prime time news with occasional but generally repetitive and uninformative specials; the Scud wars continuing apace; and all talk centering on whether or when the ground war would erupt, bringing new drama and fresh blood to the screen.[1]

Consequently, watching the Persian Gulf TV war became progressively numbing. Videocassettes of precision bombing, images of U.S. ships pounding Iraqi positions in Kuwait, and reports of coalition planes pummelling the Republican Guard, Iraqi troops, and cities normalized carnage and a culture of brutality. There were daily squabbles over bomb damage assessment, debates over the targeting and attrition of the Republican Guard, reports on the great successes of the high-tech weapon systems, the (largely imaginary) horrors of chemical weapons and terrorism, and the impact of the war on the home front. Rep. Dan Burton (R-Calif.) recommended dropping nuclear weapons on the Iraqis to limit U.S. casualties, urging this demented action on the floor of Congress and CNN's *Crossfire*. Others called for the ground war to begin, although some recommended continued pounding of the Iraqi forces in the air war so that the ground war would be a mere "mopping-up" operation.

Even the daily propaganda line became repetitive, with Bush and the Pentagon reiterating: "We are on course. We are following the plan; everything is going well." They also repeated the same Big Lies everyday: we are not targeting civilian areas; we are not planning to destroy Iraq, but merely want to get Iraqi troops out of Kuwait; we tried every diplomatic effort to negotiate a peaceful settlement; we can't pause in the bombing to negotiate a cease-fire and possible peace because this will aid the enemy; we are kind, good, and just, and our enemy is absolutely evil, so all good Americans must stand behind their country, their president, and their troops. And behind the veil of administration rhetoric, the bombing and killing continued relentlessly.

7.1 "Allied Pounding of Iraqi Targets Continues"

On February 5, NBC's Faith Daniels opened the "Today" show news summary with the simple sentence "Allied pounding of Iraqi targets continues today." A local university newspaper, the *Daily Texan,* had the headline "Allied forces continue to pummel Iraq." Throughout the day, CNN used the headline "Allied bombing of Iraq remains relentless."[2] These headlines are obviously an accurate description of what had been going on since day one of the war, and appeared to be an objective, non-controversial, and professional journalistic description of the Persian Gulf war. But what does the headline really signify? What is it communicating and what is it hiding? As an exercise in political semantics, let us unpack the sentence "Allied pounding of Iraqi targets continues" to try to reveal the horror behind the abstractions of the phrase and to see how such innocent journalistic discourse hid the suffering and death caused by the coalition bombing.

Note first the phrase "Iraqi targets," the object of the sentence. What does this mean? In itself, "target" is totally abstract: It could be referring to just about anything. But what does the phrase signify and what does it hide? George Bush and the U.S. military would no doubt read "Iraqi targets" as military targets and leave it at that. But using an article in the February 5 *New York Times* and Peter Arnett's report from CNN on that day, we might be able to get a more concrete sense of the phrase. The *New York Times* buried a story on the bottom of p. A6 with a headline: "Baghdad Jolted by Waves of B-52 Attacks." The story described heavy bombardment by three waves of allied aircraft, which "apparently included B-52 bombers, the biggest in the American arsenal." The correspondent told of antiaircraft fire piercing the sky and "terrified civilians huddled in air-raid shelters." Further,

The air strikes have crippled Iraq's infrastructure and turned life for its people into misery. There is no power and little water in any of Iraq's major cities.

The last raid began on Sunday night just before midnight. Enormous blasts shook houses on the city's fringes and sent gusts of hot air across the sprawling capital. A second wave began at 3 A.M. today and a third before dawn. "What is there left to attack?" asked a resident as he emerged from an air-raid shelter, red-eyed from lack of sleep. "Have they not destroyed everything already? Will they never stop?" . . .

On tours of several provincial cities organized by the Iraqi government, a group of international correspondents saw scenes of devastation in populated areas.

In the town of Najaf, 120 miles south of Baghdad, residents said today that planes of the alliance against Iraqi had dropped 12 bombs on a residential area some three miles from one of the holiest Shiite Muslim shrines, killing at least 20 people and wounding dozens (*New York Times,* Feb. 5, p. A6).

The *Times* story makes clear that "Iraqi targets" involve the country's economic infrastructure and civilian lives and property, as well as proper military targets. During the day of February 5, the TV networks reported repeatedly that the allied bombing campaign had involved one sortie per minute over the entirety of the war—obviously a lot of Iraqi targets were being hit. In Peter Arnett's daily CNN report on February 5, an air-raid alert went on and he noted that there had already been four raids in the early morning with major air strikes. The attacks seemed to hit targets in the suburbs and Arnett heard bombs falling in the distance. All lights were suddenly turned off in the hotel, and with a flashlight in the dark Arnett related that there was no more gasoline for sale in Iraq; pictures showed long lines of cars waiting for gas, which was abruptly cut off, forcing would-be customers to walk away with empty gas cans, while others pushed cars without gas to the sides of the street. In addition, there was no more heating oil during the coldest part of year.

The Iraqis continued to claim, Arnett reported, that the coalition forces were deliberately aiming at civilian targets. Iraqi Foreign Minister Tariq Aziz had written a letter to the UN, complaining that UN silence in the face of the bombing of Baghdad violated the UN Charter. The Iraqis claimed that the bombing had destroyed their communications centers, dams, factories, and oil refineries. There was a pall of smoke around Baghdad every day from burning oil refineries and allied bombing hit civilian targets around Baghdad constantly—a fact confirmed by international journalists, Arnett noted. As Arnett gave his report, another air-raid alert began and he stated that there was usually about ten minutes between the warning and attacks. The bombing began and the camera panned to the dark sky illuminated with sparks of flashing antiaircraft fire. Earlier, Arnett reported, the bombing had shaken his hotel and rattled the windows. The image of a flashlight pointing at Arnett's face in the darkness of Baghdad during an air attack created a surreal effect. Such reports were among live television's most memorable moments: history recorded as it happened.

Arnett recounted that in addition to the bombings and missile attacks there were reports of raids by B-52 bombers, which were portrayed as a terror bombing by the local press. To CNN anchor John Holliman, Arnett said that the bombing had moved from the center of town to the periphery. Arnett noted that he had been to places with over forty bomb craters, so that there was definitely systematic bombing of civilian targets. Holliman then brought up the argument, heard daily in the media, that the damage resulted from stray antiaircraft fire. Arnett rebutted the claim, arguing that stray "triple-A fire does not cause twenty-foot-deep craters." Despite all of the talk about precision bombing, Arnett noted, it was clear that there had been a lot of civilian damage. The Cruise missiles were especially hated by the people, who believed that the missiles were not clearly targeted. The people of Baghdad, Arnett said, felt safer when airplanes came over the city than when the Cruise missiles flew over.[3] There was tremendous bitterness in the city that the bombing war focused so relentlessly on Baghdad, although the war was supposed to be about Kuwait. People were asking Arnett: "Why here and not Kuwait?"

Thus, in both a *New York Times* article on the allied bombing of Baghdad and Peter Arnett's live CNN report the "Iraqi targets" include innocent civilians—their lives and possessions—and the social and economic as well as the military infrastructure of Iraq.[4] Civilian life had been reduced to the struggle for survival. "Iraqi targets" also included oil refineries and chemical, biological, and nuclear facilities; many believed that this bombing was producing an environmental holocaust (see 5.2, 5.3, and 10.3). The media revealed little, however, about the effects of allied bombing against the Republican Guards and Iraqi troops in Kuwait and southern Iraq. One can imagine that the bombing was fierce and took countless casualties. The United States denied that they used B-52 carpet-bombing on civilians, but they admitted, even bragged of, their heavy bombing of the Iraqi military. Indeed, the mode of destruction of the B-52 is almost exclusively carpet-bombing on a massive scale; one load of bombs can destroy an area encompassing several football fields. But many other planes and killing systems also were used, including napalm, which, like the B-52, gained notoriety during the Vietnam era. Reports began to surface around February 22 that napalm bombs were being used on Iraqi targets. Napalm is a highly controversial incendiary weapon that spreads a ball of fire over its target. It burns and defaces its survivors horribly, sticking to and eating away the skin. On February 22, BBC-1 had a report on napalm, confirming its use by the

U.S.-led coalition forces. The video footage showed a U.S. Air Force ground worker loading napalm bombs onto a plane and putting fuses into the bombs. Reporter Brian Barron stated:

> Napalm is an old and crude bomb alongside much of the allies' high-tech arsenal. But it is a terrifying weapon that kills both by burning and suffocation. Until today, there had been speculation the Americans would hold it in reserve for massive retaliation if the Iraqis carried out their threat to use chemical weapons of mass destruction.

Explaining the use of napalm, former Reagan administration official Kenneth Adelman declared on BBC-4 radio: "Well, I think the objective was to make sure that the [Iraqi military], behind the lines, er, was as wiped out as possible so that we would not risk American and British boys if we needed to go on the ground war." Adelman speculated that aversion to napalm in Vietnam resulted from the inability to tell who was the "enemy" and who were innocent peasants, but in the Gulf war, "it's quite clear, they wear uniforms, they sit in tanks, they cook over fire or whatever they do, they look like military, they are military and they're clearly identified as such. And so I think that it is proper in that time to kind of weed 'em out."

And so Iraqis conscripted by Saddam Hussein were the targets of allied bombing, "weeded out" by B-52s, napalm, and other weaponry. The *Los Angeles Times* published an article on February 24 on "Ordnance: High Tech's Gory Side" that described white phosphorus howitzer shells which burst "high-velocity, burning white phosphorus particles over a limited area. The fragments can continue to burn hours after they have penetrated a soldier's body, creating deep lesions." Other exotic devices include the Beehive system in which shells are fired out of a cannon that spits out 8,800 "tiny darts with razor edges capable of causing deep wounds." These weapons are intended to produce injuries rather than death because in the words of one munitions expert: "Injury raises hell with the enemy's logistics load. With the dead, he doesn't have to do anything. But with a wounded [soldier], he has a huge logistics problem, requiring all kinds of transportation and medical care."

Other weapons were intended, however, to maximize the kill ratio. Fuel-air explosives disperse "highly flammable liquid over a large area and then detonate it, creating a huge pressure shock that can knock down buildings and exceed the 90-pound-per-square-inch [blast pressure] lethality limit for humans." A "shape charge" is an explosive that on detonation "creates a jet traveling at up to 25,000 feet per second that cuts through armor. Once through the armor, the jet sends a blinding flash of light into the tank, followed by shattered fragments of tank armor flying at high velocity." U.S. artillery shells "contain up to 88 bomblets that cover a huge area of a battlefield. They are capable of destroying lightly armored vehicles, such as personnel carriers, with hollow-point, armor-piercing heads and of incapacitating soldiers with secondary fragmentation. ICM bomblets have an estimated 50 percent probability of killing a soldier at 15 meters. By spreading 88 submunitions, rather than a single large blast, the ICM can kill four times as many soldiers" (*Los Angeles Times,* Feb. 24, 1991).

Before the war, James Ridgeway reported that the United States was deploying antitank shells that were made out of depleted uranium (*Village Voice,* Jan. 15, 1991). His disturbing story explained that, "The U.S. Army is equipped with high-tech munitions made from nuclear wastes that can melt through the layers of armor protecting the Iraqi crews, burning them alive. Not coincidentally, those same tank-killing shells will probably turn the Iraqi desert into a permanently toxic hellhole for generations to come." The report was ignored by the mainstream media in the United States but a British TV news program in late January depicted fighter plane cannons that "shoot uranium cased shells." The Scottish church group Gulfwatch reported that these shells were made out of leftover Uranium-238, which is a byproduct of the nuclear weapons and power industry (PeaceNet, mideast.forum, Feb. 8). Gulfwatch described how they are constructed and their lethal effects, citing the Occupational Health and Radiation Safety Department at the University of Pittsburgh, which claimed: "Technically, these shells are below danger standards for nuclear material but definitely radioactive. The main environmental danger comes from the fact that in a ground war the desert may be littered with thousands of them and thus poisoned for generations. Uranium-238 is an extremely toxic chemical, and, if you survive the wound, the metal will cause kidney failure."

So the "Iraqi targets" were getting bombed by some rather fierce munitions. Now let us focus on who is doing the bombing according to the standard Persian Gulf war discourse. The headlines signify that the instigators are the "allies." This term "allies" resonates with the historical memory of World War II when an alliance of (mostly) democratic nations fought fascism in a war that most people believed was just. From the beginning of the Gulf war, the phrase "allies" was used to describe the forces that relentlessly waged war against Iraq, but the term "U.S.-led multinational coalition" is more accurate. For it was clearly George Bush who mobilized this force, whose troops organized, planned, and began the military action. Although it was UN resolutions which legitimated the attack on Iraq, the UN played no further role in the war and the coalition was totally under U.S. command, and the U.S. forces were doing most of the fighting and bombing. To be sure, the British were also deeply involved in the bombing, as were the French, Saudis, and a few other nations to a lesser extent. But the overwhelming majority of the sorties into Iraq were carried out by U.S. forces. So it was primarily the forces of Bush and the Pentagon who were pounding and pummeling Iraq and the term "the allies" obscures this crucial fact.

The discourse of the allies also refers to what most people considered a "just war" during World War II against a dangerous enemy who was a real threat to nations throughout the world. It is arguable, however, that the Gulf war was not a "just war" in the classical sense as questions were raised concerning whether the Bush administration took every possible measure to prevent the war (see 1.2) and whether the extent of the pounding of Iraq was proportionate to the threat that Iraq posed to its neighbors.[5] Indeed, it is ludicrous to compare Iraq with Nazi Germany or the Iraqi threat with that faced by the allies in World War II, who were confronting the fascist forces of Germany, Italy, and Japan.

Next, let's do a conceptual analysis of the phrase "pounding." The term has the connotation of a boxing match in which two more or less equally matched forces fight it out in the ring. The Gulf war, however, involved two of the most mismatched forces in history, in which a giant bully and its bully friends pounded on a much smaller bully. Moreover, the pounding really involved the killing and slaughter of the Iraqi people and the destruction of their economic infrastructure. Thus terms like "pounding" or "pummeling," however brutal and graphic, are really mild in comparison with the deadly destruction that was inflicted daily on Iraq.

Indeed, in both the *New York Times* and CNN Arnett report, it was noted that one type of plane bombing Iraqi targets was the fabled B-52, renowned for its Vietnam carpet-bombing (see Gibson 1986). The B-52 bomber is a rather big, slow, and clumsy plane that is distinctive for the amount of bombs that it is able to drop. ABC reported that the plane can drop twenty-five tons of bombs in one flight and all of the networks featured reports on B-52 cluster-bombing and descriptions of the tremendous damage done by B-52 attacks. Using cluster bombs, a B-52 can deliver more than 8,000 bomblets in a single mission; upon impact, the bomblets are dispersed over a wide area and then explode (Walker 1992, p. 87). But in Vietnam, as B-52s were vulnerable to antiaircraft fire, they were modified so that they could fly higher and drop their murderous loads out of the range of antiaircraft fire. This makes them not one of the precision smart-bomb delivery systems, but solely weapons of terror and death.

Yet after a B-52 crashed the weekend of February 3 on the way back to its base in Diego Garcia, the TV networks reported that B-52s were extremely old and perhaps obsolete in an era of high-tech bombing. TV also showed protests against B-52s using bases in Spain, where thousands of people demonstrated against the servicing of this death machine on Spanish soil. The British had smaller, quieter protests against the B-52s based in their country. Only after diplomatic maneuvering did France allow the plane to fly over its airspace.

To explicate further the mode of destruction in the "pounding" of Iraqi targets, we might consider a CNN interview with a British bombing crew just back from some action in Iraq. When asked about reports that they had bombed a lot of civilian targets and caused civilian casualties, a member of the crew answered: "We go about and drop our bombs and if they hit civilian targets, that's tough." The interviewer, supporting this point of view, chimed in, "That's war," and the bombardier answered, "Absolutely." So "pounding" involves killing people and destroying targets, whether military or civilian, and many of those dropping the bombs go about their daily business without a pang of conscience, with the media defending their slaughter of innocents.

During Vietnam, Gibson (1986) and others pointed out that high-tech bombing was increasingly abstract with pilots merely interacting with technology rather than perceiving the actual effects of their bombing on people and the environment. Much of the bombing in the Gulf war was even more abstract, utilizing laser-guided computers where the pilot merely pushed buttons and the weapon found its own target. The months preceding the bombing of Baghdad involved detailed "'software work' to digitally map and plot strategic installations there. The [computer] networks were then used to keep track of targets in real time, to program and guide 'precision long-range weapons,' and then to undertake 'battle damage assessment.' The whole network formed a kind of cybernetic input and feedback loop" (Robins and Levidow 1991, p. 324).

In this situation, the bombing crews were merely nodes in a system, technical operatives who pushed buttons to release bombs or missiles at targets "derealized" into mere data on a computer screen. In many cases, it was the computer program that guided the bombing "mission," so that the pilots merely flew to their site, avoided antiaircraft fire, dropped their munitions, and flew away. Moreover, the whole experience had a video game feel to it and if one had been excited by playing bombing games in simulators, the whole experience had a positive libidinal charge. In fact, some of the TV commentators and military experts seemed to be having wargasms in their ecstasies over the video bombing footage, as they "oohed" and "ahhed" over the bombing videos, as if they were getting libidinal enjoyment from watching the pornography of destruction.[6] In celebrating the technology of death, the media thus transformed the bombing into a positive and celebratory experience rather than one of tragic empathy with human suffering.

Finally, let us focus on the last term in the headline "Allied pounding of Iraqi targets continues." The verb "continues" signifies that every day since the beginning of the war, the U.S.-led coalition has carried out thousands of sorties per day, almost one every minute, the war managers bragged. The Gulf war exhibited the most massive concentration of air power and eventually involved the most massive bombing of a single target country in military history. The verb "continues" thus signifies the daily bombing assaults on Iraq which eventually unloaded tons of explosives on that country. After the war, General Merrill McPeak (1991) indicated that the U.S.-led coalition forces flew 110,000 sorties and dropped 88,500 tons of bombs: "this is about half again as much tonnage as we dropped during the entire war in Vietnam. In 43 days, we—in other words, we far exceeded our tonnage of precision-guided munitions in a war that lasted eight or nine years."

At the British military briefing on February 5, Captain Niall Irving picked up on the discourse of "continues," stating: "Allied forces are continuing to apply a grinding wheel to the Iraqi military machine." The sparks of secondary explosions signified to him that the grinding was continuously having the desired effects. Speaking of a recent massive bombing attack, Irving quoted a British source who described a massive explosion, claiming: "I think that we just woke up the whole of Iraq." In a January 30 military briefing, General Schwarzkopf bragged that a "secondary explosion we had the other day registered at 12" on a scale of 1 to 10. So continuing the bombing meant proudly bombing Iraq until it was blasted into permanent sleeplessness and reduced to rubble.

The key point, however, is that many Iraqi civilian targets were being destroyed, although the U.S. military was denying this. George Bush said repeatedly that he had no quarrel with the Iraqi people, just Saddam Hussein. Yet the U.S.-led coalition dropped tons of bombs on defenseless civilians. As Tristan Coffin put it on CNN, the Iraqis are learning what a First World power can do to a Third World power. Indeed, he was right, though this was nothing to boast about. In the Gulf war, the most heavily armed nation on earth, with the most sophisticated high-tech weapons ever, systematically destroyed the military and economic infrastructure of a Third World country equipped with a 1960s-type military apparatus of tanks, missiles, and artillery that was almost helpless against the U.S. war machine. The great military victory celebrated by the media and the public was thus really nothing more than the slaughter of a third-rate military force by the most massive and lethal military force ever assembled. Some victory.

7.2 The Bombing of Basra

On January 29, reports began circulating almost daily on the bombing of Basra, Iraq's second largest city with over 800,000 inhabitants, located in the south on the road to Kuwait City, not far from the border. Basra was a fabled ancient city, said to be the home of Sinbad the Sailor; the Tigris and Euphrates rivers join there to form the Shatt-al-Arab waterway leading to the Gulf, thus it is Iraq's most important port city. During the Iran-Iraq war it experienced significant destruction from Iranian bombing. Basra was also in the vicinity of much of Iraq's military industry and was the staging ground for Iraqi supply operations to the theater of war in Kuwait. The city was thus deemed an important military target and suffered heavy bombing in daily raids.

During the first week of February TV reports showed footage of bombed-out civilian areas of Basra and a hospital that had been bombed, and had several reports of civilian casualties. One CNN report of February 1 showed a dead child being pulled out of the rubble of a destroyed building. Hospital scenes showed large numbers of civilian casualties from the coalition bombing. A *Los Angeles Times* article (Feb. 5, 1991) interviewed refugees from the area who testified that the massive allied bombing had destroyed Basra's communication centers, oil refineries, major government buildings, and hundreds of storage facilities that contained everything from food to ammunition. Indeed, Iranian television reported in late January of powerful explosions heard in the city, the rumble of bombing, and reports of massive oil-refinery fires that shot plumes of flame and smoke high into the air. Refugees stated that the bombing "raids have left a hellish nightmare of fire and smoke so dense that the sun hasn't been clearly visible for several days at a time."

Witnesses also reported that air strikes leveled entire city blocks in civilian areas and left "bomb craters the size of football fields and an untold number of casualties" (Feb. 5, 1991). An article in the *Miami Herald* (Feb. 10, 1991, pp. A1, A23) quoted a Jordanian refugee who stated: "Basra is totally damaged. There is no petrol, no water. There are people dead in the roads and nobody is moving them. . . . People are drinking from the sewers. They have cans and they are filling them. I was driving carefully because of all the holes in the road and the dead bodies." Former U.S. attorney general Ramsey Clark reported following a trip to Iraq that:

In Basra, you can see six continuous city blocks that are almost rubble. They were homes. You'd see a guy sitting out there because they kind of watch over what's left. . . . We saw hundreds of dwellings demolished. . . . The central market in Basra has about a thousand shops—and here you see a crater that's

Victims of war. (Photo courtesy of Alan Pogue.)

bigger than the White House swimming pool, except it's round. It's right at
the entrance to the market and [the bomb] shattered everything, and it landed
right on a supermarket. It's not there anymore. I mean it's just gone. And
around, you just see damage, and there's no possible military target there.
Driving through the countryside, you see food-processing places, if they're
big, fairly systematically hit.

The mosques: We came upon one mosque in Basra—it was particularly
tragic, it was way out in the countryside. . . . There were three or four bombs
that hit around there that just kind of messed everything up. When you hit a
mosque, it's got no internal support, just this big dome, so it just comes down.
It collapses in rubble. And there was a family of 12 who had sought refuge in
there. . . . They found 10 bodies in the mosque. The minaret was still standing
there. Every type of civilian structure you could think of. (Broadcast over
WBAI-FM Radio and transcribed on PeaceNet, mideast.gulf, Feb. 12, 1991)[7]

In his Sunday, February 10, report from Baghdad, Peter Arnett noted
that the governor of the province of Basra told them that two hundred
civilians had been killed in the past few days; the journalists saw
destroyed homes, neighborhoods, and a mosque that had been bombed
out, taking video footage of this damage, but they were not allowed to
see military targets. Civil defense authorities claimed that cluster bombs
were used against civilian neighborhoods and video images showed
casings of these antipersonnel weapons that were used; the bomblets

inside explode like hand grenades. The foreign correspondents visited a hospital where they were told that sixty civilians were treated each day. Many injuries came from collapsing roofs in the poorest neighborhoods of the city. The report was illustrated by poignant pictures of women and children in a hospital, a child splattered with blood; a dazed mother in bed with bandages and her injured child beside her; pile after pile of rubble of bombed-out buildings illustrated the report. Arnett concluded that Basra was in the front line of the war, yet people were saying that they were ready to defend it and were prepared to withstand the heavy bombing raids.

After the war, Louise Cainkar, the director of the Palestine Human Rights Information Center, visited Basra and described visiting five different civilian sectors of the city that had suffered heavily from coalition bombing. She said that residents of the Ma'kel neighborhood reported 400 civilians had died from coalition bombing (1991, p. 343). According to Cainkar, "[h]ospital statistics for Basra city from the Ministry of Health show 681 civilian injury hospital admissions between January 17 and February 16, of whom 285 subsequently died. This of course reflects only a portion of civilians killed by bombs, as many never reach a hospital" (1991, p. 343).

In future histories of the Persian Gulf war, the U.S. bombing of Baghdad and Basra may be read as one of the great crimes of the century. However, the enormity of the destruction of the cities and civilians was covered over during the war by a veil of hypocrisy as U.S. officials repeated over and over that there was remarkably little civilian damage because of precise targeting and smart bombs. Yet Peter Arnett's and the other reports of the foreign correspondents in Iraq provided visual evidence refuting the claims of the war managers that they were avoiding civilian casualties.

During the weekend of February 8–9, a verbal attack by Senator Alan Simpson (R-Wyo.) on Peter Arnett was much discussed in the media.[8] Simpson had called Arnett an Iraqi "sympathizer" who had earlier "sympathized" with the communists in the Vietnam war. In a racist and McCarthyist slur, Simpson claimed that Arnett's (former) wife was Vietnamese and her brother was allegedly a Viet Cong (the latter was a lie). Although almost every major commentator in the country defended Arnett against this sleazy attack, no one stressed the close relationship between Simpson and the Bush administration, or recalled how during the Iran/Contra scandal, Simpson was a hardball defender of the Reagan administration and critic of the press. None recalled that Bush's press secretary, Marlin Fitzwater, had already taken potshots at Arnett; nor did these commentators report that there had been significant attacks on Arnett from the right since the beginning of the war, as evidenced by CNN's own letters that they read on the air as well as the attacks evident in radio and television talk shows. Simpson was thus once again a hatchet man for a Republican administration, carrying out a shoddy attack on an honorable journalist by using McCarthyist tactics as a surrogate and point man for the Bush administration.[9]

Simpson was also hypocritical because he never spoke out against Saddam Hussein before the war and was even one of those senators who had visited Iraq during the summer of 1990 when he, along with Senate Minority Leader Robert Dole, had been obsequious to Hussein. The U.S. senators visited Hussein on his birthday and may have sent a signal that he could get away with military aggression against Kuwait. Simpson denied this, but TV pictures showed him, Dole, and the others fawning over Saddam Hussein, whom they later vilified. A transcript of the visit reveals that Simpson told Hussein, "I believe that your problems lie with the Western media, and not with the U.S. government. As long as you are isolated from the media, the press—and it is a haughty and pampered press—they all consider themselves political geniuses. . . . What I advise is that you invite them to come here and see for themselves" (Simpson, in Ridgeway 1991, p. 37). Moreover, Peter Arnett revealed after the war that Simpson and other senators "upbraided" him and other journalists in Jerusalem in April 1990 "about our coverage of Hussein, who was threatening to incinerate Israel at the time. . . . We still do have the video, senator," Arnett said (*Broadcasting,* May 25, 1991, p. 91).

During the same weekend that Simpson's attack on Arnett was being discussed, Basra was suddenly very visible on U.S. television with pictures of bombing rubble and civilian casualties in hospitals appearing on CNN and other networks. The bombing of Basra was becoming a key issue in the propaganda war. During a February 11 briefing with Gen. Richard ("Butch") Neal, Charlayne Hunter-Gault of the "MacNeil/Lehrer News Hour" pointed to the pictures that showed women, children, and others hurt by the bombing campaign, and remarked that the "pictures are pretty astonishing." She asked what the coalition planned to do differently in response to these pictures. Neal repeated that they were doing everything possible to avoid civilian collateral damage, and then became agitated and incoherent. He noted that there were conflicting reports, some indicating few or no civilian casualties, while others indicated great damage to civilians. Taking the offensive, Neal argued that the press in Iraq is "censored" and one should not credit the reports of damage to civilians; as an example, he cited the story of a soldier in a hospital, who was wrapped in a blanket before the camera came, covering his uniform, so that he would appear to be a civilian casualty. "You can't credit such reports," Neal insisted and after a couple of incoherent remarks concluded: "So I'll just leave it at that."

But the reporters persevered. One indicated that Basra had almost emptied out and had become a ghost town during the Iran-Iraq war and that the allied bombing was threatening to make it a ghost town once more. With glee, Neal seized upon the great destruction it had undergone in the earlier war and suggested that the films of rubble being shown on TV were pictures left over from that war, or pictures of rubble remaining from the last war. This claim was incredible and could have easily been confirmed or disproven by the fifteen or so foreign reporters who had visited Basra. (Basra had been rebuilt after the Iran-Iraq war so that the rubble would not have been a leftover from the previous war.) Another reporter, evoking a phrase from Vietnam, suggested that if the coalition forces wished to win the "hearts and minds" of the Iraqi people, then such heavy bombing made it likely that the people being bombed would not be able to perceive the Americans as anything but callous. Neal noted that the pictures of the bombing of bridges in Baghdad pointed to the precise surgical bombing that avoided civilian casualties and hypocritically affirmed once again that with their precision bombing they were avoiding civilian casualties.

General Neal admitted that the coalition forces considered Basra a military town, suggesting that the entire area was a legitimate military target. He also admitted coalition targeting of chemical-weapons facilities and storage plants in the area. When a reporter asked about the U.S. "concern for contamination," Neal answered that the United States was trying to limit any contamination by using munitions appropriate to the targets, but then admitted: "Let's be frank, we don't put these facilities there." Thus, the coalition forces admitted bombing sensitive chemical facilities, but Neal evaded once again the question of potentially devastating chemical contamination of the environment from such bombing.

Indeed, there were many reports of significant chemical, biological, and nuclear contamination from the U.S.-led coalition bombing. As noted earlier, on January 27, brief TV reports appeared concerning the possibility of chemical contamination of northern Saudi Arabia from the bombing of weapons facilities or storage depots in Iraq. Furthermore, many independent sources provided information on contamination from the coalition bombing. For example, Environment News Service on February 11, 1991, reported:

An unknown and rapidly progressing disease has reportedly been unleashed after a bacteriological weapons production plant near the Iraqi capital of Baghdad was bombed by coalition forces. Fifty out of one hundred servicemen guarding the plant died in a Baghdad hospital shortly after being admitted. According to a report from Tass News Agency Sunday, an Egyptian physician who had been working in the hospital told a Cairo-based newspaper that the guards had lung damage and injuries to their circulatory and intestinal systems. The physician said efforts to contain the disease were unsuccessful, and it was spreading in Baghdad. (cited from PeaceNet, mideast.gulf)[10]

A reporter also noted in the February 11 briefing with General Neal that a Basra oil refinery was attacked and a lot of smoke was seen billowing over the border. Should people, the reporter asked, be advised to leave the area? Neal admitted that they attacked Iraqi oil production and storage facilities, but would not confirm the specific hit and did not provide any advice to the people of Basra as to whether they should abandon their city to escape from U.S. environmental terrorism. A reporter then came back again to the sensitive issue of chemical contamination and asked which munitions target chemical weapons facilities, and Neal answered that serious consideration was given to "sensitive type targets like that to make sure that we can minimize collateral damage," but didn't go into any details and quickly broke away from this sensitive issue.[11]

In general, TV commentators and military experts avoided the discussion of chemical, nuclear, and biological contamination like the plague, which indeed the coalition bombing may have unleashed. The network news operations almost never mentioned it: It became something that polite people did not discuss. By contrast, some of the reporters in the field seemed to be very concerned about environmental contamination, and there were reports that it was indeed a major problem that the politicians and military attempted to cover up with the ultimate complicity of the mainstream media which never systematically pursued the issue.

There was also little or no debate on the ethics of the bombing of bridges. In his WBAI radio report on his trip to Baghdad, Ramsey Clark noted:

You see extensive bombing around bridges. It's hard to hit a bridge, apparently. I even saw a U.S. Government count and they said it took 500 and some sorties to hit bridges, and they hit 31. But there are people living all around them. There's a big river through Baghdad and there are a lot of bridges across it. And people don't stay away from them. They build right up toward them. In Baghdad, the Ministry of Justice building has all its windows shattered. And right there—and I think he was trying to hit the bridge, probably, because there's just absolutely nothing else there [remaining]. But he didn't hit the bridge and he had four bombs coming in there, and he just knocked out all these—it's a poor part of town—little shops and stores. And the merchants and the people who survived, they've lost everything, and their families were killed and all. (PeaceNet, mideast.gulf, Feb. 12, 1991)

On February 11, Ramsey Clark cited on ABC the bombing of Baghdad bridges as evidence of focus on civilian targets, since people used these bridges and have their lives disrupted by the destruction of the bridges that they need to get from one part of the town to another. Peter Arnett's daily report from Baghdad that day showed the pictures of the bombed out bridges and had clips about people complaining that these attacks had killed civilians in the area. In a White House briefing the same day, Marlin Fitzwater found it "disturbing" that someone was "buying the evidence" that there was significant civilian damage in Iraq. This was in part a slam at Gorbachev who was arguing that U.S. bombing of Iraq was exceeding the UN mandate. In making the inane suggestion that the evidence of one's own eyes and the witness of reporters, day after day, was duping people to "buy into Iraqi propaganda," Fitzwater was conceding that the Iraqis were scoring points in the propaganda war with civilian "collateral damage."

Yet the deaths of innocent civilians and the destruction of the infrastructure of Iraq received little sympathy in the mainstream media, or from members of the coalition against Iraq. Moshe Arens, Israel's defense minister, told reporters after a meeting with Bush on February 10 that the Israelis were suffering from the worst bombing incurred by "Western" nations since World War II. Obviously, Vietnamese, Iraqi, and Palestinian and Lebanese people who suffered from U.S. and Israeli bombing and died in the thousands did not count. Only victims from "Western" nations presumably deserve sympathy. Indeed, there was an incredible double standard at work in the relative sympathies mustered by the network commentators toward various victims of war. Images of Israelis suffering from Iraqi Scud attacks aroused great compassion in the normally cool network anchors and correspondents. Yet, with some exceptions, the images of dead Iraqi civilians, which would become more gruesome and graphic as the war went on, were depicted as a propaganda ploy of Saddam Hussein (see 6.3).

7.3 Baghdad Atrocity

At 5:14 A.M. EST on February 13, Peter Arnett reported that during the night huge bombs had rained down on the city of Baghdad and hit a bomb shelter in a civilian area, causing many civilian deaths. The early video footage showed people milling around a huge mass of concrete and steel with smoke emerging from a hole in the ground. Around 6 A.M. EST, Arnett came on again and said that the picture was now becoming a little clearer concerning what had happened. Reporters were taken to the Amiriya area of Baghdad where hundreds of people were trapped in a bomb shelter that was directly hit by U.S. bombs. Arnett interviewed a minister of health on the scene who said that the first bomb cut a hole in the roof and the second bomb went straight through the hole and exploded, causing a massive fire in the shelter and preventing Iraqi civilian defense from rescuing the people inside. The minister claimed that the neighborhood was civilian and that the bombing attack was a "criminal, premeditated, and well-planned attack against the civilians."

The images broadcast on CNN showed people waiting anxiously outside the destroyed shelter while firemen were fighting a fire in it. Other images of the area showed houses, a school, a supermarket, and a mosque, with no evidence of military targets. Arnett reported that he and other journalists then went to a local hospital where there were bodies of thirty dead women and children, and ten more in a truck outside. The bodies were charred beyond recognition, and the Iraqis were claiming that there were as many as one thousand people sleeping in the shelter and that perhaps as many as four hundred were killed. The bombing reportedly occurred at 4:45 A.M. Baghdad time, and Arnett described the attack as part of a series of heavy bombing raids that night. Since the bombing had begun, he explained, hundreds of people had slept regularly in the bomb shelter. When the foreign correspondents arrived, one truckload of bodies had been driven away and the CNN cameraman reportedly saw many bodies dragged out of the charred remains. In response to whether the Iraqis were censoring this story, Arnett replied that they had told the correspondents for the first time that their copy would not be subject to any censorship nor would there be any Iraqi authorities with him as he gave the report. He was free to report exactly what he saw.

In their early morning news reports, ABC buried the story of the atrocity of Amiriya in the middle of their headlines and coded it as a possible propaganda ploy by the Iraqis. Mike Schneider reported that "there is a new claim now from Iraq about the allies allegedly hitting civilian areas of Baghdad. Reporters were taken today to what is left of a building in the center of the city. Iraqis say that it was a bomb shelter that was hit by allied bombs. They claim now that some four hundred people were killed in this one incident. Of course, the claims could not be independently confirmed. Keep in mind that everything that comes out of Iraq now is subject to Iraqi censorship."

The report was accompanied by obscured pictures of some twisted concrete and metal with none of the poignant images of civilian deaths shown in the CNN report. This brief news summary was followed by Schneider saying: "President Bush said that talk of civilian casualties is nothing but propaganda cooked up by Saddam Hussein," accompanied by a clip of Bush complaining. In fact, the ABC report revealed itself to be pure propaganda for the military and Bush administration. First, note how the ABC report framed the story as mere Iraqi propaganda using the terms "claim," "allegedly," and "subject to government censorship." By stating that, "of course, the claims could not be independently confirmed," one is positioned to view the report skeptically and the "of course" serves as a wink to the viewer that naturally *you* don't want to believe this Iraqi propaganda. The disclaimer that the "claims could not be independently confirmed," however, is somewhat disingenuous, as ABC could have listened to the CNN report by Peter Arnett, which was shown at least a half an hour before; they could have also asked their own correspondent on the scene what he could confirm, or cited an AP report on the bombing. And ABC could have viewed the pictures of the carnage, already on the satellite, to discern if there might actually be some "confirmation" that an atrocity had occurred.

Every war has its memorable events, those images that are seared into one's mind forever and that constitute one's picture of the war. Images of atrocities of war are especially unforgettable; during the Vietnam war, pictures of Buddhist monks burning themselves in Saigon as a protest against the war were especially powerful, as were images of U.S. soldiers torching peasant huts with cigarette lighters, of B-52 airplanes dropping high explosive bombs with great fireballs exploding below, and of a young girl running down a road with a group of refugees, her naked body scarred by napalm. These are the images of Vietnam that haunt the memory and create a picture of the horrors of war. Would the atrocities of Baghdad reach this status? Not if the Bush administration and Pentagon propaganda apparatus could help it.

The first official response came from the Pentagon with CNN reporting that the military was claiming that they had no way of determining whether the target was an air-raid shelter, if it was a civilian or a military target, and if the charred bodies were civilian or military. The Pentagon insisted that the United States was not in the practice of targeting civilians and stated that if the attack did take place, they "would feel badly about it." The Pentagon "bridles" at the suggestion that there be an "investigation" because that implied wrong-doing, though they would perform the usual "bomb damage assessment." CBS's Jim Stewart at the Pentagon said that officials were caught by surprise by the report and claimed to have no evidence of the bombing, saying that the only evidence is "Iraqi government cleared and censored film." Anchor Harry Smith in Saudi Arabia, obviously reproducing a propaganda line fed him by his U.S. military handlers, mentioned that the Iraqis had been putting military facilities in civilian areas, as if this justified bombing civilians in a bomb shelter. He generally scoffed at the claim of the bombing of a civilian target, implying that the reports were mere propaganda, thus showing himself to be eager to promote the Pentagon line from his spot in Saudi Arabia.

CBS's Randall Pinkston reported from the White House that so far there was no official U.S. reaction to the destruction of the bomb shelter in suburban Baghdad. Pinkston reproduced Pentagon sophistries that perhaps the Iraqis "placed civilians in harm's way" (in bomb shelters!) or that charred bodies were perhaps military personnel dressed up as civilians (disregarding reports that foreign reporters had seen charred bodies of women and children pulled out of the shelter). Pinkston commented that the Bush administration had been concerned about reports involving Iraqi civilian casualties as part of a "propaganda war." CBS then broadcast a series of remarks by Bush:

> February 6: "I am annoyed at the propaganda coming out of Baghdad about targeting civilians."
> February 11: "I would be remiss if I did not reassure the American people that this war was fought with high-tech."
> February 12: "I think that there is a conscientious [sic] effort on [Saddam Hussein's] part to try to raise the propaganda value, accusing us of indiscriminate bombing of civilians and it's simply not true."

Obviously, Bush's repeated disclaimers indicated that the issue of civilian casualties was a sensitive one, and the Bush administration propaganda machine now faced their greatest challenge: to put an effective spin on the Baghdad atrocities.

Although the Bush administration and the mainstream media now regularly stressed that Iraq was carrying out a "propaganda war," the latter failed to recognize the propaganda efforts of the Bush administration and Pentagon. Later in their morning show, ABC broadcast a powerful segment on the bombing by correspondent Bill Blakemore in Baghdad. Blakemore graphically described the bloody casualties that he and other reporters saw in the shelter and graphic images of bloody bodies illustrated his text. One saw Blakemore and other reporters penetrate into the smoky shelter, going as far into it "as the heat and smoke would let us." One Iraqi man told Blakemore that "I swear to God. I will get my revenge on Bush if it takes my ten generations." There were images of pools of blood on the floor and bodies and body parts "of women and children who usually sleep in the shelter at night." One man was looking for "eleven of my own" in tremendous despair. A piece of the bomb with writing in English was displayed and the report then cut to depict a collection of bodies at a hospital. An angry doctor said: "Do you call this justice? Who dares to say that 'we don't hit civilians.'" Some badly burned children who escaped and whose families had died inside the shelter were shown and interviewed. A woman screamed at the reporters: "For what? For oil, you would do this?"

Mike Schneider reminded the audience that Blakemore's report was subject to scrutiny by Iraqi government censors and then discussed the propaganda value of the pictures as well as the alleged fact that Saddam Hussein planted civilians in military targets. As it turned out, these reports were not censored by the Iraqis and to reduce these harrowing pictures to "propaganda" was obscene; earlier, Schneider had acted as if the stories of the civilian deaths were mere propaganda and when confronted with striking pictures, he continued to interpret the event as propaganda and to blame the deaths on Saddam Hussein, revealing himself to be a propaganda agent for the Bush administration and U.S. military.

Throughout the morning, the Pentagon repeated that their bombing practices and U.S. policy were to minimize civilian casualties, though they knew that there would be some such casualties. The Pentagon now also added that they were going to bomb antiaircraft artillery, even if it was to be placed in civilian areas, reversing an earlier stated policy and suggesting that the Baghdad incident was not going to temper their bombing practices. At the morning U.S. military briefing in Saudi Arabia, delayed to get its propaganda line together, Gen. Richard "Butch" Neal launched into what might be the Biggest Lie in a campaign of Big Lies. Neal appeared drawn and pinched and seemed extremely tense. His report of the dull and deadly statistics was longer than usual and appeared monstrous and inhuman in the face of the human tragedies hidden by the bland numbers of the daily kill rate. Finally, Neal commented on the "bunker strike that has had so much play over this past morning. I'm here to tell you that it was a military bunker. It was a command and control facility. . . . We have been systematically attacking these bunkers since the beginning of the campaign."

Neal went on to explain that it was an "active bunker" with a "hardened shelter," with a roof that had been recently painted to camouflage it, and that "we have no explanation why there were civilians in this bunker." He insisted that they had accurate intelligence that this was a military installation and had precisely targeted the building. Neal advised that civilians would be safer if they stayed in a residential area, though, in fact, the Amiriya shelter was built for the people in that residential area. Neal had no answer for the repeated questions concerning why, if U.S. intelligence was so great, they did not know that civilians were sleeping in the building. Neal speculated that perhaps the victims were members of the family of the military personnel who work there.

And now what would the CNN spin doctors say? Anchor Reid Collins evenhandedly noted that there were conflicting reports as to whether the building was a military or civilian shelter and CNN military "analyst" James Blackwell came on to try to put a positive Pentagon spin on the bombing. Throughout the day, Blackwell, Perry Smith, and CNN's other military commentators would do their best to argue that the shelter was a military command-and-control center, showing once again how "military analysts" were just mouthpieces for the Pentagon. Blackwell correctly noted that the military was not passing the episode off as a case of mistaken bombing. Rather, it was claiming that the building was an active target and that it had observed military personnel going in and out of the shelter and had detected electronic messages coming out that were being sent to control operations in the Kuwaiti theater. Blackwell claimed that pilots had told him that the building did not appear to be a civilian bomb shelter, at least from the air, and concluded himself that if Saddam Hussein was putting civilians in it, then that was criminal.

Reid Collins asked what if the building was a military facility during the day and a civilian shelter at night? Blackwell replied that General Neal claimed that they had no information that there were any civilians at all in the shelter. CNN Pentagon correspondent Gene Randall reasonably asked if the bombing and death toll pointed to a failure in the Pentagon's intelligence; Blackwell merely deflected the question. The rest of the day the Big Three networks returned to their regular programming of game shows and soap operas, leaving one of the major dramas of the war to play out solely on CNN. Peter Arnett reported live from Baghdad at 10:54 A.M. that 200 bodies had been taken out of the shelter and they were all women and children—he put special emphasis on the word "shelter" whereas the U.S. military apologists in the media would use the term "bunker." The manager of the shelter told Arnett that there were still about 300 more people in the building. The manager insisted that there were no military personnel or activities in it and that the shelter was purely for civilians. Indeed, no men were allowed in the shelter, which was for women and children only. The video, in fact, depicted the men waiting outside the shelter, visibly upset, in grief as they saw the charred bodies being pulled out. The report cut to an interview in the hospital with a survivor of the bombing, a young boy with severe burns who told how the bombs hit; he and a few others crawled out and he told how his mother and sisters were burned to death; he woke up on fire and turned to his mother who was already a lump of burned flesh; then he crawled out, his clothes burned off, and his body suffering from burns.

After the Saudi military briefing, which reproduced the U.S. propaganda line of the day, CNN brought on an eager Maj. Gen. Perry Smith who provided his analysis of the mystery of the bunker/shelter. Smith said that if you look at the video of the reinforced concrete, the multilayers of stairs, and the steel doors, you can see that it is a military shelter. CNN anchor Bob Cain asked if these features were not similar to a civilian shelter, and Smith answered no, that he was familiar with military bunkers and the "luxury" features were not in civilian shelters (Smith failed to specify what the luxury features were, which were certainly not visible in the video). Cain then raised the question of who the civilians might have been and Smith repeated the Pentagon line that they might have been families of the military personnel who worked in the bunker, speculating that it could also be that "he [Saddam Hussein] put a lot of civilians in there," knowing that it might be struck, to create propaganda effects around the world.

Smith's claim that this was certainly a military bunker was pure bluster. On Britain's BBC-2 (Feb. 13) a military expert, Dr. David Manley, a U.K. government's Home Office civil defence adviser, put the U.S. version in question. Manley had actually been inside both Iraqi civilian and military shelters and stated that "it was definitely a bomb-shelter. Very poorly designed and constructed—one thing, it seemed to burst open very, very easily, with these bombs. And it was penetrated very easily and from the steel and from the concrete and I would be very surprised if it was rolled steel or [that] the concrete could fetch over 50 newtons [which] is what we specify for civilian nuclear shelters. The military shelters of Saddam Hussein are very good. We do know that." The BBC interviewer went on to ask:

> Now, the suggestion is that it may have been originally a civilian shelter but that it had been converted to military purposes and perhaps it had a dual function—perhaps a civilian bomb-shelter on top and a military command and control centre underneath. Does that make sense?
>
> DR. MANLEY: No. I would not agree with that practice at all, technically. You can't just convert a civilian shelter into a military shelter. There are many, many aspects to be considered on this. I rather think that it was used for civilians. . . .
>
> PRESENTER: But the Americans say that they had good electronic intelligence that military signals were passing in and out of this bunker at an increasing frequency over the last week.
>
> DR. MANLEY: Well, it may well be so, because the communication equipment may have been stored partly in these shelters. Most countries have quite sophisticated networks of communications equipment. But I don't agree that this was one of his military shelters.

As the day went on, as we shall see, substantial evidence indicated that the bombing target was a civilian shelter and that the U.S. had massacred innocent civilians; after the war, more evidence appeared to confirm this view. Such an atrocity was bound to elicit world outrage. From the UN, CNN correspondent Jeanne Moos reported that the U.S. ambassador came with John Kelly, a big gun in the State Department, to meet with Javier Perez de Cueller, the UN Secretary General. The Cuban UN representative had said that the bombing had been going on around the clock for twenty-seven days already and had regularly been hitting populated areas and causing civilian deaths. There was a strong movement afoot in the UN to reconsider the Security Council resolution allowing force to resolve the crisis in the Gulf, and the United States was doing everything possible to head off further debate, especially in public.

Later in the morning there was an announcement by Press Secretary Marlin Fitzwater, who stated: "Last night, coalition forces bombed a military command and control center in Baghdad that, according to press reports, resulted in a number of civilian casualties. The loss of civilian lives in time of war is a truly tragic consequence. It saddens everyone to know that innocent people may have died in the course of military conflict. Americans treat human life as our most precious value." After this stunning piece of hypocrisy, Fitzwater went on to claim that the "bunker was a military target, . . . a command and control center that fed instructions directly to the Iraqi war machine," painted and camouflaged to avoid detection, and well documented as a military target. But the only "arguments" so far officially advanced was the claim that the building was camouflaged, that there were military messages transmitted from it, and that Iraqi military personnel were seen entering the building during the day.

Several TV commentators that day went to the roof of the shelter and the video showed that there was no camouflage on the shelter, that it had a merely sand and gravel flat roof; inspection of the building by journalists on the scene revealed no evidence of any communications gear or other military material in the shelter. To the U.S. claims that they detected Iraqi military personnel entering the shelter, the question was raised concerning why the same intelligence did not show civilians entering every evening and leaving every morning, as had occurred throughout the war. One military flack argued that it would be impossible to detect civilians going in at night because the U.S. satellite pictures could not detect this in the darkness, but the answer evaded the question of why the satellite did not detect civilians coming out of the shelter in the daylight and, in fact, the United States refused to answer questions concerning whether their satellite photos had a night capacity.

Fitzwater repeated that the United States did not know why civilians were in the structure, "but we do know that Saddam Hussein does not share our value in the sanctity of life." After concluding with a litany of the crimes of Saddam Hussein, including a new report that two Iraqi planes have been parked beside an ancient archaeological site, Fitzwater abruptly broke off, saying, "Thank you very much," and walked away without taking any questions, as a reporter shouted after him: "What do you mean, thank you, we want to ask you questions!"

The noon CNN telecast was headlined: "Conflicting reports out of the war zone." CNN announced that so far there were only eight survivors, and that the bombed building was just one of many targets during a twelve hour bombing raid. (Another of the bombed buildings was right across the street from the Al Rashid Hotel where the foreign journalists and Soviet diplomats were staying.) CNN then ran an ITN report by a shaken Brent Sadler who described the target as "obviously a civilian shelter" that was filled with "civilians escaping from the nightly bombing." The report contained the most graphic and horrific images so far of incinerated people, agonized families, dazed crowds, and upset journalists, powerful visual evidence that the shelter was undeniably used by civilians. One saw twisted steel and concrete with beds, obviously for sleeping. Iraqi civilian defense teams fought through the blazing fire trying to save people; one victim after another was pulled out, a blanket wrapped around their charred remains as the crowd broke into collective grief each time a new victim was brought out of the inferno.

Despite the visual evidence, CNN's military apologist, James Blackwell, came on again, determined to win points for the Pentagon, and did an "analysis" of the video clips of the building bombed to "prove" that it was a military bunker. Notice, he said, the steel doors that prevent people from coming in; look at the shelter sign in English, which looks like a Civilian Defense sign in the United States; look at the barbed wire around the building; look at the reinforced concrete—all signs, Blackwell reassured us, that it was a military bunker. He admitted that, "of course," the allies can't provide any counterevidence in the "public relations" campaign unless they release the evidence of the intelligence that established that this was a military facility, again reducing the images of Iraqi civilian casualties to propaganda. When asked why so many civilians were sleeping in the building, Blackwell repeated Perry Smith's speculation that perhaps the families of the military people who worked there slept in the bunker at night. He insisted that the bunker was like the one used by Saddam Hussein, stocked for the families of the military. But, he concluded, the more "macabre" reason for the civilian occupants might be that Saddam Hussein has pursued a new policy of moving civilians into these areas as human shields. At this point, Reid Collins cut off Blackwell's "analysis of what happened last night," while Bobby Battista looked down and away from the camera as she cut to a commercial break.

James Blackwell and Perry Smith thus not only repeated every Pentagon lie but attempted to construct "arguments" of their own concerning why the building was clearly a military shelter. None of their arguments, however, would stand up: It had been established that the shelter was built for civilians and that the dual language signs were typical in Baghdad, so there was nothing suspicious about the shelter sign being in English. The barbed-wire fence around it could be explained on the ground that there were only a few shelters in the city for civilians, that only a small percent of the people of Baghdad had access to these shelters.[12] Because of the scarcity of shelters, people in the neighborhood were given passes to sleep in them, requiring control of access via fences and entrance through a main door. Every honest reporter and all fair-minded experts who had actually visited Iraqi shelters affirmed that this was a civilian shelter, that the Iraqi military would not use such a building for its operations, that they would not allow civilians into their secret military bunkers, and that all the Pentagon arguments were mere sophistries. As Peter Arnett stated, "this is Iraq" where the military keeps their command-and-control centers away from the public and never allows the public access to sensitive facilities.

During the afternoon Pentagon military briefing in Washington, Pete Williams, Capt. Dave Herrington, and Lt. Gen. Tom Kelly repeated the old lies and added some new ones. Kelly noted that because "there has been a lot of interest" in the bombing of the facility in Baghdad, Herrington would provide a briefing on this. Herrington brought out a map of the center of Baghdad, which contained the command-and-control headquarters during the beginning of the campaign, though, he explained, because these were bombed early in the war, the Iraqis were forced out into alternate command-and-control facilities in other parts of the city, such as the Amiriya center. The next diagram contained a close-up drawing of the "bunker" bounded by a residential area, near a school and a mosque. Because the building was near civilian facilities, Herrington commented, the U.S.-led coalition chose the middle of the night for their raid and used precision weapons. Herrington emotionally stated that it "deeply hurt him as an American" that Saddam Hussein put civilians in the military facility. It seemed to be hurting the press corps in the room as Americans that they were forced to hear their government lie in such a blatant fashion; some of the military correspondents looked terribly forlorn and upset.

Herrington's "story" got somewhat out of control as he explained that the shelter was converted in the late 1980s to a military bunker. Earlier, it had been claimed that in 1985 the shelter had been upgraded to a military bunker, but now Herrington had a more elaborate story about how the shelter was hardened so that "it could even withstand a nuclear attack." This was a bit much, so Kelly had to jump in and explain that the reinforcements would protect the communications equipment from the radiation of an explosion in the area. Picking up his story, Herrington insisted that the bunker was full of military communications equipment and repeated the earlier lies that the building was a military bunker. The reporters focused on the issue of why—if the Pentagon had so much intelligence concerning this shelter—they didn't know that civilians were in the building. Kelly lamely responded that there was "no logic" in civilians going into a building with a camouflaged, painted roof and insisted, beyond logic, that the intelligence sources had never sighted any civilians going into the shelter (whereas civilians had been going into the shelter every night and leaving every morning).

The network evening news focused heavily on the story, with ABC devoting 21 minutes and 6 separate stories to the event. CBS devoted the first 9 minutes of its newscast to the bombing and had three segments on the story. NBC played the BBC version of the bombing and devoted its first 11 minutes and 3 segments to the atrocity. PBS devoted almost its entire 60 minute news program to the bombing, and though the networks tried to be even-handed, PBS was heavily slanted toward the Bush administration version.

PBS's "MacNeil/Lehrer News Hour" opened with Brent Sadler's ITN report from Baghdad, but then presented clip after clip of the Pentagon version. The "Focus" segment, "Targeting Iraq," began with clips from Dick Cheney claiming that the target was indeed a military bunker. CNN military adviser General Perry Smith repeated his arguments concerning why he believed it was not a civilian shelter, and former secretary of defense and energy, and director of the CIA, James Schlesinger implied that Saddam Hussein had consciously put civilians in the military command and control bunker to exploit the casualties, claiming that putting civilians in the facility was "a cover and deception operation by Saddam Hussein, a rather clever one." Defense establishment expert Paul Nitze was certain that it was a military command and control bunker, and correspondent Leslie Gelb stated: "None of us knows really whether it was or was not a command and control center, but I think in instances like these, our military and the Bush administration have earned credibility and, absent proof to the contrary, I am more inclined to believe them than to believe Saddam Hussein." Representative Craig Washington (D-Tx.) was a bit more skeptical but tended to go along with the consensus that the target was indeed a military one.

Soon after, varying interpretations would emerge of why the United States targeted the civilian shelter. Retired Air Force Chief Michael Dugan told the London *Times* that the military had simply made a targeting mistake and that intelligence identifying it as a military command bunker was out of date (Feb. 17, 1991, p. A1). *Newsweek* (Feb. 25, 1991, p. 20) and various commentators on CNN circulated the story that the United States believed that high-ranking Baath party officials and their families were sleeping in the shelter and that the building was targeted to eliminate the Iraqi political leadership or to give them the "message" that Saddam Hussein was threatening their survival so that they would overthrow him.[13] The *Washington Post* combined the two stories, reporting that the shelter/bunker had been placed on the U.S. military target list months ago, after intelligence experts concluded that it was a bunker designed to shelter senior Iraqi leaders but were unaware that civilians were now sleeping in it (Feb. 14, 1991). After the war, Arnett noted that "the hot rumor was that Saddam Hussein was there two hours before" the bombing, but that he could not go on the air with that information (*Broadcasting,* Mar. 25, 1991, p. 91).

ABC and some commentators on CNN proposed the "dual use" theory, suggesting that the building was both a civilian sleeping shelter and a military bunker. Ted Koppel, for instance, on the February 13 "Nightline" floated this theory, quoting a writer with the prestigious *Jane's Weekly* defense magazine, who claimed that dual use was typical of Iraqi installations. Koppel opened his program by naively stating that "there was no reason to doubt the American claim that it was a military shelter." Yet ABC's Baghdad correspondent, Bill Blakemore, had interviewed many people on the scene, all of whom assured him that civilian women and children had been sleeping in the shelter every night since the war had begun. Blakemore also insisted that he was assured by all of the people he interviewed that there was no military activity in the bunker and he commented that he had seen no evidence of any military or communications equipment.

The "dual use" theory would have to explain why the Iraqis, known for security paranoia and ultrasecret military installations, would allow civilians to sleep in a highly sensitive command-and-control center. The obvious answer was that they would not and that the Bush administration and military were simply lying. On an Arts and Entertainment cable channel (A&E) documentary series on Operation Desert Storm, produced by the BBC, the former director of the Defense Intelligence Agency (DIA), Lt. Gen. Leonard Perroots, flatly admitted that the United States made a mistake in bombing the shelter and was "without the most current information."[14] ITN journalist Nick Gowing revealed that U.S. intelligence had been at fault: "With world attention focussed elsewhere, sources have (now) told ITN that in the White House on 27th February the U.S. National Security Advisor, Brent Scowcroft, told the [British] Foreign Secretary Douglas Hurd that U.S. intelligence had been at fault.

In other words: the bunker bombing was a military mistake" (*Spectrum*, Summer 1991).

Moreover, in an interview with *USA Today* on March 19, 1991, the chief of the Air Force, Gen. Merrill McPeak, admitted that: "There is no doubt that we made some mistakes of what we bombed. I know of several. I have photographic evidence of several where the pilots just acquired the wrong target." As to whether this included the bomb shelter and infant formula factory, *USA Today* noted that McPeak "declined to give more details—mainly, he said, because he had been overruled by his superiors on talking about the matter. 'It ain't my call. I made some recommendations about this and got turned around, quite frankly'" (*USA Today*, March 19, 1991).[15]

After the war, Louise Cainkar of the Palestine Human Rights Information Center visited Baghdad and interviewed a large number of people from the neighborhood (1991, 341ff.). Her research indicated that local residents slept nightly in the shelter; males over the age of sixteen were not allowed in the shelter, with the exception of older men. The shelter held 2,000 residents and there were estimates that at least 1,600 died. During the summer of 1991, a PBS crew inspected the building and could also find no evidence that there was any military equipment in the shelter. In this *Frontline* documentary, however, Col. John Warden, the Pentagon spokesperson interviewed, continued to claim, against all evidence, that it was a military bunker. Likewise, Dick Cheney continued to claim that it was a military bunker in a 1992 documentary shown on the Discovery Channel, put together by conservative Richard Perle and the American Enterprise Institute, obviously dedicated to the enterprise of the perpetuation of Big Lies.[16]

Despite the slimness of its "evidence," the Pentagon insisted immediately and categorically that the Baghdad shelter was a military command-and-control center and has stuck with the story to the present. Throughout the Gulf war, the military adopted a policy of quick, immediate, bold, and bald-faced lies to hide their crimes. The United States wanted at all costs to maintain the illusion that their bombing was precise, based an accurate intelligence, and avoided civilian casualties. They were especially concerned to deny that they were hitting civilian targets and thus immediately claimed that Iraqi civilian targets hit were military installations when accused of hitting targets like the infant formula factory or bomb shelter. Previously, the military had attempted to manage bad news by restricting access to it, by presenting it as an isolated incident to be expected in the fog of war, and by allowing it to dribble out in a controlled seepage over a number of days or weeks. But in an age of instant information this policy was not good enough for the war image managers, so they resorted to the policy of the instant and fast lie to deal with "damage control."

The mainstream media, however, showed little interest in pursuing the story of the shelter bombing. The next morning at the military briefings the incident was not mentioned. The story was yesterday's news overcome in interest by the latest military trivia of the day. Or perhaps the press was embarrassed by the magnitude and outrageousness of the Pentagon's lying and fearful of losing contacts with the Pentagon brass, reporters simply shut up and kept their doubts to themselves. In the absence of critical media discourse, however, the policy of Big Lies to cover over major crimes seemed to work. Most of the callers to radio and TV call-in programs bought the line that the shelter was a military bunker and a legitimate military target; an ABC News/Washington Post poll on February 15, 1991, for instance, asked: "Who is most responsible for the civilian bombing deaths?" and answered: "Saddam Hussein, sixty-seven percent, Iraq, twelve percent, U.S. seven percent." The public seemed to have bought into the war aims and propaganda and was not going to be deterred in its desire for U.S. victory by mere Iraqi casualties. Bush's propaganda campaign of demonizing the Iraqis was apparently successful and the public was willing to believe the worst of them and to believe what it was told by its Masters of War, despite the facts.

While the bombing campaign was relentlessly destroying Iraq, other events were spinning out of control again in the Gulf war. Several oil spills were polluting the Gulf, some of which were attributed to the U.S. military; over fifty oil well fires burned in Kuwait and the U.S. military had admitted that coalition bombing might have caused many of the fires, though they continued to claim as well that the Iraqis were torching wells. CNN reported on February 13 that Kuwait had become a smoky hell where men and machines were being relentlessly bombed by continual coalition sorties and dozens of oil fires were burning out of control. Later that morning, another atrocity was reported: an allied bombing of a Kuwaiti bus near the border that killed thirty people, mostly refugees seeking to escape the country. Stories also began emerging from Saudi Arabia about "killing boxes": the military was dividing Kuwait into zones, or boxes, and destroying everything in the box and then going on to the next box. The coalition air war was destroying Kuwait in order to save it.[17]

7.4 Iraqi Peace Communiqué

The worst civilian bombing casualties of the war so far came at a bad time for Bush as he was torn between starting the ground war immediately and waiting for more bombing—perhaps several weeks more—to destroy to the maximum Iraq's military and industry. But the Soviets and Iraqis were floating peace initiatives, and the UN was clamoring for a public debate the very day of the Baghdad atrocity. That event only increased calls for peace and a negotiated settlement—which would rob Bush and the military of the pleasures of a decisive defeat of Saddam Hussein's military and a ground war.

On Friday morning, February 15, a startling communiqué came out of Iraq at about 5:30 A.M. EST. For the first time, it appeared that Iraq had officially agreed to withdraw from Kuwait as stipulated by UN resolution 660, which held that Iraq should unconditionally withdraw from Kuwait. The proposal included, to be sure, the usual demand for linkage with issues that Iraq wanted negotiated (withdrawal of Israel from Palestinian lands, withdrawal of Syria from Lebanon, and so on). But the key issue was that this was the first time that Iraq had ever officially agreed to begin negotiating to get out of Kuwait and to meet the UN resolutions.

Clearly, this was a big story that could be the turning point of the war: the long-awaited diplomatic breakthrough (by everyone but the Bush administration). CNN broadcast the communiqué as soon as it appeared and focused on the story for the rest of the day. From Iraq, Peter Arnett reported great excitement in the al-Raschid Hotel where news of the Iraqi offer to withdraw from Kuwait was met by "sighs of relief" and people in the street began shooting guns in celebration. Iraqi officials cautioned the news media that the communiqué was just a proposal and that people didn't understand what it meant yet, so reporters were asked to stay in the hotel and not meet with the public. Arnett stressed, however, that for the first time Iraq had agreed to withdraw from Kuwait. He suggested that the Palestinian reference and the other linkages were for "domestic consumption" and for the Arab world at large and that the communiqué signaled that the Iraqis were ready to negotiate. What was important, he insisted, was that the Iraqis had agreed to withdraw from Kuwait and to abide by UN resolution 660.

On "CBS This Morning," U.S. troops interviewed in Saudi Arabia reacted in a mixed fashion: some were joyful and eager to get home alive; others were skeptical; the hard-nosed military types who wanted the satisfaction of ground war and a decisive victory were grim and noncommittal. The Kuwaitis were also reacting variously, with some celebrating immediately and others sounding more skeptical and not trusting the Iraqis. The Saudis were ambiguous in their response and difficult to interpret. The Iraqis were cautious, waiting for the United States to respond.

Interestingly, one could easily tell that morning which network anchors, correspondents, and experts wanted negotiations and wished an end to the war, and which ones wanted to continue the war to destroy the Iraqis. NBC's "Today" host Bryant Gumbel opened by saying, "We greet you with some stunning news, some very hopeful news. Baghdad radio is reporting this morning that Iraq is prepared to withdraw from Kuwait." "CBS This Morning" co-anchor Harry Smith flatly stated, "This war, for a lot of intents and purposes, is over," adding uncouthly that the Iraqis "have had the royal snot beaten out of them." On CBS, supposed liberal Juan Williams was negative toward the peace proposal, which he saw as "very iffy," commenting that the Iraqi communiqué "adds to the sense of confusion." Neoconservative Fred Barnes cautioned that the Bush administration must handle this very carefully because Washington does not want to give Saddam a propaganda victory by making it appear that Iraq wants peace while Bush wants war. Former Carter administration official Daniel Aaron said on CBS that the Bush administration cannot act too skeptically about this, and treat it like a "dirty diaper," or Bush will come off as against peace. If Bush treated it too skeptically and then moved into a ground war, it would be received very badly politically, Aaron warned, and then pointed to the need to negotiate a cease-fire to put an end to the war.

Those who were positive and wanted peace stressed the novel elements of the Iraqi communiqué and argued that now was the time for serious negotiations and steps toward peace. Those who wanted to continue the war remarked that there was nothing new, that Saddam Hussein had always wanted linkage and had conditions for withdrawal while the Bush administration insisted on "unconditional withdrawal." The positive response was that the Iraqi communiqué should be read as a signal that Iraq was finally ready to negotiate and that now there was the need for creative ideas that would bring an end to the war. Roger Fisher of the Harvard Negotiation Project proposed that the UN meet immediately to initiate a 48-hour cease-fire to allow negotiations to begin. Quite realistically, Fisher said that "one cannot expect these people to cry Uncle! Uncle!" Instead, the governments should enter into a serious negotiating process.

Apparently, the White House and Pentagon were caught off guard by Hussein's peace feeler and the episode appeared as another Iraqi surprise. Once again, Iraq seemed to be taking the offensive in the propaganda war, saying for the first time that it would withdraw its troops from Kuwait. The Iraqi communiqué was a clever move indicating that Saddam Hussein definitely wanted to survive and was not prepared to go down in martyrdom. His timing was on target: Throughout the world, the most intense anti-American sentiment yet to emerge surfaced after the U.S. bombing of the civilian shelter in Baghdad caused hundreds of deaths. On the down side for Iraq, its military was being systematically destroyed as it was losing millions of dollars of military equipment per day by allied bombing. Indeed, the Iraqi army was perhaps on the eve of destruction. Rumors were flying fast that the ground war was imminent, that it could begin any minute, and would probably begin sooner rather than later. Obviously, Saddam had to do something to avoid a massive military defeat.

By taking the offensive in the propaganda war, Iraq put Bush in a tricky position. The coalition was showing its first cracks, with Spain demanding a halt to the bombing and the Arab masses and others outraged by U.S. killing of innocent civilians. On the other hand, the air war was proceeding brilliantly, according to the Pentagon, but there would no doubt be many forces within the coalition who would want a cease-fire and negotiations. Others, however, would prefer the total destruction of Saddam Hussein and his regime. Likewise, there were probably similar divisions within the Bush administration and within the U.S. military in Saudi Arabia, as some troops reacted positively and hopefully, while others reacted negatively and skeptically.

Reaction from the Pentagon seemed to be overwhelmingly negative and hostile to the Iraqi communiqué; the State Department at first reacted much more positively, pointing to a split within the Bush administration. The split had surfaced earlier when the State Department had floated a joint Soviet-U.S. peace initiative the night of Bush's State of the Union address, to the disgust and anger of the hawks in the Bush administration and Pentagon who wanted a smashing military victory. How, indeed, would the Bush administration respond to the Iraqi communiqué? According to CBS, the White House's first response was that it was studying the document and wanted to see the fine print, complaining that it was receiving its information third-hand from the news media. It also insisted that the prosecution of the war would not stop. CNN's Charles Bierbauer reported that there was a frenzy in the White House which had announced a briefing and then announced a slight delay, as they tried to formulate their response to the Iraqi initiative.

While waiting for the briefing, CBS's White House correspondent, Randall Pinkston, suggested that if the White House rejected the proposal out of hand, Saddam Hussein would win a propaganda victory of sorts, highlighting the Bush administration dilemma. Suddenly, Marlin Fitzwater appeared and asserted that the White House had not yet fully examined the statement, but it clearly contained conditions which are objectionable. "Promises alone are not enough," Fitzwater insisted, "there must also be concrete actions on the ground." While the CBS commentator put a positive spin on Fitzwater's reaction because he did not completely reject the Iraqi initiative, ABC's Ann Compton put an extremely negative spin on it. Compton revealed that White House officials indicated that the more they examined it, the worse it looked. They were, she explained, beginning to present it as a "real disappointment, because the statement raises the hopes of people around the world." The problem, the White House insisted to the correspondents, is the "conditions," which were turning the Bush administration more sour on the Iraqi communiqué by the moment.

In fact, such a peace proposal was the "worst nightmare" for the Bush administration, which wanted military victory to decisively defeat the Iraqis. ABC's John McWethy at the State Department also put a negative spin on it, lips more tightly pursed and forehead more wrinkled than usual for the smooth McWethy. Repeating the Pentagon/White House line of the day, McWethy said that if the Iraqis announce that they will get out of Kuwait unconditionally, the United States will stop the war, but the Bush administration totally rejects all linkage and insists that Iraqi withdrawal be unequivocal. McWethy has long been a spokesperson for the Reagan and Bush administrations, so his negative spin indicated that the administration was trying to promote a negative reaction to the Iraqi peace feeler and ultimately to sabotage it. Putting it bluntly, the Bush administration had continually done everything possible to subvert diplomatic solutions to the crisis and war and continued to pursue a military solution.

Shortly thereafter, ABC's Sam Donaldson described in Saudi Arabia rumors that the ground war was hours away and that Iraq could suffer enormous losses. Donaldson speculated that Iraq had tied the president's hand for the next phase, at least temporarily. To immediately launch a ground war would put the president in an untenable political position, if it appeared that he was launching a bloody war just when peace was possible. It was Donaldson's impression that an Iraqi withdrawal would be an enormous relief to the troops and he also believed that the commanders in the field genuinely did not want to see U.S. soldiers die.

Yet, many in the U.S. political and military establishment downplayed the positive reasons that Saddam Hussein might have to negotiate and withdraw and were wholly negative and skeptical. ABC military commentator Tony Cordesman warned that the military consequences of a cease-fire could be very serious; even a few days could give the Iraqis time to get in supplies, redeploy their troops, move mines, and change the structure of the battlefield, screwing up U.S. military intelligence. There must be an unconditional withdrawal, Cordesman insisted, or American lives will be jeopardized. Cordesman and other military "experts" continued to take this line, using it to justify the slaughter of the Iraqi troops who would soon show themselves to be totally demoralized and incapable of threatening the coalition forces (see Chapters 8 and 9).

The press and political establishment really exhibited their biases that day: Some commentators, troops, and perhaps government officials were ready for a diplomatic solution, while many in the Pentagon, Bush administration, and media wanted the ground offensive to unfold. Some individuals were speaking favorably of the peace initiative as the beginning of a diplomatic solution while others, like ABC's John McWethy, attacked the Iraqi initiative. Utilizing a highly sophistical argument, McWethy said that he was told that one key Arabic word in the Iraqi communiqué was translated as a willingness to "abide" by the UN resolution, whereas a more literal translation suggested a mere "readiness to deal with" one UN resolution, which entailed throwing out the other UN resolutions. And then McWethy went into great detail concerning the linkages demanded—precisely the point that the Bush administration would harp on themselves. Diplomatic correspondent McWethy seemed unaware that the linkages were just political rhetoric, as Arnett and others pointed out, and that one begins negotiation by seizing on positive points for negotiation. On the other hand, McWethy also failed to point out that all diplomatic negotiations depend on linkages of some sort, that linkage is part of diplomacy.

Yet, obviously, linkage in this case referred to the Palestinian question and the Bush administration was not going to allow Saddam Hussein to be perceived as the champion of their cause. For decades, the United States had sided with Israel and had opposed all efforts to negotiate a solution to the Palestinian problem which would provide them with a homeland. From the beginning of the crisis in the Gulf, Iraq had insisted that if UN resolutions concerning their actions in Kuwait should be acted upon, then, too, should the UN resolutions calling for a Palestinian homeland—resolutions which Israel had always opposed. Many Palestinians—including the leadership of the PLO—had sided with the Iraqis and Hussein was constantly evoking the issue as part of a negotiated settlement—though ultimately he would drop the issue, as we shall see in the next chapter.[18]

On CBS, White House correspondent Leslie Stahl cautioned that an overly negative reaction to the Iraqi communiqué would drive a wedge between the Bush administration, on the one hand, and the American people, many of the troops, and the coalition partners on the other. CBS correspondent Eric Engberg in Saudi Arabia, however, put a purely negative spin on the initiative, noting with a grim countenance that the list of conditions demanded were almost identical with a list from three months ago, so there was "nothing new" on Hussein's "laundry list." Engberg claimed that Iraq's making such demands when it was practically defeated was "laughable," and he suggested that Hussein was "throwing a monkey wrench in the allies' plans." Obviously promoting the position of those who sought a ground war, Engberg said that Iraq was trying to make the coalition forces "look like butchers" if they begin the war when a peace initiative was on the table. As we shall see, CBS's Engberg consistently pushed for the ground war and dutifully conveyed all the information that his Pentagon handlers wanted disseminated once the ground campaign erupted (see Chapters 8–10).

On ABC, Middle East authority William Quandt, obviously favorable to a diplomatic settlement, noted that Iraq had already taken a pounding and could not be a threat to the region, if there was a settlement limiting arms in the region. Also on ABC, Judith Kipper saw the initiative as a "real breakthrough" and predicted that over the weekend there would be some important developments coming out of Moscow, when the Iraqi foreign minister, Tariq Aziz, arrived for negotiations. ABC White House correspondent Ann Compton found a positive sign in that Marlin Fitzwater did not use the word "reject," suggesting that the "White House does not want to slam the door on this." She also speculated that President Bush was genuinely surprised by the peace proposal, as were many in Washington. She did not think that Bush would use the word "reject," which turned out to be correct but off the mark in its optimism.

7.5 A Cruel Hoax

Through the morning, the pundits provided their analyses as the world waited with great anticipation to learn George Bush's response. At 9:57 A.M., all the networks cut to Bush beginning his address to the American Academy for the Advancement of Science in Washington, so that the world could learn whether there would be war, peace, or just more confusion. Bush disclosed that when he first heard the proposal from Iraq, he was "happy that Saddam Hussein had seemed to realize that he must now withdraw unconditionally from Kuwait, in keeping with the relevant UN resolutions." Bush remarked that from what he saw on TV, there was a "celebratory atmosphere" in Baghdad and elsewhere hopes for peace. But, "regrettably," he concluded that the Iraqi communiqué was a "cruel hoax" played on the Iraqis and everyone else around the world. After closer analysis Bush found that the Iraqi proposal was full of "unacceptable old conditions," with new ones added. He had talked to members of the coalition, "and they recognize that there is nothing new here with the possible exception of [Iraq's] recognizing for the first time that [it] must leave Kuwait." Bush concluded that Iraq "must withdraw without condition. There must be full implementation of all the Security Council resolutions. And there will be no linkage to other problems in the area, and the legitimate rulers of Kuwait must be returned to Kuwait."

After demanding a "massive withdrawal" from Kuwait, Bush suggested that "there's another way for the bloodshed to stop, and that is for the Iraqi military and the Iraqi people to take matters into their own hands, to force Saddam Hussein, the dictator, to step aside." Bush stated that he "feels very sorry for the people in Iraq, and I feel sorry for the families in this country who probably felt as I did this morning when they heard the television, that maybe we really had a shot for peace today. But that's not the case, and we will continue. We will pursue our objectives with honor and decency, and we will not fail."

Bush's statement threw a wet blanket on the world's hopes for peace and made it clear that he was going to pursue a military victory. His hypocritical claim that he "regretted" that the statement was a "cruel hoax" was a sordid piece of blatant propaganda: Clearly, Bush did not want peace or a negotiated settlement. As with all of his previous efforts to block peace negotiations, Bush made categorical demands of the Iraqis (there must be massive withdrawal, no linkage, and so on), rather than sending out any signals for negotiation. Whenever the Iraqis, or the Soviets, or anyone else, put out any peace proposals, Bush invariably harped on the negative features and ignored the positive openings that might be the basis for a negotiated settlement. The rules of diplomatic negotiation, however, dictate that one ignores the negative features and begin with acceptance of the positive features. Furthermore, in the case of the Iraqi proposal, Bush upped the ante, making an aggressive move that he'd never explicitly made previously, asking the Iraqi military and citizens to overthrow Saddam Hussein—a demand that would come to haunt him later (see Chapter 10).

Bush's "feeling sorry" for the people of Baghdad and the world who wanted peace was hypocritical because if he wished, he could easily have negotiated peace. Iraq was beaten militarily and it was obviously in their interest to negotiate. And to say that the allies were pursuing their "objectives with honor and decency" was obscene in view of the killing of innocent civilians, the systematic destruction of the economic infrastructure of Iraq, and the environmental holocaust caused at least in part by allied bombing. Network commentators were visibly depressed by this incredibly hostile and aggressive response to the Iraqi peace feeler. But CBS's Harry Smith in Saudi Arabia, who during the previous hours had noted a variety of possible positive responses to the Iraqi communiqué that could bring an end to the war, gamely joined in and put a negative spin on the Iraqi communiqué, signing off with the summary that the Saudis and Kuwaitis had rejected the proposal and saw it as a deception by Saddam Hussein.

Within the framework of the propaganda war, it was obvious that Bush was trying to regain the offensive and to turn Iraq's positive initiative into something negative: a "cruel hoax." Once again, Bush pursued the course of the military hardliners by eschewing a negotiated settlement to the hostilities. Bush continued his propaganda offensive in the early afternoon with a speech at the Raytheon Patriot missile factory in Massachusetts. As the networks began to broadcast his speech, Bush was smiling and laughing. He stood up for the *Star Spangled Banner,* artificially at attention and a little too stiffly. The image framed Bush surrounded by two Patriot missiles, the flag, and Raytheon executives, who may have wanted the war to go on forever so as to keep selling their Patriot missiles. A chaplain, who was also a professor of Christian morals, was about to invoke God's blessing, but CNN cut to a Listerine ad telling the audience how to get kinder and gentler breath by buying their mouthwash, thus subverting the Bush administration's carefully orchestrated synthesis of war, business, politics, and religion.

Still holding off their live broadcast until Bush himself began to speak, CNN continued to present the linkage issue in its news summary of the day's events, failing to stress any positive features of the Iraqi communiqué. CNN thus kicked in with the warmongers and had good economic reasons to do so: Their advertising rates had increased fivefold, so they had plenty to lose from the end of war and the inevitable drop in ratings. War was good business and good television. The ground war would be very exciting, would get good ratings, and would fixate the nation once again on television as some people were beginning drift back to ordinary lives and concerns.

After its news summary, CNN cut to Bush, who was getting standing applause from the Patriot missile makers, praised by the president as "the men and women who built the Scud busters." The audience screamed with joy and collectively roared the "woof, woof, woof!" chant, which seemed to be the theme song of Operation Desert Storm. Bush told the cheering crowd how hopes were lifted in downtown Baghdad by the Iraqi initiative, but that the rising hope turned out to be a "cruel hoax, full of unacceptable old conditions," as well as new conditions. Bush affirmed that Saddam Hussein must "withdraw out of Kuwait with no conditions." The audience once again cheered and chanted "woof, woof, woof!" in neofascistic guttural harmony. Bush also repeated his proposal that the Iraqi military and citizens should step in and remove Saddam Hussein. "We have no argument with the people of Iraq. Our differences are with that brutal dictator in Baghdad." The crowd went wild chanting, "Woof, woof, woof!" as the camera shifted to frame Bush surrounded by giant Patriot missiles.

CBS cut off at this point as Bush launched into some free advertising for the Patriots, spreading again the lie of their near-perfect intercept score. But CBS's Bill Plante noted that the Soviets were starting a major peace initiative that should be watched over the weekend. As a response, the prowar crowd soon began resurrecting the cold war ideology, suggesting that all peace initiatives were a commie plot to reposition the Soviet Union in the Middle East after the war. In Israel, Tom Fenton reported that Prime Minister Shamir was upbeat and categorically rejected the Iraqi communiqué; it seemed that every politician in Israel had been brought before the U.S. television cameras that day to reject the Iraqi initiative as a mere propaganda ploy. At the UN, CBS reported that reaction ranged from negative to guardedly negative: the Kuwaiti ambassador stated his government's total rejection of the conditions and only the Yemenite and PLO ambassadors were reportedly positive. (This was a misrepresentation as CNN would repeatedly report from the UN all afternoon that there were both strongly positive and negative responses to the Iraqi communiqué.) Britain's John Major dutifully repeated Bush's propaganda line of the day by dismissing the Iraqi proposal as a "bogus sham," acting again as Bush's puppet, loyally defending Bush's every move and position.

CBS cut away at 12:59 P.M. in order to begin the next hour's soap operas (Dan Rather was in Saudi Arabia, possibly anticipating the beginning of the ground war). But ABC televised the latter part of Bush's speech where he insisted: "We will control the timetable of this engagement, not Saddam Hussein. Kuwait will be liberated!" There was wild cheering for Bush, and ABC returned to its anchors. Peter Jennings commented that Bush's pitch for a renewed strategic defense initiative (SDI) and a Patriot missile-based defense system would get some criticism in Congress, though Jennings thought that Congress and the allies would support Bush's rejection of the Iraqi communiqué, echoed by other members of the coalition. CNN's Charles Bierbauer noted that there was a moment of hope that was dashed when U.S. analysts saw what it was that Saddam Hussein was offering. Bierbauer faithfully parroted the Bush administration line: The proposal that gave rise to hope was a cruel hoax; Iraq must withdraw without condition; there must be full withdrawal from Kuwait; and there must be no linkage to other problems in the area.

Hence, the mainstream media and the coalition countries fell behind Bush immediately in rejecting the peace communiqué, as did most of Congress. The day's collective coalition marching to the White House beat was similar to the response and pulling together after the U.S. bombing of the Iraqi civilian shelter two days earlier. On Sunday, February 17, ABC's David Brinkley promoted his program by asking, "What next in the war after Saddam Hussein's phony peace offer?" The *New York Times* editorialized on February 20: "The same question can be asked about peace that is reasonable to ask about ground war: What's the rush?"

Hence, during the first few hours after the Iraqi communiqué, members of the U.S. government as well as the coalition governments responded in a mixed way, with some positive reactions, some immediately negative, and some cautious. Yet as soon as Bush came out with a total rejection, with a completely negative response, then other foreign leaders in the coalition and members of his own government kicked in behind him. And the media tended to ape the official line, assuring a ground war and thousands more Iraqi deaths as Bush's thousand points of deadly light continued to illuminate Iraq in daily and nightly bombing raids.

Notes

1. Debates centered on whether the coalition bombing had eliminated an adequate amount of Iraq's military potential to minimize coalition casualties in a ground war. CNN cited a Soviet general reporting from Iraq that 90 percent of U.S. bombs missed their targets; he also claimed that the reduction in sorties after the first week was not the result of bad weather but was caused by increasingly heavy Iraqi artillery fire. CNN also cited a French general who claimed that 30 percent of the Republican Guard military capacity had been taken out, but "Pentagon sources" doubted that much damage had been done to the Guards, and others said that it was impossible to accurately assess their "attrition." This debate concerning how much of Iraq's military capacity the air war was eliminating continued right up until the ground war itself; see the articles in the *New York Times* (Feb. 6, 1991, pp. 1A) and Knud Royce, *Newsday,* February 19, 1991, p. 4, on the battles within different U.S. intelligence agencies concerning the degree of attrition of the Iraqi military.

2. In one of the comic sections of his unintentionally humorous book, retired General Perry Smith recounts how he almost quit CNN on February 7 when he heard the headline, "Relentless Allied Air Raids on Baghdad Continue" (1991, p. 80). Smith was bothered by the use of the word "relentless." As I argue in this chapter, Smith should have been more worried about the effects of the bombing.

3. The Tomahawk Cruise missile, like the Patriot missile, was one of the systems that the Pentagon and its promoters were claiming to be highly accurate. *Newsweek* (Feb. 18, 1991) reported that the Pentagon claimed that of the first 52 Cruise missiles fired, 51 had hit their targets and that by the end of the third week 300 Cruise missiles had been fired at Iraq. At this point, the Pentagon was claiming an 85 percent accuracy rate, though outside "experts question whether these figures are inflated, and no one will really know how well the Tomahawk did for months to come" (p. 40). In one piece of free advertising for the missile system, NBC's Tom Aspell disclosed how he had seen the Cruise make a ninety-degree turn to avoid hitting the al-Raschid Hotel and then proceed to demolish its target (or so Aspell assumed). Arnett, however, was receiving many reports from Iraqis that the Cruise missiles were often unguided and missed their targets; one crashed behind the al-Raschid Hotel, smashing servants' quarters, and others hit civilian areas indiscriminately. Patrick Cockburn reported following Cruise

missile paths right after they entered Baghdad and discovering that they were hitting civilian areas (*The Irish Times,* Feb. 2, 1991). After the war, the *Washington Post* reported that classified Pentagon sources indicated that the Cruise missile hit their intended targets only slightly more than half the time, in opposition to earlier Navy claims that the missile had an 85 percent success rate (April 10, 1992, p. A1; see 4.3).

It thus appeared to the Iraqis and some journalists that the Cruise missiles were weapons of terror, much like the Scuds. The U.S. military, unwilling to admit that one of their weapons could misfire, claimed that Cruise failure to hit its target was caused by Iraqi anti-artillery fire that knocked the missile off course. If this was true, then one wonders why the Cruise missiles were fired in the daytime when Iraqi antiaircraft fire could more easily hit them, increasing the likelihood that the Cruise missiles would hit civilian areas. Finally, in February 1992, Wolf Blitzer announced on CNN that the Pentagon was suspending tests of the Cruise missile in the United States because two missiles had recently misfired and hit civilian areas.

4. A similar report is found in an article by Susan Sachs and Patrick Sloyan, "Allied Raids Taking Massive Toll on Iraq; Reports paint picture of wide devastation," *Newsday* (Feb. 6, 1991, p. 5). The authors write: "Reports from inside Iraq, from journalists, refugees and Jordanians traveling through the war zone, painted a picture of widespread damage. . . . American peace activists and refugees fleeing Iraq told reporters of feeling the thundering jolt of bombs falling in Baghdad and the southern port city of Basra, seeing bloodied children hurt by falling debris and watching clouds of black smoke from burning oil refineries and ammunition dumps blot out the sun for hours. Jordanians who had driven from Baghdad to Amman told of seeing dead drivers slumped in blazing oil trucks after air raids."

5. Two key features of classical "just war" theory require that every possible measure is taken to prevent the war and the measures taken must be proportionate to the causes of the war. Other features include: the lack of diplomatic possibilities to resolve the conflict and moral intentions; see Drinan 1991 and Elshtain et al. 1992. It is not certain that Bush exhausted diplomatic possibilities, indeed it is more likely that he blocked all diplomacy (see 1.2 and 8.1). And it is questionable whether the Bush administration's war policy was guided by moral intentions.

6. The video replays of the bombings were pornographic in that they provided thrilling voyeurism of forbidden spectacles; they provided close-ups of taboo activity, usually kept secret by the military; they were rather abstract and unemotional, providing images merely of the mechanics of destruction; and they inevitably exploded into a climax.

7. For the poignant testimony of his trip to Iraq in the form of a letter to UN Secretary-General Javier Perez de Cuellar, see Clark et al. 1992, pp. 227–235. Clark was accompanied on his trip by NBC photographer Jon Alpert, who documented the destruction. "NBC Nightly News" was going to broadcast some footage but NBC News executive vice-president Donald Browne refused to air the footage. Moreover, NBC News President Michael Gartner called in Alpert and

told him that NBC did not ever want to use anything by him again, thus terminating what had been a brilliant journalistic career for Alpert at NBC! See the account by Michael Hoyt, "Jon Alpert: NBC's Odd Man Out," *Columbia Journalism Review,* Sept.-Oct. 1991, pp. 44–47. One sees once again the effects of having corporations like GE, closely tied to the military-industrial complex, controlling broadcast institutions.

8. The public attack on Arnett began on January 21 with snipes by Tom Shales in his TV column in the *Washington Post* who wrote that "troubling questions were being raised by CNN's continuing Baghdad presence. All of Arnett's reports were now being reviewed by Iraqi censors, clouding their credibility and diluting their value" (p. C1). The ignorant Shales seemed unaware that reports from Saudi Arabia were also being reviewed by Saudi government and U.S. military censors (2.2), a fact that he never found "troubling." Shales later accused ABC Baghdad correspondent Bill Blakely of exhibiting "Arnett Syndrome," which Shales defined as "seemingly inexhaustible concern for the welfare of the Iraqis." The intrepid TV warrior Shales also claimed that the "networks may have helped Saddam Hussein" to a "propaganda victory" with their reporting on the Iraqi peace plan (see 7.4 below); quotes taken from the *Washington Post,* February 16, 1991, p. C1.

9. Not surprisingly, Senator Simpson exhibited the same McCarthyite tactics during the emotional Supreme Court hearings in October 1991 for Clarence Thomas, who was charged by his former assistant Anita Hill of sexual harassment. During the hearings, Simpson waved papers that he possessed, claiming that they were telegrams and faxes containing negative information about Hill, much as Joe McCarthy waved papers saying that he had information about communists during the witch hunts of the 1950s.

10. A note on PeaceNet on February 16 in the mideast.gulf conference indicated that "A letter from CND [Coalition for Nuclear Disarmament] in today's *Guardian* states . . . that the disease is anthrax."

11. Earlier, at a January 30 briefing, General Schwarzkopf had been asked questions about the munitions used on nuclear, biological, and chemical facilities and answered: "Every target we have attacked—be it nuclear, chemical or biological—we have very carefully selected the destruction means, okay, after a lot of advice from a lot of very, very prominent scientists. So we selected the destruction means in such a way that we absolutely, almost to a 99.9 percent have assurance [of] no contamination." Every time that Schwarzkopf resorted to such hyperbole, he was trying to conceal something, so one would like to know what "very, very prominent scientists" recommended, who they were, what actually happened, and what were the environmental consequences of the U.S. bombing of these facilities.

12. The *Los Angeles Times* had reported earlier in the war that the shelters were reserved for people of the neighborhood in which they were built. An article on January 29, 1991, described Egyptian workers who ran out of their houses when the bombs started dropping and ran to the shelters: "But there was no room in the shelters," an Egyptian said. "So we would sit beside the door. We felt safer there."

13. The weekly newsmagazines accepted the Pentagon's Big Lie. Both *Time* (Feb. 25, p. 27) and *Newsweek* (Feb. 25, p. 18) referred to the building straightforwardly as a "bunker" and failed to raise any questions concerning the Bush administration and Pentagon version.

14. Perroots also denied that the infant formula factory was a weapons factory (see 5.2). He claimed that the United States made targeting mistakes in both the infant formula factory bombing and the bomb shelter, admitting, concerning the latter, that: "There was no evidence that it was being used as a command and control bunker at the time of the attack" (*The Times,* March 25, 1991). A search of several data bases disclosed no references to Perroots in the mainstream media in the United States who thus ignored an important source who questioned the "official" U.S. version.

15. Some journalists also came to doubt the bunker story based on interviews with top government officials. *Los Angeles Times* Washington bureau chief Jack Nelson stated in a Gannett Foundation symposium: "Another doubtful piece of information concerned the so-called bunker where so many civilians were killed. I've heard it from a very good source in the government that the evidence that it was anything other than a shelter was pretty slim" (cited in LaMay et al. 1991, p. 74).

16. Mythmakers continued to parrot the U.S. government line concerning the atrocities; see Anderson and van Atta (1991) who accepted the *Newsweek* story, writing: "What is not now in doubt is that these were the families of some of the high Baathist Party and military officials. It was an exclusive air-raid shelter with a high fence to keep out the rabble. . . . It may well have hit Saddam where he would hurt the most" (p. 169). In fact, it was a neighborhood shelter with restricted access. Perry Smith (1991) continued to insist that the bomb shelter was a military bunker, repeating the arguments that had already been refuted (pp. 33ff.). Blackwell (1991), who had argued that it was a military bunker for CNN, ignores the episode in his book, attempting to cover over his participation in Pentagon lies.

17. For more accounts of atrocities committed by the U.S.-led coalition bombing, see the "Eyewitness Interviews" and other accounts in Clark et al. 1992.

18. On the intersection of the Palestinian question and the Gulf crisis and war, see the articles by Abu-Lughod, Ashrawi, and Hulaileh in Bennis and Moushabeck 1991; Shiblak in Brittain 1991; Glavanis in Bresheeth and Yuval-David 1991; and Gazilwin in Clark et al.

CHAPTER EIGHT

◆

Countdown to the Ground War

AND SO THE MEDIA propaganda war continued as the United States and Iraq struggled daily to control the flow of information. Iraq seized the offensive on February 15 by issuing its peace communiqué. This proposal created prospects for peace, giving rise to jubilation in parts of the Arab world, as well as producing hope everywhere that the human and environmental destruction would soon cease. The networks extended their morning shows, focused on the Iraqi peace initiative, and put the White House and Pentagon on the defensive. But Bush then took the offensive and gained the upper hand in the propaganda war with the complicity of his coalition partners and the media. The Iraqi peace initiative was rejected as a "cruel hoax" and the relentless pounding of Iraq continued.

8.1 Diplomatic Chess Game

There were, however, powerful forces working for peace. The Soviet Union was attempting to produce a peace plan that would bring a quick diplomatic settlement to the war. With Iraqi Foreign Minister Tariq Aziz on route to Moscow to discuss peace initiatives with the Soviets, stories circulated on February 16 that the U.S. had promised not to begin the ground war until the Soviets and Aziz had a chance to discuss Iraqi withdrawal from Kuwait. Throughout the weekend, there was thus speculation concerning a possible diplomatic settlement to the war.

The TV news headlines on February 18 focused on Aziz's meeting with the Soviets and his return to Iraq with a peace proposal from the Soviet Union. "CBS This Morning" stressed that the meeting may have been the last chance to avoid a bloody ground war, but early reports suggested that so far there were no hints of any breakthrough. Gorbachev reportedly told Aziz that Iraq's very survival depended on accepting the peace proposal. The negotiations involved, according to CBS, an all-out diplomatic effort with Gorbachev, foreign minister Alexander Bessmert-nykh, top Middle East diplomat Yevgeny Primakov, and other top Soviet officials meeting with the Iraqi foreign minister and Saadoun Hammadi, Iraq's deputy prime minister. After the initial meeting, Aziz did not tip his hand. When asked how the negotiations went, he replied, diplomatically, but somewhat grimly, "We have had cordial and objective discussions of interests of mutual importance with our Soviet friends."

"Recreating" at Kennebunkport, George Bush announced that he was not going to make any news that day and would not comment on the Soviet initiative. White House spokesman Marlin Fitzwater said at midday February 18 that they were waiting for details from the Soviets concerning the Moscow peace initiative but hadn't heard anything yet. Fitzwater added that the time for talking was over and that the United States placed all of its hopes on the coordinated land, air, and sea war that would drive Saddam Hussein out of Kuwait. The ground war had been anticipated all along, according to Fitzwater, and he threatened that the United States stood ready to begin this phase of the war. Fitzwater reiterated the (non-negotiating) U.S. position that they would accept no cease-fire and would only respond favorably if Saddam Hussein left Kuwait "unconditionally, massively, and rapidly." The United States obviously continued to maintain a tough line, blocking all diplomatic solutions.

On the February 19 "CBS This Morning" the headlines indicated that Aziz was heading to Baghdad with the Soviet peace plan, but Bush saw nothing new in the plan and the heaviest bombing of Baghdad in recent days was taking place. The morning news summary opened with Harry Smith reporting from Saudi Arabia that soldiers were poised for what may be "the biggest battle of the century" and that a last-minute Soviet peace initiative may be "too little, too late." According to Smith, Bush saw nothing in the Soviet peace proposal to prevent a ground war. A flurry of diplomatic activity continued, "but is it going anywhere?" Future journalists might note that what CBS presented as a descriptive analysis of the current state of the war was really a brief for a very specific policy proposal: Begin the ground war.

The CBS report presented the Soviet peace initiative, whose contents they didn't even know for sure, in the most negative light. Although CBS conceded that Iraq appeared to be ready to withdraw from Kuwait, they made the ridiculous suggestion that the new Soviet proposal did not differ significantly from the previous Iraqi peace proposal. Their analysis was based on leaks by the German tabloid *Bild Zeitung* that focused on alleged linkage to the Palestinian question and how the Soviet initiative would preserve Saddam Hussein's power and Iraqi borders. Thus, what masqueraded as a news report described rumored features of the Soviet peace proposal as actual fact and presented the plan in a way to make it appear unappealing to a country that still had deep suspicions of the Soviet Union and a hatred of Saddam Hussein.

The CBS report next showed Aziz meeting with Iranian President Hashemi Rafsanjani, another *bête noire* of the U.S. government and public, editorializing that since Saddam Hussein had not even seen the text of the Soviet initiative, optimism would be premature. CBS correspondent Randall Pinkston reported from the White House that optimism would be premature there, too. The Bush administration had not yet rejected the Gorbachev peace plan, but the military campaign continued apace. According to CBS, the White House claimed that the Soviets had not asked for a delay in the ground war (this was clearly mis- or disinformation, as Primakov had pleaded for a delay in the ground war the night before on ABC and CNN). The air war continued, as did preparations for a ground war, and CBS pictured troops testing weapons, reporting that "all systems are being readied" in a "ground rehearsal" for the land offensive—precisely the line that the Pentagon was putting out.

After some more news, CBS cut to Harry Smith in Saudi Arabia, interviewing Dan Rather, who, outfitted in a brown safari jacket, was serving as a booster for the Pentagon faction that wanted a ground war. Rather told Smith that by the next day a decision would be made for the ground war that would unleash the next phase of the war later in the week. He predicted that the Bush administration would wait just one day for the Soviet negotiations with Iraq to play out before deciding on the ground war and that it would then take a couple more days for the United States to organize the actual start of the battle. The CBS anchor then threw cold water on the Soviet peace proposal, saying: "Quite frankly, the deal being offered by the Soviet looks like about the same that President Bush could have gotten anytime along the way during the last months." This was the rankest nonsense, for Iraq had never before agreed to withdraw unconditionally from Kuwait and Rather had no idea what was really in the Soviet proposal.

Harry Smith then asked Rather if the United States could live with Saddam Hussein in power and Rather answered, "I doubt it," adding that Gorbachev had tried "to deal himself a pretty strong hand," positioning himself for the postwar world, and "I don't think President Bush can buy any such arrangement, but we'll see in the next 24 to 36 hours." Smith then asked, in his high-pitched, grating voice, if the Soviets were back in the "influence-peddling business." Rather answered that the Soviet military was reasserting itself again after the period of liberalization, so it's not a New World Order that Gorbachev was talking about; it's a throwback to the old world order, with the United States and Soviet Union fighting for world influence and power. Thus, Rather dismissed the Gorbachev peace plan as a mere move in world power politics between the former cold war antagonists. Returning to discuss the battlefield preparations, Smith opined that "it is amazing to think about what is amassed on the border" and wondered if the momentum for a ground war could stop. Rather deployed a poker analogy and said that Bush now has to call, raise, or fold (it would be interesting to know what Rather considered "calling," "raising" or "folding").

Continuing his sophistry and Pentagon war-faction propaganda in the analogical mode, Rather reflected, using the brutal phrase of General Powell, that "there is this great [allied] military presence in place where he [i.e., Bush] has to move it or lose it." Once again, this was absurd: Although there were arguments circulating that a military force could not maintain a high stage of readiness for more than three to seven days, to say that failing to begin the ground war immediately would cause the U.S.-led coalition to "lose" its military momentum was ludicrous. Instead, we see the extent to which some in the military were itching to fight their ground war and how some in the media, like Dan Rather and Harry Smith, were helping them. Smith closed his carefully orchestrated propaganda offensive in favor of the ground war by evoking an image of the "killing field" of Kuwait and Iraqi massacres, and he asked Rather if Bush accepted the Soviet peace proposal, presumably without destroying totally Saddam Hussein and his military, could he claim victory? Rather answered "perhaps," but then went on to imply that it would be better if the Iraqis could be defeated militarily and Saddam Hussein could be eliminated completely, so that the United States could say: "We've completed our mission; we got, by our definition, total victory," or else, Rather implied, the United States would have to "settle for something less."

In making their brief for a ground war and the elimination of Saddam Hussein, Dan Rather was overlooking the fact that such a course of action would go beyond the UN mandate, which merely sanctioned forcing the withdrawal of Saddam Hussein from Kuwait. Moreover, a ground war that invaded Iraq and got bogged down in "enemy territory" might fracture the coalition, position the United States as an aggressor, and produce immense suffering and death. But no matter, it would provide great drama, great excitement, and presumably great ratings for CBS and Dan Rather.

Indeed, why would Rather, supposedly a liberal critic of George Bush, support Bush's not-too-secret agenda to have the Soviet peace proposal fail so that the ground war could be launched? I would speculate that Rather's partisanship for the military option and expanding the U.S. war aims to the elimination of Saddam Hussein was partly opportunism and partly Rather falling prey to war fever himself. In appraising this episode, one should note that the ratings of Rather and CBS News had been steadily deteriorating throughout the Gulf war in comparison to CNN and the other networks. Just the week before, CBS News had fired one of its main news producers, and there were rumors that Rather might lose his anchor position or be forced to share it with a female co-anchor.[1] So with his very survival at stake in the competitive world of television ratings, Rather traveled to Saudi Arabia so that he could be on the scene to narrate the ground war and identify with the U.S. victory.

And so did the fundamental opportunism of commercial television show its corrupt face. Polls indicated that the audience was overwhelmingly for the war, and Rather, who seemed previously to be trying his best to do balanced, nonpartisan reporting, now began playing to the prowar audience. It was obvious that the TV audience was solidly rooting for a U.S. victory and Iraqi defeat, and Rather played to this constituency, becoming a booster for the military and all-out champion of the ground war. Consequently, Rather promoted the military line that the ground war was ready, that the troops were "good to go," "coiled to spring" (one of Rather's favorite metaphors). He therefore attacked the Soviet peace proposal on February 19, putting his prestige and power in the service of specific policy aims, taking sides in a momentous decision concerning war or peace with lives in the balance. By departing from his journalistic role as mediator, Rather disgraced CBS News in one of the most shameful episodes in the history of broadcasting, which will produce a stain on Rather's record forever.

Other networks were equally hostile to the Soviet peace initiative, thus supporting the prowar position of the Bush administration. The Soviet peace proposal was called a "tragedy" on PBS's "MacNeil/Lehrer NewsHour" and a "nightmare" and "the worst possible scenario" by Tom Brokaw on February 21 on NBC. By promoting the military option, NBC was boosting the interests of its owner, weapons producer General Electric, which obviously would profit from an all-out ground war that would deplete military stocks and provide more free advertising for military weapons systems. ABC and CNN were more even-handed in presenting the war or peace option, and on February 19 (the day of the Rather-Smith attack on the Soviet peace proposal) by the time the "CBS Evening News" came on, their report was more balanced too. Perhaps the producers in New York were appalled by Rather's performance on the CBS morning show, reined him in, and made a more balanced presentation of the options confronting the players in the Gulf war (it appeared to me, in fact, that the segments with Rather were taped that night, instead of being broadcast live as was typical, perhaps so that CBS could maintain editorial control).

On February 21, Tariq Aziz was once again in Moscow to discuss the new Soviet peace initiative. There were rumors that he carried a personal letter from Saddam Hussein to Gorbachev, and the peace camp once more hoped that this meeting would produce a diplomatic settlement. A couple of hours after the meeting began, late afternoon, EST, CNN showed a breathless and excited spokesman for Gorbachev, Vitaly Ignatenko, bursting into the press room to announce that Iraq and the Soviet Union had just agreed to an eight-point peace proposal that could form the basis for a negotiated settlement of the war. During the rest of the day the proposal was the focus of news and discussion programs and it appeared that a diplomatic settlement might be found after all.

During the morning of February 22, the seesaw between war and peace continued. Reports went back and forth between those urging a diplomatic solution and arguing that the Soviet initiative provided a rational basis for discussion contrasted to those claiming that only the decisive military victory that a ground war could bring would suffice. The debate was interrupted around 10:45 A.M. when Bush walked out of the White House toward a microphone in the Rose Garden, where he read a statement. Dan Quayle stood behind him looking vice-presidential while the war team members—Brent Scowcroft, John Sununu, and James Baker—stood in the wings looking statesmanly. Bush's eyes were down on his text throughout the reading and he appeared grim but determined. He began by stating that the United States and its allies were committed to the UN resolutions calling for Saddam Hussein to immediately and unconditionally leave Kuwait. Bush said that in view of the Soviet initiative—"which very frankly we appreciate—we wanted to set forth this morning the specific criteria that will insure Saddam Hussein complies with the UN mandate." Bush cited Hussein's defiant speech of the previous day and then his adherence to the Soviet peace proposal, which "on the face of it appears more reasonable." But, Bush argued, the Iraqis agreed to "unconditional" withdrawal only to set out a number of conditions that would be unacceptable to the coalition and to the UN resolutions.

More important and more urgently, Bush said, we have learned this morning that Saddam was launching a scorched earth policy in Kuwait, knowing perhaps that he will be forced to leave (note how Bush is reducing the Iraqis, whose military he has just ordered to be annihilated, to Saddam Hussein). He, Bush continued, is setting on fire the oil production facilities, oil terminals, and storage facilities of the country. Indeed, he is destroying the entire oil production system of Kuwait; at the same time that his foreign minister was talking peace, he was launching Scud missiles. In view of recent events, Bush affirmed, "I have decided to make public with specificity just exactly what is required of

Iraq if a ground war is to be avoided." Bush asserted that the coalition will give Saddam Hussein until noon Saturday "to do what he must do." By Saturday at 12 noon, he must begin withdrawing from Kuwait, Bush warned. Saddam Hussein must come on the radio to publicly state that he is withdrawing and that he will follow the UN resolutions. The deadline was thus set for High Noon the next day for what turned out to be the final stage of the Showdown in the Gulf.

8.2 High Noon

From the beginning of the Persian Gulf war, the U.S. military insisted that it had a "plan" to win the war, involving air, land, and sea forces, with an intent to "cut off and kill" the Iraqi forces. The U.S. military regularly claimed that it was on schedule, that all was proceeding on course, and that the air war was achieving its goals. Debates emerged as to whether the ground war was necessary to achieve victory and whether the air war had indeed "attrited" the Iraqi military sufficiently to guarantee a coalition victory with minimal casualties. While the pundits debated these issues, however, the Pentagon and Bush administration inexorably moved toward the ground war which would realize their plan.

On Saturday, February 23, the countdown began. Early reports suggested that diplomatic efforts had failed and that events were relentlessly moving toward the final ground conflict. The network news reports indicated that Tariq Aziz had left Moscow without reaching a settlement on a new plan that would mediate the differences between the Soviet and U.S. peace proposals. As the deadline approached, there were no responses from Iraq and no signs of any imminent Iraqi withdrawal.

Before leaving Moscow, Tariq Aziz and his Iraqi colleagues held a news conference and announced that they sought a peaceful resolution to the war and fully endorsed the Soviet peace plan. Shortly thereafter, Gorbachev's spokesman, Vitaly Ignatenko, held a news conference and spoke of the tragedy of the failure of negotiations. In a somber mood, he spoke of the lives that would be lost if the ground war began. Ignatenko spoke of Gorbachev's efforts to solve the problem, mentioning the intense telephone conversation between Bush and Gorbachev, and of Gorbachev's readiness to continue working to achieve peace.

In a sense, Bush's refusal to work with Gorbachev's plan to bring about a diplomatic solution to the war sealed the Soviet leader's fate. Broad segments of the Soviet power structure were outraged by Gorbachev's policies in the war. Previously, anger at Soviet Foreign Minister Eduard Shevardnadze's complicity with the UN resolutions and U.S. policy led to his resignation in December 1990. Frequent reports surfaced that the

Soviet military was outraged that one of its favorite client states, Iraq, was about to have its military forces, which the Soviets had helped to build up, destroyed. Soviet leaders were deeply upset that the United States was apparently becoming a superpower in the region, with its military forces positioned dangerously close to the Soviet border. There was worry that the war could enflame the Soviet Islamic population and drive it to revolt. And communist hardliners saw Gorbachev's capitulation to Bush as producing a dangerous situation where one dominant superpower dictated foreign policy.

The conditions for a coup and Gorbachev's overthrow were thus at hand, and Bush, instead of working with Gorbachev for a diplomatic solution, humiliated the Soviet leader, who was desperately seeking a peaceful settlement to the conflict. Bush effectively cut Gorbachev "out of the loop" in the Gulf war and made a fool out of him; while Gorbachev called for peace and negotiations Bush and his clique were planning their ground war. Although Bush and his war team presumably told other allied leaders what the real plans were, Gorbachev was kept in the dark. Gorbachev thus appeared ineffectual and irrelevant while Bush appeared as the real mover and shaker of world politics. Consequently, when the communist hardliners overthrew Gorbachev in August 1991, barely a year after Iraq's invasion of Kuwait, Bush had contributed significantly to Gorbachev's fate, weakening him to an extent that he would soon be forced out of power, thanks in part to his "friend" George Bush.

In retrospect, it is clear that Bush did not want to negotiate an end to the war; during the entire crisis in the Gulf and the Gulf war he never made any effort whatsoever to negotiate a settlement. Bush's tone, which was harsh, blunt, and unnuanced, precluded negotiation. He delivered imperatives in the ultimatum mode instead of providing positions to discuss. He imposed deadlines, one impossibly short, rather than seeking dialogue and genuine negotiation. His style was aggressive, macho, and insulting. Future students of negotiation should observe Bush's behavior as a textbook example of how not to comport oneself in situations of conflict, as a classic case of a non-negotiating stance.

There was also a question of the discourse of time in Bush's ultimatum. All forms of Bush's "diplomacy" employed the phrase that Iraq "must" withdraw "immediately" from Kuwait and at the end Bush gave the Iraqis a twenty-four hour deadline: surrender immediately or face destruction. Such a mode of temporal imperatives clashed with different rhythms of time in many parts of the world; in the Arab world, time is not parceled into well-differentiated bundles and periods, and people do not utilize such rigid time schedules. Thus, Bush was imposing his Western time and mode of discourse on a culture with a different attitude toward time. There is some question, however, as to whether Bush's ultimatum merely revealed cultural insensitivity and a failure to understand cultural differences on the part of an imperial Western ego, or whether Bush maneuvered aggressively to insure that there would be no diplomatic solution so that he could gain power and glory from a successful war.

In addition to the political and military pressures to win a total victory and destroy Iraq, there was speculation that Bush was obsessed with Saddam Hussein, that he had personalized the conflict to such an extent that he was determined to humiliate and destroy the Iraqi leader. On the February 24 "CBS Sunday Morning Show," for instance, anchor Charles Kuralt asked White House correspondent Bill Plante why the ground war was necessary, given Iraq's stated willingness to withdraw from Kuwait. Plante admitted that there was little real difference between the Soviet and U.S. proposals but claimed that without the ground war Bush would not have been able "to humiliate Saddam Hussein. He really wanted to go *mano-a-mano* [hand-to-hand] with Hussein." This is probably true, but it subjectivizes Bush's motivations for pursuing the war, thus covering over the economic and political imperatives to build up the military and his presidency, as well as the economic interests of certain corporate sectors who wanted to control the flow of oil and promote weapons sales in the area. In fact, when the war was over, Bush did not pursue the overthrow of Hussein, as we shall see in 10.4.

8.3 On the Threshold

CBS's logo "Showdown in the Gulf" highlighted the mythic frames of entertainment through which the television networks were presenting the Gulf war, and George Bush played to these frames with his noon deadline, evoking the final showdown between "good" and "evil," as in the Western classic *High Noon*. As the morning of February 22 passed and the deadline neared it was increasingly apparent that there would be no diplomatic solution. On CBS, Randall Pinkston at the White House reported that the Bush administration was stating categorically that the Soviet plan was "without effect" and "absolutely unacceptable," and that its military option was the only plan that could resolve the crisis. CBS's Betsy Aaron in Baghdad reported that thick black clouds of smoke from the previous day's bombing surrounded the city. It was a rather strange atmosphere, she said, because the radio was not telling people of the impending crisis of diplomacy, so they are going about their business as normal. Aaron stated how the foreign correspondents were taken to power plants that were first made inoperable by coalition forces using silicon and then, two days later, bombed into rubble. The message was that the allies were brutally bombing Iraqi civilian facilities, the very heart of a city, and that the facilities would take years to rebuild.

Christiane Amanpour in Baghdad reported a deep sense of pessimism in the city in her early morning CNN report of February 23. The Iraqis in Baghdad, she noted, cannot understand why there would be more war when they had agreed to the Soviet proposal. Amanpour observed that there was a major shift over the past days from optimism to pessimism, with all hopes crushed. From Saudi Arabia, CNN correspondent Rick Sallinger commented that there was no evidence that Iraq was planning any troop pullout. There was no movement of Iraqi troops, so it appeared that once again Saddam Hussein was ignoring a Bush ultimatum. There was still no schedule for a ground war, Sallinger claimed (though, in fact, the order was already in place), but the U.S. troops were ready, "even chomping at the bit," despite fear of casualties. CNN's Charles Jaco in Saudi Arabia said that military authorities warned that only if Iraqi troops packed up and left immediately would the ground war be averted. Jaco noted that the U.S. military affirmed that the ground war would be sudden, massive, and violent, "like getting hit in the face with a baseball bat."

CBS's Harry Smith reported that there were now over 150 oil wells on fire in Kuwait, and hundreds of others were mined and ready to be detonated and set aflame. Kuwaiti civilians were reportedly being rounded up, according to the Kuwaiti ambassador, and many were being executed on the spot. Bush had cited these claims the day before in order to legitimate his decision to immediately begin the ground campaign rather than to wait for the Soviet diplomatic initiative to play out. As we shall see, while the Iraqis had torched many Kuwaiti oil wells, at this point the U.S. propaganda machine was exaggerating the alleged atrocities against Kuwaitis (see 10.1). Once again, we see how Harry Smith was being used as a propaganda agent for the U.S. military, which fed him (dis)information that he dutifully reproduced for the TV audience.

Back in their studio in New York, CBS projected a computer simulation of the battlefield, and their military adviser General Crist demonstrated what the ground war might look like, using the standard images of mounds of sand dunes, called berms, fashioned into fortifications, ditches full of burning oil, barbed wire, mine fields, tank and artillery fortifications, and Iraqi troops armed with chemical weapons. For the past days, all of the networks were utilizing similar models or computer simulations of the horrible Iraqi fortifications across the border into Kuwait and throughout the country. As it would turn out, these models also were either gross exaggerations or sheer disinformation.

At midmorning, shortly before the High Noon deadline, a last-ditch hope for peace briefly flickered. CNN and CBS announced that at a UN Security Council meeting, the Soviet peace proposal would be discussed and that the Soviets were working hard to achieve a last-minute diplomatic solution. CBS reported that all day Gorbachev had been talking with world leaders to try to get support for his peace plan, arguing that with UN mediation perhaps a compromise could be worked out. It was reported that James Baker had talked at great length with Soviet Foreign Minister Bessmertnykh about the Soviet plan with Bessmertnykh arguing that the Soviet and U.S. plans were practically the same. The United States, however, reportedly insisted that there were major differences, focusing on the cancellation of some of the UN resolutions in the Soviet plan. At the UN meeting the U.S. did not want to have a showdown with the Soviets, according to the TV reports, and they praised the Soviet effort (while fearing that the Soviets could force the issue, an outcome which they viewed with some concern). CBS's Bob Fall at the UN reported that the Soviets were expected to ask for action from the Security Council, and not just a discussion of the Soviet peace proposal. The Soviets wanted to see if there was a possibility of a merger of the U.S. and Soviet proposals; several delegates were pushing this. U.S. Ambassador Thomas Pickering said that this was not what the United States wanted and ducked a question as to whether the U.S. would support a diplomatic settlement. For the next hours, there was intense speculation as to whether Aziz had agreed at the last minute to negotiate the U.S. proposals or whether the Soviets were floating a rumor to provide more time for negotiation. Typically, Dan Rather and CBS were downplaying the diplomatic side and playing up the military aspects of the ground war. In a Saturday "High Noon" "CBS News Special," Col. Mitch Mitchell stated that there was evidence that the ground offensive was rapidly approaching and that it was merely a matter of the timetable countdown. This escalation of the war was full of risks, he noted, but "with much greater gain."

CBS's Bob Schieffer claimed that the largest land battle in history was shaping up, hyping the coming massacre as a significant military engagement. CBS presented a computer simulation model of the coming ground war which was interrupted by sirens going off in Israel. CBS reported that Israel was in a state of panic and at least one Scud had been launched. The Israelis expected a major chemical attack and Tom Fenton reported that the Israelis wanted a ground war in order to destroy Saddam Hussein's military completely. Israeli officials thought that if Hussein's regime remained in power, it would constitute a great threat to Israel.[2] Dan Rather came on the screen to narrate that the decisive hour in the Persian Gulf war deadline had now passed: Baghdad was being bombed heavily; Scud attacks were hitting Israel; Kuwait was burning, a vision of hell, with 200 oil installations on fire and systematic executions taking place in the street. Meanwhile U.S. troops near the border prepared for the ground war. Rather played the drama to the hilt, acting out a countdown to war as emotionally and dramatically as he could. He obviously wanted to highlight the drama of the ground war and seemed uninterested in the diplomatic initiatives. CNN, meanwhile, played the diplomacy theme, interpreting and analyzing the Tariq Aziz response to the Soviets and following closely the activity at the UN.

NBC's Pentagon correspondent Fred Francis reported around 12:55 P.M. that the ground war had started because the United States was already jamming Iraqi radar. Some minutes later Francis broke in with the remark that General Schwarzkopf had given the order to begin the ground war. This meant, he suggested, that in the next two days the Iraqi forces in Kuwait would be circled. Francis claimed that President Bush really didn't want Iraq to withdraw because they would preserve too much military equipment and the U.S. would have to keep at least 200,000 troops in the area. In addition, Bush wanted to stop immediately the reign of terror in Kuwait City. The NBC anchors, Garrick Utley and Tom Brokaw in Saudi Arabia, then announced that the ground war had begun, though this would not be certain for some hours, and that afternoon at the Pentagon in Washington the briefers scoffed at the NBC report, which turned out to be quite accurate. At 1:00 P.M., NBC cut off its war coverage and soon ABC and CBS also concluded their morning news schedules and returned to the usual Saturday afternoon fare, so only CNN would follow the story for the rest of the afternoon. Rumors that Iraq had agreed to the Soviet peace proposal continued to circulate in the UN, but Bush released a letter saying: "We regret that Saddam Hussein took no action before the noon deadline to comply with the United Nations resolutions. We remain determined to fulfill the U.N. resolutions. Military action continues on schedule and according to plan." A bit later as the Soviets worked feverishly in the UN to integrate the U.S./Soviet peace initiatives, Marlin Fitzwater released a document pointing out that the deadline had passed and the United States had received no communication from the UN that the Iraqis planned to meet its ultimatum. Furthermore:

> Iraq continues its scorched earth policy in Kuwait, setting fire to oil facilities. It is a continuing outrage that Saddam Hussein is still intent upon destroying Kuwait and its people, still intent upon inflicting the most brutal kind of rule on his own population, yet appears to have no intention to comply with the U.N. resolutions. Indeed, Saddam Hussein's only response to the U.S. ultimatum at noon was to launch another Scud missile attack on Israel. The coalition forces have no alternative but to continue to prosecute the war.

This remarkable, terse document provided a tightly encapsulated legitimation of U.S. escalation to the ground war phase. Saddam Hussein had not yet officially responded to Bush's ultimatum (though it was not certain that the ultimatum had any legal force). Then, Fitzwater evoked the horror of Iraq torching Kuwaiti oil, destroying the very substance that the United States had, initially at least, come to recover. Next, Saddam Hussein himself was portrayed as an international outlaw, destroying Kuwait and its people, as well as a tyrant, brutally ruling his own people. The Bush administration continued its relentless demonization of Saddam Hussein, making the hated dictator the target of its terse rhetoric, and, by implication, his destruction the *raison d'etre* of the war. Its rhetoric, however, ultimately trapped the administration in a contradiction as it attacked Saddam Hussein as an oppressor of his people, thus positioning his people as victims. Yet by continuing the war it would be his people, the innocent victims of the Bush rhetoric, who would bear the brunt of the U.S.-led coalition attack.

Throughout the afternoon, there was intense UN activity to try to produce a last-minute diplomatic settlement, but the United States blocked all of these efforts. That night, after the ground war began, various UN ambassadors, such as the Yemenite one, bitterly said that the Bush administration had used and abused the UN, mobilizing support for its use of force and then relegating the UN to the sidelines. The United States, he complained, was refusing to cooperate with efforts at producing a negotiated settlement, which was precisely what the UN was intended to do. Apparently, in Bush's New World Order it was war and not diplomacy that would resolve problems, and military power would enforce security and order.

CNN military analyst retired General Perry Smith continued to misanalyze the military situation in a report on Saturday afternoon in which he stated that there had not been any surge of air strikes or massive movement of allied forces. Nor had there been any major forays into enemy territory, so he concluded that the coalition forces needed a few more days to "soften" the enemy before the ground war started. In fact, there had been forays into Kuwait and Iraq over the past days and the ground war was about to be launched as he spoke. In retrospect, it is not clear if Smith was consciously giving the Iraqis disinformation, as it was well known that Iraq constantly monitored CNN, or if he was just misinformed himself. In any case, Smith's presence raised the question of whether exmilitary men, with close connections to the military establishment, should be hired as military consultants during war as: (1) they can be expected to serve as conduits for military propaganda, as Smith constantly did; and (2) they might consciously misinform the TV audiences while giving out the disinformation that the military wants communicated.

On the "CBS Evening News," Bob Schieffer reported that everything was in place for a battle of epic proportions and that Iraq's scorched-earth policy and killing of Kuwaiti civilians gave a new urgency to launching the ground war. Schieffer claimed that the order for a ground war had gone out and it was now merely a matter of timing. CBS discussed the failed Soviet peace proposal, and the Kuwaiti ambassador stated that he would see a liberated Kuwait soon. The White House, according to CBS, believed that the ground campaign would be very, very quick, with limited casualties, and that the allies will deliver a blow from which Hussein will "never recover."

From Saudi Arabia, Dan Rather pointed out that advanced elements of the multinational forces were already in Iraq and Kuwait and that the allies were "leaning forward," preparing for the major invasion. There were reports of increased Iraqi border casualties and the constant drone of planes in a record 1,200 sorties over Kuwait, another sign that the ground war was coming quickly. Along the borders, the U.S. troops were massed for the ground war and it was now "hammer time." Rather noted again the reports of atrocities against Kuwaiti civilians, the 200 oil-field fires, and intelligence sources who mentioned a roundup of Kuwaitis. Waxing rhetorical, Rather described the roar of planes and the sound of war as planes took off in the background. The battle plan was described as fast moving, complicated, and high risk. Commanders hoped for a quick strike and a quick win. The battlefield plan included a "vertical envelopment" in which paratroopers would penetrate behind enemy lines. Pentagon officials believed that the Iraqis would be crushed, that they were on the verge of collapsing, and that massive surrenders and disorderly retreats were expected when the coalition forces went on the offensive. Rather quoted with approval a rather brutal military official who stated that the Iraqis were "on their knees and we'd like to have them flat on their backs."

Throughout the evening, CBS's Eric Engberg, reported the claims that Kuwaitis were being pulled from the streets in roundups apparently aimed at getting rid of witnesses to earlier atrocities. CBS Pentagon correspondent David Martin stated that the schedule of the ground war was moved up because of these atrocity stories. It would turn out, however, that the ground war had been scheduled for days to unfold at the day and hour that it actually started and that the atrocity stories which the media bought into were merely part of a propaganda campaign to help legitimate the coming slaughter of Iraqi troops.

In the early evening, CBS's Dan Rather described "the first video of the ground war," showing an Apache attack helicopter shooting and tearing apart Iraqi troops.[3] The ground war massacre was thus underway, though the media would celebrate it as a great victory. Around 8:30 P.M., David Martin announced that the opening phases of the ground war had begun, with U.S. troops in Kuwait where they would stay until Kuwait was liberated. Moments later, CBS's Bill Plante announced that President Bush was to arrive back into Washington shortly to make a TV address to the nation and there was no longer any doubt but that the U.S.-led coalition ground offensive was now under way.

ABC's Sam Donaldson reported from Saudi Arabia that there was a broad offensive about 2,000 kilometers [1,200 miles] along the northern Saudi Arabia and Iraqi borders that would follow "classic AirLand doctrine," which meant going after second- and third-line Iraqi troops to cut them off. It was planned to begin, he said, at 8:00 P.M. EST and as he gave his report there was a Scud attack on Saudi Arabia and ABC lost its satellite connection. ABC's Brit Hume reported that Bush's war team was assembled in the White House and that the order had been given to begin the ground war. Bush was scheduled to arrive soon to give a speech announcing and explaining the launching of the ground war. Dan Rather and Tom Brokaw were under Scud attack in Saudi Arabia and temporarily relinquished their anchor positions, and the military experts assembled to describe the AirLand war as it began to unfold.

8.4 AirLand War

For the rest of the evening, all of the networks discussed the new ground war phase of the campaign. As the military experts explained the disposition of the troops, the U.S. strategy, and the likely outcome, it was amazing how much was known in advance concerning the coalition plans and strategy. It appears that NBC and CBS had been clued in rather precisely as to the day and hour when the ground war would begin and all of their "experts" seemed to have had a good idea of the strategy, which had been leaking through the Pentagon for days and was picked up by the military analysts who had access to insider information.

All of the TV military commentators explained that the concept of an AirLand battle involved coordinated operations that use several different methods of attack at once: ground attacks, amphibious attacks, and air attacks by helicopters and multiple launch rockets, which can launch bomblets that could cover an area the size of a football field and virtually halt any kind of military action. The AirLand war doctrine had been developed to fight the Soviets in a war in Europe, or the Middle East, where the U.S. forces would face superior ground forces but would possess superior air power and high-tech weapons. The concept was the U.S. military response to the policy of gradual escalation carried out in Vietnam that had resulted in failure. AirLand battle doctrine, by contrast, was intended to overpower the enemy with a quick and massive assault that would wipe out as many enemy forces as possible during the early hours of attack. Once the enemy was initially overpowered the goal was to exterminate as many of its forces as possible, as quickly as possible. The AirLand war was thus the specific form of technowar employed in the Persian Gulf after the forty days of air war which had aimed at weakening the Iraqi troops so as to facilitate the total destruction of their forces.

Reports appeared on all of the networks that the coalition had been clearing the fields of mines over the border and that coalition troops intended to outflank the Iraqi artillery, cut them off, and destroy them with combined air and land assault. On ABC, Tony Cordesman claimed that the coalition forces had been pounding the Iraqi border positions for days and had probably destroyed much of their artillery. ABC's other military consultant, Gen. Bernard Trainor, described the variety of different operations that could be used: breaching the border, in which engineers make a path to get through mines and Iraqi troops; "sledge hammer" operations that would pound through Iraq's defenses over the Kuwait border; flanking operations; air assault attacks; air envelopment with camps set up in Iraq; and an amphibious attack from the sea. He suggested that all or most of these operations would be employed.

Cordesman claimed that with this range of strategies the coalition forces could fight the enemy at a distance, and when close range encounters occur, the coalition would prevail because its tanks had greater accuracy, velocity, visibility, and range than the Iraqi tanks and ground forces. Gen. Trainor added that Iraq had very rudimentary intelligence operations and thus wouldn't have much knowledge about what was actually going on and, consequently, would have little possibility of counterattack. As the evening proceeded, in fact, the networks provided account after account of the technological superiority of U.S. equipment and weapons which would, indeed, produce a decisive victory. Dan Rather stressed that Saddam Hussein had to fight a "one-dimensional war," having only ground forces, while the allies were multidimensional with air, sea, and ground forces. At the same time as Cordesman and Trainor on ABC were describing the U.S. plan, CBS's Rather used an even more detailed map to show the various lines of attack, pointing precisely to where different army and marine units were attacking and advancing. Rather also continually suggested that, in reference to the rumor that an amphibious assault was underway, "there is a school of thought that thinks that this might be a feint"—and indeed it was. Obviously, Rather had been rewarded for his faithful promotion of the ground war and hyping up the military with some very detailed insider information and he displayed it with great pride.

In fact, it seemed that the networks knew exactly what the order of battle was and provided remarkably accurate early reports on what the general plan was, though there would be some errors concerning alleged successes in the early reports. But the ubiquitous accounts of Iraqi chemical weapons and potential chemical attacks were exaggerated and, as it turned out, Iraq had little with which they could counter the massive allied attack. The first piece of disinformation came from NBC's Fred Francis. Either his Pentagon sources misled him or he was willingly conveying disinformation to fool the Iraqis when he reported that Failaka Island, twenty miles from Kuwait City, had been taken. For days, Francis had claimed that the allies had been dropping daisy cutter bombs on the island to drive out the perhaps 500 to 800 Iraqis who occupied it. According to Francis's sources, marines had just landed on the island and found hundreds of dead bodies. For the next day or so, others would repeat this story, which turned out to be totally false, as the Iraqi occupants of Failaka Island would not surrender until after the war was over.

In a fascinating exchange between Francis and NBC anchor Tom Brokaw, both admitted that they had known for days that the ground war would be launched on February 24. Francis chuckled with insider superiority and explained how the Bush administration had let Gorbachev "play out his hand" at diplomacy, but that the ground war was planned all along anyway and there was no desire in the Administration or Pentagon to deflect its plans. Francis noted that "the 24th was a very rich day indeed" for the invasion because the 25th is Kuwaiti independence day. This explanation, however, was rather naive and assumed that the end of the whole campaign was the liberation of Kuwait, while, as I shall argue later, there were other ultimate aims in the minds of the Bush administration and Pentagon.

Francis also indicated that he had been told by the Pentagon earlier in the week that Saturday would be the day when the ground offensive began, if the peace negotiations failed. Francis revealed that he had discussed his privileged information with Brokaw and NBC previously "so that we could make our preparations." This was a fairly astonishing revelation, indicating that the Pentagon had chosen to leak news of the coming AirLand war to NBC, the network owned by GE/RCA, two of the largest contractors of military equipment, so that they could prepare themselves for good coverage of the event. This would mean that it would be in the interest of the network to present the peace negotiations negatively and to promote the ground war, both in terms of the war contracts of the owners of NBC/RCA/GE and in terms of the ratings and prestige of their news team, which could win attention and ratings through their well-prepared war coverage.

It was likely that Dan Rather and CBS were also given fairly precise information that the ground war was on track for the weekend of February

23, and that this information might have encouraged the CBS anchor to present the peace negotiations negatively and to promote the war option so that he could have the thrill of covering the AirLand war. As we have seen, CBS was well prepared for the ground war, which gave Rather an opportunity to dramatically narrate the events, putting him in the league of Edward R. Murrow, CBS's World War II star correspondent—as well as giving Rather an opportunity to boost his ratings in the highly competitive network news game by identifying with the new patriotism and demonstrating his closeness with the military operation and personnel.

Rather claimed around 9:00 P.M. that the main coalition force was beginning to thrust deeply into Iraq, a flanking movement designed not only to encircle the Iraqi forces in Kuwait, but to ultimately bottle up the Republican Guards. Rather described the AirLand war doctrine as a plan to fight an enemy that would outnumber them, and the United States hoped that this plan would be successful in the open desert where they would face the fourth largest army in the world—a hyperbolic puffing up of the Iraqi army that occurred constantly throughout the crisis and war and that would reveal itself to be empty rhetoric. Although Rather continued to hype the war as a titanic battle between powerful forces, this puffery was highly misleading; the forces were totally unequal, and the war would result in the massacre of the Iraqi military with few U.S. casualties.

On CBS, General Crist explained that General Schwarzkopf was worried about putting together his "battlefield ballet," with sweeps going in different directions and needing to be put together in a very careful way. Crist said that his friend "Norm" [Schwarzkopf] needed to have all the sweeps work together and "if the music misses the dance step, there could be a problem," as all plans are subject to Murphy's law: If something can go wrong, it probably will. Crist believed that Schwarzkopf had been working on his plan for at least six months; if it worked it would destroy the Iraqi army with minimal U.S. casualties. Crist then described the tremendously complicated logistics that would provide supplies to the troops, especially fuel, which tanks and armored vehicles eat up quickly and which would be needed to keep the troops moving forward.

Although bad weather or strong Iraqi counterattacks might have made logistics difficult, the overall superiority of allied forces ultimately rendered them invulnerable. Serving as Pentagon PR man, Bob Schieffer gushed that the ensuing battle will be "one of the greatest land battles in the history of warfare." The entire circumference of the battlefield was one thousand miles—almost as large as World War I battlefields—with about one million troops deployed—a ridiculous exaggeration as it would turn out (see 9.3). Rather concluded by noting that the full sweep of the ground war west into southern Iraq was now underway. With this operation, the United States would try to draw the elite Republican Guard troops out to fight and would "hammer the hell out of them," Rather emphasized.

Throughout the evening, it had been announced that President Bush would appear around 10:00 P.M. to tell why he felt that it was necessary to use force, to turn to ground war, to get the Iraqis out of Kuwait, rather than continuing the air war or seeking diplomacy. At the appointed time, Bush entered the White House briefing room and stated:

> Yesterday, after conferring with my senior National Security advisers and following extensive consultation with our coalition partners, Saddam Hussein was given one last chance, set forth in very explicit terms, to do what he should have done more than six months ago: withdraw from Kuwait without conditions or further delay and comply fully with resolutions passed by the United Nations Security Council.
>
> Regrettably, the noon deadline passed without the agreement of the government of Iraq to meet demands of United Nations Security Council Resolution 660, as set forth in the specific terms spelled out by the coalition to withdraw unconditionally from Kuwait.
>
> To the contrary, what we have seen is a redoubling of Saddam Hussein's efforts to destroy completely Kuwait and its people. I have therefore directed General Norman Schwarzkopf, in conjunction with coalition forces, to use all forces available, including ground forces, to eject the Iraqi army from Kuwait. . . . The liberation of Kuwait has now entered a final phase.

It is amazing what Bush did not say in this terse speech. He did not explain in any detail why he went to the ground war and did not continue with the air war. There was nothing on why the diplomatic efforts couldn't work. His only justification for launching the ground war was that Iraq was allegedly accelerating its efforts to destroy Kuwait and its people, but Bush did not document these charges. Instead, he relied on the media propaganda apparatus to dramatize the Iraqi "scorched earth" policy and the accelerated atrocities against Kuwaiti citizens, which he briefly alluded to in his speech, knowing that the compliant mainstream media would flesh out the disinformation stories that were legitimating the ground war.

None of the network correspondents raised any questions concerning the brevity of Bush's speech or the lack of justification for launching a ground war. Note how, once again, Bush personalized the issue, attacking Saddam Hussein's failure to accept the ultimatum as well as his "redoubling" of efforts to destroy Kuwait. Note also the moralistic condemnation of Hussein not doing what "he should have done more than six months ago." And while Bush cloaked his resolution to begin the ground war with legalistic and diplomatic phrases (consultations with our coalition partners), this covered over his own rejection of diplomacy and UN mediation that was close to a settlement, to a peaceful resolution precluded by the ground war.

Instead of raising and discussing these critical issues, the compliant commentators merely praised the president, serving as a PR arm. ABC's conservative White House correspondent Brit Hume stressed how grave and serious President Bush looked, remarking that he'd never seen the president looking so grave. CBS's White House correspondent, Wyatt Andrews, ignored the substance of Bush's speech and focused on the conclusion, where Bush asked everyone to say a prayer for the troops in the Gulf. Andrews described this as "a very solemn ending," and editorialized that the president, despite having ordered a ground war, was quite worried about casualties.[4]

Dan Rather, always given to hyperbole, stated that "never since World War II has there been a night like this." He then offered a probably long-prepared and well-rehearsed panegyric on the troops in the ground war: "We can't know what it is like on the front tonight. We do know officers who can't sleep and young men who have lost what Eric Severid once called the innocence of youth, that they can't die. But now they know." Rather's military populism was getting a bit hard to stomach. On the eve of the Superbowl, he gave the troops in the desert a hearty salute, demonstrating whose side he was on. He often vigorously shook hands with the U.S. military leaders who he interviewed and fervently congratulated military commanders upon their great success in the ground war. At the end of the war, with tears welling in his eyes, Rather gushed: "There are going to be lots of people taking credit for this [the liberation of Kuwait City]. But the guys who did it are the grunts, the foot soldiers. . . . " Rather's jaw started trembling, his voice choked, and his sidekick Eric Engberg took over until the CBS anchor mastered his emotions.

At 10:30 P.M. Secretary of Defense Dick Cheney came on TV to give a briefing and announced that because allied military units were on the move, there would be a news blackout and no more briefings. He claimed that previously "we've been as forthcoming as possible about military operations," a blatant lie—Cheney had inaugurated the tightest restrictions on coverage of military actions in modern U.S. history. Henceforth, however, he ordered the regular briefing schedule to be "suspended without further notice" because we "cannot let Iraqi forces know anything." Given that the Iraqi command-and-control system had supposedly been disrupted, the question arose as to whether the news blackout was to deny the Iraqis intelligence information or the American public information. Needless to say, there was no protest from the press.[5] (And, of course, when it turned out that the news was good the next morning, the briefings were immediately reinstated so that the military could bask in the glory of their ground war victory.)

Continuing his blatant exaggeration of Iraqi military power, Cheney claimed that "casualties will be very, very, very high," as if the Iraqis had significant power to inflict casualties, which, it would soon be obvious, they did not. In the question-and-answer period, Cheney described the ground war as a "major military operation against a well-equipped and well-fortified opponent" and stated that "we do not want to underestimate the risks," but, in retrospect, there hardly appeared to be much risk against the totally demoralized and totally outclassed Iraqi army. Cheney admitted that there was "a planning date and a planning hour when General Schwarzkopf thought that his forces were ready" for the ground war, a date "subject to change based on weather or changes in the diplomatic situation." Bush had approved the original date, which had been "for some period of time . . . this particular day and hour."

Soon after Cheney's speech, Dan Rather appeared in dawn's early light in Saudi Arabia and reported that the troops had been fighting through the night and now that it was dawn, they could see what they'd been doing. Rather announced that one coalition column was going up the superhighway, past Khafji into Kuwait. The Pentagon claimed that they had cut Iraq's fiberoptic cable from the Iraqi military command so that Iraq couldn't talk to its commanders in the field, and thus "must communicate in the clear" (i.e., through shortwave radio), which the United States could intercept; this "keeps him dumb and blind." From one mile from the border of Kuwait, CBS correspondent Bob McKeown informed viewers that bombardment of the Iraqis in Kuwait from every direction shook the earth and that, under that cover, allied tanks moved up to the sand wall and crossed the border into Kuwait. This radio account was presented as the "first report from the battlefield behind the allied line," where McKeown was positioned with Saudi and Qatari Arab forces. No one ever convincingly explained how McKeown got up there and was allowed to continue broadcasting, eventually becoming the first correspondent to reach Kuwait City. Was this a military payoff to CBS for such fine cheerleading or an example of innovative reporting?

McKeown reported that it had been initially presumed that the first Iraqi defense line was eight miles from the border with the classic defense system of trenches, mines, and artillery, but that coalition forces had quickly moved eight to ten miles over the border without meeting any resistance. He described how the ground shook under constant bombardment during the night when bombs hit and concluded that coalition planes and ships were delivering their ordnance on Iraqi positions. Saudi TV revealed that allied forces had crossed the border into Kuwait and were approaching the al-Wafra area. Later in the evening, it was claimed that French legionnaires had thrust twelve miles into Iraq, meeting little resistance. Cairo radio said that Egyptian forces had entered Kuwait. An all-out ground war was thus on, ranging over the full extent of the Saudi and Kuwaiti border, stretching west into Iraq.

Dan Rather concluded his report with a summary of the U.S. troops' movement into Kuwait and southern Iraq and cited a statement from Dick Cheney claiming that it was not a matter of objective policy to change the government of Iraq, that the United States was committed militarily only to getting the Iraqis out of Kuwait. CBS Pentagon correspondent David Martin, either naively or apologetically, said that this makes the ground war pursue a much more limited objective: "the expulsion of Iraqi soldiers from Kuwait with a minimum loss of American life." This was only half true, as would soon be clear. Although the U.S.-led coalition did not go to Baghdad to overthrow Saddam Hussein, it was soon evident that the goal of the war was to destroy the Iraqi military and not just to liberate Kuwait.

Around 11:00 P.M., the networks signed off and it was up to CNN to report the progress of the war. Very little hard information came through that night and, for the most part, CNN merely recycled the evening's momentous news without much analysis, interpretation, or discussion. In a late night report from the Pentagon, CNN's Candy Crowley reported that the Pentagon was presenting the ground war as a major military offensive against a well-armed and a well-fortified enemy and was not underestimating the difficulty involved and would thus block out all news to protect the troops. CNN anchorperson Susan Rook brought up the question of the extent of Iraqi resistance, mentioning the recent report that the French forces had penetrated deep into Iraq without meeting any resistance, and Crowley replied that the Pentagon had admitted that many Iraqi troops were surrendering, but that more resistance would take place farther within Kuwait. Thus, the Pentagon and its defenders were continuing to project an image of a strong enemy and the possibility of significant resistance by the Iraqis, a picture that would be shattered by the next day.

8.5 Cake Walk

Overnight, bits and pieces of information were dribbling in. Early in the morning of February 24, CNN reported that allied forces had penetrated deep into Iraq and were taking hundreds of prisoners. Coalition forces continued to rush through the gaps in Iraqi defenses prepared by the army engineers. Kuwaiti news agencies claimed that coalition troops had taken the city of Jahruh, outside of Kuwait City, on the road to Basra.

The report of the seizure of Failaka Island continued to circulate, though CNN indicated that it was "unconfirmed." It was also announced that amphibious troops had already begun an invasion of Kuwait and that allied paratroopers had landed in Kuwait City; these latter reports turned out to be wrong: although some paratroopers may have landed in Kuwait City, they were not an invasion force. Moreover, the amphibious forces were used as a deception to tie down Iraqi troops on the Gulf shore.

The first video pictures of the ground war were presented in a pool report by ITN's Sandy Gall who portrayed coalition forces going across Saddam Hussein's "much vaunted sand fortifications." Gall reported that coalition bombardment of Iraqi positions preceded the incursion of Kuwaiti and Saudi vehicles ten to fifteen miles into Kuwait in the direction of Kuwait City, where the troops "advanced like clockwork." There were no trenches of burning oil, and only a lone Saudi foxhole and broken artillery gun, though some Iraqi prisoners were captured about ten miles in. This first report showed no real opposition from Iraqi forces and the so-called "Saddam line" was appearing to be a myth.

ITN's Jeremy Thompson presented a pool report with the first eyewitness account of the battle area, interviewing U.S. F-15 pilots who described activity all along the border area and fires throughout Kuwait. According to Thompson, coalition troops were racing across the desert in a very broad area with no resistance, while British artillery shelled Iraqi positions. Over 200 burning oil fields created the background to the battle, a scene one U.S. pilot described as "looking like hell." Apache helicopters flew into Iraqi-held territory and used laser-guided technology to find their targets, proving to be very effective tank killers.[6] The British "Desert Rats" (an elite infantry unit) were said to be racing across the desert in the West, and multiple rocket launchers were reportedly firing at Iraqi positions. Thompson concluded that "the full force of Desert Storm is now being unleashed."

Another ITN report, by Geoffrey Archer, described the preparation of the battlefield by fuel-air bombs and napalm and indicated that coalition forces were easily progressing toward Kuwait City through "Iraq's static defenses." Other coalition forces within Iraq were proceeding toward Republican Guard forces, with one division racing as far north as the Euphrates. A Kuwaiti exile claimed that Kuwait City would be liberated by the next day—its independence day. Reports indicated that Iraqi soldiers were surrendering by the thousands.

So far, then, all reports were extremely upbeat, though there was some exaggeration. The first sign that things were going *really well,* however, was an unscheduled press conference by General Schwarzkopf. Although a news blackout was in effect, obviously Schwarzkopf had some good news and couldn't wait to brag about the success of his operation. In addition, as CBS correspondent Susan Spencer would report later in the morning, Schwarzkopf broke the announced forty-eight-hour news blackout immediately in order to upstage the Pentagon and be the first to provide the good news. CNN reported later that Schwarzkopf was also concerned because British and French military authorities were giving briefings that gave the impression that they were doing splendidly in conquering Iraqi forces with a little help from the Americans.

So about 9:00 A.M., EST, General Schwarzkopf strode confidently into the briefing room and stated that he would provide a brief assessment of the progress of the ground campaign. Schwarzkopf claimed that the coalition forces had reached all of their first-day objectives and were continuing their attack, speeding to their destinations. With one exception, contact with enemy forces could be characterized as light. A marine task force was counterattacked by enemy armor, but the enemy quickly retreated when fire was returned. Ten hours into the offensive, more than 500 Iraqi prisoners have been taken and "friendly casualties are remarkably light." Schwarzkopf cautioned that the U.S.-led forces were doing very well, but the war was not over yet. Opposition was light, Schwarzkopf conjectured, because of the "excellent job in preparing the battlefield." So far the general was delighted with the progress of the campaign.

The usually loquacious Schwarzkopf answered questions brusquely in a shot-gun fashion and rudely refused any followups, controlling the media as totally as he controlled his troops. Stormin' Norman was also continuing to present the misleading impression that his goal was merely to get Iraqi troops out of Kuwait; indeed in his next major briefing he would concede that his goal was much greater (see 9.3). When asked if the reason that the Iraqi opposition was so light was that allied troops were avoiding a frontal confrontation with the Iraqis, Schwarzkopf answered brutally that: "We're going to go around, over, through, on top, underneath, and any other way it takes to beat them." It would soon appear for anyone with the eyes to see, that the allied troops were merely advancing without opposition and massacring anything in its way in a total slaughter of the Iraqi army that didn't have a chance against the high-tech military forces arrayed against them (see Chapters 9 and 10.2 for details of the carnage).

At this point, however, one did not know whether one should believe Schwarzkopf or not in light of the greatly exaggerated success stories of the first night of the air war when a Pentagon disinformation source claimed that the U.S.-led coalition was winning an overwhelming victory and that the war would soon be over. This time, however, it turned out that Schwarzkopf's confidence and optimism were justified. In retrospect, it would be interesting to know the extent to which the Pentagon knew in advance that they were assured of an easy victory over a demoralized and outclassed Iraqi army, or if they themselves were surprised at the ease of the victory.

CNN's Perry Smith explained that Schwarzkopf was running "a very fast campaign" that would go quickly to victory. It is "more impressive," General Smith enthused, "than anything we've seen in history, even more impressive than the 1967 Israeli campaign" (the Six-Day War). In fact, it is "one of the most impressive campaigns in history" and would be over in just a matter of days. And so Smith continued his rhetoric in praise of the wonders of the U.S. military, repeated his belief that the first four to six hours were the key, and as the initial phase went so well, the ground war would be an easy "mopping-up operation," and it turned out this time that he was correct. Obviously, Smith's friends in the Pentagon had told him that a rout was at hand and he was able to hype the massacre as a brilliant military victory, continuing his PR work for the Pentagon.

Reporting from Saudi Arabia on the "CBS Sunday Morning" show hosted by Charles Kuralt, Dan Rather followed General Schwarzkopf's briefing with the first footage of surrendering Iraqi soldiers, which showed a couple of scared and hungry-looking fellows who had been dropped into the desert and subjected to incredibly heavy bombardment. Eric Engberg recounted that there were reports from military sources that Kuwait City was now in the hands of the allies. Rather pointed out that the first reports of this success came from Kuwaiti news sources, but now military reports also confirmed this. According to Engberg, U.S. paratroopers made a drop into Kuwait City and the "shock power that airborne forces bring to the battlefield" supposedly overpowered the Iraqis. This was total disinformation as it would take a couple more days to occupy Kuwait City. Engberg then circulated once more the propaganda line of the day concerning the atrocity stories and Iraqi scorched earth policy that he claimed might have encouraged the president to undertake the ground war—this also was total nonsense as the ground war had been planned for weeks and would have taken place independent of alleged Iraqi atrocities, propaganda that the United States was spreading. The compliant Engberg disseminated the horror stories without raising a shadow of doubt, though Dan Rather had to caution him about accepting at face value all of the stories he was being told by Kuwaiti sources.

There was, Engberg continued, no word of any amphibious assault, though there were 17,000 marines either proceeding with the assault or holding back. In sum, the coalition offensive was proceeding very smoothly and was encountering only light resistance. After this cheery report, Engberg, who earlier in the week came off as a great enthusiast for the ground war and a great hater of peace talk, put his glasses on, squinted at his list of Pentagon fed "information," and, satisfied that he had presented his "information" as fully as possible, grinned and took his glasses off again. CBS's military analyst, General Dugan, stated that the whole range of operations were now engaged and were moving forward "forcibly." He claimed that the areas that the allies were fighting in were "well prepared." Dan Rather, waxing poetical, described the Kuwaiti battlefield as an eerie sight as the sun went down, because of the dark, hazy sky produced by over 300 burning oil wells. Using sports metaphors once again, Rather praised General Schwarzkopf's "fast break offensive" and "quick lightning strike for a lightning win." Schwarzkopf would utilize the football metaphor the next day when he described his strategy as a "Hail Mary" play whereby all forces go racing down the field as fast as they can from all sides to score a big win (see 9.3). Rather said that the Iraqis were being "wiped out" by the allied invasion, which was a "blowup" for the allied forces, and if this held up, the war could be over very quickly. Engberg commented that this was precisely the plan—to use armored forces to overpower the Iraqis quickly and drive them to surrender. The cake walk was on and would continue until the high-tech massacre was over.

As the morning proceeded, a significant flow of video came in via pool footage, cleared by military censors, sent up quickly to the satellites, and the networks were airing all footage of the theater of war immediately. Countless replays of desert footage showed forlorn Iraqi prisoners, a few abandoned foxholes, fires burning in oil wells, and allied forces racing unimpeded through Kuwait. Iraqi soldiers were depicted waiting throughout the desert with white flags, ready to surrender, and the allied forces were portrayed rushing through the desert meeting little or no resistance. The "Saddam Line" had turned out to be a fraud promoted equally by the Iraqis and the U.S. military and their compliant media.

In an interesting exchange, ABC military expert Bernard Trainor told Peter Jennings that he was surprised that the Iraqis had shown so little resistance and that the allies punched through their fortifications with "such alacrity." Based on his scrutiny of "unclassified satellite photos," Trainor was led to believe that Iraq had stronger fortifications, even on the front line (though obviously these Iraqi positions had been "attrited" from the heavy bombing). The question that no one posed, though, was whether Schwarzkopf and his commanders, and Bush and his war team, knew all along that the ground war would be a massacre with few casualties or if they too were genuinely surprised.

Later in the morning, CBS's Jim Stewart at the Pentagon advised that reports of Kuwait City's liberation were premature, though allied forces were actually outside of the city. NBC continued to beat the drum of the dramatic success of the AirLand war plan that was meeting little or no resistance, and added that Iraqi soldiers were eager to surrender. ABC's Sam Donaldson narrated a video of Saudi Arabian troops going through the sand fortifications into Kuwait, and the images showed miserable Iraqi bunkers and dejected prisoners of war about ten miles inside Kuwait. In a British ITN report that followed on ABC, the Iraqi defenses looked totally inadequate and Sandy Gall pointed out that there was no flaming oil and no Iraqi resistance, not even any troops. The question at this point was whether all Iraqi frontline defenses had moved back to second and third lines of defense or whether their military had simply collapsed.

After an incredible segment celebrating George Bush (see 10.4), NBC's Pentagon correspondent Fred Francis came on to report that General Powell had just called the president to say that "things are going very well, extremely well." Following this line, Francis claimed that "things are moving very fast, much better than we expected" (note the "we" identifying Francis with the Pentagon). There has been "very little resistance" and "we have so many prisoners that we don't know what to do with them all." The plan, Francis confided, was to go north of the Republican Guard to destroy them or to force a surrender. Once again, a Pentagon insider made it clear that the U.S. military was not just content to drive Iraqis out of Kuwait, but intended to cut off and destroy the Republican Guard, the heart of the Iraqi military.

CBS Pentagon correspondent David Martin supported this appraisal and announced that his sources in the Pentagon claimed that in the first three hours of the war, U.S. casualties were "in the single digits," though Martin warned that the Republican Guards had not been engaged and so things might turn more difficult at this point. Martin noted that the Pentagon was claiming that the Iraqi communication system had been destroyed and that the Iraqi military, including the Republican Guards, did not know what was going on and were thus effectively "shut down" as a coherent fighting force—though this remained to be confirmed. Charles Kuralt, giving away again the true end of the operation, noted that the Republican Guards were going to be surprised when the allied troops "swung down on them." Martin admitted that the whole operation was designed to engage the Republican Guards, saying that the Republican Guards were the "center of gravity" and that the operation was designed to draw them out and to destroy them.

On ABC, military analyst Tony Cordesman indicated that the theater of operations was now cut in half, and both the Republican Guards and Iraqi forces in Kuwait were being encircled for the kill. Peter Jennings asked if perhaps the commentators were not "speaking about this too quickly" and Cordesman admitted that this might be true. Cordesman— who had been one of the major promoters of the ferocious Iraqi troops armed with powerful fortifications, artillery, and chemical weapons—admitted finally that the first line of defenses was obviously weak. He now believed the Iraqi troops had retreated to the second line of defenses or were killed or captured (as it would turn out, the Iraqis had practically no lines of defense after forty days of fierce pounding). The town of al-Jahra was a key goal, Cordesman explained, as this would provide easy access to Kuwait City and would block any escape (earlier CNN had reported, following Kuwaiti sources, that al-Jahra was seized, but there was no official confirmation). Gen. Bernard Trainor came on and indicated that it appeared that the allies had cut off various avenues of retreat for the Iraqi army, both in Kuwait and southern Iraq, and that they were moving as far north as the Euphrates River to cut off retreating Iraqis from escaping north to Baghdad.

Jennings concluded the ABC report by noting that we were now seeing for the first time the face of the Iraqi army and its suffering on the battlefield. The video images presented the Iraqis as rather wretched and hardly threatening; one clip, shown by ABC on this segment and rerun throughout the day, showed an Iraqi soldier about to collapse and kissing his Egyptian captor; another would show surrendering Iraqis kissing the hand of an embarrassed American. In his wrap-up, Jennings summarized the events, citing General Schwarzkopf's claims that everywhere the allied forces had met their first day's objectives with "astonishingly light" casualties and no indications of chemical weapons.

CBS's Eric Engberg described how "Task Force Ripper" easily penetrated Iraqi defenses that were "only lightly defended." The U.S.-led coalition forces also found poorly maintained mine fields and fortifications, which they had easily breached, and quickly moved to the second line of Iraqi defensive fortifications. Things were going equally well here with air power being used to pummel Iraqi troops, making it easy for coalition ground forces to advance. The emphasis now, Engberg claimed, was to shift to close air support for the ground troops as they advanced. The level of sorties had been stepped up, with numerous missions flown in support of marines as they advanced, as well as against Republican Guards in southern Iraq. So, in short, Engberg concluded, there was less trouble getting through Iraqi fortifications than anticipated and Dan Rather summed up the Iraqi plight: "low maintenance, low morale."

Rather concluded by noting that there were many pool reports of penetration into Kuwait by coalition forces, but what the large U.S.-led forces were doing in southern Iraq had been "shrouded in mystery": the forty-eight-hour battle plan was still unfolding and "the questions in the air" concerned how far north into Iraq coalition forces were advancing, whether a deep air envelopment was being employed, where and when coalition forces would turn on the Republican Guard, and whether the

Republican Guards would resist. Continuing to play up the drama of the situation, Rather presented the war as an exciting story which would be continued the next day, advising the audience to stay tuned to CBS for any new developments.

In addition to the special news programs covering the ground war, the usual Sunday morning talk programs, such as "This Week With David Brinkley," focused on the Gulf war. On a stunningly ideological episode on Brinkley's program, Jack Smith provided a documentary summary of the week's events that could easily have been produced by the White House, it so perfectly reproduced their propaganda lines. The episode began with images of Iraq's "scorched earth" policy in Kuwait and reports of Iraqi atrocities that legitimated moving into the ground war. Smith presented the week's diplomatic activity, precisely as the Bush administration did, with the Soviets and Iraqis proposing intolerable preconditions that would save Saddam Hussein's face, regime, and military. The Bush administration refusal to negotiate was presented as manly, and Henry Kissinger came on to indicate that it was necessary to have a "decisive military victory," so that "it is absolutely clear who won and lost."

The message was that Saddam Hussein's survival would be tolerable only if he was totally diminished and his military was destroyed. In the United States, Jack Smith reported, the whole country was behind the war effort and wanted victory. David Gergin of *U.S. News and World Report,* Reagan's former media director, exulted that "I think now that whatever apprehensions people have had, they are willing to put them aside for the point that we have to finish the job, that we're on the verge of victory, we're about to crush the enemy." In other words, enjoy the slaughter and put all moral concern aside. Smith concluded his report with exultation in the coalition victory and the smashing defeat of Saddam Hussein. The end was near and as we shall see in the next two chapters it would be a bloody one that would be celebrated as a great victory by the U.S. and its coalition allies.

Notes

1. See the *Wall Street Journal,* Feb. 7, 1991, pp. A1 and A6. Rather had shot down the earlier Iraqi-Soviet peace proposal on February 12 by stating jocularly, "If you consider this a kind of Iraqi-Soviet Scud, . . . Marlin Fitzwater at the White House has fired what amounts to a diplomatic Patriot at it." Thus does Rather imply that a peace proposal is threatening and dangerous and that shooting it down is patriotic.

2. Curiously, twice during the afternoon, a hysterical Tom Fenton reported for CBS from Tel Aviv that Saddam Hussein had accepted the ultimatum, as if a diplomatic solution was indeed at hand; oddly, Dan Rather did not correct him.

3. This and some other brutal videos showing Iraqis being massacred were shown to reporters but not to the public. After the war, the Canadian Broadcasting Corporation (CBC) aired some tapes showing U.S. pilots exulting in the destruction of Iraqi tanks and other targets, but I have seen no such tapes aired on U.S. television. A documentary shown on the Arts and Entertainment (A&E) network, "Journals of War," on May 16, 1992, revealed U.S. military personnel describing the slaughter of Iraqi troops in the ground war, including the burying of live Iraqis in ditches and bunkers with bulldozers, which a U.S. officer described as a "good tactic"; see the further discussion of the ground war in Chapters 9 and 10.

4. It seems that the networks are choosing more conservative personnel to serve as White House correspondents. During the Bush era, for example, ABC replaced Sam Donaldson with Brit Hume, and CBS replaced liberal Leslie Stahl with the more conservative Wyatt Andrews. For examples of Hume's liberal bashing, see the right-wing journal *Insight,* July 29, 1991, pp. 33ff.

5. Later, a right-wing critique of press control emerged evident in the *U.S. News and World Report* book *Triumph Without Victory* (1992) which argued that the public was denied access to the heroic achievements of the U.S. military due to the tight censorship of images and news from the front. Actually, the U.S. military has plenty of official tapes and pictures of the ground war which have not yet been released. The high-tech massacre of the Iraqis would no doubt make a popular series of horror movies, *Desert Slaughter* I-XVI.

6. In fact, there was a great debate after the war concerning whether the Apaches were or were not such great tank killers (see 4.3).

CHAPTER NINE

◆

Endgame

AND SO THE BUSH administration rejected any diplomatic conclusion to the Gulf war, and the AirLand war began hours after the deadline. As the ground war began, the TV networks revealed that during the visit of Colin Powell and Dick Cheney to Saudi Arabia on the weekend of February 9 a decision had been made that 8:00 P.M. February 23 would be the "go date." Consequently, during the time of the Soviet/Iraqi peace negotiations, Bush decided that if he was to carry out the Pentagon's plan, he would have to set an ultimatum for noon Saturday, so as not to postpone the ground offensive. Schwarzkopf therefore had the go-ahead in his hand, and the White House and the Pentagon were just waiting for the deadline to pass in order to begin the AirLand war. Thus, the Soviet and Iraqi peace initiatives were just a sideshow that the war planners sabotaged by delivering an ultimatum that it would be impossible for the Iraqis to accept.

9.1 The Destruction of Iraq

By noon on February 24, twenty-four hours after Bush's deadline and sixteen hours into the ground war, it was obvious that the U.S. strategy was not just to drive the Iraqis out of Kuwait, but to annihilate Saddam Hussein's military. This was clear from pronouncements from the Bush administration war team who spoke on the Sunday morning talk shows and from listening carefully to the military experts as well as looking at the maps of U.S. troop movements into southern Iraq aimed at cutting off the Republican Guards. Indeed, the allied offensive made no sense whatsoever as a plan to drive the Iraqis out of Kuwait, though it could be seen as a comprehensive plan to cut off and destroy Iraq's military. The French offensive in western Iraq, the U.S. envelopment of the Republican Guard, and the British forces' advance toward the Euphrates River in a bid to cut off Iraqi forces in Kuwait from Baghdad, as well as the establishment of a large refueling and supply base in western Iraq, all seemed aimed at cutting off and destroying the Republican Guard rather than facilitating the liberation of Kuwait.

Thus, everything that the Bush administration said about the liberation of Kuwait was camouflage, an ideological veil, for the final phase in the destruction of the Iraqi army. The term "liberation of Kuwait" was indeed hypocritical, for the Bush administration never supported democracy in the country and was in effect returning Kuwait to a feudal monarchy. Indeed, the "liberation" of Kuwait was a mere excuse for the destruction of the infrastructure of Iraq and the Iraqi military, especially the Republican Guard. The U.S. rejection of Iraq's February 15 offer to leave Kuwait, of the Soviet proposal of February 22, and of Gorbachev's proposal to let the UN mediate between the Soviet and U.S. peace proposals on the eve of the ground war made it clear that the U.S. did not seek a diplomatic settlement, or merely the departure of Iraqi troops from Kuwait, but a decisive military victory and the destruction of the Iraqi military. Those in the Congress and the media pundits, as well as U.S. allies, who believed that the Gulf war was about the liberation of Kuwait were duped and taken in by U.S. rhetoric that stated over and over that they were "only" aiming at the liberation of Kuwait, that they were enforcing UN resolutions, and thus were pursuing limited goals when actually they had a much more ambitious program in mind. It seemed that for the U.S. government only a goal so significant as the destruction of Iraqi power and the establishment of George Bush and the U.S. military as the superpowers of the world would justify such an enormous undertaking. Merely pushing Saddam Hussein out of Kuwait could hardly justify such an overwhelming marshaling of resources, expense, and the risks involved in carrying through an all-out war.

The goal of destroying Iraq and its military power explains why the bombing campaign was so long, why Iraq's economic and communications infrastructure was destroyed, why much in Iraq was reduced to rubble, and why the ground war was the necessary culmination of the massacre. If the goal had been merely to push the Iraqis out of Kuwait, this could have been easily achieved diplomatically, or much earlier with military force. If the goal had been merely the liberation of Kuwait, all of the coalition's firepower could have been aimed at Kuwait City and Iraqi troop formations within Kuwait. Had the liberation of Kuwait been the goal, the incredible concentration of coalition military power could have also been aimed at liberating oil wells and other economic sites within Kuwait. In fact, the liberation of Kuwait with military force could have been accomplished weeks earlier and presumably have saved Kuwait much property and many lives, and perhaps have avoided the environmental catastrophe from the burning Kuwaiti oil wells. But, no, this was not what the Gulf war was all about and, as we shall see, George Bush and his team were perfectly willing to sacrifice Kuwait to achieve their goals.

Thus, the stakes were much higher than the Bush administration and media let on. Destroying the Iraqi military would be harder to achieve and more risky than simply liberating Kuwait, which, after twenty-four hours of the ground campaign, was looking relatively easy. The elite of the British, French, and U.S. coalition forces had embarked on a danger-ous mission within Iraq itself, in desert country without a water supply, full of dangerous diseases, and possible environmental contamination from the destruction of its nuclear, biological, and chemical weapons facilities. The season of monsoon rains and sandstorms was approaching and the coalition forces could have been overpowered by the unpredict-able forces of nature, impervious to the control of the war managers. There were also thousands of Republican Guards and other hostile forces who could harm the coalition troops as they rushed to cut off the Iraqi military from escape to northern Iraq and as they prepared to draw them out to fight and annihilate them. Obviously, the plan was to use U.S.-led coalition troops as a bait to draw out the Republican Guards so that coalition air and ground power could exterminate them. But it remained to be seen whether the Republican Guards were paper tigers, whether they had been destroyed beyond the point where they could mount an effective offensive, inflict heavy casualties on the coalition forces, or even defend themselves.

Neither the escalation of the war goals nor the risks involved in invading and occupying Iraq were discussed in the mainstream media. The coalition propaganda apparatus was well organized, and one ob-served throughout the day of February 24 a significant mobilization of world public opinion behind Bush's unilateral decision to launch a ground war. The British prime minister, John Major, taped a message affirming the need to enter the ground war phase, and Queen Elizabeth made the first royal speech in favor of war since World War II. As we have seen, the stakes were much higher than the befogged publics were aware, and an all-out propaganda offensive was orchestrated by the White House. France's President Mitterrand chimed in with some banalities about how the ground war was inevitable, and at least some of the Arab allies—the Saudis, Kuwaitis, and the Turks—came out in favor of the ground war. It was striking that the coalition forces all said more or less the same thing, repeating the propaganda line of the White House.

I analyzed earlier how the White House propaganda apparatus mobi-lized the U.S. government, its domestic friends, and coalition forces to support the propaganda line of the day (Chapter 5). The goal now was to mobilize the entire alliance behind the ground war. The mainstream media, especially television, served this purpose with hardly any voices questioning Bush's escalation of the war. The ground war began and Congress, the media, and much of the public simply accepted and even welcomed it. The only discordant voices which appeared in the mainstream media were the muted Soviet objections to the ground campaign. Although the Soviets were probably extremely angry at Bush's rejection of Gorbachev's peace plan, they bit their tongues, put on a good face, and muttered banalities about the need to maintain good superpower relations.[1] The only criticisms of the ground war came from Iraq's allies— Yemen, Cuba, and Jordan—positioning any opponent of the ground war as pro-Iraqi. One would see few, if any, media images of antiwar demonstrations or hear any voices of dissent from this position until the end of the war, though there were, in fact, many demonstrations and dissenters in the United States and elsewhere. The media pulled behind the Bush administration and Pentagon and faithfully advanced their war policies until the end, compliant servants of power.

The dominant theme was the propaganda of an easy ground war and quick victory for the allied forces—propaganda that accurately portrayed the outcome. The notion of a quick victory was mobilized by the discourse of the application of sudden and massive air, land, and sea power which would overwhelm the Iraqis. The networks had prepared this concept by talking of the greatest mobilization of military force in history. The rhetoric of the overwhelming military firepower assembled was supported by their early claims about "remarkable successes," "amazingly low casualties," and "meeting little Iraqi resistance." In retrospect, it was fairly certain that this would be the case, as the Iraqi forces within Kuwait were either destroyed or totally demoralized after weeks of bombing. Thus, it was reasonably certain that the U.S. war managers could justifiably assure the public of rapid success in the opening phase of the ground war.

The image of an easy AirLand war victory was bolstered by pictures of a blitzkrieg across the Kuwaiti border and a triumphant march toward Kuwait City with little or no resistance. There were numerous video reports of coalition forces racing across the border uncontested. There were frequent images of Iraqi POW's surrendering, including a striking picture of what looked like hundreds of Iraqi prisoners marching single file across the desert with their hands over their heads. Images of an Iraqi prisoner kissing an Egyptian soldier before collapsing were shown repeatedly, as were pictures of a group of surrendering Iraqis kissing the hands of their U.S. captors and breaking into tears. The administration/ media line was that Iraqi troop morale was totally destroyed and that victory would be easy—a discourse that turned out to be true this time.

But, in a sense, the images of the blitzkrieg into Kuwait made it appear too easy and could have raised the question as to whether the entire ground war was a propaganda set-up, a cake walk carefully orchestrated and hyped by the U.S. war managers and their media allies. In retrospect, the media greatly exaggerated what forces the coalition troops would face as they crossed the Kuwaiti border. Repeatedly, TV viewers saw graphics, sketches, and computer simulations that portrayed the sand fortifications (berms), mines, barbed wire, ditches of burning oil, tanks, and well-armed Iraqi troops armed with powerful armor, artillery, and chemical weapons. For months, military "experts" had pontificated about the "battle-hardened Iraqi army" and their "elite Republican Guards." What one saw, by contrast, in the first video footage of the allied invasion of Kuwait, was an almost empty desert with Iraqi fox holes and primitive bunkers, scattered mines, a few ditches with oil, and some abandoned rusty Iraqi tanks and vehicles.

In interpreting the significance of the initial pictures of great numbers of Iraqi prisoners, reportedly thousands in the first two days, commentators indicated that the frontline Iraqi troops were cannon fodder: conscripts, who were poorly trained, unmotivated, and miserable after months in the harsh desert. They were poorly fed, though they did not appear to be starving, and had been subject to weeks of bombing and torment. It was certain that thousands of these Iraqi conscripts would surrender and it turned out that many of them were Shiite and Kurdish troops hardly eager to fight for the Hussein regime. General Schwarzkopf and his crew must have known this, as they had total air supremacy and could fly over this region at will with their reconnaissance flights. The coalition troops had also already taken thousands of prisoners, or deserters, who had no doubt given them information on the pathetic state of the Iraqi troops in Kuwait. Moreover, Schwarzkopf and his war team must have known that these surrenders would create positive images of a quick allied victory.

Reports had emerged by the third week of the war that more than a quarter of the positions in Iraq's regular army in Kuwait were deserted and that an estimated one-fourth to one-third of the troops in Iraq's regular army in Kuwait had either defected, been taken prisoner, killed, or simply fled their positions (*Los Angeles Times,* Feb. 7, 1991). Many of these conscript troops returned to the cities from which they were drafted, or went into hiding. But these reports referred only to the regular Iraqi army in Kuwait and not to the Republican Guards or the Iraqi troops who were currently fighting the U.S.-led invaders in their own country. Would they, too, be such push-overs? And Kuwait City itself? Would the Iraqis abandon it without a fight? What would be the fate of the coalition forces in occupied Iraq and how and when would the liberation of

Kuwait be achieved? These were the questions that would be raised and answered during the next days.

9.2 Desert Slaughter

After the early morning news reports of February 24, there was no more significant news the rest of the day. The information cap was so tight that even the evening news programs had little new to report. Obviously, the opening day's incursion into Kuwait went extremely well, but it was not yet clear how the allied troops were faring in southern Iraq. For the next several days, the U.S. military tightly controlled the flow of news from this field of operations, so as to conceal the magnitude of the slaughter of Iraqi forces.

On February 25, Day 40 in the Persian Gulf war, CNN depicted Marlin Fitzwater saying that White House officials were suffering "the anxiety that comes with war." One imagined that the coalition soldiers, spending the night in an unfamiliar and dangerous desert environment were also feeling some anxiety, as were their loved ones on the home front. CNN reported that Kuwaiti troops were celebrating their independence day in Kuwait and hoping for the liberation of their country that day. Saudi radio reported that Arab troops and U.S. Marines were on the edge of Kuwait City. Images showed the relentless U.S.-led coalition advance with troops moving across the border, clearing mines, and inexorably moving toward Kuwait City. There were images of long lines of Iraqi prisoners of war marching through the desert, hungry, in poor physical shape and dejected. Fourteen thousand Iraqi soldiers had reportedly been taken prisoner and no chemical weapons had been used. Allied petroleum and supply lines were having trouble keeping up with the allied tanks because the advance was so fast. The report once again was upbeat.

In the first live Pentagon report of the day, CNN's Gene Randall recounted that the news blackout was still in force, but a briefing would be coming up in the morning. Randall noted that there was the prospect of heavy fighting ahead, as it had long been thought that the Republican Guards would put up fierce resistance. The Iraqis had fired a Silkwood missile at U.S. ships but missed (later, the British claimed that their antimissile forces destroyed it). In a report a bit later in the morning, Randall noted that the Republican Guard was moving out and that this may be "the defining moment of the war" with a major battle ahead. He indicated that one incident could bring significant casualties and warned against premature euphoria.

CNN's correspondent Greg LaMotte reported from Saudi Arabia that Saddam Hussein had launched three Scud attacks on the desert kingdom, but the Scuds did not seem to be working—they exploded in the air and caused no damage. In a report by Jeremy Thompson from ITN, it was evident how easy it had been for the coalition forces on the way up the road to Kuwait City. The video showed carcasses of Iraqi vehicles littering the way, just fifty miles from Kuwait City. There was an abandoned trench full of oil and Thompson reported that "Saddam's army had fled without even lighting the fires." The allied forces have, he said, charged forward meeting little resistance; British pilots were amazed by the rate of the movement of Iraqi targets, fleeing from the allies. There was little resistance from the Iraqis, and U.S. Apache helicopters were said to have played a key role in destroying Iraqi equipment and troops, using Hellfire missiles to ravage tanks at night. The passage through the mine fields had been carefully marked by allied engineers and was not proving to be particularly difficult; furthermore, the mine fields were in disrepair.

CNN's Mike Chinoy reported from Saudi Arabia that up to eighty tanks of the elite Republican Guards appeared to be coming out to fight in southern Iraq, according to coalition pilots who had flown over them. This might be the long promised great tank battle, hyped constantly as "the greatest since World War II." But it would also bring the Iraqi tanks out into the open, which was what the U.S.-led coalition wanted: Once the Republican Guard moved out of their bunkers, Chinoy explained, coalition air power could bomb them. The Republican Guard was reportedly moving out and the coalition forces were preparing for the great battle.

Throughout the day, CNN provided continuing reports of allied advances to Kuwait City. So far, however, there was no amphibious landing, though the TV networks dutifully reported that preparations continued on the boats off the coast. Marines were ready and in position if called on. There were repetitive accounts of remarkably large numbers of POWs, and Iraqis continuing to emerge from bunkers waving white flags. Brian Jenkins of CNN reported from the border area that he saw 500 Iraqi POWs who had been brought to his area; Jenkins had hooked up with Saudi forces who were moving into Kuwait and provided, first, live satellite radio reports and, then, live satellite TV reports. The Iraqi POWs, he claimed, were kneeling and didn't look frightened, but resigned and almost happy, now that the fighting was over. Jenkins was twenty miles inside Kuwait and stated that resistance, based on the evidence of burned-out Iraqi vehicles, was not as fierce as might have been expected, though the frontline Iraqis might be third stringers and not Iraq's best.

At 8:00 A.M., on "CBS This Morning," Paula Zahn reported that allied forces were within "striking distance" of Kuwait City and could take it "within hours." CBS had hooked up correspondent Bob McKeown with coalition Arab forces going into Kuwait who had just experienced an artillery battle. He reported that the coalition convoy was stopped when pockets of Iraqis resisted with artillery fire, but U.S. air power came in to destroy the Iraqis. McKeown described how there was some Iraqi artillery fire when they crossed the border in the early morning, but that it was quickly silenced. He indicated that there were mines and unexploded cluster bombs everywhere; Saudi troops had been clearing the mines, and helicopters were also clearing mines by exploding them from the air. The whole landscape appeared desolate in the satellite TV footage, showing burned out vehicles, bombed roads, and downed power lines. There were paths beside the road formed by Saudi engineers, and McKeown's convoy was staying close to this safe path.

CBS reported that the Republican Guards and allied forces may have been clashing already. CBS's Robert Krulwich speculated that the Republican Guards may have sent out a feinting force to fight so that the rest could escape, but CBS military adviser Gen. Bob Wagner smiled and claimed that they cannot escape, that Iraqi troops are trapped in both Kuwait and southern Iraq; they are "sealed off, blocked off." A major battle was shaping up and Wagner claimed that "it will be a great success for our side." He believed that there was probably already contact between the Republican Guards and coalition forces in southern Iraq and that the battle for Kuwait City had also probably begun, and that these would be the two battles to follow.

On NBC's "Today," the headlines predicted that Kuwait City would be liberated by the end of the day by 30,000 U.S. marines and paratroopers, who along with Kuwaiti and Saudi forces, prepared to invade the city. Although allied forces had met some resistance, they were still moving quickly toward Kuwait City and amphibious feints by marines were continuing along the coast to keep the Iraqis guessing. Conflicting reports, however, continued to circulate about the movements of the Republican Guards. CBS's Jim Stewart reported that eighty-nine Republican Guard tanks were advancing and that perhaps as much as a division of the Republican Guard was moving toward a major confrontation and that this would be the first time that U.S. forces were taking on the best of the Iraqi armies.

Contradictory information emerged shortly thereafter from NBC's Jim Miklasewski who said that the Pentagon now claimed that the Republican Guards had not yet come out to fight, that the earlier reports were false. NBC's Tom Aspell observed from Baghdad that Iraq claimed that the reports about the capture of Failaka Island by coalition forces were also false and that it was occupied by 4,000 well-armed Iraqi troops; later, it would turn out that this was true. CBS predicted that the liberation of Kuwait City would not take place that day and was most likely at least a day away. These slightly different spins on events raised questions as to what was really going on and the suspicion that once again the U.S. military was greatly exaggerating its early successes or covering over setbacks. This time, however, it really was winning big and was engaging in a desert slaughter of the Iraqi forces.

The next day the *New York Times* reported, that "Air Force officers at a higher level said they doubted that the tanks spotted on the move belonged to the [Republican] Guards" (Feb. 26, 1991, p. A7). Despite this denial, most of the network correspondents and anchors continued to chatter throughout the day about the great tank battle occurring between the coalition forces and the Republican Guards. The media pundits had not yet figured out that there would be no great battles in this war, that it was a one-sided slaughter and not a war where opposing troops actually engaged and killed each other in combat.

Stories of Iraqi crimes in Kuwait began early in the morning of February 25 and multiplied throughout the day. Early telecasts repeated the stories of the previous day, and, during the Saudi briefing, General Khalid, Schwarzkopf's Saudi counterpart in girth, ego, and instrumental relation to truth, reported that Iraqis in Kuwait were "doing horrible things": "I hate to say it, but they are killing people by axes, they rape females, cut certain parts of them and hang them in every street" (see 10.1 for critique of these claims). Khalid, whose own people still had courts of Islamic justice that sentence thieves to have their hands cut off and adulterous women to be stoned to death,[2] summoned up great moral indignation and threatened that Iraqis who commit atrocities will be tried as war criminals. Bush's national security adviser, Brent Scowcroft, appeared in news clips saying that the "Iraqis were virtually producing genocide in Kuwait City."

There was some skepticism, however. When told by ABC's Sam Donaldson that a fax from the Free Kuwait group in London was circulating in Saudi Arabia indicating that the coalition forces had captured and liberated Kuwait City, Peter Jennings said that they had received a similar fax that they were dismissing. Reports from inside Kuwait, Jennings pointed out, were "fairly dicey." CBS's Dan Rather also had to warn his correspondent Eric Engberg that the reports of Iraqi atrocities inside Kuwait City were not reliable. Yet these reports continued to circulate through the day. General Neal reported in his U.S. military briefing in Saudi Arabia that Iraq was carrying out systematic terrorism against economic sites in Kuwait and destroying buildings in Kuwait City. Throughout the afternoon of February 25, CNN said that "reasonably reliable sources" indicated that Iraq had orders to destroy 180 buildings in Kuwait City, including the presidential palace (though that was already reported as destroyed), and that Iraqi troops were destroying hospitals, schools, and grocery stores. Obviously, the CNN news readers did not know that they were in an intense propaganda war as well as a ground war.³

Raising suspicions that coalition war aims were being dramatically escalated, speculation began to circulate as to whether the elimination of Saddam Hussein and his regime was now the goal of the war. On the early morning ABC news program, Mike Schneider asked White House correspondent Ann Compton, "if this is going as well as it appears, might they not expand their objectives?" (that is, beyond merely taking Kuwait). Compton replied that the United States had expanded its objectives long ago, they just hadn't announced them publicly. ABC happy-talk host Charlie Gibson also made a point of asking most of his guests if the elimination of Saddam Hussein was not necessary to claim victory, as did NBC "Today" host Bryant Gumbel. Most guests, such as a conservative British member of Parliament who appeared on NBC, claimed that it would be necessary to remove Saddam Hussein in order to declare victory and that this removal was a valid goal.

The military news was generally upbeat. At the U.S. military briefing in Saudi Arabia, General Neal, gaunt and unsmiling, described the battlefield as "dynamic and ever changing." He claimed that during the second day of the ground campaign the allies continued to attack Iraqi forces and continued to encounter only light to moderate resistance, while engaging Iraqi armor and ground forces with "tremendous success" in ongoing fights. Neal claimed the destruction of 270 Iraqi tanks in the past two days with over 18,000 Iraqis surrendering and few U.S. casualties (4 Americans killed and 21 wounded).

As the afternoon of February 25 progressed, the news got better and better. CNN reported on tremendous successes with U.S. forces preparing to engage the Republican Guards. The French claimed to have totally "neutralized" an entire division of Iraqi troops, and allied troops were reportedly marching on Kuwait City. But then the greatest tragedy of the war for the U.S. forces occurred. A Scud missile hit a residential complex outside of Dhahran where U.S. soldiers were residing, producing a huge explosion and a tremendous fire. In the initial report, Reuters claimed that twelve were killed and many were injured; eventually, the death count rose to twenty-eight.⁴ Mike Chinoy of CNN said that he had talked to a Saudi who witnessed the event and personally claimed to have pulled the bodies of four dead U.S. soldiers out of the rubble and that many were seriously wounded. A Patriot was said to have been fired at the Scud, but it was not yet certain if it hit or not, and obviously an "intercepted" Scud, Chinoy explained, can be very lethal. Later, the U.S. military claimed that the Scud broke up in the air so that no Patriot was fired, and then that the Scud was out of the Patriot's defense perimeter.

Finally, after floating these two lies, the U.S. military admitted that the Patriot computer system was down in the missile batteries that were supposed to protect the region of the city in which the Scud landed (*New York Times,* May 20, 1991, p. A1).

At 5:44 P.M., CNN interrupted its newscast to say that they had just received an AP report of Baghdad radio announcing that Saddam Hussein had ordered his troops out of Kuwait. Jeanne Moos reported on CNN from the UN that the Soviet ambassador had stated that Iraq was ready to withdraw from Kuwait in a short time, with no preconditions and with a stop in the fighting. Moos reported that this made little sense to the U.S. officials who said that they wanted to hear this directly from the Iraqis. Apparently, then, the Baghdad radio report was the way of making public the resolve of the Iraqis to leave Kuwait and to bring the war to a close. Moments thereafter, CNN transmitted an AP report that Tariq Aziz had communicated to the Soviet leadership that Iraq was ready to start an immediate and unconditional withdrawal. The endgame was beginning.

The United States, however, had more in mind than merely driving the Iraqis out of Kuwait and continued to fiercely keep up its military offensive, slaughtering Iraqi troops even when they were fleeing. There was no way that the Bush administration was going to allow Iraq's army to escape and its Republican Guards to be preserved. On the other hand, it was now clear that Saddam Hussein was a survivor after all, who finally saw that even in a ground war he could not really achieve any success against the high-tech coalition forces. After the announcement of the Iraqi retreat from Kuwait was broadcast, CNN, in the interests of promoting rational discourse, cut to a congressman who was promoting a bill to allow the assassination of Saddam Hussein. Rep. Bob McEwen (R-Ohio) denounced the "evil" Iraqi president, attacked Gorbachev and the Soviets, and said that the Soviet peace plan was totally unacceptable. McEwen failed to perceive that Iraq had announced its withdrawal and willingness to follow the key UN resolution concerning unconditional withdrawal from Kuwait; in effect, Iraq was admitting defeat and was surrendering. For McEwen, however, nothing except the statement, "I surrender" would do. McEwen also worried about the specter of the Soviet Union selling military hardware to Saddam in the future. Tobe Gati of the UN Association informed McEwen that in effect Saddam was saying "I surrender" and that this should wrap it up. Moreover, she argued, the goal of the UN resolutions was the liberation of Kuwait and not to go to Baghdad to get Saddam Hussein. McEwen responded that he himself did not hear Saddam say "I surrender" and then added that Saddam should be brought immediately to Arab justice.

And so once more Iraq had the Bush administration in a quandary. If Iraq started pulling out its forces from Kuwait unconditionally, what should be the U.S. response? The initial White House (non)reaction to the announcement of the Iraqi withdrawal was typical; Marlin Fitzwater said, "We know nothing about it. We've just heard the press reports." But the White House, Pentagon, State Department, and U.S. UN delegation immediately began planning their spin on the latest surprise move of Saddam Hussein.

At 6:00 P.M., CNN White House correspondent Frank Sesno reported that he had been told by a Bush administration official that large numbers of Iraqi tanks, troops, and equipment *were* withdrawing from Kuwait, that the United States was trying to "engage" the retreating Iraqi troops, but that bad weather was "preventing a full engagement" of the sort "that we usually enjoy." When asked why the U.S. military was still attacking the fleeing Iraqis, a "senior official" joked that "we are trying to destroy them. This will spur them along." Sesno claimed that President Bush wanted a "public avowal" of "total capitulation" from Iraq in order to end the war. Operation Desert Storm had obviously metamorphized into Operation Desert Slaughter.

From within Kuwait, Charles Jaco interviewed some marine grunts preparing for the battle for Kuwait City; they were pleased to hear the news but a couple of them said that there could be no victory without "taking out" Saddam Hussein. A Kuwaiti told Jaco that "Saddam Hussein has never told the truth" so we don't know if we can believe him. But, the Kuwaiti acknowledged that Hussein understood power, and that he probably understood that his soldiers were about to get destroyed, so it would be reasonable to conclude that he would actually accept the UN conditions to save his own skin and that of his retreating troops. CNN then reported that orders were given to the Iraqi armed forces to return to the positions where they had been stationed before August 1, 1990, and confirmed again that Iraqi troops were fleeing the country. But this would not be enough for George Bush and his war team.

CNN's Charles Bierbauer reported from the White House that Marlin Fitzwater was complaining that there was nothing that the Bush administration could respond to, "no authoritative contact," and so "the war goes on." Baghdad radio, he suggested, was not to be trusted. Bush was playing racquetball at the time, and Brent Scowcroft stated that they had heard nothing to stop them from prosecuting the war as planned. A senior White House official had told Bierbauer that allied troops were already in Iraq planning to engage the Republican Guard troops and that the destruction of the Republican Guard was a "de facto objective," admitting that once the ground war began, there was an "escalation in goals." The official also admitted to Bierbauer that toppling Saddam Hussein, though not a written objective, was "another de facto objective."

And so, off the record, the White House was now admitting that its true goals were the destruction of the Republican Guard and Saddam Hussein—though this could have been merely a ploy to temporarily placate public opinion which was overwhelmingly in favor of removing Hussein as the ultimate goal of the war. Wolf Blitzer of CNN reported from the Pentagon that there was no official response to the Iraqi withdrawal and that the war was continuing well ahead of schedule. The Pentagon claimed that the Iraqis have not been able to organize any significant counteroffensive. The Pentagon asserted that 300 Iraqi tanks had been destroyed since the beginning of the AirLand war and that over 25,000 POWs had been taken. It also acknowledged concern that the retreating Iraqi troops might be marching to engage the coalition troops in Iraq who were poised to destroy the Republican Guards. Later, it was revealed, however, that the Iraqi retreat was a complete rout and posed no military threat to the multinational forces whatsoever, suggesting that the U.S. military was using this hypothetical to legitimate the slaughter of the retreating Iraqi troops.

The Kuwaiti ambassador, a member of the al-Sabah family, Kuwait's ruling oligarchy, came on CNN to state that the Iraqi withdrawal was "too little, too late." This cliche, no doubt written by the U.S. propaganda managers or his own PR firm Hill and Knowlton, became the order of day and was repeated by Kuwaiti, Saudi, and other parrots of the U.S. military machine throughout the night. The only reason that the Iraqis were making such overtures, according to the Kuwaiti ambassador, was that they were trying to "sow confusion." The Kuwaiti implied that the Iraqis were trying to bring back the Soviet initiative, which all coalition forces had rejected. From a tactical point of view, he said, they were trying to escape before they were surrounded, and so the war should go on to destroy the Iraqis. Getting indignant, he exclaimed that too many lives have been lost, so we should not get excited about this peace proposal. We should instead, he advised, keep the war going, because, in effect, Saddam "has to surrender to the allied forces in Kuwait." The Kuwaiti then went through his litany of atrocities and claimed that he had himself seen security reports of fires and murder in the city. Once the city was liberated, it would be revealed that the Kuwaiti propaganda apparatus greatly exaggerated the damage and violence committed by the Iraqis during the last days of the occupation (see 10.1). Admittedly, the Iraqis had greatly harmed Kuwait and committed many criminal acts against its people, as George Bush and his military had been doing and would continue to do in the theater of war.

9.3 The War According to Schwarzkopf

By February 25, it was clear that the Iraqis were leaving Kuwait en masse and that the war for all practical purposes was over. The U.S. military, however, said that the Iraqi army was in a "fighting retreat" and was thus a legitimate military target as they continued systematically to slaughter them. On the evening of February 25, some hours after the Iraqis announced their retreat, the TV networks showed Bush's war team arriving at the White House for a meeting; soon after Marlin Fitzwater stated: "We will continue to prosecute the war," thus robbing Iraqi mothers and wives of many more sons and husbands. Fitzwater did say that "unarmed soldiers in retreat" would be spared, but "retreating combat units" would be dealt with as combat units and handled accordingly (that is, exterminated). As it turned out, the U.S. military massacred everything in sight, including some British troops mistaken for Iraqis, U.S. troops wiped out by "friendly fire," scores of Kuwaitis and others who had been taken as hostages by the fleeing Iraqis, and Palestinians and others who chose to flee with the Iraqis (see 10.2).

During the evening on the CNN talk shows, the two CNN military advisers, James Blackwell and Perry Smith, urged on the coalition forces to more slaughter of Iraqis, as did former Secretary of Defense Harold Brown and an apologist for the massacre, Michael Mandelbaum of Johns Hopkins University. Over the next couple of days as the Pentagon continued to annihilate fleeing Iraqis and as the Iraqis, with Soviet support, continued to affirm adherence to the UN resolutions, there were debates about whether the coalition forces could legitimately fire on a retreating army. The "official" position seemed to be that until a cease-fire was declared, the massacre of fleeing Iraqis was perfectly legitimate, though some reporters and media commentators had some doubts about its legality and morality. Interestingly, in a CBS report of February 25, CBS Pentagon correspondent David Martin pointed out that the Pentagon had said repeatedly that they would "not shoot retreating Iraqi soldiers in the back," although that was what they did. On my satellite dish that night, I picked up the feed of a reporter who had been told by a "Pentagon official": "We can shoot them in the ass as well as we can shoot them in the head." For the next few days, the U.S. forces would indeed shoot and kill fleeing Iraqis from the head to the toes, annihilating many of them with fuel air explosives, carpet bombing, and missiles, as well as burying alive hundreds more in trenches (see 9.4 and 10.2).

During February 26, Saddam Hussein himself made a public commitment to withdraw from Kuwait and to meet the UN resolution. This was, of course, not enough for George Bush, who pressed for unconditional surrender and ordered his forces to continue attacking Iraqi troops, which were now in total disarray. By February 27, it was announced that the U.S.-led coalition forces had blocked off Iraqi escape routes and were engaged in two major battles with Iraqi forces. These were hyped in the same terms as the opening day of the ground war as "ferocious," with "tremendous fighting," "the fiercest tank battles since World War II," but like the earlier "battles" of the ground fighting, it was really a Desert Slaughter, with the coalition forces systematically annihilating the out-gunned and demoralized Iraqis. And yet during the two days since the Iraqis began fleeing from Kuwait, there had been little hard information, not much new video, and obviously the military was not revealing what they were doing because they were engaged in one of the greatest massacres in history, the details of which would only trickle out in the days to come. It would be up to General Norman Schwarzkopf to provide a triumphant version of this brutal episode in U.S. military history, and Stormin' Norman was once again up to the task.

Wednesday evening, Saudi time, on February 27, Schwarzkopf began a briefing to describe the course of the war. Pleased as punch with himself and his punchy allied forces, he stomped in with his charts to brief the world concerning the marvelous success of the allied military operation. Schwarzkopf began with a highly dubious statement, claiming that "what we started out against was a couple of hundred thousand Iraqis that were in the Kuwait theater of operations." As I indicated in Chapter 1, commercial satellite photos and independent analyses of these photos suggested that there were far fewer Iraqi troops in Kuwait than the United States claimed. By saying at this late date that the Iraqis had a "couple of hundred thousand" troops, Schwarzkopf doubled the number of estimated Iraqi troops that were claimed to be in Saudi Arabia on August 7 when the U.S. troops officially began arriving (see 1.1).

Schwarzkopf then stated that in the middle of November the decision was made to increase the U.S. forces in Saudi Arabia "because by that time huge numbers of Iraqi forces had flowed in the area . . . and therefore, we increased the forces and built up more forces." This claim also is highly dubious, as if the buildup was a defensive move. Instead, if the commercial satellite photos were accurate, it could be that Iraq increased their forces in the Gulf as a response to the U.S. troop buildup; this point can and should be verified by independent analyses and sources. There was good reason to believe that at the time of the initial U.S. troop deployment, Iraq saw clearly that it faced a massive military force as well as an international economic embargo and that it would be suicidal to act in an offensive manner. There is also good reason to believe that the U.S. had decided to go to war and destroy Iraq and that the additional forces were sent over for this purpose. Senator Sam Nunn (D-Ga.) and others began to speak at this time of the U.S. forces switching from a defensive to an offensive posture, and a congressional debate ensued as to whether a Persian Gulf war was a good idea, with Bush and the Pentagon winning the debate. Thus, it appears that a decision was made that double the number of troops were needed, in order to quickly and decisively defeat Iraq.

In his briefing, General Schwarzkopf stated that he aligned his forces against Iraqi forces stationed in Kuwait and built up a strong naval presence. He bragged how he made it a key point to call attention to the naval forces in order to utilize a threat of a naval amphibious operation to draw the Iraqis to fortify the shore, and later described the feigned amphibious landing as a ploy to draw Iraqi troops to the coastal region. Schwarzkopf may or may not have been telling the truth here. Perhaps a failure to adequately clear the coastal region of mines prevented the amphibious troops from participating; interviews with the potential amphibious forces revealed that they were deeply disappointed that they were not able to participate in the AirLand war. There is good reason to believe that they were actually intended to participate and that their inability to sweep the mine fields in a timely fashion prevented their deployment. Obviously, all the major military forces would have liked to participate in the AirLand war and the lack of participation of the amphibious forces could have been due more to operational difficulties than to a conscious ploy by Schwarzkopf to deceive Iraqi defensive positions.[5]

Trying to make it appear that a fair fight was in the making, Schwarzkopf then claimed:

> Basically, the problem we were faced with was this: When you looked at the troop numbers, they really outnumbered us about 3 to 2. And when you consider the number of combat service support people we had, that's logisticians and that sort of thing, our armed forces, as far as fighting troops, we were really outnumbered 2 to 1. In addition to that, they had 4,700 tanks versus our 3,500 when the buildup was complete, and they had a great many more artillery then we do.
>
> I think any student of military strategy would tell you that in order to attack a position, you should have a ratio of approximately 3 to 1 in favor of the attacker. And in order to attack a position that is heavily dug in and barricaded, such as the one we had here, you should have a ratio of 5 to 1 in the way of troops in the favor of the attacker. . . . We were outnumbered at a minimum 3 to 2 as far as troops were concerned, we were outnumbered as far as tanks were concerned, and we had to come up with some way to make up the difference.

Once again, Schwarzkopf's figures were highly dubious. BBC reporter John Simpson argued that although the U.S. was claiming that the number of Iraqi troops in the theater of war was over 540,000: "After the war was over it became known that, when the Iraqi army was at full strength in early January, there were fewer than half that number: approximately 260,000. Once the bombing began, the desertions began in earnest. Tens of thousands simply headed home. In the front line among the conscripted men the desertion rate was sometimes more than 30 percent" (1991, p. 332). Thus Simpson concluded that by the time the ground offensive began, the Iraqi strength might have fallen below 200,000 compared to 525,000 coalition forces, giving the coalition forces a 2 to 2½ to 1 advantage.[6] Moreover, the quality of the Iraqi forces was vastly inferior. They had little or no intelligence capacity; much of their equipment was obsolete or nonfunctional; their troops were poorly trained and motivated; and there were even reports after the war that senior Iraqi officers taken prisoner had indicated that the Iraqi army had no battle plan because their officers believed that Iraq would pull out of Kuwait and there would be no war (*Newsday,* Mar. 26, 1991, p. 5).

Thus, Schwarzkopf's presentation of seemingly superior Iraqi military forces confronting underdog allied forces was highly misleading. Indeed, a House Armed Service Committee report released in April 1992, claimed that the coalition forces outnumbered the Iraqis on the eve of the ground war by a 5 to 1 margin, rather than being outnumbered 3 to 2 as Schwarzkopf was claiming (see note 6). Moreover, Schwarzkopf's numbers also ignored the decisive fact that U.S. air superiority made it possible to demolish almost any Iraqi military target and thus to easily decimate and demoralize the Iraqi forces, as actually happened. Schwarzkopf next explained that the air campaign was to isolate the Kuwaiti theater of operations by taking out bridges and supply lines that ran between the northern and southern part of Iraq. "That was to prevent reinforcements and supplies coming down into the southern part of Iraq and the Kuwaiti theater of operations. It was necessary to reduce these forces down to a strength that made them weaker, particularly along the frontline barrier that we had to go through." This analysis was also propaganda, which legitimated the vicious destruction of Iraq's economic and social as well as its military infrastructure. Schwarzkopf justified the destruction of Iraq's infrastructure on military terms, claiming that the destruction of Iraq's roads, bridges, communications facilities, power plants, and industrial infrastructure would make it impossible for Iraq to supply its troops in Kuwait. Critics of the U.S. bombing argued that the massive destruction of Iraq's infrastructure was not justified militarily and in fact constituted an excessive and criminal overkill, waging war against the Iraqi people and not just their military.[7]

In any case, it was clear that if Schwarzkopf merely wanted to get the Iraqis out of Kuwait, he could simply have used his massive air power to bombard the front-line Iraqi troops in Kuwait until they were destroyed or ready to surrender, and then invade Kuwait with ground forces to finish off the job. But instead Schwarzkopf's goal, which his comments here conceal, was the destruction of the Iraqi military and its power in the region. He would later admit this himself in the question-and-answer session; when asked if the war was now over in the light of the Iraqi withdrawal from Kuwait, General Schwarzkopf responded:

> I would say that there's a lot more purpose to this war than just to get the Iraqis out of Kuwait. The purpose of this war was to enforce the resolutions of the United Nations. There are some 12 different resolutions of the United Nations, not all of which have been accepted by Iraq to date, as I understand it. . . . What else needs to be done? If I am to render the mission which I've been given, we need to put the Republican Guard out of business.

Here the blunt Schwarzkopf admitted that his mission was not merely the UN mission of getting the Iraqis out of Kuwait, but to destroy the Iraqi military, especially the Republican Guard, and he would proceed to attempt to do precisely that. When describing his campaign to sweep into Iraq to envelop and destroy the Iraqi military, Schwarzkopf once again employed hyperbole. After they eradicated the Iraqi Air Force, Schwarzkopf explained, the coalition forces had eliminated his ability to see what the forces were doing. Once "we took out his eyes," the coalition forces were able to send a massive movement of troops to the far west, beyond where Iraqi troops were deployed, for an invasion of southern Iraq. Schwarzkopf bragged that this was "absolutely an extraordinary move, I must tell you. I can't recall any time in the annals of military history when this number of forces have moved over this distance to put themselves in a position to be able to attack." Employing a dubious football metaphor, Schwarzkopf then compared his move to a "Hail Mary" play in which the quarterback throws the ball downfield as far as possible and all the receivers race toward the end zone as fast as they can in the hope that someone can catch it in the scramble. This is, to say the least, a highly bizarre metaphor, though no one pointed this out. One employs the "Hail Mary" play in football as a desperate last ditch attempt to pull victory from defeat. There was no chance of defeat in this case, so Schwarzkopf's metaphor was completely misleading. Furthermore, the "Hail Mary" play is a fundamentally irrational attempt to gain a last minute victory. Schwarzkopf's technowar, by contrast, was a methodically planned and incremental, highly rationalized destruction of Iraqi troops and equipment.

Schwarzkopf next described how the AirLand war began with an assault on the barrier at the Kuwaiti/Saudi border, which Saddam Hussein described, according to Schwarzkopf, "as an absolutely impenetrable tank barrier that no one would ever get through." At 4:00 A.M., on February 24, some marines launched attacks through the barrier system and were accompanied by some army brigades on their flank, with Saudi forces advancing on the easternmost front. Meanwhile a French armored division launched an overland attack on the west to take the al-Salman airfield, deep into southern Iraq. And by 8:00 A.M., the 101st Airborne launched an air assault deep into southern Iraq to establish a supply base within Iraq to service the occupying allied forces.

Schwarzkopf then went through each of these moves, describing the brilliance and heroism in hyperbolic terms, leaving out some of the gorier details that would later surface (see 9.4). As one saw on television, there were really no Iraqi forces in any condition to resist and the invasion was simply a cake walk in military lingo (see 8.5). Thus it is hard to imagine what was so brilliant or heroic about the invasion of Kuwait in the face of visual evidence that showed forlorn Iraqis in pitiful fox holes, surrendering by the hundreds. When a reporter raised this question, Schwarzkopf exploded with anger, asking the poor fellow if he'd "ever been in a mine field?" Schwarzkopf then recounted a Vietnam experience in which he told of being stuck in a mine field under attack and watched a young soldier get blown up by a mine. In the video footage, one did see plenty of mines in the desert but the coalition forces had sufficient equipment to clear these mines. There were few casualties from Iraqi mines, so Schwarzkopf's bluster merely exaggerated the invasion of Kuwait as far more dangerous and difficult than it really was. Indeed, television had shown reports of the various ways in which mine fields had been cleared, ranging from B-52 cluster bombing, fuel air bombs, and Miclic mine-sweeping machines to other devices. Praising the Saudis, apparently for political purposes, Schwarzkopf claimed:

> First of all, the Saudis over here on the east coast [he said pointing to a map] did a terrific job. They went up against a very, very tough barrier system. They breached the barrier very, very effectively. They moved out aggressively and continued their attack up the coast.

TV images, by contrast, showed no barrier system whatsoever but some isolated foxholes, deserted trench positions, some mines that hadn't been exploded, and some barbed wire. The TV reports indicated that the Saudis penetrated about eight miles across the border before they drew any artillery fire from the Iraqis. Allied planes then quickly took out the artillery and the Saudis moved on. So again, Schwarzkopf's version of the Gulf war was pure bombast and propaganda. He then lavished praise on the U.S. Marines:

I can't say enough about the two Marine divisions. If I use words like brilliant, it would really be an underdescription of the absolutely superb job that they did in breaching the so-called impenetrable barrier. It was a classic, absolutely classic, military breaching of a very, very tough minefield, barbed wire, fire-trenches-type barrier. They went through the first barrier like it was water. They went across into the second barrier line, even though they were under artillery fire at the time. They continued to open up that breach. And then they brought both divisions streaming through that breach. Absolutely superb operation, a textbook [case], and I think it'll be studied for many, many years to come as the way to do it.

Once again, Schwarzkopf was elevating a cake walk into a brilliant military achievement, and the media and TV audience fell for his bluster. The first barrier, as was widely reported, had no Iraqi troops defending it and when the marines encountered fire in the second barrier, coalition air forces eliminated the Iraqi artillery readily and quickly. Some of Schwarzkopf's own troops described the invasion as less dangerous and difficult than many of their training missions. Had there been more defensive power on the Iraqi side, obviously there would have been more casualties of the invading forces. The low casualties clearly attested to the fact that the Iraqis were already licked and all the coalition forces needed to do was to walk across the border, collect dazed and grateful Iraqi soldiers as POWs, and kill anyone who put up a fight. All during the day of the "brilliant" battle narrated by Schwarzkopf, pitiful Iraqis in isolated foxholes in the desert surrendered to anyone, whether military or journalists.

Moreover, the Iraqis obviously had no capability to counter the allied flanking operation. Numbers released by the Saudi government indicated that by February 23, Iraqi front units were 50 percent below capacity and second units were reduced to 50–70 percent and cut off from all reinforcements. Schwarzkopf also admitted that as soon as the allied troops crossed the border "we started getting a large number of surrenders," a point dramatically illustrated by the TV images of capitulating Iraqis. Previously, in a couple of border forays, Iraqi troops had given up almost immediately without a fight and with almost no casualties for the allied forces who engaged in operations behind enemy lines just before the AirLand war. The United States also, as Schwarzkopf now admitted, put special forces deep into enemy territory to reconnoiter and to carry out special tasks like helping establish the U.S. logistics base or to hunt for Scud missiles.

Over and over, the Pentagon praised the high level of its intelligence capabilities and thus it knew perfectly well that it was going to achieve an extremely easy victory in the AirLand war. Schwarzkopf told reporters a few days before the ground war began that "[t]he Iraqi army was overrated and on the verge of collapse" (quoted on ABC, Feb. 25, 1991). But in his briefing, Schwarzkopf dissembled the ease with which the rout of the Iraqis took place, with few allied casualties and a slaughter of Iraqi troops. Continuing his fable, Schwarzkopf narrated how on the morning of February 24th, the coalition started to move its forces into the most heavily defended area, starting with the marines, who rapidly went north, and the Saudi forces on the east coast who were "also moving rapidly to the north and making very, very good progress." More Egyptian, Syrian, and Saudi forces went across the border into Kuwait at this time making "a headlong assault into a very, very tough barrier system, a very, very tough mission for these folks here." Whenever, Schwarzkopf multiplied his adjectives or adverbs, or used nouns like "brilliant," he was invariably hyping his operation and covering over the ease with which the coalition forces destroyed the hapless Iraqis.

Schwarzkopf then described in more detail the French, British, and U.S. invasion of southern Iraq, noting that the French penetrated deep into the west of southern Iraq and the 101st Airborne Division went as far as the Euphrates valley.

> [W]e were 150 miles away from Baghdad and there was nobody between us and Baghdad. If it had been our intention to take Iraq, if it had been our intention to destroy the country, if it had been our intention to overrun the country, we could have done it unopposed for all intents and purposes from this position at that time. But that was not our intention. We had never said it was our intention. Our intention was purely to eject the Iraqis out of Kuwait and to destroy the military power that had come in here.

It is not clear what the consequences would have been of an allied incursion into Baghdad, but it is interesting that in this set of remarks Schwarzkopf revealed the true intention and limitations of the entire "plan" when he indicated that the goal was "to destroy the [Iraqi] military power" and not to march to Baghdad to overthrow Saddam Hussein. On one hand, Schwarzkopf admitted in his briefing that the goal of the U.S. administration was not merely the liberation of Kuwait but the destruction of the Iraqi military. On the other hand, he made it clear here that the overthrow of Saddam Hussein was not part of the U.S. agenda, that they were prepared to allow Hussein to survive. Indeed, in the eventual cease-fire negotiations and weeks following the cessation of military hostilities, the United States allowed Hussein to reestablish power in the face of powerful opposition throughout his country, to the disgust of many who had previously wholeheartedly supported the Bush administration's war policies.

Moreover, it is significant that Schwarzkopf did not describe the details of the destruction of the Iraqi military, much of which was going on as he was speaking and which we shall analyze in as much detail as sources allow in later sections. In fact, it is interesting that Schwarzkopf gave his briefing before the slaughter of the Iraqi army was completed and before any details had been revealed. Thus, there was little questioning concerning whether there was overkill, excess, and a downright massacre in his attempted destruction of the Iraqi army. Instead of going into the details and extent of the slaughter, he quickly pointed to areas of movement of the Saudi and U.S. marine progress on the eastern front, which had already taken over Kuwait City after the Iraqis had fled. He then pointed on his map to the forces in southern Iraq who were fighting the Republican Guard and to the 24th Infantry Division, who "made an unbelievable move all the way across into the Tigris and Euphrates valley, and proceeded in blocking this avenue of egress out of, which was the only avenue of egress left because we continued to make sure that the bridges stayed down. So there was no way out."

This turned out to be only partially true. The U.S. forces had blocked major avenues of retreat from Kuwait into Iraq and would thus be able to wipe out without impunity much of the retreating Iraqi forces in what pilots described as "a turkey shoot." After the war, it was claimed on March 1 that the United States had destroyed thirty-one out of thirty-two Iraqi divisions and had destroyed completely the Republican Guard. Later these figures would be contested when thousands of Guards appeared to put down Shiite and Kurdish rebellions in March and April. Thus, many more Iraqi troops and tanks escaped than Schwarzkopf admitted, so there obviously was a "way out" for these troops, who later helped Saddam Hussein suppress rebellion against his regime (10.4).[8] Thus, Schwarzkopf consistently exaggerated the extent of his destruction of the Iraqi military apparatus, while at the same time trying to cover over the slaughter of Iraqi troops: "To date, we have destroyed over 29 [Iraqi divisions]—destroyed or rendered inoperable; I don't like to say 'destroyed' because that gives you the vision of absolutely killing everyone, and that's not what we are doing, but we have rendered completely ineffective over 29 Iraqi divisions, and the gates are closed."

"Peace is not without its cost," Schwarzkopf admitted, and then detailed some of the U.S. casualties—a total of seventy-nine killed in action. Schwarzkopf claimed that while the loss of one single life was intolerable, casualties of that order of magnitude were "almost miraculous." When asked what happened to the rest of the reported 200,000 Iraqi troops in the border area, Schwarzkopf answered:

There were a very, very large number of dead in these units, a very, very large number of dead. We even found them when we went into the units ourselves and found them in the trench lines. There were very heavy desertions. At one point, we had reports of desertion rates of more than 30 percent of the units that were along the front here. As you know, we had quite a large number of POWs that came across, and so I think it's a combination of desertions, it's a combination of people that were killed, there's a combination of the people that we captured and there's a combination of some other people who are just flat still running.

The most interesting points here involve the heavy desertions of Iraqi troops, "perhaps 30 percent" along the front, and the miraculously low number of allied casualties. This statement seems to verify that the forces were totally unbalanced and that the whole ground war involved the exaggeration of Iraqi forces to hype the coalition victory and to conceal the desert slaughter.

During the question part of the briefing, the reporters, by now putty in Schwarzkopf's hands or intimidated by his bravado, asked their tame questions, giving Schwarzkopf the opportunity to insult Saddam Hussein as a military strategist, extol the brilliance of his plan, and assure the reporters that chemical weapons hadn't been used. Schwarzkopf also made himself an agent once again of the propaganda war, claiming that there were rumors of 40,000 Kuwaiti hostages, which "pales to insignificance in the face of the Iraqi atrocities of the last week," though he refused to give any details. He asserted that people who could commit atrocities like the Iraqis "weren't members of the same human race as the rest of us," again involving himself in racist hyperbole. As it turned out, the stories of Iraqi atrocities in Kuwait City during the last days of the occupation were greatly exaggerated, part of the propaganda war, though the fleeing Iraqi troops did take many Kuwaiti hostages, many of whom were perhaps slaughtered by Schwarzkopf's own forces, which seemed to be killing everything in sight—an event that the Kuwaiti government and media never explored and that I shall discuss in the next chapter (10.2).

During his briefing, Schwarzkopf attempted to shape the historical record and journalistic account of the war much as he shaped the battlefield: to use brute power to impose his will upon the terrain. In retrospect, it is striking the extent to which the Bush administration and Pentagon followed the politics of lying in their discourses during the Gulf war. Throughout the war, lying was as aggressive, systematic, and outrageous as in Vietnam and I have documented a series of these lies in this book. Of course, Pentagon lying was merely following the example of the Bush administration which lied about: (1) the reason for sending U.S. troops to the Gulf in the first place (i.e., to protect Saudi Arabia from Iraqi invasion whereas there is no evidence that Iraq intended this;

see 1.1); (2) the claim that it was seeking diplomatic settlements when obviously it desired war (see 1.2); and (3) its orchestration of the propaganda campaigns condemning Iraqi environmental terrorism (much of which coalition forces were responsible for), Iraqi mistreatment of POWs (all of which returned safe and sound), and denials of causing Iraqi civilian casualties, despite much evidence to the contrary (see Chapters 4–7).

U.S. hypocrisy and lying to cover over the fruits of its bombing missions could be contrasted with the British, who openly admitted the failure of a precision bomb after the worst civilian atrocities caused by their bombing. Some days after the Amiraia bombing, the British attempted to bomb a bridge in the city of Falluija and a precision bomb went astray and hit a market place in the vicinity of the bridge. Rather than deny their complicity in these civilian deaths, the British admitted that their bomb went astray, even showing the videotape of a bomb veering away from its target and exploding off-camera on the other side of the river. Unlike the U.S. military briefers, the British were capable of admitting a mistake and apologizing.

9.4 Days of Shame

Meanwhile, the diplomatic charade continued and Bush refused to negotiate a settlement as the ground war entered its fourth day. The Iraqis had proclaimed their willingness to abide by the UN resolution to withdraw from Kuwait and actually begin withdrawal on February 25; every day thereafter the Iraqis repeated their willingness to abide by the UN resolutions, but every day, the Bush administration rejected Iraqi and UN pleas for a cease-fire. Instead, as the U.S. military briefer General Neal put it on February 26, coalition forces would continue to "attack and attack and attack," using "every means available to destroy" fleeing Iraqis.

The mainstream media consistently legitimated the U.S. high-tech massacre during this time. On February 25, "CBS This Morning" host Harry Smith announced to Dan Rather that the Iraqis were "turning tail and heading for their homeland," but were leaving with their weapons. Rather commented that their destruction was justified because they were taking their weapons with them and that the United States was currently encircling the Republican Guards in order to destroy them. "The idea," Rather explained, was not to leave "Saddam Hussein's power base intact" and that Bush was saying that "we're not letting you come this far and when we have a hammerlock on you say 'OK, you can go home.'" On ABC, Tony Cordesman argued that, according to the "normal customs of war," the United States "has been generous" in allowing Iraqis to "put down their guns and withdraw" and that the Soviet effort to push for a cease-fire in the United Nations was "totally unacceptable." "The absolute custom and law of war," Cordesman said, "is that the state involved must sue for a ceasefire or a surrender itself." On NBC, Faith Daniels reported that the judgment in Washington was that "this [that is, the Iraqi retreat] is a ruse, they're not sincere, they are just regrouping." When asked if the U.S.-led coalition forces should go to Baghdad to take out Saddam Hussein, NBC military consultant James Dunnigan insisted that the problem in the Middle East was the "socialist Baath party" and that this cancer would have to be ripped out (of Iraq and Syria!) before the region would be safe from subversion.

Meanwhile, as the media pundits tried to justify the high-tech massacre of the fleeing Iraqis, General Schwarzkopf's troops appeared to be under orders to destroy everything in sight. *Newsday* revealed on September 12, 1991, that "[t]he U.S. Army division that broke through Saddam Hussein's defensive frontline used plows mounted on tanks and combat earthmovers to bury thousands of Iraqi soldiers—some alive and firing their weapons—in more than 70 miles of trenches, according to U.S. Army officials" (p. A1). In a grisly story based on eyewitness accounts, Patrick Sloyan described how the U.S. division "The Big Red One" destroyed trenches and bunkers being defended by more than 8,000 Iraqi soldiers with a combination of airpower, artillery, tanks, and vehicles with plows that buried alive hundreds, perhaps thousands, of hapless Iraqi conscripts, placed in the harsh deserts without adequate training or weapons. The U.S. soldiers interviewed indicated how defenseless the Iraqis were, with one stating: "What you saw was a bunch of buried trenches with people's arms and things sticking out of them." There were no U.S. casualties in the slaughter, though Pfc. Joe Queen remarked: "A lot of guys were scared. But I enjoyed it."

At the height of the ground war, the U.S.-led forces were, according to official figures, killing 100 tanks per day and countless Iraqi soldiers. Not only did the U.S. use new high-tech precision weapons but they used new "area-impact munitions" to annihilate the Iraqi army.[9] In addition to napalm, which explodes and hideously burns human flesh, the U.S. used fuel-air explosive bombs, "daisy cutters," and multiple launch rocket systems to obliterate the Iraqis. Fuel-air explosives utilize high-energy fuels such as butane which are dispersed from canisters to produce aerosol clouds which then explode rather than just burn. The resulting blasts are several times greater than conventional weapons and have a devastating effect on bunkers, silos, and people; they are sometimes referred to as "the poor man's nuclear weapons." "Daisycutters" are 15,000 pound bombs which contain explosives that can produce blasts almost in the nuclear weapon range. Cluster bombs and missiles can spread 247 bomblets over more than an acre, generating nearly 500,000 high-velocity shrapnel fragments. Cruise missiles could also deliver a version of cluster bombs and B-52s could drop a tremendous amount of munitions on an area the size of four football fields. Finally, multiple-launch rocket systems carry two pods of six missiles that can deliver nearly 8,000 bomblets over 60 acres in one salvo. British arms expert Paul Rogers (1991) pointed out that during the closing stages of the war, the U.S. and British armies fired a thousand salvoes, or 12,000 missiles from their systems. These attacks were extremely lethal and a British reporter describing shelling of Iraqi positions during the ground war claimed: "It was this as much as the weeks of pounding from the air by the American B-52 bombers and fighter-bombers that shattered the nerve of the Iraqis. An Iraqi company commander captured after the first day's action said the rockets had killed all but seven of his command of 250 in less than 10 minutes. A captured artillery brigadier said fewer than 20 of his heavy guns had been knocked out in the weeks of air raids, but the artillery bombardment had put paid to the rest, all but six, in an hour" (in MacArthur 1991, p. 221).

On April 8, the *New York Times* published an article on a battle that the United States had fought on February 27, the day of Schwarzkopf's briefing and the day before the cessation of military activity. According to Michael Gordon, "When the 40 minute battle was over, American tanks and aircraft had destroyed 60 T-72 tanks, 9 Iraqi T-55 tanks and 38 armored personnel carriers" (p. A6). It was impossible to know how many Iraqi casualties there were because, in the words of Col. Montgomery Meiggs, the tanks "exploded and burned fiercely" so that "there were not a whole lot of bodies." The *Times* article described the massacre as "a showcase for the superiority of American-made weapons and tactics over Iraq's Soviet-designed arms and static defense." It was "a one-sided victory . . . an impressive tableau of destruction." Many U.S. soldiers were horrified by the slaughter, however. According to Gordon, "Young American soldiers, accustomed to destroying wooden tank targets at test ranges said they were astounded to see the Iraqi tanks turn into fireballs." Sgt. Larry Porter noted, "We have all had a chance to call our wives and most of the guys could not talk about it to them. I don't think my wife needs to know what took place out here. I do not want her to know that side of me."

During the same period U.S. forces killed ten British troops, and CNN reported on September 17, 1991, that on February 27, 1992, an undisclosed number of U.S. troops were killed by "friendly fire." But probably the most appalling episode in the shameful Persian Gulf war was the systematic destruction of the Iraqi army as its individual soldiers desperately fled from Kuwait and southern Iraq (see 10.2). General Schwarzkopf mentioned a couple of brief details of the slaughter on February 27 when he claimed that there "was no way out" and "the gates are closed," though none of the reporters followed up on it, thus failing to gain insight into what was probably the most significant military action going on during the ground war: the attempt to systematically destroy the Iraqi army.

As usual, the Bush administration and Pentagon created specious rationalizations for the continued brutality and, as usual, their defenders in the media went along with their actions and statements. In the debate concerning whether the U.S.-led massacre of the retreating Iraqis—who were pleading for a cease-fire and who had indeed left Kuwait—was "legitimate," the *New York Times* published on February 27, 1991, an article by John X. Crossman, Jr., headlined: "Experts Back U.S. on Rules of War. They Assert Allies Have Clear Right to Attack Retreating Iraqis Carrying Arms." With historical examples going back to the Middle Ages and through the Civil War, the 1907 Hague Convention, and the Geneva Convention of 1949, the *Times's* rationalization of the slaughter indicated that it was clearly within the rules of war to massacre retreating Iraqis (p. A8). But against such rationalizations stands the fact that the Iraqi army was already decisively defeated and clearly had no will to fight.[10] The Iraqis had clearly appealed for a cease-fire through their official state radio, their UN representative, their head of state, and the Soviet Union, which tried to negotiate a cease-fire in the United Nations, but which was blocked by the Bush administration. Instead, Bush's plan was apparently to annihilate the Iraqi army, to inflict the maximum amount of destruction on the Iraqis to establish U.S. military power as fearsome and relentless, and thus to punish the Iraqis for refusing to bend to the will of the neoimperialist superpower. Bush made his point and thousands of Iraqis died as a result.

Seeking to replace Henry Kissinger and Jeane Kirkpatrick as intellectual of choice to justify the unjustifiable, Thomas Friedman, a former CIA intern and James Baker's occasional tennis partner, wrote a front-page *New York Times* story titled "The Rout Bush Wants. A Disorderly, Humiliating Iraqi Surrender Will End Hussein's Power, Officials Believe" (Feb. 27, p. A1). The slaughter was justified by Friedman on the (dubious) grounds that only "unconditional surrender" and the devastation of the Iraqi army would end Saddam Hussein's power and eliminate Iraq as a military threat. This will help, Friedman wrote, pleasantly conveying the official Bush administration line, "speed the withdrawal of most of the 537,000 American troops in the gulf, and to make sure that they will not have to come back to fight again some day." Friedman, of course, neglected the fact that the massacre was intended to ratify the U.S.

superpower status in the region and he failed to discuss the messy facts concerning the bloody slaughter of the retreating Iraqis. Instead, he provided a rationalization for Bush administration policy. Such were the ways that "journalists" and "scholars" compromised and sold themselves to the victorious forces, helping to hide the brutality of the war.

To get some sense of the magnitude of the massacre that Friedman was politely justifying, one merely had to turn to the lead news story in the same day's edition of the *New York Times*:

> All night long, American warplanes pummeled Iraqi tanks, armored personnel carriers and trucks on the road leading north from Kuwait City as they sought to reach Basra, pilots said. The movement created a column 25 to 30 miles long, three or four abreast in place, and except for a few surface-to-air missiles, they were defenseless against the F-15, F-11 and F-16 fighter bombers that came at them, wave after wave, along with Navy planes.
>
> In the wind and driving rain, "it was close to Armageddon," an Air Force officer said. (Feb. 27, p. A1)

And that's it. Armageddon for the Iraqis but no details, no follow ups, and certainly no outrage. Indeed, the only critical view of the Desert Slaughter on network television during the Days of Shame was the pained anger of an Arab, Hisham Sharabi, on the February 27 "MacNeil/Lehrer News Hour." Instead, television focused on the glories of the liberation of Kuwait and the atrocities of the Iraqis in Kuwait. No one bothered to focus on the atrocities of the U.S. slaughter of the Iraqis. In the February 28 *New York Times*, there was a mention in the lead story that Bush's speech to end the war was an attempt to balance the U.S. position "that Iraq could not get off too easily, with mounting international pressures to stop the assaults on an obviously defeated army." There was no discussion of the international pressures by civilized nations in regard to the U.S.'s barbaric behavior nor were there any details on the slaughter of the Iraqis, except for a brief mention of it at the end of a story glorifying the U.S. taking of central Iraq:

> Once the barriers were up, the troops zeroed in on a "killing zone" and blasted anything that tried to drive through, including a truck filled with sacks of flour. But most of the traffic was soldiers in civilian cars, heading away from Kuwait, many carrying televisions, boxes of women's clothes and other looted goods. On Tuesday night, the explosives arrived and bridges and other parts of the road were blown up. (*New York Times*, Feb. 28, p. A7)

The Persian Gulf TV war thus ended up being a massacre of the Iraqi military in a total mismatch through which the most powerful high-tech military machine ever assembled slaughtered a Third World army. Those

Corpses of Iraqi soldiers.

The real war—what the official reports rarely showed. (Photos courtesy of Alan Pogue.)

U.S. authorities who were privy to military intelligence knew full well that the Iraqi army was incapable of fighting back. A *Newsday* dispatch from Susan Sachs indicated that the Pentagon consistently and intentionally overestimated Iraqi capabilities (Mar. 3, 1991). Lt. Gen. Walter Boomer told Sachs that they had "known for weeks that the [Iraqi] lines weren't that formidable. . . . But we wanted to let Iraqis think we still thought they were big." This is nonsense as obviously the military wanted the public to think that the Iraqis were "big" to enhance the Pentagon's victory. Sachs indicated that one "senior commander agreed that the information about Iraqi defenses . . . was highly exaggerated. 'There was a great disinformation campaign surrounding the war,' he said, with some satisfaction."

Throughout the war, the Bush administration and Pentagon consistently exaggerated the power, the evil, and the magnitude of the Iraqi military which was obviously out of its league militarily. The Iraqi army was hyped up as the "fourth most powerful in the world" and its "battle-hardened troops," "elite Republican Guard," and massive array of weapons were constantly extolled in the media. Even the highly touted Republican Guard were overblown in the media discourse. As Simpson explained, "The Republican Guard, which journalists and politicians insisted on describing as 'elite', was increased by several divisions during the period of the crisis, largely by means of taking men from regular units and giving them red berets. Anyone who could march in step was considered eligible. The officers of the Republican Guard were usually better trained, but that generally meant that they too had to be taken from other units. The mass dilution meant that the Republican Guards' standards, which in the war against Iran had been above average, were little different from those of the rest of the Iraqi army" (1991, p. 334).

In fact, many U.S. soldiers indicated to journalists their surprise that the Iraqi army collapsed so quickly and one imagines that the front-line soldiers honestly did not know that they were facing such badly outpowered and demoralized forces. A British soldier told reporter Robert Fox that, "It was more like an exercise with enemy in it than anything I had expected. A bit like a stroll in the park" (in MacArthur 1991, p. 225). One U.S. soldier said that their practice exercises were more difficult and dangerous than the actual fighting, constantly described by Dan Rather and the media puff patrol as "fierce," or "ferocious." The Pentagon hyped the "formidable Iraqi enemy" primarily for its own bureaucratic purposes. By having in place the image of a strong Iraqi opponent they could thus puff up and promote their great victory, they could produce the image of a "brilliant" campaign, and would thus boost their own careers and prestige. In so doing, they inflicted needless suffering on the families of allied troops and the public deeply concerned about the well-being of the U.S. forces in the Gulf. Indeed, both the military and media should be severely criticized for their exaggeration of the dangers faced, thus terrorizing unnecessarily the public worried about the fate of the troops, as well as needlessly terrorizing the troops themselves.

9.5 The Perfect War

The United States and George Bush emerged from the Gulf massacre as leaders of a Neoimperialist World Order. At a speech at an American Legion convention on February 27, Dick Cheney praised the leadership of George Bush, saying that the "bottom line is that this whole effort has been put together and held together by the leadership of the United States" and that the man who provided the leadership for the U.S. and the whole world in "rolling back the aggression of Saddam Hussein" was George Bush. "This was one of the most successful achievements, not only from a military but also from a diplomatic and a political standpoint, that this country has ever seen." If the systematic destruction of a small country and systematic lying, manipulating, and killing is one of the greatest achievements of a country, then that country is in bad shape. But neither imperialism nor neoimperialism has ever been ashamed to cover over crimes and aggression with the most bald-faced lies and blatant hypocrisy.

I am using the highly charged term "neoimperialist" quite deliberately. Susan Sontag once wrote that during the Vietnam war, it became possible, even mandatory, to use the word "imperialism" in light of the massive U.S. assault on Vietnam, thousands of miles away from the United States. From a more technical standpoint of political theory, however, neither Vietnam nor the Persian Gulf war were classical imperialist wars. Classical imperialism involved a stage of capitalism in which the capitalist superpowers occupied foreign countries to directly exploit their labor power, resources, and markets. Classical imperialism usually involved the imposition of a government administered by the imperialist country, supported by a military force from the occupying power, often bolstered by "native" forces and sometimes administrators. Neoimperialism, by contrast, involves the control of markets, politics, and sociocultural developments through a combination of military, political, and cultural power. Neoimperialism corresponds to the stage of capitalism in which transnational corporations and superpower nation states attempt to dominate the economic and political destinies of nations throughout the world by a combination of military threats, covert actions, political diplomacy, and cultural hegemony.

Indeed, one of the hidden agendas of the Persian Gulf adventure from the beginning was to establish the United States decisively as the world's number-one superpower based on the application of crushing military power as an instrument of imposing political will and domination on smaller countries who would not conform to the interests of the hegemonic neoimperialist powers. To effectively carry through this object lesson, the United States had to demonstrate an ability to assemble, organize, and carry through an impressive demonstration of military power. To make this lesson dramatically, Iraq had to be presented as a dangerous enemy and then destroyed, and this was the goal of the war from the beginning. Successful accomplishment would establish the U.S. as the most powerful military force in the world and would demonstrate the threat of the use of military power to establish U.S. political hegemony.

For Bush and his ilk, the most important result of the victory in the Persian Gulf war was that it would once and for all allow the United States to overcome the "Vietnam syndrome." During a "power walk" in Maine on Sunday, February 17, about a week before the ground war and on the day that his church service was interrupted by an antiwar protester, Bush explicitly claimed that the coming U.S. victory in the Gulf war would overcome the Vietnam syndrome. In one of his first speeches after the war, he exulted: "By God, we've kicked this Vietnam syndrome forever!" By "Vietnam syndrome," Bush meant the unwillingness to commit U.S. military power for political objectives on account of fear of failure, thus repeating the Vietnam debacle. In fact, however, if one sees the Vietnam syndrome as a disease, as the proclivity to use U.S. military power to solve political problems, then the Gulf massacre was a classic expression of the Vietnam syndrome, of a militarist compulsion to use U.S. military power to resolve political conflicts.

Iraq was the victim, therefore, of a neoimperialist attempt to control its destiny. Iraq refused to submit to the will of the Western neoimperialist superpower and its allies, who responded violently and with determined resolution to pound Iraq into submission. The Persian Gulf massacre made clear to upstart Third World countries that if they refuse to play by the rules established by the capitalist superpowers, they will be crushed by military force. The Gulf technowar also demonstrated the efficacy of U.S. high-tech weapons systems and military power. Indeed, the deserts of the Middle East were a perfect testing ground for new high-tech weapons and military strategies that could restore U.S. military prestige and establish the superiority of U.S. military technology and personnel.

Bill Gibson, whose work has greatly influenced the present one, called his book on Vietnam, *The Perfect War: Technowar in Vietnam*. In conversations with him I argued against this title on the grounds that the Vietnam war was messy, convoluted, out of control, and ultimately a resounding defeat for the technowar managers; Gibson, of course, intended his title ironically and used it to expose the hubris of the war managers who thought that Vietnam would be the perfect war to test their new weapons systems and counterinsurgency doctrines and techniques. They failed in this earlier venture and needed a smashing victory to reestablish their "credibility" and prestige. The Persian Gulf war, by contrast, *was* the perfect war: it had the perfect enemy in the Iraqi president who was the perfect villain whom the propaganda apparatus could demonize. Iraq possessed a Third World army that appeared threatening in view of the magnitude of men, tanks, artillery, and weapons, but which, in fact, was a pushover, guaranteeing a sure win. In addition, the U.S. orchestrated a media propaganda war with spin control for every eventuality and had at its disposal a compliant media not only willing to transmit its every lie, piece of disinformation, and propaganda, but positively affirming and celebrating the war machine's every move.

The Gulf war was celebrated by some commentators as a successful attempt to reinvigorate the American psyche, to overcome doubts and confusions, and to ally national anxieties. The *Wall Street Journal* commented that success in the Gulf war "should create a new, upbeat temperament in a populace that has been in the dumps since the 1960s" (cited in the *Progressive,* Mar. 1991, p. 10). There can be no doubt that people in the U.S. were angry and confused, looking for someone or something to blame for their worries and troubles. Saddam Hussein and Iraq were the perfect scapegoat and the Bush administration exploited this to the maximum. As the *Progressive* put it, "War offers an ideal scapegoat and escape. Saddam Hussein can be pressed into service as the new Willie Horton, a focal point for the politics of resentment that is built on cheap sloganeering" (Mar. 1991, p. 10). In this interpretation, the war served as a handy substitute for the collapse of the Soviet empire, providing a new target for domestic fears and hatred.

The Persian Gulf war was thus the perfect war to test Pentagon weapons and strategies; to deplete their overstocked supply of weapons and to create the need for new ones; to reestablish the prestige of the military against future budget cuts; to militarize the culture and create new military myths and ideology; to advance the careers of officers who could pose as heroes; and to promote the fortunes of George Bush and his war team. But this was not the perfect war for the people and culture of Iraq, the environment of the Persian Gulf, or any of the people who had to pay, and will have to pay, with their lives and livelihoods. The war was hardly perfect or beneficial for the casualties of the war on all sides: the foreign workers and other refugees thrown out of Iraq, Kuwait, and Saudi Arabia, many of whom are now condemned to a life of misery and perhaps horrible death; and Arabs who had to experience yet another humiliation in their history of defeat by Western powers.

Other victims of the war include those in the U.S. who will have to live in a culture of militarism with declining social programs, a declining standard of living, and increased public squalor for all. Indeed, although the troops of the Persian Gulf were celebrated as national heroes who returned to hyped up parades and victory celebrations, costing millions of dollars, they too were victims of George Bush's Gulf war. Many had to spend months in the burning and then freezing Saudi Arabian deserts, subject to incredible discomfort and horrendous fears. Many reservists had to leave jobs and families, incurring tremendous financial and emotional burdens, while being exposed to injury and death. Their families at home experienced severe hardship with fathers or mothers gone, leaving the other spouse and children at home, suffering many emotional traumas, which were sometimes documented in the media. Many marriages broke up from the strain and divorce rates for Gulf war troops were over 50 percent in many areas of heavy military concentration.[11]

In addition, the troops in the desert were exploited in one of the largest medical experiments in history, in which they served as guinea pigs for untested drugs against chemical warfare agents.[12] According to Laurie Tormey Hasbrook (see Note 12), several soldiers died from these experiments and many are now sick from various diseases which they contracted in the Gulf region. Joel Bleifuss discussed the administration of untested drugs on the Gulf military guinea pigs, reporting that the "Health Alert" section in the latest Military Families Support Network (MFSN) indicates that at least a dozen military wives who got pregnant after their husbands returned from the Gulf have had miscarriages. When one of the soldiers asked whether his wife's miscarriage could be related to the experimental drugs he took, he was told that the military was "not allowed to discuss the drugs" *(In These Times,* Dec. 18, 1991, p. 4). Bleifuss also notes that the MFSN reports that Gulf war veterans are already starting to turn up in shelters for the homeless. The *New York Times* reported on November 13 (p. A11) that the military has stopped accepting blood donations from Persian Gulf war veterans because of a rare parasite brought home from the region caused by bites from sand flies.

Thus George Bush's war took a heavy toll on the domestic population as well as the people of Iraq and other populations in the area. It was not, in the final analysis, a perfect war at all, but just another filthy war expressive of a world without logos and without the ability to resolve conflicts without violence. Like all wars, it was therefore barbaric, primitive, and vicious without, as I shall argue in the next chapter, any redeeming features at all.

Notes

1. The Soviet media, however, expressed outrage over the U.S. refusal to work with the Soviet government to negotiate a diplomatic solution. The Soviet news agency Tass commented on February 24 that "this unique chance [offered by the Soviet peace plan] was allowed to slip away and the tragedy began fraught with great bloodshed." The commentary stated that the coalition forces wanted above all "to destroy fully Iraq's military-industrial potential and state structures to ensure a privileged position for the United States and its allies in the postwar arrangements." The milder official Soviet reaction the same day stated: "The instinct to rely on the military solution prevailed, despite the fact that Iraq's agreement to withdraw its forces from Kuwait in keeping with the United Nations Security Council Resolution No. 660 has created a basically new situation, clearing the way to transferring the Gulf conflict to the footing of a political settlement." The Soviet military and hardliners were even more outraged, and this rage contributed to the abortive coup attempt against Gorbachev some months later. Thus, Bush's refusal to negotiate a settlement risked the survival of Gorbachev's regime and could have destroyed perestroika and produced a new cold war. Bush thus appears as a gambler every bit as reckless as Saddam Hussein, but luckier.

2. The Associated Press reported on June 15, 1991, that the Saudi executioner was once again a busy man after the departure of Westerners. The report indicated that public executions had resumed in Saudi Arabia after a ten-month break during the time that Western reporters and troops were in the country. "The executions were stopped in order to avoid upsetting Western public opinion," the director of Middle East Watch, Andrew Whitley noted. "That to our minds, is a cynical manipulation of the legal process."

3. Interestingly, a caller from San Diego on the CNN "Larry King Live" show made the point that the Kuwaitis had hired a public relations firm and that these reports were carefully orchestrated propaganda. King cut her off and the issue was not discussed.

4. Dan Rather of CBS described the Scud attack as a "terrorist counterattack" and CBS correspondent Harry Smith described it as "Saddam Hussein's act of terrorism." It is not clear why Iraq's firing of a missile at Saudi Arabia during war was "terrorism" while the U.S. bombing of Iraq and slaughter of the fleeing Iraqi troops was good, clean war.

5. It could also have been the case that the United States noted that Iraqi defenses were too strong on the Kuwaiti shore and that an amphibious operation would have sustained intolerably high casualties. After the war, the TV networks showed models of impressive Iraqi fortifications along the shoreline, which could have produced many coalition casualties. The April 1992 Pentagon report conceded that as late as February 10, U.S. commanders planned to mount an amphibious attack south of Kuwait City. But damage to two U.S. warships from Iraqi mines and uncertainty about how many more mines might be in the waters along the Kuwaiti coastline forced planners to abandon the option. The Marines remained on their ships off the coast to deceive the Iraqis into thinking they were coming ashore and were reportedly unhappy that they were deprived of the joys of an amphibious attack.

6. A Finnish military expert, Pekka Visuri, also independently estimated that there was "at most only about half of the 500,000 Iraqi troops purported by American officials or Western media" (Luostarinen 1991, p. 11). In addition, *U.S. News and World Report* estimated in *Triumph Without Victory* that Iraq probably only had 300,000 troops in the field, and perhaps as few as 200,000 (1992, p. 405). In a report on the Gulf war released on April 23, 1992, the House Armed Services Committee concluded that U.S. and allied troops held an overwhelming 5-to-1 advantage at the start of the ground war. Although the Pentagon claimed that Iraqi forces in the region totaled more than 500,000, the House report claimed there may have been as few as 180,000 Iraqi troops in the region. The committee concluded that the 42 Iraqi divisions were severely undermanned at the beginning of the conflict and depleted by desertions, deaths, and injuries during the intense 40-day aerial bombardment that preceded the ground attack. Congressmen Aspin and Dickinson said a more reliable figure for the initial Iraqi force was 361,000, which was depleted by some 153,000 desertions and 26,000 killed and wounded during the air war. Schwarzkopf was thus constantly guilty of transmitting "shamelessly doctored" statistics (Pierre Sprey) during the Gulf war and the shameless mainstream media let him get away with it to the shame of the nation.

7. Joshua Epstein claimed on ABC in February that the U.S.-led coalition's destruction of Iraq's economic infrastructure was totally unnecessary to the military campaign. The 1992 Pentagon Report admitted that bombing of Iraq's electrical system was excessive and unnecessary to the war effort. Ramsey Clark would later carry out a War Crimes Tribunal claiming that Bush and his war team violated international law in their bombing of Iraq's civilian infrastructure and murder of civilians; see Clark et al. 1992. A November 1991 report by Middle East Watch claimed that both sides in the Gulf war committed "serious violations of the laws of war" and that "many hundreds of civilians needlessly lost their lives because U.S.-led coalition commanders failed to abide by the laws of armed conflict." Repeated U.S. violations included: daytime attacks on military targets in urban areas; excessive collateral damage; and systematic attacks on food, agricultural, and water-treatment facilities "appear to have violated laws against hitting targets that have no apparent military value." Similarly, attacks on Iraq's electrical system "may also have resulted in excessive civilian costs compared to the concrete and direct military advantage anticipated. . . . [T]he lack of electricity in Iraq has exacerbated food shortages, crippled the country's sewage-treatment and water-purification systems, badly hurt the medical apparatus, and impaired much of its ability to produce its own food." Finally, U.S. forces "appear to have repeatedly and indiscriminately attacked civilian vehicles on Iraqi highways and bedouin tents in Western Iraq, where they were seeking out Scud missile sites" (Middle East Watch 1991).

8. Defense Intelligence Agency and CIA estimates "suggest that about 1,430 of Iraq's armored personnel carriers got away, where originally it was believed that no more than 500 did. Similarly about 700 of Iraq's estimated 4,550 tanks in southern Iraq escaped, against an earlier estimate of between 500 and 600" (Cohen and Gatti 1991, pp. 296–297). The 1992 Pentagon report conceded that it had overestimated the number of Iraqi armored personnel vehicles destroyed, revising the number from claims of 2,400 destroyed to 1,450 (see 4.3).

9. The following discussion is indebted to Paul Rogers, "The Myth of the Clean War," *Covert Action Information Bulletin,* No. 37 (Summer 1991), pp. 26–30 and to the transcription of an interview with Rogers on WBAI radio, September 16, 1991, transcribed in the PeaceNet bulletin board, misc.activism.progressive, Feb. 8, 1992. See also Paul Walker, "The Myth of Surgical Bombing in Iraq," in Clark et al. 1992, pp. 83–89.

10. The counterargument against the morality and legality of the slaughter is found throughout Clark et al. 1992 and Middle East Watch 1991b.

11. See the article in the *New York Times,* (July 16, 1991), the *Los Angeles Times* (Jan. 15, 1992), and *USA Today* (Jan. 16, 1992). The *Boston Globe* had an article on Gulf vets and homelessness, indicating that many were seeking refuge in homeless shelters (Jan. 16, 1992).

12. See the *Los Angeles Times,* Jan. 1, 1991, which had a brief notice "Unapproved Drugs Cleared for Troops." The Military Families Support Network newsletter *Newswire,* Vol. 2, No. 1 (Feb. 1992) documented the parasitic diseases found among Gulf vets, the administration of untested or not fully approved drugs, and other health and readjustment problems. Laurie Tormey Hasbrook, in

a talk at the November 1991 Midwest Radical Scholars and Activist conference, claimed that this was the largest experimental use of untested drugs in history. Hasbrook had been interviewing a group of Gulf war veterans who had served months in the Gulf and who had then entered Kuwait but did not directly participate in ground war fighting. One member of the group had committed suicide, another had a nervous breakdown, and as many as 50 percent were suffering traumas from their experiences, though many were not seeking psychological help as they feared this would harm their military careers.

CHAPTER TEN

◆

Aftermath

ON FEBRUARY 26, after Iraqi troops had already fled the country, coalition forces entered Kuwait City, where they were met by a jubilant crowd. They were accompanied, of course, by television crews and soon live satellite feeds from Kuwait City were broadcast by CBS, CNN, ABC, and finally NBC. CBS's Dan Rather, his eyes moist with tears, vigorously shook the hand of an American officer, saying, "Congratulations for a job well done." The media had well served the Pentagon during the war and enthusiastically participated in the ecstasy of victory. The March 11 *Newsweek* had a laughing Norman Schwarzkopf on its cover with the triumphant inscription "VICTORY!" while *U.S. News and World Report* scripted "KNOCKOUT!" above the pictures of a moving tank. *Time* magazine showed victorious U.S. troops in Kuwait City on their March 11 cover and then portrayed a joyous homecoming on their March 18 cover, providing a fitting closure to the U.S. triumph (see Figure 10.1).

Excited Kuwaitis greeted the troops and media crews as conquering heroes, and Kuwaiti citizens, resistance fighters, and foreign citizens who had been trapped in the city all had their fifteen minutes of media celebrity. Atrocity stories were told, hatred of the Iraqis was expressed repeatedly, and Kuwaitis happily waved pictures of the emir. Kuwaitis also chanted the name of George Bush, whose country eventually won billions of dollars worth of contracts to rebuild the country. Of course, Bush could have easily liberated Kuwait as early as August through pursuing a diplomatic settlement, and could have pursued the Iraqi or Soviet peace initiatives of the past weeks, saving the country and environment much destruction. The "liberation" of Kuwait was as phony and hypocritical as the Gulf war itself.

On February 27, George Bush appeared on television to halt the U.S.-led extermination of Iraqi troops. He declared Kuwait liberated and Iraq defeated. In the mode of control characteristic of technowar, Bush dictated stiff terms for a full cease-fire and so was able to impose his will on the defeated and massively overpowered Iraqis. The Gulf war was a great triumph for George Bush, establishing him as the leader of the Neoimperialist World Order. In the aftermath of the Gulf war, however, there was a brief revelation of the U.S. high-tech massacre of the fleeing Iraqis during the last two days of the war (10.2). But the liberation of Kuwait and revelation of Iraqi atrocities against Kuwaitis during the occupation (10.1) conveniently pushed U.S. atrocities out of the news and produced a climate in which Bush could bask in the warm glow of victory and win the highest approval ratings for a U.S. president in modern history. The war thus ended with a series of propaganda victories in addition to the military victory.

The ecological consequences of the war, however, were impossible to control completely (10.3), as were the turbulent passions unleashed by the Pandora's box of the Persian Gulf war (10.4). Consequently, unpleasant news continued to emanate from Kuwait and Iraq for some time after military hostilities ceased. Uprisings by rebel forces in southern Iraq and Kurdish forces in northern Iraq were violently suppressed by Saddam Hussein and his military, which was not rendered as ineffectual as Schwarzkopf had claimed. Moreover, eventually the popularity of George Bush and the war would fade and people would see that the U.S. military adventure really produced little of value for the people of the United States and the Middle East (10.5). As the days and months went by, Hussein seemed as firmly in control as ever. Moreover, suspicions emerged in July 1991, concerning whether the U.S.-led coalition had destroyed his nuclear, biological, and chemical weapons programs to the extent previously asserted by Schwarzkopf and his minions. Reports also began surfacing of the horrible suffering of the Iraqi people caused by the U.S.-led coalition bombing as epidemics, lack of medical care, and malnutrition threatened to take hundreds of thousands more lives in addition to the civilian and military casualties already inflicted. The Kuwaiti oil fires threatened the health and environment of the region and many forecasted a "nuclear winter" effect, if the fires were not extinguished and if the smoke blocked out the sun and disrupted weather patterns across the planet. Hence, the people and environment of the region continued to suffer the violence of the war long after the euphoria of the U.S. victory had subsided.

In this chapter, I shall argue that the aftermath of the Gulf war reveals that little of value was gained by this human and environmental holocaust. *Time* magazine posed the question "Was It Worth It?" on its August 5, 1991, cover. The aftermath of the war left Saddam Hussein in power and many people concluded that the affair had produced nothing but new regional instability, the slaughter of tens of thousands of Iraqis, and "near apocalyptic conditions" in Iraq, as well as one of the worst

Figure 10.1   Celebration.

INSIDE KUWAIT: Anger and Chaos

TIME

A Moment To Savor

And the lessons of victory

environmental disasters in history. Millions of people had been displaced by the crisis and war, Kuwait was in ruin and chaos, and the whole episode wasted hundreds of billions of dollars (see Note 2 in the Preface for figures). In addition, the Gulf war brutalized U.S. culture and created the conditions for a resurgence of militarism that deflected attention from pressing social and economic problems (10.5). The experience also brutalized Kuwait and the aftermath of its "liberation" was extremely unpleasant, as we shall see in the next section.

10.1 Torture and Other Atrocities

During the period from the eve of the ground war through the end of the war, a propaganda campaign circulated stories concerning Iraqi atrocities against Kuwaitis. On February 23, the day that the ground war began, Gen. Butch Neal continued to lie dutifully for his country, claiming that "[t]here seems to be a systematic campaign of execution, particularly people that they [the Iraqis] may have tortured previously. They're sort of destroying the evidence, I guess, for lack of a better term." Robert Gates, Bush's deputy national security adviser, and current head of the CIA, said in a February 24 interview on CNN that there were "large scale executions and torture, mutilation" and other atrocities being committed in Kuwait: "we are hearing that they may be setting fire to Kuwait City itself, large sections of the city are in flames. This is a sort of a medieval practice."[1]

Continuing the propaganda campaign, Saudi General Khalid reported on February 25 that Iraqis in Kuwait were committing "unspeakable acts," including smashing heads in with axes, rape, and dismembering Kuwaitis and hanging their parts in public places. General Schwarzkopf also spoke in his briefing of February 27 of "unspeakable atrocities" that reporters would discover in Kuwait City and claimed that the Iraqis had taken "up to 40,000 [hostages]." The television networks circulated these stories without much skepticism. CNN was particularly guilty and CBS's Dan Rather once had to remind correspondent Eric Engberg that one should not always accept such stories at face value as Engberg was enthusiastically rattling off a list of recent Iraqi horrors fed to him by his military handlers.

More skeptically, the *New York Times* of February 26 cited Andrew Whitly, director of Middle East Watch, an independent human-rights group, who warned about "the self-interested nature of the sources and the timing of their announcements" (p. A10). The *Times* also cited refugees from Kuwait who had just arrived at the Jordanian border and "said they saw no evidence of the widescale atrocities alleged by Kuwaiti exile groups and some American officials." One refugee, Ghazi Hijazi, a businessman, said that, "Iraqi troops are treating people well. They are not bothering them" (p. A10). National Public Radio's John Hockenberry interviewed refugees from Kuwait City in Amman, Jordan, on February 26 who said that they had not seen the alleged burning buildings and murdered civilians. Some Iraqi atrocities were documented when coalition troops entered the city, but it was discovered that the atrocity stories were greatly exaggerated,[2] though the TV networks continued to circulate them daily, falling prey to another Kuwaiti/U.S. disinformation campaign (see 2.1 for discussion of the earlier campaigns during the crisis in the Gulf).

On February 28, ABC's "Nightline" had a segment on the Iraqi atrocities against Kuwaitis. Host Ted Koppel recalled an episode after the Iraqi invasion in September when a young woman called him from Kuwait to tell of the atrocities being committed against the Kuwaiti people. Koppel claimed that he had reason to believe that this woman was captured, tortured, and killed by the Iraqis. After playing a tape of his earlier telephone interview with the woman, Koppel brought on a Kuwaiti "doctor," who was allegedly a resistance fighter, to detail her fate which the "doctor" described as "the worst I've seen all through the last six-and-a-half months."[3] The "doctor" then depicted in detail her torture and mutilation, with her head cut by an axe into three pieces, and the depositing of her body in front of her house.

The doctor's face was concealed with the *gutras,* a Kuwaiti headdress, wrapped around it and when asked why he was hiding his identity, he replied that Kuwait City was still not completely safe. This claim was suspicious because everyone else in Kuwait City seemed eager to tell his or her story of the Iraqi occupation directly to the camera. Finally, the "doctor" provided details of other Iraqi torture and execution of Kuwaitis illustrated by pictures that the doctor had allegedly taken himself in hospitals and the morgue, to document the atrocities. The pictures looked suspiciously like the ones used by the Free Kuwait and Hill and Knowlton cabal at the UN and Congressional exhibitions of Iraqi atrocities.

The Kuwaiti doctor may have been part of a propaganda campaign, first, because he was quick to tell Ted Koppel exactly the story about the young Kuwaiti resistance fighter that fit into Koppel's videotape of her call to his show earlier when she revealed the Iraqi atrocities in Kuwait City. Moreover, the "doctor's" example of atrocities was suspicious in that the Iraqis splitting a head into three pieces with an axe was precisely the grisly example referred to by General Khalid at the Saudi briefing a few days before. The "doctor's" hiding of his identity was also suspicious, repeating the ploy of the "doctor" who had earlier told the much-publicized and then discredited story of the Iraqis killing premature babies by robbing their incubators. His pictures of Kuwaitis tortured by Iraqis appeared quite similar to the ones presented at the UN and Congress by the Kuwaiti exile movement (see 2.1). It was therefore entirely possible that the "doctor" was part of a Kuwaiti-U.S. propaganda campaign to dramatize atrocities for a world ready to believe anything about the demonized Iraqis.[4]

The "doctor" recounted additional horror stories and said that tortured and executed victims numbered in the hundreds and those who were tortured, imprisoned, and released totaled in the thousands. When asked if Kuwaitis wanted to exact revenge from the Iraqis who were imprisoned in Kuwait, he answered that they were treating the Iraqi prisoners humanely and even giving them medical treatment, precisely the Kuwaiti government line of the moment. Within a few days, however, it was revealed that Kuwaitis were at that very moment systematically killing Iraqis and Palestinians suspected of being collaborators in extremely brutal ways, so the "doctor" here might have been producing propaganda to deflect attention from Kuwaiti atrocities to Iraqi ones.

Furthermore, the "doctor" claimed that the health conditions for the Kuwaiti people were currently very poor because of the Iraqi destruction of the water desalination plant (earlier said to have been destroyed by the oil spill), but that water was being brought in and in general they were overall "in good shape" (again, the line being advanced by the Kuwaiti government). The "doctor" appeared the next morning on ABC's "Good Morning America" where he was interviewed, still hiding his identity, about Iraqi crimes during the occupation.

This episode raises questions concerning the responsibilities of TV networks in serving as conduits for propaganda of the U.S. or foreign governments and the precautions that they should take. Did ABC attempt to discover if the woman resistance fighter actually existed or whether she was an invention of a Kuwaiti exile propaganda group? What efforts did ABC take to check into the identity of the "doctor" and what evidence did they have that his testimony was genuine? Instead of exhibiting any skepticism, Koppel and ABC presented the "doctor" simply as an objective authority, eyewitness to the truth concerning Iraqi brutality. They raised no questions concerning his authenticity and the accuracy of these reports and simply conveyed his assertions as facts, thus potentially falling prey to a Kuwaiti propaganda campaign. ABC also failed to note the similarity of the pictures of Kuwaiti torture victims that the "doctor" allegedly took to the ones displayed in Washington and New York during the congressional and UN hearings when the Free Kuwait group submitted evidence of Iraqi atrocities.

Thus, it appears that ABC became part of a highly orchestrated propaganda campaign to circulate stories of Iraqi atrocities, as did other television networks, which were also quick to circulate such stories without checking their veracity or raising any questions concerning their authenticity. Charles Jaco of CNN, closely connected to the Kuwaiti resistance throughout the war, was especially susceptible to Kuwaiti propaganda stories concerning the Iraqis. In his reports from "liberated" Kuwait City, he presented the stories of his sources, who recounted Iraqi atrocities simply as fact, thus becoming a vehicle for the positions that the Kuwaiti government wanted circulated.

The *New York Times* on February 28 did deflate the Iraqi atrocity story favored by George Bush, Dan Quayle, and several high-ranking generals who repeated incessantly the story of how Iraq entered a hospital after the war and took premature babies out of incubators, throwing them on the floor and leaving them to die, so that the incubators could be used in Iraq (see 2.1). The *Times* reported: "Some of the atrocities that had been reported, such as the killing of infants in the main hospitals shortly after the invasion, are untrue or have been exaggerated, Kuwaitis said. Hospital officials, for instance, said that stories circulated about the killing of 300 children were incorrect" (Feb. 28, 1991, p. A6). ABC's John Martin did a follow-up on the story on March 15, interviewing doctors in the hospitals where the alleged Iraqi crimes took place. One doctor showed Martin the incubators which hospital officials had hidden during the Iraqi occupation and other doctors indicated that there were "no nurses to take care of these babies and that's why they died."[5]

Martin also revealed in his ABC report that reports of Iraqi hostage taking were exaggerated. While General Schwarzkopf claimed in his February 27 briefing that 40,000 Kuwaitis were taken prisoner, Kuwaiti authorities later stated that the numbers were more like 1,500–3,000. On the other hand, the figure of 4,000 hostages cited by the BBC continued to circulate and Susan Sachs reported on July 28, 1991 that, "The whereabouts of some 4,000 Kuwaitis arrested by Iraqi occupation troops are still unknown" (*Newsday*, p. 39). Hence, Kuwaiti authorities might have wanted to play down the number of Kuwaitis taken hostage by the fleeing Iraqis and quite probably slaughtered with the Iraqi army fleeing Kuwait (see 10.2). Finally, Martin claimed that the reports of thousands of Kuwaitis executed by Iraqi soldiers, circulated by U.S., Saudi, and other authorities, were also exaggerated and that the "real number" is "something around a little bit over 300." Likewise, Humans Rights Watch concluded: "In total, 320 people are known to have been killed by Iraqi forces during the occupation of Kuwait, from August 2, 1990 to February 25, 1991" (1991a, p. 3).

Reporters found that the claims of Robert Gates and others concerning widespread damage to the city were also highly exaggerated. There was extensive damage to the city, but much of it could be attributed to coalition bombing or the Kuwaiti resistance.[6] A *Washington Post* reporter observed that, "Throughout the city, destruction was spotty. Windows of some stores, such as jewelry and watch shops, were smashed and the contents looted. Many others were left untouched. Gaping holes yawned in the sides of several posh hotels. . . . Overall, however, most buildings throughout the city remained undisturbed" (Feb. 28, 1991). By March 1, gas was available and the Kuwaiti interior minister stated on March 4 that electricity and water could be restored to the city in a few days. *Newsweek* reported that the airport was functional, roads and water system were basically in good shape, and that backup electrical generators were available to restore power. One military official told the magazine a week after the cease-fire that, " '[t]he bottom line is that damage is not as extensive as had been thought' " (March 11, 1991, p. 33).

On March 4, the first member of the Royal Family returned to Kuwait; Crown Prince Sheik Saad al-Abdullah al-Sabah kissed the ground and declared a return to the official rule by his family. CNN's Tom Mintier reported that the Kuwaiti resistance movement announced that it was turning in its weapons. According to Mintier (and this is pure disinformation), the resistance forces were planning to officially disband and give power back to the former government. And then, in an episode on March 4 that suggested more propaganda, an alleged member of the resistance came on camera, his face shrouded with his shawl and thick glasses. The "resistance fighter" proclaimed that the Kuwaiti resistance was giving up its weapons and "will have democracy peacefully and without guns." Obviously, the Kuwaiti government wanted the resistance to give up their guns and it used the bait of promised democracy to get them to surrender their weapons and dissolve the resistance organizations, which constituted a threat to the autocratic policies of the al-Sabah family.[7]

The early pictures of the resistance fighters showed courageous and heroic young men and women, armed, fighting for the liberation of their country, arresting Iraqis, and policing the area, while protecting its citizens. During the occupation, they had provided food, medical aid, security, and hope to the Kuwaitis who suffered the Iraqi occupation. They were organized in small, well-disciplined cells and risked their lives to preserve their country and people while the rich Kuwaiti exiles frolicked in Monte Carlo, London, or other comfortable locales.

The resistance members were now, however, an impediment to the Kuwaiti Royal Family, who wished to reestablish its autocratic rule. The resistance was experienced in the art of self-government; many were genuine champions of democracy who took responsibility for the well-being and survival of their people in an incredibly difficult situation. They were freedom fighters who wanted democracy and had the prestige and the military skills to demand it. The resistance fighters thus posed a significant challenge to the ruling family, which had already announced that it would impose martial law for three months and would not recall the Kuwaiti parliament or give women rights, as they had promised earlier, "until things are better." The former Kuwaiti regime thus had the interest of first disarming and then marginalizing the Kuwaiti resistance forces so as to secure their own continued authoritarian rule; the U.S. media, with some exceptions, were furthering this goal.

Indeed, the U.S. government was siding, as conservative governments usually do, with the Kuwaiti ruling family. The U.S. government was keenly interested in securing lucrative contracts (estimated at $100 to $200 billion) for U.S. firms to help rebuild Kuwait, and early estimates indicated that U.S. corporations received over 70 percent of the initial contracts.[8] The U.S. government and its corporations could best do business with the former Kuwaiti ruling circles and were probably not particularly interested in democracy and the fate of the Kuwaiti resistance. U.S. officials pay lip service to democracy, but do business with the autocrats. Indeed, while the United States pretends to be committed to democracy, the primary national allegiance, particularly of the Bush administration, is to capitalism (see Kellner 1990). Therefore, the U.S. corporations and the capitalist state were eager to do business with the ruling elite with whom U.S. business interests already had relations and who could be counted on to provide lucrative deals.

In helping promote the Kuwaiti government line that the resistance should surrender their arms and submit to the al-Sabah's rule, the media were thus promoting the interests of the U.S. government and those firms seeking to do business with the Royal Family. However, on March 4 and 5, there were some TV stories critical of the al-Sabah family, and some positive stories on the Kuwaiti resistance and its demands for democratization aired. ABC's "Nightline" of March 4 featured an interview with a prominent Kuwaiti businessman who accused the al-Sabah family of hiring assassination squads to murder members of the Kuwaiti resistance. Host Ted Koppel also interviewed a leading member of the prodemocracy movement who had been shot by a Kuwaiti in his house and was now paralyzed. As Koppel held his hand in a hospital-bed interview, the Kuwaiti democrat told him that the shooting was deliberate, though he hesitated to name his assassin.

The Kuwaiti UN ambassador, a member of the al-Sabah family, vehemently denied that his family was involved in political assassinations. He claimed that members of his family had stayed in Kuwait and struggled in the resistance, attempting to undermine the distinction being made by resistance members between those who stayed and struggled and those who left the country. The ambassador defended the three-month imposition of martial law and then promised that there would be democratization, though by summer 1992 no democratic reforms had yet materialized.[9]

Early in the morning on March 5, CNN featured stories of prodemocracy Kuwaiti resistance forces, who did not want to surrender their guns and were calling for democratization. A male professor urged more democracy and a female resistance fighter argued for equal rights for women, who had served heroically in the resistance. The episode also showed resistance members continuing to police streets, "often meting out their own justice," which involved assassination of Iraqi secret police, Palestinian collaborators, and those involved in atrocities against Kuwaitis, as the mainstream media was beginning to report. Both members of the resistance movement and Kuwaiti troops who were now occupying the city were carrying out vigilante actions, which the U.S. media noted but did not investigate.

However, CNN continued to circulate daily Iraqi atrocity stories, including the incubator story, which had been thoroughly discredited. On both March 5 and 6, CNN ran a story about grave diggers in Kuwait who allegedly buried over forty victims of the incubator atrocity in mass graves. This was somewhat astonishing in the light of the exposure of the story and showed the extent to which CNN was manipulated by Kuwaiti disinformation campaigns.

In any case, Kuwait was now "liberated" and the old ruling powers returned to consolidate their autocratic rule. The country suffered under martial law and a primitive form of "justice" in which those who were suspected of collaboration with the Iraqis were summarily executed. Robert Fisk, a reporter for the British *Independent,* told of U.S. Special Forces troops looking on as Kuwaitis brutalized Iraqis and Palestinians. When Fisk and an associate tried to intervene when three Kuwaiti soldiers were beating up a Palestinian boy, the U.S. troops pushed him aside, telling him, "This is martial law, boy. Fuck off." Then, smiling, the U.S. soldier told him to "have a nice day" (*The Independent,* Mar. 4, 1991). Undeniably, there was a rash of vigilante executions of Iraqis and those suspected of collaborating with the Iraqi regime during the occupation in the days after the liberation.[10] Mass graves, holding up to fifty-four "unidentified bodies" of people who appeared to have died since March, indicated organized and "official" mass murder by Kuwaiti authorities. Kenneth Roth, deputy director of Human Rights Watch, stated in a *New York Times* Op-Ed piece that other documented "post-liberation killings of people in police and military custody substantiates this view" (June 11, 1991).

The return of Kuwaiti "legal" institutions did not help matters much. During a series of well-publicized "trials" in June 1991, individuals were sentenced to long prison terms and sometimes death on the word of informers. Those charged with collaboration were denied access to lawyers and one young man was sentenced to twenty years imprisonment for wearing a T-shirt embroidered with the figure of Saddam Hussein; he claimed that he had owned it before the war and merely slept in it occasionally. Women employed as servants of Kuwaitis complained of a dramatic increase in rape, often by Kuwaiti soldiers. Seven entertainers were sentenced to life in prison for "taking part in an Iraqi-established union for artists" and for "propagandizing" in their profession. The government seemed incapable of getting the country running again, and pollution from oil fires rendered the country virtually unlivable (10.3). Talk of democratic reform subsided and U.S. corporations greedily competed for contracts.

In a speech to Congress on March 6, George Bush orated that we will "forge a future that should never again be held hostage to the darker side of human nature. . . . A world in which freedom and respect for human rights find a home among all nations. The Gulf war put this new world to its first test, and, my fellow Americans, we passed the test." At the time of his speech, mass arrests, street executions, torture, and rape were the order of the day in "liberated" Kuwait. Oppression continued and Bush supported the nondemocratic government forces by stating during a July 1, 1991, press conference in response to a reporter's question about repression in Kuwait, "The war was not fought about democracy in Kuwait. . . . I think we're expecting a little much if we're asking the people of Kuwait to take kindly to those that had spied on their countrymen that were left there, that had brutalized their families there and things of that nature." Showing their appreciation, the Kuwaiti government daily *Sawt al-Kuwan* ran these comments on its front page July 3, 1991: "Bush declares his understanding of Kuwait's attitude towards collaborators" (Middle East Watch 1991a). Business had returned to usual—but worse.

Kuwait refused to let many of its citizens back in the country after its liberation, including many who were visiting Iraq, in some cases, visiting relatives taken hostage during the crisis. Kuwait also refused to let many foreign workers return, including Egyptians and workers from other members of the coalition. Susan Sachs reported on June 9, 1991, that "Miffed at the gulf states' ambivalence about keeping wartime promises of jobs and financial aid, Egypt and Syria are withdrawing troops that were supposed to form the core of a new gulf security force. . . . An underlying theme is that Kuwaitis are ungrateful" (*Newsday,* p. 13). And greedy: "Recent advertisements by landlords in Kuwait, including one member of the ruling al-Sabah family, warn displaced tenants to pay rent for the months of Iraqi occupation in five days or lose the belongings left in their Kuwait apartments" (*Newsday,* p. 13).

10.2 High-Tech Massacre

Meanwhile, as the hoards of reporters invaded Kuwait, images began to emerge of the extent of massacre of Iraqis by the U.S.-led coalition forces. Few scenes shown of actual fighting in the Kuwaiti and Iraqi theaters of death appeared during the last several days of the war. The pool system had assured that the military would control what images would be shown of the combat. Although there were a few images of wounded U.S. troops, there were no images of the slaughter of Iraqis by the U.S.-led coalition. There was also little discussion of the extent of Iraqi casualties in the mainstream media. Schwarzkopf and other coalition military leaders refused to speculate on the number of Iraqi dead, and there were few mainstream media inquiries into the topic.

The *New York Times* published an article on March 1 which minimized Iraqi casualties. A front-page story by John H. Cushman, Jr., was headlined: "Military Experts See a Death Toll of 25,000 to 50,000 Iraqi troops."[11] Note that Iraqi casualties went down already from the 85,000–100,000 casualty figures cited by the Saudis the day before, suggesting that a sanitizing process was underway. Cushman's sources were "military experts," probably the most vacuous sources imaginable. The story then cited several other estimates, with the largest being the 85,000–100,000 Saudi estimate. But there was no discussion of how these estimates were reached. Cushman did quote General Schwarzkopf who said that there would be no official counting of Iraqi casualties, which he contrasted with a report that President Bush had ordered General Powell to undertake an analysis of the number of Iraqis killed as the war progressed. If the process will be similar to the report undertaken of casualties during the Panama invasion, one could expect more lies and another cover-up.[12]

At the afternoon Pentagon briefing on March 1, Lt. Gen. Thomas Kelly said bluntly that the United States was not in the game of counting casualties and when pushed said that they had "killed an entire army."[13] Details of the magnitude of the systematic annihilation of the Iraqis emerged, however, when reporters journeyed up the highway leading from Kuwait City to Iraq, and about twenty miles from the city found evidence of a tremendous slaughter of Iraqis who were fleeing from Kuwait. The first report on what became known as "the Highway of Death" was broadcast on CNN during the morning of March 1, which showed pictures of the road from Kuwait City to the Iraqi border. According to CNN correspondent Tom Mintier, video had just surfaced of a scene outside of Kuwait City depicting "vehicles who were going nowhere." The fleeing Iraqis took any vehicles that they could find to drive to Iraq and when they got outside of the city the allies put a pincer movement on them. They were hit by allied aircraft and artillery in place along the highway, producing a massive traffic jam and subsequent slaughter. The vehicles included civilian cars, buses, trucks, tanks, fire engines, and armored vehicles, some of which burned together as they caught fire and then exploded, producing a conflagration from which few, if any, escaped. There were hundreds of victims, Mintier reported, and charred bodies, burned beyond recognition, were evident inside and around the vehicles.

The video showed pictures of a highway littered with civilian and military vehicles that had been destroyed in one of the most massive slaughters by air power in history. There were images of one vehicle after another, mile after mile, piled upon each other, evoking a picture of a giant traffic jam in which planes bombed and destroyed anything below themselves. Mintier stated that there may have been heavy civilian casualties, and it was not certain if the victims were Iraqis, their Kuwaiti hostages, or fleeing Palestinians.

CNN then cut to a piece on the opening of the U.S. embassy in Kuwait and next to a story of Iraqi atrocities in Kuwait, as if to justify the slaughter. As the story was developed through the day, more legitimations of the systematic killing were produced by CNN and the other television networks. A CNN report cut to a U.S. soldier on the highway who laughed and smiled, saying, "This is absolute chaos. This is ridiculous." He indicated that all of the vehicles were stolen and that the cars were full of military gear and stolen consumer goods, such as television sets and other items. Thereafter, the official U.S. military pushed the line that the corpses littering the highway or burned in their vehicles were thieves fleeing the city in stolen vehicles full of contraband goods.

For the rest of the day the theme of the looters getting their due punishment was privileged by the networks; one soldier remarked: "They're just looters, not fighters" and this quote was repeated endlessly by CNN and the other networks. All of the major network evening news accounts covered the story, though none featured it and they all tended to play it down.[14] The segment was generally framed by stories of Iraqi atrocities, which presented the Iraqis as subhuman monsters and thus seemingly excused the slaughter as just punishment. While there were, no doubt, torturers and even killers among the fleeing crowd, there were also young Iraqi conscripts who were in Kuwait against their will, as well as Kuwaitis, Palestinians, and civilian forces in the masses of fleeing people slaughtered in a high-tech massacre.

The CBS reporting was especially apologetic. On March 1, CBS reported that the pictures of mile after mile of wreckage were "evidence of the panic of a fleeing army." The report then focused on Kuwaitis who were venturing back onto the road: Some came to see the wreckage, while others came to see the dead soldiers. "They got what they deserved. They are not human beings," a Kuwaiti said on camera. The CBS report concluded that the area was still a "dangerous place" with munitions and artillery pointed at Kuwait City (which subliminally suggested that the slaughtered individuals were engaged in a military operation against Kuwait City and thus deserved to die). The report quickly cut back to Kuwait City with mobs of people surrounding the news crew to joyfully chant "U.S.A! U.S.A!"

On March 2, CBS ran an even more appalling justification for the Highway of Death. A report by Eric Engberg featured Gen. Walter Boomer who justified the slaughter on the Highway of Death: "In addition to being thoroughly incompetent, they were thieves as well as murderers." A blonde crew-cut soldier stated: "Seeing all the damage that we did to these guys, it almost made it worth while for all the time we spent here." This disgusting report shows the mechanisms of denial and projection at work, in which the U.S. military and their complicit media accomplices deny coalition crimes and project all evil on the Iraqis. CBS's effort to justify the unjustifiable in this segment shows the depth of complicity of the media in covering over and justifying U.S. crimes.

Mainstream newspapers tended to downplay the story. The March 2 *New York Times* inserted a couple of brief paragraphs concerning what was arguably one of the major stories of the war in the middle of an article by R. A. Apple, who tersely described the basic facts and, like the TV reporters, stressed the "looters" angle (p. 6A).[15] The mainstream media in Britain, however, were more critical of the desert slaughter. A BBC report mentioned that the vehicles taken out of Kuwait City were mostly civilian vehicles and that there were very few tanks or artillery on the Highway of Death, raising the question whether the fleeing Iraqis with their hostages were a legitimate military target. The BBC's Stephen Sackur also discerned evidence of cluster bombs, antipersonnel weapons that are designed to break up into hundreds of little bomblets to maximize damage to both humans and machines. Sackur wrote: "It was the scale of the American attack that took my breath away. Was it necessary to bomb the entire convoy? What threat could these pathetic remnants of Saddam Hussein's beaten army have posed? Wasn't it obvious that the people of the convoy would have given themselves up willingly without the application of such ferocious weaponry?" (in MacArthur 1991, p. 265).

On the March 3, "This Week With David Brinkley" program, correspondent Sam Donaldson had the bad manners to ask Bush's national security adviser, Brent Scowcroft, a question concerning what he described as the "annihilation" of the fleeing Iraqis north of Kuwait City. Scowcroft, showing no remorse and offering no real explanation, answered that "our objective was not to kill people but to destroy the offensive capability of Iraq." Donaldson made the point, forgotten in the other media stories, that thousands of Kuwaiti civilians were fleeing with the Iraqis, taken as hostages.[16] Scowcroft's stunning answer was that "I think that our bombing—first of all, remember, Sam, that our bombing is unlike bombing in any other conflict. We're talking precision. We're talking you shoot at tanks, you hit the tank. For the people in it, of course, it's the same, but for the people who may be innocent bystanders going along in convoy, it is not the same." This answer is incredible because it exemplifies the claim that the high-tech precision bombing was able to cleanly destroy military equipment while avoiding civilian casualties. It is also disingenuous because during the massacre on the Highway of Death, the bombing was systematic, with Scowcroft's warriors brutally wiping out everything in their kill zones with methodical precision (though some Brits, Kuwaitis, and coalition "friendlies" were accidentally killed as well). But in the case of the Highway of Death there was ample evidence that the Iraqis were taking Kuwaiti hostages with them, though that didn't stop the U.S. military from ordering and condoning the massacre.

Donaldson let Scowcroft get away with his hypocritical non sequitur answer and conservative ideologue George Will quickly changed the subject.[17] Scowcroft relaxed, knowing that all he had to do was equivocate and the question would be dropped. Watching Brent Scowcroft answer, or rather evade, Donaldson's question, allowed one to see the cold demeanor of an individual whose sense of national security is military security and who all of the insider accounts of the genesis of the Gulf war suggest was, along with Bush, the most resolute in pushing the war option and refusing all diplomatic solutions (see 1.3).[18]

There was very little mainstream media discussion or commentary on the full scope of the high-tech massacre. One report observed that Marine Gen. Walter Boomer passed along a message to his commanders from Norman Schwarzkopf "not to let anybody or anything out of Kuwait" (Bill Gannon, *Newark Star-Ledger,* Feb. 27, 1991). The Highway of Death was briefly featured but there were few reports on the other killing fields of the ground war. The other major route out of Kuwait to Iraq was a coastal route running north to the Iraqi border city of Umm Qasr and according to an Army officer on the scene there was " 'nothing but shit strewn everywhere, five to seven miles of just solid bombed-out vehicles.

The U.S. Air Force,' he said, 'had been given the word to work over that entire area, to find anything that was moving and take it out'" (Michael Kelly, *The New Republic,* Apr. 1, 1991, p. 12). A Navy A-6 pilot noted that the convoy consisted of "a 20-mile nose-to-tail jam" (Mike Gaines, *Flight International,* Mar. 6–12, p. 8).

A powerful account of the carnage on the road to Umm Qasr, Kuwait, was found in the *Los Angeles Times* in a story by Bob Drogin (Mar. 10, 1991) which contained much graphic detail.

> For 60 miles, hundreds of Iraqi tanks and armored cars, howitzers and antiaircraft guns, ammunition trucks and ambulances were strafed, smashed and burned beyond belief. Scores of soldiers lie in and around the vehicles, mangled and bloated in the drifting desert sands. . . . Every truck is riddled with shrapnel. No looting by the dead soldiers was evident. No survivors are known or likely. . . . At one spot, snarling wild dogs have reduced two corpses to bare ribs. Giant carrion birds claw and pick at another; only a boot-clad foot and eyeless skull are recognizable (p. A1). (See also the graphic account by Michael Kelly in the *New Republic,* Apr. 1, 1991.)

During the high-tech massacre, U.S. air activity was frenzied and air controllers were worried about collisions in the air. A report was dispatched from the USS *Ranger* by Randall Richard of the *Providence Journal* that: "Air strikes against Iraqi troops retreating from Kuwait were being launched so feverishly from this carrier today that pilots said they took whatever bombs happened to be closest to the flight deck. The crews, working to the strains of the Lone Ranger theme, often passed up the projectile of choice . . . because it took too long to load." A BBC radio report indicated that U.S. fighter planes were lining up to take off from their aircraft carriers to the strains of the William Tell Overture over the loudspeakers to go on what they called "The Turkey Shoot." British military officials were quick to point out that they did not participate in the Desert Slaughter and were perhaps embarrassed by the excesses of their U.S. comrades-in-arms. Indeed, the metaphor of the hunt was appropriate for the massacre. One pilot said that it "was like shooting fish in a barrel," and Squadron leader Cmdr. Frank Sweigert said that their human targets were "basically just sitting ducks" (*Washington Post,* Feb. 27, 1991).

C-SPAN broadcast an interview with two F-10 pilots, "Fish" and "Karl," on February 27, taken from military pool footage.[19] They described their pleasure in killing tank after tank, with Fish exploding in wargasmic ecstasy when he described what it was like to see his target explode. From the ground, the sight was not so pretty. London *Independent* reporter Richard Dowden stated in a televised interview, "The lorries further down the line would have tried to crash off the motorway and just get away, just get off the road and [the coalition pilots] would have chased them, and you saw them in the desert, and then you would see bodies going from those lorries so they'd actually hunted down people who were just running away" (PeaceNet, mideast.gulf, Feb. 27, 1991). The highway was literally awash with blood, with one reporter writing, "As we drove slowly through the wreckage, our armored personnel carrier's tracks splashed through great pools of bloody water. We passed dead soldiers lying, as if resting, without a mark on them. We found others cut up so badly, a pair of legs in its trousers would be 50 yards from the top half of the body. Four soldiers had died under a truck where they had sought protection" (*Newsweek,* Mar. 11, 1991, p. 25).

In the days following the end of the war, there were isolated reports of other massacres of fleeing Iraqi troops throughout northern Kuwait and southern Iraq. On March 1, a convoy of Iraqi troops allegedly fired at U.S. troops and the valiant warriors destroyed hundreds of Iraqi tanks and vehicles, while slaughtering over 2,000 Iraqi soldiers, two days after Bush had called a halt to military activities. In a report published in the May 8, 1991, *Newsday,* Patrick Sloyan claimed that Schwarzkopf had ordered the massacre, described as "the biggest clash of the gulf war's ground campaign," even though fighting had ceased. Although the U.S. military briefer had claimed that day that U.S. forces were using loud-speakers "to tell the Iraqis that a ceasefire had occurred," no loudspeakers were used in this specific postwar massacre. Apache helicopters armed with laser-guided Hellfire missiles slaughtered the Iraqi troops and the army footage of the fight obtained by *Newsday* recorded one U.S. soldier joking, "Say hello to Allah" as he fired a hellfire missile.

To cover over the carnage, Saudi "mortuary platoons" quickly moved to bury the bodies without ascertaining whether the bodies were Iraqi, Kuwaiti, Palestinian, or Asian guest-workers.[20] An episode shown on CNN on March 11 depicted the digging of mass graves for the massacred Iraqi troops, reduced to burnt-out corpses. But the mainstream media did little after the initial reports to investigate the Desert Slaughter, ranging from the bombing of Iraqis fleeing north to Baghdad or Basra, to those caught on the Highway of Death and other killing fields in Kuwait. No discussion took place either concerning who was responsible for the desert slaughter. Schwarzkopf had ordered at the start of the ground war "not to let anybody or anything out of Kuwait City" (*Newark Star-Ledger,* Feb. 27, 1991) and after the war Air Force General Merrill McPeak (1991) stated: "I think we have tried to disarm the Iraqi Army as humanely as possible." But then he admitted that: "It's during this phase that the true fruits of victory are achieved from combat, when the enemy's disorganized" (1991). Yet what military "fruits" were realized in these senseless slaughters?

Reports indicated that many of those retreating from Kuwait City had put white flags on their vehicles which were visible to U.S. pilots (Rowan Scarborough, "Pool Report Aboard the USS *Blue Ridge*," *Washington Times*, Feb. 27, 1991) and, as noted, there were many reports that Kuwaitis, Palestinians, and other civilians were massacred by U.S. forces. Consequently, there were claims that the slaughter of retreating Iraqis and others constituted a war crime, violating "the Geneva Conventions of 1949, Common Article III, which outlaws the killing of soldiers who are out of combat" (Joyce Chediac, "The Massacre of Withdrawing Soldiers on 'The Highway of Death,'" in Clark et al. 1992, p. 91). The Bush administration claimed that the Iraqi troops were retreating to regroup and were thus in "fighting retreat," but, in fact, they were a "fleeing rabble," as the Pentagon would eventually admit.

Thus the high-tech massacre of the fleeing Iraqis stands as an example of systematic extermination and is the perfect expression of technocratic war, of systematically annihilating the enemy by wiping out anything that moves. This was the fruit of U.S. technowar: the massive production of death and extermination of the Iraqi military and whoever happened to be in the way of the U.S. Armada of Winged Death. The Highway of Death thus served as the most dramatic demonstration of U.S. killing power and provided a fitting and necessary ending to a war dedicated from the beginning to the destruction of the Iraqi military and to the demonstration of U.S. military power.

The Desert Slaughter clearly demonstrated that (1) war *is* hell; (2) war is *not* a viable solution to political conflicts; and (3) thus war is obsolete as a mode of contemporary conflict resolution. The Gulf war vividly demonstrated the lethality of high-tech weapons systems and the tremendous damage that they are capable of inflicting on the social-industrial infrastructure of a system, the environment, and human life. Although the claims for precision and cleanness of the high-tech weapons systems were surely exaggerated, in fact the United States proved that it could systematically slaughter a fleeing army and destroy the economic and social infrastructure of a country. The Gulf war also clearly discloses the tremendous environmental damage which high-tech weapons systems inflict on the environment, suggesting that modern warfare is a form of environmental terrorism and even ecocide.

10.3 Environmental Holocaust

In addition to the human holocaust produced by the massacre of Iraqis by the U.S.-led coalition and the systematic destruction of Iraq's infrastructure, the Gulf war also produced an environmental holocaust. It resulted from the U.S.-led coalition bombing of oil wells and oil tankers in Iraq and Kuwait, Iraq's torching of oil wells and deliberate pouring of oil into the Gulf, and coalition bombing of nuclear, chemical, and biological weapons facilities in Iraq. Every day, during the last week of the war and for weeks thereafter, there were TV images of the pollution of the Gulf and, especially, images of the polluted air from the burning oil wells.

On a March 1 CNN report, Reid Collins noted that Iraq had set explosives on all 900 oil fields in Kuwait and that allied bombings had set some of them off, causing a portion of the oil fires. He cited Kuwaiti government officials who claimed that even though the Iraqis had torched many of the wells as they were leaving the country, if the coalition forces had acted sooner they could have saved some of them. This story, however, of Kuwaitis criticizing the U.S. prosecution of the war, was quick to disappear and did not surface in the *New York Times* or most other mainstream media sources.

In retrospect, if Bush had chosen to negotiate a diplomatic settlement to end the war, most of the oil fires could have been prevented. In fact, the entire environmental holocaust was directly a result of Bush's decision to pursue a military solution to the crisis in the Gulf by launching an air war and ground war, and to refuse any negotiated settlement. At major environmental conferences before the war began, it was argued that if war broke out in such an ecologically sensitive area, there was sure to be an environmental catastrophe and this was undeniably what resulted. Furthermore, had Bush not insisted on the ground war, a settlement could have been negotiated that would have saved the Kuwaiti oil wells and the Gulf environment from the ensuing holocaust. George Bush and Saddam Hussein thus emerge from the Gulf war as two of the greatest environmental terrorists in history.

News reports of March 1 contained disturbing new details concerning the ecological holocaust caused by the Gulf war.[21] CNN reported through the day that the black, sooty smoke and toxic acid rain from the burning oil wells caused concern about the health of children, the aged, and those vulnerable to pollution in what one ecologist called: "A very, very difficult and perhaps dangerous situation." Other reports described the plumes of black acrid smoke filled with sulfur that made day look like night and made it hard to breath in some places in Kuwait and Saudi Arabia. The pollution was already producing acid rain throughout the area, with smoke rising to 10,000 feet, but the real danger would appear if the smoke rose to 30,000 feet, where it could hit the jet stream and travel around the earth. Substantial fear existed that warmer weather in the summer would make this possible, which could bring falling temperatures and acid rain that could destroy rice crops and other agriculture in India and Southeast Asia. Another expert saw the effects of the fires limited to the area; he didn't see the pollution effecting India or Southeast Asia. Work was soon to begin on dealing with the oil fires as three Texas firms were contracted to put them out, a process that could have taken from one to six years.

As it turned out, the Kuwaiti government initially gave contracts to extinguish the oil fires only to U.S. firms and put Bechtal corporation in charge of hiring companies to squelch the fires. Various Australian, German, Japanese, and other companies wanted to participate in the process, but the Kuwaiti government and their American friends prevented them from sharing in the activity.[22] This obstacle obviously inhibited and delayed the extinction of the fires, and reports began to circulate of pollution from the fires ranging from India to China to Germany. By September 1991 there were reports that the pollution from the oil fires, combined with volcanic ash from Mt. Pinitubo in the Philippines, had circled the earth in a sooty haze and threatened to create a nuclear winter, lowering the temperature of the earth and perhaps producing an environmental catastrophe of cataclysmic proportions.[23]

Although the oil fires were reportedly extinguished by November 1991, concerns continued to mount concerning the large number of uncapped high-pressure wells still spewing fountains of oil into the air, producing rivers and lakes of oil throughout Kuwait, up to a mile long (Tokar 1991). The National Oceanic and Atmospheric Administration chief scientist, Dr. John Robinson, "announced at a September [1991] briefing that there are an almost unbelievable 175 million barrels worth of oil (over seven *billion* gallons of oil at 42 gallons per barrel) lying on the ground in Kuwait. Oil is still pouring out of the ruptured underground casings of many of the extinguished wells. The Hawaiian wildlife protection group Earthtrust reports that migrating birds often mistake the oil lakes for water, facing almost certain death once they come into contact with the toxic pools" (Tokar 1991, p. 58). The British journal *New Scientist* reported (November 9, 1991) on the danger that the deluge of oil might wash into the Gulf and there was also dangers of the oil polluting the water supply and invisible poisonous vapors emanating from evaporating oil (see Vialls 1991). These sources indicate that the lakes of oil make it difficult to stem the flow of oil from the high-pressure wells, and it is thus still uncertain to what extent the out-of-control Kuwait oil wells will destroy the environment of Kuwait and the surrounding Gulf.

There was also the question of environmental contamination by coalition bombing of Iraqi oil refineries, factories, and their nuclear, chemical, and biological weapons industries (see 5.3). On March 2, C-SPAN cablecast a press conference with the Worldwatch Institute where two environmentalists answered questions on the environmental implications of the Persian Gulf war. Christopher Flavin noted that it was certain that there would be significant contamination of the immediate environment through the bombing of these facilities. The key questions, however, concerned the extent of the contamination and its nature. Obviously, the water supply could be threatened by potential contamination, and agriculture might also be affected. Yet as of this writing, although there has been a significant UN effort to inspect whether Iraq is continuing its biological, chemical, and nuclear weapons programs, there have been no official reports released on environmental contamination by the coalition bombing.

As it turned out, Iraq had moved much of the crucial nuclear material which escaped the allied bombing so that the bombing of Iraq's nuclear facilities merely risked an environmental holocaust with little benefit. Obviously, nuclear, chemical, and biological weapons are a menace, but it is arguable that the issue could be better dealt with through negotiations calling for dismantlement of unconventional weapons programs and through UN-imposed restrictions on nuclear, chemical, and biological weapons production throughout the world. In this way, there could be an international boycott imposed against supplying Iraq's and other nuclear, biological, and chemical weapons programs, with strict inspection to guarantee compliance. The United States, by contrast, dropped tons of bombs on Iraq's weapons facilities, causing a level of environmental contamination that is still unascertained, while falsely claiming that the bombing had eliminated Iraq's unconventional weapons capacities. Further, George Bush has yet to support limiting military sales to the Middle East, raising suspicions that part of the motivation for the Gulf war was precisely to increase U.S. arms sales to the region.

Discussion began after the war concerning the need to develop stricter environmental laws during wartime and the need to have something like a Geneva Convention for environmental crimes by ecoterrorists.[24] The Gulf war revealed once again that the imperialist and militarist mind, has no environmental consciousness. Technowar utilizes advanced informational and military technology to carry out systematic destruction of enemy troops and to dominate the battlefield. Technowar is the latest project in what the Frankfurt school called the domination of nature, a project that inexorably results in social domination and ecological destruction of the environment (Kellner 1989a). Technowar disregards the environment in its war plans and does not concern itself with ecological issues except as they impinge on warfare and politics. The military perspective does not recognize embeddedness in nature but, like modern science and technology, is concerned with the sovereignty of the subject over nature. The Other, be it people or the environment, is conceived of as the stuff of domination, mere matter to be controlled or destroyed. The madness of this project was clearly revealed in the Gulf war in the wanton destruction of the environment by both sides.

Thus, the devastation of the Persian Gulf shows the need to avoid wars, which in an era of high-tech warfare constitute a form of environmental terrorism. I have noted that early in the war Bush removed all environmental restraints on the Pentagon and blocked government agencies from revealing information concerning the environmental effects of the Gulf war. Thus, we see in retrospect, and too late, that "untying the hands" of the Pentagon meant in practice giving them unrestricted power to wreak maximum destruction on the environment and human beings. The Gulf war showed once again the disregard for the environment within the military and political establishments in the United States and elsewhere, as well as the need to abolish war in the contemporary era as a mode of conflict resolution.

10.4 Iraq Explodes; Saddam Hangs On

While George Bush won tremendous acclaim for his "victory" in the Gulf war,[25] Saddam Hussein was forced to struggle for his very survival. Hussein faced a relentless propaganda war against him in the West and internal unrest and eventually upheaval at home. At the end of the war, all the TV networks featured talk shows on what to do about Saddam Hussein. One of the favorite topics was whether war crimes trials should be instituted against him, and the advisability of assassinating him was also discussed. Another preferred genre was commentary on the fate of fallen tyrants, although such obituaries were somewhat premature because—to the summer of 1992 at least—Hussein has managed to hold onto power. On February 28, for instance, CNN raised the question "what's next for Saddam Hussein?" CNN described him as joining "a long list of dictators who were brought down" and offered a CNN perspective by Bill Moyers.

Moyers intoned that it was good that the world was rid of another dictator whom the United States supported and then had to be taken down—Batista, Somoza, Marcos, the shah of Iran, and Noriega. Saddam is next, Moyers opined, one more Frankenstein monster rampaging out of the laboratory who had to be hunted down. Moyers recalled that Reagan and Bush supported Saddam during the Iraq/Iran war, as did "armchair warriors" Sen. Alan Simpson (R-Wyo.) and Rep. Stephen Solarz (D-N.Y.) who gained political capital in attacking Saddam Hussein during the Persian Gulf war, but who earlier groveled in his presence when he was "just our bad guy." They armed him and allowed him to become the neighborhood bully, Moyers explained.

Although Moyers's portrait of the fallen dictator was premature, his Frankenstein metaphor was apt because it implied that there were creators of the Iraqi military machine who should be held responsible (though one could question whether monster metaphors promote intelligent political discourse). Moyers then pointed out that the Gulf war was not an even match: Iraq is about the size of Texas and has about as many people. Its military was exhausted by the Iran/Iraq war and it had no air force willing to fight. Its front-line troops were dragged off the streets of Baghdad and put in the desert with ill-fitted uniforms and no training, and, as for his doomsday weapons, "the better grandma to fool you." The truth, Moyers argued, was that Iraq was a Third World country with a fifth-rate economy. After this accurate analysis, Moyers then called Saddam Hussein "a world class psychopath" who "could play Rambo against Kuwait, but in confronting the allied military, he was just the mouse that roared." The sooner he's gone the better, Moyers concluded, though many of those now chasing him had encouraged him in the first place.

All day on March 1, the networks floated a story published in France's prestigious paper *Le Monde* that Saddam Hussein was going to flee to Algeria and that the Algerian government was cutting a deal for his escape. Even after the Algerian ambassador to the U.S. and the Bush administration denied the story, CNN and the other networks continued running it. For the next week, stories of domestic opposition to Saddam were highlighted in the U.S. media. It was hard to distinguish disinformation from genuine rebellion, but the flood of refugees from Basra and southern Iraq gave credence to stories that there was significant opposition to Hussein's rule (obviously, one could not trust anything that the U.S. military or Bush administration might say about Hussein or Iraq). There were repeated stories that rebellions were exploding: in the north of Iraq by Kurds and in the south by disgruntled military, townspeople who had suffered during the war, and fundamentalist Shiite Moslems, encouraged by Iran, who opposed Hussein's Baath party and Sunni Moslem regime.[26] Some of these stories were clear exaggeration, mixing information with disinformation: CNN and the other TV networks reported in the days following the war that the Kurds completely controlled the north of Iraq, that Hussein's son was killed in Basra along with other leaders of his regime, that oppositional forces controlled cities throughout southern Iraq, and that Hussein had been assassinated. In fact, Hussein's son was not killed and although rebel forces were in control of large amounts of the country, government forces were able to regain the initiative—thanks largely to the inactivity of Bush who failed to support the rebellions he had called for.[27]

The recurrent stories of fighting in the south of Iraq indicated that there was genuine insurrectionary turmoil in Iraq, and its decision to eject all foreign journalists on March 6 suggested that Iraq was preparing to deal with this turmoil violently—as they did. Reuters reported that the Republican Guards were on patrol in the streets of Baghdad and that road blocks had been put up on the approaches to the city in order to tighten security and to prevent rebellion from breaking out in the capital. CNN also reported on March 6 that Saddam Hussein had appointed his cousin as internal security minister. Hussein's relative, Ali Hassan al-Majid, had brutally suppressed Kurdish rebellions in the 1980s and was in charge of the Iraqi occupation of Kuwait during a period of many atrocities.

Commentators saw these moves as a show of force, indicating that Hussein was acting decisively to maintain his regime. Many commented that while Hussein was obviously unable to successfully fight tremendously superior U.S.-led coalition forces, he was able to maintain order and power in his own country. Thus the *New York Times* reported on March 7: "Despite Western assessments of the Republican Guard's disarray, Western officials in Saudi Arabia said loyalist troops had apparently put down an Islamic revolt in Basra, Iraq's second largest city, where rebellious Shiites claimed to have control over the weekend" (p. A8). In fact, it was later reported that the elite Republican Guard was "virtually intact" after the cease-fire and that reports of its destruction were greatly exaggerated (*Newsday,* July 7, 1991, p. 7).

For the first time, Iraqi and Kurdish oppositional leaders were shown on U.S. TV. Although they repeated the standard attacks on Saddam Hussein, the Iraqi opposition seemed to have had no coherent program, no unity among their ranks, and no organized movement inside or outside Iraq. They continued to bicker among themselves and no viable Iraqi opposition emerged to replace Hussein and his regime. The U.S. had apparently done nothing to try to help organize a democratic opposition to Hussein and never made the democratization of Iraq a war aim.

Yet during the war, the Bush administration had urged the Iraqis to overthrow Saddam Hussein and in the aftermath CIA and covert forces were urging them to do so.[28] Thus, it appeared that systematic efforts were underway throughout Iraq to topple Hussein's regime.

But the Bush administration backed off in their campaign against Hussein precisely when these rebellions appeared potentially able to eliminate the Iraqi government. While Bush and his team had repeatedly urged Hussein's overthrow, they were not taking any public position on the unrest in Iraq and did nothing to publicly encourage oppositional forces. Perhaps they could find no cohesive oppositional forces to support and perhaps they simply did not have a coherent policy to deal with Iraq after the war. No doubt, the Bush administration worried about Shiite forces taking over southern Iraq and pursuing a fundamentalist Islamic revolution in the Iranian mode. Although one could do business with a Saddam Hussein, buying his oil and selling him arms, it was not certain that Islamic revolution in the Gulf would serve U.S. interests.

After putting down the rebellions in the south, Hussein sent his forces north to crush Kurdish rebellions. The Kurds were driven out of their homeland and sought refuge in the harsh mountain region near the border with Turkey and a desolate border region near Iran. Bush's failure to respond to the suffering of the Kurds, Shiites, and other forces rebelling against the regime of Saddam Hussein exposed the phoniness of his highly touted New World Order. To those who hoped that henceforth the superpowers would promote justice, democracy, and the cause of oppressed peoples against brutal domination, Bush clearly demonstrated that for him the New World Order was merely an order of Realpolitik, of selfishly following his own perceived interests with little concern for the suffering or just causes of others.

Kuwait was of concern to the Bush administration because of the economic and geopolitical interests involved, as well as the benefits that Bush, the Pentagon, and the military-industrial complex would reap from a successful war. But the fate of the Kurds and the Iraqi people obviously meant nothing to Bush who seemed not have an idealistic impulse in his personality. When Bush appealed to lofty moral principles during the Gulf crisis and war, this was sheer hypocrisy for there is little or no evidence that George Bush has ever exhibited a consistent adherence to moral principles. He is the paradigm of the narrow, opportunistic, and insincere politician who solely follows his own interests and those of his class while caring nothing for the unfortunate and oppressed. His lack of concern for principle was clearly evident on television during March and April. When he went on vacation in April, TV juxtaposed images of fleeing and dying Kurds with pictures of Bush playing golf and "recreating" in his upper-class life-style. Images of Bush joggin', fishin', and playin' tennis juxtaposed with images of thousands of Kurdish refugees freezing, starving, and dying on the Turkish and Iranian border area was truly repellent. Consequently, many commentators saw Bush's inaction as moral bankruptcy and political failure of nerve. As Doug Ireland put it:

> If, as Bush claimed, Saddam really was the "new Hitler," and the need to emasculate him the most important moral issue since World War II, the logic of the administration's policy would have dictated some form of intervention at the first signs of revolt, when it could have aided those who responded to America's call with a minimum of direct military involvement—keeping Saddam's air arms from the skies, for example, while offering weapons,

training, military counsel, and food and medical aid to the rebel coalition, through client states if necessary (a long-standing U.S. practice around the world in other, less urgent circumstances). Bush's failure to do so reveals that the administration's rationale for his bloody war—with its hundred of thousands of casualties, most of them morally innocent conscripts or civilians— was a lie from the gitgo (*Village Voice,* Apr. 16, 1991, p. 8)

This raises the question of why Bush chose to end the war when he did and why he did not go further in destroying the Iraqi military and overthrowing Saddam Hussein. In a March 27 interview with David Frost on PBS, General Schwarzkopf said that he personally wanted to continue fighting, to pursue a "war of annihiliation."[29] A rightwing critique of the end of the war has emerged, presented by *U.S. News and World Report* in their book *Triumph Without Victory* (1992), that criticizes the premature ending of the war. The team that produced the book claimed that the war had been originally planned for 144 hours but was halted after 100 hours, primarily because of pressure by Arab coalition partners who did not want to see Iraq dismembered and a radical Shiite regime emerge in the south and an autonomous Kurdish republic emerge in the north (1992, pp. 395ff.). This led to a failure of nerve on Bush's account and a "tragic conclusion" to the Gulf war (1992, p. 400).

Arab pressure on Bush to end the war and U.S. and Arab aversion to seeing a radical Shiite regime emerge might have been part of the reason for Bush ending the war, but, like the causes of the war, the conclusion too is overdetermined and requires a multi-causal analysis (see 1.3). Bulloch (1991) argues that Bush had won an adequate victory with minimum losses and did not want to risk losing further troops in a battle for Baghdad or the annihilation of the Iraqi army; consequently, many Iraqi divisions survived intact. On a 1992 Discovery Channel documentary organized by the American Enterprise Institute, Assistant Secretary of State Paul Wolfowitz said that reports of the slaughter of the fleeing Iraqis had produced revulsion in the Pentagon and Powell called the operation to a halt, not wanting to produce the appearance of the U.S. forces "piling on," to use Wolfowitz's football metaphor. Others claim that the U.S. had faulty intelligence that led them to believe that the Iraqis would definitely overthrow Saddam Hussein and end his regime (interview with Garth Jowett who cited discussions with U.S. government sources, Houston, Mar. 9, 1992).

No doubt at least some of these considerations influenced the decision to end the war, but there might have also been a cunning and cynical calculation that Saddam Hussein's continuation in power might be useful. The survival of Saddam Hussein provided an enemy and bogeyman in the area to legitimate keeping U.S. military forces in the Middle East and to help keep up the military budget to deal with such villainous threats to U.S. interests. In addition, a threatening Hussein could help promote the sale of U.S. arms to the region. Perhaps Saddam Hussein was more useful to George Bush alive than dead or disposed of.[30] If Bush fell behind in the 1992 election, he could always mount a strike against Hussein and mobilize popular support for the action. If he won the presidency and found the economy in a slump and his popularity slumping, he could mount a war against Iraq to generate public support.

Whatever Bush's motivations for ending the war when he did, Hussein's military slaughtered rebels by the scores in southern Iraq, often within kilometers of U.S. military forces, while the United States sat back and allowed the slaughter to take place. Eventually, the TV coverage of the plight of the Kurds, however, was so heart-wrenching that U.S. forces were sent to northern Iraq so that the Kurds, starving and freezing in inhospitable refuges in Turkey and Iran, could return home under the protection of the U.S.-led coalition forces.[31] Obviously, at any time Bush could have ordered U.S. troops to create a buffer zone to protect the Kurds from the Iraqi army and his failure to do so clearly revealed his lack of moral fiber. Indeed, even some of his strongest defenders in the Gulf war such as columnists William Safire and Jim Hoagland severely criticized Bush's inaction.

But during the summer of 1991, the U.S. troops pulled out of northern and southern Iraq and Saddam Hussein continued to rule the country. Consequently, the Gulf war produced nothing for Iraq but incredible misery. A UN team described the appalling conditions in most of the country, with massive disease, malnutrition, lack of adequate medical care, and primitive conditions:

> Nothing that we had seen or read had quite prepared us for the particular form of devastation which has now befallen the country. The recent conflict has wrought near-apocalyptic results upon the economic infrastructure of what had been, until January 1991, a rather highly urbanized and mechanized society. Now most means of modern life support have been destroyed or rendered tenuous. Iraq has, for some time to come, been relegated to a pre-industrial age, but with all the disabilities of post-industrial dependency on an intensive use of energy and technology. (Ahtisaari in Clark et al. 1992, pp. 237–238)

During the rest of 1991, reports continued to circulate of growing health problems, starvation, economic collapse, and hopelessness in Iraq.[32] The U.S. policy of "bomb now, die later" produced for the Iraqi people epidemics of cholera, typhoid, and other deadly diseases and the lack of medicine and medical equipment to deal with even minor problems. Iraqi children were dying of starvation and disease, and Bush continued to insist on an economic boycott of Iraq. Saddam Hussein built up Baghdad and strengthened his military and security apparatus. The Gulf war had brought nothing but incredible suffering to the Iraqi people while failing to destroy the regime of Saddam Hussein or to bring peace and stability to the region.

10.5 The Militarization of U.S. Culture and Society

In retrospect, only George Bush, the U.S. military, some sectors of the economy, and the military-industrial complex benefitted from the Gulf war. Kotz and Larudee (1991) noted: "After years of lackluster performance, eight of the leading U.S. arms contractors saw their stock value rise by $5.3 billion in the month after the war began" (p. 17). Moreover, White House Budget Director Richard Darman said that arms inventories would be restored to their level before the war, leading Sen. Tom Harkins (D-Ia.) to complain that the Pentagon planned to buy 500 more Patriot missiles although only 160 were fired (p. 17). The *Wall Street Journal* reported on February 27, 1991, that the Bush administration wanted to place the $54.5 billion pledged by coalition allies to underwrite the U.S. Gulf war effort, along with $15 billion in U.S. funds, into an account that it could spend without pesky congressional oversight.

The Gulf war also greatly helped promote foreign arms sales.[33] The *Toronto Star* (Aug. 12, 1991, p. A3) reported the "U.S. [was] tops in supplying Third World weaponry" in 1990, increasing arms sales from nearly $8 billion in 1989 to $18.5 billion in 1990. Sales to Middle Eastern countries produced the dramatic upsurge. The success of new military technologies in the Gulf war led the Bush administration to push anew their Strategic Defense Initiative, popularly known as Star Wars. In his March 6 speech to Congress, Bush called for expansion of the program and has continued urging the development of high-tech weapons systems against congressional pressure for deeper military cuts. Tom Wicker wrote in an August 2, 1991, syndicated column that "the Pentagon still is seeking more than $500 billion of taxpayers' money for 'about 100 major weapons-acquisitions programs.'"

And so George Bush, the U.S. military, and the military-industrial complex were the immediate beneficiaries of the Gulf war.[34] Bush was transformed from wimp to warrior and the U.S. military was able to overcome its humiliation in Vietnam and its past failures. The U.S. appeared to be the world's sole remaining superpower, a high-tech military colossus dominating Bush's New World Order.[35] On the whole, the military had not gotten such good press and PR since World War II.

From the beginning through the aftermath of the war, nightly newscasts interviewed military spokespeople and defenders, presented positive images of military hardware and troops, and legitimated the alleged need for a strong military. The military was concerned with overcoming the "Vietnam syndrome" and restoring their credibility. Television coverage of the crisis and the war enabled the military to gain prestige lost during the Vietnam debacle and the criticisms of military spending and incompetency during the previous decade.

The military also regained dominion over the press with the success of their pool system (see 2.2), allowing them to control which members of the media gained direct access to the troops and ensuring that military officials always accompanied media representatives when they talked to the troops, thus curtailing the amount of critical discourse emanating from the front. But the mainstream media also presented incredible PR for the military, inundating the country with images of war and the new high-tech military for months, while the brutality of war was normalized and even glamorized in the uncritical media coverage. Throughout the Persian Gulf TV war, the culture of militarism became *the* mainstream culture after a period when war and the military were in disfavor. After Vietnam, people were sick of the military, sick of death, sick of destruction, and sick of war; the military was relegated to the sidelines of U.S. culture and even the doghouse. During the Persian Gulf TV war, the military returned to the front and center stage of the culture, producing a striking, albeit short-lived, militarization of the media and culture in the United States.

It became increasingly apparent during the Gulf war that the U.S. military was attempting to impose its worldview, language, and fundamental project—war—on the public in order to increase the military's social prestige and to ensure their continued domination of social wealth. The war accordingly produced a militarization of the mainstream media, especially news and information. During the Gulf war, TV news coverage was dominated by war news; discussion of war and military discourse colonized TV and radio talk shows; and, cumulatively, images and thoughts of war saturated the national consciousness.

Some intellectuals, unknown before the war, attained cult status or at least impressive influence. Tony Cordesman of ABC was obsequiously and deferentially treated by anchor Peter Jennings and widely cited by "Gulfie" commentators in the press and TV talk shows. Revealing his status as a champion of the military-industrial complex, Cordesman published an Op-Ed piece in the *New York Times* right after the war calling for resistance against calls for cuts in military spending (Feb. 28, 1991). Cordesman praised the U.S.'s new "combat culture," which enabled it to win a decisive victory in the Gulf war, and concluded that the

United States was the only country in the world with the force to serve as the world's "policeman." At a symposium after the war at the Brookings Institute, Cordesman said that people should not feel sorry for the suffering and murdered Iraqis because they had tolerated Saddam Hussein and thus deserved their punishment. Cordesman was established as a media celebrity. Yet during the war he said nothing that revealed any real insight and constantly harped on the motif of Iraqi chemical weapons, which were never used, while hyping the destructive capacity of the Iraqi military, which ultimately proved to be no match for the U.S.-led coalition.[36] Cordesman mainly served to terrorize viewers into supporting the Bush administration and Pentagon, who would protect them from the threats that Cordesman so effectively evoked.

Each network had at least two generals employed as military commentators, and CNN managed to find numerous military hacks who predictably took the military point of view and rarely provided any original insight or perspective on the war, serving instead merely to put the Pentagon spin on the events of the war. By contrast, peace groups and antiwar spokespeople almost disappeared from TV coverage after the first week of the war. As the war progressed, the media allowed fewer and fewer anti-war voices to spoil the Great Celebration. A survey by the media watch group FAIR indicated that only 1.5 percent of the voices present in the TV discourse during the first two weeks of the war articulated an antiwar position, and, as the war went on, these voices were even more infrequent. The hysterical supporters of the Gulf war, who were terrorized into an irrational war psychosis, viciously attacked the networks that portrayed antiwar demonstrations or allowed antiwar perspectives. Fearing a loss of ratings and revenues, the TV networks cut back on the antiwar and peace segments.

During the Gulf war, hysteria permeated the country (see Chapter 6), and after the war the euphoria of victory made it appear that the entire country was in the grips of rampant militarization. The euphoria concerning the military victory continued through the parades welcoming veterans of the Gulf war home and celebrating the war and its "heroes." Big and little cities all over the country prepared for celebrations to welcome back the troops and to celebrate their victory. In New York City, Washington, D.C., and smaller cities throughout the country millions of dollars were lavished on victory parades and celebrations and thousands of homeless and millions of unemployed workers were given circuses rather than bread.

In the months after the war, General Schwarzkopf addressed Congress; received high military honors from the Queen of England, the King of Saudi Arabia, the Emir of Kuwait, and other feudal powers who seemed to admire the general's authoritarian demeanor and military achievements; and won his greatest victory of all—a $5.5 million contract for a book. George Bush had a flutter of the heart from an overactive thyroid condition that pundits suggested might have led him to such extremes of brutality against the Iraqis. Medicine soon slowed down his heartbeat and metabolism to a manageable level and it appeared certain that Bush would run for re-election in 1992.

Yet the old economic and social problems reappeared and George Bush did nothing to address them. Negative images continued to flow from the Middle East and as disillusionment with the war set in, the rampant nationalism and militarism of the spring and early summer subsided. During the summer of 1991, Bush's administration was involved in several controversies. Robert Gates, one of the inner circle of Bush's war team, was nominated to head the CIA, and his confirmation was temporarily threatened because of his role in the Iran/Contra scandals, the arming of Iraq, and the CIA scandals of the Casey era. Gates had obviously doctored intelligence information to serve the political ends of his bosses and had been wrong on the Soviet Union, continuing to push the "evil empire" line at the moment when the Soviet empire was disintegrating and the Soviets were beginning to reform their society. Gates had opposed sanctions against Saddam Hussein's regime, despite its human rights record, and had been in favor of arms sales to Iraq. No matter. Bush was able to get his crony Gates confirmed as head of the CIA, as the Congress allowed Bush to get away once again with unconscionable political choices. Likewise, Bush's nomination for the Supreme Court, Clarence Thomas, appeared to be totally unqualified for the position and was caught up in dramatic charges of sexual harassment by one of his former employees, Anita Hill. Yet, he too was appointed after extremely divisive hearings and congressional debate.

On August 5, 1991, Congress announced that it would undertake formal inquiries into claims that the 1980 Reagan/Bush election team, including George Bush, had met with Iranians to hold U.S. hostages in Tehran until after the election, a treasonous act, which, if true, would be the greatest political scandal of the century. Gary Sick's *The October Surprise,* published in the fall of 1991 documented the scandal and questions were raised concerning the role of Bush in the Reagan administration and its many scandals.

By the fall of 1991, it appeared that the U.S. "victory" was pyrrhic and short lived. Bush's popularity slowly but steadily declined and questions were raised in Congress and the press concerning the level of U.S. military spending. The collapse of the Soviet Union and waning of militarism led to some cutbacks in defense spending in 1992, including cancellation of some major weapons programs and a decision to concentrate on research and development rather than weapons production (see *New York Times,*

Jan. 24, 1991, p. A1). The U.S. military budget was steadily reduced and new weapons systems were canceled. Further, the U.S. seemed unable to affect the course of world events after the war. There was no solution to any of the problems in the Middle East in the aftermath of the war, Japan became increasingly aggressive in asserting its own interests, and the United States seemed strangely irrelevant to the collapse of the Soviet Union and the moves toward European economic and political union. The Gulf war thus appeared to be a short-term solution to the political problems of George Bush and the U.S. military that affected no significant change in the U.S. economy or world politics.

As Bush's popularity dramatically declined and his presidency appeared threatened in the upcoming 1992 election, his administration leaked plans to topple Saddam Hussein, with the aid of U.S. military power, and the possibility of dramatic military action to save his failing presidency was a distinct possibility in 1992 (see the *New York Times*, Jan. 19, 1992, p. A1). In the February 18, 1992, New Hampshire primary Bush received the worst primary vote of any Republican president in history, with his opponent, columnist Patrick Buchanan, receiving 37 percent of the vote and about 20 percent write-in ballots for other candidates indicated widespread disgust with Bush, even in his own party. Bush's primary campaigning was lackluster and he seemed to have no focus or message. By July 1992, Bush trailed Texan billionaire Ross Perot in polls in many parts of the country, despite the fact that Perot had not even formally announced his candidacy.

By 1992, the Bush administration was plagued by a scandal called "Iraqgate." It was alleged that $5 billion in loans to purchase agricultural goods approved by the Reagan and Bush administrations had been used to help finance Saddam Hussein's military machine.[37] It was also alleged that the agricultural aid program involved bribes, financial improprieties, doctored documents, lies to Congress, and a major cover-up by Bush administration officials. In addition, it was claimed that George Bush himself had been a major supporter of the aid for Iraq program, both as Vice-President and as President, urging banks to provide credit for Iraq and strongly supporting the aid program over objections within governmental circles concerning Iraq's ability to pay back the loans and its deplorable human rights record. Despite these objections, Bush had signed a National Security Directive in 1989 approving the program, which cost U.S. taxpayers $2 billion in defaulted loans and which helped build up the Iraqi military machine that the U.S. faced in the Gulf war.

In May 1992, Henry B. Gonzalez (D-Tx.) held Congressional hearings on the Iraqi aid program, and in June 1992, Jack Brooks (D-Tx.) held hearings to determine if a special prosecutor should be established to determine if high-level crimes had been committed by the U.S. government. Increased criticism circulated concerning Bush's prewar activities toward Iraq, and his Gulf war policy was no longer taken to be a brilliant exercise in Presidential politics. Although the Bush team had planned to use dramatic footage of the Gulf war as a major part of the re-election campaign, the war was no longer resonating positively with voters. A June 27, 1992, *New York Times* story, "Bush's Greatest Glory Fades as Questions on Iraq Persist," raised questions about the Bush administration's Iraq policy and reported that before Bush appeared at a National-American Wholesale Grocers' Association conference in March, the audience was shown a film about the Gulf war "that was filled with images of the President reviewing and honoring American troops. When the film ended, the audience responded with total silence" (p. A8). Bush's Gulf war triumph was no longer a political plus, and emboldened Democrats began actively criticizing Bush's supposed competency in foreign policy.

The U.S. economy had been gravely weakened by decades of excessive military spending and a gigantic deficit to finance it. Indeed, there are arguably two losers in the cold war: the United States, the Soviet Union, whose economies were severely harmed by decades of military spending (while the two losers of World War II, Japan and Germany, have prospered). The enormous military spending in the U.S. has caused a tremendous drain of resources toward the military which has contributed to an imbalanced economy and public squalor, with a disproportionate amount of economic activity and public funds going to the military. Although the Gulf war might have arguably enabled military spending to bolster the economy in the short term, the militarization of the economy has blocked desperately needed changes of budget priorities.

During the Gulf war, the United States proved that it could destroy the highways of Iraq, but it could have used its resources to rebuild its own system of highways. Bush showed that the U.S. military could destroy the cities of Iraq, but meanwhile cities in the United States are decaying and deteriorating. The U.S. bombing created conditions for health epidemics in Iraq, but during the same period it was painfully clear that the country could not offer adequate health care to its own people. The U.S. government attacked Iraqi treatment of Kurds, Shiites, and other minorities, but offered nothing to improve race relations in the U.S. Indeed, the "smart bombs" used in the Gulf war will not help end illiteracy in the U.S. or educate the youth. The high-tech bombing programs will not help develop software for environmental protection or urban planning. The medical experiments to develop antidotes to chemical and biological weapons will not help the fight against AIDS and cancer. The temporary jobs created to produce military equipment and supplies for the Gulf did not translate into permanent jobs. Allowing women to serve in the Gulf did not help with child care, the feminization of poverty, and women's rights in the workplace. Controlling alcohol and drug use in Saudi Arabia did not solve the problems of drugs and alcohol abuse in the United States. Providing homes for half-a-million soldiers in the desert did not help produce homes for the homeless in the United States.

In short, the Gulf war was a temporary diversion from the acute problems facing U.S. society, problems exacerbated if not created by over a decade of the economic policies of Reagan and Bush. Despite Bush's demagogic claim to "have drawn a line in the sand" against unemployment in his State of the Union message during January 1992 and his demagogic shout that "This shall not stand!" (repeating his slogans of the Gulf crisis), in fact Bush has no policies for unemployment or to strengthen the economy and produce jobs. As Carl Boggs (1991) has argued: "While the Pentagon has devoured nearly $8 trillion since 1950 (now more than $300 billion annually) to support American power around the world, the social infrastructure deteriorates at an ever faster rate. The U.S. military can annihilate the Iraqi armed forces with sophisticated missiles, planes, and tanks, but the U.S. economy cannot begin to solve basic problems of education, housing, health care, the environment, and urban violence. With the economic system in decline, this imbalance has gotten so out of control that public needs are now being systematically and flagrantly neglected."

The militarization of society has drastic implications for democracy in the United States. With the concentration of so many resources and power in the military sector, what Eisenhower called "the military-industrial complex" has come to control state priorities and to render social and cultural needs of secondary importance. Military spending tends to be highly undemocratic with large budgets for secret projects and, as Melman (1991) has argued, for decades only a small number of corporations benefit in a sector that produces few jobs or public goods. Moreover, the militarization of culture has meant that the military has come to dominate ever more realms of popular culture, ranging from movies, TV shows, video and computer games, and toys to trading cards.[38] In addition, the military got splendid free advertising for its wares from the positive media presentation of their high-tech weapons systems and "precision" bombing.

The Gulf war dramatized the two main problems of U.S. society: militarism and excessive concentration of corporate, state, and media power. The same ruling interests came to control the state, the economy, and the media during the 1980s and 1990s with Ronald Reagan and George Bush pursuing policies that primarily benefitted the corporate elite and the military-industrial complex, while the media were taken over by giant corporate conglomerates that tended to favor the Reagan and Bush administrations and military events which promoted the interests of the arms industries. All of the Big Three TV networks were connected with the defense industry, oil corporations, big banks, and other corporate sectors which benefitted from the Gulf war and all the mainstream media promoted the war policies of the Bush administration and U.S. military technology, prowess, and achievements. The result was complicity of the media, the state, and the military in the promotion of a highly destructive war that only benefitted a few groups and individuals.

Indeed, Danny Schechter (1991) suggests that one of the reasons why the TV networks were so uncritical of the Bush administration policy and disinformation during the Gulf war was because at that time the networks were "engaged in a massive lobbying effort to change the FCC's Financial Syndication rules. Those rules passed at a time when the public airwaves were thought fit for regulation in the public interest and limited the networks' rights to own and market their own programming, ostensibly to limit their power to totally monopolize the marketplace. This meant that program suppliers, not the networks, would forever make the big money when the 'Cosby Show' and others went into syndication" (p. 25). Schechter notes that one of the Federal Communications Commissioners, James Quello, who was "network point person on the issue," had "made a very public point of criticizing aggressive questioning at Pentagon Press briefings as unpatriotic in a speech to the Indiana Broadcasters Association. Schechter indicated that he spoke to a top network producer who explained that there was no way that the TV networks could debate Bush administration war policy "when the networks had such an important economic agenda under consideration in Washington. There is no way to confirm this story," Schechter notes, "but other journalists I've talked to say it 'sounds right'" (ibid).

Sounds right to me as well. In my book *Television and the Crisis of Democracy,* I cited the November 1985 *Mother Jones* story by Mark Dowdie who noted how ABC spiked controversial stories concerning close friends of Ronald Reagan just before the 1984 election because ABC was interested in a lucrative merger it was negotiating (Kellner 1990, pp. 172–173). I also speculated that the network's interest in having the Financial Syndication rules repealed might have led the networks to favor Bush during the 1988 election, knowing that the Republican president would be more likely to support the deregulation of television carried through so aggressively during the Reagan administration (Kellner 1990, Chapter 4). When it comes to economics, the commercial TV networks will always sacrifice journalism and favor a political status quo that supports their own interests.

Thus the crisis of democracy intensified during the Gulf war and it remains to be seen if democracy can be restored in the United States. There can be no genuine democracy without an informed public, and the mainstream media has consistently failed to promote vigorous public debate concerning the policies of the Reagan and Bush administrations. Especially during the Gulf war, the corporate media merely promoted the Bush administration policies and since the end of the war, the mainstream corporate media have failed to reopen a debate concerning whether the Gulf war was worth it, why the war that didn't have to be took place, what interests were served by the war, and what its consequences have been.

The mainstream media generally fails to contextualize events and to make the links between the U.S. complicity in militarizing Iraq, Bush's motivation for pursuing the Gulf war, and the new post–cold war era which requires a National Security State to undertake new adventures to survive threatened cuts in its budget. The mainstream media has never explored fully Bush's links to the October Surprise, the Iran/Contra affair, Noriega, the CIA, and the National Security State (Kellner 1990). It is no accident that there have been two wars during the first two years of Bush's presidency and that Bush and his inner circle have been desperately trying to preserve the military-industrial complex during an era when it is becoming increasingly obsolete and dangerous. Yet the same mainstream media that made George Bush a world celebrity through their puffery of the Gulf war could just as easily unmake him. Or the U.S. media could continue covering up Bush's complicity in some of the greatest scandals and crimes of the century. Time will tell.

Since 1980, conservative forces have controlled economic, political, and cultural power, using this power to promote their own agendas at the expense of the general public. Concentrating more power in the hands of conservative and militarist social forces could spell the end of American democracy and an unending cycle of wars, military interventions, social squalor, and economic depression which will make Orwell's *1984* appear as a utopia. There is the clear and present danger that George Bush, Brent Scowcroft, Dick Cheney, Robert Gates, Dan Quayle, and other representatives of the military-industrial complex and National Security State will do anything—even undertaking a potentially catastrophic war—to further their interests.

Reversing the slide toward militarism and overturning the conservative hegemony of the past years will require rethinking the cold war, the Vietnam and Gulf wars, the Reagan-Bush era, and the bitter fruits of U.S. foreign policy over the past several decades. Failure to do so and to reverse the current direction of U.S. society will certainly be a disaster. A democratic society cannot allow a small group of people to break the law, subvert the rules of politics, and engage in wars and covert actions to promote their ideological, political, and economic agendas. If democracy is to thrive in the United States, individuals and social movements must struggle to reinvigorate a democratization of society. What was once the Soviet Union has been at least attempting to democratize their society and this effort is also needed in the United States.

Notes

1. Gates's fantasy was published in the *Washington Times,* Feb. 25, 1991, p. 9. During the Reagan years when Gates was employed by the CIA, he constantly exaggerated the military threat of the Soviet Union, doctoring figures and facts to serve the requirements of his boss William Casey. While working for Bush, Gates continued to disseminate disinformation and lies to support the policies of the administration, revealing a total disregard for truth and accuracy. During his confirmation hearings as CIA director, critics noted his propensity to politicize information, but nonetheless he was confirmed, showing the general level of corruption and disregard for truth and lack of integrity during the Reagan and Bush years.

2. Bruce Wallace reported that, "The extent of [Iraqi] violence is still unknown. Some Kuwaitis said that allied forces had exaggerated atrocities in order to demonize the Iraqi armed forces." Wallace also found that the Iraqi secret police, and not the military, was responsible for much of the torture and violence. See "Joy Among the Ruins," *MacLean's,* March 11, 1991, p. 24.

3. Recall that during the UN hearings on Iraqi atrocities against Kuwait in November 1990, another "doctor" appeared, also hiding his identity with a headdress, claiming that he had helped bury forty babies murdered by Iraqis who stole their incubators—a story that turned out to be sheer propaganda (see 2.1). Using "doctors" as witnesses provided the aura of a professional, disinterested, "expert" authority. These "doctors," however, were part of a propaganda campaign organized by Kuwaiti government forces.

4. The "doctor" also appeared to a *Time* magazine reporter who wrote: "A Kuwaiti doctor too nervous to give his name told arriving journalists that Iraqis often dismembered prisoners before killing them. 'Some of the bodies were missing noses,' he said. 'Some had their eyes taken out. What the Iraqis did was beyond belief'" (Mar. 11, 1991, p. 39).

5. Alexander Cockburn had earlier questioned the veracity of the alleged Iraqi baby incubator atrocities; see *The Nation,* Feb. 4, 1991, p. 114. Cockburn cited a variety of Kuwaiti doctors and nurses who disputed the story, which was disseminated by Amnesty International, the mainstream media, and George Bush who referred to the story six times in one month (see 2.1).

6. Greenpeace researchers noted that from the beginning of the air war, attacks "were made on 'strategic' targets in Kuwait, including communications and transportation related facilities. A *Newsweek* pool reporter observed that 'several industrial plants on the outskirts of the city had been severely mauled by allied attacks including a Hyundai headquarters'" (Feb. 26, 1991). The *Washington Times* wrote on 4 March that the "city's AT&T phone system required only moderate repairs and adjustments after the air strikes of Operation Desert Storm."

The firing of coalition 16-inch artillery rounds also had significant impact on Kuwait's civil infrastructure (Arkin, Durrant, and Cherni 1991, pp. 54–55).

The Greenpeace team also noted that it was difficult to sort out who was responsible for some of the major damage to Kuwaiti facilities. "There were reports, for instance, that the communications ministry, 'had been heavily damaged by the Kuwaiti resistance in an effort to cut off the Iraqis' telephone-monitoring ability.' Other reports are circulating within the Defense Department of sabotage of communications facilities in Kuwait by the resistance (some of whom were assisted by US special operations forces" (1991, p. 54). Finally, they concluded that much of the damage was caused during the last week of the occupation, putting in question the lurid claims of extensive damage to Kuwait by the Iraqis from the beginning of the occupation.

7. On March 5, CNN carried a live report by Tom Mintier, who interviewed an alleged resistance fighter who also took the progovernment position that it was time for the resistance to lay down its guns, return to civilian life, and allow the government to take over all power—precisely what the Kuwaiti government was urging. Others in the Kuwaiti resistance movement, however, were urging democratic reforms, though CNN and Mintier privileged the progovernment sources during the first days after the "liberation."

8. See *New York Times* (Feb. 28, 1991, p. A11) and *Time* (March 11, 1991, pp. 42–43).

9. On February 28, 1992, "Nightline" had a one-year anniversary program on the liberation of Kuwait that was highly critical of the lack of democratic reform, the corruption in granting contracts for Kuwait's reconstruction, and the general greed and corruption of the Kuwaiti government.

10. Middle East Watch put out a report titled "A Victory Turned Sour: Human Rights in Kuwait Since Liberation," which indicated that of about 5,800 persons detained by the Kuwaiti government since the "liberation," at least 3,000 remained in detention by late 1991. Many were tortured and killed and more than 1,500 Palestinians and others were summarily deported. About half of the 180,000 Palestinians fled during the Iraqi occupation, and although this is evidence that they did not collaborate, they have not been allowed to return. Thousands of Bedouins were also stranded outside of Kuwait and have not been allowed to return. See Middle East Watch 1991a and the summary by Aryeh Neier in *The Nation,* Sept. 23, 1991, p. 327. See the testimony in Clark et al. concerning claims that U.S. special forces were present during the torture of Palestinians and others in Kuwait after the war (1992, pp. 125f. and pp. 140ff.) .

11. It was Cushman who some days earlier had produced the story suggesting that according to military law it was perfectly appropriate for the U.S. to slaughter fleeing Iraqi soldiers, despite the fact that their government had indicated a willingness to meet all UN resolutions (see *New York Times,* Feb. 27, 1991, p. A8).

12. An April 1992 House Armed Services Committee Report estimated that of the 183,000 Iraqi soldiers in Kuwait at the start of the ground war, about 63,000 were captured and 120,000 either fled or were slain. Of that 120,000, about 100,000 Iraqi soldiers were thought to have escaped (according to one U.S.

intelligence estimate), leaving a ballpark figure of 20,000 Iraqi soldiers killed during the ground war, plus 9,000 reported killed by allied air attacks before the ground attack began. The House study gave no figures on civilian dead. During the Panama invasion, official military reports concluded that 220 Panamanian civilians were killed, while Catholic and Episcopal churches estimate that more than 3,000 died, many of them in the barrio of El Chorillo, close to Noriega's headquarters; see Alexander Cockburn, *In These Times,* June 6, 1990. Cockburn points out that the Commission for the Defense of Human Rights in Central America stated in a March 1, 1990, report that "the actual death toll has been obscured through U.S. military practices, including: (1) incineration of corpses without prior identification; (2) burial of remains in common graves without identification; (3) U.S. military control of administrative offices of hospitals and morgues, permitting the removal of all registries to U.S. military bases." A "60 Minutes" episode on September 30, 1990, revealed the discovery and exhuming of mass graves and estimated that approximately 4,000 Panamanians were killed in the U.S. invasion.

13. It should be noted that it is still not certain how many Iraqi troops and civilians were killed in the war. The bloody civil war after the cessation of U.S.-led military activity and the thousands of deaths from disease and lack of adequate medical service make it difficult to know for sure the number of deaths. Greenpeace estimates that from 100,000 to 120,000 thousand Iraqi military were killed during the air and ground war (Press Release, Aug. 13, 1991), a figure close to numbers leaked by U.S. military sources. Alexander Cockburn, however, claimed that the U.S. military exaggerated the figures to hype their success and that more "plausible estimates are probably in the region of 25,000 military casualties . . . plus some 4,500 civilian casualties from the bombing" (*Statesman and Society,* Jan. 10, 1992, p. 12). Many more were killed, he noted, in the civil war afterwards and from diseases and primitive conditions caused by the bombing. Patrick Cockburn claimed that recent figures suggest that as few as 8,000–15,000 Iraqi soldiers were killed on the battlefield based on interviews in Iraq with medical personnel, Iraqi soldiers, and villagers who report far fewer deaths from their villages than were expected (*The Independent,* Feb. 5, 1992, p. 11). *U.S. News and World Report's Triumph Without Victory* also suggests estimates of 8,000–18,000 killed, according to U.S. sources that question the previous DIA estimates of 100,000 Iraqi troops killed, which could be revised up to 50 percent in either direction (1992, pp. 404 and 408). Yet all of these estimates could be disinformation, either trying to inflate the achievement of U.S. military body counts or to cover over the extent of the carnage—a cover-up that could be both in the interests of the U.S. military and Iraqi regime.

14. U.S. television tended to sanitize the pictures of the Highway of Death by removing troubling images of burned and mutilated bodies. Moreover, photographs of the episode were pulled from distribution to try to erase the memory of the unsavory episode. An image of an Iraqi soldier burnt to a crisp in the Desert Slaughter was published by the British *Guardian* on March 3 and created a great uproar; see the discussion in MacArthur 1992, pp. 255ff.

15. It is symptomatic that the *New York Times* did not dedicate a complete story to the episode or even to the slaughter of the fleeing Iraqis throughout the

theater of war. The *Times* frequently takes the most scandalous and explosive information that involves key figures, policies, and events concerning the U.S. political establishment and presents this information in a condensed and truncated form; this way it can salve its journalistic conscience by printing "all the news that's fit to print" while remaining a stolid and reliable pillar of the established order. Throughout the Gulf war, it buried the most explosive information in stories positioned in the middle of the paper, as when it revealed information concerning the coalition force's responsibility for much of the Gulf oil spills or as it did in the Highway of Death story. None of the mainstream media linked the desert slaughter to Bush's refusal to allow a cease-fire.

16. BBC Television News reported on March 5: "The Kuwaitis fear that many of the hostages taken from Kuwait by retreating Iraqi troops may have died in allied air attacks. Hundreds of the vehicles they used were trapped and bombed at the Mutla Gap as they poured out of Kuwait City, heading north on the main road to Basra." Reporter Michael Macmillan noted that Kuwaitis were concerned that buses like those in which the Iraqis rounded up Kuwaitis, taken as hostages the last days of the war, were found on the road to Basra. ABC "Nightline," in fact, on March 1 showed a bus full of passengers burnt to crisp ash, but did not mention that these might be Kuwaiti hostages; a CBS News report on March 2 showed a number of buses destroyed by U.S. bombing, without mentioning that Kuwaitis might have been inside. The BBC report concluded by noting that U.S. soldiers had supervised the burial of the dead in mass graves and that the Kuwaitis feared that perhaps thousands of the five thousand Kuwaitis taken hostage in the last days of the war might be buried in those graves. Stephen Sackur of the BBC reported that among the dead on the highway were contract workers from the Indian subcontinent as well as Palestinians fleeing oppression from a "liberated" Kuwait (1991). As of the present, there is no evidence that the Kuwaiti government investigated this episode and discovered how many Kuwaitis were killed with the Iraqis and whoever else was unfortunate enough to have been on the road; no doubt the results would be too embarrassing for their U.S. "liberators."

17. During the early morning hours of January 18, 1991, on ABC, George Will urged escalating the war aims to the destruction of Saddam Hussein after barely one day of war! Yet in April 1991, when there was pressure to intervene against Hussein on behalf of the Kurds, the opportunistic Will argued against U.S. intervention, supporting Bush's line of the moment. During the Reagan years, the bow-tied warrior called for a U.S. invasion of Nicaragua to overthrow the Sandinista government. Indeed, Will helped prep Ronald Reagan for debate in 1980 with a debate book stolen from the Carter campaign and then was allowed to comment on the debate for ABC! In any case, Will can always be counted on to support the most reactionary policies and forces at any given moment and it is incredible that ABC allows this right-wing ideologue to serve as a "commentator."

18. The lack of any serious investigations of Brent Scowcroft's past, economic and political interests and agenda, and activities during the Gulf war is a testament to the poverty of the mainstream media.

19. "Fish" was the code name for pilot Eric Salomonson whose last name was close to Salmon while "Karl" was the code name for a pilot whose last name was

Marks so he became "Karl" after Karl Marx. An unnamed pilot (Fish, I think) was cited on BBC Radio 4 on February 27 saying: "I just spot the tank, it's nothing real cosmic, . . . lock it up, good lock, let her rip! It's the biggest Fourth of July show you've ever seen! And to see those tanks just boom! And more stuff just keeps spewing out over and the shells flying on the ground. And they just become white hot. It's wonderful!"

20. Strictly speaking, this procedure was, Middle East Watch director Aryeh Neier states, a war crime "in violation of Geneva Convention requirements that they be identified, the cause of death established, their interment conducted honorably and according to their religion, their graves marked and information provided to their families so as to permit exhumation and reburial" (*The Nation,* Sept. 23, 1991). All of the mass burials of Iraqi dead by U.S. forces as well as the bull-dozing of Iraq troops under sand were war crimes under this convention.

21. On February 28, the previous evening, Ted Koppel told on ABC's "Nightline" how a trip by heliocopter from Saudi Arabia to Kuwait City was aborted because of the intensity of the oil pollution which reduced visibility to 500 meters; his footage showed incredibly thick, dark smoke that blocked out the sun during day time.

22. See the article by Joe Vialls published in *The Guardian* on August 21, 1991, and posted in PeaceNet, mideast.forum, August 16, 1991.

23. In several bulletin boards in PeaceNet during the summer and fall of 1991, intense attention was focused on what might have been the ultimate disaster produced by the Gulf war. It was reported that scientists in China were arguing that the oil fires were causing heavy rains, and astronauts observed that the entire earth was circled in a haze and that parts of the earth couldn't even be seen because of the thickness of the black smoke (PeaceNet, en.climate, Aug. 6, 1991). Michael Adams, a military scientist doing research on the effects of the oil fires, claimed that the U.S. government and military, with the complicity of the mainstream media, were concealing the extent of the disaster (PeaceNet, en.climate, Sept. 4). In an article in the *New York Times* on Oct. 19, 1991, p. A1, however, Youssef Ibrahim asserted that "a senior Kuwaiti oil executive said in a telephone interview" that there were only 87 oil wells still on fire and that all of the fires in the region would be extinguished soon. Soon after, it was claimed that all of the oil fires were extinguished. Yet, as I report below, there were fears that the oil lakes and rivers formed by wells that continued to spew forth torrents of oil also constituted a serious environmental threat. On the Gulf war environmental damage, see André Carothers, "After Desert Storm the Deluge," *Greenpeace,* Oct./Nov./Dec. 1991, pp. 14ff. This account is highly skeptical of U.S. government claims concerning the environmental damage. See also the Greenpeace report of the environmental damage to the Gulf put together by Arkin, Durrant, and Cherni (1991) and the January 1992 Greenpeace Report, "The Environmental Legacy of the Gulf War" (thanks to Bill Arkin for making this information available to me).

24. The *New York Times* reported on March 11, 1991: "Greenpeace Wants to Outlaw Making War on the Environment" (p. A7).

25. Before the war was even over, the Republican party network, NBC, presented a puff-piece on Bush on their February 24 Sunday morning show,

which magnified him as a "great president" with footage and accolades that could easily be used by his 1992 reelection campaign. Maureen Dowd published a PR piece on Bush in the *New York Times* on March 2 titled, "War Introduces Nation to a Tougher Bush." Bush's popularity ratings soared, he was visited by major world leaders after the war, and addressed Congress on March 6, receiving tumultuous applause and a hero's welcome.

26. The media tended to reduce the southern Iraqi rebellions to Shiite fundamentalist revolts, but other sources indicated that a variety of forces in opposition to Saddam's regime were involved in the rebellions. See *Anarchy* No. 30, Fall 1991, pp. 4ff., which stressed the proletarian nature of the revolts.

27. During the rebellions there were stories that the U.S. blew up Iraqi munitions rather than allowing the rebels to use these weapons against Hussein's regime and that the U.S. refused the rebels all military aid. On a January 16, 1992, "ABC World News Tonight," Sheila MacVicar interviewed an Iraqi rebel officer who complained about begging for U.S. military support and being turned down. She concluded: "The American and other allied forces were under orders not to help the rebels. Days later, as Saddam Hussein moved to crush the uprising, the officer and others fled into exile." No coherent explanation has yet emerged from the Bush administration concerning why they did not give at least minimal military aid to the rebels trying to overthrow Saddam Hussein.

28. See the article on CIA encouragement for Iraqi rebel forces in the *Washington Post,* April 3, 1991. The *New York Times* also published articles indicating that a Kurdish broadcast facility calling for the overthrow of Hussein was linked to the CIA (April 6, 1991) and that another clandestine radio station that had been urging the Iraqi people to revolt against Hussein's regime was also connected to the CIA (April 16, 1991).

29. Within two days, Schwarzkopf backed off this story and the White House claimed that Schwarzkopf himself had ordered cessation to military activities and that there was no debate over whether the war should or should not end. Schwarzkopf also insisted in his interview with Frost that he had been "suckered" by the Iraqis into letting them keep their helicopters, which they used to crush the rebellions against Hussein's regime. Yet there was nothing to keep the United States from renegotiating the terms of the cessation of hostilities (the cease-fire had yet to be negotiated). Hence, Schwarzkopf's feeble excuse for nonintervention is just another example of the lies and hypocrisy that governed U.S. discourse during the Persian Gulf massacre.

30. The *International Herald-Tribune* reported on May 4–5, 1991, that the "U.S. Bungled Chance to Oust Hussein." According to a U.S. Senate Foreign Relations Committee staff report, rebellious Iraqi military officers had sent out feelers asking for U.S. support for a coup against Saddam Hussein in March 1990. However, the Bush administration rebuffed them and the coup did not come off. Hence, there was a long-time policy of Bush administration failure to help overthrow Saddam Hussein.

31. Daniel Schorr documents how Bush reacted to the Kurdish plight as a response to an outraged public, which was shocked by nightly images of Kurdish suffering. See "Ten Days That Shook the White House," *Columbia Journalism*

Review, July/August 1991, pp. 21–23. On the plight of the Kurds, see the poignant accounts in MacArthur 1991, pp. 333–371; Simpson 1991, pp. 365ff.; Susan Sachs's April 1991 articles in *Newsday*; and Robert Fisk's articles in the *Independent.*

32. See the reports by Hooglund and Hiltermann in *Middle East Report,* July/ August 1991; by Cainkar in Bennis and Moushabeck 1991; Arkin, Durrant, and Cherni 1991; Middle East Watch 1991b; and Clark et al. 1992.

33. Kotz and Larudee (1991) report that Raytheon's order backlog of $2.3 billion for Patriot missiles at the end of 1990 "was likely to rise to $5 billion by the end of 1991 because of new orders from Saudi Arabia, Israel, Turkey, and Greece. Loral, maker of electronic components for missiles and aircraft, expects at least $1.3 billion of foreign sales . . . Saudi Arabia has expressed interest in buying $20 billion of U.S. weapons, including at least 24 F-15 fighter planes and 235 M-1 tanks over and above the 465 tanks previously ordered. Last September, after Turkey joined the coalition against Iraq and agreed to let the United States use its air bases, the U.S. Export-Import Bank approved a $1.37 billion loan guarantee for Turkey to buy 200 military-type helicopters—the largest single transaction in the history of the bank" (p. 17).

34. U.S. banks also benefitted from the Gulf war. Kotz and Larudee (1991) point out that the tremendous petrodollar surpluses from Saudi Arabia and Kuwait will "flow even more heavily into American banks. The American banking system has been sorely ailing from its inability to raise capital. A joke circulating in recent weeks said the alliance between the U.S. and Kuwait was fortuitous because Kuwait was a banking system without a country, while the U.S. was a country without a banking system. Citicorp got a taste of the benefits of this alliance when, in late 1990, Saudi Prince al Waleed bin Talal paid $590 million to buy 4.9 percent of its common stock. This was a sizable fraction of the $1 billion to $1.5 billion in capital that Citicorp needed to raise" (p. 17).

35. The *New York Times* published excerpts from a Defense Department document that indicated that the U.S. was developing a strategy "to insure that no rival superpower is allowed to emerge in Western Europe, Asia or the territory of the former Soviet Union" (March 8, 1991, p. A1). The document rejected the strategy of collective internationalism developed after World War II and projected a vision of the future with U.S. military power serving as the policeman of the world. The plan envisaged the possibility of unilateral U.S. military action against Iraq, North Korea, Pakistan, and India "to prevent the development of weapons of mass destruction." Presumably, Israel was safe from a preemptive U.S. strike.

36. On February 21, Cordesman appeared on ABC's "Nightline" and provided a harrowing and detailed account of the Iraqi military horrors assembled behind the Kuwaiti border which the coalition troops would face in a ground war. As it turned out, this was mere hyperbole and Cordesman had either fallen for U.S. military disinformation or disseminated it himself so that the slaughter of Iraqis during the ground war would appear as a brilliant military victory. After the war, Cordesman traveled for ABC to Saudi Arabia and Kuwait in March 1991, and revealed his surprise that Iraqi fortifications were so primitive.

37. The story was first broken in the *Los Angeles Times* in a series of stories by Douglas Frantz and Murray Waas (see Chapter 1, n. 3), which drew upon

House speeches of Henry B. Gonzalez (D-Tx.). It was followed by *U.S. News and World Report* in a May 18, 1992, cover story and by articles in the *Washington Times,* May 13, 1992; the *Chicago Tribune,* May 14, 1992; and the *New Republic,* June 1, 1992. "Iraqgate" was discussed throughout the summer in major newspapers and journals, but mainstream television had not investigated the scandal in any detail at the time this book went to press, outside of one episode of ABC's *Nightline* in June.

38. On November 10, 1991, ABC played a TV movie *Heroes of Desert Storm,* which was introduced by George Bush. Many movies on the war are in the works as well. Desert Storm board games, computer and video games, trading cards, and other artifacts have become a small growth industry.

Bibliography

THE BIBLIOGRAPHY CONTAINS works that I cited more than once or that have contributed to the theoretical and political analysis in this study. Newspaper and other sources that merely document facts are cited in the text.

Agee, Philip (1990). "Producing the Proper Crisis," *Z Magazine,* November, pp. 53–60.

Aguilar, Salvador et al. (1991). *Las Mentiras de Una Guerra. Desinformación y Censura en el Conflicto del Golfo.* Barcelona: Deriva Editorial.

Aksoy, Asu, and Kevin Robins (1991). "Exterminating Angels. Morality, Violence and Technology in the Gulf War," *Science as Culture,* No. 12, pp. 322–336.

Althusser, Louis (1969). *For Marx.* New York: Pantheon.

Anderson, Jack, and Dale Van Atta (1991). *Stormin' Norman.* New York: Zebra.

Anderson, Robin (1991). "The Press, the Public and the New World Order," *Media Development,* October, pp. 20–26.

Arkin, William, Damian Durrant, and Marianne Cherni (1991). *On Impact: Modern Warfare and the Environment. A Case Study of the Gulf War.* Washington, D.C.: Greenpeace; short version in *Greenpeace,* May, pp. 90–112.

Armstrong, Scott (1990). "Iraqnophobia," *Mother Jones,* Nov.-Dec., pp. 24–27, 68.

————— . (1991). "Eye of the Storm," *Mother Jones,* Nov.-Dec., pp. 30–35, 75–76.

Bagdikian, Ben (1990). *The Media Monopoly,* 3rd ed. Boston: Beacon Press.

Barthes, Roland (1972) *Mythologies.* New York: Hill and Wang.

Bennis, Phillys, and Michel Moushabeck, eds. (1991). *Beyond the Storm. A Gulf Crisis Reader.* Brooklyn, N.Y.: Olive Branch Press.

Blackwell, James (1991). *Thunder in the Desert.* New York: Bantam Books.

Boggs, Carl (1991). "Social Movements and Political Strategy in the Aftermath of the Gulf War" (unpublished MS).

Bresheeth, Haim, and Nira Yuval-Davis, eds. (1991). *The Gulf War and the New World Order.* London and Atlantic Highlands, New Jersey: Zed Books.

Briemberg, Mordecai, ed. (1992). *It Was, It Was Not.* Vancouver: New Star Books.

Brittain, Victoria, ed. (1991). *The Gulf Between Us.* London: Virago.

Browne, Malcom W. (1991). "The Military vs. the Press," *New York Times Magazine,* March 3, pp. 27ff.

Bruck, Peter A., ed. (1991). *Medien im Krieg. Die zugesplitzte Normalität.* Salzburg, Austria: Osterreichische Gesellschaft fur Kommunikationsfragen.

Bulloch, John (1991). "How Bush Lost the Gulf War," *The Independent,* Dec. 8, p. 10 (Sunday Review Page).

Bulloch, John, and Harvey Morris (1991). *Saddam's War: The Origins of the Kuwait Conflict and the International Response.* London: Faber.

Cagan, Leslie (1992). "Reflections of a National Organizer," in Peters 1992, pp. 373–386.

Cainkar, Louise (1991). "Desert Sin," in Bennis and Moushabeck 1991.

Chomsky, Noam (1987). *Pirates and Emperors.* Montreal: Black Rose Books.

———. (1989). *Necessary Illusions.* Boston: South End Press.

———. (1990). "Nefarious Aggression," *Zeta Magazine,* October, pp. 18–29.

———. (1991). "Aftermath: Voices From Below," *Z Magazine* (October), pp. 19–28.

———. (1992). "'What We Say Goes': The Middle East in the New World Order," in Peters 1992, pp. 49–92.

Clark, Ramsey, et al. (1992). *War Crimes. A Report on United States War Crimes Against Iraq.* Washington: Maisonnneuve.

Cleaver, Harry (1991). *The Political Economy of the Persian Gulf Crisis.* Austin, Tex.: Pamphlet Press.

Cockburn, Alexander, and Andrew Cohen, "The Unnecessary War," in Brittain 1991, pp. 1–26.

Cohen, Roger, and Claudio Gatti (1991). *In the Eye of the Storm. The Life of General H. Norman Schwarzkopf.* New York: Farrar, Straus and Giroux.

Colodny, Len, and Robert Gettlin (1991). *Secret Coup.* New York: Saint Martin's Press.

Czitrom, Daniel J. (1982). *Media and the American Mind.* Chapel Hill: University of North Carolina Press.

Darwish, Adel, and Gregory Alexander (1991). *Unholy Babylon.* New York: Saint Martin's Press.

Draper, Theodore (1991). "The Gulf War Reconsidered," *New York Review of Books* (Jan. 16), pp. 46–53.

Draper, Theodore (1991). "The True History of the Gulf War," *New York Review of Books* (Jan. 30), pp. 38–45.

Drinin, Robert (1991). "Persian Gulf War Fails to Qualify as Just," *National Catholic Reporter,* Feb. 8, p. 2.

Dunnigan, James F., and Austin Bay (1992). *From Shield to Storm: High-Tech Weapons, Military Strategy, and Coalition Warfare in the Persian Gulf.* New York: Morrow.

Ellul, Jacques (1965). *Propaganda.* New York: Random House.

Emery, Michael (1991). "How Mr. Bush Got His War: Deceptions, Double-Standards & Disinformation." Westfield, N.J.: Open Magazine Pamphlet Series; originally published in the *Village Voice,* March 5, 1991, pp. 22–27.

Emery, Michael, and Edwin Emery (1992). *The Press and America: An Interpretive History of the Mass Media.* 7th ed. Englewood Cliffs: Prentice-Hall.

Enloe, Cynthia (1992). "The Gendered Gulf," in Peters 1992, pp. 93–110.

Elshtain, Jean Bethke, et al. (1992). *But Was It Just? Reflections on the Morality of the Persian Gulf War.* New York: Doubleday.

FAIR (1990). *Critique of MacNeil-Lehrer News Hour.* New York.

———. (1991). Press Release on Gulf War Coverage. New York.

Farouk-Sluglett, Marion, and Peter Sluglett (1990). "Iraq Since 1986: The Strengthening of Saddam," *Middle East Report,* No. 167, pp. 19–24.

Fialka, John J. (1992). *Hotel Warriors: Covering the Gulf War.* Washington, D.C.: The Media Studies Project/Woodrow Wilson Center.

Fox, Thomas C. (1991). *Iraq: Military Victory, Moral Defeat.* Kansas City, Mo.: Sheed & Ward.

Frank, Andre Gunder (1991). "Third World War: A Political Economy of the Gulf War and New World Order," in *The Gulf War and the New World Order.* Amsterdam: Notebooks for Study and Research, #14.

Friedman, Norman (1991). *Desert Victory.* Annapolis, Md.: Naval Institute Press.

Fromm, Erich (1941). *Escape from Freedom.* New York: Holt, Rinehart and Winston.

Gerbner, George (1992). "Persian Gulf War: The Movie," in Mowlana, Gerbner, and Schiller 1992.

Gerbner, George, and Larry Gross (1976). "Living with Television: The Violence Profile," *Journal of Communications* (Spring), pp. 173–199.

Gibson, James William (1986). *The Perfect War. Technowar in Vietnam.* Boston and New York: The Atlantic Monthly Press.

Gittings, John (1991). *Beyond the Gulf War: the Middle East and the New World Order.* London: Catholic Institute for International Relations.

Graubard, Stephen R. (1992). *Mr. Bush's War.* New York: Hill and Wang.

Greer, Edward (1991). "The Hidden History of the Iraq War," *Monthly Review,* May, pp. 1–14.

Gross, Bertram (1980). *Friendly Fascism.* Boston: South End Press.

Habermas, Jürgen (1975). *Legitimation Crisis.* Boston: Beacon Press.

Halberstam, David (1973). *The Brightest and the Best.* New York: Random House.

Henderson, Simon (1991). *Instant Empire: Saddam Hussein's Ambition for Iraq.* San Franciso: Mercury House.

Henson, Scott (1991). "Entangling Alliances," *The Texas Observer,* Jan. 25, pp. 5–8.

Herman, Edward, and Noam Chomsky (1988). *Manufacturing Consent.* New York: Pantheon.

Herr, Michael (1967). *Dispatches.* New York: Alfred A. Knopf.

Hilop, Diro (1990). *The Longest War.* London: Paladin Books.

Jaber, Saleh (1991). "The New Imperialist Crusade," in *The Gulf War and the New World Order,* Notebooks for Study and Research, #14.

Jewett, Robert, and John Lawrence (1988). *The American Monomyth,* 2d edition. Lanham, Md.: University Press of America.

Jin, Khoo Khay, ed., (1991). *Whose War? What Peace? Reflections on the Gulf Conflict.* Penang: Aliran Kesedaran Malaysia.

Johnson, James Turner, and George Weigel (1991). *Just War and the Gulf War.* Lanham, Md.: University Press of America.

Joseph, William K. (1991). "Right on Schedule," *The Journal of Psychohistory,* 19 (1), pp. 23–33.

Jowett, Garth, and Victoria O'Donnell (1992). *Propaganda and Persuasion.* Newbury Park, Calif.: Sage.

Karsh, Efraim, and Inari Rautski (1991). *Saddam Hussein. A Political Biography.* New York: The Free Press.

Kashmeri, Zuhair (1991). *The Gulf Within: Canadian Arabs, Racism and the Gulf War.* Toronto: James Lorimer & Co.

Keen, Sam (1986). *Faces of the Enemy.* New York: Harper and Row.

Kellner, Douglas (1978). "Ideology, Marxism, and Advanced Capitalism," *Socialist Review* 42 (Nov.-Dec.), pp. 37–65.

_____. (1979). "TV, Ideology and Emancipatory Popular Culture," *Socialist Review* 45 (May-June), pp. 13–53.

_____. (1984). *Herbert Marcuse and the Crisis of Marxism.* London: Macmillan Press and Berkeley: University of California Press.

_____. (1989a). *Critical Theory, Marxism, and Modernity.* Cambridge and Baltimore: Polity Press and Johns Hopkins University Press.

_____. (1989b). "From *1984* to *One-Dimensional Man*: Reflections on Orwell and Marcuse," *Current Perspectives in Social Theory,* Vol. 10, pp. 223–252.

_____. (1990). *Television and the Crisis of Democracy.* Boulder, Col.: Westview.

_____. (forthcoming). "Film, Politics, and Ideology: Toward a Multiperspectival Film Theory," in *Movies and Politics,* ed., James Combs (New York: Garland, in press).

Kellner, Douglas, and Michael Ryan (1988). *Camera Politica: The Politics and Ideology of Contemporary Hollywood Film.* Bloomington, Ind.: University of Indiana Press.

Kelly, John (1990). "Hearing Before the Subcommittee on Europe and the Middle East of the Committee on Foreign Affairs, House of Representatives," April 26, 1990. Washington: U.S. Government Printing Office.

al-Khalil, Samir (1989). *Republic of Fear.* Berkeley: University of California Press.

Klare, Michael (1990). "Policing the Gulf—and the World," *The Nation,* Oct. 15, p. 413, 416–420.

_____. (1991). "Fueling the Fire: How We Armed the Middle East," *The Bulletin of Atomic Scientists,* Jan./Feb., pp. 19–26.

Knightly, Phillip (1975). *The First Casualty.* New York and London: Harcourt Brace Jovanovich.

Kolko, Gabriel (1991). "Obsessed with Military 'Credibility,'" *The Progressive,* March, pp. 24–26.

Kotz, David, and Mehrene Larudee (1991). "Settling Accounts: Who Gets What in the Post-war Grab for Contracts and Oil?" *In These Times* (March 27, 1991), p. 17

LaMay, Craig et al. (1991). *The Media at War.* New York: Gannett Foundation Media Center.

Lang, Curtis (1991). "It's Oil in the Family," *Village Voice,* February 5, p. 32–33.

Lasswell, Harold D. (1971). *Propaganda Technique in World War I.* Cambridge, Mass.: MIT Press.

Lee, Martin A., and Norman Solomon (1991). *Unreliable Sources.* 2nd ed. New York: Lyle Stuart.

Luostarinen, Heikki (1991). "Innovations of Moral Policy in the Gulf War," *Media Development,* October, pp. 10–14.

MacArthur, Brian, ed. (1991). *Despatches from the Gulf War.* London: Bloomsbury.

MacArthur, John R. (1992). *Second Front: Censorship and Propaganda in the Gulf War.* New York: Hill and Wang.

Malek, Abbas, and Lisa Leidig (1991). "US press coverage of the Gulf War," *Media Development,* October, pp. 15–19.

McPeak, Merrill (1991). "Special Defense Department Briefing." Washington, D.C.: Federal Information Systems Corporation, March 15.

Melman, Seymour (1991). "Military State Capitalism," *The Nation,* May 20, p. 66.

Middle East Watch/Human Rights Watch (1991a). *A Victory Turned Sour: Human Rights in Kuwait Since Liberation.* New York: Human Rights Watch.

Middle East Watch/Human Rights Watch (1991b). *Needless Deaths in the Gulf War: Civilian Casualties During the Air Campaign and Violations of the Laws of War.* New York.

Miller, Judith, and Laurie Mylroie (1990). *Saddam Hussein and the Crisis in the Gulf.* New York: Times Books.

Miller, Mark Crispin (1992). *Spectacle: Operation Desert Storm and the Triumph of Illusion.* New York: Poseidon/Simon and Schuster.

Mowlana, Hamid, George Gerbner, and Herbert I. Schiller (1992). *Triumph of the Image: The Media's War in the Persian Gulf—A Global Perspective.* Boulder, Colo.: Westview.

Owen, Roger (1991). "Epilogue: Making Sense of an Earthquake," in Brittain 1991, pp. 159–178.

Peters, Cynthia (1992). *Collateral Damage. The New World Order At Home & Abroad.* Boston: South End Press.

Postol, Theodore A. (1991). House Armed Services Committee, Washington, D.C.: Federal Information Systems Corporation, April 16.

Postol, Theodore A. (1991–1992). "Lessons of the Gulf War Experience with Patriot," *International Security,* Vol. 16, No. 3 (Winter), pp. 119–171.

Pratt, Ray (1991). "Manipulated Public or Nation in 'Denial'?" (unpublished Ms.).

Ridgeway, James, ed. (1991). *The Rush to War.* New York: Four Walls Eight Windows.

Roach, Colleen (1991). "Feminism, Peace, and Culture," *Media Development* (in press).

Robins, Kevin, and Les Levidow (1991). "The Eye of the Storm," *Screen,* Vol. 32, No. 3 (Autumn), pp. 324–328.

Rogin, Michael (1987). *Ronald Reagan: The Movie.* Berkeley: University of California Press.

Ruffini, Gene (1991). "Press Fails to Challenge the Rush to War," *Washington Journalism Review,* March, pp. 21–23.

Sackur, Stephen (1992). *On the Basra Road.* London: London Review of Books.

Said, Edward (1978). *Orientalism.* New York: Random House.

———. (1981). *Covering Islam.* New York: Random House.

Salinger, Pierre, and Eric Laurent (1991). *Secret Dossier: The Hidden Agenda Behind the Gulf War.* New York: Penguin Books.

Sasson, Jean P. (1991). *The Rape of Kuwait.* New York: Knightsbridge.

Schanberg, Sydney H. (1991). "Censoring for Military Political Security," *Washington Journalism Review,* March, pp. 23–26.

Schechter, Danny (1991). "Gulf War Coverage," *Z Magazine,* December, pp. 22–25.

Schiller, Herbert (1989). *Culture, Inc.: The Corporate Takeover of Public Expression.* New York: Oxford University Press.

Sciolino, Elaine (1991). *The Outlaw State.* New York: John Wiley.

Shaheen, Jack G. (1984). *The TV Arab.* Bowling Green, Ohio: Popular Press.

Sick, Gary (1991). *The October Surprise.* New York: Random House.

Sifry, Micah L., and Christopher Cerf, eds. (1991). *The Gulf War Reader.* New York: Random House.

Simon, Bob (1992). *Forty Days.* New York: G.P. Putnam's Sons.

Simpson, John (1991). *From the House of War.* London: Arrow Books.

Slotkin, Richard (1973). *Regeneration Through Violence: The Mythology of the American Frontier.* Middletown: Wesleyan University Press.

Smith, Jean Edward (1992). *George Bush's War.* New York: Holt.

Smith, Perry (1991). *How CNN Fought the War.* New York: Birch Lane Press.

Sprey, Pierre, and Bill Perry (1991). House Armed Services Committee, Washington, D.C.: Federal Information Systems Corporation, April 22.

Stockwell, John (1978). *In Search of Enemies.* New York: Norton.

———. (1991). *The Praetorian Guard.* Boston: South End Press.

Taylor, Philip M. (1992). *War and the Media: Propaganda and Persuasion in the Gulf War.* New York: Saint Martin's Press.

Timmerman, Kenneth R. (1991). *The Death Lobby: How The West Armed Iraq.* Boston: Houghton Mifflin.

Tokar, Brian (1991). "Disaster in the Gulf and Poison at Home," *Z Magazine,* December, pp. 57–60.

Umberson, Debra, and Kristin Henderson (1991). "The Social Construction of Death in the Gulf War" (unpublished Ms.).

U.S. News and World Report (1992). *Triumph Without Victory.* New York: Random House.

Yant, Martin (1991). *Desert Mirage: The True Story of the Gulf War.* Buffalo, NY: Prometheus Books.

Vialls, Joe (1991). "Kuwait Oil Volcanos Still Active," PeaceNet, mideast.gulf, Dec. 1.

Vidal, John (1991). "Poisoned Sand and Seas," in Brittain 1991, pp. 133–142.

Waas, Murray (1990). "What We Gave Saddam for Christmas: The Secret History of How the United States and Its Allies Armed Iraq," *Village Voice,* Dec. 18.

Waas, Murray (1991). "Who Lost Kuwait?" *Village Voice,* Jan. 16–22, pp. 60ff.

Walter, Paul (1992). "The Myth of Surgical Bombing," in Clark et al. 1992.

Weiner, Jon (1991). "Domestic Political Incentives for the Gulf War," *New Left Review* (May/June), pp. 72–78.

Weiner, Robert (1992). *Live From Baghdad.* New York: Doubleday.

Whittemore, Hank (1990). *CNN: The Inside Story.* Boston: Little, Brown and Company.

Winter, James (1991). "Truth as the First Casualty: Mainstream Media Portrayal of the Gulf War," *The Electronic Journal of Communication,* Vol. 2, No. 2 (Fall).

Wolton, Dominique (1991). *War Game.* Paris: Flammarion.

Woodward, Bob (1991). *The Commanders.* New York: Simon and Schuster.

About the Book and Author

Douglas Kellner's *Persian Gulf TV War* attacks the myths, disinformation, and propaganda disseminated during the Gulf war. At once a work of social theory, media criticism, and political history, this book demonstrates how television served as a conduit for George Bush's war policies while silencing antiwar voices and foregoing spirited discussion of the complex issues involved. In so doing, the medium failed to assume its democratic responsibilities of adequately informing the American public and debating issues of common concern.

Kellner analyzes the dominant frames through which television presented the war and focuses on the propaganda that sold the war to the public—one of the great media spectacles and public relations campaigns of the post–World War II era. In the spirit of Orwell and Marcuse, Kellner studies the language surrounding the Gulf war and the cynical politics of distortion and disinformation that shaped the mainstream media version of the war, how the Bush administration and Pentagon manipulated the media, and why a majority of the American public accepted the war as just and moral.

Douglas Kellner is professor of philosophy at the University of Texas–Austin and author of *Television and the Crisis of Democracy* (1990).

Index